THE HISTORIAN AS DETECTIVE

THE HISTORIAN AS DETECTIVE

ESSAYS ON EVIDENCE

Robin W. Winks, EDITOR

HARPER TORCHBOOKS
Harper & Row, Publishers
New York, Hagerstown, San Francisco, London

The Introduction first appeared, in slightly different form, in *The Texas Quarterly,* XI, Winter, 1968.

LIBRARY OF CONGRESS CATALOG CARD NUMBER: 67-22522
ISBN: 0-06-131933-3
80 12 11 10 9

To Raymond Kierstead, Edmund Morgan, Robert Olson, and Christopher Wrenwood, colleagues and addicts too

Contents

Acknowledgments xi

Introduction xiii

PART I. VIGILANTE JUSTICE?

1. What Is Evidence? The Relativist View—"Everyman His Own Historian," by Carl L. Becker 3
2. On Believing What One Reads: The Dangers of Popular Revisionism—from *American Attitudes Toward History,* by C. Vann Woodward 24
3. Who Killed John Doe? The Problem of Testimony—from *The Idea of History,* by Robin G. Collingwood 39
4. Tracer of Missing Persons: Biographer and Autobiographer —from *An Autobiography,* by Theodore Roosevelt, and *Theodore Roosevelt: A Biography,* by Henry F. Pringle 61

PART II. HABEAS CORPUS

5. The Secret of the Ebony Cabinet: A Search for "Lost" Manuscripts—from the Preface to *Boswell's London Journal (1762–1763)*, by Christopher Morley 89
6. The Mystery of Marie Roget, and Other Diversions: Another Search for Lost Manuscripts—from *The Scholar Adventurers,* by Richard D. Altick 104
7. The Case of the Man in Love: Forgery, Impure and Simple —"The Minor Collection: A Criticism," by Paul M. Angle 127
8. The Case of the Men Who Weren't There: Problems of Local Pride—"The Mystery of the Horn Papers," by Arthur Pierce Middleton and Douglass Adair 142

PART III. THE ADVERSARY METHOD

9. The Case of the Eyewitnesses: "A lie is a lie, even in Latin" —from *Aspects of the Study of Roman History,* by Thomas Spencer Jerome 181

10. The Case of the Cheating Documents: False Authority and the Problem of Surmise—from *The Gateway to History,* by Allan Nevins 192

11. A Medley of Mysteries: A Number of Dogs That Didn't Bark—from *The Modern Researcher,* by Jacques Barzun and Henry F. Graff 213

12. The Case of the Mysterious Diary: Evidence Over Time— "Has the Mystery of 'A Public Man' Been Solved?," by Roy N. Lokken, and "A Rejoinder," by Frank Maloy Anderson 232

13. The Case of the Harried Scholars: Of the World That Is Too Much with Us—from *The Dead Sea Scrolls,* by Millar Burrows 257

PART IV. THE CASE METHOD

14. The Case of the Needless Death: Reconstructing the Scene —"The Death of Captain Cook," by J. C. Beaglehole 279

15. The Private Eye: Going Over the Ground—from *Ulysses Found,* by Ernle Bradford, and *Testaments of Time,* by Leo Deuel 303

16. The Case of the Missing Telegrams: Suppressing Evidence —"The Missing Telegrams and the Jameson Raid," by C. M. Woodhouse 317

17. The Case of the Very Minor Matter: Inadvertent Error— "An Alleged Hysterical Outburst of Richard II," by L. C. Hector 341

18. The Case of the Feigning Man: Medical-Psychological Evidence—from *Charles Sumner and the Coming of the Civil War,* by David Donald 347

PART V. ALLIES

19. The Case of the Grassy Knoll: The Romance of Conspiracy —"The Assassins," by John Kaplan 371

20. The Roman Coin Mystery: The Romance of Objects—from *Paths to the Ancient Past,* by Tom B. Jones 420

21. The Case of the Silent Witnesses: The Romance of Gadgetry —from *Stonehenge Decoded,* by Gerald S. Hawkins and John B. White 432

22. The Case of the Fit in the Choir: The Application of Psychoanalysis—from *Young Man Luther,* by Erik H. Erikson 460

PART VI. VERDICTS

23. The Strange Nature of Pure Joy: The Historian's Pleasure Principle—"The Psychiatrist, the Historian, and General Clinton," by William B. Willcox 497

24. The Pleasures of Doubt: Re-enacting the Crime—"The Limits of Historical Knowledge," by Robin G. Collingwood 513

25. The Problem of Hope: Contemporary History—"On the Inscrutability of History," by Arthur Schlesinger, Jr. 523

26. Conclusion—A Letter to Groucho Marx, by Russell Baker 537

Bibliography 541

Acknowledgments

Detective-fiction buffs are an obsessive lot, devouring great quantities of such books, but it has been my experience that they seldom care to talk about what they read, or why, perhaps being vaguely ashamed of doing so. With the exception of the selection of one essay, since rejected from the anthology, the pleasant task of ferreting out examples to illustrate the several points I wished to make therefore fell entirely to me. This does not mean that I have failed to gain from chance conversations with friends about the genre, just as I have gained far more from historians with a similar interest in historical method. I am grateful to all who share either or both pleasures.

I should like to acknowledge the help of my parents—of my mother, who as an English teacher did not allow herself to become unduly dismayed when I chose to read Ellery Queen and Carl Sandburg rather than *Silas Marner,* and of my father, who as a scientist and football coach, expressed only mild disapproval over my unconcern with some primitive double helix and only modest disappointment that I passed through John R. Tunis to read Manning Coles and Arthur Bryant. My wife, although clearly preferring that I should relax with port and Milton, has settled for beer and Chandler. As an undergraduate, I learned much from a man who will not remember me, James Sandoe, long a reviewer of detective stories, and later Anthony Boucher helped me, after I had sent him an Indonesian translation of Conan Doyle. Most of all, I wish to thank the editors of the *New York Times,* who, by making their Sunday edition so intolerably fat, have driven me away from wasting my time over its pages, so that I might have a few precious hours for learning more about Hercule Poirot.

A NOTE TO THE PAPERBACK EDITION

Neither the historian nor the detective has been without fault. I am happy to take advantage of the reprinting of this book for its paperback edition to correct four minor errors which had crept past my proofreading eye in the first version, and to add two new titles to the Bibliography. I should also like to draw attention to a particularly fine example of the type of detective fiction to which the Introduction refers, Eric Ambler's *The Intercom Conspiracy,* based on an ingenious use of a discovered manuscript, and to mention *The Armchair Detective,* a quarterly journal devoted to crime fiction.

Introduction

I have compiled this book of essays for fun, and I claim no other high purpose for it. My vocation as a professional historian often leads me to deal with questions of evidence. The historian must collect, interpret, and then explain his evidence by methods which are not greatly different from those techniques employed by the detective, or at least the detective of fiction. It is not surprising, then, that historians often seem to relax with a so-called detective story, or that certain English dons and American professors are known not only to be addicts of the genre but sometimes even contribute to the literature. Perhaps the real detective trusts more to luck, or to gadgetry, or to informers than does the fictional hero, who, for reasons of plot construction, must be driven through a series of narrow escapes, up a number of false paths, and at last, by doggedness, intuition, and a certain intelligence, to the dénouement. Obviously the author of such fiction does not construct his work as the historian does, for to one the outcome is known and to the other that outcome is at best guessed at. But the reasoning processes are similar enough to be intriguing. What I have tried to explore in this anthology is the relationship between the colorful world of fictional intrigue, then, and the good gray world of professional scholarship, and to show how much of the excitement, the joy, and even the color properly belongs to the latter.

Recently a student asked me to defend "the social utility of the historian." One could do so, I believe, but not here, any more than I would wish to write on the social utility of Agatha Christie. In any case, a graduate student at the Université de Montréal composed a master's thesis on the ethics of the good Hercule Poirot, and the Uppsala Studies in English, an archly scholarly Swedish series, include a volume on the grammatical structure of Miss Christie's prose, so she has not been overlooked entirely. Perhaps the social utility of history is little more than that implied by William Haggard's Colonel Russell, fictitious head of England's not quite fictitious Security Executive, or (John) Ross MacDonald's hard-boiled sentimentalist, Lew Archer: someone ought to be interested in finding out the truth about things, for the truth ought to matter. My same student also told me that he could never be a historian, for the life was far too lonely. One does not wish to romanticize the historian by belaboring his aloneness, but in the final analysis he is probably the least able of all scholars to work for a team, the least willing to collaborate, to co-author, to engage in public testimony and debate. One wonders whether the discipline makes the historian remote or whether it merely attracts those who already are so inclined. Still, whatever compulsions are at work, the historian remains a private person, unwilling to reveal much of himself in his written word. His individuality is to be discovered, rather, in the range of topics on which he chooses to write, in the way in which he gathers evidence, in his conception of peripheral as opposed to central questions, in the very style of his expression. In history perhaps more than in any other discipline, the book is the man, the medium is the message, and the understanding of evidence and how to employ it is one's closest approach to that truth others seek in churches.

Nevertheless, historians are teachers as well as researchers and writers. In seeking out answers to questions which historians or other scholars frame, in pursuing the data which will provide partial answers to those questions, in ordering the data in a sequence that is both meaningful and true, and in evaluating the validity, importance, and causal relationships of the data, the writer employs certain commonly accepted canons of his profession. However, as a teacher, the historian seldom has occasion to raise the more difficult problems of evidence and evaluation, especially for undergraduates who infrequently have need for specialized skills, for paleography, for linguistics, or even for the ability to read an old map sufficiently well to draw at least as much information from its dimmed lines as the cartographer intended.

When one speaks of evidence to an undergraduate, or to a lay reader of history, one generally means: How do we know that something is true? That it happened when, or how, or where the press, or a text, or a friend, or a parent, or an encyclopedia said that it did? In other words, while the professional historian frequently is engaged in judging the credibility of a witness, in attempting to gauge the bias that will be present in the account of a contemporary involved in the events he describes, the lay reader more often is concerned with assessing the credibility of a printed record, of one book's account against another's. Both levels of assessment involve the problem of evidence.

Evidence means different things to different people, of course. The historian tends to think mainly in terms of documents. A lawyer will mean something rather different by the word, as will a sociologist, or a physicist, or a geologist, or a police officer at the moment of making an arrest. For certain problems evidence must be "hard," while for others it may be "soft." Even if no acceptable or agreed-upon definitions of evidence may be given, most of us recognize intuitively what we mean when we use the word.

Very possibly the historian thinks of evidence more intuitively than most other people do, and for this reason he has worried the word about until it may have taken on more functions than its fragile origins will bear. Increasingly, social scientists think of evidence, or of data, as quantitative; that is, as something that can be counted. To such scholars, the historian's tendency toward vague and admittedly intuitive conclusions arising from a systematic but often unstructured examination of the evidence is an annoying sign of an anti-theoretical bent. "Many Colonial American newspapers appear to have turned against the British Crown by 1775" is a less satisfying statement than is the apparent certitude of a clear calculation: "Of 27 Colonial newspapers examined, 19 show—by virtue of giving over more than 457 column inches of space to anti-Parliamentary comment—that they had turned against the Mother Country by mid-1775." Both statements may well arise from an examination of "the evidence," but one appears to be more scientific than the other.

These two quotations, which are, incidentally, quite fictitious although representative of two techniques for generalizing among historians, involve a "leap of faith" between evidence (the data) and conclusion (the generalization). This "leap of faith," as the theologian calls the intuitive process, is more frequently covered up by the historian as a "legitimate inference." But inferences remain incapable of final proof, and thus evidence and its evaluation remain inexact for the historian, whether he be of the school that insists that history is a humanity or of the school that thinks it is a social science. Because historians deal with the inexact, they have developed certain common-sense rules for evaluating evidence in terms of its reliability, its relevance, its significance, and its singularity.

Inference is notoriously unreliable, as are eyewitnesses, memories of old men, judgments of mothers about first children, letters written for publication, and garbage collectors. At the moment, I drive a much-battered 1954 Cadillac, full of wayward lurchings, unidentifiable rattles, and unpredictable ways upon the road. Recently I shifted a shovel, which I carry in the trunk as proof against New England snows, to a new position. No sooner had I closed the lid than a new and penetrating noise arose from the back of the car which clearly was a metal shovel bouncing about within a trunk. My inference was that this was so, and for a week I drove without investigating the noise. Then the gas tank fell off, proving my inference wrong. The reader may infer that I plan to use the royalties from this book to buy a new car. If he does, he will be right.

We all make inferences daily, and we all collect, sift, evaluate, and then act upon evidence. Our alarm clocks, the toothpaste tube without a cap, warm milk at the breakfast table, and the bus that is ten minutes late provide us with evidence from which we infer certain unseen actions. The historian must reconstruct events often hundreds of years in the past, on the basis of equally homely although presumably more significant data, when the full evidence will never be recoverable and, for that portion of it recovered, when it may have meanings other than we would attach to similar evidence today. Thus the historian has evolved his standards of inquiry, of thoroughness, and of judgment to provide him with a *modus operandi.*

Historians pose to themselves difficult, even impossibly difficult, questions. Since they are reasonably intelligent and inquiring and since they do not wish to spend their lives upon a single question or line of investigation, they normally impose a time limit upon a given project or book (or the time limit is imposed for them by a "publish or perish" environment). They will invariably encounter numerous unforeseen difficulties because of missing papers, closed collections, new questions, and tangential problems; and the search through the archive, the chase after the single hoped-to-be-vital manuscript, has an excitement of its own, for that dénouement, the discovery, an answer may—one always hopes—lie in the next folio, in the next collection, in the next archive.

Much of the historian's work, then, like that of the insurance investigator, the fingerprint man, or the coroner, may to the outsider seem to consist of deadening routine. Many miles of intellectual shoe leather will be used, for many metaphorical laundry lists, uninformative diaries, blank checkbooks, old telephone directories, and other trivia will stand between the researcher and his answer. Yet the routine must be pursued or the clue may be missed; the apparently false trail must be followed in order to be certain that it is false; the mute witnesses must be asked the reasons for their silence, for the piece of evidence that is missing from where one might reasonably expect to find it is, after all, a form of evidence in itself.

Precisely because the historian must turn to all possible witnesses, he is the most bookish of men. For him, no printed statement is without its interest. For him, the destruction of old cookbooks, gazetteers, road maps, Sears, Roebuck catalogues, children's books, railway timetables, or drafts of printed manuscripts, is the loss of potential evidence. Does one wish to know how the mail-order business operated or how a Nebraska farmer might have dressed in 1930? Look to those catalogues. Does one wish to know whether a man from Washington just might have been in New York on a day in 1861 when it can be proved that he was in the capital on the day before and the day after? The timetables will help tell us of the opportunity. Does one wish to see the growth of new highways, the spread of asphalt into a neglected corner of Colorado, or Indiana, or Maine during the Depression years? Oil-company road maps will help. Does one wish to know what kinds of ideas a Theodore Roosevelt, or a Clement Attlee, or a John F. Kennedy may have fed upon as children? Back files of *St. Nicholas,* or *Boy's Own,* or even *Superman* will be relevant. And thus one also needs to know who collects what: that the University of Syracuse houses children's literature, that Cornell holds on to its railway timetables, or that Yale keeps old road maps.

Of course one applies these notions of relevancy outside book-lined rooms, too, and the historian needs to be the most practical of men as well. One, of my acquaintance, worked with Marine intelligence during World War II. He was asked to help judge how many Japanese had dug in on one of the strategically crucial South Pacific islands, an island which the Marine Corps planned to make their own, whatever the losses, within a few days. No Japanese could be seen from aerial reconnaissance, since their camouflage was nearly perfect. The historian provided an accurate figure, however, for he noted from aerial photographs that particularly dark patches could be identified as latrines, and upon consulting a captured Japanese manual, he learned how many latrines were to be dug per unit of men. The rest was so simple a matter of calculation that even the historian could provide an answer without the aid of a computer.

Clearly, then, the historian needs to assess evidence against a reasonably well-informed background. Is one writing of the Pullman Strike of 1894? One must, obviously, know quite a bit about general labor conditions, about business management, about employment opportunities and the nature of the economy, about Chicago and its environs, and about the railroad industry. But since many of the strikers were Welshmen, one needs also to know something of contrasting work conditions in that part of Wales from which the workmen came. Since the strike was compounded by inept police and militia work, one needs to know about the nature of such work in Illinois and, comparatively, elsewhere. One needs to investigate the judicial system, the rôle of President Grover Cleveland, the powers open to Governor John P. Altgeld, the ideas of Eugene V. Debs, and the effects of the Chicago World's Fair, which brought hundreds of drifters into the metropolitan area to contribute to the violence associated with the strike. Since the strike disrupted mail service throughout the nation, forcing letters north onto Canadian tracks, one needs to investigate at least briefly the Canadian rail network, the relationship with railwaymen elsewhere, and the applicability of the secondary boycott.

One needs to know much of the general climate of opinion at the time to assess the meaning of the strike. One needs to look at company, city, union, judicial, militia, post-office, Presidential, legal, and gubernatorial records; at the private papers of Cleveland, Altgeld, Pullman, Debs; at the papers of the judges, magistrates, and strikers, if they can be found and, when found, if one can gain access to them. Much that one learns on such journeys will never appear in the final book, but every nuance, every sentence, will be better informed, closer to the truth, more protected against one's own biases (which can never be totally blocked out, and no responsible historian claims that they can be), than if such journeys were not taken at all.

The historian of the United States is in a particularly favorable situation in that he will have more data, more evidence, more rewarding journeys, than any other national historian. From the outset, the Puritans knew that they were on an errand into the wilderness, to build "a city upon a hill" which one day the world would wish to emulate or, at the very least, to study. They were historically minded, and one legacy of that conviction is the system of magnificent national, state, and local archives across the United States.

Every one of the fifty states has an archive, ranging from the superbly organized depositories of Massachusetts, Pennsylvania, and Illinois to the tiny but valuable archives of Arkansas, Alaska, and Delaware. There are over two thousand local historical societies that preserve materials; hundreds of university and college libraries; hundreds more of public and private libraries. There are over five hundred historical journals devoted largely to American history alone, and there are organizations of historians who give much of their time to writing about such specialized subjects as textiles, aviation, or cotton. There is a *Labor History* review, an *Agricultural History*, a *Business History Review;* there is a peace-research junta, a *Journal of Conflict Resolution,* a *Newsletter* on the history of the Second World War, and dozens of scholarly outlets for work in diplomatic and political history. There is a historical journal for Westchester County, New York, and one for Cowlitz County, Washington, a Catholic, a Jewish, a Presbyterian, a Methodist, a Quaker historical journal: a *Journal of Negro History, a Scan-*

dinavian-American Review; there are a dozen railway-history journals, the Canal Society of New York publishes a piquantly named quarterly, *Bottoming Out;* there is a journal devoted to the history of libraries and another to the history of journals. The historian must search through these to find relevant materials, and although most of the search will be unrewarding, since most such articles are antiquarian scissors-and-paste, these articles may supply the clue that leads one on to a collection of virtually untapped original source materials.

By a "source" the historian means material that is contemporary to the events being examined. Such sources include, among other things, diaries, letters, newspapers, magazine articles, tape recordings, pictures, and maps. Such material may have appeared in print before, edited or unedited, and still be a source. The term is meant to be restrictive rather than inclusive, in that it attempts to indicate that works of secondary scholarship, or synthesis, are not sources, since the data have been distilled by another person. More of this distinction, which is an important one, will become apparent from the essays that follow. One good way for the novice historian to lose Brownie points among his serious-minded fellows is to call a biography of George Washington or an analysis of the Magna Charta a "source." (While on niceties of the totem pole, one may also add for the cognoscenti that an "antiquarian" is one who merely gathers and records data, while a historian likes to think that he goes beyond these steps to order and interpret data.) If the historian who prefers to work largely at the interpretive level wishes to condemn a work as unimaginative fact-grubbing, he will call it "solidly researched," while if a scholar who is primarily archive-oriented wishes to damn his more introspective colleague with faint praise, he will say that the book under review "takes up the Big Questions." Readers new to the game of academic criticism should be aware that cream sometimes passes for skim milk. Of all things one must not be called, merely "competent" is among the most damning. On the other hand, to be a "seminal writer" does not mean one's work is destined for the Grove Press but, rather, that one has lots of ideas which cause other people to have lots more ideas. Whether the ideas are good or not is another question entirely.

Obviously one man's scholarship is another man's pedantry, and the point here is merely to say that with sufficient diligence American historians can expect to find the answer—or at least *an* answer—to most factual or non-value questions they may choose to put to themselves. As a result, American researchers tend to begin with the questions they wish to entertain first (Did failed farmers truly move West to begin life anew in the eighteen-forties? Did immigrants reinforce older patterns of life or create new ones?), confident that the data can be found. European historians, on the other hand, are likely to begin with the available source materials first, and then look to see what legitimate questions they might ask of those sources. (Here are the private papers of Joseph Chamberlain, or of Gladstone, or of Disraeli. What do they tell me of British politics? Of Queen Victoria? Of the Jameson Raid? Of the development of British tariff policy? Of Colonial affairs? Of Ireland?) The result is, as the following essays will help show, that scholars of different nations do approach the problem of evidence somewhat differently—as surely any reader of detective fiction, aware of the differences between the American procedures in Elizabeth Linington's Los Angeles Police Department and Ed McBain's 87th Precinct and the British procedural school of fiction in J. J. Marric's Gideon of Scotland Yard and Maurice Procter's Inspector Martineau of Granchester, ought well to know.

Nor would I mean for my parallels between historical research and detective fiction to be taken too literally. There obviously is a gap between them, just as there is a gap between politics and scholarship. Dean Rusk, once an academician, has reminded us of the latter gap by pointing out that while scholars argue toward conclusions, those in positions to determine policy must argue to decisions. Most detective fiction moves toward a conviction, just as most spy thrillers involve some concept of retribution arising from betrayal. The historian is not particularly interested in retribution, a point on which he is rather inclined to remember the Biblical injunction. There are a few historians who enter a room with all guns blazing, and some few who think they are judge and jury, but most are content to take the amoral path which leads to Finding Out and to Explaining Why but not necessarily to What It All Means.

One should not expect too much of history or of detective fiction but one need not apologize for reading either. My wife, it is true, does not like to see me engrossed with Charlotte Jay, even though my scholarly bailiwick is supposed to include Pakistan and New Guinea, both brought to life in Miss Jay's excellent mysteries. My wife once read a mystery story and didn't like it. Edmund Wilson also once read three or four and didn't like them, but one cannot always expect to agree with even so astute a figure as our senior critic, much less our wives, and if pressed to the wall, one can probably mention a few acceptable critical types who have admitted to enjoying a little murder now and then.

Wilson's criticism, to be fair, was against the stylistic crudities of most detective fiction, and he undoubtedly is right. Few members of the mystery guild can write really well, although to imitate the conversational gambits of Archie Goodwin in one of Rex Stout's orchidaceous Nero Wolfe escapades is no mean feat, and I would happily put some of the authors cited in the source notes to the selections which follow up against some of the more arcane Canadian authors of whom Mr. Wilson has recently approved. Words do count in detective fiction, of course—the murder of Miss Christie's Roger Ackroyd turns on the fact that the guilty party did exactly what he said he did—and perhaps historians enjoy, and fairly readily solve, the formal puzzles of the genre simply because they are attuned to a careful examination of each word that they read. Perhaps this is also one reason why the short story seems ill-suited to such fiction: there simply is not space for enough words to build character, obfuscate motive, and weave plot. Thackeray once said of Macaulay that the latter read "twenty books to write a sentence; he travels a hundred miles to make a line of description," and this sense of necessary excess is what makes the historian what he is.

Why try to explain away an addiction, in any case? Graham Greene, who wisely calls what he apparently thinks his lesser efforts "entertainments," suggests that thrillers are not meant to do much more than that (although his *Brighton Rock,* for example, surely does much more). Perhaps one reads thrillers, spy fiction, counterspy stories, mysteries, and the entire gamut of such high-level rubbish simply because one has been to the Topkapi Palace and knows that the thieves in Eric Ambler's *The Light of Day* can't get away with it, since the jewel room differs in fact in one crucial detail from Ambler's description of it. Perhaps one reads F. W. Bronson's Yale-based *The Bulldog Has the Key,* not a good book at all, simply because a room directly above one's own office figures prominently in the narrative. Perhaps one reads MacInnes, Leasor, Mather, Buchan, or Adam Hall simply because they invoke places one has been to or, *sacrebleu,* like Casablanca, wishes to go to. Perhaps one reads them because, as Joan Kahn, the editor of the Harper Novels of Suspense, has remarked, mystery readers are brighter than the average (average what she does not say). Why, after all, does one write history? Perhaps, as Bach is supposed to have answered when asked why he composed, for the greater glory of God—and because we enjoy it.

A final warning is necessary. There are many quite important questions of evidence that the following essays do not touch upon. In some instances recent research has served to modify the conclusions of a few of the essays themselves. Several problems in research are unrepresented. In one or two instances I was unable to secure permission to reprint an essay that better makes the point I wished to see made, and a less central demonstration has been substituted. I feel no sense of guilt about these omissions, any more than I think anyone has a moral duty to purchase or to read historical material that does not interest him simply because someone deems it culturally worth while. This book is not meant to be a Baedeker, a Barzun and Graff, a Vincent Starrett, or an Anthony Boucher for "the historian on evidence." It is meant to be a collection of essays that are interesting in themselves and which, sometimes rather incidentally, demonstrate different ways in which a historian's mind may work, or should work, or can work. There are no conclusions to be drawn about any particular historian or school of historians, any more than one would draw conclusions about skiing holidays in the Adirondacks from reading too many books that deal with multiple murders in snowed-in mountain cabins. The book was meant to give me some modest fun between other more self-consciously serious tasks, and if it does not provide the same for the reader, then we have both made unfortunate choices.

I have selected, and edited, all the essays that follow in order to point up the element of evidence within them, to emphasize leads and clues, straight tips and false rumors, and the mischief wrought by time. Where any material, within footnotes as well as within text or interior quotations, has been omitted, I have supplied ellipses. I hope that none of the authors represented here will feel that I have done an injustice to his argument by using excerpts rather than an entire article or chapter; I freely admit that I have used the essays to speak to my points rather than to those which the authors may originally have intended. Most of the essays included voluminous documentation, the great majority of which I have removed; those footnotes retained have, of course, been renumbered. Readers who wish to see the complete documentation should consult the originals, to which full citations are provided. Material inserted in brackets was supplied by the editor, and any footnotes which I have added are clearly indicated. Notes have been regularized where necessary to the usual American model, and printers' errors have been quietly corrected without intruding *sic*. Some of the original essays included illustrations, which have been eliminated, as have most of the subheadings, interior divisions, and variant spacings. The detective and spy stories mentioned in the source notes and in my own brief connective essays were chosen because I thought they represented a close fictional parallel to the historical problem under discussion, and also because I enjoyed reading them. Some closer parallels which I found crashing bores are not cited. Several favorite historians are not included, for when I first assembled the essays I wished to use, I found that I had enough for over three volumes of the length of the present one. Prudence, the publisher, and the fact that my Puritan conscience would permit me to work on this collection only while on Cape Cod vacations, which come but once a year, dictated that I slash viciously, retaining only passing references to the titles I should have liked to have included. These, which appear in the opening note to each selection, will offer the reader much more evidence on the historian as detective.

ROBIN W. WINKS

Great Sand Lakes
Massachusetts

PART I

VIGILANTE JUSTICE?

1. What Is Evidence?

The Relativist View

ONE OF THE MASTERS OF ROMANTIC SPY FICTION, JOHN Buchan, once observed that only two ingredients were essential to the successful thriller writer: an ability to create likable characters and a feel for landscape. The author could then propel his figures across that landscape in pursuit of some secret of deadly import to the world, or at least to the British nation, which was much the same thing. An element of suspense was added by requiring the hero to move from point A to point Z in a specified period of time, and then by placing numerous time-consuming and dangerous obstacles across his path. The secret of Buchan's success was that he thus spoke to Everyman, for he satisfied one's longing for men who could make clear-cut moral decisions in a world which, for the reader, was becoming less and less clearly defined; he satisfied the armchair traveler's hunger for a sense of place, for a knowledge of what a night spent in the open in the Scottish Highlands must be like; and he satisfied our own sure knowledge that if time eventually runs out for most of us, it does not run out for our heroes. Buchan, as did Ian Fleming a generation later, knew that men enjoy esoteric information and that the human mind closes almost joyfully upon facts, upon presumed technical and sophisticated expertise. If James Bond was an authority on Martinis, Aston Martins, and the women of beautiful firm breasts, Buchan's Richard Hannay also knew how to kill a man by pressing him just *so,* there, behind the left (never the right) ear, or how to catch a thrown dagger between his lips—old African tricks picked up in Hannay's youth. Everyman could be a spy, too, for if he could not know the secret path that lay above the Khyber Pass, he did know the lay-by just off the M1 on the way to Birmingham.

We are all detectives, of course, in that at one time or another we all have had to engage in some genuine deductive routine. Each day we do so, if only in small ways. By the same token, we are all historians, in that we reconstruct past events from present evidence, and perhaps we build usable generalizations upon those reconstructions. There, just *so,* that stain on the carpet is a historical reminder that our good friend Jim can't hold his drinks past his third one, and so we conclude that hereafter Jim's dosage will have to be counted. More important, most of us tend to generate assorted operable truths from our past experiences, whether about our abilities to balance our personal budgets, the effects of particular medicines, or God's operations or lack of them in our daily lives. These truths are merely useful, not necessarily true, in that they help us to decide what to do next; that is, they ingrain within us, almost unconsciously, a sequential pattern of thought. In order to think in sequences, we also learn to discard irrelevancies and to give priorities to the data that remain, so that we see, if we have learned to think clearly at all, which facts are most important in making a decision (to buy this car, to go to that movie, to choose that college, to burn or not to burn our draft cards); that is, which facts are dominant, as opposed to those facts which, although relevant, may nonetheless be set aside for a lower order of priorities. As we do this, we are thinking as the historian thinks, generating our operable truths, our hypotheses for daily life and yearly self-evaluation, embracing those "vital lies," in historian Hans Kohn's phrase, which become beliefs that, whether capable of proof or not, we feel we must live by. We are then, however gross our own thought processes, on the path to becoming intellectual historians.

The professional scholar who best expressed how Everyman is his own historian was Carl L. Becker. A Professor of History at Cornell University, Becker was and is regarded as one of the most luminous writers that the guild of American historians has ever produced. He wrote on politics in pre-Revolutionary New York, on the Enlightenment thought of the French *philosophes,* and on a variety of other subjects, always with clarity, wit, and insight. In 1931, as President of the American Historical Association, he delivered an address which continues to be an excellent statement of the relativist point of view. This essay, "Everyman His Own Historian," is the best place to begin learning how we all, with and without academic training, use (and abuse) evidence. One could hardly do better than to read Becker in connection with that odd little Canadian mystery story by John Buell, *The Pyx,* in which the deductions of Everyman lead to both use and abuse of man's spiritual nature. Both Buell and Becker know how to reduce complex problems to their lowest terms without any loss of sophistication.

♦ ♦ ♦

Once upon a time, long long ago, I learned how to reduce a fraction to its lowest terms. Whether I could still perform that operation is uncertain; but the discipline involved in early training had its uses, since it taught me that in order to understand the essential nature of anything it is well to strip it of all superficial and irrelevant accretions—in short, to reduce it to its lowest terms. That

---

FROM Carl L. Becker, "Everyman His Own Historian," *American Historical Review,* XXXVII (January, 1932), 221–36. Copyright 1932 by American Historical Association. Reprinted with permission. The address was delivered at Minneapolis on December 29, 1931.

For additional reading: If one finds Becker's ideas of interest, a further infusion is recommended. Another classic essay of his appeared in the October, 1910, issue of the *Atlantic Monthly,* as "Detachment and the Writing of History." This article and many others have been reprinted by the Cornell University Press (Ithaca, 1958) in a volume of that title, edited by Phil L. Snyder. And if one wishes to pursue this problem of relativity further in the realm of detective fiction, Anthony Burgess's perverse *Tremor of Intent* follows nicely upon John Buell.

operation I now venture, with some apprehension and all due apologies, to perform on the subject of history.

I ought first of all to explain that when I use the term history I mean knowledge of history. No doubt throughout all past time there actually occurred a series of events which, whether we know what it was or not, constitutes history in some ultimate sense. Nevertheless, much the greater part of these events we can know nothing about, not even that they occurred; many of them we can know only imperfectly; and even the few events that we think we know for sure we can never be absolutely certain of, since we can never revive them, never observe or test them directly. The event itself once occurred, but as an actual event it has disappeared; so that in dealing with it the only objective reality we can observe or test is some material trace which the event has left—usually a written document. With these traces of vanished events, these documents, we must be content since they are all we have; from them we infer what the event was, we affirm that it is a fact that the event was so and so. We do not say "Lincoln is assassinated"; we say "It is a fact that Lincoln was assassinated." The event *was,* but is no longer; it is only the affirmed fact about the event that *is,* that persists, and will persist until we discover that our affirmation is wrong or inadequate. Let us then admit that there are two histories: the actual series of events that once occurred; and the ideal series that we affirm and hold in memory. The first is absolute and unchanged —it was what it was whatever we do or say about it; the second is relative, always changing in response to the increase or refinement of knowledge. The two series correspond more or less; it is our aim to make the correspondence as exact as possible; but the actual series of events exists for us only in terms of the ideal series which we affirm and hold in memory. This is why I am forced to identify history with knowledge of history. For all practical purposes history is, for us and for the time being, what we know it to be.

It is history in this sense that I wish to reduce to its lowest terms. In order to do that I need a very simple definition. I once read that "history is the knowledge of events that have occurred in the past." That is a simple definition, but not simple enough. It contains three words that require examination. The first is knowledge. Knowledge is a formidable word. I always think of knowledge as something that is stored up in the *Encyclopaedia Britannica* or the *Summa Theologica:* something difficult to acquire, something at all events that I have not. Resenting a definition that denies me the title of historian, I therefore ask what is most essential to knowledge. Well, memory, I should think (and I mean memory in the broad sense, the memory of events inferred as well as the memory of events observed); other things are necessary too, but memory is fundamental: without memory no knowledge. So our definition becomes, "History is the memory of events that have occurred in the past." But events—the word carries an implication of something grand, like the taking of the Bastille or the Spanish-American War. An occurrence need not be spectacular to be an event. If I drive a motor car down the crooked streets of Ithaca, that is an event—something done; if the traffic cop bawls me out, that is an event—something said; if I have evil thoughts of him for so doing, that is an event—something thought. In truth anything done, said, or thought is an event, important or not as may turn out. But since we do not ordinarily speak without thinking, at least in some rudimentary way, and since the psychologists tell us that we can not think without speaking, or at least not without having anticipatory vibrations in the larynx, we may well combine thought events and speech events under one term; and so our definition becomes, "History is the memory of things said and done in the past." But the past—the word is both misleading and unnecessary: misleading, because the past, used in connection with history, seems to imply the distant past, as if history ceased before we were born; unnecessary, because after all everything said or done is already in the past as soon as it is said or done. Therefore I will omit that word, and our definition becomes, "History is the memory of things said and done." This is a definition that reduces history to its lowest terms, and yet includes everything that is essential to understanding what it really is.

If the essence of history is the memory of things said and done, then it is obvious that every normal person, Mr. Everyman, knows some history. Of course we do what we can to conceal this invidious truth. Assuming a professional manner, we say that so-and-so knows no history, when we mean no more than that he failed to pass the examinations set for a higher degree; and simple-minded persons, undergraduates and others, taken in by academic classifications of knowledge, think they know no history because they have never taken a course in history in college, or have never read Gibbon's *Decline and Fall of the Roman Empire*. No doubt the academic convention has its uses, but it is one of the superficial accretions that must be stripped off if we would understand history reduced to its lowest terms. Mr. Everyman, as well as you and I, remembers things said and done, and must do so at every waking moment. Suppose Mr. Everyman to have awakened this morning unable to remember anything said or done. He would be a lost soul indeed. This has happened, this sudden loss of all historical knowledge. But normally it does not happen. Normally the memory of Mr. Everyman, when he awakens in the morning, reaches out into the country of the past and of distant places and instantaneously recreates his little world of endeavor, pulls together as it were things said and done in his yesterdays, and coördinates them with his present perceptions and with things to be said and done in his to-morrows. Without this historical knowledge, this memory of things said and done, his to-day would be aimless and his to-morrow without significance.

Since we are concerned with history in its lowest terms, we will suppose that Mr. Everyman is not a professor of history, but just an ordinary citizen without excess knowledge. Not having a lecture to prepare, his memory of things said and done, when he awakened this morning, presumably did not drag into consciousness any events connected with the Liman von Sanders mission or the Pseudo-Isidorian Decretals; it presumably dragged into consciousness an image of things said and done yesterday in the office, the highly significant fact that General Motors had dropped three points, a conference arranged for ten o'clock in the morning, a promise to play nine holes at four-thirty in the afternoon, and other historical events of similar import. Mr. Everyman knows more history than this, but at the moment of awakening this is sufficient; memory of things said and done, history functioning, at seven-thirty in the morning, in its very lowest terms, has effectively oriented Mr. Everyman in his little world of endeavor.

Yet not quite effectively after all perhaps; for unaided memory is notoriously fickle; and it may happen that Mr. Everyman, as he drinks his coffee, is uneasily aware of something said or done that he fails now to recall. A common enough occurrence, as we all know to our sorrow—this remembering, not the historical event, but only that there was an event which we ought to remember but can not. This is Mr. Everyman's difficulty, a bit of history lies dead and inert in the sources, unable to do any work for Mr. Everyman because his memory refuses to bring it alive in consciousness. What then does Mr. Everyman do? He does what any historian would do: he does a bit of historical research in the sources. From his little Private Record Office (I mean his vest pocket) he takes a book in MS., volume XXXV, it may be, and turns to page 23, and there he reads: "December 29, pay Smith's coal bill, 20 tons, $1017.20." Instantaneously a series of historical events comes to life in Mr. Everyman's mind. He has an image of himself ordering twenty tons of coal from Smith last summer, of Smith's wagons driving up to his house, and of the precious coal sliding dustily through the cellar window. Historical events, these are, not so important as the forging of the Isidorian Decretals, but still important to Mr. Everyman: historical events which he was not present to observe, but which, by an artificial extension of memory, he can form a clear picture of, because he has done a little original research in the manuscripts preserved in his Private Record Office.

The picture Mr. Everyman forms of Smith's wagons delivering the coal at his house is a picture of things said and done in the past. But it does not stand alone, it is not a pure antiquarian image to be enjoyed for its own sake; on the contrary, it is associated with a picture of things to be said and done in the future; so that throughout the day Mr. Everyman intermittently holds in mind, together with a picture of Smith's coal wagons, a picture of himself going at four o'clock in the afternoon to Smith's office in order to pay his bill. At four o'clock Mr. Everyman is accordingly at Smith's office. "I wish to pay that coal bill," he says. Smith looks dubious and disappointed, takes down a ledger (or a filing case), does a bit of original research in his Private Record Office, and announces: "You don't owe me any money, Mr. Everyman. You ordered the coal here all right, but I didn't have the kind you wanted, and so turned the order over to Brown. It was Brown delivered your coal; he's the man you owe." Whereupon Mr. Everyman goes to Brown's office; and Brown takes down a ledger, does a bit of original research in his Private Record Office, which happily confirms the researches of Smith; and Mr. Everyman pays his bill, and in the evening, after returning from the Country Club, makes a further search in another collection of documents, where, sure enough, he finds a bill from Brown, properly drawn, for twenty tons of stove coal, $1017.20. The research is now completed. Since his mind rests satisfied, Mr. Everyman has found the explanation of the series of events that concerned him.

Mr. Everyman would be astonished to learn that he is an historian, yet it is obvious, isn't it, that he has performed all the essential operations involved in historical research. Needing or wanting to do something (which happened to be, not to deliver a lecture or write a book, but to pay a bill; and this is what misleads him and us as to what he is really doing), the first step was to recall things said and done. Unaided memory proving inadequate, a further step was essential—the examination of certain documents in order to discover the necessary but as yet unknown facts. Unhappily the documents were found to give conflicting reports, so that a critical comparison of the texts had to be instituted in order to eliminate error. All this having been satisfactorily accomplished, Mr. Everyman is ready for the final operation—the formation in his mind, by an artificial extension of memory, of a picture, a definitive picture let us hope, of a selected series of historical events—of himself ordering coal from Smith, of Smith turning the order over to Brown, and of Brown delivering the coal at his house. In the light of this picture Mr. Everyman could, and did, pay his bill. If Mr. Everyman had undertaken these researches in order to write a book instead of to pay a bill, no one would think of denying that he was an historian.

I have tried to reduce history to its lowest terms, first by defining it as the memory of things said and done, second by showing concretely how the memory of things said and done is essential to the performance of the simplest acts of daily life. I wish now to note the more general implications of Mr. Everyman's activities. In the realm of affairs Mr. Everyman has been paying his coal bill; in the realm of consciousness he has been doing that fundamental thing which enables man alone to have, properly speaking, a history: he has been reënforcing and enriching his immediate perceptions to the end that he may live in a world of semblance more spacious and satisfying than is to be found within the narrow confines of the fleeting present moment.

We are apt to think of the past as dead, the future as nonexistent, the present alone as real; and prematurely wise or disillusioned counselors have urged us to burn always with "a hard, gemlike flame" in order to give "the highest quality to the moments as they pass, and simply for those moments' sake." This no doubt is what the glowworm does; but I think that man, who alone is properly aware that the present moment passes, can for that very reason make no good use of the present moment simply for its own sake. Strictly speaking, the present doesn't exist for us, or is at best no more than an infinitesimal point in time, gone before we can note it as present. Nevertheless, we must have a present; and so we create one by robbing the past, by holding on to the most recent events and pretending that they all belong to our immediate perceptions. If, for example, I raise my arm, the total event is a series of occurrences of which the first are past before the last have taken place; and yet you perceive it as a single movement executed in one present instant. This telescoping of successive events into a single instant philosophers call the "specious present." Doubtless they would assign rather narrow limits to the specious present; but I will willfully make a free use of it, and say that we can extend the specious present as much as we like. In common speech we do so: we speak of the "present hour," the "present year," the "present generation." Perhaps all living creatures have a specious present; but man has this superiority, as [Blaise] Pascal says, that he is aware of himself and the universe, can as it were hold himself at arm's length and with some measure of objectivity watch himself and his fellows functioning in the world during a brief span of allotted years. Of all the creatures, man alone has a specious present that may be deliberately and purposefully enlarged and diversified and enriched.

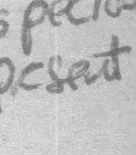

The extent to which the specious present may thus be enlarged and enriched will depend upon knowledge, the artificial extension of memory, the memory of things said and done in the past and distant places. But not upon knowledge alone; rather upon knowledge directed by purpose. The specious present is an unstable pattern of thought, incessantly changing in response to our immediate perceptions and the purposes that arise therefrom. At any given moment each one of us (professional historian no less than Mr. Everyman) weaves into this unstable pattern such actual or artificial memories as may be necessary to orient us in our little world of endeavor. But to be oriented in our little world of endeavor we must be prepared for what is coming to us (the payment of a coal bill, the delivery of a presidential address, the establishment of a League of Nations, or whatever); and to be prepared for what is coming to us it is necessary, not only to recall certain past events, but to anticipate (note I do not say predict) the future. Thus from the specious present, which always includes more or less of the past, the future refuses to be excluded; and the more of the past we drag into the specious present, the more an hypothetical, patterned future is likely to crowd into it also. Which comes first, which is cause and which effect, whether our memories construct a pattern of past events at the behest of our desires and hopes, or whether our desires and hopes spring from a pattern of past events imposed upon us by experience and knowledge, I shall not attempt to say. What I suspect is that memory of past and anticipation of future events work together, go hand in hand as it were in a friendly way, without disputing over priority and leadership.

At all events they go together, so that in a very real sense it is impossible to divorce history from life: Mr. Everyman can not do what he needs or desires to do without recalling past events; he can not recall past events without in some subtle fashion relating them to what he needs or desires to do. This is the natural function of history, of history reduced to its lowest terms, of history conceived as the memory of things said and done: memory of things said and done (whether in our immediate yesterdays or in the long past of mankind), running hand in hand with the anticipation of things to be said and done, enables us, each to the extent of his knowledge and imagination, to be intelligent, to push back the narrow confines of the fleeting present moment so that what we are doing may be judged in the light of what we have done and what we hope to do. In this sense all *living* history, as [Benedetto] Croce says, is contemporaneous: in so far as we think the past (and otherwise the past, however fully related in documents, is nothing to us) it becomes an integral and living part of our present world of semblance.

It must then be obvious that living history, the ideal series of events that we affirm and hold in memory, since it is so intimately associated with what we are doing and with what we hope to do, can not be precisely the same for all at any given time, or the same for one generation as for another. History in this sense can not be reduced to a verifiable set of statistics or formulated in terms of universally valid mathematical formulas. It is rather an imaginative creation, a personal possession which each one of us, Mr. Everyman, fashions out of his individual experience, adapts to his practical or emotional needs, and adorns as well as may be to suit his aesthetic tastes. In thus creating his own history, there are, nevertheless, limits which Mr. Everyman may not overstep without incurring penalties. The limits are set by his fellows. If Mr. Everyman lived quite alone in an unconditioned world he would be free to affirm and hold in memory any ideal series of events that struck his fancy, and thus create a world of semblance quite in accord with the heart's desire. Unfortunately, Mr. Everyman has to live in a world of Browns and Smiths; a sad experience, which has taught him the expediency of recalling certain events with much exactness. In all the immediately practical affairs of life Mr. Everyman is a good historian, as expert, in conducting the researches necessary for paying his coal bill, as need be. His expertness comes partly from long practice, but chiefly from the circumstance that his researches are prescribed and guided by very definite and practical objects which concern him intimately. The problem of what documents to consult, what facts to select, troubles Mr. Everyman not at all. Since he is not writing a book on "Some Aspects of the Coal Industry Objectively Considered," it does not occur to him to collect all the facts and let them speak for themselves. Wishing merely to pay his coal bill, he selects only such facts as may be relevant; and not wishing to pay it twice, he is sufficiently aware, without ever having read Bernheim's *Lehrbuch,*[1] that the relevant facts

[1] *Lehrbuch der historischen Methode,* by Ernst Bernheim (Leipzig, 1889),

must be clearly established by the testimony of independent witnesses not self-deceived. He does not know, or need to know, that his personal interest in the performance is a disturbing bias which will prevent him from learning the whole truth or arriving at ultimate causes. Mr. Everyman does not wish to learn the whole truth or to arrive at ultimate causes. He wishes to pay his coal bill. That is to say, he wishes to adjust himself to a practical situation, and on that low pragmatic level he is a good historian precisely because he is not disinterested: he will solve his problems, if he does solve them, by virtue of his intelligence and not by virtue of his indifference.

Nevertheless, Mr. Everyman does not live by bread alone; and on all proper occasions his memory of things said and done, easily enlarging his specious present beyond the narrow circle of daily affairs, will, must inevitably, in mere compensation for the intolerable dullness and vexation of the fleeting present moment, fashion for him a more spacious world than that of the immediately practical. He can readily recall the days of his youth, the places he has lived in, the ventures he has made, the adventures he has had—all the crowded events of a lifetime; and beyond and around this central pattern of personally experienced events, there will be embroidered a more dimly seen pattern of artificial memories, memories of things reputed to have been said and done in past times which he has not known, in distant places which he has not seen. This outer pattern of remembered events that encloses and completes the central pattern of his personal experience Mr. Everyman has woven, he could not tell you how, out of the most diverse threads of information, picked up in the most casual way, from the most unrelated sources—from things learned at home and in school, from knowledge gained in business or profession, from newspapers glanced at, from books (yes, even history books) read or heard of, from remembered scraps of newsreels or educational films or *ex-cathedra* utterances of presidents and kings, from fifteen-minute discourses on the history of civilization broadcast by the courtesy (it may be) of Pepsodent, the Bulova Watch Company, or the Shepard Stores in Boston. Daily and hourly, from a thousand

was the basic manual on historical method in use until World War I. [Editor's note.]

unnoted sources, there is lodged in Mr. Everyman's mind a mass of unrelated and related information and misinformation, of impressions and images, out of which he somehow manages, undeliberately for the most part, to fashion a history, a patterned picture of remembered things said and done in past times and distant places. It is not possible, it is not essential, that this picture should be complete or completely true: it is essential that it should be useful to Mr. Everyman; and that it may be useful to him he will hold in memory, of all the things he might hold in memory, those things only which can be related with some reasonable degree of relevance and harmony to his idea of himself and of what he is doing in the world and what he hopes to do.

In constructing this more remote and far-flung pattern of remembered things, Mr. Everyman works with something of the freedom of a creative artist; the history which he imaginatively recreates as an artificial extension of his personal experience will inevitably be an engaging blend of fact and fancy, a mythical adaptation of that which actually happened. In part it will be true, in part false; as a whole perhaps neither true nor false, but only the most convenient form of error. Not that Mr. Everyman wishes or intends to deceive himself or others. Mr. Everyman has a wholesome respect for cold, hard facts, never suspecting how malleable they are, how easy it is to coax and cajole them; but he necessarily takes the facts as they come to him, and is enamored of those that seem best suited to his interests or promise most in the way of emotional satisfaction. The exact truth of remembered events he has in any ease no time, and no need, to curiously question or meticulously verify. No doubt he can, if he be an American, call up an image of the signing of the Declaration of Independence in 1776 as readily as he can call up an image of Smith's coal wagons creaking up the hill last summer. He suspects the one image no more than the other; but the signing of the Declaration, touching not his practical interests, calls for no careful historical research on his part. He may perhaps, without knowing why, affirm and hold in memory that the Declaration was signed by the members of the Continental Congress on the fourth of July. It is a vivid and sufficient image which Mr. Everyman may hold to the end of his days without incurring penalties. Neither Brown nor Smith has any interest in setting him right; nor will any court ever send him a summons for failing to recall that the Declaration, "being engrossed and compared at the table, was signed by the members" on the second of August. As an actual event, the signing of the Declaration was what it was; as a remembered event it will be, for Mr. Everyman, what Mr. Everyman contrives to make it: will have for him significance and magic, much or little or none at all, as it fits well or ill into his little world of interests and aspirations and emotional comforts.

What then of us, historians by profession? What have we to do with Mr. Everyman, or he with us? More, I venture to believe, than we are apt to think. For each of us is Mr. Everyman too. Each of us is subject to the limitations of time and place; and for each of us, no less than for the Browns and Smiths of the world, the pattern of remembered things said and done will be woven, safeguard the process how we may, at the behest of circumstance and purpose.

True it is that although each of us is Mr. Everyman, each is something more than his own historian. Mr. Everyman, being but an informal historian, is under no bond to remember what is irrelevant to his personal affairs. But we are historians by profession. Our profession, less intimately bound up with the practical activities, is to be directly concerned with the ideal series of events that is only of casual or occasional import to others; it is our business in life to be ever preoccupied with that far-flung pattern of artificial memories that encloses and completes the central pattern of individual experience. We are Mr. Everybody's historian as well as our own, since our histories serve the double purpose, which written histories have always served, of keeping alive the recollection of memorable men and events. We are thus of that ancient and honorable company of wise men of the tribe, of bards and storytellers and minstrels, of soothsayers and priests, to whom in successive ages has been entrusted the keeping of the useful myths. Let not the harmless, necessary word "myth" put us out of countenance. In the history of history a myth is a once valid but now discarded version of the human story, as our now valid versions will in due course be relegated to the category of discarded myths.

With our predecessors, the bards and story-tellers and priests, we have therefore this in common: that it is our function, as it was theirs, not to create, but to preserve and perpetuate the social tradition; to harmonize, as well as ignorance and prejudice permit, the actual and the remembered series of events; to enlarge and enrich the specious present common to us all to the end that "society" (the tribe, the nation, or all mankind) may judge of what it is doing in the light of what it has done and what it hopes to do.

History as the artificial extension of the social memory (and I willingly concede that there are other appropriate ways of apprehending human experience) is an art of long standing, necessarily so since it springs instinctively from the impulse to enlarge the range of immediate experience; and however camouflaged by the disfiguring jargon of science, it is still in essence what it has always been. History in this sense is story, in aim always a true story; a story that employs all the devices of literary art (statement and generalization, narration and description, comparison and comment and analogy) to present the succession of events in the life of man, and from the succession of events thus presented to derive a satisfactory meaning. The history written by historians, like the history informally fashioned by Mr. Everyman, is thus a convenient blend of truth and fancy, of what we commonly distinguish as "fact" and "interpretation." In primitive times, when tradition is orally transmitted, bards and story-tellers frankly embroider or improvise the facts to heighten the dramatic import of the story. With the use of written records, history, gradually differentiated from fiction, is understood as the story of events that actually occurred; and with the increase and refinement of knowledge the historian recognizes that his first duty is to be sure of his facts, let their meaning be what it may. Nevertheless, in every age history is taken to be a story of actual events from which a significant meaning may be derived; and in every age the illusion is that the present version is valid because the related facts are true, whereas former versions are invalid because based upon inaccurate or inadequate facts.

Never was this conviction more impressively displayed than in our own time—that age of erudition in which we live, or from which we are perhaps just emerging. Finding the course of history littered with the *débris* of exploded philosophies, the historians of the last century, unwilling to be forever duped, turned away (as they fondly hoped) from "interpretation" to the rigorous examination of the factual event, just as it occurred. Perfecting the technique of investigation, they laboriously collected and edited the sources of information, and with incredible persistence and ingenuity ran illusive error to earth, letting the significance of the Middle Ages wait until it was certainly known "whether Charles the Fat was at Ingelheim or Lustnau on July 1, 887," shedding their "life-blood," in many a hard-fought battle, "for the sublime truths of Sac and Soc." I have no quarrel with this so great concern with hoti's business. One of the first duties of man is not to be duped, to be aware of his world; and to derive the significance of human experience from events that never occurred is surely an enterprise of doubtful value. To establish the facts is always in order, and is indeed the first duty of the historian; but to suppose that the facts, once established in all their fullness, will "speak for themselves" is an illusion. It was perhaps peculiarly the illusion of those historians of the last century who found some special magic in the word "scientific." The scientific historian, it seems, was one who set forth the facts without injecting any extraneous meaning into them. He was the objective man whom Nietzsche described—"a mirror: accustomed to prostration before something that wants to be known, . . . he waits until something comes, and then expands himself sensitively, so that even the light footsteps and gliding past of spiritual things may not be lost in his surface and film."[2] "It is not I who speak, but history which speaks through me," was Fustel [de Coulange]'s reproof to applauding students. "If a certain philosophy emerges from this scientific history, it must be permitted to emerge naturally, of its own accord, all but independently of the will of the historian."[3] Thus the scientific historian deliberately renounced philosophy only to submit to it without being aware. His philosophy was just this, that by not taking thought a cubit would be added to his stature. With no other preconception than the will to know, the historian would reflect in his surface and film the "order of events throughout past times in all

[2] *Beyond Good and Evil* [(London ed., 1914)], p. 140.
[3] Quoted in *English Historical Review,* V, 1.

places"; so that, in the fullness of time, when innumerable patient expert scholars, by "exhausting the sources," should have reflected without refracting the truth of all the facts, the definitive and impregnable meaning of human experience would emerge of its own accord to enlighten and emancipate mankind. Hoping to find something without looking for it, expecting to obtain final answers to life's riddle by resolutely refusing to ask questions—it was surely the most romantic species of realism yet invented, the oddest attempt ever made to get something for nothing!

That mood is passing. The fullness of time is not yet, overmuch learning proves a weariness to the flesh, and a younger generation that knows not [Leopold] Von Ranke is eager to believe that Fustel's counsel, if one of perfection, is equally one of futility. Even the most disinterested historian has at least one preconception, which is the fixed idea that he has none. The facts of history are already set forth, implicitly, in the sources; and the historian who could restate without reshaping them would, by submerging and suffocating the mind in diffuse existence, accomplish the superfluous task of depriving human experience of all significance. Left to themselves, the facts do not speak; left to themselves they do not exist, not really, since for all practical purposes there is no fact until some one affirms it. The least the historian can do with any historical fact is to select and affirm it. To select and affirm even the simplest complex of facts is to give them a certain place in a certain pattern of ideas, and this alone is sufficient to give them a special meaning. However "hard" or "cold" they may be, historical facts are after all not material substances which, like bricks or scantlings, possess definite shape and clear, persistent outline. To set forth historical facts is not comparable to dumping a barrow of bricks. A brick retains its form and pressure wherever placed; but the form and substance of historical facts, having a negotiable existence only in literary discourse, vary with the words employed to convey them. Since history is not part of the external material world, but an imaginative reconstruction of vanished events, its form and substance are inseparable: in the realm of literary discourse substance, being an idea, *is* form; and form, conveying the idea, *is* substance. It is thus not the undiscriminated fact, but the perceiving mind of the historian that speaks: the special meaning which the facts are made to convey emerges from the substance-form which the historian employs to recreate imaginatively a series of events not present to perception.

In constructing this substance-form of vanished events, the historian, like Mr. Everyman, like the bards and story-tellers of an earlier time, will be conditioned by the specious present in which alone he can be aware of his world. Being neither omniscient nor omnipresent, the historian is not the same person always and everywhere; and for him, as for Mr. Everyman, the form and significance of remembered events, like the extension and velocity of physical objects, will vary with the time and place of the observer. After fifty years we can clearly see that it was not history which spoke through Fustel, but Fustel who spoke through history. We see less clearly perhaps that the voice of Fustel was the voice, amplified and freed from static as one may say, of Mr. Everyman; what the admiring students applauded on that famous occasion was neither history nor Fustel, but a deftly colored pattern of selected events which Fustel fashioned, all the more skillfully for not being aware of doing so, in the service of Mr. Everyman's emotional needs—the emotional satisfaction, so essential to Frenchmen at that time, of perceiving that French institutions were not of German origin. And so it must always be. Played upon by all the diverse, unnoted influences of his own time, the historian will elicit history out of documents by the same principle, however more consciously and expertly applied, that Mr. Everyman employs to breed legends out of remembered episodes and oral tradition.

Berate him as we will for not reading our books, Mr. Everyman is stronger than we are, and sooner or later we must adapt our knowledge to his necessities. Otherwise he will leave us to our own devices, leave us it may be to cultivate a species of dry professional arrogance growing out of the thin soil of antiquarian research. Such research, valuable not in itself but for some ulterior purpose, will be of little import except in so far as it is transmuted into common knowledge. The history that lies inert in unread books does no work in the world. The history that does work in the world, the history that influences the course of history, is living history, that pattern of remembered events, whether true or false, that enlarges and enriches the collective specious present, the specious present of Mr. Everyman. It is for this reason that the history of history is a record of the "new history" that in every age rises to confound and supplant the old. It should be a relief to us to renounce omniscience, to recognize that every generation, our own included, will, must inevitably, understand the past and anticipate the future in the light of its own restricted experience, must inevitably play on the dead whatever tricks it finds necessary for its own peace of mind. The appropriate trick for any age is not a malicious invention designed to take anyone in, but an unconscious and necessary effort on the part of "society" to understand what it is doing in the light of what it has done and what it hopes to do. We, historians by profession, share in this necessary effort. But we do not impose our version of the human story on Mr. Everyman; in the end it is rather Mr. Everyman who imposes his version on us—compelling us, in an age of political revolution, to see that history is past politics, in an age of social stress and conflict to search for the economic interpretation. If we remain too long recalcitrant, Mr. Everyman will ignore us, shelving our recondite works behind glass doors rarely opened. Our proper function is not to repeat the past but to make use of it, to correct and rationalize for common use Mr. Everyman's mythological adaptation of what actually happened. We are surely under bond to be as honest and as intelligent as human frailty permits; but the secret of our success in the long run is in conforming to the temper of Mr. Everyman, which we seem to guide only because we are so sure, eventually, to follow it.

Neither the value nor the dignity of history need suffer by regarding it as a foreshortened and incomplete representation of the reality that once was, an unstable pattern of remembered things redesigned and newly colored to suit the convenience of those who make use of it. Nor need our labors be the less highly prized because our task is limited, our contributions of incidental and temporary significance. History is an indispensable even though not the highest form of intellectual endeavor, since it makes, as Santayana says, a gift of "great interests . . . to the heart. A barbarian is no less subject to the past than is the civic man who knows what the past is and means to be loyal to it; but the barbarian, for want of a transpersonal memory, crawls among superstitions which he cannot understand or revoke and among people whom he may hate or love, but whom he can never think of raising to a higher plane, to the level of a purer happiness. The whole dignity of human endeavor is thus bound up with historic issues, and as conscience needs to be controlled by experience if it is to become rational, so personal experience itself needs to be enlarged ideally if the failures and successes it reports are to touch impersonal interests."[4]

I do not present this view of history as one that is stable and must prevail. Whatever validity it may claim, it is certain, on its own premises, to be supplanted; for its premises, imposed upon us by the climate of opinion in which we live and think, predispose us to regard all things, and all principles of things, as no more than "inconsistent modes or fashions," as but the "concurrence, renewed from moment to moment, of forces parting sooner or later on their way." It is the limitation of the genetic approach to human experience that it must be content to transform problems since it can never solve them. However accurately we may determine the "facts" of history, the facts themselves and our interpretations of them, and our interpretation of our own interpretations, will be seen in a different perspective or a less vivid light as mankind moves into the unknown future. Regarded historically, as a process of becoming, man and his world can obviously be understood only tentatively, since it is by definition something still in the making, something as yet unfinished. Unfortunately for the permanent contribution and the universally valid philosophy, time passes: time, the enemy of man as the Greeks thought; to-morrow and to-morrow and to-morrow creeps in this petty pace, and all our yesterdays diminish and grow dim: so that, in the lengthening perspective of the centuries, even the most striking events (the Declaration of Independence, the French Revolution, the Great War itself; like the Diet of Worms before them, like the signing of the Magna Carta and the coronation of Charlemagne and the crossing of the Rubicon and the battle of Marathon) must in-

[4] *The Life of Reason* [5 vols. (New York, 1905–6)], V, 68.

evitably, for posterity, fade away into pale replicas of the original picture, for each succeeding generation losing, as they recede into a more distant past, some significance that once was noted in them, some quality of enchantment that once was theirs.

2. On Believing What One Reads:

The Dangers of Popular Revisionism

In the hands of the unsophisticated, or of True Believers who would wish to reshape the past for their own purposes, historical relativism is a dangerous weapon. In truth, not every man can be his own historian, for the gap between decisions made within one's private life and those decisions made in one's public capacity is often dangerously narrow. If, as an individual, I decide that I dislike most people who speak with a particular accent, such an irrational fancy is my business; but if, as a teacher, I decide to bar from my class those same people, my fancy has become the public's business. The historian must keep open the channels for disagreement and reinterpretation, but his professional training, if not his common sense, will also remind him that revisionism has natural limits—limits imposed by the evidence. He will resist attempts to read into evidence interpretations that are insupportable, to rewrite the history of a people in order to favor an ascendant group (as in Stalin's Russia). In short, one must remember that it is usually the victor who writes the histories, both to account for the triumphs and to help sustain them. The historian, by his nature, must speak for the historical underdog—for those who have not survived to tell their tales, as well as for the victor.

Between historical relativism and historical positivism falls a shadow, a shadow which darkens the ground most commonly sought by historians when they turn to assessing the meaning of the evidence they find and of the experiences they describe. This consensus school recognizes that history is neither an art nor a science in the usual meanings of the words, and that, in the hands of those who demand justification from their history, it too often is akin to a religion. Armed with a healthy skepticism, such historians ask, "Can we believe our own history?" as C. Vann Woodward does in the following essay. Woodward, now Sterling Professor of History at Yale University, is a noted student of the South. Born in Arkansas, educated in Georgia and North Carolina, but with teaching experience in the West as well as the North, Woodward has been able to see America's regional identities in the larger national perspective. As he concludes here—in an address originally delivered at Johns Hopkins University, where for fifteen years Dr. Woodward trained graduate students—we must remember that, however relatively we may view it, the past was real. We seek to understand both that real past, as it actually occurred, and also to understand the myths that have fed on that past, since the latter are a part of our intellectual history as well. Evidence, therefore, consists not only of "hard facts" but also of beliefs, for myths widely enough entertained have ways of becoming true.

♦ ♦ ♦

Americans, no less than other people, have expected too much of history. They have made too many demands upon it and put it to

---

FROM C. Vann Woodward, *American Attitudes Toward History* (Oxford: Clarendon Press, 1955), pp. 1–20, reprinted with the permission of Professor Woodward. This was his Harold Vyvyan Harmsworth Professorship Inaugural Lecture, delivered before Oxford University on February 22, 1955. The address appears in a somewhat different form in the *Johns Hopkins Magazine*, V (February, 1954), 1–6, 16, © 1955 by C. Vann Woodward.

For additional reading: To follow further the problem of history as both a humanity and a social science, the reader will enjoy a collection of wise addresses by H. Stuart Hughes, of Harvard University, brought together under the title *History as Art and as Science: Twin Vistas on the Past* (New York, 1964). The advantages of skepticism and self-doubt are obvious themes in detective fiction as well, of course; a notable example is Robert van Gulik's tale of his T'ang Empire protagonist, Judge Dee, in *The Chinese Nail Murders,* which draws upon van Gulik's own scholarly research into early Chinese administrative history.

too many questionable uses. In fact, it is probable that Americans have for certain reasons made more exorbitant demands upon history than have other peoples.

For one thing, history has had to serve Americans as a source of the folk-lore, myth, and legend that seems essential to the spiritual comfort of a people in time of stress. Other nations were born with the heritage of a long and misty prehistoric past that served as a limitless source of myth and legend. Even Israel, the youngest of nations, was endowed with a rich heritage of this sort and has lost no time in exploiting it. Soviet Russia in time of national crisis and invasion could supplement her dialectical myth with legend from an heroic age. But the American past fell entirely within the historic era, from the age of discovery, exploration, and settlement on down to the present. What prehistory there was belonged rightfully to the red Indian, and remained about the only part of his heritage the white man has left him. After celebrating their independence from the mother country the Americans felt a little lonely in their wilderness. As Lloyd Lewis remarked, they discovered that having banished King George they had lost King Arthur, and along with him a host of patron saints and familiar deities. Likewise the immigrants from Northern Europe and the Mediterranean who cast their lot with the Anglo-Americans also found themselves bereft of their hero gods and folk-legends.

Myth-hungry and legend-starved, the Americans set about peopling their wilderness with folk-gods constructed from their own history. The tall tales and credulous minds of the American frontier were fruitful sources of myth. Popular leaders became folk-legends before they were good and dead. Political hagiography preceded political biography in America, and the two were sometimes confused.

The most elaborate creation of American political hagiography is the Abraham Lincoln legend. It required 1,079 pages of bibliography merely to list the books and pamphlets published by 1939 on the Civil War President. Since his death in 1865 an average of more than fifty books and pamphlets a year have been published on Lincoln. The industry is still expanding. . . .

Towering bibliographical monuments to other historical figures are still under construction. Unprecedented among editions of the works of modern political figures for completeness and thoroughness is a forty-volume shelf of the papers of Thomas Jefferson, now in process of appearing. An elaborate edition of the works of Benjamin Franklin has been undertaken on a comparable scale. The space crisis that plagues librarians has been augmented by thirty-nine volumes of the writings of George Washington, and monumental editions of the works of the two Roosevelt Presidents. A National Historical Publications Commission has recommended to President Eisenhower government publication of the papers of 361 American leaders. New-model American biographies threaten to surpass the three-decker model of Victorian England in size and length of shelf covered if in nothing else. . . . American biographers have difficulty living long enough to complete works of the size now projected. Douglas Southall Freeman did complete seven volumes on Robert E. Lee and his lieutenants, but died . . . after publishing only five of the seven huge volumes of the life of Washington he planned. James G. Randall died after only three of his volumes on Lincoln had appeared.

By no means all the examples I have cited can be classified as American hagiography, for they include some of our finest historical scholarship. But the sheer scale of these works, the zest and devotion of rival schools of interpretation, and the dedicated zeal with which scholars dig for minutiae and debate fine points, cannot be fully explained without taking into account the impulse of filial piety. One is at a loss to find a counterpart for this activity in modern times apart from Russia, and the Russians are handicapped by having only one generation of post-Revolutionary history upon which to operate and by an appalling turnover of saints in an already thinly populated pantheon.

Americans use their history not only as a source of myth and an object of filial piety, but as a substitute for political theory. Developing this thesis in a recent book, Daniel Boorstin has pointed out that America has never produced a political theorist of first rank, and that as a people they have exhibited a singular indifference to political theory and dogma. Instead they have sought their values, the meaning of their experience, and a chart for their future in their history. The assumption has always been that there is in their past a sort of proto-American theory that, if properly understood, will prove adequate to all exigencies. If it is flouted or ignored, on the other hand, the result will be disaster or peril. Any flouting of it is labelled "un-American." And any new policy or legislation or administrative change must be squared somehow with this proto-American theory before it is acceptable.

The American Clio has been placed in the role of a sacred oracle from whom the meaning of events and the pathway of the future are periodically sought. The answers the oracle has given have been in the form of reinterpretations of American history. And the interpreters of the Oracle have not always belonged to Clio's ordained priesthood of historians.

One of the major official interpreters of the Oracle is the Supreme Court of the United States. Although that august body is concerned with the interpretation of a written constitution, it has not considered itself bound by earlier opinions. It has felt free to overrule former decisions, to re-examine the words of the Founding Fathers, and to discover in them different and hitherto unsuspected meanings, remarkably applicable to the issues of the moment. By this means an eighteenth-century document, the oldest written constitution in existence, has been found to anticipate magically the strange and sudden shifts of policy and the unforeseeable needs of the nineteenth and twentieth centuries.

Similarly the framers of our foreign policy have diligently consulted the Oracle. Washington's Farewell Address and Monroe's Doctrine have been found to mean one thing at one time and another at another time. Sacred text has been used to sanction both isolationism and, within a very brief interval, interventionism and internationalism as well.

When Americans fall upon hard times and it becomes clear that drastic remedies must be used, as in the late depression, they do not evolve theories of revolution to justify change, but reinterpret their past and seek therein precedent and sanction for radical experiment with old institutions. In this manner little difficulty has been encountered in finding sanction for such diverse movements as Jacksonian Democracy, Reconstruction, Theodore Roosevelt's Square Deal, Wilson's New Freedom, Franklin Roosevelt's New Deal, and Truman's Fair Deal. All have been found to be orthodox and to square with the proto-American theory. In fact American radicalism has typically, though not always, rallied to the cry of restoring the true faith and throwing the corrupters out of the temple. The American Revolutionists, with assistance from Burke, proclaimed their cause to be the protection of constitutional rights against English innovators. Abolitionism made little headway so long as its leaders believed in burning the Constitution, and succeeded only when Lincoln presented it as a means of conserving the system which, in his words, "our fathers brought forth on this continent" some "four score and seven years ago"! During the American Civil War both North and South declared themselves to be fighting to preserve the true interpretation of the Constitution, the *true* faith.

In moods of disenchantment and cynicism and self-criticism Americans have not contrived nihilistic or anarchist theories but have reinterpreted their past again, this time in an iconoclastic spirit, debunked their heroes, ridiculed the Puritan theocracy, and dwelt on the human motives of the Founding Fathers and Constitution Framers. Other moods, ranging from complacency to hysterical insecurity, have registered themselves in laboured reinterpretations of American history.

These habits of mind contrast strongly with an old and widely accepted stereotype about America, that originated in Europe, but one in which Americans themselves have sometimes believed. The European stereotype is that America is a country without respect for tradition and ties with the past, where anything new can happen and utopias breed like flies. The fact is that so far as political institutions are concerned something like the reverse is true—that Europe since 1789, and especially in the twentieth century, is a continent of broken historical continuity where the ties of tradition have not prevented vacillations from one extreme dogma to its opposite. And in the meantime America has contrived to live since 1789 in an historical continuum in which tradition has been the very life of the political system.

There are those who would congratulate Americans upon their attitude toward history as the secret which has rendered them immune from the poisonous dogmas of extreme right and extreme left, which have infected a good part of the rest of the world. On this point, however, there is ground for serious doubt. For a facility in the manipulation of the past is a two-edged weapon, a weapon that the dogmatists have used with greater effect than the traditionalists. Americans, as we have seen, have acquired over the years a rather dangerous dependence upon this weapon. It is of dubious value in the defence of freedom. There is reason to believe, in fact, that it is better adapted to the uses of the enemies than to the purposes of the friends of free society.

Those who have read George Orwell's *1984* will recall a scene between the Commissar and Winston Smith, a sort of archivist in the Ministry of Truth whose job it was to keep the records in conformity with the changing party line. He had faltered in the faith and the Commissar instructed him forceably in these words: "We the Party, control all records, and we control all memories. Then we control the past, do we not?" The Commissar then quoted a party slogan: "Who controls the past controls the future; who controls the present controls the past."

Now the year 1984 was by no means the first in which "the Party" sought to control the past. It is a practice at least as old as recorded history. Those who control the present have always found it expedient to extend their control in some measure over the past. Americans, with their special sensitivity to history, and their old habit of manipulating it, have not been at all backward in this enterprise.

In 1776, when the Founding Fathers took the path of treason and revolution, their first care was to seize control of the history of colonial America. Thomas Jefferson pictured it in the Declaration as "a history of repeated injuries and usurpations" that included "works of death, desolation, and tyranny" as well as "cruelty and perfidy scarcely paralleled in the most barbarous ages." He specified a staggering series of atrocities in support of his conclusion that "a prince, whose character is thus marked by every act which may define a tyrant, is unfit to be the ruler of a free people." So much for George III. It was a long time before it was entirely safe for an American historian to point out that George was a comparatively mild monarch, that British rule of the American colonies was exceptionally liberal, and that it was not very consistent of the colonists to enlist as an ally in their crusade against monarchy the much more absolute monarch of France.

In 1787, when the Federalists resolved to overthrow the first American constitution and impose the present one, their first endeavor and main reliance in propaganda was to control the public memory of the history of the Confederation. So successful were they in blackening the record of our first constitutional government that to this day the period of the Confederation is popularly conceived of as a time of confusion, bankruptcy, anarchy, and disgrace. A century and a half was to elapse before investigation revealed that it was instead a period of growing prosperity, rapid reconstruction, and peaceful contentment—save on the part of an ambitious minority.

In 1798 a powerful faction of the party that had overthrown the Confederation and established the new government wished to drag the country into a war against France. Party propagandists fell vigorously to the work of manipulating the past and revising history to suit the party line. They systematically obscured in the public mind the memory of America's debt to France, the alliance of 1778, and the French military aid that saved their skins and won the Revolution. They also sought to destroy the pro-French sympathy that had swept America in 1789, when their popular ally followed their example and joined the ranks of revolutionary republican governments. In place of all this, enterprising Federalist controllers of the past substituted an image of a treacherous France, led by sinister revolutionists and filthy Jacobin atheists, enemies of mankind, bent upon undermining morals and subverting all order. French nationals were made subject to deportation or imprisonment. Americans of the Jeffersonian party were smeared with guilt by association, charged with sympathy for Jacobin principles, with promoting the cause of Jacobinism, with reading Jacobin literature, with dining in private with Jacobin agents.

Skipping two generations that are by no means barren of additional instances of this American proclivity for controlling the past, I turn for my next illustration to the period of sectional struggle preceding the Civil War. This great struggle for the control of the American future was preceded by a struggle for the control of the American past. Embarking upon a contest for power that would not be complete until the North had subjected the South to military conquest and then imposed its political and economic system upon the conquered people by dictatorship, the aggressive party in the North required strong justification for its course. This entailed an elaborate revision of the whole history of the South. The latter revision eventually conjured up a long-term conspiracy of treacherous men bent upon subverting the Constitution. They were the Lords of the Lash, as domineering, licentious, and impenitently wicked a crew as ever disgraced the human form. Their cruelty and brutality were said to exceed human limits. . . .

Once the Southerners united and rallied in a struggle to overthrow Northern control imposed by Reconstruction, they all but outdid the North in their wholesale revision of history. So thorough a job did they do of picturing Reconstruction as a reign of absolute terror, of black evil triumphant over white virtue, of barbarism lording it over civilization, that the North itself came to accept the propaganda as truth. One Northern historian writes of the Reconstruction period that "Never have American public men in responsible positions . . . been so brutal, hypocritical, and corrupt. . . . Brutal men, inspired by personal ambition or party motives, assumed the pose of philanthropists and patriots, and thus deceived and misguided vast numbers of well-meaning people in the North." Such history as this gave to international usage the word "carpetbagger" and made it a synonym of all that is despicable in public life. History such as this also left the hapless Negro with a heritage of propagandistic odium that still handicaps his struggle for basic rights.

Neither the North's image of the South's past nor the South's image of the North's past bears more than slight resemblance to the truth unearthed by historians after years of investigation. Yet each image persists fragmentarily in the public mind and furnishes additional evidence that those who control the past control the future.

A more recent example is the campaign of the American Communist party to capture strategic areas of the American past. Shrewdly grasping the American weakness for the historical approach, the party leaders adopted the slogan, "Communism is Twentieth-Century Americanism." Identifying Communism as a new-fangled Americanism, they took pains to identify it also with old-fangled Americanism. Carefully they selected edifying episodes to be rendered into parables of the class struggle. National heroes were selected to be arrayed in the garments of dialectical materialism as class leaders—for example, Tom Paine, Sam Adams, John Brown, Abraham Lincoln, and John Peter Altgeld. Biographies, monographs, pamphlets, articles, and collections of suitable source materials and documents rolled from the party presses. Strange figures from the American backwoods began to parade through the pages of history carrying the hammer and sickle. The party headquarters were adorned with portraits of the Great Emancipator, and at a Lincoln-Lenin rally in New York, Earl Browder said, "The times call again for a Lincoln, for a new party, for a new program." The campaign, as it turned out, proved abortive, but the strategy was orthodox and the American precedents were numerous.

There was nothing at all unusual about the Communists claiming Lincoln. They were merely following standard American political practice. As David Donald has pointed out, at the same time as the Communists were claiming him, Lincoln was also hailed as patron saint by the socialists, the prohibitionists, and a proponent of Union Now—not to mention the Republicans and Democrats. In the 1948 election, not only the Dewey Republicans and the Truman Democrats, but the Henry Wallace Progressives and the Dixiecrats were all for Lincoln. As Senator Everett Dirksen solemnly adjured his Republican colleagues, the first task of the politician is "to get right with . . . Lincoln."

Obviously the Communists did not originate the tactics of controlling the past. Nor did the American politicians either, for that matter. It is a device as old as history.

It is especially in periods when there occur sudden and dramatic reversals of policy on the part of major powers that the crisis in the control of the past—in other words the crisis in the integrity of history—is acute. Such a period is most certainly our own—a period which, for sudden and complete reversals of foreign policy, is comparable with few in modern history of which I am aware.

If the American Communists were embarrassed and caught off guard when Russia suddenly allied herself with Hitler's Germany, American anti-Communists were equally embarrassed when a year and a half later they suddenly found themselves embracing Russia as an ally. Then for four years America shed blood, sweat, and tears in behalf of Russia and other allies, poured out life and treasure in the common cause, rejoicing at every advance of the Red Army, cheering every victory, and bemoaning every setback. We can recall the pictures of VE Day representing laughing American soldiers stretching hands eagerly to laughing and eager Russian troops at the juncture of the two armies. That was in 1945. Then suddenly before the year was out the roles had changed again. Within a brief five years Russia was transformed by the vicissitudes of power politics from black villain to sterling hero and back again to black villain and public enemy. And the American press responded promptly with suitable sentiment and emotion. I am not suggesting that there were not understandable reasons for change in attitudes and policy, but I *am* concerned with the intellectual consequences.

One recalls Orwell's book again—the scene of the huge party rally in support of the war against Urasia. The party orator in the midst of a flight of eloquence, a tirade of hate against Urasia, is handed a dispatch saying that Urasia had suddenly switched from enemy to ally, and the former ally East Asia was now the enemy. The party orator, without changing syntax or missing a beat in his hymn of hate, in the very midst of a sentence, turned his speech into support of the new party policy of hate East Asia and love Urasia.

China is another instance of the modern magic of power politics —as witness the transformation of these brown brothers of the Orient, the darlings of missionaries, philanthropists, and capitalists, from friendly, smiling protégés into oriental monsters of unspeakable brutality and cruelty. And while this Aladdin-like magic transpired on one side of the China Sea, on the opposite side the Genie of power politics was transforming the Japanese from hideous oriental monsters of unspeakable brutality and cruelty into friendly, smiling little brown protégés.

Simultaneously, on the other side of the globe, other public enemies of yesterday were being converted with bewildering haste into cherished friends and allies. The Germans, for example, found themselves shifted overnight from the role of malevolent fiends and enemies of mankind into the champions of freedom and the bastion of defence against our former allies, the Russians. . . .

These confusing transitions in foreign policy have their counterpart in domestic affairs. Witness, for instance, what has happened to the popular esteem and affection in which the New Deal was once held. For twenty years it was a sure winner to rally majorities at the polls. In four successive presidential elections and twice that number of congressional elections, overwhelming majorities of the electorate marched to the polls in its support. In 1936 the New Deal ticket won majorities in all the forty-eight states but two. Then suddenly the New Deal became an opprobrious epithet, a smear word often sufficient to damn a man politically, and sometimes enough to call in question his loyalty and his very integrity.

Contemporaneously with sudden transitions in foreign and domestic policy there has taken place among public figures—and among some intellectuals as well—a hurried turning of coats, a lot of hasty conversions and quick changes of allegiance. Isolationists turned into interventionists, radicals into reactionaries, fellow travellers into informers, Russophobes into Russophiles and back into Russophobes. Among the professors there was a flurry of revising the textbooks and lectures, of "bringing the material up to date," of "cleaning up the new revision." One heard a good deal about "new points of view," "new schools of thought." Historians were perhaps less prone to this tendency than others, but one heard them assure each other emphatically that each generation had to rewrite history, that the old interpretations were outmoded. . . .

Orwell pictured the crude and ruthless methods his Brave New World employed to control the past. In the Ministry of Truth, it was the job of his pathetic hero, Winston Smith, the new-style historian, to revise the files of old newspapers to keep them in conformity with the ever-changing party line, to alter documents, destroy photographs, delete names, and revise reputations. At convenient intervals along the streets and in public buildings were installed "Memory Tubes," suction devices into which it was the duty of all loyal citizens to thrust any piece of historical evidence or scrap of record that deviated in any way from the current party line. This simple and direct way of controlling the past is the way of the dictatorships, which painstakingly revise history to obliterate from memory public figures, heroes, events, platforms, and policies that are inconvenient.

But there are subtler, more oblique ways of controlling the past and controlling the historian who writes about the past. These are ways whose purposes are rarely admitted, ways often designed for different purposes. At least four such ways are currently familiar to historians, especially those dealing with recent history. . . .

The first of these is the classification of documents. Obviously governments must make use of some such system to defend national security. But everyone acquainted with military or government offices will be aware of how easy it is to abuse and misuse this device. The security and welfare of national interest for which classification of documents is officially intended is sometimes confused with the security and welfare of individual, bureaucratic, or private interest. And it *can* be used to protect those interests—sometimes against national interests—by the suppression of evidence through classification into confidential, secret, or top-secret categories.

A second device is the control of archives. Most familiar in the case of private papers and records of business firms, it is found useful by governments as well. Sometimes archives are closed entirely for periods, but more often they are restricted to those who have been, to use a familiar expression, "cleared as a security risk." Thus, instead of screening the records—as in the case of classification—this device screens the historians.

A third device is putting the historian on the pay-roll. More and more often the historian is found writing the history of an institution that is paying him for his work. The independent scholar at grips with a period of the past is becoming somewhat rarer. Instead he often joins a team and works on a history of the air force, the navy, army, marines, or of government bureaus, agencies, and commissions; or of corporations, philanthropic foundations, railroads, churches, and colleges. I am not impugning the integrity of historians so employed. I have been so employed myself on occasion. But just because of that I am conscious of the abuses of which such employment is capable.

Fourth among these new ways of controlling the past is the publication of archives of selected evidence and testimony. The big congressional investigation is one American instrument for this purpose. In this manner huge shelves of volumes have been published on Pearl Harbor, State Department, foreign policies, China policy, public servants, diplomats, writers, and college professors of unpopular views. By this means, those who control the present can extend their control in some measure to the past. They can submerge large areas of history that embarrass present policy. They can also discredit public servants or intellectuals in disfavour by citing out of context opinions shared widely by informed and responsible people a few years back, opinions embodying the felt necessities of an earlier time, or public policies widely supported but which are now discredited because of changed conditions or shifts in public opinion.

Let me finally recall the corollary of the dictum that "who controls the present controls the past": it was that "who controls the past controls the future." Under this rule, Voltaire's definition of history as "a pack of tricks we play upon the dead" could be altered to read, "History is a travesty upon the unborn." As custodian of the past and keeper of the public memory, the historian under modern conditions fulfils an even more responsible and vital role—that of guardian of the future. To defend the integrity of history, as well as his own integrity, the historian must, therefore, forever contest with "those who control the present" the control of the past.

In the main, I think the historians in America have shown a commendable fortitude in their contest with those who control the present. Scarcely any popular leader in our history has been able to secure acquiescence of the historical guild in his enterprise of controlling the past. Such leaders have repeatedly met with resistance from the historians. The national trait that I have attempted to describe has been more characteristic of the popular mind than of the professional historian.

The historian's duty, however, has been rendered doubly difficult by the long-standing habit his fellow countrymen have formed of insisting that precedent and sanction must be found in their past for any departure or experiment that necessity might dictate at a given moment. His function is complicated by their custom of regarding history as an oracle that has an answer appropriate to every occasion, and by their faith in a proto-American doctrine of the Founding Fathers adequate to every exigency in the shifting fortunes of domestic and foreign politics.

The historian's defence of the integrity of American history is further complicated by the popular construction placed on the doctrine of historical relativism propounded by such influential members of his own craft as Carl Becker and Charles Beard. I raise no question with regard to the scholarship of these two historians, both of whom I greatly admire. But Becker's doctrine of "Everyman His Own Historian" and Beard's doctrine of "History as an Act of Faith" are capable, when loosely construed, of breeding mischief of a serious character among the laity. In some ways Becker and Beard could be pictured as the Martin Luther and Philipp Melanchthon of the American faith. They preached a sort of secular Reformation of relativism, a new Protestantism that gives licence to the layman to consult the sacred text for himself and seek out its meaning without mediation of the priesthood.

I am not preaching a counter-reformation against Becker and Beard, but as one of the priesthood I am expressing some misgivings regarding the popular consequences of their relativist reformation, and also some misgivings concerning the American Everyman as his own historian.

Whatever concessions the historian is prepared to make to the doctrine of relativism, he must retain a fundamentally unshakable conviction that the past is real—however hard it may be to define its nature and write an unbiased record of it. Fully conceding those difficulties, the historian must never concede that the past is alterable to conform with present convenience, with the party line, with mass prejudice, or with the ambitions of powerful popular leaders.

3. Who Killed John Doe?

The Problem of Testimony

THE PAST WAS REAL, YET TRUTH IS RELATIVE. TO MANY this will be a counsel of despair, but neither Woodward nor Becker intend such small-beer truths as these. The one does not wish us to overlook the ways in which our natural desire to show how the past is relevant to the present may lead us to distort that past, while the other wishes us to recognize that the process of historical inquiry, although not the data themselves, can quite legitimately serve present purposes. The two views are not at all incompatible, as much of Professor Woodward's own work shows, for in all his books, most notably his most famous, *The Strange Career of Jim Crow,* he demonstrates how widely-believed lies about the past have shaped Southern opinions about the future.

Both authors would agree that the historian's tasks are to formulate important—that is to say, relevant—questions, to seek out means of providing answers to those questions, and to draw interpretive conclusions from the answers. The central methodological problem for the historian, then, is to know how to interrogate witnesses, how to test evidence, how to assess the reliability and the relevance of testimony. But this does not mean, contrary to much opinion and unfortunately much practice as well, that the historian merely sets one testimony against another and applies a rigorous set of rules by which he roots out the contradictions between the witnesses. The historian, as an interrogator, wishes to know what fact may lie behind an untruth rather than merely to prove the statement to be untrue.

We can now come full circle. Properly the historian does also, for he must get back to his starting point, touching bases as he goes. I can now introduce an analysis of the problems of evidence and testimony, and the involvement of the self in both, that is rather more difficult than I would have dared to begin with. It is relevant to how the historian works as a detective, but even more relevant to how the historian also seeks for himself within his work. The final mystery, as in Muriel Sparks' *The Mandelbaum Gate,* Raymond Postgate's *Verdict of Twelve,* or Walter Van Tilburg Clark's *Ox-Bow Incident,* rests not in event but in character, and if the historian is to tell it like it happened, the character he must understand best is his own.

This is a problem to be stalked rather than met head-on. Robin G. Collingwood was concerned with the problem, which he approaches in his brilliantly written and cogently argued book, *The Idea of History,* a work of art and (although he would have rejected the term, since he disliked professional logicians) of logic which will repay close attention. He presents his argument by borrowing from the detective fiction which English dons (for such he was) are said to dote upon, that fiction of suspicious vicars, peculiar happenings within the college walls at night, and gargoyles that look down upon the Oxford Broad. After several important preliminary observations, Collingwood solves the murder of John Doe for us, much in the manner of the leisurely English detectives, almost always small town and amateur, of the nineteen-thirties. Collingwood was a historian noted for his splendid work on Roman Britain, and held the Waynflete Professorship of Metaphysical Philosophy in Oxford University.

Collingwood obviously disagrees with Carl Becker. In his perceptive and yet often curiously blind *Autobiography,* Collingwood further unfolded the growth of one man's thought, writing a history of the mind. He refuted the canard that the past was dead and discussed the dangers arising from what he called "the tiger in the grass"—the problem of deciding which tools to use for which purpose, and the related problem of understanding why history does not give us tools for several practical needs to which the demagogue, the absolutist, and the social dropout would attempt to bend the discipline. The historian, Collingwood wrote, must be able to spy the tiger in the grass, as a woodsman can find the less obvious features hidden from the careless eye of the traveler. To those who complain that there is little point to finding the tiger unless one is to be given a rifle with which to shoot him, Collingwood replied that there were two answers:

> The first is this. You want a rifle? Then go where rifles are to be had. Go to the gunsmith's. But do not expect the gunsmith to sell you a rifle which can see tigers as well as shoot them. For that, you must learn woodcraft. . . .
>
> The second is this. If you are sure that the thing you are going to see in the grass is going to be a tiger, and if your only idea about tigers is that they are things to shoot, take a rifle with you. But are you sure? What if it turns out to be your own child playing Indians?

Let us see how Collingwood uses that rifle against the murderer of John Doe.

♦ ♦ ♦

When John Doe was found, early one Sunday morning, lying across his desk with a dagger through his back, no one expected that the question who did it would be settled by means of testimony. It was

---

FROM Robin G. Collingwood, *The Idea of History* (New York: Oxford University Press, Galaxy ed., 1956), pp. 249–80. Printed with permission of Clarendon Press, Oxford.

For additional reading: I confess to a strong bias in favor of Collingwood and feel that the interested reader should see far more of him than can be given here. *An Autobiography* (London, 1939), unfortunately out of print, is a startling self-analysis, and Collingwood's own foray into applying his theories of history, in *Roman Britain* (Oxford, 1932), is exciting reading. As to the leisurely pace of John Doe and Detective-Inspector Jenkins, may I suggest to the reader R. T. Campbell's *Bodies in a Bookshop* or any of the tales of either Freeman Wills Crofts or Gladys Mitchell? Several excellent books by Ngaio Marsh might be cited here as well.

not likely that anyone saw the murder being done. It was even less likely that someone in the murderer's confidence would give him away. It was least likely of all that the murderer would walk into the village police-station and denounce himself. In spite of this, the public demanded that he should be brought to justice, and the police had hopes of doing it; though the only clue was a little fresh green paint on the handle of the dagger, like the fresh green paint on the iron gate between John Doe's garden and the rector's.

This was not because they hoped that, in time, testimony would be forthcoming. On the contrary, when it did come, in the shape of a visit from an elderly neighbouring spinster asserting that she killed John Doe with her own hand because he had made a dastardly attempt upon her virtue, even the village constable (not an exceptionally bright lad, but kindly) advised her to go home and have some aspirin. Later in the day the village poacher came along and said that he had seen the squire's gamekeeper climbing in at John Doe's study window; testimony which was treated with even less deference. Finally the rector's daughter, in a state of great agitation, rushed in and said she had done it herself; the only effect of which was to make the village constable ring up the local Inspector and remind him that the girl's young man, Richard Roe, was a medical student, and presumably knew where to find a man's heart; and that he had spent Saturday night at the rectory, within a stone's throw of the dead man's house.

There had been a thunderstorm that night, with heavy rain, between twelve and one; and the Inspector, when he questioned the rectory parlour-maid (for the living was a good one), was told that Mr. Roe's shoes had been very wet in the morning. Questioned, Richard admitted having gone out in the middle of the night, but refused to say where or why.

John Doe was a blackmailer. For years he had been blackmailing the rector, threatening to publish the facts about a certain youthful escapade of his dead wife. Of this escapade the rector's supposed daughter, born six months after marriage, was the fruit; and John Doe had letters in his possession that proved it. By now he had absorbed the whole of the rector's private fortune, and on the morning of the fatal Saturday he demanded an instalment of his wife's, which she had left to him in trust for her child. The rector made up his mind to end it. He knew that John Doe sat at his desk late into the night; he knew that behind him, as he sat, there was a french window on the left and a trophy of Eastern weapons on the right; and that on hot nights the window was left open until he went to bed. At midnight, wearing gloves, he slipped out; but Richard, who had noticed his state of mind and was troubled about it, happened to be leaning out of his window and saw the rector cross the garden. He hurried into his clothes and followed; but by the time he reached the garden the rector was gone. At this moment the thunderstorm broke. Meanwhile the rector's plan had succeeded perfectly. John Doe was asleep, his head fallen forward on a pile of old letters. Only after the dagger had reached his heart did the rector look at them, and see his wife's handwriting. The envelopes were addressed "John Doe, Esq." Until that moment, he had never known who his wife's seducer had been.

It was Detective-Inspector Jenkins of Scotland Yard, called in by the Chief Constable at the entreaty of his old friend's little girl, who found in the rectory dustbin a lot of ashes, mostly from writing paper, but including some from leather, probably a pair of gloves. The wet paint on John Doe's garden gate—he had painted it himself that day, after tea—explained why the gloves might have been destroyed; and among the ashes were metal buttons bearing the name of a famous glove-maker in Oxford Street whom the rector always patronized. More of John Doe's paint was found on the right cuff of a jacket, ruined as to shape by a recent wetting, which on Monday the rector bestowed on a deserving parishioner. The Detective-Inspector was severely blamed, later on, for allowing the rector to see in what direction his inquiries were tending, and thus giving him an opportunity to take cyanide and cheat the hangman.

The methods of criminal detection are not at every point identical with those of scientific history, because their ultimate purpose is not the same. A criminal court has in its hands the life and liberty of a citizen, and in a country where the citizen is regarded as having rights the court is therefore bound to do something and do it quickly. The time taken to arrive at a decision is a factor in the value (that is, the justice) of the decision itself. If any juror says: "I feel certain that a year hence, when we have all reflected on the evidence at leisure, we shall be in a better position to see what it means," the reply will be: "There is something in what you say; but what you propose is impossible. Your business is not just to give a verdict; it is to give a verdict now; and here you stay until you do it." This is why a jury has to content itself with something less than scientific (historical) proof, namely with that degree of assurance or belief which would satisfy it in any of the practical affairs of daily life.

The student of historical method will hardly find it worth his while, therefore, to go closely into the rules of evidence, as these are recognized in courts of law. For the historian is under no obligation to make up his mind within any stated time. Nothing matters to him except that his decision, when he reaches it, shall be right: which means, for him, that it shall follow inevitably from the evidence.

So long as this is borne in mind, however, the analogy between legal methods and historical methods is of some value for the understanding of history; of sufficient value, I think, to justify my having put before the reader in outline the above sample of a literary genre which in the absence of any such motive it would, of course, be beneath his dignity to notice. . . .

"History," said [J. B.] Bury, "is a science; no less, and no more." Perhaps it is no less: that depends on what you mean by a science. There is a slang usage, like that for which "hall" means a music-hall or "pictures" moving pictures, according to which "science" means natural science. Whether history is a science in that sense of the word, however, need not be asked; for in the tradition of European speech . . . the word "science" means any organized body of knowledge. If that is what the word means, Bury is so far incontestably right, that history is a science, nothing less.

But if it is no less, it is certainly more. For anything that is a science at all must be more than merely a science; it must be a science of some special kind. A body of knowledge is never merely organized, it is always organized in some particular way. Some bodies of knowledge, like meteorology, are organized by collecting observations concerned with events of a certain kind which the scientist can watch as they happen, though he cannot produce them at will. Others, like chemistry, are organized not only by observing events as they happen, but by making them happen under strictly controlled conditions. Others again are organized not by observing events at all, but by making certain assumptions and proceeding with the utmost exactitude to argue out their consequences.

History is organized in none of these ways. Wars and revolutions, and the other events with which it deals, are not deliberately produced by historians under laboratory conditions in order to be studied with scientific precision. Nor are they even observed by historians, in the sense in which events are observed by natural scientists. Meteorologists and astronomers will make arduous and expensive journeys in order to observe for themselves events of the kinds in which they are interested, because their standard of observation is such that they cannot be satisfied with descriptions by inexpert witnesses; but historians do not fit out expeditions to countries where wars and revolutions are going on. And this is not because historians are less energetic or courageous than natural scientists, or less able to obtain the money such expeditions would cost. It is because the facts which might be learned through such expeditions, like the facts which might be learned through the deliberate fomenting of a war or a revolution at home, would not teach historians anything they want to know.

The sciences of observation and experiment are alike in this, that their aim is to detect the constant or recurring features in all events of a certain kind. A meteorologist studies one cyclone in order to compare it with others; and by studying a number of them he hopes to find out what features in them are constant, that is, to find out what cyclones as such are like. But the historian has no such aim. If you find him on a certain occasion studying the Hundred Years War or the Revolution of 1688, you cannot infer that he is in the preliminary stages of an inquiry whose ultimate aim is to reach conclusions about wars or revolutions as such. If he is in the preliminary stages of any inquiry, it is more likely to be a general study of the Middle Ages or the seventeenth century. This is because the sciences of observation and experiment are organized in one way and history is organized in another. In the organization of meteorology, the ulterior value of what has been observed about one cyclone is conditioned by its relation to what has been observed about other cyclones. In the organization of history, the ulterior value of what is known about the Hundred Years War is conditioned, not by its relation to what is known about other wars, but by its relation to what is known about other things that people did in the Middle Ages.

Equally obvious is the difference between the organization of history and that of the "exact" sciences. It is true that in history, as in exact science, the normal process of thought is inferential; that is to say, it begins by asserting this or that, and goes on to ask what it proves. But the starting-points are of very different kinds. In exact science they are assumptions, and the traditional way of expressing them is in sentences beginning with a word of command prescribing that a certain assumption be made: "Let ABC be a triangle, and let AB=AC." In history they are not assumptions, they are facts, and facts coming under the historian's observation, such as, that on the page open before him there is printed what purports to be a charter by which a certain king grants certain lands to a certain monastery. The conclusions, too, are of different kinds. In exact science, they are conclusions about things which have no special habitation in space or time: if they are anywhere, they are everywhere, and if they are at any time, they are at all times. In history, they are conclusions about events, each having a place and date of its own. The exactitude with which place and date are known to the historian is variable; but he always knows that there were both a place and a date, and within limits he always knows what they were; this knowledge being part of the conclusion to which he is led by arguing from the facts before him.

These differences in starting-point and conclusion imply a difference in the entire organization of the respective sciences. When a mathematician has made up his mind what the problem is which he desires to solve, the next step before him is to make assumptions which will enable him to solve it; and this involves an appeal to his powers of invention. When an historian has similarly made up his mind, his next business is to place himself in a position where he can say: "The facts which I am now observing are the facts from which I can infer the solution of my problem." His business is not to invent anything, it is to discover something. And the finished products, too, are differently organized. The scheme upon which exact sciences have been traditionally arranged depends on relations of logical priority and posteriority: one proposition is placed before a second, if understanding of the first is needed in order that the second should be understood; the traditional scheme of arrangement in history is a chronological scheme, in which one event is placed before a second if it happened at an earlier time.

History, then, is a science, but a science of a special kind. It is a science whose business is to study events not accessible to our observation, and to study these events inferentially, arguing to them from something else which is accessible to our observation, and which the historian calls "evidence" for the events in which he is interested. . . .

Francis Bacon, lawyer and philosopher, laid it down in one of his memorable phrases that the natural scientist must "put Nature to the question." What he was denying, when he wrote this, was that the scientist's attitude towards nature should be one of respectful attentiveness, waiting upon her utterances and building his theories on the basis of what she chose to vouchsafe him. What he was asserting was two things at once: first, that the scientist must take the initiative, deciding for himself what he wants to know and formulating this in his own mind in the shape of a question; and secondly, that he must find means of compelling nature to answer, devising tortures under which she can no longer hold her tongue. Here, in a single brief epigram, Bacon laid down once for all the true theory of experimental science.

It is also, though Bacon did not know this, the true theory of historical method. In scissors-and-paste history the historian takes up a pre-Baconian position. His attitude towards his authorities, as the very word shows, is one of respectful attentiveness. He waits to hear what they choose to tell him, and lets them tell it in their own way and at their own time. Even when he has invented historical criticism, and his authorities have become mere sources, this attitude is at bottom unchanged. There is a change, but it is only superficial. It consists merely in the adoption of a technique for dividing witnesses into sheep and goats. One class is disqualified from giving testimony; the other is treated exactly as authorities were treated under the old dispensation. But in scientific history, or history proper, the Baconian revolution has been accomplished. The scientific historian no doubt spends a great deal of time reading the same books that the scissors-and-paste historian used to read—Herodotus, Thucydides, Livy, Tacitus, and so forth—but he reads them in an entirely different spirit; in fact, a Baconian spirit. The scissors-and-paste historian reads them in a simply receptive spirit, to find out what they said. The scientific historian reads them with a question in his mind, having taken the initiative by deciding for himself what he wants to find out from them. Further, the scissors-and-paste historian reads them on the understanding that what they did not tell him in so many words he would never find out from them at all; the scientific historian puts them to the torture, twisting a passage ostensibly about something quite different into an answer to the question he has decided to ask. Where the scissors-and-paste historian said quite confidently "There is nothing in such-and-such an author about such-and-such a subject," the scientific or Baconian historian will reply "Oh, isn't there? Do you not see that in this passage about a totally different matter it is implied that the author took such-and-such a view of the subject about which you say his text contains nothing?"

To illustrate from my fable. The village constable does not arrest the rector's daughter and beat her periodically with a rubber truncheon until she tells him that she thinks Richard did the murder. What he tortures is not her body, but her statement that she killed John Doe. He begins by using the methods of critical history. He says to himself: "The murder was done by somebody with a good deal of strength and some knowledge of anatomy. This girl certainly hasn't the first, and probably hasn't the second; at any rate, I know she has never attended ambulance classes. Further, if she had done it she wouldn't be in such a hurry to accuse herself. The story is a lie."

At this point the critical historian would lose interest in the story and throw it in the waste-paper basket: the scientific historian begins to be interested in it, and tests it for chemical reactions. This he is able to do because, being a scientific thinker, he knows what questions to ask. "Why is she telling a lie? Because she is shielding someone. Whom is she shielding? Either her father or her young man. Is it her father? No; fancy the rector! Therefore it is her young man. Are her suspicions of him well founded? They might be; he was here at the time; he is strong enough; and he knows enough anatomy." The reader will recollect that in criminal detection probability is required, of a degree sufficient for the conduct of daily life, whereas in history we demand certainty. Apart from that, the parallel is complete. The village constable (not a clever lad, as I explained; but a scientific thinker does not have to be clever, he has to know his job, that is, know what questions to ask) has been trained in the elements of police work, and this training enables him to know what questions to ask and thus to interpret the untrue statement that she did it herself into evidence for the true conclusion that she suspects Richard Roe.

The constable's only mistake was that in the excitement of answering the question "Whom does this girl suspect?" he lost sight of the question "Who killed John Doe?" This is where Inspector Jenkins, not so much because he was a cleverer man as because he had learned the job more thoroughly, had the advantage of him. The way I see the Inspector going to work is like this.

"Why does the rector's daughter suspect Richard Roe? Probably because she knows that he was involved in something queer which happened at the rectory that night. We know that one queer thing happened at the rectory: Richard was out in the storm, and that was quite enough to make the girl suspicious. But what we want to know is, did he kill John Doe? If he did, when did he do it? After the thunderstorm broke, or before? Not before, because here are his tracks going both ways in the mud of the rectory garden path: you see them beginning a few yards from the garden door, going away from the house; so that is where he was, and that is the direction he was going in, when the downpour began. Well, did he carry mud into John Doe's study? No: none there. Did he take off his shoes before going in? Think a moment. What position was John Doe in when he was stabbed? Was he leaning back or sitting upright in his chair? No; because the chair would have protected his back. He must have been leaning right forward. Possibly, indeed probably, asleep in the position in which he still lies. How exactly did the murderer proceed? If Doe was asleep, nothing easier: step quietly inside, take the dagger and in it goes. If Doe was awake and merely leaning forward, the same might be done, but not so easily. Now, did the murderer pause outside to take off his shoes? Impossible. In either case, speed was the first thing necessary: the job had to be done before he leaned back, or woke up. So the absence of mud in the study lets Richard out.

"Then, once more, why did he go into the garden? For a walk? Not with that thunderstorm growling about. For a smoke? They smoke all over the house. To meet the girl? No signs that she was in the garden; and why should he? They had had the drawing-room to themselves ever since dinner, and the rector isn't one to shoo young people off to bed. Broad-minded sort of chap. Had trouble, I shouldn't wonder. Now, why did young Richard go into that garden? Something must have been going on there. Something queer. A second queer thing that night at the rectory, one we don't know about.

"What could it have been? If the murderer had come from the rectory, which that paint suggests he did, and if Richard saw him from his window, it might have been that; because the murderer got to Doe's house before the rain began, and Richard was caught in it ten yards from the garden door. Just time. Let's see what would follow, if the murderer did come from the rectory. Probably he went back there afterwards. No tracks in the mud; why? Because he knew the garden well enough to keep on the grass all the way, even in that pitch darkness. If so, he knew the rectory very well and also spent the night there. Was it the rector himself?

"Now, why does Richard refuse to say what made him go into the garden? It must be to keep somebody out of trouble; almost certainly, trouble about the murder. Not himself, because I've told him we know he didn't do it. Somebody else. Who? Might be the rector. Can't think of anybody else it might be. Suppose it was the rector; how would he have worked it? Very easy. Go out about midnight, in tennis shoes and gloves. Quite silent on the rectory paths—no gravel on them. Reach that little iron gate into John Doe's garden. Does he know it's wet paint? Probably not; it was only painted after tea. So he grabs it. Paint on glove. Probably paint on jacket too. Walk on the grass to Doe's study window. Doe is leaning forward in his chair, or likelier asleep. Now for a bit of quick work, easy for a good tennis-player. Left foot inside, right foot to the right, grab that dagger thing, left foot forward, in it goes.

"But what had John Doe been doing at that desk? Nothing on it, you know. Queer. Does a man spend the evening sitting at an empty desk? There must have been something there. What do we know about the chap at the Yard? Blackmailer, that's it. Had he been blackmailing the rector? and gloating over the letters, or what not, all evening? And did the rector, if it was the rector, find him asleep on top of them? Well, that's not our business. We'll pass it on to the defence, for what it's worth. I'd rather not use a motive like that in prosecution.

"Now then, Jonathan, don't go ahead too fast. You've got him in there, you've got to get him out again. What exactly does he do? About now it begins to rain cats and dogs. Back he goes through it. More paint at the gate. Walk on grass, no mud brought in. Back in the house. All soaked: gloves covered with paint, too. Wipe paint off door-knob. Lock up. Put letters (if it was letters), and anyhow gloves, in the hot-water furnace—the ashes may be in the dustbin now. Put all clothes in the bathroom cupboard; they will be dry by morning. And so they are; but the jacket will be hopelessly out of shape. Now what did he do with that jacket? First, he'd look for paint on it. If he found paint, he'd have to destroy the thing; and I pity the man who tries to destroy a jacket in a house overrun with women. If he didn't find any, he would certainly give it away on the quiet to a poor man.

"Well, well: there's a pretty story for you; but how can we tell whether it's true or not? There are two questions we've got to ask. First: can we find the ashes of those gloves? And the metal buttons, if they are like most of his gloves? If we can, the story is true. And if we can find a lot of writing-paper ash as well, the blackmail bit is true, too. Second: where is that jacket? Because if we can find the tiniest speck of John Doe's paint on it, there's our case."

I have gone to some length in this analysis because I wish to bring home to the reader the following points about the questioning activity which is the dominant factor in history, as it is in all scientific work.

(1) Every step in the argument depends on asking a question. The question is the charge of gas, exploded in the cylinder-head, which is the motive force of every piston-stroke. But the metaphor is not adequate, because each new piston-stroke is produced not by exploding another charge of the same old mixture but by exploding a charge of a new kind. No one with any grasp of method will go on asking the same question all the time, "Who killed John Doe?" He asks a new question every time. And it is not enough to cover the ground by having a catalogue of all the questions that have to be asked, and asking every one of them sooner or later: they must be asked in the right order. . . .

(2) These questions are not put by one man to another man, in the hope that the second man will enlighten the first man's ignorance by answering them. They are put, like all scientific questions, to the scientist by himself. This is the Socratic idea which Plato was to express by defining thought as "the dialogue of the soul with itself," where Plato's own literary practice makes it clear that by dialogue he meant a process of question and answer. When Socrates taught his young pupils by asking them questions, he was teaching them how to ask questions of themselves, and showing them by examples how amazingly the obscurest subjects can be illuminated by asking oneself intelligent questions about them instead of simply gaping at them . . . , in the hope that when we have made our minds a perfect blank we shall "apprehend the facts."

It is characteristic of scissors-and-paste history, from its least critical to its most critical form, that it has to do with ready-made statements, and that the historian's problem about any one of these statements is whether he shall accept it or not: where accepting it means reasserting it as a part of his own historical knowledge. Essentially, history for the scissors-and-paste historian means repeating statements that other people have made before him. Hence he can get to work only when he is supplied with ready-made statements on the subjects about which he wants to think, write, and so forth. It is the fact that these statements have to be found by him ready-made in his sources that makes it impossible for the scissors-and-paste historian to claim the title of a scientific thinker, for this fact makes it impossible to attribute to him that autonomy which is everywhere essential to scientific thought; where by autonomy I mean the condition of being one's own authority, making statements or taking action on one's own initiative and not because those statements or actions are authorized or prescribed by anyone else.

It follows that scientific history contains no ready-made statements at all. The act of incorporating a ready-made statement into the body of his own historical knowledge is an act which, for a scientific historian, is impossible. Confronted with a ready-made statement about the subject he is studying, the scientific historian never asks himself: "Is this statement true or false?," in other words "Shall I incorporate it in my history of that subject or not?" The question he asks himself is: "What does this statement mean?" And this is not equivalent to the question "What did the person who made it mean by it?," although that is doubtless a question that the historian must ask, and must be able to answer. It is equivalent, rather, to the question "What light is thrown on the subject in which I am interested by the fact that this person made this statement, meaning by it what he did mean?" This might be expressed by saying that the scientific historian does not treat statements as statements but as evidence: not as true or false accounts of the facts of which they profess to be accounts, but as other facts which, if he knows the right questions to ask about them, may throw light on those facts. Thus in my fable the rector's daughter tells the constable that she killed John Doe. As a scientific historian, he begins attending seriously to this statement at the point where he stops treating it as a statement, that is, as a true or false account of her having done the murder, and begins treating the fact that she makes it as a fact which may be of service to him. It is of service to him because he knows what questions to ask about it, beginning with the question: "Now, why does she tell this story?" The scissors-and-paste historian is interested in the "content," as it is called, of statements: he is interested in what they state. The scientific historian is interested in the fact that they are made.

A statement to which an historian listens, or one which he reads, is to him a ready-made statement. But the statement that such a statement is being made is not a ready-made statement. If he says to himself "I am now reading or hearing a statement to such-and-such effect," he is himself making a statement; but it is not a second-hand statement, it is autonomous. He makes it on his own authority. And it is this autonomous statement that is the scientific historian's starting-point. The evidence from which the constable infers that the rector's daughter suspects Richard Roe is not her statement "I killed John Doe," but his own statement "The rector's daughter tells me that she killed John Doe."

If the scientific historian gets his conclusions not from the statement that he finds ready-made, but from his own autonomous statement of the fact that such statements are made, he can get conclusions even when no statements are made to him. The premisses of his argument are his own autonomous statements: there is no need for these autonomous statements to be themselves statements about other statements. To illustrate once more from the story of John Doe. The premisses from which the Detective-Inspector argued to the innocence of Richard Roe were all premisses of the Detective-Inspector's own stating, autonomous statements resting on no authority but his own: and not one of them was a statement about statements made by anybody else. The essential points were that Richard Roe had got his shoes muddy while going away from the rectory, that no mud was to be seen in John Doe's study, and that the circumstances of the murder had been such that he would not have stopped to clean or remove his shoes. Each of these three points, in its turn, was the conclusion of an inference, and the statements upon which they severally rested were no more statements about other people's statements than were these three points themselves. Again: the ultimate case against the rector did not logically depend upon any statements made by the Detective-Inspector about statements made by other persons. It depended upon the presence of certain objects in a certain dustbin, and of certain paint-smears on the cuff of a jacket made in the conventional clerical style and shrunk by wetting; and these facts were vouched for by his own observation. I do not mean that the scientific historian can work better when no statements are made to him about the subjects on which he is working; it would be a pedantical way of avoiding scissors-and-paste history, to avoid occasions of this type which might be a trap for the weaker brethren; what I mean is that he is not dependent on such statements being made.

This is important because it settles by appeal to principle a controversy which, even if it is no longer so urgent as it was, has not yet ceased to echo in the minds of historians. This was the controversy between those who maintained that history was ultimately dependent on "written sources," and those who maintained that it could also be constructed from "unwritten sources." The terms were unhappily chosen. "Written sources" were not conceived as excluding oral sources, or as having any special connexion with handwriting as distinct from chiselling in stone or the like. "Written sources," in fact, meant sources containing ready-made statements asserting or implying alleged facts belonging to the subject in which the historian was interested. "Unwritten sources" meant archaeological material, potsherds, and so forth, connected with the same subject. Of course, the word "source" was in no sense applicable to these, for a source means something from which water or the like is drawn ready made; in the case of history, something from which the historian's statements are drawn ready made, and the point of describing potsherds as "unwritten sources" was to indicate that, not being texts, they contained no ready-made statements and were therefore not sources. . . .

If history means scissors-and-paste history, where the historian depends on ready-made statements for all his knowledge about his subject, and where the texts in which he finds these statements are called his sources, it is easy to define a source in a way which has some practical utility. A source is a text containing a statement or statements about the subject; and this definition has some practical utility because it helps the historian to divide the whole of extant literature, once he has determined his subject, into texts which might serve him as sources, and must therefore be looked at, and those which cannot, and may therefore be ignored. What he has to do is to run over his library shelves, or his bibliography of the period, asking himself at every title: "Could this contain anything about my subject?" And, in case he cannot give the answer out of his head, aids of several kinds have been provided: notably indexes and specialized or classified bibliographies. Even with all these aids, he may still miss an important piece of testimony, and thus provide sport for his friends; but on any given question the amount of testimony that exists is a finite quantity, and it is theoretically possible to exhaust it.

Theoretically, but not always practically: for the amount may be so large, and some parts of it so difficult of access, that no historian can hope to see it all. And one sometimes hears people complaining that nowadays so much raw material for history is being preserved that the task of using it is becoming impossible; and sighing for the good old days when books were few and libraries small, and an historian could hope to master his subject. What these complaints mean is that the scissors-and-paste historian is on the horns of a dilemma. If he possesses only a small amount of testimony about his subject, he wants more; because any new piece of testimony about it would, if really new, throw new light on it, and might make the view he is actually putting forward untenable. So, however much testimony he has, his zeal as an historian makes him want more. But if he has a large amount of testimony, it becomes so difficult to manipulate and work up into a convincing narrative that, speaking as a mere weak mortal, he wishes he had less.

Consciousness of this dilemma has often driven men into scepticism about the very possibility of historical knowledge. And quite rightly, if knowledge means scientific knowledge and history means scissors-and-paste history. Scissors-and-paste historians who brush the dilemma aside with the blessed word "hypercriticism" are only confessing that in their own professional practice they do not find that it troubles them, because they work to such a low standard of scientific cogency that their consciences become anaesthetized. Such cases in contemporary life are highly interesting, because in the history of science one often meets with them and wonders how such extraordinary blindness was possible. The answer is that the people who exhibit it have committed themselves to an impossible task, in this case the task of scissors-and-paste history, and since for practical reasons they cannot back out of it they have to blind themselves to its impossibility. The scissors-and-paste historian protects himself from seeing the truth about his own methods by carefully choosing subjects which he is able to "get away" with, exactly as the nineteenth-century landscape-painter protected himself from seeing that his theory of landscape was all wrong by choosing what he called paintable subjects. The subjects must be those about which a certain amount of testimony is accessible, not too little and not too much; not so uniform as to give the historian nothing to do, not so divergent as to baffle his endeavours to do it. Practised on these principles, history was at worst a parlour game, and at best an elegant accomplishment. I have used the past tense; I leave it to the conscience of historians who are capable of self-criticism to decide how far I might justly have used the present.

If history means scientific history, for "source" we must read "evidence." And when we try to define "evidence" in the same spirit in which we defined "sources," we find it very difficult. There is no short and easy test by which we can decide whether a given book is or is not capable of providing evidence about a given subject, and indeed no reason why we should limit our search to books. Indexes and bibliographies of sources are of no use at all to a scientific historian. This is not to say that he cannot use indexes and bibliographies; he can and does; but they are indexes and bibliographies not of sources but of monographs or the like: not of evidence, but of previous discussions which he can take as a starting-point for his own. Consequently, whereas the books mentioned in a bibliography for the use of a scissors-and-paste historian will be, roughly speaking, valuable in direct proportion to their antiquity, those mentioned in a bibliography for the use of a scientific historian will be, roughly speaking, valuable in direct proportion to their newness.

In my fable there is only one obvious characteristic common to all the pieces of evidence used by the Detective-Inspector in his argument: they are all things observed by himself. If we ask what kind of things, it is not easy to give an answer. They include such things as the existence of certain footprints in certain mud, their number, position, and direction, their resemblance to prints produced by a certain pair of shoes, and the absence of any others; the absence of mud on the floor of a certain room; the position of a dead body, the position of a dagger in its back, and the shape of the chair in which it is sitting; and so on, a most variegated collection. This, I think, we can safely say about it: that no one could possibly know what could or could not find a place in it until he had got all his questions not only formulated but answered. In scientific history anything is evidence which is used as evidence, and no one can know what is going to be useful as evidence until he has had occasion to use it.

Let us put this by saying that in scissors-and-paste history, if we allow ourselves to describe testimony—loosely, I admit—by the name of evidence, there is potential evidence and there is actual evidence. The potential evidence about a subject is all the extant statements about it. The actual evidence is that part of these statements which we decide to accept. But in scientific history the idea of potential evidence disappears; or, if we like to put the same fact in these other words, everything in the world is potential evidence for any subject whatever. This will be a distressing idea to anyone whose notions of historical method are fixed in a scissors-and-paste mould; for how, he will ask, are we to discover what facts are actually of service to us, unless we can first of all round up the facts that might be of service to us? To a person who understands the nature of scientific thinking, whether historical or any other, it will present no difficulty. He will realize that, every time the historian asks a question, he asks it because he thinks he can answer it: that is to say, he has already in his mind a preliminary and tentative idea of the evidence he will be able to use. Not a definite idea about potential evidence, but an indefinite idea about actual evidence. To ask questions which you see no prospect of answering is the fundamental sin in science, like giving orders which you do not think will be obeyed in politics, or praying for what you do not think God will give you in religion. Question and evidence, in history, are correlative. Anything is evidence which enables you to answer your question—the question you are asking now. A sensible question (the only kind of question that a scientifically competent man will ask) is a question which you think you have or are going to have evidence for answering. If you think you have it here and now, the question is an actual question, like the question "What position was John Doe in when he was stabbed?" If you think you are going to have it, the question is a deferred question, like the question "Who killed John Doe?"

It was a correct understanding of this truth that underlay Lord Acton's great precept, "Study problems, not periods." Scissors-and-paste historians study periods; they collect all the extant testimony about a certain limited group of events, and hope in vain that something will come of it. Scientific historians study problems: they ask questions, and if they are good historians they ask questions which they see their way to answering. It was a correct understanding of the same truth that led [Agatha Christie's] Monsieur Hercule Poirot to pour scorn on the "human bloodhound" who crawls about the floor trying to collect everything, no matter what, which might conceivably turn out to be a clue; and to insist that the secret of detection was to use what, with possibly wearisome iteration, he called "the little grey cells." You can't collect your evidence before you begin thinking, he meant: because thinking means asking questions . . . and nothing is evidence except in relation to some definite question. The difference between Poirot and Holmes in this respect is deeply significant of the change that has taken place in the understanding of historical method in the last forty years. Lord Acton was preaching his doctrine in the heyday of Sherlock Holmes, in his inaugural lecture at Cambridge in 1895; but it was caviare to the general. In Monsieur Poirot's time, to judge by his sales, the general cannot have too much of it. The revolution which dethroned the principles of scissors-and-paste history, and replaced them by those of scientific history, had become common property. . . .

To be sure, many professional and highly honored historians disagree with Collingwood's strictures against Big Think generalizations, and there are many who find his description of scissors-and-paste history—that which "depends altogether upon the testimony of authorities"—not entirely fair. "Scientific history" too often is taken by the unsuspecting to mean totally objective history, which nearly all historians except the pathetically amateur and the irrevocably Marxist realize is unobtainable. On occasion Collingwood, because of his approving references to "scientific history," is hit by flak sent up against other targets. But Collingwood did not equate "scientific" with "objective," in the sense of hoping to arrive at a fullness of truth, for he recognized that the full truth about the past can never be recovered. One of the reasons this is so, of course, is that we can never know the full truth about ourselves, the investigators, while the natural human tendency to be avengers of ourselves and our allegiances gets in the way. Self-knowledge, therefore, takes pre-eminence among the historian's tools. H. Stuart Hughes, himself a leading student of modern European social and intellectual history, has even recommended that doctoral candidates in history should include psychoanalysis among their bag of tricks,[1] and while few historians are as yet prepared to see self-inquiry formalized in this way, most recognize the need for tracing the missing person within themselves. Autobiography and biography, after all, are very different things.

[1] See Hughes, *History as Art and as Science: Twin Vistas on the Past* (New York, 1965), pp. 42–66.

4. Tracer of Missing Persons:

Biographer and Autobiographer

THE ONE PERSON THE HISTORIAN CANNOT AFFORD TO HAVE missing is himself. This sounds sophomoric, but many sophomores are more intelligent than many adults I know. In the final analysis, as Collingwood showed, no one can write of others without being alert to his own idiosyncrasies and being prepared, to the best of his ability, to guard against them. One cannot totally separate personality from history as it is written, and probably one should not try. Observably, historians tend to take on the mannerisms and intonations of the subjects and periods they study: American historians of England often are tweedy types with needless patches on the elbows of their jackets, given to pronouncing "schedule" without the "c," and if historians of modern American politics sometimes seem to be politicians, no one should be surprised.

On the whole historians have not cared to inquire too deeply into their personal motivations for being historians. I have often wondered (would that a foundation would support me in finding out) whether a particular discipline attracts certain people because they already have personality traits that are in affinity, or whether they develop those personality traits as a result of a lifetime in the discipline. I think the former, and child psychology would bear me out, just as I suspect that certain universities have self-weeding devices that tend to eliminate the majority of those who do not share the institution's ethos. Surely so, one says, and but of course. But since historians have not cared to look closely at themselves, perhaps because of their own conception of time (one is still referred to as "a rising young historian" until at least a fiftieth birthday, and to write of living historians in personal terms is not always thought to be in the best of taste), they have failed to explore a genuinely major dimension of their subject. Most, I suspect, would be shocked at Professor Hughes's suggestion that they submit to psychoanalysis. Yet one must admit that few historians have managed to see themselves either plain or even significantly, at least on paper. Gibbon's *Autobiography* is exciting in its way but is scarcely the whole man. G. G. Coulton, the English medievalist, hides more than he reveals in his *Fourscore Years*. E. L. Woodward, in *Short Journey,* suggests rather less than a novel by C. P. Snow does about the corridors of academic power, although more charmingly. G. M. Trevelyan, in his brief autobiography, reminds us of the books he wrote and of some of the people he knew. Arthur M. Schlesinger, Sr., throughout *In Retrospect: The History of a Historian,* reveals almost nothing about why a boy who delivered newspapers in Xenia, Ohio, should have died an honored scholar at Harvard University. Paul Knaplund, who at the University of Wisconsin became America's leading student of the British Empire, tells us in *Moorings Old and New* of his Norwegian background but very little about why he chose to become a historian, and one of an empire he had never known. Roy Frank Nichols, *A Historian's Progress,* and John Hicks, *My Life with History,* are equally unrevealing.

Indeed, I know of no historian's autobiography that is successful, at least in the way in which Roy Pascal means "successful." Professor Pascal, of the Department of Germanic Literature in the University of Birmingham, England, has argued that the only truthful autobiography is one in which the author perceptively grows because of the act of writing—because of reliving and therefore rethinking past events. In this he is close to Collingwood's notion of encapsulating the past through empathy, through what

Herman Melville's Pierre felt when he looked up to the great mountain before him. Most autobiographies are static, as though the past had fallen into place only to be recorded without further reflection—almost as though the agonizing reappraisals inherent in all writing were mysteriously set aside when accounting to oneself. In truth, growth within the individual in the act of writing, visible change between the first and the last chapter of an autobiography, and a growing self-awareness must be present, or one might as well say of the autobiographer as the Duke of Rockingham said of the industrious historian of the Roman Empire, "Ah! Scribble, scribble, eh, Mr. Gibbon?"

The exercise of self-discipline involved in autobiography has thus defeated most people. Perhaps the task is an impossible one. Even Henry Adams, whose own maturation he watches over so carefully in his *Education,* grows rather too self-consciously for some historians' tastes. To be by oneself surprised may require a naïveté against which all of the historian's other traits will fight.

One of the first lessons that the historian, and the detective, learns is that men do not see themselves as others see them. For some time now I have been taking pleasure in comparing biographies with their subjects' autobiographies, for the contrast is invariably instructive, both for the craft of history and for the subjects themselves. The two selections which follow offer an opportunity to see how Theodore Roosevelt described his years as a member of the police board of New York City, in his *Autobiography,* and how these same years appeared to the first good biographer of T. R., Henry F. Pringle. Roosevelt's book was written in 1913, after he had been President of the United States but while he still expected to be a force in future politics, and perhaps even President again; Pringle's book, the work of a newspaperman whose two-volume biography of William Howard Taft also won wide acceptance in the groves of academe, was written in 1931, when many in the nation were longing again for a vigorous President.

Roosevelt is speaking:

♦ ♦ ♦

In the spring of 1895 I was appointed by Mayor [William L.] Strong Police Commissioner, and I served as president of the Police Commission of New York for the two following years. Mayor Strong had been elected mayor the preceding fall, when the general anti-Democratic wave of that year coincided with one of the city's occasional insurrections of virtue and consequent turning out of Tammany from municipal control. He had been elected on a non-partisan ticket—usually (although not always) the right kind of ticket in municipal affairs, provided it represents not a bargain among factions but genuine non-partisanship with the genuine purpose to get the right men in control of the city government on a platform which deals with the needs of the average men and women, the men and women who work hard and who too often live hard. I was appointed with the distinct understanding that I was to administer the Police Department with entire disregard of

---

FROM *Theodore Roosevelt: An Autobiography* (New York: Macmillan Co., 1913), pp. 186–90, 205–6, 208, 210–11, 218–21 (reprinted with permission of Charles Scribner's Sons; copyright 1913 Charles Scribner's Sons, renewed 1941 Edith K. Carow Roosevelt); and from Henry F. Pringle, *Theodore Roosevelt: A Biography* (New York: Harcourt, Brace & Co., 1931), pp. 132–50 (copyright © 1931, 1956 by Henry F. Pringle, reprinted by permission of Harcourt, Brace & World, Inc.).

For additional reading: Pascal's book is *Design and Truth in Autobiography* (Cambridge, Mass., 1960); another fascinating study in self-evaluation as opposed to posthumous discovery is R. C. H. Catterall, "The Credibility of Marat," in the *American Historical Review,* XVI (October, 1910), 24–35. The number of detective stories dealing with this theme is great, for the case of the lying witness is commonplace in the genre. Perhaps the best on self-delusion are the several novels of Margaret Millar, the Canadian-born wife of psychiatrist Kenneth Millar, who writes of similar themes under his mid-career pseudonym of John Ross MacDonald. A book which attempts to examine the influences upon the lives of seven outstanding contemporary historians, as well as six who are no longer writing, is Marcus Cunliffe and Robin W. Winks, editors, *Pastmasters: Some Essays on American Historians* (New York, 1969).

partisan politics, and only from the standpoint of a good citizen interested in promoting the welfare of all good citizens. My task, therefore, was really simple. Mayor Strong had already offered me the Street-Cleaning Department. For this work I did not feel that I had any especial fitness. . . .

The man who was closest to me throughout my two years in the Police Department was Jacob Riis. By this time, as I have said, I was getting our social, industrial, and political needs into pretty fair perspective. I was still ignorant of the extent to which big men of great wealth played a mischievous part in our industrial and social life, but I was well awake to the need of making ours in good faith both an economic and an industrial as well as a political democracy. I already knew Jake Riis, because his book "How the Other Half Lives" had been to me both an enlightenment and an inspiration for which I felt I could never be too grateful. Soon after it was written I had called at his office to tell him how deeply impressed I was by the book, and that I wished to help him in any practical way to try to make things a little better. I have always had a horror of words that are not translated into deeds, of speech that does not result in action—in other words, I believe in realizable ideals and in realizing them, in preaching what can be practised and then in practising it. Jacob Riis had drawn an indictment of the things that were wrong, pitifully and dreadfully wrong, with the tenement homes and the tenement lives of our wage-workers. In his book he had pointed out how the city government, and especially those connected with the departments of police and health, could aid in remedying some of the wrongs.

As president of the Police Board I was also a member of the Health Board. In both positions I felt that with Jacob Riis's guidance I would be able to put a goodly number of his principles into actual effect. He and I looked at life and its problems from substantially the same standpoint. Our ideals and principles and purposes, and our beliefs as to the methods necessary to realize them, were alike.

. . . As I viewed it, there were two sides to the work: first, the actual handling of the Police Department; second, using my position to help in making the city a better place in which to live and work for those to whom the conditions of life and labor were hardest. The two problems were closely connected; for one thing never to be forgotten in striving to better the conditions of the New York police force is the connection between the standard of morals and behavior in that force and the general standard of morals and behavior in the city at large. The form of government of the Police Department at that time was such as to make it a matter of extreme difficulty to get good results. It represented that device of old-school American political thought, the desire to establish checks and balances so elaborate that no man shall have power enough to do anything very bad. In practice this always means that no man has power enough to do anything good, and that what is bad is done anyhow.

In most positions the "division of powers" theory works unmitigated mischief. The only way to get good service is to give somebody power to render it, facing the fact that power which will enable a man to do a job well will also necessarily enable him to do it ill if he is the wrong kind of man. What is normally needed is the concentration in the hands of one man, or of a very small body of men, of ample power to enable him or them to do the work that is necessary; and then the devising of means to hold these men fully responsible for the exercise of that power by the people. This of course means that, if the people are willing to see power misused, it will be misused. But it also means that if, as we hold, the people are fit for self-government—if, in other words, our talk and our institutions are not shams—we will get good government. . . .

The first fight I made was to keep politics absolutely out of the force; and not only politics, but every kind of improper favoritism. Doubtless in making thousands of appointments and hundreds of promotions there were men who contrived to use influence of which I was ignorant. But these cases must have been few and far between. As far as was humanly possible, the appointments and promotions were made without regard to any question except the fitness of the man and the needs of the service. As Civil Service Commissioner I had been instructing heads of departments and bureaus how to get men appointed without regard to politics, and assuring them that by following our methods they would obtain first-class results. As police commissioner I was able practically to apply my own teachings. . . .

The many-sided ethnic character of the force now and then gives rise to, or affords opportunity for, queer happenings. Occasionally it enables one to meet emergencies in the best possible fashion. While I was Police Commissioner an anti-Semitic preacher from Berlin, Rector [Wilhelm] Ahlwardt, came over to New York to preach a crusade against the Jews. Many of the New York Jews were much excited and asked me to prevent him from speaking and not to give him police protection. This, I told them, was impossible; and if possible would have been undesirable because it would have made him a martyr. The proper thing to do was to make him ridiculous. Accordingly I detailed for his protection a Jew sergeant and a score or two of Jew policemen. He made his harangue against the Jews under the active protection of some forty policemen, every one of them a Jew! It was the most effective possible answer; and incidentally it was an object-lesson to our people, whose greatest need it is to learn that there must be no division by class hatred, whether this hatred be that of creed against creed, nationality against nationality, section against section, or men of one social or industrial condition against men of another social or industrial condition. . . .

There was in New York City a strong sentiment in favor of honesty in politics; there was also a strong sentiment in favor of opening the saloons on Sundays; and, finally, there was a strong sentiment in favor of keeping the saloons closed on Sunday. Unfortunately, many of the men who favored honest government nevertheless preferred keeping the saloons open to having honest government; and many others among the men who favored honest government put it second to keeping the saloons closed. Moreover, among the people who wished the law obeyed and the saloons closed there were plenty who objected strongly to every step necessary to accomplish the result, although they also insisted that the result should be accomplished. . . .

This was the situation that confronted me when I came to Mulberry Street. The saloon was the chief source of mischief. It was with the saloon that I had to deal, and there was only one way to deal with it. That was to enforce the law. The howl that rose was deafening. The professional politicians raved. The yellow press surpassed themselves in clamor and mendacity. A favorite assertion was that I was enforcing a "blue" law, an obsolete law that had never before been enforced. As a matter of fact, I was only enforcing honestly a law that had hitherto been enforced dishonestly. There was very little increase in the number of arrests made for violating the Sunday law. Indeed, there were weeks when the number of arrests went down. The only difference was that there was no protected class. Everybody was arrested alike, and I took especial pains to see that there was no discrimination, and that the big men and the men with political influence were treated like everyone else. The immediate effect was wholly good. I had been told that it was not possible to close the saloons on Sunday and that I could not succeed. However, I did succeed. The warden of Bellevue Hospital reported, two or three weeks after we had begun, that for the first time in its existence there had not been a case due to a drunken brawl in the hospital all Monday. The police courts gave the same testimony, while savings-banks recorded increased deposits and pawn-shops hard times. The most touching of all things was the fact that we received letters, literally by the hundred, from mothers in tenement-houses who had never been allowed to take their children to the country in the wide-open days, and who now found their husbands willing to take them and their families for an outing on Sunday. . . .

During the two years that we were in office things never slipped back to anything like what they had been before. But we did not succeed in keeping them quite as highly keyed as during these first weeks. As regards the Sunday-closing law, this was partly because public sentiment was not really with us. The people who had demanded honesty, but who did not like to pay for it by the loss of illegal pleasure, joined the openly dishonest in attacking us. Moreover, all kinds of ways of evading the law were tried, and some of them were successful. The statute, for instance, permitted any man to take liquor with meals. After two or three months a magistrate was found who decided judicially that seventeen beers and one pretzel made a meal—after which decision joy again became unconfined in at least some of the saloons, and the yellow press gleefully announced that my "tyranny" had been curbed. . . .

In company with Jacob Riis, I did much work that was not connected with the actual discipline of the force or indeed with the actual work of the force. There was one thing which he and I abolished—police lodging-houses, which were simply tramp lodging-houses, and a fruitful encouragement to vagrancy. Those who read Mr. Riis's story of his own life will remember the incidents that gave him from actual personal experience his horror of these tramp lodging-houses. As member of the Health Board I was brought into very close relations with the conditions of life in the tenement-house districts. Here again I used to visit the different tenement-house regions, usually in company with Riis, to see for myself what the conditions were. It was largely this personal experience that enabled me while on the Health Board to struggle not only zealously, but with reasonable efficiency and success, to improve conditions. . . .

The midnight trips that Riis and I took enabled me to see what the Police Department was doing, and also gave me personal insight into some of the problems of city life. It is one thing to listen in perfunctory fashion to tales of overcrowded tenements, and it is quite another actually to see what that overcrowding means, some hot summer night, by even a single inspection during the hours of darkness. There was a very hot spell one midsummer while I was police commissioner, and most of each night I spent walking through the tenement-house districts and visiting police stations to see what was being done. It was a tragic week. We did everything possible to alleviate the suffering. Much of it was heartbreaking, especially the gasping misery of the little children and of the worn-out mothers. Every resource of the Health Department, of the Police Department, and even the Fire Department (which flooded the hot streets) was taxed in the effort to render service. The heat killed such multitudes of horses that the means at our disposal for removing the poor dead beasts proved quite inadequate, although every nerve was strained to the limit. In consequence we received scores of complaints from persons before whose doors dead horses had remained, festering in the heat, for two or three days. One irascible man sent us furious denunciations, until we were at last able to send a big dray to drag away the horse that lay dead before his shop-door. The huge dray already contained eleven other dead horses, and when it reached this particular door it broke down, and it was hours before it could be moved. The unfortunate man who had thus been cursed with a granted wish closed his doors in despair and wrote us a final pathetic letter in which he requested us to remove either the horses or his shop, he didn't care which. . . .

Occasionally during the two years we had to put a stop to riotous violence, and now and then on these occasions some of the labor-union leaders protested against the actions of the police. By this time I was becoming a strong believer in labor-unions, a strong believer in the rights of labor. For that very reason I was all the more bound to see that lawlessness and disorder were put down, and that no rioter was permitted to masquerade under the guise of being a friend of labor or a sympathizer with labor. I was scrupulous to see that the labor men had fair play; that, for instance, they were allowed to picket just so far as under the law picketing could be permitted, so that the strikers had ample opportunity peacefully to persuade other labor men not to take their places. But I made it clearly and definitely understood that under no circumstances would I permit violence or fail to insist upon the keeping of order. If there were wrongs, I would join with a full heart in striving to have them corrected. But where there was violence all other questions had to drop until order was restored. This is a democracy, and the people have the power, if they choose to exercise it, to make conditions as they ought to be made, and to do this strictly within the law; and therefore the first duty of the true democrat, of the man really loyal to the principles of popular government, is to see that law is enforced and order upheld. . . .

Roosevelt's ideas about power and duty, indeed much of his political philosophy, come through clearly enough from his personal account. Yet if one contrasts the autobiography with the best analysis of his political principles, John Morton Blum's *The Republican Roosevelt* (Cambridge, Mass., 1954), one finds that T.R. was a more subtle and imaginative thinker than his stress upon the strenuous life would suggest. But let us turn to Pringle's biography (where the forthright word "prostitution" is used for Roosevelt's euphemism "vagrancy") to see how the strenuous life influenced the people of New York.

The appointment of Theodore Roosevelt in 1895 to the police board of New York, which brought friction and fighting enough to surfeit even his restless spirit, may be traced back to two events some years before. The first was a legislative investigation in 1884, which initiated Roosevelt into certain irregularities practiced by guardians of the law. The second took place on Sunday, February 14, 1892, when the Rev. Charles H. Parkhurst told his congregation that New York was "a very hotbed of knavery, debauchery and bestiality." Subsequent fulminations by the pastor of the Madison Square Church resulted in 1894 in the momentary downfall of Tammany Hall.

A member of the State legislature in 1884, Roosevelt had led in the fight for the passage of four or five bills backed by civic organizations in New York. It was their hope, as it has been the hope of similar organizations ever since, that the legislation would put an end to graft and corruption in police and other municipal circles. Enthusiastic rallies were held at which orators pointed to Assemblyman Roosevelt as their champion. Upon his "young shoulders were carried the earnestness and the wisdom of years."[1] One of the reform bills called, specifically, for an inquiry into the city's police force. In due time Roosevelt was presiding over hearings conducted in the ornate parlor of the old Metropolitan Hotel, once owned by Boss Tweed, and before him passed witnesses who told unsavory stories of police incapacity and dishonesty.

Roosevelt was convinced, after the hearings in 1884, that police reform was vitally needed in New York. His reports to the legislature called for civil service and for a single police commissioner to take the place of the bipartisan board of four members. These Utopian changes were slow in coming, however. The bipartisan board, of two Republicans and two Democrats, still existed when Roosevelt was appointed eleven years later. The police alliances with vice and crime were as strong as ever.

Ultimately, feeling the stings of Dr. Parkhurst's shafts himself,

[1] *New York Times,* March 28, 1884.

Roosevelt's enthusiasm for this extremely active clergyman began to cool and he referred to him as "that goose." But for a time their relations were most cordial, and Roosevelt watched with approval the pastor's efficient campaign against Tammany and sin, which started in 1892. Parkhurst was a handsome man of fifty when he fired his first salvos. . . .

No restraints clouded the meaning of the sermons in which he described disorderly houses and gambling dens that "flourish . . . almost as thick as the roses of Sharon." A few members of the congregation stirred uneasily as he named names and described plush and gold interiors. . . . The Parkhurst exposures resulted in the appointment of another legislative committee, the famous Lexow tribunal, and this proved far more effective than the one Roosevelt had commanded in 1884. Its hearings substantiated, with additional lurid details, the charges that Parkhurst had made, and in 1894 the prophets of Tammany Hall foretold defeat. William L. Strong, a respected businessman, received fusion support and was elected mayor of New York. He found it an unhappy rôle and a brief one; reform mayors of New York usually find it so.

Roosevelt's letters to Henry Cabot Lodge reveal that the mayoralty nomination had been offered to him before it had gone to Strong, but it is not clear whether the suggestion came from [Thomas] Platt and the Republican machine or from the far less influential fusion leaders. Not improbably, Platt would have preferred Roosevelt to Strong, whom he viewed with suspicion as "another of the fellows who wore a little bunch of whiskers under his chin." Strong was a man of standing, whose place in the community had long since been assured. Roosevelt was young and ambitious. This might make him more amenable to party discipline.

But Roosevelt was in no position to accept the nomination. He had no money for campaign purposes, and so he watched the contest with deep interest from Washington. "The stars in their courses fight for us," he told Lodge, and perhaps found satisfaction in the knowledge that Strong, if elected, would doubtless offer some appointment. He declined a first suggestion, to become street cleaning commissioner, because he felt no special qualification for the post. On the other hand, the "work of the Police Department . . . was in my line. . . . I was glad to undertake it."

Police headquarters was still on Mulberry Street in 1895, a gloomy building with subterranean dungeons where rats and vermin assisted the persuasive effectiveness of the third degree. The patrolman of the day was usually abnormally fat and usually abnormally stupid. He could barely read and write. His convenient conscience made strict obedience to the commands of his political sponsor easy. Sometimes he was honest enough. More often, he saw that wealth and a life of ease could be achieved by emulating the accepted methods of grafting upon saloon-keepers, gamblers, and prostitutes. New York in the '90's was outwardly respectable. Divorce was a social disgrace. The home was the citadel of virtue, and all wives were chaste. But there was a furtive world beyond the home, and in this world the police moved like very corporeal shadows. Their uniformed commander, as Roosevelt took office, was the famous Tom Byrnes, then holding the title of superintendent of police and only nominally subordinate to the four civilian commissioners. During the Lexow Committee investigation Byrnes admitted to a fortune of $300,000, but offered the moral excuse that he had made this in Wall Street, with the assistance of Jay Gould.

The arrival at Mulberry Street of any new commissioner was a crisis in police circles. It meant promotions and demotions, and the shifting of favorites from warm inside posts to pounding of cold pavements. The arrival of Roosevelt in May, 1895, was doubly unsettling because it was known that Mayor Strong desired his selection as president of the police board. Too, there were rumors of his incorruptibility, his daring courage, and his independence. Naturally enough, his appointment had been viewed with mixed emotions. To Tom Byrnes, it was the end of happy, influential days. To Jacob Riis, whose excursions into New York's slums had produced *How the Other Half Lives,* the appointment seemed divine deliverance from an era of corruption. Riis was a newspaper reporter at headquarters. He told his fellow journalists excitedly: "Theodore Roosevelt is the man for the president of the Police Board, and God will attend to his appointment. That's all I want to know. I don't care who the other commissioners are."

The Lord's plan was carried out at the first meeting of the new board, and Roosevelt became its president. It was the other commissioners, however, who blocked his program. Before two years of his five-year term had ended he was weary and discouraged and was hoping that William McKinley, now President of the United States, would call him back to Washington. At first, though, every one was optimistic. The New York *World* proclaimed "the substitution of the reform idea for the spoils system."

The general approbation did not extend to the other three members of the board; Frederick D. Grant, son of the Civil War general, Andrew D. Parker, an anti-Tammany Democrat, and Avery D. Andrews, the second Democratic member. Roosevelt got along amicably with Andrews; the two men became close friends. Parker, however, was to be his bitter opponent, and Grant he considered easily misled. For the bipartisan board, destined to be the center of unending friction, only the politicians had any use.

A secondary cause of disharmony in the police board was the spotlight focused on Roosevelt, a spotlight so white and continuous that the other three commissioners found themselves in comparative shadow. The new president of the board was none too considerate of the feelings of his colleagues. He came rushing into headquarters on the first day, had himself elected chairman, and demanded as soon as he could get his breath, "What'll we do now?" He assumed, from the start, that his position was superior to the standing of the other three commissioners, although, in law and in fact, each had equal power.

But Roosevelt could not be blamed, at the beginning, for the public attention he attracted. Later he may have been responsible, because of his Haroun-al-Raschid prowlings through the city, often accompanied by a reporter. He had no way of avoiding the pen portraits of such journalists as Arthur Brisbane, then a feature-writer on the New York *World*. "Sing, heavenly muse," began Brisbane's prose poem, "the sad dejection of our poor policemen. We have a real Police Commissioner. . . . His teeth are big and white, his eyes are small and piercing, his voice is rasping. . . . His heart is full of reform, and a policeman in full uniform, with helmet, revolver and night club, is no more to him than a plain, every day human being. . . . The new commissioner cannot be described as an intellectual type . . . but he does look like a determined man."[2] Another writer was impressed by Roosevelt's ear,

[2] New York *World,* May 17, 1895.

a feature neglected by historians. It was "probably the smallest ear on any full-grown man in New York. . . . If a small ear . . . means anything, Mr. Roosevelt's ear means a lot." The journalist failed to explain, however, exactly what this did signify; although it was presumably in Roosevelt's favor, for he then told of a scar under the ear. This, too, has been ignored by other writers; there is no mention of it elsewhere. But the reporter who discovered it said that the men at headquarters believed the gash had been suffered "fighting an Indian out West."

Every one agreed that the new police head had brought a note of action to Mulberry Street. He was noisy, effusive, and picturesque, and his flair for dressing up led him to wear, on hot summer days, a remarkable black silk sash in place of a vest. This, combined with a pink shirt and with its tasseled ends dangling to his knees, was a constant source of astonishment to visitors at headquarters. In May, 1895, Roosevelt was not quite thirty-seven years old. He was heavier than he had been before, a development that worried him a good deal. But his health was excellent; he was determined to make good, and he saw in the post of police commissioner the opportunity for limitless pleasant excitement.

"The peculiarity about him," wrote Joseph Bucklin Bishop, later his official biographer but then a newspaper writer, "is that he has what is essentially a boy's mind." . . .

The first crisis faced by the new board lay in the person of Byrnes. "I think I shall move against Byrnes at once," Roosevelt wrote Lodge on May 18. Less than ten days later the policeman who had been in the department since 1863, who had caught the notorious Manhattan Bank robbers, and who had earned the gratitude of prominent financiers by orders that thieves were not to operate, as such, in Wall Street, packed his things and departed. Inspector Peter Conlin, who was ultimately to protest that he was weary of "being used as a missile, thrown by one commissioner at the other," was made acting chief. Conlin, too, quickly fell under Rooseveltian disapproval.

Mr. Brisbane had judged Roosevelt correctly; it proved to be true that the new commissioner talked to his men "as patronizingly as they have always talked to the public." It was early in the police commissioner days that Roosevelt's teeth, "almost as big as colt's teeth," according to Mr. Brisbane, grew famous. It became part of the New York credo that delinquent patrolmen watched uneasily for the approach at night of a dark figure with gleaming molars. Walt McDougall, the cartoonist, made a drawing for the New York *Recorder* in which a bluecoat was being scared half out of his meager wits by the realistic combination, in front of a building on his beat, of a hanging optician's sign, in the shape of eyeglasses, with under it a dentist's advertisement in the form of a set of teeth. Some time passed before Roosevelt appreciated the humor in this, and he was also offended when some reporter disguised himself with a broad-brimmed hat and circled the town frightening policemen by chattering his teeth at them. Still later, peddlers appeared with small whistles supposed to be replicas of "Teddy's Teeth," and a loyal policeman arrested one of the hawkers for *lèse majesté*. But by this time, Roosevelt's sense of humor had returned and when shown one of the novelties he remarked that they were "very pretty."

"I suppose it is more habit than anything else," said Roosevelt in 1900, when asked to explain his extraordinary dental display. "All short-sighted men have some facial characteristic of which they are unconscious. I cannot be blamed for having good teeth, or this characteristic of a short-sighted man."

The unhappy police considered Roosevelt's eyesight all too good during the summer of 1895. He arrived one drowsy June afternoon at a station house in the lower part of the city, and interrupted the meditations of the sergeant on the desk. He watched appreciatively while an ambulance surgeon sewed up the cuts in the hand of a Mr. John Sullivan, suddenly brought in. This diversion over, the commissioner went back, with the sergeant as a nervous escort, to the cell block in the rear of the station house. In one of the cells was an intoxicated woman engaged in the absorbing occupation of hauling on a string which disappeared out of a window. While the sergeant watched in horror, and Roosevelt very sternly, a whisky flask appeared on the end of the string. But the sergeant was a man of action. He entered the cell, battled with the inebriated lady, and emerged with the remnants of the bottle and a badly cut hand. Roosevelt made a note of his heroism and departed, remarking that he had had "a very pleasant time." This was life in the raw.

The excursions at night gave Roosevelt the greatest pleasure. There was a fantastic note to the program of dining at some one's home and then, at midnight, sallying forth with a black cloak over his evening clothes and a wide-brimmed hat pulled down over his face. He prowled through dark streets in the hope of finding a patrolman asleep, off his beat, or engaged in diverting conversation with a friendly prostitute. Disguised as he was, the commissioner could often lead some unwary patrolman into insolent defiance when questioned. Then Roosevelt would reduce the wretch to incoherent servility by explaining that he was president of the police board. . . .

. . . So the ramblings would continue until well toward dawn. Then Roosevelt would appear at Mike Lyons's restaurant on the Bowery, eat a hearty meal of ham and eggs, and retire to a couch at his office near-by for an hour or two of sleep. By 10 o'clock he was refreshed and energetic once more, ready to pass judgment on the trembling victims of the night's excursion.

The citizens of New York, as they read of these exploits, glowed with vicarious satisfaction. They had yearned to humble insolent policemen themselves. The approval was entirely unanimous and Roosevelt was the subject of commendatory comment in Philadelphia, Chicago, Baltimore, and other cities. The Chicago *Times-Herald* said he was the biggest man in New York "if not the most interesting man in public life." The Ithaca (New York) *Daily News* declared him its candidate for the Republican presidential nomination in 1896. Before the end of the year, Cabot Lodge was painting alluring pictures of the United States Senate, of the White House itself.

But in New York, at least, the applause began to die when Roosevelt announced that he intended to enforce the Sunday excise law and that, in due time, even beer would be impossible to obtain on the Sabbath. This was not reform; it was interference with personal liberty.

Fundamentally, Roosevelt was not a prohibitionist nor did he really care whether beer or anything else was sold on Sunday. He started with the sound position that violations of the excise law led to extortion by the police and that if the department was to be cleansed, it was necessary to enforce the law. He soon became enmeshed in a web of inaccurate thinking, however, and he demanded that all laws, good and bad, be enforced. He delivered himself into the hands of his enemies, because of this surplus of zeal, and his career as police commissioner ended largely in failure.

Roosevelt's views on prohibition itself can, fortunately, be set forth in his own words. He expressed himself as forcibly opposed on at least three occasions while in public life; in 1884, in 1905, and in 1908. It was not until the last year or so of his life that Roosevelt was persuaded to endorse the dry movement and he then did so with qualifications and misgivings. . . .

But the struggle for morality by legislative fiat gathered force. The support of the churches had soon been enlisted and the alarm of the politicians increased. Curiously enough Roosevelt, whose paternalistic tendencies were pronounced and who believed in a Federal divorce law, continued to feel that alcohol was an individual problem. On August 10, 1905, he addressed the Catholic Total Abstinence Society in convention at Wilkes-Barre, Pennsylvania, and emphatically approved its purpose. Excessive use of intoxicants caused untold evil in the life of any man, but "in the last analysis the factor most influential . . . must be the sum of that man's own qualities. . . . I believe in the work of these great temperance organizations. . . . But most of all I believe in the efficacy of the man himself." . . .

. . . But [Roosevelt] was facing a situation, not a theory, and it was an extremely complicated situation. New York had been drifting along comfortably under a law that forbade the sale of liquor on Sunday. The front doors of the saloons were closed, but the workingman knew that a side or rear door would swing hospitably inward at the slightest touch. Virtuous vestrymen, passing the corner saloon on their way to church, saw with satisfaction that all was outwardly decorous. They knew that at their clubs, after the morning service, refreshment could be obtained. Despite this tranquillity, however, the Sunday closing law was a source of evil; the police enforced it against the saloon-keepers who refused to buy protection. Roosevelt had not been in office for more than a few weeks before he attempted to solve the insoluble. . . .

Accompanied by columns of newspaper prediction that the day would be dry, the Roosevelt program of enforcement started on Sunday, June 23, 1895. Early on that day a small steamer, the

S.S. *Sarah,* anchored in the Harlem River with a large sign over the side bearing the words: "No Whisky or Beer Aboard, but Plenty of Water. Try the Water. It's the Kind You Like." Whether word of this prehistoric Rum Row had been passed about, or whether they were merely curious, large numbers of men were soon pulling for the vessel in rowboats, and three stout policemen in uniform promptly hired a skiff of their own. The skipper of the *Sarah* saw them, however, and pulled anchor in time to steam away. Later in the day he returned, probably for additional customers anxious to sample the water. This time Roosevelt's men used guile. In plain clothes they rowed to the *Sarah* once more, boarded her, and made their arrests.

By the middle of July, 1895, the uproar was incessant, and Roosevelt had been transformed into an extremely unpopular figure. His men continued to arrest saloon-keepers, the town was measurably more arid than it had been, and the weather was exceedingly hot. The workingman, deprived of his beer, demanded to know why the upper classes, enjoying the cool recesses of the Union League Club, could obtain anything they wanted to drink. They could also patronize hotels, and order liquor with their meals; the poor man could not afford this. Each Sunday, the ferries to Hoboken and other New Jersey oases were crowded, and United States Senator [David B.] Hill of New York, aware that political capital lay in denouncing the Roosevelt program, said that the Democrats constituted the only hope of the wets. The watchword among the "friends of personal liberty," he declared, was "Organize! Organize! Organize!" . . .

At first, Roosevelt was dubious regarding the Sunday closing law. On June 30, 1895, he wrote his older sister that it was "altogether too strict," but that enforcement was the only alternative. Before the end of August, however, he had lost sight of his original beliefs, and told Lodge that "I have now begun to think that we ought not to have the saloons open on Sunday." He had forgotten, also, that during the Assembly debate in 1884 he had voiced an emphatic defense of beer-drinkers as "decent and reputable citizens . . . you will find that the Germans, who are the main beer drinkers, furnish to the criminal class a smaller percentage than . . . they form of the whole population."

The Sunday closing law, like the Federal prohibition amendment that was to follow it, struck at the beer-drinker more than at the whisky-drinker. The saloon-keeper could sell a quart of hard liquor to be smuggled home. The man with the tin pail known as a "growler" was certain to be caught emerging from the side door. The beer-drinker of the '90's faced perils, in fact, that no longer exist, for his long mustaches offered a clue to what went on behind the swinging doors. The police waited in plain clothes on the corner near a suspected saloon; when a citizen appeared wiping his mustaches with the back of his hand, they made a raid.

That New York was much more dry on Sunday during that summer is undoubtedly true. That it was as dry as Roosevelt believed it—"I have, for once, absolutely enforced the law in New York"—is improbable. That it was dry enough to irritate the citizenry to new heights of indignation is clear. Roosevelt's law-abiding Germans were particularly outraged. Favorite beer parlors and gardens, where they had spent quiet days with their wives and children, were closed. After an unhappy summer, and knowing that the State elections were but a few weeks distant, they organized a parade of protest. It was scheduled for September 25, 1895. It was known that the atmosphere would be stolidly hostile. But some one made the mistake of sending an invitation to Roosevelt, supposing that he would appreciate the heavy sarcasm implied and would decline. Instead, he promptly accepted. It was a tactical error on the part of the Germans, for Roosevelt enjoyed himself hugely and, with the amazing talent for the picturesque that helped carry him to the White House, the police commissioner transformed the angry demonstration into a minor personal triumph.

He laughed uproariously when a coffin labeled "Teddyism" was trundled by, when signs appeared proclaiming "Roosevelt's Razzle Dazzle Reform Racket," when Germanic drinking societies solemnly held empty beer steins aloft. One float represented several men in evening dress, seated at a table and drinking champagne, and bore the sign, "Millionaire's Club." Other placards were: "Good Morning. Have You Seen Roosevelt's Name in Print?," "Liberty, Priceless Gem, Where Hast Thou Flown? To Hoboken!," "Roosevelt's Russian Rule." Then a rotund German, his blue eyes peering through heavy lenses, trudged past and, looking up at the reviewing stand, asked in a loud tone,

"Wo ist der Roosevelt?"

The police commissioner leaned far over, grinned his dental grin, and screamed back:

"Hier bin Ich!"

There was a burst of laughter, from marchers and spectators alike. Next day's newspapers agreed that Roosevelt had survived his supposed ordeal very well indeed.

But the enemies of reform had, before this, devised a master stroke which spelled ultimate defeat. It aggravated the growing friction in the police board. It supplied ammunition that even Roosevelt's personality could not turn aside. Their latest move, Roosevelt wrote on July 14, 1895, "has been, through various lawyers, to revive obsolete blue laws, and bring cases before magistrates. . . . The blue law business is puzzling." Instead of ignoring the ordinances against soda fountains, florists, delicatessen keepers, and bootblacks, Roosevelt vacillated between agreeing that these ancient statutes must be enforced and insisting that he was not interested. He told a Good Government Club on July 16 that "the law will be enforced in every particular." He permitted the police to close soda water parlors. He indignantly denounced as a lie the story that orders had gone out against flower-selling; but so friendly a journal as the New York *Times* commented on the arrest of a peddler who had sold five cents' worth of violets to a detective.

Tammany Hall was probably back of these arrests, made to embarrass Roosevelt. He had placed himself in a position where such blows could be struck. It was next rumored that ice could no longer be sold on Sunday, and Charles F. Murphy, then a Tammany leader on the East Side, dispensed ice water free of charge from two liquor stores on Avenue A. The attacks went to the extreme of stating that ice was being denied the sick and dying, and Joseph Pulitzer's New York *Evening World* thereupon reached a new low mark in journalistic depravity. It published an account, giving neither names nor dates nor place, of a mother who had vainly sought a small piece of ice for her sick child. The dealer had declined to sell, since it was a Sunday morning, but had given the woman some ice. At this moment a patrolman came by, refused to listen to their stories, and took them both to court. The *Evening World* concluded this obvious fabrication by describing the mother's return to the bedside of her child.[3]

> "I was kept away, darling. I couldn't get the ice because . . ."
> Suddenly the words died on her lips. She knelt by the bed and took a little wasted hand in hers. Then, raising her face, she gazed up with dry eyes that yet saw nothing and whispered:
> "Thy will be done, O God! Thou knowest best!"
> For the child was dead!

. . . The reform element, once his stanch allies, was irritated by the constant bickerings at meetings of the police board. Welfare workers were horrified when he sanctioned the use of a small boy to obtain evidence against a saloon where liquor was sold to minors. Sporting enthusiasts were indignant over his attempts to control conditions in the prize ring; even more furious protests arose in conservative circles when he went to a prize fight himself and said he enjoyed it because it had been an honest contest. Mayor Strong, who had appointed Roosevelt to office, had meanwhile grown weary of the blue-law and excise activities, as he made clear in an address at the Waldorf-Astoria on December 11, 1895. The mayor remarked, with a trace of bitterness, that in New York the police commissioners were more important than the mayor. He said that a citizen of an upstate town had recently asked whether one of the four heads of the department could not be lent to assist in cleaning up a local crime wave.

"I told him," the mayor said, "all four were busy watching the girls who sold flowers and the poor devils who sold ice on Sunday."

Roosevelt declined to reply to this, saying he knew that the mayor could not be serious. But as early as October he had been writing to Lodge that Strong had been asking him "to let up on the saloon, and impliedly threatening to turn me out if I refused!" The cruelest defection was that of Dr. Parkhurst himself. In September, 1895, he had promised to stand by Roosevelt "until death." In January, 1897, he was scolding him for his part in the police board quarrels and insisting that the board, "by the indignity of its de-

[3] *Ibid.*, August 26, 1895.

meanor . . . is doing more to depress than elevate the tone of the force." . . .

The year [1895] ended with open disagreement over excise enforcement, with Mayor Strong urging Roosevelt to soften his blows. But in April, 1896, a still more serious complication arose through the passage at Albany of the Raines Law, a statute which turned out to be the greatest boon to commercialized vice in the history of New York. Ostensibly a liquor-control measure, the Raines Law continued the provision that hotels could serve liquor on Sunday and defined a hotel as a structure with ten bedrooms and facilities for serving meals. Soon hotels were springing into existence at an astonishing rate. Competition became excessively keen as hundreds of new ones appeared; the ten rooms required by law were used for prostitution in order to pay the overhead. Previously Roosevelt's problem had been merely to see whether, in places where intoxicants were served, there had actually been dining-rooms. Now his men had to judge whether the hotels themselves were genuine. That many were not was indicated by the offer of a furniture firm to furnish all of the ten rooms for $81.20.

Roosevelt failed utterly to realize the significance of the new law, and was inclined to praise it. The defects, however, were promptly called to his attention. In November, 1896, Chief Conlin reported that criminals were opening these places and could not be controlled. Roosevelt then complained that the word "hotel" had been put into the law with "utter laxness of definition." In December it was estimated that 2,000 new hotels had been started and Roosevelt, making a tour of inspection, found ample evidence that a crisis had arrived. One of the "hotels" on the Bowery had stable stalls roofed over with wire for rooms. Over the bar at this inn was a sign reading: "Sleeping in This Hotel Positively Prohibited." There were other places as bad, or worse.

Had Roosevelt begun a crusade against this evil, a drive as vigorous as his excise campaign of the year before, he would have found public opinion squarely behind him. Commercialized vice, even in the '90's, was far different from beer-drinking on Sunday. But Roosevelt, it would seem, had no heart for another fight. He had been pulling wires for some weeks in the hope of an appointment from President McKinley. His effectiveness, also, had been further damaged by violent quarrels with Comptroller Ashbel P. Fitch, who had objected to the manner in which certain police funds had been allocated. At a city hall hearing on May 5, 1896, Roosevelt had exploded that Fitch was no fighter and would run away. The following intellectual exchange then ensued:[4]

Fitch: I would never run away from you!
Roosevelt: You would not fight.
Fitch: What shall it be, pistols or—
Roosevelt: Pistols or anything you wish.
Mayor Strong: Come, come. If this does not stop I will put you both under arrest.

The year closed, and 1897 began, very much on this note. . . . The last few months of 1896 were devoted by Roosevelt almost entirely to the campaign against [William Jennings] Bryan and to negotiations for appointment as Assistant Secretary of the Navy. On April 17, 1897, his letter of resignation from the police board went to Mayor Strong. It contained the usual insincere phrases: ". . . deep appreciation of your attitude . . . very much has been accomplished . . . we have warred against crime and vice more effectively than ever before." . . .

The police commissioner years were years of immaturity, but there was growth, too. If they ended in a degree of failure, they were not without influence on Roosevelt and his career. Of chief importance is the fact that he came into contact, for the first time, with social problems on an extended scale. It was during the Mulberry Street days that Roosevelt absorbed so much of the philosophy of Jacob Riis and abandoned the attitude of aloof noninterference that had marked his legislative years. He became "more set than ever in my distrust of those men, whether business men or lawyers, judges, legislators or executive officers, who seek to make of the Constitution a fetich for the prevention of work of social reform." . . .

Years of immaturity and years of growth: Pringle characterized Roosevelt's period as a member of New York's police board in this way, and he could have written in the

[4] New York *Tribune,* May 6, 1896.

same vein of the historian himself. Obviously the mature scholar's work differs from that of the young man first attempting to prove himself entitled to be heard, and equally obviously one would not wish to read any history book without knowing something of its author, his background, age, and affiliations at the time he wrote. Historiography, as distinct from history, concerns itself in part with the study of the many pressures upon the historian as he selects topics about which to write and then attempts to tell his story. Wallace Stegner, in *Wolf Willow,* his autobiography, spoke of a "pontoon bridge" the scholar must build between his past self and his present work, of how he must begin with his personal "question mark in the circle."

But no one would wish for the historian to indulge in lengthy self-analysis within the pages of a work entitled *The Dissolution of the Monasteries,* for it is the monasteries, and not the author's attitude toward Roman Catholicism, that will most concern the majority of readers of such a book. Still, one might hope to find a brief preface in which the author tells us something of himself, whether it is as Dom David Knowles writing on those monasteries or Arthur Schlesinger, Jr., writing on the Age of Roosevelt—Franklin, not Theodore.

The fetish that is perhaps most damaging to the historian is the notion that one can be a self-made man. There is no more boring and boorish businessman than he who reminds us of how he climbed from rags to riches, but at least such a tale is seldom socially dangerous. The historian who forgets that he is the product of an intricate, deeply personal interaction between himself and many environments soils by arrogance that which he would persuade us to accept by mock humility. One might make a good case against those historians who have known but one intellectual environment—all England and all Oxford, or all New England and all Ivy—but there are too many good historians of whom this is true. The environmental range, therefore, is one more of the mind than of place, and in his search for evidence, for the corpus upon which the historian will work, one may expect a variety of mental experiences that rival a Don Quixote. Enough, then, of warnings against vigilante justice, whether from the hands of a political party, a religious body, a social or racial group, or merely oneself—let us turn to the actual act of finding the evidence, to the historian in his private rôle as investigator.

PART II

HABEAS CORPUS

5. The Secret of the Ebony Cabinet:

A Search for "Lost" Manuscripts

THE SCHOLAR'S FIRST TASK IS TO FIND THE EVIDENCE, AND often this is the most exciting part of his work. It is the dream of every Civil War historian to discover in some virgin treasure-trove *the* document that will prove, beyond the shadow of a doubt, that John Wilkes Booth did (or did not, for that matter) kill Abraham Lincoln, and that Lincoln's Secretary of War, Edwin M. Stanton, was or was not party to the plot. But that single piece of evidence, by which a lifetime of research falls into place, seldom exists, for the historian does not make his case, plea for his defendant, or prosecute his master villain on the basis of one discovery. The historian works by accretion, adding a bit here and a piece there, until a reasonable likeness of the subject of his pursuit begins to emerge. He constructs an Identikit, and to do so he must have all possible evidence—not just that which, with prior logic, seems most important, but that which, before examination, may be presumed not to be important at all. The historian must find not one Lincoln letter but thousands of Lincoln letters if he is to construct an approximate truth. Nor does the historian defend or prosecute, in fact, for just as the detective leaves such judgments to the courts, so, too, does the researcher need most of all to get his man. Like Sergeant Friday, he only wants to get the facts.

The facts arise from verifiable data, and verifiable data most often consist of manuscript records. The diaries, journals, letters sent and received, even Becker's check stubs and Collingwood's paint-smeared jacket, are the subjects of the scholar's attention, and they must be the initial objects of his quest. In a sense, Buchan's plot outline is true for the scholar, since he pursues a collection of documents which may or may not exist from continent to continent under the pressure of time: of weeks grasped from a so-called vacation period, of sabbaticals slowly squeezed from one's employer, of the awareness of one's own shortening time, shortening patience, even shortening interest. The following essay, written by Christopher Morley as a Preface to the first full publication of *Boswell's London Journal,* captures the excitement of the chase and the pleasures of discovery fulfilled.

♦ ♦ ♦

As the express trains between London and Liverpool go racing across the Midlands, the passenger can see, for a minute or so, the noble bulk of Lichfield Cathedral. It rises above the green fields

---

FROM *Boswell's London Journal, 1762–1763* (New York: McGraw-Hill, 1950), edited by F. A. Pottle. Copyright 1950 by Yale University. Used with permission of McGraw-Hill Book Company.

For additional reading: One of the most interesting recent quests has been that carried out by two scholars working independently of each other to identify the factual sources for Joseph Conrad's *Lord Jim,* and to find the present-day geographical sites for those in the novel. The two books, Jerry Allen's *The Sea Years of Joseph Conrad* (New York, 1965) and Norman Sherry's *Conrad's Eastern World* (Cambridge, 1965), while reaching similar conclusions, do so by somewhat different paths. An interesting scholarly controversy has developed between the two writers, and in particular over Miss Allen's contention that "by definition a discovery can be made but once" and that the principal discoveries were hers; the reader may wish to read Miss Allen's article, "Conrad's River," in the *Columbia University Forum,* V (Winter, 1962), and the illuminating controversial review and letters which appeared on the subject in the *Times Literary Supplement* in London on November 3, 10, and 24, 1966, and in the *Spectator,* a London weekly, on August 5, 1966. The theme of a search for lost manuscripts also numbers among the clichés of detective and spy fiction; interesting variants on the theme, which are outstanding novels in their own right, include Eric Ambler's *The Schirmer Inheritance* and James Hall Roberts' *The Q Document,* one of the best books of its kind ever written.

of Staffordshire, a couple of miles west of the line, landmark of the town where Samuel Johnson was born. I'm afraid many travellers miss that glimpse, and I know I have caused puzzled looks by nudging attention to it; but there must also be others who, when they see the spire, think momentarily of the extraordinary life, and the endless fountain of ink, that began below it. When I last saw it (autumn, 1949), on account of some weakness in the great flèche, it was "reticulated and decussated" in steel scaffold, fine as cobweb, hardly less spectacular than the cathedral itself.

I remember that glimpse as an emblem of the work, patient these many years, of scholars and collectors who, before they are done, will have given us exciting new perspectives not only on Johnson, but . . . on his friend and biographer, James Boswell. With equal craft and judgment the scholars and collectors have clustered about a famous edifice, mending, supporting, renewing the tall spire. The parable is not exact: there was certainly no instability in the great Cathedral of Biography, *The Life of Samuel Johnson:* but that masterpiece begins to emerge, from devoted masonry and restoration, taller and more decorative than ever. . . .

Perennially, fact reasserts prevalence over fiction. It would be impossible to invent any detective story so fantastic as the history of the Boswell Papers, running through five generations from Scotland to Ireland, and from their initial suppression and neglect by those most intimately concerned, to their discovery, a century and a half later, their purchase by an American, and then their eventual transfer to a safe new haven in the vaults of the Yale University Library. To understand what happened we must go back to Boswell's strict Presbyterian family.

From the first, Boswell's family had disapproved of his association with Johnson, and even more of his profligate way of life. At twenty-one he had fathered an illegitimate child; afterwards his amorous escapades had been both numerous and notorious; still later, though devoted to his wife ("that valuable woman"), he had been incapable of remaining faithful to her. Small wonder, then, that by the time he died he was already a legend of impropriety, which death transmuted to the skeleton in the family closet. The papers he left—and especially the uninhibited journals . . . served only to confirm this impression of him within the home circle at

Auchinleck; and later events, as we shall see, reinforced it further. So it would appear that the family legend of Boswell as an ancestor to be on the defensive about, and therefore to be kept under cover, took firm hold and was passed on from generation to generation.

But "his chosen lifework," as Professor Chauncey B. Tinker has said of Boswell, was "defeating the forces of oblivion." Even Tinker, at that moment (1922), did not know how decisively Boswell had defeated them. The process took a long time, but at his death, in 1795, it was already well begun. Being both a canny Scot and a lawyer with an eye to the future, Boswell left a will in which he named three of his friends as trustees of his unpublished manuscripts: Sir William Forbes, the Reverend W. J. Temple, and Edmond Malone. The fact that he took this precaution is proof enough that Boswell attached considerable importance to his papers, no matter what his immediate heirs may have thought.

Temple died in 1796, only a year after Boswell, without having seen the papers. Forbes was evidently alarmed by the nature of the manuscripts. He considered them unpublishable, but equally undestroyable. He died ten years later, in 1806. So far as we know, his only editorial contribution to the problem was to insert at various places in the journals markers bearing the note: "Exceptionable Passage" or "Reprehensible Passage."

The third executor, the Irishman Malone, was of a different sort. Distinguished scholar and analyst of Shakespeare, he had recently (1790) published his famous edition of the plays; perhaps he yearned, as a born editor would, for another job equally severe. It was Malone who with kindness and wisdom had kept poor split-minded Boswell to the great task he had to finish before he died. The deuce with the law, Malone must have said; the deuce with standing for Parliament; and the deuce also (in moderation) with wine and women. Get on with the *Life*. Night after night, in his "elegant library," Malone corked the decanter and uncorked Boswell's portfolio of scrawl-handed memos.

It had taken Boswell more than twenty years to assemble these multifarious and multitudinous jottings about Johnson, and now the exhausting compilation had to be carried through by a breaking man, ridiculed by paragraphers and cartoonists, half-crazed by melancholia, dissipation, disappointment in law and politics, the death of his wife, and perplexities of money and his children's education. But he had Malone to keep him at it. Together, they went over the collected material. . . . Boswell was the curator of Johnson's memory, but Malone, in those last bewildered years, was curator of Boswell. . . .

So, even after death, Boswell had his usual luck. Of his chosen executors, Forbes was a busy banker in Edinburgh and probably as easily shocked as bankers have to be. Temple was a parson in remote Cornwall, less shockable than a banker, but urn-buried in family pains of his own. But the third was the exceptional Malone, acute and experienced editor. So far as we can guess at this distance, he did all that friend and critic can. Though he did not advise publication of the papers (resistance by Boswell's family would have been too strong to permit it anyhow), he saw to it that they were preserved.

The reproach used to be that Boswell's executors never met to discute their problem. If not, so much the better: none felt free to destroy anything. We know that Forbes and Malone corresponded and sent boxes of the papers to and fro by wagon. The upshot was that they decided (since the papers had been willed for the benefit of Boswell's younger children; the heir, Sir Alexander, had the estate) to wait until the younger son, James Boswell, Jr., who had more of his father's tastes than Alexander, would be old enough to offer mature opinion. Malone was left with the belief that most of the manuscripts had been returned to Auchinleck.

But at this point Malone's handwriting becomes an element in the story. It has been ingeniously suggested: Did Malone write of a certain manuscript that it "had been *burned* in a mass of papers," or "*buried* in a mass of papers"? That is one of the small red herrings that have slipped through the seines of scholarship. We know the answer now, or at least the major answer; but for years it was assumed, on the authority of Malone's possibly misread word, that at least a part and probably all of Boswell's papers had been destroyed. What seems likely is that whoever found himself in possession of any of the notes and journals took one horrified and fascinated look, and shoved them into the nearest closet.

Malone died in 1812. Both the Boswell sons, Sir Alexander

(familiarly known as Sandy) and Jamie the Younger, died in 1822. James, Jr., died of illness, and Sandy was killed in a duel shortly afterwards.[1]

The mansion at Auchinleck was left to a group of semi-noble dames who were naturally timorous of anything associated with their great-grandfather. The portrait of Johnson by Sir Joshua Reynolds, so Sir Walter Scott said, was moved from the drawing room to the attic, face to the wall. The papers, if any, were presumed destroyed. This attitude need not surprise us. There are still plenty of well-bred people who prefer life to turn its face to the wall.

But even in the dampest closets the bony pattern of Old Mortality is durable. Never did any skeleton resume so much mortal flesh so many years later.

To ramify the history of the papers and the Boswell family tree, through its failure of heirs male and marriages in the distaff, is a

[1] Alexander Boswell . . . was, like his father, a passionate Tory. He contributed to a rather disreputable Tory newspaper bitter anonymous attacks on one James Stuart of Dunearn, a lawyer in Edinburgh, a man with whom he was outwardly on good terms. These attacks were witty but outrageous, and especially charged Stuart with cowardice. (Stuart, who was a man of family, was treated with contempt for having embraced the lucrative profession of solicitor rather than the gentlemanly one of barrister. Alexander Boswell, among other things, called him a "fat coward" and said he would draw "bills, wills, and petitions" or *"aught* but a trigger.") Stuart got hold of the office papers of the newspaper and found from the manuscripts of the articles that Alexander Boswell was the author. When Sir Alexander returned from London after James's funeral, he found a card waiting for him, and two days later received a challenge. He refused to apologize, and met Stuart in a duel at the farm of Balbarton, an ancient Boswell property. Sir Alexander, a good shot, fired into the air; Stuart, who had never fired a pistol before, fired without taking aim and wounded Sir Alexander mortally. The spinal cord was severed just below the neck. He was carried to the near-by house of his elderly cousin Claud Boswell, Lord Balmuto. The family was in the midst of a house-cleaning, and a portrait of Sir Alexander's grandfather, Lord Auchinleck, was lying on the bed where Sir Alexander was to be placed. The men who removed the picture from the bed had Sir Alexander's blood on their hands, and it is said that the back of the picture still shows the stains. Sir Alexander, who was of course completely paralyzed, died next day. When Stuart was tried for murder, Lord Jeffrey, his chief counsel, read to the Court those passages of Boswell's *Life of Johnson* in which Johnson defends duelling as a form of self-defence, and Boswell admits that if he himself were affronted, he would think it necessary to fight. The jury acquitted the accused without leaving the room.

pleasure for specialists. Abridgement for the amateur need mention only the great turn-points in the century and a half after Boswell's death.

First, there was [Thomas Babington] Macaulay's extraordinary essay and the condensed version of its characterization of Boswell included in his "Life of Johnson" in the *Encyclopædia Britannica,* a work spread in millions as a class room text. It was impressed on every schoolboy, in Macaulay's gorgeous rhetoric, that the greatest of all biographies outside Holy Writ was the work of a clown, zany, screwball, and buffoon. As *soutenance de thèse,* Macaulay's essay can never be surpassed; and never, by Boswellians, quite forgiven. No wonder the Boswell family, hypersensitive as only Scottish heirs can be, encouraged the notion that the reliques of their freakish ancestor had perished. Perhaps the wish was father to the thought: by now they may even have believed it.

Then happened a strange adventure. About 1840—no one has ever been able to tell me the precise date and circumstance—an English traveller, one Major Stone of the East India Company, was making purchases in the shop of Madame Noël in Boulogne. Major Stone found his supplies, whatever they were, wrapped in pages of manuscript signed with the large and legible name, *James Boswell.* All Madame Noël knew was that they were part of a bale of scrap she had bought from a junk-pedlar. Major Stone was smart enough to buy all that remained. They proved to be near one hundred letters written to the Reverend William Temple.

How did they happen to turn up in this unlikely place and fashion? For answer we go back to Boswell.

Of the many friendships in Boswell's life, two were critical. A man of temperament has friendships reaching many ways. There was the great one, world-known, reaching upward to Johnson; and another, candid and laxative—and in the long run no less significant—downward to his lifelong confidant, the parson Temple. To Temple he always told all. How comforting it is to have a confessor of one's own age. To Temple he confessed what he would never have mentioned to Johnson. This being the basis of their friendship, Temple cherished Boswell's letters and preserved them. But Temple had a daughter who married a too-lavish parson, Mr. Powlett, whom Boswell had once invited to breakfast and found congenial. Perhaps it was Powlett's memory of Boswell's charm that caused him, when he shot the moon and moved to France to escape creditors, to take with him his father-in-law's papers. And in due course, all unknowing, Madame Noël came into possession of the letters, presumably dispersed on Powlett's death, which occurred in 1834.

After Major Stone acquired them they circulated among various hands and were eventually published (sharply "castrated," as scholars say) in 1857. Eventually they came to safe-deposit in the Pierpont Morgan Library in New York, and were first published in full by Professor Tinker in 1924. I imagine the ghost of Boswell, relaxing into the Doric accent: "Heave awa', lads, I'm no deid yet."

Another cusp in the graph was drawn when great-granddaughter Emily Boswell, in 1873, married one of the ancient and noble family of Talbot, seated at Malahide Castle outside Dublin. Emily's sister and co-heir Julia, Mrs. Mounsey, had married a mayor of Carlisle, of which Border stronghold Boswell himself had once been Recorder. Mrs. Mounsey may seem unimportant to the Common Reader (as Johnson called us), but the fact of her existence was to prove of great cost and circumstance some seventy years later.

The Common Reader, privileged and otiose person, looks with most uncommon calm on the toils of scholars. Even this casual summary of better men's devotions must, however, mention the great and still laureate edition of the *Life* by George Birkbeck Hill (Oxford, 1887). This, and his succeeding collections of ana, were the primer and cornerstone of all modern reference. Dr. Hill, who relished most his honorary fellowship at Pembroke College, Oxford, Johnson's own "nest of singing birds," was refused entrance to Auchinleck, and harpooned the family in an essay in *The Atlantic Monthly;* this did not make access any easier for later pilgrims.

In 1905, ob. old Mrs. Mounsey, and the Auchinleck property and archives passed to the Hon. James Boswell Talbot, great-great-grandson, and heir of Malahide. Just when the papers were moved to Ireland I don't know. It must have been some forty years ago. Except for a sheaf of chance-choice items in an Ebony Cabinet (an heirloom to Boswell from a great-grandmother), they simply passed from one attic to another. They were shoved away anywhere convenient—some in a croquet box which afterwards became famous.

In 1921, the heir, James Boswell Talbot, succeeded to the title and castle of Malahide: a kindly man, interested in sports and horses and the estate; not much curious about papers, dimly rumoured disreputable, that had come down through his mother's family. He married, in middle life, a highly intelligent and sprightly lady of a theatrical background and with the keen sense of actuality and box-office that the stage implants. Soon after Lord Talbot's marriage, Professor Tinker's *Letters of James Boswell* (1924) was being widely reviewed in the press, and the remote observer begins to see the diagram of destiny taking shape.

Professor Tinker was one of the earliest of scholars to estimate Boswell, with magical Powder of Sympathy, as a phenomenon in himself even if he had never known Johnson. The eventual publication of all the Boswell Papers . . . will provide overwhelming corroborative evidence to prove it.

On July 29, 1920, Tinker had written to the great Tom Tiddler's Ground of bibliography, the London *Times Literary Supplement,* asking if anyone knew of any letters of Boswell in private custody. *The Times* of London is not only the best printed newspaper in the world, it is the only one in which anything whatever printed causes eventual ricochet. One issue, regardless of date, is as good as another; it is printed on paper too asbestic for good kindling, so it is rarely destroyed. And it is read, not in a hurry, by the kind of elderly dons, parsons, eccentrics, to whom reading is dram and drug. In this instance, reply was prompt and explicit: Professor Tinker got an anonymous communication: "Try Malahide Castle." He looked up *Burke's Peerage* and noted the Boswell connection.

By felicitous coincidence the United States Consul General in Dublin at the time was a college classmate, Yale '99, and intimate friend of Tinker's, Mr. Charles Hathaway. With his aid and that of others, including the Ven. the Archdeacon of Dublin, discreet *pourparlers* were arranged. After some delay, the Consul and the Professor were invited to tea at Malahide. One loves to conceive the kind of letter Boswell himself would have written if he had wanted to crash the castle. Those who know his immortal brass in gaining access to Rousseau and Voltaire can well imagine it. . . .

In a memorandum tenderly Boswellian in tone, Professor Tinker has recorded his visit, which took place June 30, 1925.

"I was accompanied by the Consul General on the fateful Tuesday. . . . I took with me, as a propitiatory offering, a copy of my edition of *Boswell's Letters,* published the year before. The gift was accepted, but without enthusiasm. It served only to increase the natural suspicions of my intentions."

One doubts whether Professor Tinker, *molto agitato,* really did justice to his tea and cucumber-and-cress sandwiches and caraway cake. It was finally Lord Talbot, puzzled and bored, who suggested the guests be taken to the next room to see the Ebony Cabinet. "I recall," says Tinker, "a magnificent escritoire of black oak, but of course one must make allowance for the tendency to heighten and colour memories now twenty-five years old." He saw, and was allowed to handle, "papers in a drawer stuffed full of manuscripts. There were letters of Boswell to his son Sandy—some manuscript sheets of the *Life*—a number of volumes of a diary—Lady Talbot told me that parts of it were not suitable for print."

There were also, the Talbots told the stricken scholar, at least two boxes of papers from Auchinleck that had never been opened. When was student ever so tortured? But Tinker pays honourable tribute to Lady Talbot's understandable coolness. "There was no reason why she should be well-disposed to an American who arrived wishing to know the nature and extent of the family papers. As the state of affairs was slowly disclosed to me, my dismay mounted with my fascinated attention. The mere existence of such treasures made my edition of the *Letters* seem *passé*. I saw that all that had been said and written about Boswell must now be revised. My state of mind was not happy.

"When we left, Lord Talbot descended the castle stairway with us, and held the door of the taxi for me to enter. He suggested that perhaps we might be inclined to visit Dublin again in the autumn, for the races. . . . I told my friend that I had seen the Valley of Rubies."

That one glimpse was all that Tinker was to be granted as long as the papers remained at Malahide. But he came away with precious knowledge which others before him had sought in vain. He knew that the Boswell Papers—or at least a part of them—still survived; and he knew where they were. The news was revealed to few people, but of course spread. A famous American collector of rare manuscripts made a courageous effort. He sent a cable to Lord Talbot offering £50,000 for the papers. This was approximately a quarter of a million dollars at the then rate of exchange. Lord Talbot took umbrage that such an offer had been made for the family papers by a stranger, and he did not answer the cable. That was the end of that chapter.

Tinker also told his friend A. Edward Newton, and Newton next had a go at the papers. Again the stone wall. So when Newton saw that he, too, could get nowhere, he encouraged a friend of his to try his luck. There was nothing to lose by trying, and Newton told his friend that if anyone could succeed where others had failed and given up, he was the man.

Now enters the remarkable character of Lieutenant-Colonel Ralph Heyward Isham, who possessed precisely those qualities that our history requires. Not in any sense an academic person, he had nevertheless long been a student of the eighteenth century, and he was already a well-known Johnson collector. He had also, desirable for collectors, considerable funds. Though an American, he had lived much abroad, and had served a notable career in the British Army, rising to staff officer in the First World War. Courageous, gay, and reckless of wit, he had done champion service in humouring and restoring order among disaffected troops growling to be demobbed in 1919. Above all, perhaps, he knew that a straight line is not always the shortest distance between two points.

Through proper channels, Colonel Isham made his identity known to Lord Talbot, and expressed a wish to visit Malahide to see the Boswell Papers. No word or hint of wanting to buy them, you understand; he just wanted to look at them. And in due course, again through channels, Lord Talbot sent his answer: he would be glad to receive Colonel Isham at the castle if he chanced to be in the neighbourhood. Well, it just so happened that he chanced to be in the neighbourhood with reasonable but not unseemly haste. This was in 1926. He was received, he saw some of the papers, and the sequel proves that he got on well with Lord and Lady Talbot. He was invited to return, and later he spent several days as house-guest at the castle.

Only Colonel Isham . . . can tell the complete details of what happened from this point on. For present purposes all we need to know is that, as Chaucer said somewhere in the glorious *Troilus:* "to fisshen then he leyde out hooke and line." And who has more fun: the fisherman in planning his lures, or the fish in being caught by the perfect angler? Here there is legitimate question as to who was fish, who fisherman. For, after cordial relationship had been won, it was Lady Talbot who made the first cast. Did Colonel Isham think the papers had real value? Oh yes, said he; no doubt of it.

That was the right answer. Lady Talbot could not have helped hearing of occasional auction sales at Sotheby's or elsewhere, and of casual Boswell holographs that had brought considerable guineas. As the Prayer Book says, she marked and inwardly digested. Then, too, there was that other American who had cabled his offer of £50,000 for the papers, sight unseen. Perhaps that meant they were worth even more.

So, the Colonel having given the right answer, a basis for fair dealing was established. It took many months of negotiation, but in the end, as Colonel Isham tells it, Lady Talbot persuaded him that they ought to sell the papers. In 1928, then, he was able to take title to the biggest single catch in literary angling. It included many treasures: some leaves of the manuscript of the *Life,* some letters to and from Boswell, and the journals—not, however, including the [*London Journal* for 1762–1763], which had never been at Malahide and was not then known to have survived.

In a story so replete with the incredible, one learns not to be surprised by anything—which is just as well, for the unexpected went on happening to the very end. An old box, supposed to contain a set of croquet implements, was found stuffed with manuscripts in 1930. Again, in 1937, Isham made personal search of the castle and turned up some remarkable things, including a pathetically intimate diary of Dr. Johnson's private anxieties. Then, in 1940, when the Government was looking for places to store food in wartime, the loft of a disused stable or outhouse at Malahide was cleared for this purpose—and what should turn up but two chests containing Boswell archives.

To a relic-destroying and apartment-living generation these repeated discoveries may seem beyond belief. Yet they happened. Malahide is an ancient moated castle with stone turrets and battlements; and in such a sprawling structure there are always innumerable garrets, cellars, cupboards, ancient chests, and similar depositories for any kind of plunder that one wants to put out of sight and yet cannot bear to part with. So it is perhaps not so fantastic after all that the papers, once their value was established, continued to turn up. At any rate, Colonel Isham, having started on the trail, had no choice but to follow the spoor to the very bottom of his bank account.

In the mean time, no less astounding was the adventure of Professor Claude Colleer Abbott, then Lecturer in English at the University of Aberdeen. Perhaps he is the best example in our time of Walpole's serendipity, characteristic of one who finds something he wasn't looking for. What Professor Abbott was actually looking for was material for a new life of James Beattie, an eighteenth-century Scottish philosopher, a friend of both Boswell and Johnson, but quite forgettable now. Abbott found it necessary to examine papers preserved at Fettercairn House, not far from Aberdeen, an estate of Lord Clinton. Lord Clinton is the direct descendant of Sir William Forbes, one of Boswell's literary executors. To his amazement, going through a capharnaum of miscellany (this was October, 1930, to January, 1931), Professor Abbott found what completely side-tracked him from Beattie. In bags, bundles, bean sacks, and helter-skelter through the closets and attics of an ancient house, he found some sixteen hundred letters and manuscripts and documents to, from, and by Johnson, Boswell, and their friends. Among them was the [London] journal. . . . Presumably Forbes had examined these papers during his executorship and had not got around to returning them to Auchinleck before he died.

Professor Abbott's catalogue of the Fettercairn papers took time to prepare. Announcement of his discovery was not published until 1936 and immediately precipitated a legal battle.

Boswell, as a Scottish advocate, would have been professionally excited by the great lawsuit to determine the ownership of these Fettercairn papers. I can see him, with fresh-powdered wig, listening ghostlike to the argument. The cause was throng with claimants, eventually reduced to four: among them Colonel Isham, who had secured an assignment of the claim of Lord Talbot. Another was the residuary legatee of Mrs. Mounsey, the Cumberland Infirmary.

Experts have often told us that there is nothing so traditionally special as Scottish law. The cause, which fell into the ancient classification of multiplepoinding ("poinding" is pronounced "pinding"), was pleaded before the Court of Session in Edinburgh, which awarded the property in equal shares to Colonel Isham and to the Cumberland Infirmary as claimants deriving their interests from the sisters Emily and Julia, Boswell's great-granddaughters.

Legally, this settlement was quite correct. Practically, it presented a dilemma. For how are equal shares to be apportioned when the thing to be divided is, not money, but 1,607 items of literary material, the value of which still remains to be determined? The Cumberland Infirmary was for having the papers sold at auction and dividing the proceeds. But Colonel Isham wanted the papers themselves. In the end, after much negotiation, he succeeded in persuading the Cumberland Infirmary to sell its half interest to him; the price was agreed upon and the money paid. What with lawyers' fees, court expenses, and all the rest of it, old Mrs. Mounsey had cost the Colonel dear.

Colonel Isham had to wait until the Second World War was over to take possession of his new treasure. But at last came October 23, 1948, when a few friends assembled in his apartment in New York to celebrate the opening of the boxes from Fettercairn (which one of the Colonel's sons had super-cargoed across the Atlantic). With a keen sense of chronology, the evening was linked with October 23, 1773, when Johnson and Boswell, after passing sea-dangers, sat down in the inn at Inveraray; and the usually abstemious Doctor called for "some of that stuff that makes Scotchmen happy." Colonel Isham, looking taller and more lean than ever, was certainly happy on this occasion; but afterwards, realizing that his successful quest had sapped his fortune, he began groping for a possible and seemly redemption. You will find his solution in a headline on the front page of *The New York Times* for August 1, 1949: "Yale Gets Boswell Papers."

The news account told how Boswell's archives had found permanent sanctuary at Yale through a gift from the Old Dominion Foundation of Washington, established by Paul W. Mellon, and through purchase of all the publishing rights by the McGraw-Hill Book Company.

Here the story seemed to end. But wonders never cease, and there is always room for a postscript. . . . Lord Talbot died without issue. His title and the castle at Malahide passed to a relative who had no Boswell blood in his veins. The widowed Lady Talbot had to choose another residence; and the new Lord Talbot, in house-cleaning, found—what else but more Boswell papers? Not having any claim on them, he sent them to Lady Talbot; and, even as these lines are written, negotiations have been concluded for their acquisition by Colonel Isham and for their transfer to Yale.

So endeth the fantastic history of the Private Papers of James Boswell. . . .

6. The Mystery of Marie Roget, and Other Diversions:

Another Search for Lost Manuscripts

THE WORLD OF LITERARY SCHOLARSHIP IS FULL OF MANY no less fantastic adventures. Scholars who are dependent upon manuscript material for their work have learned that archives, however well organized and however vigorously curators pursue their records for deposit, often do not contain the most needed data. This is especially so in countries frequently devastated by war, in the tropics where worm and dust corrupt, or in newly-developing nations which have yet to turn their attention to their past. The search, it is true, begins with the archives—with national, state, and local historical societies and depositories—but more often than not it must also branch out into private homes, company records, and the fading memories of participants in the past one seeks to recapture.

As we have observed, students of American history are more fortunate than others, for American records are uncommonly well preserved. The Puritans kept records of their materials intact—here a record of the purchase of a cow, there an account of a conversion, or of evidence of an outward sign of the inward grace. The American Revolution gave added strength to the conviction that we would be called upon to tell our story. The Civil War engendered an obsessive historical consciousness in the South. With the New Deal, a magnificent national archive was constructed to house yet more of the nation's treasures. Taught in every school and college, history became a story of progress, and so that we might look down on the rungs of the ladder we were ascending, we developed a national attic unmatched, in relation to our short history, by that of any other people. Local societies, microfilms, reprint houses, and journals add to the staggering bulk with which the American historian must contend. Do you want to know of the rise of the penny dreadful? Read the *Journal of Popular Culture*. Do the Great Lakes interest you? Read *Inland Seas*. Is the city of Buffalo your unlikely concern? See *Niagara Frontier*. Airplanes? There is a journal. Exploration? There is a journal. Canada's Grand Manan Island, off the coast of Maine? The Grand Manan Historical Society publishes an occasional journal. And where there are journals there are museums, libraries, and archives, each with its unique treasures.

In the United States, then, as we have seen, the historian may say to himself, "What questions would I like to ask?" He may, with a considerable degree of confidence, anticipate finding the answers before he has exhausted all the available material. But in new nations, in Malaysia or Ghana, each with an excellently managed archive, or even in England, with the vast storehouses of the British Museum, the Public Record Office, the Bodleian Library at Oxford, and hundreds of antiquarian societies and private muniment rooms, the historian nonetheless must reverse the procedure. "What manuscript collections exist?" he asks. Only then does he move on to the second stage, "What questions may I most fruitfully direct to these manuscripts?" The search for the manuscripts becomes the first task, and the techniques to be used differ neither in kind nor in degree from the dogged legwork of the insurance investigator, the tracer of missing persons (or "skip-tracer"), or the detective routinely pursuing leads which, he hopes, will unfold like nesting boxes to reveal a kernel of evidence. The historian enters the phase of his work so ably, if scathingly, described by Henry James in *The Aspern Papers*.

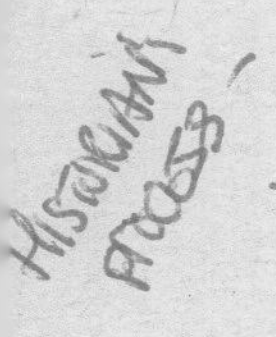

The search for manuscripts thereby raises one of the historian's earliest moral dilemmas. James's protagonist felt justified in misleading his Mrs. Prest, Juliana Bordereau, and even the pathetic niece, Miss Tina, because he thought the public deserved Jeffrey Aspern's papers. In fact, he was that public, for he wanted a bundle of the Aspern letters more than the answer to the riddle of the universe (surely more beneficial to that anonymous public he used to rationalize his actions), and he came armed with visiting cards bearing a *nom de guerre*.

Yet all of us, from motives no more harmful than courtesy, may pretend an interest in a subject that bores us. Where is the line to be drawn? I once asked a graduate student in the midst of her oral examination whether, in order to get access to the records of a Roman Catholic missionary order in Africa, she would pretend to be a Catholic. She pointed out realistically that the question might not arise, since her name was French and the brotherhood might assume that she was of the faith. But what if they asked, and in their asking made it clear that were she not a Catholic, she would be barred from the papers? She answered with the only permissible reply: that she would honestly admit that she was of Protestant background, although scarcely a believer in any organized religion any longer, and she would hope to persuade the members of the order that she would be fully as objective as any other researcher—in truth, more objective than a Roman Catholic from a different order or, indeed, from the same order. In short, she would trust to the sophistication of her audience to see that for the trained historian one's personal background could be made reasonably irrelevant.

Yet what if the audience is not sophisticated? Seventeen years ago I was pursuing the official records of the Ringatu Church, a quasi-Christian movement among the Maori of New Zealand. The New Zealand government did not recognize the Church at the time, for its injecting a unique Maori figure, the Glorious Niu, into the Godhead and thus being Quadrinitarian. Furthermore, it was believed to have descended directly from a nineteenth-century cannibalistic movement. The Ringatu understandably were suspicious of all whites. I could demonstrate my sympathy to their point of view if they would give me time—I had learned Maori, was moving through the country on foot, and knew their history reasonably well. But without seeing their records I could not say that my conclusions would be favorable to the Church.

As it happened, I found the records and was given permission to copy them, dragged out one by one from under the bed of the *poutikanga* (president) of the Church. A moralist may have found my course to the papers objectionable, or entirely too Jesuitical, but upon reflection I do not. Because I was an American, and because the Maori of New Zealand's East Cape had met few Americans who were not Mormons—a group then and since most active in missionary work in the area—all thought I was, as they said, "a saint." By chance my senior thesis in college had been on the Mormon church, and I had no difficulty in speaking the necessary theological language. Because the Ringatu faith had drawn upon that of the Mormons for a portion of its doctrine, I was passed from hand to hand until I met the *poutikanga*. No one asked me whether I was, in fact, a Mormon and I volunteered no information. The *poutikanga* asked only whether I liked to fish, and asked me to accompany him on his daily fishing round. I hate fishing, I become violently seasick even on Long Island Sound; I nonetheless went fishing for three days in a tiny open boat. On the last day we fished among the rocks off a small inlet, where my now Maori friend wrenched small octopuses loose from the undersides of the stones to which they clung with their suction disks. These he threw to me, alive, to put in a basket. I have a childhood fear of crawling things, but I caught them and nursed them through a long, hot afternoon. That evening he began to bring out the papers, dating back to the eighteen-nineties, and within ten days I had copied them all—the only white person at that time to have done so.

The major point of this personal tale is yet to be made. The *poutikanga* permitted me to copy the records only upon my promise not to publish them until after his death. The promise was made, the records were copied, and they remain to this day unpublished, for that hardy fisherman, then—in 1952—in his seventies, is still alive. The material was to have been used in a Master's thesis but it was not and a different thesis was written; one day the material will help to make a good book. To obtain the materials by pretending to an interest that was not really my own seemed to me permissible; to publish them against a clearly given promise and a clearly expressed desire is not. If in order to talk at ease with someone whose confidence I wish to earn I spend a day or so of intensive study on, let us say, Sikkimese royal titles, the knowledge I have and use is real—only the interest is assumed. Yet all of us learn many things because they will be useful, candidly admitting to ourselves that they are not in themselves interesting. It is a thin line between guile and courtesy, and no doubt many historians have crossed it, or would place the line elsewhere. Yet surely there is some difference between the *nom de guerre* and *savoir de guerre*.

The following essay reveals a number of ways in which scholars have searched out and obtained admission to resources of indisputable importance. "The Scholar Adventurers," its author, Richard D. Altick, a Professor of English at Ohio State University, calls them. He shows how techniques of the search may be enhanced by a study of the interests and emotions of the quarry.

♦ ♦ ♦

There is not a single figure in the history of English or American literature whose biography may be sealed up and labeled "Completed." Year after year we learn more about the personal lives, the characters, and the literary careers of scores of great writers—and are forced to unlearn much that we had previously believed true. In the past thirty years thousands of letters written by Swift, Addison, Steele, Boswell, Johnson, Walpole, Scott, Lamb, Wordsworth, Coleridge, Byron, Shelley, the Brownings, Dickens, Emerson, and Thackeray have been published for the first time, with thousands more still to come. Our view of these men naturally must be revised in the light of the new information contained in their letters. Similarly, new scholarly editions of the works of the great English and American men of letters are revealing a great deal about the methods of composition and revision that lay behind the text of the earlier editions. Not until 1926, for instance, were we able to read Wordsworth's great philosophical poem, *The Prelude,* in the form in which the poet had first written it in 1805–06; until that time we knew the poem only in the much altered version which was published in 1850. A comparison of the original text with one that was the result of forty years of tinkering enables us to view with fresh insight the great changes Wordsworth's philosophical attitudes underwent as he grew older. . . . The manuscripts of Nathaniel Hawthorne's *English* and *American Notebooks* tell us much more about England and America—and about Hawthorne—than his widow felt it proper to reveal in 1870. It is scarcely an exaggeration to say that our present methods of scholarship are turning up so much new material that if the present rate of discovery continues, every generation will find it necessary to rewrite the history of English literature and the biographies of many of its principal ornaments.

FROM Richard D. Altick, *The Scholar Adventurers* (New York: Macmillan Co., 1950), pp. 86–104. Reprinted with permission of the Macmillan Company from *The Scholar Adventurers* by Richard D. Altick. Copyright 1950 by Richard D. Altick.

For additional reading: The whole of Altick's admirable book is well worth reading, and it is available again in an inexpensive paperback edition (New York: Free Press, 1966). I adapted my title to the previous essay on the Malahide Castle find from it. Altick's bibliography will lead the reader to many other equally fascinating detective stories. A similar work, less sprightly but full of accounts of this nature, is William Leo Lucey, *History: Methods and Interpretation* (Chicago, 1958). Again, much detective fiction parallels the stories given in both books, although the hunt-and-find private detective traditionally must meet with assorted mayhem along the path to discovery; but then so, too, does the scholar, when he turns to the reviews of his published work. Three British authors who come readily to mind, in the ways they employ the techniques discussed in Altick's book, are the two Smiths, Clark (try *The Case of Torches*) and Godfrey (see *The Flaw in the Crystal*), and Mary Kelly, especially in *The Spoilt Kill,* the last a pun upon "kiln."

All sorts of specialized scholars have, of course, contributed to this steady increase of literary information. But no one has more adventures in the course of his work than the manuscript hunter, the man who tracks down the raw materials of literary biography. He may not always travel in distant countries, as hundreds of scholars have done in an attempt to overtake the ghost of a footloose author or his equally nomadic descendants. But he is guaranteed his moments of suspense and frustration and profound perplexity and occasional exultation. He meets all sorts of people; he finds himself in all sorts of interesting situations; and with all of them he must be equipped to deal.

The quarry is Literary Documents—a generic term which includes all kinds of written records that throw light on some aspect of a literary figure's life and work: the successive drafts and revisions of his writings; his diaries, letters, and autobiographical fragments; the letters and reminiscences of members of his family and his friends; legal records such as affidavits, deeds, and wills. The ultimate aim is twofold: first, to discover facts which previously have been unknown; second, to check the statements and quotations of earlier biographers and editors by going back to the original sources. . . .

At the outset, the routine of the manuscript hunter is fairly well established. He goes to the most obvious places first. He consults a great array of scholarly reference books, such as the catalogues of manuscripts owned by the British Museum and the various libraries at Oxford and Cambridge. He writes to, or visits, all the large libraries that have manuscript collections. If he is lucky, he may discover that the papers of the author in whom he is interested have been preserved intact by his family and have eventually found their way to a library or a museum. The late Gordon Wordsworth, a direct descendant of the poet, some years ago gave his family archives to the Wordsworth Museum at Grasmere, in the Lake District. Scott's journal, a great mass of his correspondence, and many of his other papers are preserved at his famous home, Abbotsford. The main bulk of the papers of Longfellow is to be found at his old home, Craigie House, in Cambridge, Mass. The papers of Henry James and Emerson are now in the Harvard

Library; those of Sherwood Anderson are in the Newberry Library, Chicago; and so on.

Or our scholar may find that though his author's papers once were widely scattered, some collector has devoted his life and fortune to reassembling them. This was the case with the Brontë material that was collected by a wealthy Philadelphian, Henry H. Bonnell, who generously returned it to the town of Haworth in Yorkshire; and with many of the papers of Leigh Hunt, which were amassed by Luther A. Brewer of Cedar Rapids, Iowa, and presented upon his death to the University of Iowa. Baylor University in Texas is world-famous for its rich Browning collection, the fruit of many years of devoted work by Professor A. J. Armstrong. One of the finest Keats collections in the world was amassed by the poet Amy Lowell, who bequeathed it to the Harvard University Library, where it was joined not long ago by the equally rich one of the Marquis of Crewe. The great manuscript collection of Dickens's friend and biographer John Forster, now in the Victoria and Albert Museum in London, is a starting-point for scholars wishing to do research on figures so diverse as Samuel Richardson and Dickens himself.

But there is no such thing as an even "reasonably" complete manuscript collection relating to a single author. A scholar working on Scott, for example, though he may find much to detain him at Abbotsford, must supplement what he learns there by examining the quantities of Scott manuscripts held by the British Museum, the University of Edinburgh, the National Library of Scotland, and a host of private collectors.

When, as happens more often than not, a scholar establishes with virtual certainty that there is no major concentration of the papers associated with his author, he must abandon his lazy man's dream of having his materials borne to him upon a silver platter, to the sound of trumpets, and get down to real work. He must comb every library, large and small, every archive, every institution where manuscripts may conceivably be kept; he must go through innumerable catalogues of book dealers and auctioneers to find out what manuscripts have turned up for sale in the last hundred years or so, and then try to trace them as they passed from collector to collector; he must try to communicate with every single person or institution that would have any reason for being interested in acquiring or preserving the manuscript relics of his author. It takes years of steady work to exhaust such possibilities. . . .

As if it were not enough to have to write and visit hundreds of libraries and private collectors in quest of the elusive document, the lot of the manuscript hunter is made harder by a persistent suspicion that librarians and collectors, however systematic their cataloguing methods, often do not know what they actually possess. Such a suspicion arises less from an innate cynicism on the part of the scholar than from his own and his colleagues' actual experiences. One thinks, for instance, of the recent case of Dr. Campbell's diary. In the year 1854 there was published, in Sydney, Australia, a little book called *A Diary of a Visit to England in 1775, by an Irishman* (*The Reverend Doctor Thomas Campbell*). Its principal interest lay in its descriptions of meetings with Dr. Johnson, to whom Boswell introduced Campbell. The reviewers were skeptical about the book. For one thing, the history of the manuscript was disturbingly vague. The sponsor of the 1854 edition, an official of the Supreme Court of New South Wales, said that the manuscript had been found behind an old cupboard in one of the offices of his court. Without impugning the sincerity of the sponsor, it was pointed out that any common forgery could be "discovered" in the same way. Again, the diary, as published, contained little that was not already known about Johnson. But after considerable debate the English Johnsonians of mid-Victorian days decided, without having seen the manuscript, to accept the diary as genuine.

In the early 1930's, Professor James L. Clifford, who is now on the graduate faculty at Columbia University, decided to look into the question afresh. He faced difficulties at the very outset, for he could not find a copy of the 1854 volume anywhere in the United States; and only after extensive advertising in Australian papers was he able to locate a copy for sale. The next step was to try to discover the manuscript diary itself, in order to learn whether it contained material, omitted from the printed version, which would establish its authenticity beyond question. By diligent inquiry,

Clifford found that the manuscript had long ago been given to the Mitchell Library in Sydney. But after making a thorough search the librarians reported that they could find no trace of it. Clifford then resigned himself to another advertising campaign in Australia; if the Mitchell Library did not have the diary, presumably someone did, and he was out to find who it was. But just as his campaign was getting under way he received an excited and somewhat apologetic letter from the officials of the Mitchell Library. The manuscript diary (genuine beyond doubt) had been discovered, quite by accident, in a long-neglected drawer in the library!

Neglected drawers are, indeed, the despair of manuscript hunters—the more so because, as in Clifford's case, it is not easy to persuade one's correspondents, who may be halfway round the earth, that they have not looked everywhere that they should. Fortunate is the man who can examine drawers and closets and cupboards for himself. Mason Wade, when he was working on his biography of Francis Parkman, was puzzled to be unable to find any trace of the journals the historian wrote during his far-reaching travels in the great West. He knew that such journals had once existed, because two earlier writers on Parkman had drawn upon them. Parkman's historical papers had gone to the Massachusetts Historical Society, and his books to Harvard, while his descendants retained his personal papers; but none of the owners could locate the journals. Finally Wade, taking a long chance, went to the old house at 50 Chestnut Street, Boston, where Parkman had spent his later years. The attic study the historian had used, a romantic room decorated with Indian trophies and lined with books by Scott and Byron and Cooper, had not been disturbed since his death in 1893. In the center of the dusty, silent room stood Parkman's desk. Wade pulled out one row of drawers. All that they contained was the wire grid which the nearly blind Parkman had used to guide his handwriting. But when he pulled out the drawers on the other side of the desk the long-lost journals, together with a mass of other papers, lay revealed. Presumably Parkman's family, when they had gone through his effects to gather the material he had willed to the Historical Society and to Harvard, had overlooked those laden drawers.

But to return to the matter of hunting manuscripts in libraries.

Americans especially, accustomed to the staggeringly efficient cataloguing systems of their great public and university libraries, find it hard to believe that hidden treasures still turn up in institutions specifically devoted to the care of books. Yet just at the moment that I am revising this chapter, the newspapers relate the story of a young library-school student who discovered a copy of the extremely rare first edition of Handel's *Messiah* blushing unseen on the shelves of the public library at Johnstown, Pennsylvania. An even greater find occurred recently at the public library in Sheffield, England. For centuries there had accumulated, in the muniment rooms of the mansion at Wentworth Woodhouse, papers of the utmost value to literary and political history; for the Straffords, Rockinghams, and Fitzwilliams, whose seat it has been, were prominent in public affairs from the time of the English Civil War. Some of the papers had been examined in the past by scholars working on particular phases of history; but they had never been generally available, let alone catalogued.

In the summer of 1949 the whole collection was transferred to the Sheffield library in three furniture vans, and scholars immediately flocked to the feast. Among them was Professor Thomas W. Copeland of the University of Chicago, who knew that it included many papers relating to Edmund Burke, whose patron, the second Marquis of Rockingham, had once owned Wentworth Woodhouse. While Copeland was at work on the Burke manuscripts that had already been sorted out, an assistant of his arrived from America. In order to familiarize him with the state of the papers, Professor [George Reuben] Potter, a historian from the University of Sheffield who was supervising the opening of the collection, took him into the basement strong room where various boxes of materials were lying about. But let Copeland himself tell the story:

"This is the way these things looked when we first opened them up," Potter said, lighting on a box which had not yet been opened and was covered with a century's dust. "You see, the contents are tied up in dozens of little packets thrown in in no kind of order." He picked out a packet, wiped the dust off it, and undid the ribbon around it. By chance it was a packet of letters to Burke. He took out another packet —and then it turned out that the entire box was filled with packets just like it: about seven or eight hundred letters that had been overlooked in all previous hunts for Burke materials, some of them by Johnson, Boswell, Garrick, Reynolds, and other notables!

That story, of course, implies no reflection on the Sheffield cataloguing system, because it is a task of years to classify so enormous an aggregation of manuscripts, and rather than bar access to them until the job was finished (as some librarians would) the Sheffield authorities generously threw open the collection to impatient scholars who could therefore have their extra thrill of discovery. Even when manuscripts have been properly catalogued, however, it sometimes happens that scholars overlook them. Professor Leslie Marchand during his "Byron pilgrimage" . . . dropped into the library of Trinity College, Cambridge, where young Byron had lived the life of a lord from 1805 to 1808. He scarcely expected to find anything there, because he assumed that every Byron scholar would have examined the manuscripts as a matter of course. But when he took down the catalogue of the library's manuscript collection, he found that Trinity College owned half a dozen Byron letters of whose existence no previous student seemed ever to have been aware. And then there was the embarrassing experience of the scholars who produced the great edition of Milton published by Columbia University. During their comprehensive search for every bit of material Milton had ever written, they ran across a reference, in an old catalogue of a London bookseller, to a manuscript that contained some unprinted Milton writings. Try as they would, they could not learn where the manuscript had gone after it was sold. Finally they wrote the bookseller, begging him to reveal who had bought it from him. Dealers often decline to give out such information, for some collectors of rare literary material, partly to avoid being bothered by curious scholars, do not like to have news of their purchases get abroad. But in this case there was no difficulty; the bookseller, hard pressed to conceal his unholy glee, was happy to inform them that the Milton manuscript had been bought years ago by the Columbia University Library!

After ruefully telling me this story Professor Thomas O. Mabbott pointed the moral that they had learned the hard way: "If you are searching for something, the first place to look is where it should be." The Columbia University Library may not have been the most obvious place, but there is no denying that it was the nearest. He hastened to add: "If it isn't there, the next place to look is somewhere it *shouldn't* be. Guessing the 'shouldn't' of course is pure luck or something like telepathy."

But before telepathy or extrasensory perception is brought into play, there is one more course of action, intellectually the most challenged of all. The manuscript hunter who has failed to attain his goal through a systematic canvassing of libraries and private collections—the places where his quarry *should* be—does, in effect, what Sherlock Holmes was wont to do when he faced a blank wall. He may not recline the whole night long upon a pile of cushions, choking the room with clouds of strong tobacco smoke and sawing upon the fiddle that he has thrown across his knees; but his mental processes are the same. In a word, our scholar now employs the Science of Deduction.

He may be looking for particular items, such as a journal or one side of an extended correspondence, or an unpublished essay, or an earlier version of a famous poem, which he knows once existed but has now dropped completely from view. Or he may not be looking for anything in particular; his search may be motivated simply by the circumstance that fewer papers of his author are known to exist than is quite reasonable, and that therefore more are awaiting rescue. In either case, once he is satisfied that whatever he is seeking is not to be found in any of the more or less logical places, he abandons the present and goes back to the past—to the time when his author died. What happened to the man's papers then? Who inherited them? What did he do with them? Or did the author somehow dispose of his manuscripts during his own lifetime? If so, where did they go?

The possibilities are as diverse as life itself. By the use of a great variety of tools—genealogical works, voluminous histories of small British and American localities, church records, post-office directories, alumni rolls of schools and universities, records of the probate courts, newspaper and magazine obituaries, the printed memoirs of everyone who had some association with the author or his family—the scholar begins the long, tortuous search for clues. If his author died, let us say, in 1750, he is sometimes obliged to completely reconstruct the history of the man's family, and often of the families of all his correspondents and publishers and biographers, for two centuries. In the history of the families involved he must take note of every occasion on which property may conceivably have changed hands—events such as marriages, removals, bankruptcies, financial settlements, and deaths. As he works out the early history of the family and its manuscript possessions, our scholar may be dismayed to see the original archives partitioned before his very eyes, one parcel of letters going to a biographer in 1840, a manuscript diary given to a souvenir collector in 1850, an unpublished autobiography disappearing during a family moving in 1860. . . . His problem is not unlike that of an observer who tries to follow the progress of fifty or a hundred selected ants through a swarming anthill. Here are only a few of the fates a certain lot of manuscripts may have met:

(1) The family which inherited them from the author preserved them, say, through the next two generations. But then the family disappeared into the mists of time. Perhaps it died out. If so, did the last survivor still possess the manuscripts? Then what happened to them? The researcher must find his will, ascertain the testator's heirs, and begin to trace them and their heirs and assigns in turn. Or perhaps only the family name died out, through the childlessness of the sons and the marriage of the daughters. The daughters' families must be traced down through the years. Perhaps they in turn died out, and their property went to a distant cousin. The cousin's family must be traced . . . and so on, almost *ad infinitum.*

(2) But suppose the author's immediate descendants had some reason, real or imaginary, to regret bearing his name—perhaps he had embraced an unpopular political cause, or had committed some moral indiscretions. They would not have been so careful to preserve his papers. Indeed, they might have chosen to destroy them—a deed which was long but unjustly imputed to Boswell's embarrassed Victorian descendants. Or at best they would have let the papers fall into dust, or casually given them away to anyone so eccentric as to want to possess the relics of a misspent life.

(3) Or perhaps the family needed money and was forced to sell

its hero's papers. Who bought them? Heaven grant that they were sold *en bloc* rather than auctioned in parcels, like the papers of Garrick and Walpole! Even if they were bought as a whole, what happened to them on the death of the original purchaser?

(4) If some later generation left the family house, what happened to the papers? Scholars have found that it always pays to visit every house known to have been occupied by the family of a man of letters; there is always the chance that they left some papers behind that later occupants have never discovered or have failed to recognize at their true value.

(5) There is always the possibility that the appalled scholar will find that the family who owned the papers migrated to one of the outposts of the British Empire—taking the papers with them. Then what? The weary manuscript hunter faces some really first-class complications. Yet potentially there may be riches in store for him. It is an endlessly tantalizing thought that in obscure towns in Australia and Canada, even in the remote hills of India, today may rest documents of untold value for English literary history. Perhaps one of the most dramatic scholarly discoveries of the next few years will occur there—it is not at all impossible.

(6) The family may have held the papers until they were borrowed for use by an early biographer of the author. The biographer, in the easy-going way of Victorian gentlemen-scholars, may have failed to return them. What became of them? Did they pass down through his own family?

(7) The author in question may have left his papers to a friend, perhaps his literary executor. Who were his friend's heirs? What did they do with the papers? (It was the strange failure of Boswell and Johnson scholars to ask this question that delayed until 1930 the discovery of the great cache of papers at Fettercairn House—the home of the son of one of Boswell's executors.)

This by no means exhausts the possibilities which the scholar must canvass for clues to the present location of his author's manuscripts. He must, indeed, follow the same process in the case of everyone who had some connection with the author. He must try to find the little notebook filled with personal reminiscences which was said to have been written late in life by the author's school friend. He must look up the family of every man with whom the author carried on a correspondence. He must try to discover whether the papers of our author's publishers are still extant; if so, they may contain not merely important letters but actual manuscripts and proof sheets. If the author contributed to periodicals, the scholar must explore the correspondence files of the publishers of the periodicals. But, as the leading authority on American author-publisher relations has discovered to his sorrow, nineteenth-century editors often regarded such correspondence as their personal property, and when they resigned their posts took along the files to add to their personal archives. Which means that the scholar must then proceed to trace down the editors' heirs.

Nor should lawyers' offices be neglected. Here is a good case in point. Everyone knows that in the eighteenth-century British theater Shakespeare's plays underwent all sorts of radical changes. None of these changes were for the better, and some of them were as dreadful as Nahum Tate's "improvement" of *King Lear,* which managed to provide a romantic love-affair between Edgar and Cordelia as well as a beatifically happy ending.

Now one of the most ruthless "improvers" of Shakespeare in the middle of the eighteenth century was the great actor David Garrick. From his own time down to 1933, the list of Garrick's sins against the integrity of Shakespeare was headed by his revision of *Hamlet.* The actual text of that version was supposed to be destroyed, but all evidence pointed to its having been a perfectly dastardly offense, with the single aim of fattening still further the part of Hamlet, which was played by Garrick himself. Since Hamlet's role, as Shakespeare originally wrote it, is probably the fattest in dramatic literature, one may guess that Garrick was either a megalomaniac or a glutton for punishment. At any rate, the tradition of the outrageous liberties which Garrick had taken with *Hamlet* began with his first biographer and was repeated down through the whole of the nineteenth century and the first third of the twentieth.

Meanwhile the manuscript which would have proved the truth or error of the whole tradition was, unknown to everyone, still in existence. After Garrick's death in 1779 his rich dramatic library had passed down through his family until it was dispersed at public auction in 1823. In this sale, however, certain of the actor's manuscripts, among them that of his *Hamlet,* were not included, either through an oversight or because those in charge of the sale considered them too trivial to bother about. These neglected items were put into the hands of solicitors to be sold at some future date.

But the profession of law in England at this time was in the leisurely mood in which Dickens's *Bleak House* depicts it, and nothing was done. Instead, the manuscript was stored in a box along with the other unsold relics; and there it slumbered in perfect peace for seventy-five years, until, in 1900, the building which contained the firm's offices was marked for demolition. When, in the ensuing housecleaning, the box was examined, an alert partner recognized the value of its contents, which were sent to a dealer for rather belated auction. There H. C. Folger's agent brought the Garrick *Hamlet* manuscript, and it went across the sea to Brooklyn, where, evidently without having been even cursorily examined, it promptly went back to sleep in one of Folger's fabulous warehouses of literary treasure-trove. Only after his death, when the accumulations of his warehouses were taken to the new Folger Shakespeare Library at Washington and there revealed, did anyone have an opportunity to examine the manuscript. Professor G. W. Stone of George Washington University promptly seized the opportunity, and discovered that tradition had been all wrong. Garrick's contemporaries, and following them his biographers, had done him an injustice. Compared with the other versions of *Hamlet* that were current in the eighteenth century, Garrick's is good Shakespeare.

Speaking of lawyers' offices and the unsuspected literary information they may contain, it is exciting to recall that a few years ago the office of a well known legal firm in New York turned out to hold what may be an essential clue to a famous real-life mystery which Edgar Allan Poe "solved" in one of his classic stories.

In 1841 a young tobacconist named John Anderson operated at 319 Broadway, New York City, one of the most prosperous cigar stores of the time. The merchandise it stocked no doubt was excellent, but, until the previous year, its success had been chiefly due to the presence behind the counter of an unusually beautiful girl. Her name was Mary Rogers.

On Sunday, July 25, 1841, Mary left her mother's house on what she said was a visit to her aunt. Not long afterward she was seen in the company of a tall, dark, well dressed young man aboard a ferry bound for Hoboken. Later in the same day the two stopped at a Hoboken tavern operated by one Mrs. Loss. Thereafter nothing was seen of Mary until the following Wednesday, when her body, bearing signs of violence, was found floating in the Hudson. Her clothing subsequently was discovered in a thicket near Mrs. Loss's tavern.

The mysterious death of Mary Rogers soon became one of the *causes célèbres* of the century. The New York newspapers rivaled one another in the fullness of their reports and the enterprise with which their reporters tried to dig up new information. The air was full of theories and rumors; but no positive solution was ever forthcoming. Some held to the belief that she had been raped and murdered by one or another of the gangs of ruffians who then frequented Hoboken. Others—probably the majority—maintained that she had died as the result of an abortion performed in the tavern. This latter view was based primarily upon a reported statement by Mrs. Loss as she lay dying not long afterward. It is doubtful that Mrs. Loss ever made any such statement, although the district attorney himself seems to have been partial to the abortion theory, perhaps on the basis of other, undisclosed evidence.

A year and a half later an American magazine, the *Ladies' Companion,* published "The Mystery of Marie Roget," by the young journalist Edgar Allan Poe. In this story, one of the first classics of detective literature, Poe set forth his solution of the mystery. Partly for prudential reasons, and partly because he had already created the character of Dupin, the sedentary French detective, he transferred the locale to Paris and made his characters French; but the disguise was purely perfunctory. Everyone knew he was really telling the story of Mary Rogers—and it is even clearer now that diligent investigators have read the files of all the New York papers of the time and shown that the lengthy excerpts from the "Paris" papers from which Dupin derived his facts were almost completely based upon the actual journalistic reports of the Rogers case. Poe himself was no mean researcher.

Poe's own solution, reached after a brilliant but not always cogent exercise of what he loved to call "ratiocination," was that Mary Rogers died during or after an abortion performed at Mrs.

Loss's tavern. The man on the ferry he identified as the mysterious young naval man who had figured conspicuously in the newspaper speculations at the time. Such a man was known to have been an admirer of Mary's, and the heaviest suspicion had fallen upon him, although no prosecution was ever brought against him or anyone else.

Among those who were *not* suspected, at least so far as the newspapers knew, was Mary's former employer, John Anderson. Even though deprived of her glamour behind the counter, his business continued to flourish. His tobacco was sold in enormous quantities to the soldiers in the Mexican War, and later he branched out with equal success into real estate speculation, eventually becoming a millionaire. After his death in Paris in 1881, his heirs began a long drawn-out litigation over his will. During the various trials it was revealed (and reported in the newspapers) that Anderson often recalled that in the years immediately following Mary's death he "had had many, *very* many unhappy days and nights in regard to her," and had been in frequent communication with her spirit.

In December of 1891, the litigation entered the phase known to the legal records as Laura V. Appleton *v.* The New York Life Insurance Company and Frederick A. Hammond. In this action, brought before the Supreme Court of New York County, Anderson's daughter sought to break her father's will on the ground that when he had signed it he was mentally incompetent.

Now students who were intrigued by the mystery of Mary Rogers knew of this case, and suspected that in the course of the trial further evidence might have been heard relating to Anderson's preoccupation with the fate of his unfortunate shopgirl. No actual record of the testimony, however, was known to exist, because the case had been settled out of court and the official record ordered destroyed. But Samuel Copp Worthen, a lawyer closely associated with Mrs. Appleton, had been a student of one of the first reliable biographers of Poe, George Edward Woodberry of Columbia University, and had never lost his interest in literature, and specifically in Poe. He knew that in the testimony during the trial in 1891 there had been important revelations—and he also knew that his firm had retained in its files a copy of that testimony. Worthen kept his secret for almost fifty years; but in 1948 he decided that the time had come to reveal it, and he wrote an article for the scholarly periodical *American Literature*. This is what he reported.

Mrs. Appleton's lawyers had gone to much trouble to bring before the court and jury testimony that would tend to prove Anderson's mental incompetence. Perhaps that part which related to Anderson's communion with Mary Rogers's ghost did have such a tendency. But why had Anderson been so disturbed over her death if he had merely been her employer? The answer was provided in the testimony of acquaintances to whom he had talked about his connection with the case. To them he revealed that after Mary's body was found he had been arrested and examined, but released for want of evidence. This, apparently, had never got into the papers; but the fact of his arrest became known to several persons, including James Gordon Bennett, the famous editor of the *New York Herald,* and the resultant damage to his reputation preyed on his mind. Years later, after Anderson became prominent, the reigning Tammany boss, Fernando Wood, asked him to be a candidate for mayor of New York; but, fearing what might be said during the campaign about his connection with the Rogers case, he refused to run.

And then the testimony in 1891 brought out the most startling fact of all—one that previously had been completely unknown. Anderson, it was deposed, had confessed to his friends that before Mary's death he had paid for an abortion she had had, and that he had got "in some trouble over it." But apart from that earlier episode, he had continued, he had not had "anything, *directly, himself,*" to do with Mary Rogers's difficulties. Note the significant qualifications.

Whether Anderson was reporting the actual truth in these statements is, of course, open to question. If his mental balance was sufficiently precarious to substantiate a lengthy attempt to break his will, his credibility must not be accepted without reservation. Yet Worthen, a man of long legal experience, felt that he was speaking the truth. His reconstruction of Anderson's part in the Mary Rogers mystery was this. Anderson, according to his own statement, had already financed one abortion for Mary. (Whether or not he was responsible for her pregnancy on that occasion or the subsequent one is a matter upon which scholarship feels itself incompetent to pronounce.)

When in 1841, after she had left his employ, she again found herself in what would then have been called "an interesting condition," she appealed to him for help; and, if only for the reason that the prosperity of his cigar store owed a great deal to her bewitching presence, he again came to the rescue. The tall, dark man on the ferryboat therefore would have been the abortionist. After Mary's death in Mrs. Loss's tavern he, or Mrs. Loss's sons, disposed of her body in the river and arranged her clothing in the thicket so as to give rise to the theory that a felonious gang had done her to death.

If Worthen's theory based on this newly revealed evidence is correct, then Poe hit upon the right solution in his story. His chief error was in eliminating Anderson from suspicion of complicity; but it was an error common to all who followed the case while it was unfolding in the newspapers. Neither he nor anyone else, with the possible exception of the authorities who arrested Anderson for questioning, knew that the young tobacconist had abetted the earlier abortion.[1]

But we have spent enough time in lawyers' offices, which are, after all, only one of the many places where documents of importance to literary history lie.

There remain, for example, the unknown potentialities of official archives—not only the best known ones like the vast collection at the Public Record Office in London, but the multitude of local record collections in England and America and every other country where English-speaking men of letters have been. If our author was once a soldier or a sailor, there are undoubtedly some records of him and, if he had a responsible position, even detailed files of his reports in the War and Admiralty offices in London and the corresponding departments in Washington. The records of the American Adjutant General, for example, have yielded information on Poe's brief and unhappy career as a soldier; and in the archives of the Ministère de la Marine in Paris Professor Charles R. Anderson

[1] For a recent book on this subject, see John Walsh, *Poe the Detective: The Curious Circumstances Behind "The Mystery of Marie Roget"* (New Brunswick, N.J., 1967). [Editor's note.]

found the logbook of the French frigate whose cutter had quelled the South Sea island brawl Melville describes in *Omoo,* and in whose brig Melville and his companions were allowed to cool off. If the author worked for a governmental or quasi-governmental agency—like Anthony Trollope as an inspector for the British Post Office, or Charles Lamb as a clerk in the East India Office, or Walt Whitman as an employee of the United States Department of the Interior—the thorough scholar must not neglect the chance that in those voluminous archives are hidden papers which may by no means be restricted in their interest to the narrowly workaday side of the author's life. If he was an American diplomat, like Washington Irving or Nathaniel Hawthorne or James Russell Lowell or Bret Harte, the records of the State Department must be searched. And even if he was a more or less common citizen, he may have had financial dealings or legal complications whose trail can be followed with profit by a diligent inquirer. A few years ago Professor Dixon Wecter threw valuable new light on Edmund Burke by pursuing such a superficially unpromising lead.

Even more recently, the late Professor Newman Ivey White made one of the most provocative finds in the history of Shelley scholarship by a search of public records. Among the perplexing mysteries of Shelley's life has always been the identity of the "Neapolitan ward" who is mentioned briefly and evasively in one or two of his letters in 1820. The child remained a vague wraith until White in 1936, through the American consul-general at Naples, engaged an Italian professor, Alberto Tortaglione, to search the records in Naples for documentary evidence of the child's birth and its parentage. Tortaglione discovered a document certifying that on December 27, 1818, a daughter, Elena Adelaide, was born to Shelley and "Maria Padurin, his legitimate wife," as well as a death certificate for the child, dated some fifteen months later and repeating the same information except that the Italian version of Mary Godwin's name had become "Maria Gebuin." Since it is plain from Mrs. Shelley's journal and other evidence that she did not bear a child in December, 1818, Shelley obviously perpetrated a fraud upon the authorities.

Who was Elena Adelaide? Shelley's daughter by someone else? The illegitimate child of a maidservant in Shelley's household?

And why did Shelley perjure himself in order to adopt her? In 1820, the Shelley-Byron circle was thrown into an uproar by the maidservant's story that the baby was Shelley's child by Jane Clairmont, who earlier had been Byron's mistress. Since one of the meager clues we possess in the case is a statement in Mary Shelley's journal that Jane was ill on the day on which Elena is supposed to have been born, Professor White examined Jane Clairmont's unpublished diary, then in the library of Thomas J. Wise. In the pages referring to the period when the maidservant was accusing Jane of being Elena's mother, White found several passages carefully crossed out. Hoping for some clue in the deletions, he placed the pages under the infrared lamp; but he found no allusion to the "Neapolitan affair." His discovery of the birth and death records, far from solving the mystery, has served only to muddy the swirling waters of controversy over Elena's identity. Shelley scholars still may be conveniently divided into those who think that Shelley was the child's father, and those who think he was not; and those who think that Jane Clairmont was her mother, and those who think not.

From what has been said thus far, it should be fairly obvious that hunting for manuscripts is not a profession for a lazy man. . . .

7. The Case of the Man in Love:

Forgery, Impure and Simple

NOR MAY A MAN BECOME LAZY ONCE THOSE MANUSCRIPTS are found, for they may be forgeries, whole or in part, consciously or unconsciously, for financial gain or for personal satisfaction, but lying witnesses nonetheless. Carter Dickson's charge to his audience, *The Reader is Warned,* is to be kept in mind by any historian or by anyone who would read history. The scholar must first test for authenticity those precious manuscripts he has found, and he will wish to test them doubly if they were found for him, perhaps too fortuitously.

This is especially so when a public figure is involved. Forged Lincoln signatures are legion. Accordingly, public interest was great, and scholarly skepticism ready, when a body of papers, known as "the Minor collection," began to appear in print late in 1928, apparently throwing additional light upon Lincoln and Ann Rutledge. Although given the prestigious vehicle of the *Atlantic Monthly* for first publication, historians were quick to close in on the Minor papers, riddling them with revelations of anachronisms, improbabilities, and other peculiarities. The following essay, on discovery dashed and villains foiled, was written for the *Atlantic* by a leading Lincoln scholar, Paul M. Angle of Chicago.

♦ ♦ ♦

Those of us who engage in historical research are likely to assume that everyone will know what tests to apply in order to establish the authenticity of a series of historical documents, and will possess the knowledge necessary for the successful application of those tests. The assumption is unwarranted, of course. Rarely will all possible criteria suggest themselves even to highly intelligent persons without historical training, and more rarely still will they possess the specialized knowledge without which the criteria are useless.

In view of this fact it will be worth while at least to itemize the tests which a collection, such as the alleged Lincoln documents published serially in the *Atlantic* . . . , should pass before its genuineness can be accepted. First come the purely physical criteria: Is the paper of the proper age, and is the ink that of the period in which the documents are supposed to have been written? Next, the soundness of the collection's pedigree, so to speak: Has it come down through a line of well-authenticated, reputable owners? Then, if the documents purport to be the work of a well-known character, comes the question of handwriting. Does it resemble that of letters and papers of undoubted genuineness? More intangible, but very important, is the question of general content. Are the sentiments expressed in any given document in harmony with the known views of the person who is supposed to have written it, or even with his general character as established beyond dispute? Finally, do specific incidents mentioned in the challenged documents check with demonstrable historical fact?

It is not often that all of these tests can be brought to bear against a body of material so effectively as in the case of the Minor collection. Almost every item revealed such serious flaws that belief in the genuineness of the entire group became untenable. Recognizing this, the editor of the *Atlantic* not only published a statement withdrawing former expressions of confidence in the collec-

---

FROM Paul M. Angle, "The Minor Collection: A Criticism," copyright 1929 by the Atlantic Monthly Company, Boston, Massachusetts. Reprinted with permission.

For additional reading: A closely argued, scholarly inquiry into a ninth-century forgery is Walter Goffart's *The Le Mans Forgeries: A Chapter from the History of Church Property in the Ninth Century* (Cambridge, Mass., 1966). A spy story turning upon this theme, in part, is Adam Hall's *The Quiller Memorandum.*

tion, but asked me, as one of those active in attacking its claims to credence, to state the case against it. . . .

As soon as the collection was presented for publication, the *Atlantic* submitted specimens of the paper to a distinguished chemist for analysis. The report described it as "pure linen with a trace of cotton." Since modern paper is largely made from wood pulp, the presumption was that the paper of these documents was of sufficient age.

However, that is not a fact of positive importance. The first concern of every forger is to secure old paper, and on the whole it is easily accomplished. In this case a suspicious resemblance to the flyleaves of old books suggests the source from which it was obtained. There is another disquieting feature of physical appearance. Several of the documents are written in green ink. Green ink usually has an aniline dye as a coloring agent, and aniline dyes were not in use prior to the second half of the nineteenth century. However, the color of the ink could do no more than arouse suspicion, since inks of all colors have long been used to some extent.

When the line of descent of the Minor collection was critically examined serious weaknesses appeared. The story of its formation and transmission was related with considerable explicitness. For various plausible reasons Lincoln and Ann Rutledge gave each other's letters to a common friend, Matilda Cameron. Matilda added her own diary, and the collection passed to Sally Calhoun, described as the daughter of John Calhoun, Lincoln's friend and benefactor. Sally added memoranda of conversations with her father and letters from Lincoln, and gave the entire group of documents to two friends, Margaret Morrison and Elizabeth Hirth. In time these joint owners transferred it to Elizabeth's brother, Frederick Hirth. With the addition of a letter Hirth is supposed to have received from Lincoln it attained its final form, and descended through Hirth's widow and Miss Minor's own mother to the present owner.

Examination, however, fails to reveal satisfactory evidence that the first two reputed owners of the collection, Matilda Cameron and Sally Calhoun, ever actually existed. Matilda is described as one of the eleven daughters of John Cameron of New Salem, and Ann's cousin as well as bosom friend. But the page from the Cameron family Bible on which the names and birth dates of the children were inscribed, now in the possession of Mrs. Edna Orendorff Macpherson of the Illinois State Historical Library, fails to record a Matilda among them.

However, in the family record only the first names and middle initials are given, and for three of the girls the middle initial was M. Might not that have stood, in one case, for Matilda? Matilda's diary destroys the possibility. In the entry dated July 10, 1833, occurs this statement: "I will keep everything in my box James giv me last crismas. my first bow wuz James and *now Sam* Anns wuz first John and now Abe. she wuz 17 when she met John and I wuz 19 when I first met James." Since James and Matilda were lovers "last crismas," their first meeting could not have occurred later than 1832. If Matilda was then nineteen, she must have been born not later than 1813. But Vicana M., the second of the Cameron girls and the first to bear the middle initial M., was born on December 31, 1815. A daughter was born in 1813, but her name was Elizabeth P.

Equally conclusive is the argument against the existence of Sally Calhoun. John Calhoun, whose daughter she is supposed to have been, was born in Boston, Massachusetts, in either 1806 or 1808—both dates are given in different accounts. He came to Springfield, Illinois, in 1830, and on December 29 of the following year married Sarah Cutter. According to John Carroll Power's *History of the Early Settlers of Sangamon County, Illinois,* he had nine children, but among them a Sally or Sarah is not to be discovered.

However, it has been pointed out that the birth dates of two of Calhoun's children, as recorded in this volume, are three months apart; and it is argued that if his account is in error in this respect it is not unreasonable to doubt the infallibility of his list of the children's names. The fact remains, however, that in spite of this error—probably a printer's mistake—Power's *History* is a very reliable compilation, so reliable that it is constantly used by Springfield lawyers in the examination of abstracts, and readily accepted in court as furnishing satisfactory proof of heirship.

But the case against the existence of Sally rests on other evidence than Power's *History*. In a letter written from St. Joseph, Missouri, December 12, 1928, Mrs. Adele P. McCord, the only living grandchild of John Calhoun, stated: "I was an only grandchild on her side of the family & very fond of my Grandmother Sarah Cutter Calhoun. I became closely associated with her & my Aunts, and never once did I hear any of them called Sally." Mrs. McCord added that Mrs. Mary W. Inslee Kerr, of St. Joseph, Missouri, was the only person still alive who would have first-hand knowledge of the Calhoun family, and stated that she would get in touch with her if possible. In due time Mrs. Kerr's daughter answered on behalf of her mother, now ill. "General John Calhoun and his family," the letter reads, "were intimate friends of hers and there was never a daughter named, or called, Sally Calhoun."

Analysis of physical qualities and examination of the manner in which it was preserved are the only standards by which the Minor collection as a whole can be judged. In describing the outcome of tests other than these, it will be an advantage to divide the collection into several parts: (1) the Lincoln letters, (2) the books bearing Lincoln marginalia, (3) the Ann Rutledge letters, (4) Matilda Cameron's diary, and (5) Sally Calhoun's memoranda.

Since no unchallenged specimen of Ann Rutledge's writing is known to have been preserved, and since the very existence of Matilda Cameron and Sally Calhoun is at best doubtful, it is obvious that only the Lincoln letters and the books which he is supposed to have annotated can be judged on the score of handwriting. Yet the test is of the utmost significance. If the handwriting of the Lincoln documents in the Minor collection is indistinguishable from that of genuine Lincoln letters of the same approximate date, the presumption of authenticity is strong; but if it is markedly different, then all other flaws do no more than make the proof of spuriousness overwhelming.

Important as handwriting may be, however, there is little one can say about it. Actual comparison of specimens is the only test. Nevertheless, it may be worth while to point out one or two features of general appearance which can be reported in words. In the letters from the Minor collection Lincoln is frequently made to begin sentences with small letters. Letters of known authenticity never show this feature. Moreover, until the last few years of his life Lincoln usually—not always, of course—employed a short dash in place of a period. But in the Minor documents dashes are used only to indicate breaks—not terminations—of the thought.

In explaining the rakish, uneven appearance of the handwriting of these letters it has been argued that "Lincoln had two definitely distinct styles of writing his name—the formal signature, identified with legal documents or public business, and the more rambling and haphazard hand of friendly and familiar intercourse. The letters in this collection were of the second category. . . ."

This statement is true only to the extent that, in signing official papers as President, Lincoln usually wrote his name "Abraham Lincoln," while he signed letters of all descriptions with the familiar "A. Lincoln." Legal pleadings were generally signed "Lincoln," followed either by *"p. q."* (*pro querente*) or *"p. d."* (*pro defendant*). So far as the character of the handwriting is concerned, there is no distinction, beyond that due to a greater or lesser degree of haste, between that to be found in the body of public and legal documents and that to be found in the body of letters.

It is true that not all specimens of Lincoln's writing are exactly similar, but the variations are the result of the writer's age rather than the character of the subject matter. Thus the handwriting of his youth shows immaturities not discernible in that of middle age, while letters written as President show clearly the effect of advancing age and mental strain. But the widest variations from these natural causes are as nothing compared with the difference between two intimate letters of the same approximate date, one from the Minor collection, the other indisputably genuine.

But in ruling out the Lincoln letters we need not depend on handwriting alone, conclusive as that should be. There is the evidence from "known character," so to speak. Does the Lincoln of the Minor letters harmonize with the Lincoln of historical fact? Or are they two different, distinct individuals—so different and distinct as not to be explained as variant phases of the same person?

In answering these questions I shall disregard, as being in the last analysis a matter of opinion, my belief that the distorted and unnatural individual pictured as the writer of the letters in the Minor collection does not square at all with the Lincoln of historical fact. Instead, I shall quote, for the reader's own comparison, two expressions on the same subject—slavery.

In one of the letters to John Calhoun, printed in the *Atlantic* for December 1928 (undated, but presumably written during his term in Congress), Lincoln is made to recount a conversation with a slave at the time of one of his two visits to New Orleans. Asked whether he was happy in slavery, the black had raised "a face of hopeless resignation" and answered, "No—no Marse I nevah is happy no mo. whippins is things that black folks nevah can stop remembrin about—they hurt so." Lincoln then reminds his correspondent: "this is one I forgot to tell you before. but John I guess it takes a queer fellow like me to sympathise with the put upon and down trodden. those blacks John dont live—they simply *exist.* I never trapped an animal in my life and slavery to me is just *that* both filling my soul with abhorrence."

Compare the foregoing with the following extract from a letter to Mary Speed, the sister of the one man with whom Lincoln's intimacy is unquestioned:

> By the way, a fine example was presented on board the boat [Lincoln was describing his return from a visit at the Speed home] for contemplating the effect of condition upon human happiness. A gentleman had purchased twelve negroes in different parts of Kentucky, and was taking them to a farm in the South. They were chained six and six together. . . . In this condition they were being separated forever from the scenes of their childhood, their friends, their fathers and mothers, and brothers and sisters, and many of them from their wives and children, and going into perpetual slavery, where the lash of the master is proverbially more ruthless and unrelenting than any other where; and yet amid all these distressing circumstances, as we would think them, they were the most cheerful and apparently happy creatures on board. One whose offense for which he had been sold was an over-fondness for his wife, played the fiddle almost continually, and the others danced, sang, cracked jokes, and played various games with cards from day to day. How true it is that "God tempers the wind to the shorn lamb," or in other words, that he renders the worst of human conditions tolerable, while he permits the best to be nothing better than tolerable.

It is only fair to point out that in 1855 Lincoln described this incident less amiably, calling slavery a "continued torment." My own belief is that this quickened perception of slavery's evil was a direct result of the agitation caused by the repeal of the Missouri

Compromise in 1854. In any event, comparison of the two passages suggests, at least, the argument which could be built upon stylistic differences if space permitted. Is it possible for a man to write clear, easy prose in 1841, and seven years later to be guilty of verbiage resembling the stilted effort of a high-school freshman?

So much for the general character of the Minor letters from Lincoln in Washington to Calhoun in Springfield. The difference between the Lincoln of these letters and the Lincoln of historical fact is great enough to make a careful student skeptical, even if disquieting suspicions have not previously been aroused. And a skeptical student, if competent, will at once commence the most exacting, and most exciting, of all tests—the search for errors of specific fact.

The method consists in the critical examination of every fact which admits of independent verification. As this examination largely concerns John Calhoun and his relations with Lincoln, some comment upon him is necessary.

John Calhoun came to Springfield in 1830, and continued a resident of the town until his appointment as Surveyor-General of Kansas and Nebraska in 1854. From 1832 until 1835 he was Surveyor of Sangamon County. The county, then considerably larger than now, was being settled rapidly, and the demand for a surveyor's services was greater than one man could satisfy. At the instance of mutual friends Calhoun appointed Lincoln his deputy, with the specific duty of making surveys in the northwestern part of Sangamon County, now the separate county of Menard.

As time went on, Calhoun occupied other public offices. In 1838 he was elected to the legislature from Sangamon County. Four years later he was appointed Clerk of the Circuit Court and held the position until 1848, serving simultaneously as trustee of the defunct State Bank. As Lincoln advanced to a prominent position in local Whig circles, Calhoun gained place in the Democratic Party, becoming one of [Stephen A.] Douglas's trusted lieutenants when that leader rose to national prominence. Frequently Lincoln and Calhoun clashed in debate, and local tradition, well supported, has it that Lincoln feared no one, Douglas not excepted, more than Calhoun.

With these facts in mind, let us examine closely the letter of

July 22, 1848. Aside from the fact that it implies a degree of political accord which did not exist, it contains several historical inconsistencies. "Jed was here and called on me about a month ago. he told me of your trip to Gentryville and your clearing the boundries, titles etc."—so Lincoln is made to write. Calhoun's trip must have taken place in 1848, or Lincoln, who took his seat in Congress in December 1847, would have known about it. But in 1848 Calhoun was Clerk of the Circuit Court, and the records show that he was performing the duties of that office in person. Relatively few legal papers for 1848 remain in the court files, but those that do contain his signature under the file date. Several were filed every month—frequently every week—during the entire year. For the month of May—the time most likely, according to the letter, for Calhoun to have made his Gentryville trip—the record is especially complete.

Moreover, even if Calhoun had gone to Gentryville, he could not have had for the reason of his visit that alleged in the letter. "He told me of your trip to Gentryville and your clearing the boundries, titles etc; Dear John at this time I want to extend my deepest gratitude for the service rendred my Mother," etc. The inference that Calhoun cleared "boundries, titles etc." for Lincoln's mother is inescapable. But in 1848 Lincoln's mother had no interest in any land at Gentryville. When Thomas Lincoln had removed from Kentucky to Indiana he entered one hundred and sixty acres near the present town of that name, but he never succeeded in obtaining a patent to more than eighty acres. This holding he sold to James Gentry in the winter of 1829–1830, shortly before removing to Illinois.

The last sentence of the letter is also open to suspicion. "Mary is well thank the Lord and joins in love to you and yours," Lincoln is supposed to have concluded. That Mrs. Lincoln was in Washington is a necessary inference. That she actually was in Washington is extremely doubtful. She had accompanied Lincoln there in the winter of 1847, but in the following spring she and the children had returned to the family home at Lexington, Kentucky. Her own letters show that she contemplated remaining there during July and August, and Lincoln's letters, particularly one dated July 2, show that he was fully conversant with her plans, and did not expect her to join him soon. There is no direct evidence of Mrs. Lincoln's movements from early July until mid-October, but all the information accessible indicates that her presence in Washington on July 22, 1848, is highly improbable.

So much for the letter of July 22, 1848. That to Calhoun of May 9, 1834, offers even greater inconsistencies, one in particular admitting no explanation of any sort. "There seems some controversy," Lincoln writes, "between him and Green concerning that North East quarter of Section 40—you remember?" Since 1785 the government system of surveys had provided for townships divided into thirty-six sections, numbered consecutively from one to thirty-six. Natural irregularities occasionally resulted in townships with fewer than thirty-six sections, but never in one with more than that number. For Lincoln to have inquired of Calhoun—both men being official surveyors—regarding a "Section 40" is unthinkable.

In the same letter Lincoln remarks that "the Bixbys are leaving this week for some place in Kansas." Kansas, however, was not open for white settlement until twenty years after the date of this letter. A few squatters, guides, and Indian traders were clustered about its military posts at an earlier date, but that was all. It is doubtful whether even the word "Kansas" was in common use as designating the region it now describes. Most maps of the period referred to describe the vast territory west of Missouri and north of Arkansas Territory simply as "Missouri Territory" or "Indian Territory," while the gazetteers list the word only as the name of a river.

The books bearing Lincoln marginalia in the Minor collection are no more worthy of credence than the letters. The handwriting is equally unlike that which is indisputably his. In addition, there is no indication that Lincoln was in the habit of underlining and commenting upon passages in the books he owned. Many books from his library are in existence, but not one whose authenticity is above suspicion contains any writing other than his name or a simple presentation inscription.

Moreover, no reliance need be placed upon these general considerations to prove spurious the notations in at least one of the volumes of the collection. This is [Samuel Phillips] Newman's [*A*] *Practical System of Rhetoric,* containing many underscorings and comments. The book was published in 1829 at Andover, Massachusetts. On the flyleaf is the name of its original owner: "Miss Susan Y. Baker, March 15 Eastport Academy." At the bottom of the title-page is the signature, "A. Lincoln; Gentryville." At the top of the page, in the same handwriting, are a few lines expressing gratitude to Miss Baker for her gift of the book. All seems regular enough (the handwriting always excepted) until one discovers that the preface of the book is dated, in type, May 1829. Consequently Miss Baker's inscription, 'March 15,' could not have been written earlier than 1830. And on March 15, 1830, Abraham Lincoln was not residing in Indiana, having, according to his own statement, departed for Illinois some two weeks before that time.

When these specific discrepancies are added to the evidence of spuriousness which the examination of handwriting, general content, and documentary history amassed, proof becomes overwhelming. No matter what the character of the rest of the collection, the Lincoln documents are worthless.

The other items in the Minor collection contain even more historical inconsistencies than the Lincoln material. Two grave errors are to be found in the Ann Rutledge letters alone.

Twice Ann refers to the New Salem schoolmaster as "Newton Graham." The name, in fact, was Mentor Graham. In the Illinois State Historical Library are poll books for the year 1834 signed Mentor Graham. In the Menard County records at Petersburg, Illinois, are several legal documents in which the name is given as Mentor Graham; and Mrs. Henry Bradley, a granddaughter living at Greenview, Illinois, has two deeds and three promissory notes so signed. Moreover, Mrs. Bradley, who knew Graham before his death, never heard him called by any other name than Mentor. Her recollection is supported by several other members of the family who were in close contact with him for several years, and who also state that they never knew of his using any other name than Mentor.

More conclusive, however, than a mistake in a name is the following sentence from one of Ann's letters to Lincoln. "I am greatfull," the writer says, "for the Spencers copy-book I copy frum that every time I can spair." Since Ann Rutledge died on August 25, 1835—the date is recorded in the family Bible—this letter was written prior to that time. But [P. R.] Spencer's first publication on penmanship, under the title of *Spencer and Rice's System of Business and Ladies' Penmanship,* was not issued until 1848.

It has been suggested, nevertheless, that although Spencer's first formal treatise on penmanship was not published until 1848 he might have been issuing copy books or leaflets many years before that time, all trace of which has since disappeared. As a matter of fact, the work here mentioned was not a formal treatise, but exactly the sort of publication contemplated in the suggestion I have stated. It consisted of small slips of paper with mottoes lithographed in Spencerian writing, each packet of slips being enclosed in a long envelope similar to those in ordinary use to-day.

I have already referred, in connection with the question of whether or not Matilda Cameron was a real person, to one grave error in her diary. There are others. Twice she writes of boats from Springfield. On July 10, 1833, she states that her church got the first *Missouri Harmony Hymn Book* "last boat from Springfield"; while a later entry records that "the boat being du Satiday cum in while we wuz by the mill." Both references indicate plainly that boats carrying passengers were running between Springfield and New Salem on a regular schedule.

To anyone familiar with the Sangamon River, and the country through which it passes, the idea is absurd. The river swings around Springfield in a rough semicircle, coming no nearer than five miles at any point. Besides, it is called a "river" more by courtesy than because the size of the stream merits the description. Generally it is no larger than a good-sized creek, and in July—when, according to Matilda, boats were running regularly—it will hardly float a canoe. Moreover, it meanders from Springfield to New Salem in wide curves, probably running a course of fifty miles between the two towns, less than twenty miles distant by air line. Under these circumstances, a packet line was simply impossible.

Lincoln's published correspondence reveals a second flaw in the Cameron diary. One of Matilda's boats—the one which was "du Satiday"—brought "Dave turnham a frend of Abes from gentryville" to New Salem. This was the same Turnham to whom Lincoln, on October 23, 1860, wrote a letter in which the following statement occurs: "I well remember when you and I last met, after a separation of fourteen years, at the cross-road voting place in the fall of 1844." Thus we have Lincoln's own word that he had not seen Turnham from the time he left Indiana in 1830 until he made a campaign trip to the vicinity of his old home in the fall of 1844.

Another entry in the diary commences with the statement, "Marthy Calhone teched Ann sum new patern of kroshay and she is going to tech me." This entry must have been dated 1835 or earlier, yet Martha Calhoun, sixth child of John Calhoun, was not born until January 9, 1843. This somewhat startling weakness in chronology has been explained on the ground that Calhoun had a sister Martha, to whom the reference might naturally apply. The explanation is possible, of course, but very unlikely. In the first place, if Calhoun's sister Martha was living with him she would not have been at New Salem—a misapprehension which runs through all these documents—but at Springfield. In the second place, Calhoun's father was a prosperous Eastern merchant, well able to support his family. It hardly seems likely that a young woman would have left a comfortable home in an established community for the hardships of life in a raw Illinois village.

One more observation, and we are done with Matilda Cameron. Her final diary entry, dated March 12, 1836, contains the following statement: "sum folks has left Sand Ridge and also a lot in Salem. . . . John Calhone and family has al-reddy gone. Abe is tendin surveying for him hear what litle ther is to do." The statement contains two errors of fact. Never having lived in New Salem, John Calhoun of course had not migrated. In 1836, as for the past six years, he was living in Springfield. And whatever surveying Lincoln was doing was for Thomas M. Neale, not Calhoun, who had resigned his position the previous year. I have not been able to find the exact date of Calhoun's resignation, but as early as September 26, 1835, Neale was signing surveys as Surveyor of Sangamon County.

Only the memoranda of Sally Calhoun remain. Several of the objections raised against the other documents apply here with equal force—the failure of the picture of Lincoln there drawn to harmonize with his known character, the improbability of an interest in Lincoln great enough to have led Calhoun to dictate these reminiscences, the frequent use of the name "Newton Graham." Most important, however, is the fact that the memoranda, dated St. Joseph, Missouri, imply the presence of Calhoun, although Calhoun—be it insisted yet once more—was still living in Springfield. It is useless to cite evidence proving that Calhoun was actually in Springfield on certain dates, for only one of Sally's memoranda is dated. That one was supposedly written on June 2, 1848. On May 29 Calhoun put his file mark and signature on legal papers in Springfield, and it was practically impossible for him to have been in St. Joseph four days later. Even if, by strenuous traveling, he had succeeded in making the trip in that time, it is straining credulity too far to believe that he would at once have put his daughter to recording incidents in the early life of Lincoln.

Thus every test except that of the fitness of the paper has found the Minor collection defective. Critical examination showed glaring weaknesses in the line according to which the collection is supposed to have descended. The handwriting of the items which purport to have been written by Lincoln bears no resemblance to that of authentic documents. The content of the Lincoln letters is not in complete harmony with his known ideas on one subject at least, slavery, and it is difficult to believe that such wide stylistic differences as have been pointed out can occur in the writing of the same individual. And the number of historical inconsistencies, some of which admit no possible explanation, is very large. By no possibility can the Minor collection be genuine.

Then who fabricated it? We know what sort of person the forger was, for in these documents he has drawn the outlines of his own character. Considerable cleverness dictated the explanation of the collection's formation and descent to the present. The character of Matilda Cameron, exceedingly well drawn, indicates no small degree of creative ability. Wide though superficial reading provided enough information about Lincoln's life to deceive those whose knowledge was not fairly extensive. Only when cleverness, artistic skill, and general information could no longer suffice, and sound knowledge became indispensable, did the forger fail. Certainly he—or she—was not familiar with Lincoln's correspondence, either in its original or in its published form. Complete ignorance of the geographical setting of the story was coupled with defective knowledge of the minor characters. Under the circumstances it was only natural that the forger, like an amateur playwright, should overdraw his Lincoln, emphasizing too strongly his best-known traits.

That exposure followed quickly should cause no regret, for the Lincoln of the Minor collection was, after all, a sorry character. What he wrote was full of inflated sentimentality, and the manner in which he wrote it suggested a man no more than half literate. To me, at least, a belief in the common authorship of these documents and the Gettysburg Address was impossible—and I much prefer the Gettysburg Address.

Is the case here against the Minor collection proven? Virtually but not entirely must be the reply. Much that Angle has said is based on surmise, the historian's equivalent of circumstantial evidence. In all probability a jury would convict. Nonetheless, one might well object that Angle relies a little too heavily upon the authority of John Carroll Power's *History of the Early Settlers of Sangamon County,* using it to refute various points of detail in the Minor papers, without putting Power to the test as well. Nor does the argument about Lincoln's known views of slavery go down smoothly, for Lincoln said many apparently contradictory things about the subject. And while the specific copy of Newman's *Practical System of Rhetoric* to which the article refers may have been published in Andover in 1829, an early edition appeared in Portland, Maine, in 1827. Angle does not rest his case on these three points alone—points which a clever defense lawyer might be able to persuade a jury to disregard—and in the totality of his argument it is impossible not to find for him and against the defendant. Yet, as we shall next see, printed histories of local events are not invariably to be trusted.

8. The Case of the Men Who Weren't There:

Problems of Local Pride

PERHAPS THE MOST FAMOUS INQUIRY INTO THE AUTHENticity of an entire set of primary source materials was one undertaken by a committee sponsored by the Institute of Early American History and Culture. The object of the investigation was a body of documents known as "the Horn Papers" which purported to reveal much that was new and to answer many old and perplexing questions about the settlement of western Pennsylvania. What was extraordinary about the Horn Papers was that they were handsomely published, with no thought of profit on the part of their owner, editor, or sponsors, and that they were issued with the apparent imprimatur of a respected local history society. In addition, the papers were unusually well bolstered, it seemed, by the presence of contemporary maps, lead plates, arrowheads, tools, and a "mountain of artifacts."

The resulting investigation cut deeply into the quiet of Greene County, Pennsylvania, setting friends against each other and bringing otherwise obscure historical problems into national prominence. Ellery Queen's *Glass Village* springs to mind, except that in Greene County there were no villains and, at least at the outset, there was no plot. All except one of the participants in the bizarre events that followed undoubtedly were sincere and honest men, and even that one may well have been both, within the limits of his own definitions of the terms. Certainly, it seems clear, that man had no intention to defraud anyone when he began upon the course that led to the mystery of the Horn Papers, for neither he nor anyone else stood to gain in any tangible way. Gain may be measured in other ways, however, and perhaps the search for motivation in this instance is best left to each reader of the following essay.

Although the essay is long, I print most of it here, for the investigation was closely warped and woofed into the total body of Horn evidence. The article, by two historians, Arthur Pierce Middleton and the late Douglass Adair, both then of Williamsburg, Virginia, is based on the report of the Institute's committee. It first appeared in 1947 in a journal affiliated with the Institute, the *William and Mary Quarterly,* which specializes in Colonial American history. Middleton was associated with the Mariners' Museum in Newport News, Virginia; Adair edited the *Quarterly* and was at the time of his death a professor of history in the Claremont Graduate School in Claremont, California. A restrained account, the essay might well end, as it raises the question of motivation, with the common technique of some mystery novels of the nineteen-twenties in which the penultimate chapter was called "Let the Reader Decide."

♦ ♦ ♦

Almost anyone who saw the substantial three volumes entitled *The Horn Papers: Early Westward Movement on the Monongahela and Upper Ohio, 1765–1795* lying on a library table probably accepted them as an unusually impressive collection of data on local history.

FROM Arthur Pierce Middleton and Douglass Adair, "The Mystery of the Horn Papers," *William and Mary Quarterly,* 3rd series, IV (October, 1947), 409–43. Copyright 1947 by Douglass Adair. Reprinted by permission.

For additional reading: On a similar problem, see Raymond Walters, Jr., "The James Gallatin Diary: A Fraud?," *American Historical Review,* LXII (July, 1957). Two detective stories which deal with the disruption of a town because of outside investigators are Dashiell Hammett's classic, *Red Harvest,* and Judson Philips' *Whisper Town.*

The respectable bulk of the books, the discreet gold lettering of the title on the black cover give no hint of the furor excited by their publication. Everything about their external appearance is reassuringly undramatic. Yet the printing of these solid-looking volumes divided a local community into opposing camps, agitated an entire region in fierce partisan debate, and, in time, attracted the incredulous attention of the whole American historical profession.

If our same hypothetical observer, in idle curiosity, had leafed through the first two volumes of *The Horn Papers*—the volumes that provoked the bitter controversy—he still would have seen little to arouse his excitement. Here he would have found the diaries of Jacob Horn and his son Christopher whose entries, dated from 1735 to 1795, fill approximately sixty printed pages. Published with the diaries is the fifty-page court docket, dated 1772–1779, of what is described as "the first English court held west of the mountains." . . . Also printed here are miscellaneous papers, court orders and maps of the Ohio region during the last half of the eighteenth century. The last 265 pages of Volume I of *The Horn Papers* contain fifteen chapters written by W. F. Horn (a descendant of the abovementioned diary-writing pioneers who now lives in Topeka, Kansas) on the early history of southwest Pennsylvania and the adjacent counties of northwest Virginia and Maryland. These chapters . . . are based in large part on the data contained in the diaries and court records printed in the first 140 pages of the volume. Volume II is made up of more than 500 family histories and genealogies of the early settlers in the region and these, too, depend on the Horn diaries and records for their validity. On cursory examination, therefore, *The Horn Papers* look like just another example of the standard type of local history issued by so many county and state historical societies during the last century. As such *The Horn Papers* appeared to be an extremely valuable publication, not only for students of local history but also for professional scholars who draw much material required for building up a more comprehensive picture of the American past from works of this type.

Nevertheless the appearance in print of these innocuous-seeming historical data in 1945 drew forth a charge almost unprecedented in the annals of American scholarship. Made by Mr. Julian

P. Boyd, Librarian of Princeton and recognized authority on the history of western Pennsylvania, this charge appeared in the July, 1946, issue of the *American Historical Review* which as the official publication of the American Historical Association is the most influential historical journal in the United States. Mr. Boyd wrote, after a careful examination of *The Horn Papers,* "I think the conclusion is inescapable that large parts of the documentary materials in the first two volumes, including diaries, maps, court records, memorandums, and even lead plates and hieroglyphs, are sheer fabrications. I do not know of any similar publication of fabricated documents among all the thousands of documentary publications issued by American historical societies."

This suspicion of forgery—the most serious charge that can be leveled at any historical writing—focused attention on the mystery of *The Horn Papers;* but it did not solve that mystery. Mr. Boyd felt sure that part of the materials was manufactured—but some of the documents had the ring of authenticity, and he confessed that the true and the false were so intermingled that it was difficult to separate them. The situation was further complicated by the opinion of two other professional historians—also experts on frontier history—Dr. Paul Gates and Dr. Julian P. Bretz who rejected the idea that the Horn documents were fabrications. There was no reason to doubt that in the main they were authentic eighteenth-century documents, badly edited by amateurs whose chief sin was lack of scholarly training. It was this slovenly editing, Mr. Bretz and Mr. Gates believed, that had misled Mr. Boyd and aroused his suspicions. . . .

The obvious solution to this scholarly impasse was independently proposed by both Mr. Boyd of Princeton and Dr. A. P. James of the University of Pittsburgh. Each suggested that a careful investigation of *The Horn Papers* by some official body was urgently required. Such an investigation would apply to the disputed materials all the various skills and techniques available to historians in dealing with questioned documents and artifacts. During the summer of 1946 with the approval and aid of Dr. Guy Stanton Ford, editor of *The American Historical Review,* a committee to investigate *The Horn Papers* was organized under the sponsorship of the Institute of Early American History and Culture at Williamsburg.

Since the challenged material dealt with the early history of western Pennsylvania, Virginia, Maryland and West Virginia, historical societies of those states were asked to appoint representatives to the investigating committee. Dr. Solon J. Buck, Archivist of the United States, whose published works on western Pennsylvania history and long experience in dealing with dubious documents ideally fitted him for the post, agreed to act as chairman. Dr. Arthur Pierce Middleton, trained and experienced in the skills of both archeology and history, was appointed as full-time executive secretary of the Committee. . . .

So began the search for that elusive thing called historical truth in the matter of *The Horn Papers*. Mr. Boyd's letter had posed two major questions for an investigating committee to answer. First, were *The Horn Papers* authentic? If not, what portions had been fabricated? In the second place, if lack of authenticity was clearly proved, what was the motive for the publication of spurious documents? Every historian has heard of fake Washington signatures or of Lincoln letters sold for the pecuniary advantage of the faker; but clearly this was a case of a different sort. At no time was there ever any hint that *The Horn Papers* were printed with intent to defraud anyone or to make money for anyone. It was equally clear that *The Papers* were not intended as a hoax or a mischievous prank. . . .

And now that the task is finished, has truth been captured and exhibited so that all can agree on her features? The members of the Committee hesitate to make such a triumphant claim. Unfortunately for any who desire a complete and total solution neatly tied up in a tight package the Committee could not follow the pattern of the fictional detective story where *all* ambiguity is miraculously dissolved in the last five pages by the phenomenal deductions of a Sherlock Holmes. The most they can say is that they have apprehended certain aspects of truth: certain facts in regard to the diaries and papers attributed to Jacob and Christopher Horn have now been established beyond question or cavil. After the events leading up to the publication of the Horn documents have been described, therefore, and after the various steps taken by the Committee to test the diaries and artifacts have been set forth, it will remain for you, the reader, to judge if what has been learned during the investigation is sufficient to solve the mystery of *The Horn Papers* once and for all.

The Horn Papers first became a matter of public record in 1932 when the editors of the Washington, Pennsylvania, *Observer* and the Waynesburg, Pennsylvania, *Democrat-Messenger* each received letters from an unknown correspondent in Topeka, Kansas. Although letters to the editor are normally not saved by newspaper offices the one received by the *Observer* was so unusual that it is still carefully preserved today, fifteen years after its receipt. Since it is the earliest public announcement concerning *The Horn Papers* yet discovered, a transcript of the neatly written, long-hand original, in which punctuation and spelling are exactly duplicated, is presented here:

Topeka, Kansas,
Aug. 15th, 1932

Editor "Washington Observer,"
Washington, Pa.

Dear Sir:

I have in my possession several pages of interesting historical notes relating to the early history of what is now Washington, County Pa., and I am writing to ask you if the "Observer" will be interested in publishing a some what lengthy article, if I prepare the article from the manuscripts which I copied in 1891, from the original diaries kept by Jacob. Horn and Christopher Gist, from 1750, to 1767, from the Diaries, and Note Books kept by John and Christopher Horn under dates from 1773, to 1798, and the same kept by John Horn, son of Christopher Horn, under dates from 1785, to 1838, with years of research work, among the records at Williamsburgh, Va, at Philadelphia, Harrisburg, and some reviews in the Carnegie Library in Pittsburgh, I have much original "data Matter" that relates to the times, and events that took place in old Augusta County, afterwards the District of West Augusta, then finally, Yohogania County, Va, before Washington County was organized in March 1781.

These original papers containing many interesting historical accounts of events were recorded in the days of which the events took place, and give a detailed account of the life and home of Jacob. Horn, at Snow Creek Virginia, of Christopher Gist, Jacob Horn, and the two French surveyors, trip from Snow Creek, to Camp Cat Fish 1, at "Spirit" Spring, on Cat Fish Run on North Tingooqua Creek, (North Ten Mile Creek) in June, 1751. *"The planting of the French Lead Plates* on *Dunkard Creek,* at the *Mouth* of *Casteel Run* in Morgan township, Greene, Co. The life and much history of John Canon's Career in Washington County prior to his founding Canonsburg, in 1787.

These records give a pretty clear account of the Jacob Horn Block House at Camp Cat Fish 1. at "Spirit" Spring and of *his Court held there in September, 1773,* and in *June, 1774,* thence the *removal* to the *Heath's homestead,* the *division of the Court there,* the Court brought back to the home of John Canon, at Augusta town, in *September, 1775,* then the building of the Augusta Town Court House in the spring of 1776, by John Horn and Abiga Hough.

The *description* of *Augusta Town is Complete* with "*plat* and *Chart*" also a *description* of *Razortown in 1780.*

There are a score of other matters, and persons, mentioned that I cannot enumerate here, but which I would wish to include, if, I prepare the article as several of your City, and County people have ask me to do.

None of this has ever been published, and while much of it agrees with Boyd Crumrine's History, but goes on to clear up many things that he does not clearly settle in regard to the old Virginia Courts, &c. in the days prior to 1781.

Now if the "Observer" feels that the people of present Washington County, will be interested in obtaining a fairly clear knowledge of the "first days" in the settlement of the County *from these records.* please let me know soon, and I will prepare the article stating only varified facts, with Charts, notes, and dates of all events which the records Mentions in references.

I have been in Communication with your fellow man, Hon. J. F. Mc Farland, in relation to the relocation of the Jacob Horn homestead which to my surprise is a lost location, and while I do not know exactly where the Block House stood, My father, the late S. R. Horn, had seen it and the graves of Jacob Horn, wife, daughter, and John Hardtman, on two different occasions, in 1839, and in 1848.

Please inform me as to the wishes in this matter and I will act in accordance. also as to whether the Copy should be type written, or left in my own hand writing.

Thanking you for the favor of an early reply. I remain

Very Sincerely

W. F. Horn

2325 Topeka Ave.

It is hard for anyone unfamiliar with the local history of southwestern Pennsylvania to appreciate the impact of Mr. Horn's offer on historically minded residents of Washington and Greene counties, and to understand why his articles created such a stir as soon as they began to appear in print. In effect his manuscripts, as he described them, offered solutions for a series of problems that local historians had puzzled over for years. Augusta Town and Razortown were famous "lost towns" that preceded the establishment of the present Washington; even their locality was a question of debate, and now Mr. Horn said he had a "plat and Chart" of one, and a contemporary description of the other. In like manner his proffered account of the courts held at Camp Cat Fish and at Spirit Spring in 1773 and 1774 promised to be historical dynamite, for previously the earliest court in the region was thought to have been held in 1776. In 1905 the Washington County Historical Society had ceremoniously set up a granite monument marking the site of this court and describing it as the "FIRST COURT HELD BY ANY ENGLISH SPEAKING PEOPLE WEST OF THE MONONGAHELA RIVER." Mr. Horn's report of two earlier courts would therefore require the demolition of this memorial and the erection of another. In fact the Horn manuscripts, on the basis of Mr. Horn's description, would do much more than "clear up" (to use his own words) the lacunae of Boyd Crumrine's justly famous history of the region —they would require its complete revision. . . .

In many parts of the United States a threat to revise drastically long cherished local traditions or to rewrite local history would hardly cause a ripple of interest except among a tiny group. This was not the case in Greene and Washington counties. The visitor to this region cannot but be impressed by the consciousness and deep-rooted pride of the local people in their own rich heritage from the past. Washington and Jefferson and Waynesburg colleges are centers of local historical interest. Each of the counties has a flourishing historical society made up of active members greatly concerned with the region's history. . . . [A] large percentage of the present landowners are descendants of the settlers who first entered the territory at the end of the eighteenth century. . . .

The editor of the *Observer,* however, delayed about accepting Mr. Horn's offer. It was, therefore, the neighboring newspaper at Waynesburg, the *Democrat-Messenger,* that printed, during 1933–1934, excerpts from the diaries and manuscripts in Mr. Horn's possession. These short samples immediately proved so popular and created so much excitement in both Greene and Washington counties that the *Observer* took up the tale. From May, 1935, through January, 1936, lengthy installments of *The Horn Papers* appeared as a regular Saturday feature.

The newspaper publication of the Horn articles and manuscripts in the *Democrat-Messenger* acted as a local introduction—or rather as a reintroduction—for Mr. W. F. Horn himself, who now returned to his ancestral home as something of a local celebrity. Waynesburg became his headquarters, and he regularly visited that town through the remainder of the 1930's and early 1940's, sometimes staying several months at a time. He reknit old friendships, among them one with A. L. Moredock, President of the Greene County Historical Society, and gained many new friends through his infectious enthusiasm for the region's history and his knowledge of its past. Inevitably he was asked to lecture on Waynesburg's history and here his success was marked. He was always willing to help any local person trace a genealogy; nor did he charge fees for such services even though he would spend much time and fill many sheets of paper with his fine copperplate writing in working out a complete family line. Mr. Horn's "historical walks," or exploring trips, through the hills and along the old paths of the area also became locally famous. Even individuals who are not personally friendly with the man speak of his ability to make the past come alive, to recreate the drama of pioneer days as he walked along pointing out the ancient landmarks of the region. Although Mr. Horn was not a young man his energy never seemed to flag on these expeditions nor did his ability to hold an audience enthralled ever fail. By 1935, just three short years after his initial letter to the newspapers, Mr. Horn was widely accepted as the historical oracle of the Greene County Historical Society and though he still maintained his chief residence in Topeka, Kansas, he had also become a leading citizen of Waynesburg.

Nor did his fame remain merely local. In 1939 Mr. Horn was called to Uniontown to act as historical adviser in excavating what he identified as French fortifications constructed in 1747–1748 just before the outbreak of the French and Indian War. In 1942 he was invited to Hagerstown, Maryland, where he lectured on the colonial history of western Maryland and received an ovation. In 1945 he made the first of several speeches before the Marion County Historical Society of Fairmont, West Virginia, on the early explorations of that region. Here, too, his audiences were spellbound. In the words of the vice-president of that Society, "Mr. Horn was a wonder."

Few historians and few historical documents ever generate such intense and widespread enthusiasm as this. The Horn documents, however, had certain unusual features that were sure to win them acclaim wherever Mr. Horn exhibited them. One quality that struck everyone who heard him lecture from his ancestors' journals was the amazing wealth of detail provided on the "common man"—to use a modern term—of frontier history, the obscure individual in the rank and file of the westward movement whose only historical record, before *The Horn Papers* were discovered, was a name on a deed, on a petition, in a tax list, or in a family Bible. It is not surprising therefore that, as one listener reports, the Marion County Historical Society was overwhelmed by the body of explicit information on early settlers presented by Mr. Horn, and thought him "a wonder" when he "could give dates, day, month and year, on which pioneers from whom our members descended had come into this section."

Another feature that helped guarantee *The Horn Papers* instantaneous popularity was the unique documentation they provided for famous events and figures in frontier history. Jonathan Hager, Christopher Gist, John Canon, and Thomas Cresap were far from being obscure pioneers. They were the generals and chiefs-of-staff of the westward movement. Nevertheless historians have been baffled in trying to trace the careers of these prominent men. For certain periods in their lives there are more than adequate records, they act their historic roles on a stage brightly illuminated by contemporary documents. But for each there are periods of absolute darkness, gaps in our knowledge of where they were, or of what they were doing, or why, blank spots that historians deemed it impossible to fill. In instance after instance, however, *The Horn Papers* plugged these holes. . . .

A scarcely less popular feature of *The Horn Papers* was the supplementary collection of artifacts and relics of pioneer life that had been preserved with the manuscripts. In 1942 when Mr. Horn spoke before three hundred people at a Hagerstown luncheon he read excerpts from the Jacob Horn diary, which described his ancestor's visit to "the fur trade house" of one "Jean Le Beau" on March 19, 1739, and Le Beau's gift to Jacob of a marble cross which the latter had admired. Mr. Horn, from the details in his great-great-great-grandfather's diary, then identified Le Beau's house as the old ferry house situated across the Potomac from Williamsport, Maryland, a landmark known throughout the neighborhood. Finally, as a dramatic climax to his talk Mr. Horn presented Le Beau's cross, which he said had been preserved for two hundred years in his family, to the president of the local historical society. At the same time Mr. Horn gave to the Hagerstown Museum another valued relic mentioned in Jacob's diary: one of the "4 new Virginia Colonial Coins" that Jacob speaks of having received from Jonathan Hager on March 4, 1740. This coin like the cross, Mr. Horn reported, had been preserved by his family all these years.

The mementos presented at Hagerstown were probably the most striking example of Mr. Horn's generosity with historical artifacts. This munificence was matched on a lesser scale everywhere he went lecturing on his ancestors' documents. In West Virginia he gave arrowheads from the battlefield of Flint Top (mentioned in both the Jacob and Christopher Horn diaries); and the Waynesburg Museum was the recipient of a large collection of frontier relics. Everywhere—in Maryland, Pennsylvania, and West Virginia—these historic objects, tangibly linking the persons and events mentioned in *The Horn Papers* with the present, aroused almost as much interest as the diaries themselves. . . .

Still another element in the popularity and enthusiastic acceptance of *The Horn Papers* was the appeal it made to the local pride and patriotism in those areas where Jacob and Christopher Horn's activities had centered. If one wished to write a regional folk drama or pageant based on the Horn manuscripts, there are at least four clearly discernible dramatic themes woven into the texture of the diaries. The first of these is the clash of pioneer and Indian; the second, the contest between French and English for control of the strategic Ohio area; the third, the theme of American patriot *v.* England; and finally there is the conflict between the virile western frontiersman and the tidewater settler east of the mountains. Each of these themes has its quota of heroes and villains; each has at least one scene which in a pageant would make a magnificent set piece. . . .

It would be hard to devise a record better calculated than *The Horn Papers* to promote the historical pride of the inhabitants dwelling beside the headwaters of the Ohio River. . . .

If the story of *The Horn Papers* was in the main a ten-year record of dazzling success, nevertheless, a minor current of criticism and disbelief existed from the first report of the documents in 1933. Indeed the original hesitation of the Washington *Observer,* in 1932, about printing the manuscripts is evidence of an initial scepticism which increased with time. In the beginning this criticism centered in the Washington County (Pennsylvania) Historical Society whose members, as semi-official custodians of the county's historic tradition found the Horn documents and Mr. Horn's newspaper articles disturbing, if only because these were so greatly at variance with long established local history. Mr. Horn himself and his sibylline books might very well be accepted as the new oracle in Waynesburg, but Crumrine's *History* had been the bible of Washington County for more than half a century. It was too highly regarded to be upset by any series of newspaper articles. Thus a counter-current of opinion concerning *The Horn Papers* developed in opposition to the rising tide of approval and praise. . . .

The Horn critics, necessarily basing their strictures on the newspaper excerpts of the manuscripts and on Mr. Horn's articles and lectures, focused on two major points: the doubtfulness of certain facts related in the diaries themselves; and the impossibility of tracing any of the supplementary authorities that Mr. Horn adduced to buttress his ancestors' journals.

The anti-Horn group were further disquieted by what they deemed the cavalier way in which their objections were brushed aside when they asked that the startling new history presented by the Horn journals be substantiated by other records. It is reported that Mr. Horn's usual reply was that since the data were in his ancestors' manuscripts no other authentication was necessary. Moreover, since part of the Horn materials *did* square with the established record, the pro-Horn group argued that those pages which gave a unique account of persons and events and which therefore could not be tested against unimpeachable contemporary records should also be accepted.

When urged to explain why the massacre of 12,000 Indians at the Battle of Flint Top in 1748 (reported only in *The Horn Papers*), and the planting of three French lead plates in Greene and Washington counties (reported only in *The Horn Papers*) were not mentioned by a single contemporary document and why no nineteenth-century historian hinted at their occurrence, Mr. Horn did provide supplementary authority.[1] He referred the sceptics to "Andrea's, Early History of Northwest Virginia, 1760–1780," a copy of which had been in his own library until 1882. A lengthy quotation from it was printed in the *Observer* (July 13, 1935) for his critics to read. Further to document the diary's record of the French plates, Mr. Horn cited what he described as the "eminent authority" on eighteenth-century Anglo-French relations "Mrs. M. E. Gail" of Paris whose work in the Quebec and Paris archives, he said, fully corroborated the diarist's account of the planting of the plates. For critics who questioned genealogical data in *The Horn Papers* he produced long typewritten reports he had received from "The International Genealogical Society" of London and Philadelphia and "The American Genealogical Society." Mr. Horn suggested that anyone interested could write to these organizations and obtain verification of the accuracy of the Horn journals.

There is no record as to whether any of Mr. Horn's critics ever tried to do this, but they did make every possible effort to obtain a copy of "Andrea's History of Northwest Virginia." The effort was unavailing—neither its author nor its title nor date and place of publication could be traced in any bibliography, list of copyrights, library catalogue, or rare-book dealer's inventory. However the failure to discover this nineteenth-century account of the lead plates seemed of minor importance when two lead plates dated 1795

[1] That the French did, on the other hand, plant lead plates in the Ohio Valley in 1749 to establish their claim to the area is well known and can be documented by scores of contemporary accounts. That plate-laying expedition was commanded by M. Céloron, and one of the plates that he buried has been on exhibit in the Virginia Historical Society for over a hundred years. . . .

were excavated on August 11, 1936, just where the maps in *The Horn Papers* indicated they would be found.

The discovery of the two lead plates, though it did not completely silence Mr. Horn's opponents, in effect reduced their criticisms to offstage mutterings. Although the plates were *not* the French plates described in the Horn diaries as having been planted in 1751, and although there were ambiguous circumstances about their excavation,[2] Mr. Horn's supporters could henceforth quote the newspaper account of the discovery to all who doubted. The plates which had been found, said the *Observer* report on August 12, "seemed to prove almost conclusively that the French plates had existed." Nearly ten years later when, according to Mr. Horn, the original 1751 plate with the French inscription on it was found among the effects of a deceased sister, this second discovery served further to confirm the earlier more dramatic find.

The exhumation of the lead plates in 1936 did more than fortify the faith of the Greene County Historical Society in Mr. Horn's manuscripts. The members of the Society were now so thoroughly convinced of the value and importance of *The Horn Papers* that they determined to issue them in book form. This idea, it should be noted, was not originally suggested by Mr. Horn himself; all evidence points to the fact that when he first unveiled the manuscripts in 1932 he expected only newspaper publication in the *Observer* or the *Democrat-Messenger*. Now, however, under the enthusiastic urging of his Waynesburg friends he acceded to their plan of issuing *The Horn Papers* in a permanent form.

[2] The newspaper accounts of the excavation of the plates as well as the account in *The Horn Papers* . . . would indicate that the W.P.A. diggers under the direction of Mr. F. B. Jones, Archeologist and Curator of the Greene County Historical Society, found them. Actually they were unearthed by Mr. Horn himself during a two-hour period while the director was away. Dr. Mary Butler Lewis to Julian P. Boyd, Media, Pa., November 22, 1946. At the time Dr. Butler was assistant state archeologist of Pennsylvania. In the excitement of the moment Mr. Horn rushed to clean up his find in a nearby creek and the exact position of the plates was forgotten. This was brought out when Mr. Jones later tried to take photographs. Members of the Greene County Historical Society were distressed that Mr. Horn had washed the plates and destroyed the archeological evidence but, as they later reported, he was so happy and excited by his discovery "skipping and dancing about like a kid" that they didn't have the heart to chide him. Statement of Mr. Jones, to Messrs. Middleton and Adair, January, 1947.

The account of the struggle to get *The Horn Papers* published is a minor epic of historiography—an amazing story of resoluteness in the face of seemingly insurmountable obstacles. Almost the entire burden of preparing the Horn manuscripts for the press and of raising the money to publish them fell on the shoulders of Mr. A. L. Moredock and of the late Mr. J. L. Fulton, President and leading member respectively of the Greene County Historical Society.[3] The record of their efforts is a tale of determination, and self-sacrifice, in which any historical society could legitimately take pride.

In the beginning it was hoped that the Greene County Committee could interest either a university press or a commercial publisher in printing *The Papers*. The University of Pittsburgh, however, declined on the ground that the cost of verifying the questionable statements would be prohibitive. This discouraging reply was partly offset when a New York publisher agreed to print the book, if the Greene County Historical Society would underwrite the venture. Mr. Moredock and Mr. Fulton finally resolved to finance the enterprise to the extent of their own resources, and to seek the additional funds necessary by securing prepublication subscriptions from libraries, historical societies and interested individuals. In 1938 a series of brochures was circulated for this purpose. With heartbreaking slowness the money was gradually secured.

Paralleling the difficulties of the Greene County Historical Society in raising funds were the problems of editing the manuscript which Mr. Horn turned over to them. Originally the Society supposed there would be enough material for only one volume. Additional material however, produced along with the transcript of the diaries, twenty-two maps and numerous artifacts to be photographed, and the mass of letters, reports of speeches, and genealogical data, necessitated a two-volume work. . . .

After enlarging the scope of the work, the Greene County Committee found themselves saddled with an incredibly difficult edi-

[3] Technically *The Horn Papers* were issued by a "Committee for the Greene County Historical Society," the copyright being held in the names of W. F. Horn, J. L. Fulton, and A. L. Moredock. However *The Papers* were generally spoken of as a Society publication, just as Mr. Horn himself was described in newspaper accounts as "Historian of the Greene County Historical Society."

torial task. Neither Mr. Moredock nor Mr. Fulton had any editorial experience in preparing historical documents for the press. Moreover the manuscripts to be edited were in such condition that they would have baffled a veteran editor. The copies of the diaries that Mr. Horn told them he had made in 1891 were in great confusion. Written on discolored, worn paper of every conceivable size and shape, they lacked any continuity of arrangement, and the editors had to put them together like a jigsaw puzzle. Mr. Moredock stated that on several occasions Mr. Horn carried off, to show to interested friends, documents or pages of the transcript that were being worked on and forgot to return them. Under these discouraging circumstances the Greene County Committee tackled the editing of the documents and began to work out rule of thumb editorial procedures. As an additional editorial burden Mr. Moredock and Mr. Fulton assumed the task of acquiring specialized knowledge in eighteenth-century American history outside the western Pennsylvania field.

Even before publication was undertaken the members of the Greene County Committee were sensitive about the charges that *The Horn Papers* were full of errors. They became even more sensitive as the work progressed. Laboring over the manuscripts they discovered contradictions in dates, biographical anomalies, and other errors. At the same time they found themselves exposed to a new challenge, this time from university scholars and professional historians who heard about *The Horn Papers* as a result of the publication program. Without exception, the professionals to whom the papers were submitted for opinion cautioned against publication unless the dubious parts could be verified. In spite of professional discouragement Mr. Moredock and Mr. Fulton felt committed to publication: *The Papers* had already been advertised and subscriptions accepted. Moreover, the experts while pointing to errors in *The Papers* had not denied that much of the data when tested by the scholars' own standards might be authenticated. Because scholars had produced no documents that explicitly discredited them, an impressive additional body of facts was presumed to be correct.

Under the circumstances what the editorial committee did is perfectly understandable. Where the manuscripts showed internal inconsistencies and contradictions they attempted to establish the correct reading on the basis of supplementary research. They also decided to publish with *The Horn Papers* additional historical material of unquestioned value, although these extra documents added appreciably to the cost of printing and although they were not an integral part of the Horn manuscripts. Preparations were therefore made to print in Volume II the 1790 census of heads of families of Washington County; in like manner plans were matured to issue a third volume containing maps of Washington and Greene counties prepared by the Pennsylvania Land Office.

Mr. Moredock has testified to the perplexed state of mind in which the Greene County publication committee found itself as the editorial work progressed. They tried in as many ways as they could think of to test the accuracy of *The Papers* as they became fully conscious of the many scattered "errors." In Mr. Moredock's words, the committee was "well aware there are some controversial matters" that inevitably would appear in print. The editors believed, however, that the deciding factor was the need "to preserve the material for the future." Drawing an analogy from the career of the famous collector, Lyman C. Draper, who accumulated thousands of manuscripts on western history but, paralyzed by his ideal of completeness and the hope of finding one more relevant paper, never published a page of his projected history of the pioneers, Mr. Moredock observed: "Had Mr. Draper proceeded in this way [i.e. as did the Greene County Historical Society] and made available to the general public the sources as he gathered them, a great benefit to history would have resulted. Perhaps some controversial matters would have been found. Even so, could we say such would have destroyed their value?"

And so, what can only be described as the prodigious efforts of the Greene County Committee went on in the face of mounting financial demands, inadequate clerical assistance, wartime paper shortages, refractory printers, and their own doubts about portions of the manuscript they were editing. Throughout they were sustained by the certainty that they were rendering an important service to their own neighborhood and to the historical profession generally. At last, after nine years of editorial work and after the expenditure of approximately $20,000 (a sizable proportion of which they had advanced themselves), Mr. Moredock and Mr. Fulton saw with pride the three impressive volumes of *The Horn Papers* issue from the press in December, 1945.

Six months later Mr. Boyd focused national attention on *The Papers* by branding them fabrications, and calling for an investigation by an impartial committee.

The Committee appointed to investigate *The Horn Papers* began their analysis of the published volumes with an impartial mind. It was soon discovered that the materials published in Volumes I and II furnished internal evidence that bore out Mr. Boyd's judgment.[4]

The *prima facie* reasons why portions of the documentary material in *The Horn Papers* appeared to be spurious are: (1) evidences of ineptitude in copying the original manuscripts; (2) anachronistic and doubtful words and phrases; (3) biographical anomalies; (4) historically incorrect or doubtful statements; (5) internal discrepancies; and (6) internal similarities of documents purporting to be of different authorship.

A glance at *The Horn Papers* reveals that the documentary material was carelessly presented. Although the original manuscripts are said by Mr. Horn to have been in very poor condition and partially illegible when he copied them in 1891, there are few or no indications of omissions, of conjectural reconstructions of damaged pages, or of illegible or doubtful words. These deficiencies, although more heinous in connection with the documentary material, are by no means confined to it. The secondary material containing many quotations from supposed primary sources is usually without citation, and never with an adequate citation. This leads one to

[4] The Committee unfortunately was unable to communicate directly with Mr. Horn. His daughter, Miss Mae B. Horn, in a letter to Arthur Pierce Middleton, Topeka, Kansas, February 24, 1947, informed the Committee that her father was too ill to reply. Miss Horn enclosed a certificate from Mr. Horn's physician, George W. B. Beverley, dated February 22, 1947. Mr. Horn, however, has continued his correspondence with other interested persons. As recently as August, 1947, a correspondent in Fairmont is reported to have received a letter "in which Mr. Horn was quoted as saying that . . . he no longer was interested in what was done about the Horn Papers." E. E. Meredith to Arthur Pierce Middleton, Fairmont, West Virginia, August 11, 1947.

surmise either that the copyist was completely unfamiliar with accepted editorial techniques, or that he had reason to conceal the source of his information.

Although editorial ineptitude puts the careful scholar on his guard when considering specific details, it is not necessarily evidence against the authenticity of a document as a whole. Much more important evidence is the frequent appearance of anachronistic and doubtful words and phrases, for it is well known that "anachronisms are the rock on which counterfeit works always run most risk of shipwreck."[5] The documentary material in *The Horn Papers* abounds in such words and phrases, some of them quite impossible for the eighteenth century[6] and many others highly dubious.[7] Scarcely a page is devoid of them. Similarly, many passages in the diaries have the ring of nineteenth rather than of eighteenth-century phraseology. . . .

An authentic diary would be true throughout, not just in a majority of its entries. It would be true, in all instances where the writer was in a position to know the truth. A genuine diary might, indeed, contain a false statement because the writer was misinformed, because he recorded hearsay that was in error, or because his judgment was faulty. But an authentic diary would under no circumstances record the appearance and activities in the writer's company of a person when that person is known to have been elsewhere or after he is known to have died. A single instance of this kind would cast doubt on the authenticity of a diary even though every other entry were correct, for it would unquestionably demon-

[5] James Anson Farrer, *Literary Forgeries* (London, 1907), p. 2.

[6] Examples: "trail," used frequently in the Horn diaries as early as 1735, to mean a path or road, belongs to a later period—the earliest reference to it in the *Oxford English Dictionary* and the *Dictionary of American English* is dated 1807; the word "stow[a]way," used in the Jacob Horn diary in an entry for 1738, first appears in the *Oxford English Dictionary* in a reference dated 1854. Other undoubtedly anachronistic words and phrases in the Horn documents are "tepee" (1740), "Virginia Blue-bloods" (1748), "braves" (1748) for Indian warriors, and "Ranch" (1748) in the expression "Gist's Mule Ranch."

[7] Examples of doubtful words and expressions: "hometown" (1736), "fur trade house" (1739), "frontire spirit" (1739), "the wilds of Baltimore's Colony" (1739), "race hatred" (1772). The Committee has on file a full list of such anachronisms of which the above is but a small sampling.

strate that the document had been tampered with. *The Horn Papers* contain not one but many such biographical irregularities, and they form, perhaps, the most important single body of *prima facie* evidence against the manuscripts.[8] Closely associated with biographical errors are the many historically incorrect or doubtful statements in the Horn documents which, though too numerous to consider individually, have the cumulative effect of discrediting them. . . . .

Also damaging to *The Horn Papers* are the internal contradictions in the documentary material. Christopher Horn variously recorded Gist's death as having occurred from November, 1768 to October, 1770. The references to the date of the battle of Flint Top reveal that the author of both the Jacob and Christopher Horn diaries was completely unfamiliar with the Julian Calendar (in universal use in the British colonies until 1752) and that, as a result, the references are considerably at variance. Moreover, the ignorance of the calendar change resulted in situations such as the appearance in Williamsburg of Buck Eckerlin and his brother in October, 1748, after having witnessed a battle on the frontier that was not supposed to have taken place until the following month.

From a purely stylistic point of view, there is evidence that the diary of Jacob Horn, the notes of Christopher Horn, the diary and daybook of John Horn the elder, and the Camp Cat Fish docket were probably written by the same person. In the writings of both Jacob and Christopher Horn the eccentricities are identical: the same misspellings, the same use of anachronistic words, the same use of doubtful words and phrases, and the same historically incorrect or dubious statements. Another similarity between the Jacob Horn diary and the Christopher Horn notes is the fondness of both for recording prophetic words of Gist and Canon. On the other hand, each of these documents is written in the same peculiar lit-

[8] Christopher Gist appears frequently in the Horn diaries during the years 1759–1769, and his death from eating a surfeit of wild grapes and red plums is recorded at "Laurel Hill, or Little Haystack Knob" in 1769. But from unimpeachable contemporary documents we know that Gist died of smallpox *en route* from Williamsburg to Winchester, Virginia, in 1759. Other biographical impossibilities in *The Horn Papers* involve Thomas Cresap, John Canon, Dr. Samuel Eckerlin, and Jonathan Hager.

erary style—an ill-matched combination of extraordinary linguistic crudities or pseudo-archaisms and outbursts of romantic sentiment couched in graceful nineteenth-century language.

On the other hand there was a weight of evidence favorable to *The Horn Papers,* otherwise there would have been no disagreement about them. The mere bulk and complexity of the collection of papers, the impressive number of collateral artifacts, the absence of any pecuniary or other compelling motive for forgery, the unquestioned sincerity of the sponsoring society, the many statements in the manuscripts that agree with generally accepted facts all strengthened the opinion that some of the Horn documents were genuine.

In view of this conflicting testimony the investigation entered a second phase. *The Horn Papers* certainly could not be accepted as genuine in their entirety. The search now concentrated on the problem of discovering if any were unimpeachable. It was hoped by expert examination of the physical objects—the eighteenth-century manuscripts, the lead plates, the maps, the other artifacts—to rescue some *bona fide* material.

The original papers upon which *The Horn Papers* are based were, according to Mr. W. F. Horn, boxed up by Christopher Horn in 1795 and the chest handed down in 1809 to his son, John, and by him in 1856 to his grandson, Solomon. In 1882, Solomon Horn moved west and took it with him to Doniphan County, Kansas. Mr. Horn reported that when the chest was opened in 1891 at Troy, Kansas, by his father and himself, it was found to contain the family records and maps as well as a number of artifacts—small wooden boxes, tools, objects of shell and stone, and glassware. Mr. Horn also asserted that the papers, being . . . "very much moth-eaten"—were partially illegible. But the introduction of *The Horn Papers* states that "Many, including the court docket, were preserved," and the impression that a substantial portion of the original manuscripts had survived was sustained by statements in the promotional literature. The Committee, however, learned from the President of the Greene County Historical Society that only the court docket and three of the maps purported to be original; everything else in the Society's possession was a copy made by W. F. Horn in 1891 of original papers no longer extant.

In addition the Society had had two supposedly original items: (1) a torn portion of Lord Dunmore's receipt to Jacob Horn for the return of his commission as justice at Camp Cat Fish; and (2) a perspective map on birch bark of the site of Turkey Foot Rock made by Jacob Horn in 1751. Shortly after the Horn papers were deposited with the Society, the surviving fragment of the receipt vanished. Thereafter, the Society took steps to reproduce photographically the remaining papers, a timely precaution, for almost immediately thereafter the birch bark map also disappeared in an inexplicable manner. That left only the court docket, the three maps and the artifacts. . . .

The court docket together with several maps and a number of sheets of Mr. Horn's transcript of 1891 were accordingly sent by the Greene County Historical Society at the Committee's request to Mr. Arthur E. Kimberly, of Washington, D. C., for scientific analysis. Mr. Kimberly's report [concluded that] . . .

(1) The docket and maps were not produced during the period 1760-1800 as stated but were manufactured at a considerably later date.
(2) One person . . . produced all of the items examined.
(3) Although the precise determination of the age of ink inscriptions of this type is difficult, it is most probable that these writings were produced no earlier than 1930. . . .

Extraordinary from many points of view, *The Horn Papers* are unique in the annals of American historiography in the sheer quantity of collateral artifacts advanced to substantiate them. In addition to the voluminous papers, there are three lead plates bearing inscriptions and dates, and thirty or forty objects of wood, glass, metal, hide, flax, shell, and stone, besides rifles, carpenter and cooper's tools, drawing instruments, cannon balls, and a large collection of arrowheads and other Indian relics. . . .

To silence the sceptical, apparently, several of the artifacts were provided with labels (in handwriting similar to that appearing in the court docket and on the maps formerly thought to be original) attesting the date and maker. Other objects, without benefit of label, were ascribed to particular persons, years, and places: a wall bracket was made by Jacob Horn in 1745; a wooden potato masher in 1750; a spool and flax thread in 1760; a rifle made at

Augusta Town in 1776 used by Christopher Horn during the Revolution; a bell-metal brace made at Razortown in 1783; and a surveyor's plumb bob made at Augusta Town in 1777 used in extending the Mason-Dixon Line in 1784 and in laying out Greene County in 1796.

Because of the bulk of the collateral artifact material, it was not feasible for the Committee to include every known piece in its intensive investigation. In addition to the lead plates, about a third of the collection was examined and submitted to experts for opinion. This group included the objects mentioned in the Jacob Horn diary, the glassware supposed to have come from the Christopher Horn chest, and several objects that bore inscriptions purporting to be of the eighteenth century.[9] (1) The copper coin (diameter 13/16 inch) dated 1734 was the only object that was clearly of eighteenth-century origin, but instead of being a Virginia colonial coin, as alleged by Mr. Horn, it is a Dutch duit (eighth of a stuiver). The obverse bears a crowned shield with the lion rampant of the province of Holland and the reverse a large V with the letters O and C superimposed upon the arms of the V, and the date 1734. The VOC monogram, common on Dutch coins of the seventeenth and eighteenth centuries, was probably misconstrued to mean "Colony of Virginia." The Virginia statute authorizing the first issue of coins was passed in 1773. (2) The stone cross (length 4″, cross piece 2¼″) is of a white marble of wide distribution. It is crudely made, the sides shaped with a metal file. As the expert lapidary asserted that this kind of stone darkens upon exposure to air and to contact with other materials, the complete absence of stain on the surface clearly indicates that the cross is of recent manufacture. (3) The two pieces of glassware said to have been in the Christopher Horn chest, and therefore to antedate 1795, are quite obviously spurious. One is a pressed-glass sherbet glass (4″ high, 3½″ in diameter); the other is a small glass (2½″ high, 2″ in diameter)—probably a toothpick-holder—with a ruby-glass rim. The latter is mounted upon a white marble base

[9] These objects were examined by Mr. James L. Cogar, curator of Colonial Williamsburg, Inc., and by Mr. Minor Wine Thomas, archeologist of Colonial Williamsburg, Inc. The stone cross was examined by Mr. George C. Barclay, of Barclay & Sons, certified gemnologists, Newport News, Va.

of two steps (2¾″ x 2¼″). Even a novice at glass collecting would know that such items are of the late nineteenth century, if not of the early twentieth century. (4) The wooden razor box (9½″ x 3¼″ x 2¼″) with brass hinges and a wooden latch. The cover of the inside compartment bears a label reading: "PENN INN—PENNS POINT MDCCXXXVII I JACOB HORN MADE THIS RAZOR BOX AT CONWELLS SHOP THIS SAME MONTH BY HIS CONSENT." (All block capitals except the letters "s" which are script and long, even when they appear as final letters of words.) Mr. Kimberly in a report dated May 8, 1947, asserts that the ink on the label is the same type used in the court docket and "1891" transcript, that it was written with a steel pen, and that the top handle of the razor box is attached with machine-made brads and that the screws used in fastening the hinges appear to be of modern manufacture. It is Mr. Kimberly's opinion that the razor box is spurious.

The most significant objects in the Horn collection were three lead plates. Two of these—the American plates of 1795—had been unearthed by the archeological expedition of 1936. These plates had been advanced as the strongest proof that there had been French plates buried in Greene County as the Horn diaries reported. In 1945 the third plate, this one with a French inscription and the date 1751, turned up in Kansas among the effects of Mr. Horn's deceased sister, Miss Dora Horn.

At the same time that the manuscript court docket and maps were sent to Washington for expert appraisal, the Greene County Historical Society sent two lead plates to the research laboratories of the National Lead Company for spectrographic analysis. One plate sent was the recently-recovered French plate of 1751, the other was one of the American plates of 1795. At the same time the Virginia Historical Society generously loaned for comparative analysis the Céloron plate which had unquestionably been buried in the Ohio Valley by a French expedition in 1749.

The spectro-chemical analysis of the three plates was revealing. The Céloron plate differed markedly both from the plate dated 1751 and that dated 1795. Both of the latter contained some nickel and a high content of silver and copper. Mr. [E. J.] Dunn, expert spectroscopist of the National Lead Company, for this reason attributed the lead to southeastern Missouri, the only source of lead known to him that contains nickel. Although the French had mined lead in what is now Missouri prior to 1750, the mines were not then operating nor had they been for some time previous. Moreover, the decided difference in composition of the lead plate dated 1751 from the genuine French plate is peculiar, especially in view of the chemical similarity of the two plates dated 1751 and 1795. The spectrographic analysis also disposed of the American plate of 1795, because the inhabitants of western Pennsylvania at that date could hardly have had access to Missouri lead.

If Mr. Dunn's report on the lead plate of 1751 left its status undetermined, the analysis of the French inscription on its face left no doubt of its spuriousness. The letter "Q" appearing in the text, for example, is a modern type form not used in French inscriptions until nearly three quarters of a century after 1751.[10] Moreover, the text of the inscription is not in eighteenth-century French, indeed, it was most certainly not written by a Frenchman in any century. . . .

But what of the numerous statements in *The Horn Papers* that are demonstrably correct, or at least plausible, and what of the occasional authentic ring that led Mr. Boyd of Princeton and other specialists in western [Pennsylvania] history to suppose that they contained genuine as well as counterfeit parts? The answer was not easy to find, but once found seems clear. The perpetrator of a forgery would quite naturally be led to incorporate a number of true facts and authentic phrases in his fabricated documents. And it can be shown that the forger of the Horn manuscripts drew heavily on such works as Boyd Crumrine's *Old Virginia Court House at Augusta Town, Near Washington, Pennsylvania, 1776–1777* (1905). Crumrine proved to be an excellent quarry for material: he was candid enough to admit the extent of every hiatus in his knowledge of the history of the period and region about which he wrote, thereby virtually inviting a creative artist to fill

[10] This form of "Q" appears no earlier than 1818 in "Comparative Table of Types used by the French National Printing House from its Foundation to 1825," in Daniel B. Updike, *Printing Types* (Cambridge, Mass., 1927), II, plate 327, opp. p. 187. Sol Hess, art director, Lanston Monotype Machine Company, to Arthur Pierce Middleton, Philadelphia, August 6, 1947, is also of this opinion.

gaps with imaginary data. Moreover Crumrine provided suggestions that were elaborated upon by the author of the Horn saga. . . . The product when threshed was one single grain of Boyd Crumrine wheat and a ton of Jacob Horn chaff.

Throughout the early stages of *The Horn Papers* controversy, the protagonists derived great comfort from the geographic accuracy of the diaries and the physiographic exactitude of the Horn maps. Their owner on being taken through Tygart's Valley for the first time was able to identify and impute historic associations to tributaries, hills, Indian sites and paths to the amazement of his guides, who had hunted and fished along the river all their lives. This exact geographic information was attributed solely to the Jacob Horn diary, which was found by the local people to be so full of explicit and accurate details that Mr. Charles Snyder of Fairmont was able to trace the day-to-day progress of Jacob's alleged exploring trip of 1750 on the modern, large-scale map in the Monongahela Power Company's office. Similarly, the President of the Greene County Historical Society asserted in a public address that the Horn maps must have been drawn by someone familiar with the territory because one of them revealed "the nearness of head springs of Muddy Creek to the main stream of South Ten Mile, *something not recognized by cartographers until the United States Geological survey was made*."[11] But in view of what is now known about *The Horn Papers,* it is apparent that the creator of the diaries and the maps carefully worked over the modern geological survey maps and may even have traced portions of them. Moreover there is evidence that details were added to the maps after 1930. In consequence, the fabrications assumed accuracy and minuteness of detail that astounded and delighted the believers in the Horn documents, who in their enthusiasm lost sight of the fact that genuine maps and diaries of the period seldom contain such details. Consequently, they quite understandably construed this feature of *The Papers* to be one of the strongest proofs of the authenticity of the manuscripts whereas, in reality, the very profusion of accurate topographical detail was one of the most convincing proofs that they were counterfeit.

[11] Address by A. L. Moredock, President of the Greene County Historical Society, at Morgantown, W. Va., June 8, 1946. The italics are ours.

Here then is the account of the mystery of *The Horn Papers* as it developed in its fantastic form for more than ten years; and here, too, is the account of the scholarly investigation of that mystery which extended over another year. But the story of *The Horn Papers* is still not ended, for the noxious influences of *The Papers* are already fermenting and will continue to work for an indeterminate time. Many genealogists have already incorporated Horn data in their reports of various family lines, and as a result the national headquarters of the Daughters of the American Revolution has had to take precautions to cope with them. The praiseworthy campaign to raise funds to restore the Jonathan Hager House in Hagerstown, Maryland, is meeting opposition from individuals, who were *always* against expending money on such projects, and who now cite *The Horn Papers* affair as reason for noncooperation.[12] Thus the poison works on. And, undoubtedly, for years to come some unwary individuals will continue to be misled by the documents' fascinating historical fictions, and other persons will continue to use the story of the false diaries as a weapon against legitimate and valuable historical enterprise.

The Horn Papers will also live on in another fashion, as will the reputation of the mysterious creator of the Horn saga.[13] The fantastic counterfeiter, whoever he was, and whatever his genuine abilities as a student of regional history were, is henceforth disqualified among scholars. His creative feat, however, may well be regarded by posterity as ranking him in that fascinating and devious company which includes [many forgers who created exciting, if false, accounts of the past]. Beyond a doubt, also, the impressive first and second volumes of *The Horn Papers* which, by reason of this investigation, now seem worthless to their purchasers will in time become collectors' items in the field of literary curiosities. As such, their pecuniary value will very likely exceed the original purchase price, for they will be sought and treasured with comparable fabrications on the grand scale—fabrications which possess

[12] The house was preserved. [Editor's note.]

[13] Mr. Moredock in January, 1947, advanced the hypothesis that "Old John" Horn, the grandfather of Mr. W. F. Horn, possibly fabricated some of the Horn documents as a joke on his own family. Since Mr. W. F. Horn was too ill to communicate with the Committee, it has been impossible to learn his opinion of this theory.

the peculiar worth such efforts have in illuminating the strange uses to which some men put their talents. . . .

Often the search for evidence does not involve manuscripts, fabrications upon site and situation factors, or the testing of alleged genealogies but merely the identification of an author. That "merely" creeps subtly past many a reader, however, who assumes that pseudonyms are easily cracked. But why does a writer take a pseudonym? To avoid detection, of course, and normally he will make that detection as difficult as possible. Writers of detective fiction themselves have been known to seek out the anonymity of a pseudonym—Josephine Bell, Josephine Tey, Patricia Wentworth, H. Baldwin Taylor, Simon Harvester, James Munro, William Haggard, (John) Ross MacDonald, Carter Dickson, Andrew Garve, Robert L. Pike, and B. Traven (is he really Berick Traven Torsvan?) are all names you will not find on any mailbox. Usually, given modern methods of research, record-keeping, and invading privacy, it is true that such pseudonyms cannot remain pseudo for long: the pseudonymous Helen Hudson, who recently wrote of a Gothic-embowered Ivy League university in her thinly veiled *Tell the Time to None,* cannot have thought the truth would not out (especially when one of the more cretinous figures in the novel was a certain "little Dr. Winks," a name not so common as to have prevented first thoughts of libel in the patronymical possessor, until he reflected that he was not, he hoped, cretinous, and certainly, he knew, not little).

The pseudonym is essential to detective fiction—could we do without secret agents named Roger Winthrop who turn out to be that master of disguise, the Baron Hugo von Berchtesgaden, or without numbered bank accounts in Switzerland, or James Bond's unflappable boss, M? But in real life, out there in the world where royalties have to be paid and books have to be shelved, such devices are difficult to protect. One need not be a historian or a detective to go to the card catalogue of the nearest library, there to read that Manning Coles, the author of those classics of the pre-Bond period of spy fiction, *Drink to Yesterday* and *Toast to Tomorrow,* was two people, Cyril Henry Coles and, as the card says with relentless fullness, Adelaide Frances Oke Manning. Another flick of the wrist brings us the knowledge that Ellery Queen, the American master of them all, unless your ballot goes to Erle Stanley Gardner, is also two people, Manfred Bennington Lee and Frederic Dannay.

Both these instances raise an interesting question of internal evidence: it would be apparent, I think, to most careful readers that Coles and Queen each were two or more persons. A single author's skills may flag across the years but on the whole they will flag in consistent ways. The skill of two authors will change at different rates, and the interaction between them will also change in ways producing yet other alterations in the character of their writing. In recent years, Manning Coles has not written anything approaching the quality of the first two novels, products of the nineteen-forties, and it comes as no surprise to learn that one of the partners died and that the other has carried on alone. And, to my taste, Queen has written little that is satisfying since 1954. I know nothing about Messrs. Lee and Dannay but I suspect that one is responsible for the plotting and dialogue and that the other is responsible for working out the formal puzzle represented by each book. While the intricacy of the puzzles has not changed, both plot and dialogue have ceased to have much for which we can commend them.

A single writer occasionally may write a book well below his standards, too. Lionel Davidson, one of the few authors potentially able to step into Eric Ambler's shoes, wrote two books of exceptional quality, *Night of Wenceslas* and *The Rose of Tibet,* before letting his guard down a bit in *A Long Way to Shiloh* (which, its American publishers fearing that Civil War buffs would buy it and be disappointed, was called *The Menorah Men* in the United States, confusing yet a different audience). But these three books were published within six years, just as fourteen of the books of Bond were written across thirteen years, and the pace may have been too fast rather than the talent foreshortened. Philip MacDonald wrote nothing so good as *Warrant for X* until *The List of Adrian Messenger,* twenty-one years apart. Hillary Waugh, whose Police Chief Fred Fellows of Stockport, Connecticut (Guilford? Branford? Shelton?), is a small-town answer to the naturalistic episodes that Ed McBain (Evan Hunter) unfolds within the confines of Riverharb's 87th Precinct, has also written as H. Baldwin Taylor but far less well, while John Creasey seems to put more effort into his plotting when he abandons the unconvincing Superintendent "Handsome" West for the fiction of J. J. Marric, one of his pseudonyms, and Marric's Commander Gideon, although both are "of Scotland Yard." Robert L. Pike writes badly and Robert L. Fish writes well, although they are the same person. Obviously all these writers conceive of their task and of their audience differently as they assume their pseudonyms. Or perhaps they feel trapped by one or the other of the names into writing stereotyped material.

Many an author writing under his own name has ceased to grow as he has discovered just what it is that his audience will and will not buy. Critics often remark that an author's second work is not as original as his first. This is scarcely surprising, since a first book, like a first child, is truly first-born. There is no audience to please; there are only the writer and his integrity. But if that first book is an overwhelming success, the temptation to repeat that success by repeating the techniques that produced it is strong. Among writers of recent times who all too clearly became the victims of their own successes have been, in descending order, John D. Macdonald, Ian Fleming, Donald Hamilton, Brett Halliday, Desmond Cory (Shaun McCarthy), Carter Brown, and Richard Prather. Even Raymond Chandler flagged at the end. To resist repeating oneself, to risk offending a cozy and dependable market, takes added courage if one has created a series figure, one who, like Leslie Charteris's The Saint or Erle Stanley Gardner's Perry Mason, is expected to conform to a pattern of thought and performance (and who, in the latter case, now looks like Raymond Burr). Innovation and growth then become more difficult since character development is unlikely, leaving only scene, plot, and dialogue open to genuine experimentation. No wonder Sir Arthur Conan Doyle wanted to kill off Sherlock Holmes so that he might sleep nights. By 1961 Halliday had written thirty-three Michael Shayne books, and by 1966 Gardner had dictated sixty-four episodes for Perry Mason! Even Sir H. Rider Haggard had given up his Allan Quatermain after fourteen adventures.

Success corrupts, and absolute success corrupts absolutely, to coin a phrase. In 1942 Marshal Hermann Göring paid nearly £165,000 for a remarkable painting by the great Dutch artist Vermeer. At the end of World War II the Dutch authorities sought to prosecute the seller for trading with the enemy. But when found, the seller, a Dutchman named Van Meegeren, confessed that he had painted the picture himself, together with five other presumed Vermeers and two De Hooghs, for which he had been paid £734,000. Did Van Meegeren do wrong to cheat his nation's enemy of a fortune? How did he succeed in hoodwinking some of Europe's leading art critics? Why did he wish to do so? Why did he continue doing so? This case, the Horn Papers of the art world, has been retold in detail by Lord Kilbracken in a book, *Van Meegeren,* which is as rich as any of its kind in historical literature.

Historians, too, must face the danger of audience entrapment, although the problem takes different forms. During the long Civil War Centennial we saw many good men repeat themselves time and again. Some scholars, perhaps "tempted by flattering offers," as Orin Grant Libby once wrote of David Ramsay, "the plagiarist" of eighteenth-century American historical scholarship,[14] seem to have

[14] *American Historical Review,* VII (July, 1902). [Editor's note.]

turned increasingly to editing books of readings (this book is one example), almost as though they confused a pair of scissors and a Xerox machine for pen and paper. Yet another form of entrapment, especially in those universities where "publish or perish" (a not indefensible practice, be it said) is the motto, arises from the presumed necessity to select subjects for research which may be brought to fruition within a predictable number of years. The result is that many young scholars, with first book—usually their doctoral dissertation—safely in press, turn to a project not unlike the dissertation itself, proving again that they possess skills the dissertation was meant to demonstrate. This is known as "taking possession of a field," and it may go on even to a third book. Not until canonization, in some quarters called tenure, do such scholars feel free to experiment with techniques and subjects which may yield no early return.

Of course, one may become captive to more than audience, fame, method, or income. One may be trapped by the comfort of the library, by polished brass, old leather, and soft armchairs, into thinking that one need not cover the actual ground of history, without going over the actual scenes of which one must write, seeing for oneself (if those Conrad scholars) the River Berau, just as Gibbon walked the ground of his Roman ruins. As the great British historian noted in his autobiography, "It was at Rome, on the fifteenth of October, 1764, as I sat musing amidst the ruins of the Capitol, while the barefooted fryars were singing Vespers in the temple of Jupiter, that the idea of writing the decline and fall of the City first started to my mind." There is a sense of nuance, an eye and an ear for place, which must infuse the best historical writing (of a Macaulay, or a Garrett Mattingly, or a Parkman), which can alone be gained by pursuing the place as well as the document. Does not our sense of that classic struggle between Holmes and Moriarty quicken if we have seen the Reichenbach Falls, above the Englischer Hof? Is not Margery Perham's magisterial biography of the greatest of

British imperialists, Lord Lugard, given a portion of its authority because of Miss Perham's own experience as a colonial administrator in Nigeria? Do not Gavin Black's Malaysian-based espionage stories read better because he (and his reader) clearly knows Kuala Lumpur and, indeed, even Kenny Hill, where the hero hides within his fortress estate? Bruce Catton, the master worker over the already much-trod ground of the battles of the Civil War, has obviously walked those grounds. In an age of pseudo-travel through magazines, radio, and film, the historian should not be satisfied to settle for what Daniel Boorstin has called *The Image;* he must seek the substance of place.

One of my own special pleasures is to read novels while in the locale they describe. I walked the streets of Halifax one snow-laden February day with Hugh MacLennan's *Barometer Rising* in my hand. This, surely the best novel yet to have come out of Canada, and a thriller of a high order, describes in accurate detail the great explosion within the narrows of Halifax's harbor in February of 1917, an explosion which leveled the old city below its protective Citadel and took over a thousand lives. I had read the novel before and had not been moved but as I stood above Bedford Basin and saw the *Imo* (of the novel) bear suddenly down upon the *Mont Blanc* (of reality), filled with a hundred tons of picric acid and TNT, I saw the novelist as historian. Henry Fauconnier's *Soul of Malaya* came alive to me while I was sitting in the shade of a rubber plantation that looked out across his House of Palms, now reconstructed after it was destroyed by the Japanese, a home Fauconnier built in Selangor. D. H. Lawrence's *Kangaroo* takes on new importance as one walks the beaches near Thirroul, south of Sydney, where he wrote. Much of Charles Dickens suddenly became meaningful after living for six months in that part of the London he knew best, just as a visit to Robert Louis Stevenson's birthplace in Edinburgh and to his grave in Apia both gave new excitement, for me, to *The Master of Ballantrae* or even *Treasure Island.* Nor does one need to read only those authors given the imprimatur of scholarly study to recognize this quality of verisimilitude: George R. Stewart's *Storm,* one of the finest evocations of weather, as well as one of the better contemporary restatements of Melville's theme of the interrelatedness of events and men, as shown in "The Try-Works" in *Moby Dick,* does not demand that one have been snowed in on Donner Pass to understand it—but it helps. The pleasure of Helen MacInnis's *Decision at Delphi* was enhanced by reading it at a café table overlooking the great valley below those ruins, and (to turn again to our detective fiction) Maurice Procter's superb portraits of Granchester, *The Big Smoke,* which is either Birmingham or Manchester, cannot fail to bring the Midlands to life. In an essay that follows in Part IV, David Donald brilliantly reconstructs an event within the halls of Congress by a detailed investigation of a scene he himself has quite literally measured, just as an American colonialist proved, a few years ago, that the number of British troops on Bunker Hill (i.e., at Dorchester Heights) could not have been as legend reports, by measuring the actual space upon the hill and calculating how many men could stand shoulder-to-shoulder upon it.

Another form of captivity, more subtle than the brandy glass and good cigar at home, more dangerous than entrapment by one's audience, and ultimately more corrosive to history, if not to the historian, is that which arises from a misplaced sense of patriotic duty. Jared Sparks, a Harvard-trained theologian and the owner of the *North American Review,* who was one of the earliest native-born American historians, was also one of our first unclean chimney sweeps. Between 1834 and 1837 he published *The Writings of George Washington* in twelve volumes. Later he also edited four volumes of letters written to Washington. Never a person who wanted to offend those more highly placed than he, Sparks edited out of Washington's papers nearly all the references that were derogatory to New Englanders. Sparks also argued, perhaps correctly, that since the average nineteenth-century reader did not realize how many acceptable forms of spelling prevailed in the previous century, his audience might think Washington illiterate if he did not alter the General's spelling and grammar. In order not to offend public sensibilities, Sparks also omitted Washington's earthier phrases. And, as a patriot, the editor noted that he was "persuaded that every American reader will be pleased to see the name of Washington associated with any historical illustrations tending to establish truth and justice." An Englishman, P. H. Stanhope, Lord Mahon, wrote an open letter to Sparks in 1852 to protest editorial methods which attempted to preserve a purely Olympian image for the Father of His Country, and Sparks replied to Lord Mahon's strictures in the same year with a sweeping defense of patriotic history, a defense I do not print here because of its length, but one which all might read with profit. Will our historians of the Bay of Pigs or Britain's writers on Suez do any better, one wonders? What will we read of the war in Vietnam twenty years from now?

This is not to say that Sparks was a bad historian but, rather, that he was as good as he could be within the confines of his own conception of his task, his audience, and his subject, and that this conception is one with which most professional scholars today would disagree, at least publicly. Sparks, after all, was one of the first to carry out multi-archival research, long before most scholars began to insist that peripheral archives should be investigated. He also knew that simple legwork, the ferreting out of relevant books, was not in itself research. (How many free-lance authors grace themselves with the title "researcher" by virtue of a few strenuous weeks spent ferreting out books in the New York Public Library, a task which is necessary but nonetheless only the preliminary to research itself. Many do much legwork but very little research indeed. Of course, if *Time* magazine wishes to call those miniskirted girls who pull almanacs off the shelf to verify the population of Ottumwa "researchers," that is their prerogative—they're paying them, after all.) But Sparks thought of himself as a guardian of the nation's treasure, and when the historian begins to put on the mantle of Guardian, he is forgetting that it is not his task to defend, but to reveal. The historian is no one's friend at court, even though he must often borrow from the court of law. Most often he borrows the adversary method of questioning. And if detectives have their manuals, their Prestwich on Poison or their Pearson on Perfect Crimes, historians also have their instruction books. It is to some of these—the general and theoretical studies of historical methodology—that we must now more fully turn.

PART III

THE ADVERSARY METHOD

9. The Case of the Eyewitnesses:

"A lie is a lie, even in Latin"

WHAT KINDS OF PEOPLE MAKE THE BEST WITNESSES? Grown men? Women? Children? Psychologists would suggest that each makes a reliable witness with respect to certain types of data, but that each may also be totally unreliable about other data. Rôle psychology, in particular, would seem to indicate that when a witness is forced into playing two rôles simultaneously—that of teacher and student, for example, or that of father and son, as when three generations are present in a single household—he will remember one type of evidence with greater clarity than another. One must know the witness well to know which rôle may be dominant in his moment of observation. We might assume, for example, that a member of a minority group will recall with greater clarity events touching upon his minority status. But this clearly may not be true: he may repress those events, he may color them with emotion, or he may not even be aware that he is a member of the minority to which the investigator assigns him. For we all are members of minorities in one way or another—if not in color, or in religion, or in place of residence, or by virtue of a regional accent, then perhaps through education or the lack of it, or because of the kind of work we do, or because we are albinos. How is the reader of an inert eyewitness account to know to which of these minority positions the author of the account was most sensitive? We all know the danger of ascribing to a person particular actions because of his color when, in fact, we reason that his actions were a function of his educational level, but how are we to know that the environmental assumption which replaces the hereditary one is correct? Especially how is one to know when the eyewitness lived over two thousand years ago?

The following essay on the credibility of testimony is taken from *Aspects of the Study of Roman History,* a series of lectures by Thomas Spencer Jerome, first published in 1923, nine years after his death. Jerome was a Harvard graduate and lawyer who served as American consular agent at Capri, in Italy. His assertion that "the basis of all right knowledge about anything is accuracy and completeness of observation" is not to go unchallenged, however, as we will recall from Robin G. Collingwood. Jerome is concerned here with the problem of confidence.

♦ ♦ ♦

The student of Roman history is confronted at the outset by the general problem of the degree of confidence which may justly be felt regarding information based on human testimony. There have been many indeed who have gloomily questioned the extent of our knowledge of the past of human societies. [J. L.] Motley asserted that "the record of our race is essentially unwritten. What we call history is but made up of a few scattered fragments, while it is scarcely given to human intelligence to comprehend the great

---

FROM Thomas Spencer Jerome, *Aspects of the Study of Roman History* (New York: Capricorn Books reprint ed., 1962), pp. 27–34, 39–42, 51–52, 43–45, and 47–49 (in that order). Originally published by G. P. Putnam's Sons, 1923.

For additional reading: A detailed examination of the contradictions inherent in testimony is provided by Bernhard Knollenberg in "Bunker Hill Re-viewed: A Study in the Conflict of Historical Evidence," *Proceedings of the Massachusetts Historical Society,* LXXII (October, 1957–December, 1960) [Boston, 1963], 84–100. Gullibility is treated with respect to the so-called Mecklenburg Declaration by A. S. Salley in "The Mecklenburg Declaration: The Present Status of the Question," *American Historical Review,* XIII (October, 1907), 16–43. Three unusually fine works of fiction, which may roughly be classified as spy stories, and which show how complex testimony may be, especially as misinterpreted by the reader, are Uwe Johnson's *Speculations about Jakob,* R. Vernon Beste's *Repeat the Instructions,* and Francis Clifford's superb *All Men Are Lonely Now.*

whole."[1] And [J. A.] Froude, with what some scholars would call his own method in mind, declared that "it often seems to me as if History was like a child's box of letters, with which we can spell any word we please. We have only to pick out such letters as we want, arrange them as we like, and say nothing about those which do not suit our purpose."[2]

The scholar is bound to weigh his evidence with the utmost care, for the testimony may be either deliberately or unconsciously falsified. It is evident, for example, that [Mason Locke] Weems, the Plutarch-like biographer of Washington, invented out of whole cloth the tale of the cherry tree, and that, being animated by the same exalted principles as his amiable Greek predecessor, his intention was not "to give information about George Washington but to suggest virtuous conduct to young Americans."[3] . . .

In addition to evidence . . . deliberately manufactured, there is also testimony which has been unconsciously falsified through defects of observation, imagination, and memory. For instance, in 1911 there appeared in a small English magazine, which shall remain unnamed, a description by an eye-witness of the eruption of Vesuvius in 1906. The most interesting feature of this article was that it contained, with the exception of the eruption and of the writer's presence in Capri, practically not a single correct statement of the events observed; and the defect extended to very simple matters of fact about which there ought to have been no question of interpretation. It was said, for example, that just before the eruption the volcano seemed on the point of extinction, whereas the "smoke" had been gradually increasing for three years; that the sea became too rough to permit crossing to Naples, and that for over a week no mail or news was received from the mainland. As a matter of fact, no day passed without at least one mail boat, and the weather was continuously calm. Capri, the writer of the article went on to say, was buried under the volcanic ash; "our roof and garden were covered to the depth of half a metre"; whereas the fall of ash would have been considerably overestimated if put at

[1] *The United Netherlands* (New York, 1868), III, 477.

[2] J. A. Froude, *Short Studies on Great Subjects* (*The Science of History*), I (New York, 1876), 1.

[3] A. B. Hart, *American Historical Review*, XV (1910), 242.

half an inch. And yet the article, I have reason to believe, was written by a young man whose good faith was not open to question. If the memory could thus go wrong in five years, we cannot wholly avoid the suspicion that the famous letters of Pliny the Younger, written some twenty-five or thirty years after the catastrophe which overwhelmed Pompeii, may contain elements due to a similar defective recollection.

But selected episodes, however valuable they may be as illustrations of an established proposition, possess little probative force; at most they serve to indicate merely that many false stories obtain currency—a matter of common knowledge. What is needed for our purposes is a class of cases obtained under strict control from identical objective data, and sufficiently numerous to furnish us with averages and percentages, so that we may see, not simply that human minds are sometimes inaccurate—everyone knows that—but rather in what proportion such inaccuracies exist, and how profound they are. Such cases should also have the characteristic of relation to minds which for the time being had no motive to misstate and presumably were endeavoring to bear true testimony as to simple objective facts.

For material of this sort recourse must be taken to the researches of certain scholars, chiefly Continental, who of late years have made careful investigations into the psychology of testimony. A glance at the results obtained in a few cases will furnish some idea of the difficulties which beset a student whose material is derived from human testimony.

One of the simplest experiments was that carried out by M. [Alfred] Binet with children.[4] A new reddish-brown French two centimes stamp together with some other simple objects—we confine our attention to the stamp—was pasted on a piece of cardboard and shown to twenty-four children for a space of twelve seconds, and they were then separately interrogated about what had been

[4] *L'Année Psychologique* [Paris], XII (1906), 161ff; XI (1905), 128ff. Dr. [Hans] Gross, after a careful examination of the subject, reached the conclusion that a healthy child, at least a boy, is one of the best witnesses to simple events, and that the errors of children, while different from those of adults, are neither more gross nor more frequent than those of their elders. See H. Gross, *Zur Frage der Zeugenaussage, Archiv für Kriminal-Anthropologie und Kriminalistik,* XXXVI (1910), 372–82.

exhibited. Four questions were asked about the stamp. All but three of the children said it was a French and not a foreign stamp. Only nine, however, stated its color correctly, although either red or brown was taken as a correct answer. The false answers were with one exception given positively. The blue of the fifteen centimes stamp was perhaps most familiar to the children, and six of them declared this stamp was blue; three said green; four said rose, and even white had its witness. Nine out of the twenty-four gave the correct denomination of the stamp, which was plainly marked on it. There was noticed a correlation between mistakes of color and of denomination. Thirteen answered correctly that the stamp was an unused one. One intelligent boy declared it was a used stamp; and being asked how he had reached this opinion, said that he saw that the gum had been removed; yet the stamp was pasted upon a card. Four asserted positively that it had been used, alleging that they were able to see distinctly the cancelling stamp, and they described its location. One of the older pupils even saw the letters "RIS"—the last letters of the word Paris—in the cancelling mark. The experimenter calls attention to the precision of these false memories as showing that a very positive statement given without the least hesitation can be entirely false. So also the descriptions were generally exact on one point and false on another: few were erroneous in all particulars. When experiments of this sort were carried on by means of leading questions, the percentage of errors was much greater, and similar results were obtained with students from sixteen to nineteen years of age. Where a written description of an object seen was required, only one-sixth of the observers made no mistakes. It was abundantly shown in all these cases that positiveness on the part of the witness and presence of detail in his answers gave no assurances whatever of their correctness.

One of [William] Stern's tests was slightly more complicated.[5] He had three simple pictures in black and white, which he exhibited for forty-five seconds each to about thirty cultivated adults who immediately wrote down what they had seen in each picture, and thereafter at certain intervals of time again submitted written statements. Such parts of their depositions as they were willing to take oath upon were indicated by underlining. Without going into de-

[5] Compare *L'Année Psychologique,* XII (1906), 168ff.

tails, it may be said that the results were not of a nature calculated to give one great confidence in the value of testimony. Error was not the exception, but the rule. Out of two hundred and eighty-two depositions only seventeen were entirely correct; and of these seventeen, fifteen were among the statements written down immediately. By the fifth day even, the proportion of misstatements reached about a quarter of all the details submitted. In the depositions containing indications of matters on which the observer was willing to take an oath, only thirteen out of sixty-three failed to contain false statements, to all of which however the witnesses were prepared to swear. Many of these were cases of the introduction of elements which were absolutely absent from the picture. So one student wrote three weeks after the event: "The picture shows an old man seated on a wooden bench. A small boy is standing at his left. *He is looking at the old man who is feeding a pigeon. On the roof is perched another pigeon which is preparing to fly to the ground to get its share of the food."* The italicized statements were wholly incorrect: there were no pigeons in the picture. Perhaps the figure of a cat in the scene may have suggested the idea of a bird to the observer. In this, as in other cases, the testimony of women revealed more, but less exact, remembrance than that of men.

A third class of experiments is that of a representation before spectators who do not suspect the fictitious character of the scene, of a short but striking event carefully prepared beforehand. For instance, at a Psychological Congress at Göttingen before witnesses who were psychologists, jurists, and physicians, and therefore presumably more skilled in observation and statement than ordinary persons, the following carefully prepared experiment was tried.[6]

Not far from the hall of meeting of the Congress, a public festival and masquerade ball were in progress. Suddenly the door of the hall opened and a clown rushed madly in, pursued by a negro with a revolver in his hand. They stopped in the middle of the hall, reviled one another; the clown fell, the negro leaped upon him, fired, and then suddenly both ran out of the room. The whole affair had lasted barely twenty seconds. The presiding officer requested the members present to write out, severally, statements of the affair, since doubtless there would be a judicial investigation. Forty reports were made out. Only

[6] A. van Gennep, *La Formation des Légendes* (Paris, 1910), pp. 158–59.

one had less than twenty per cent of errors, fourteen had from twenty to forty per cent of errors, twelve from forty to fifty per cent, and thirteen more than fifty per cent. Furthermore, in twenty-four reports, ten per cent of the details were pure inventions, and the proportion of inventions surpassed that figure in ten other reports. . . . It goes without saying that the entire scene had been arranged and even photographed in advance. The ten false reports are then to be put in the category of fables and legends, the twenty-four are semi-legendary, and six only can be regarded as having approximately the value of exact testimony. But with an ordinary public, the proportions are different, and one may estimate the percentage of pure inventions at fifty per cent at least.

It will appear from these and similar experiments that erroneous testimony was given in simple matters of direct, personal observation by witnesses who were not influenced by any conscious pre-existing emotion or prepossession, and who were actuated by a desire to give an exact and truthful narrative. Yet the results were not encouraging. It is evident, as scholars who have conducted or studied such experiments have shown, that good faith, the desire to tell the truth, and the certainty that the testimony is true, as well as the opportunity to secure correct information, and the absence of prepossessions, are far from affording adequate guarantees that the truth will be told. The most honest witness may misstate; the worst may tell the truth. Entirely faithful testimony is not the rule but rather a rare exception. . . .

The basis of all right knowledge about anything is accuracy and completeness of observation. A highly developed power of ratiocination, if not based on precise and correct data, is simply an additional cause of error, since it is more misleading to take the wrong path and follow it rigorously than to keep on making errors which may, and sometimes do, cancel one another, and eventually bring one out into the right path. But precision and accuracy require a mental effort which fatigues and pains one unaccustomed to it.

It is [as Spencer says] impossible to get accuracy from undeveloped minds; and undeveloped minds dislike prescribed ways of obtaining accuracy. Cooks hate weights and scales—prefer handfuls and pinches; and consider it an imputation on their skill if you suggest that definite measures would be better. There are uneducated men who trust their own sensations rather than the scale of a thermometer—will even sometimes say that the thermometer is wrong, because it does not agree with their sensations. The like holds with language. You cannot get uncultivated people, or indeed the great mass of people called cultivated, to tell you neither more nor less than the fact. Always they either overstate or understate, and regard criticism or qualification of their strong words as rude or perverse. . . .[7]

Another significant factor in impairing the validity of testimony is that of language. The failure on the part of a writer to interpret correctly events of another age and sometimes of another *milieu,* frequently rests upon the imprecision of language. Words often change their meaning with the lapse of years, and expressions which are figurative or symbolic may mislead the commentator of a later day. It is evident that later writers on religion went astray in their interpretations of earlier religious thought, and it is probable that in the controversy between Gaius and the Jews each party misinterpreted the other's language. We should know more than we do now about the Roman census, if we were quite sure of the exact meaning of such expressions as *capite censi.* . . . Ferrero has pointed out that what a Roman writer calls corruption, we generally call progress.[8] Again, had the word *tyrant* possessed a distinct and unchanging significance, certain pages of ancient history would have been less misunderstood. Language, indeed, often obscures rather than elucidates the facts lying back of it; for, as [Thomas] Hobbes says: "words are wise men's counters, they do but reckon by them: but they are the mony of fooles." . . .

One of the prime requisites of a historian, it will generally be conceded, is a thorough knowledge of the intellectual habits of the people and age whose life he seeks to reconstruct. He will recognize the fact that language is an unfailing index of intellectual capacity and moral attainment; that it is never a static thing; that there are always particular modes or fashions of expression which, if widely spread and long continued, are embodied in literature,

7 Herbert Spencer, *The Principles of Psychology* (New York, II, 1910), 388.

8 [Guglielmo] Ferrero, *Characters and Events of Roman History* (New York, 1909), pp. 3–35.

and that a period becomes distinctive by the use and abuse of certain words and phrases as surely as it does by dress. To be ignorant of the language of the literary remains of an age is no greater disqualification for one who seeks to interpret them correctly than to be ignorant of how that language was used—what the public sentiment of the times tolerated, expected or approved as mere *façons de parler;* what expressions were recognized as being no more than figurative and not to be understood literally; what touches were simply established conventions; what allowances contemporary readers were prepared to make; what differences in form of composition, if any, there were between a positive, honest assertion of fact, and a bit of badinage or politeness or general abuse. . . .

The foregoing are some of the difficulties which beset the mind in the correct ascertainment of facts; but there are further difficulties to be encountered before a truthful narrative emerges. The mind is not a phonograph which repeats in testimony what it takes in from the senses; and in the manipulation and transformation which experience undergoes before it reappears in evidence, there participates a whole brood of sophistries and fallacies, blunders and botches of intellection, which play their part in distorting and confusing the original facts. In much of what commonly passes for reasoning there is less logic than dreaming. Careful reflection and close reasoning require too much effort. Men "guess at results," said Spencer. . . . It is much easier to argue from extreme facts than to weigh carefully and to avoid hasty generalizations. This is a sturdy and shameless fallacy, much esteemed by controversialists, and ancient writers afford some striking instances of it. Many of them were prone to confuse judgments of facts with judgments of value, and to present what were really only expressions of personal tastes, ideals, or interests, in the guise of objective facts. . . .

. . . [W]hen the mind has accumulated a stock of experiences, it has learned that the arrangement and order of thoughts do not always correspond to the arrangement and order of objective things. It is at this point that the desire of the bard to please the assembled warriors by singing of their extraordinary prowess, or of the historian to inculcate virtue by glorifying the records of his race, or of the witness in the box to save his case, leads to what may fairly be called mendacity. Indeed, so ingrained is the practice of gratifying the feeling and desire which initiate thinking that conventional fictions are apt to be less misleading than scrupulously exact statements. We may imagine the misunderstandings which would be caused by a refusal to adopt the common mendacities of polite society. In the more serious field of statecraft, Bismarck is said to have found that nothing so deceived his adversaries as to tell them the truth.

In conclusion, the matter comes down to this, that the human mind is not primarily an organ by which man determines the real objective truth of things and gives utterance to it, but is rather a tool by which one accomplishes one's desires. As this intelligence grows, man comes to know to a greater or less degree that inanimate nature, as well as the lower animals, has uniform modes of reaction, and that his desires in regard to them can be effected only by real knowledge; hence he abandons magic for science when dealing with them and tries to think clearly and accurately. But his fellow men he finds more complex problems. They can be deceived to his profit; they can be entertained by fictions to his profit; they can be coerced by threats to his profit; and in these various ways of extracting profit from them, his language will be guided by dominating principles other than a desire to give them truthful information. He finds furthermore that there are various sorts of obligations laid upon him to refrain from truth-telling under divers penalties. He is a member of a state, a church, a party, a class, a clique, a family, and in all these relations he is virtually obliged to see things as they are not, and to speak that which is false, under penalties varying from execution down to mere inarticulate unpopularity, most difficult to be borne. Acting in these various capacities he is constantly trained in juggling testimony, in judicious blindness, in expressing opinions he does not feel, in bringing his words and actions and thoughts, if possible, into conformity with something other than real facts; and all the while he sees those who are most completely and skilfully disingenuous reaping rewards, or what he has been taught to regard as such, in private and public life. Apart from certain occupations where he is brought into contact with something other than human nature, he finds little to encourage resolute veracity of thought and speech; and many forms of declension from this ideal he is taught to hold as very precious virtues—many aspects of loyalty and patriotism, or of orthodoxy; much of conventional morality, politeness, tact, *savoir-faire,* and the like. . . .

Enough of these perturbations arise about the threshold of consciousness, but many more lurk beneath and affect what is said and written, even when there is a desire to tell the simple truth. Fortunately, mixed up with them is a great measure of truth which, hostile to dominant prepossessions, has been thrust into the background, but which nevertheless frequently crops out to give the lie to mendacity itself. It is the problem of the historical student to identify these unconscious fidelities to fact, and to extract them from the mass of conscious or unconscious perversions, clear them up, link them together, and establish the real situation. And the first principle to be observed is that when a document from the distant past is under consideration, we have not made the first step towards its interpretation until we have recognized that although it is in a learned tongue, it is none the less a human document. Only so can we dismiss from our minds the powerful prepossession of man's childhood—a blind reverence for the written word.

10. The Case of the Cheating Documents:

False Authority and the Problem of Surmise

MUCH OF WHAT WE ARE TAUGHT SEEMS DESIGNED TO INculcate precisely the reverence for the written word of which Jerome so justly complains in the preceding chapter. Historians, or at least teachers of history, are not free of this trait, for all too often history is taught as though it were a body of facts to be gathered from an attic of patriotic knowledge essential to Americanization and memorized. Nor are teachers in other nations any more likely to wish to reveal to their charges that so much of history is a mere matter of opinion, for to open such a Pandora's box in the midst of a classroom, and especially in one which must, as in some countries, march to the tune of a nationally prescribed syllabus, is to disrupt tempers, schedules, and indoctrination. Of course, one must find some middle ground between blind acceptance and utter rejection of that which is put before us as history. It may be Justice who wears the blindfold but it is Clio, the Muse of history, who seems to have needed it. If in Tennessee one could not until 1967 or later teach as fact that man evolved from some lower order of being, one still may not teach it in Arkansas. Even Wisconsin, that home of progressive enlightenment and of a truly great state university, once proposed to pass a pure-history law which prohibited teaching anything that would tend to lower the Founding Fathers in the esteem of schoolchildren. "But what are we to tell the children?" is not a question asked only upon divorce. What we must tell them sometime, however, is that history is more akin to philosophy than it is to grammar. Of course, as we have seen before, myths held long enough have a way of becoming true, just as wants entertained long enough (especially by small children) tend to become genuine needs.

The historian psychologically reacts badly to anyone who says "History tells us," for the historian knows that history tells us nothing: we must painfully extract every message from Clio, for she is mute. The historian also is likely to seem somewhat agitated when someone justifies a conclusion, or a value judgment, by saying that he "read it in the newspapers." Newspapers are not only the products of fallible men; they are the products of fallible men under pressure and they are owned, on occasion, by men who would use them for their, or even their advertisers', purposes. Everyone remembers the 1948 headlines which proclaimed Dewey's victory over Truman; similar errors creep daily onto the pages of even the best newspapers. The historian knows just how fallible his daily paper may be (although there are many who seem to feel that they cannot be certain whether it is raining or snowing until the *New York Times* has told them so), and so he is doubly conscious of the errors of fact, as well as of the distortions of opinion and the misquotations of authority, that lie in wait for the unwary researcher in nineteenth-century sheets, in an age when journalism was yellow, as they say, as well as red, white, and blue.

Today we suggest to students that they not treat any story as true until they have seen it reported in roughly the same factual form by more than one wire service, in more than one newspaper, and in the latest edition of that newspaper. We also suggest that they read the "Letters to the Editor" column for several days after each event in order to pick up corrections suggested by participants. Most important, we suggest that they study the newspaper for general credibility before they attempt to use it as a source. The *Christian Science Monitor* is a remarkably accurate paper on national events, and often on international matters as well—its reporter was the first in Indonesia to write of Sukarno's decline—but one might not wish to trust its reports on fluoridation any more than one would want to rely solely on the *Wall Street Journal,* also a highly reliable paper, when reading of the Dixon-Yates affair. The venerable *Times* of London has been known to distort the truth now and then (more now than then if one is of the Labour persuasion), and *Time* magazine has been suspected of viewing life Lucely on occasion (even to its weekly way of finding some means, however irrelevant, to mention a certain Ivy League university). Why, then, should a researcher trust all that he finds in a once-forgotten file of the Rochester (New York) *Daily Democrat & American* for the eighteen-sixties?

One newspaperman who should know the answer to this and similar questions is Allan Nevins. For years the doyen of American historians, an author in the grand tradition, Nevins has been so productive, so prodigious in his research, and so efficient as to qualify for the title, "the Last Victorian," which I mean entirely in praise. Nevins began as a newspaperman—as have several other fine American historians, such as Bruce Catton, W. J. Cash, and George Fort Milton—and became one of the leading scholars of the Civil War, of American business history, of Rockefeller, Ford, Hamilton Fish, and Grover Cleveland. Until recently he was a professor of history at Columbia University; he is now a research associate of the Huntington Library in California. When he was at the height of his powers he wrote a charming, wry, and witty book which is still an excellent guide through the gateway to history, and from it I take the following selection, as well as the title for this portion, "The Case of the Cheating Documents."

♦ ♦ ♦

Mankind dearly loves a good story, and dearly loves to believe it true. Before any tale can greatly please the hearer thereof, it must have some degree of verisimilitude; it must conquer part of our faith. Many of the earliest masters of fiction dressed it as absolute fact, and were credited beyond their expectation. Thus multitudes have accepted [Daniel] Defoe's *Memoirs of a Cavalier* as a true history—Lord Chatham did so; and even astute critics, impressed by the wealth of circumstantial detail in Defoe's *Journal of the Plague Year,* have declared that it must have been based on some work by an actual observer. In daily social intercourse and in literature, an artistic lie is sooner swallowed than a clumsy truth. Indeed, many people insist through thick and thin on having the artistic lie in place of the bald and unattractive fact. Historians may explain a thousand times that Wellington never exclaimed, "Up, Guards, and at them!" and that C. C. Pinckney never blazed, "Millions for defense, but not one cent for tribute." These supposed ejaculations will nevertheless remain immortal. Sober critics have now labored for generations to show that Tacitus's portrait of Tiberius is cruelly unjust; but its vigor and artistic unity render it indestructible. Legends often become a point of faith. . . .

Credulity is pleasant; we all like to be cozened a bit. We love to cover the harsh gray stone of the everyday world with the moss and ivy of fancy. And it must be added that pleasing inventions fly like gossamer before the wind. Mr. H. L. Mencken early in his career wrote an article on the bathtub, in which he asserted with plausible historical detail that it had been invented in the 1840's, that Millard Fillmore had been the first to install one in the White House, that the medical profession and public long regarded it with deep suspicion, and that laws had been passed against the perilous contraption by Virginia, Pennsylvania, and Massachusetts. He was astonished to find this *jeu d'esprit* accepted by most readers at face value. He was still more astonished to find newspapers and magazines copying these "facts" in ever-widening circles, so that they cropped up

---

FROM Allan Nevins, *The Gateway to History* (Boston: D. C. Heath & Co., 1938, 1962), pp. 119–34, 137–45, 149–54, 159–61, 163–67. Reprinted by permission.

For additional reading: Another good and more recent book of this sort is Norman Cantor and Richard I. Schneider, *How to Study History* (New York, 1967). The equivalent in detective fiction is Howard Haycraft, *Murder for Pleasure: The Life and Times of the Detective Story* (New York, 1941).

year after year in the most dignified periodicals. This naïveté of humankind has its humorous side. But to historians it is not quite so amusing.

Our simple forefathers drank delightedly at many fountains on which modern scholarship long ago pinned up the harsh placard "Condemned." Take as an example that ingratiating old book called Sir John Mandeville's *Travels.* Sir John saw many wonderful matters in his Eastern journeys, and heard of more—the monarch Prester John; a haunted valley in Armenia; two-headed monsters; the dragon of Cos; the castle of the sparrow-hawks; and miracles aplenty. Long after his marvels began to be taken with large pinches of salt, men still believed him a reality and his travels a fact. But he has melted to nothingness like a ghost in sunshine. Critics now doubt whether there ever was a Mandeville, a knight, or even an Englishman connected with the book's composition. Possibly one John Burgoyne, living at Liège under the name of Jean de Bourgogne, was the author. But author is not the correct word, for the volume is an arrant jackdaw's nest. It was stolen in bits from other writings, among which may be named Brunetto Latini's *Tresor,* Albert of Aix's chronicle of the first crusade, the *Speculum* of Vincent de Beauvais, and works by Jacques de Vitry, Piano Carpini, Petrus Comestor, and Hayton the Armenian. Tracing the origins of this pastiche has furnished no little amusement to scholars.

Or consider the delight with which our forefathers read Parson Weems's *Life of George Washington,* first issued in 1800 and greatly expanded by anecdotal material in successive editions. Mason Locke Weems was part clergyman, part book-agent, part schoolmaster in northern Virginia, and probably held occasional services in Pohick Church, where Washington had once worshipped. Upon this he based his title of "formerly rector of Mount Vernon Parish." In its original form the *Life* was a brief, inaccurate, and highly rhetorical record of Washington's military career. Subsequently Weems added many homely stories which, if not true, were at least *ben trovato.* Each carried an ostentatious moral. His immortal tale of George, the hatchet, and the cherry tree was introduced as "too true to be doubted," though his only authority was an "aged lady" who as a "distant relative" had sometimes visited the Washingtons. Like the book's long dialogues and set speeches, it was obviously invented. According to a grandson of Weems, it was probably suggested by the fact that one of his own children had cut down a "Pride of China" tree and frankly confessed his misdeed. But multitudes have believed it:

> One day in the garden where he often amused himself hacking his mother's pea-sticks he unluckily tried the edge of his hatchet on the body of a beautiful young English cherry-tree, which he barked so terribly that I don't believe the tree ever got the better of it. The next morning the old gentleman, finding out what had befallen his tree, which by the way was a great favorite, came into the house; and with much warmth asked for the mischievous author, declaring at the same time that he would not have taken five guineas for his tree. Nobody would tell him anything about it. Presently George and his hatchet made their appearance. *"George,"* said his father, "do you know who killed that beautiful little cherry-tree yonder in the garden?" This was a *tough question;* and George staggered under it for a moment, but quickly recovered himself, and, looking at his father, with the sweet face of youth brightened with the inexpressible charm of all-conquering truth, he bravely cried out: "I can't tell a lie, pa; you know I can't tell a lie. I did cut it with my hatchet."

Forgery is in fact one of the oldest and commonest of human offenses. In ancient India grants of land made by rulers for sacerdotal purposes were often defined in inscriptions upon plates of copper. But implicit reliance cannot be placed upon these records. As early as the time of the lawgiver Manu punishments were decreed for the falsification of grants, and copper plates have been found which are barefaced forgeries. In this instance the motive was venal in the lowest sense, and the action untouched by artistry. Forgeries committed by politicians who wish to damage an opponent, such as the famous "Morey letter" falsely attributed to [James] Garfield in 1880—a letter approving the importation of Chinese labor—are equally devoid of dignity. Much more dangerous are those forgeries in which a skilled hand attempts to supply the market for writings by famous men. One of the first warnings the teacher of Renaissance history must give students of Luther, Erasmus, and numerous other figures is to beware of the stream of manufactured documents attributed to them. The forgery of letters purporting to be by Marie Antoinette has long been a thriving industry, and still continues. In Americana, the New York Public Library maintains a large collection—a veritable museum—of false autographic material. As spurious letters of Franklin, Washington, Jefferson, Lincoln, Poe, and other famous figures come up for sale and are recognized, dealers turn many over to the library. The most notorious of American autograph forgers, Robert Spring, a bookdealer in Philadelphia just before and after the Civil War, turned out hundreds of skilful forgeries to supply the market. His fictitious documents are more plentiful today than his own genuine letters. . . . Manufactured Lincoln letters have found their way even into printed compilations of his papers.

The most dangerous and vicious of all forgeries are those committed in behalf of a cause—the cause of a nation, of an institution, or of a leader—and intended to bring about a permanent falsification of history. Perhaps preëminent among such forgeries stands the so-called Donation of Constantine. This was a supposed grant by the Emperor Constantine to Pope Silvester and his successors. In gratitude for his conversion to Christianity, Constantine according to this document not only recognized the spiritual supremacy of the Roman pontiffs over the other patriarchates of the church in all that pertained to faith and worship, but also gave them temporal sovereignty over Rome, parts of Italy, and all provinces and places of "the western regions." This document was forged sometime between 750 and 800 A.D. During the ninth century the ecclesiastical writer now called the Pseudo-Isidore included it in the collection known as the False Decretals; and in time, with the authority of Pope Nicholas, it was accepted as part of the canons of the church. Gibbon pointed out that in his own day it was still formally "enrolled among the decrees of the canon law." Throughout the Middle Ages adherents of both popes and emperors regarded it as genuine. Two early popes, Silvester II and Gregory V, used it to support important territorial claims, and in 1050 Leo IX employed it in his controversy with the Byzantines involving still larger papal pretensions. During the twelfth century and afterward it became a powerful engine of the church in its contest with the political rulers of Europe, the partisans of the Holy Roman Empire regarding it with dread and hatred, and the partisans of the Pope somewhat cautiously employing it. Dante regarded it as genuine, and as a good Guelph execrated Constantine for the supposed grant as a source of enormous evils. But Laurentius Valla critically assailed the Donation in 1440, and though the controversy persisted until the close of the eighteenth century, its fraudulent character was at last completely demonstrated.

In this instance the forgery, which long imposed upon chroniclers and historians as well as ecclesiastical authorities, which indeed enjoyed almost six centuries of unchallenged vitality, was at last consigned to outer darkness. Discussion has long since shifted to the question of its authorship, some Catholic writers attempting to prove that the church had no hand in it. The best evidence is that it was executed in the papal chancery about 775, partly as a defense of the papal possessions, and partly as a means of attacking Byzantine heresy. The wonder is that it had so stubborn a life. . . .

In one striking instance the debate as to whether certain documents represent a political forgery still rages. Men even yet take sides heatedly on the question of the "Casket Letters." These letters, together with a sonnet-sequence, Mary Queen of Scots is accused of having written to her lover [the Earl of] Bothwell in 1566–67. They have long ago disappeared. Their very disappearance is a mystery, some students believing that Mary's royal son James obtained and destroyed them. But the text remains, and if authentic, offers incontrovertible proof that Mary was an accomplice in the murder of her husband [Lord] Darnley. If authentic! The controversy revolves chiefly about the second or "Glasgow letter," a long and peculiar epistle. If even the compromising parts of it were genuine, Mary was certainly guilty. But her accusers, the men who first produced the letters and pushed their evidence vigorously, were completely lacking in veracity. The Earl of Morton and the Regent Moray cannot be believed upon oath; they lied, they contradicted themselves, and throughout the episode they behaved most disingenuously. Nevertheless, the ablest student of the subject, Andrew Lang, concludes that the whole "Glasgow letter" was written by Mary. Some German writers, applying the principles of the higher criticism of Homer and the Bible, conclude that the documents are of composite origin, being partly letters by Mary and partly a diary, combined and edited by other hands. Still other writers attack the letters as wholly or largely false. . . . In this instance the problem of authenticity is of vital importance to our view of a great historical figure—and yet it is probably insoluble. . . .

Even when the falsity of a document has been amply proved it frequently makes so striking an impression upon the public mind that, as we have said, vestiges of belief in it linger for many years. In 1781 the Reverend Samuel A. Peters, publishing *A General History of Connecticut,* gave it a memorable bit of spice by inserting a table of "Laws made by this independent Dominion, and denominated Blue Laws by the neighboring colonies." His cloth made it seem impossible that he should prevaricate. Indeed, the laws that he quoted had a certain ring of truth, for they chimed with the popular idea of Puritan severity. Other writers began to accept them, and for decades a belief in the inhuman blue laws of The Land of Steady Habits was almost universal. But experts on colonial law and history presently began scrutinizing Peter's list with a suspicious eye. One alleged law made it criminal for a mother to kiss her infant on the Sabbath, and others had a very queer look:

> No one shall run on the Sabbath day, or walk in his garden or elsewhere, except reverently to and from meeting.
>
> No one shall travel, cook victuals, make beds, sweep house, cut hair, or shave on the Sabbath or fasting day.
>
> No one shall read Common Prayer, keep Christmas or Saints'-days, make minced pies, dance, play cards, or play on any instrument of music, except the drum, trumpet, and jews'-harp.
>
> Married persons must live together, or be imprisoned.

Peters had attempted to protect himself by stating that this code, which even regulated the style of the hair and the mode of crossing streams, was "never suffered to be printed." Indeed it was not, for it never really existed. Various sets of Connecticut laws were published; and while they do offer some basis for a large majority of the forty-five statutes which he cited, they fall far short of the grim picture he drew. The laws of 1650 did not even provide penalties for Sabbath-breaking. Yet a general impression that Connecticut had a frightful code of interferences with personal liberty, based upon or fortified by Peter's inventions, persists in quarters which wish to think ill of Puritanism.

Some minor forgeries, indeed, are impossible to kill. It is of course a mere misattribution which leads many people, year after year, to declare that Washington warned the country against "entangling alliances"; the truth being that Jefferson expressed that particular warning. But outright invention is responsible for a quotation which American protectionists, decade after decade, have put into the mouth of Abraham Lincoln. "I do not know much about the tariff," Lincoln is quoted as saying, "but I know this much, when we buy manufactured goods abroad, we get the goods and the manufacturer gets the money. When we buy manufactured goods at home, we get both the goods and the money. When an American paid $20 for steel rails to an English manufacturer, America had the steel and England the $20. But when he paid $20 for the steel to an American manufacturer, America had both the steel and the $20." There are three reasons for our certainty that Lincoln was not the author of this quotation: (1) Lincoln was too sagacious to make a statement containing so much economic folly. (2) The most thorough ransacking of Lincoln's speeches and writings reveals no such statement. (3) Lincoln was shot April 14, 1865, and the first steel rail was not rolled in America until May, 1865. Yet this barefaced forgery, in behalf of the high-tariff interest, was repeated as Lincoln's by no less a person than Alfred E. Smith [in] 1934. . . .

Invention, indeed, runs a strange and wonderful gamut. It may be used to cast discredit upon a whole race, as in the forgery of the so-called Protocols of the Wise Men of Zion, purporting to lay bare a Machiavellian plan for Jewish world-dominion. It may originate, on the other hand, in a trifling private jest. "This day," writes Samuel Pepys on August 28, 1661, "I counterfeited a letter to Sir W. Pen, as from the thiefe that stole his tankard lately, only to abuse and laugh at him." Or it may be employed in the Las Casas style to give verisimilitude to an otherwise bare and unconvincing narrative. Thus A. C. Buell published in 1900 a two-volume life of John Paul Jones which was praised by the *American Historical Review,* accepted as an authority in various universities, and recommended to students of the Naval Academy at Annapolis. It seemed sober history; it was actually a mixture of authentic and manufactured materials. When his sources ran thin, Mr. Buell calmly manufactured new ones. He invented a French memoir upon Jones by Adrien de Cappelle, a volume of papers by the North Carolina worthy Joseph Hewes, and a printed French collection of Jones's own papers, drawing "facts" liberally from these imagined storehouses. He invented collections of papers by Robert Morris and Gouverneur Morris in places where they had never existed, and so obtained more "facts." He invented a will by William Jones of North Carolina in order to give John Paul an estate, and had Jones deposit 900 guineas in the Bank of North America in 1776—a wonderful feat, for the Bank was not established until 1781. In short, as Albert Bushnell Hart has written, this inventor of materials recalls Mark Twain's praise of the duckbilled platypus, so versatile and gay. "If he wanted eggs," remarked Mark Twain, "he laid them."

Invention has even been used to gain a few dollars by spurious contributions to a biographical dictionary. A long-standard and still-useful compilation, *Appleton's Cyclopaedia of American Biography,* is disfigured by not less than forty-seven sketches, and probably many more, of men who never existed. The unknown author of these sketches was paid by space, and to obtain a larger remuneration coolly created heroes out of thin air. He gave the world an explorer, Bernhard Hühne, who discovered a good part of the coast of California; a botanist, Oscar Hjorn, whose book on *Les Legumineuses Arborescentes de l'Amérique du Sud* produced a "sensation" when published; an industrialist, Penanster, who in 1755 broke up the Spanish monopoly of the cochineal dye industry; and a French scientist, Henrion, who won fame by combatting the Asiatic cholera in South America in 1783, fifty-two years before it first appeared there. It appears that the editorial work on this *Cyclopaedia* was somewhat lax; contributors were free to suggest names not included in the original lists, and their sketches were not verified, and not revised save for literary form. But the large body of excellent material in the compilation has floated the spurious articles, so that many writers have been led astray by the misinformation—the errors being repeated from book to book, even in our own day. . . .

While the forgery is entirely false and dishonest, a far larger body of materials are only partially false, and of these many are not dishonest by intention at all—that is, do not contain any conscious dishonesty. The very fact that a document is entirely and deliberately spurious often makes its character easy to detect. But when truth and misstatements are mingled, both emanating from some writer known to be sincere, discovery becomes difficult. Many a letter, a document, a piece of autobiography, originally quite genuine and candid, all its parts possessing the same general value as evidence, has been revised, amended, or otherwise so tampered with that some parts become untrustworthy. In other words, its integrity has been destroyed. Again, students of history must deal with a large class of documents which are quite frankly composite in character, proceeding from various hands or sources. The task of discriminating among the different parts of these composite documents, and determining which are most valuable and why, requires the use of tests as searching as those which determine the integrity of a document—indeed, even more searching.

A simple and picturesque example of a problem in the integrity of documentary sources is offered by a comparison of Captain John Smith's first and second versions of his adventures in Virginia. As the whole world knows, Smith helped to obtain the charter of the London Company, arrived in Virginia with the colonists early in 1607, traded with the Indians for provisions, and when Jamestown fell into grave difficulties, took charge of the colony and by decision and resourcefulness saved it. He restored discipline, set everyone to work, and made it self-supporting. In his volume *A True Relation,* written in Virginia and published in England in 1608, he recounted his early exploits and adventures. He told how, making an excursion to the Chickahominy, he was surrounded by two hundred hostile Indians, and after bemiring himself in a swamp, was captured. They carried him before an Indian king. Smith showed this monarch his compass, and so won his favor. Thence taken before the "emperor" Powhatan, he was in danger of being killed by certain Indians whose relatives he had slain, but was saved by his guards. After he had treated Powhatan to a long discourse on the greatness of the British king, the mightiness of his navy, and "the noyes of Trumpets and terrible manner of fighting" in Europe, he was sent back to Jamestown. In this book he barely mentions Pocahontas, then a maiden of perhaps twelve. But in 1616, about the time that John Rolfe brought Pocahontas as a bride to England, he wrote a letter to King James's queen, Anne of Denmark, in which he asserted: "After some ix weeks fatting among these salvage countries, at the minute of my execution, she hazarded the beating out of her own brains to save mine." And he soon went still further.

In 1624, in his *Generall Historie,* Smith rewrote his early narrative of Virginia adventures. This time the two hundred hostile Indians became three hundred. This time he recalled a picturesque detail, the exhibition by the Indians of a bag of gunpowder which they proposed to plant the following spring. Above all, he recounted in more dramatic form the tale of Pocahontas's gallantry. He described the grim and dusky Powhatan in the centre of the stage, himself in the foreground, fettered but undaunted, and the lovely Pocahontas suddenly emerging at the climactic instant:

> A long consultation was held, but the conclusion was two great stones were brought before Powhatan; then as many as could layd hands on him, dragged him to them, and thereon layd his head, and being ready with their clubs, prepared to beate out his braines. Pocahontas, the King's dearest daughter, when no entreaty could prevaile, got his head in her armes, and laid her own upon his to save him from death; whereat the Emperour was contented he should live.

It is not strange that this story has inspired conflicting views among students.[1] . . . Henry Adams and Edward Channing assail the story, but Charles M. Andrews accepts it. A pretty question of the integrity of a source is involved.

If John Smith retouched his narrative to make a good story better, he did simply what many raconteurs do. Sir Walter Scott confessed a weakness for dressing up his old anecdotes with new cocked hat and walking stick. His motive was artistic. But that of many a man who renders an old tale more dramatic is vanity. In each new version, oral or printed, the teller's rôle becomes a little more witty, heroic, or resourceful. George IV asserted so often (without impolite contradiction) that he had been at the

[1] See Marshall W. Fishwick, "Was John Smith a Liar?," *American Heritage,* IX (October, 1958), 28–33, 110–11. [Editor's note.]

battle of Waterloo that he at last really believed he had taken an important part there. When the first two volumes of *The Intimate Papers of Colonel* [E. M.] *House*, edited by Charles Seymour, appeared in 1926, most readers gave them the value of an autobiography buttressed by a huge variety of letters and memoranda. Mr. House had chosen his editor carefully; it was incredible that he had not read every line of the work in manuscript or proof. These volumes claimed for him a decisive part in the shaping of the Federal Reserve Act of 1913. It was not difficult for ex-Secretary Carter H. Glass, in *An Adventure in Constructive Finance,* to riddle this pretension and show that Mr. House had played no real part whatever. The claim made by him was undoubtedly an instance of self-deception. It was not essentially different from Tartarin of Tarascon's story of his heroic exploits in the repulse of Tartar raids in China; the sole basis for which was that as a young man he had been offered a clerkship in the Orient, which he had refused! . . .

Sometimes a published book bears frank evidence that the text belongs to two or more very different dates. David F. Houston, successively head of the Department of Agriculture and of the Treasury under President Wilson, published in 1926 his valuable *Eight Years with President Wilson's Cabinet.* This work is written in two tenses, past and present, which alternate in the most disconcerting fashion. Frequently the two tenses appear on the same page. It is obvious that matter in the present tense was lifted more or less verbatim from Mr. Houston's diary, and that in the past tense was supplied years later. But the line between them is far from clear, while nobody knows just how great were the liberties taken with the text of the diary. To the student of history it is of the utmost importance to learn whether the opinion Mr. Houston gives of Secretary [of State William Jennings] Bryan, of the Federal Reserve Act, or of Wilson's neutrality policies, is his opinion of 1914, his opinion of 1926, or a nondescript combination of the two. The published volume leaves us in the dark. This medley of contemporaneous and reminiscent matter, annoying to the general reader, is maddening to the historian, who never knows whether a statement upon a man or transaction is authentically of the period, or embodies later reflections.

But while Mr. Houston made no effort to conceal his mixture of two different points of view, one during and one after the event, many a personal chronicler has tried to palm off his late-learned wisdom as early sagacity. Most diarists write consciously or subconsciously for publication. They are acutely alive to the impression they will make on posterity. It is difficult to resist the temptation to strike out faulty judgments, or to add new and better strokes to the old picture. . . .

No memoir or autobiography should be used without an effort to make certain that judgments stated as belonging to a particular date have not actually been colored or wholly shaped by subsequent occurrences. No diary or volume of letters should be used without a watchful eye for telltale evidence that the text has been altered before publication to delete entries that have become absurd, or to insert material which will reflect credit on the writer's shrewdness and insight. The more naïveté in a diary, the better the historian likes it! . . .

No composite histories are more familiar, and none more interesting, than the three Synoptic Gospels of Matthew, Mark, and Luke. None has ever been given more penetrating and exhaustive study than they. It is obvious to anyone who examines the New Testament in critical spirit that the value of its different parts to students of the past is far from uniform. It is a highly varied collection of narratives, letters, homilies, and prophecies. Some historical inconsistencies of the Gospels have been very unfairly exploited by hostile critics like Thomas Paine and Robert G. Ingersoll. Matthew and Luke, while giving accounts of the virgin birth, yet trace the genealogy of Jesus up through Joseph. Matthew declares that the Holy Family went at once into Egypt to escape Herod, while Luke states categorically that it stayed in Bethlehem forty days, then went to Jerusalem, and then to Nazareth. We are given more or less discrepant accounts of the Sermon on the Mount, the anointing of Jesus, the betrayal of Judas, the trial scene, and even in some details of the crucifixion; while at many points the narratives are vague. The attempt to wring out of the Gospels their exact historical values is full of interest. How vast an effort has been concentrated into that attempt can be understood only by those who have studied Christian Hermeneutics and what was once termed the higher criticism. It represents, in all probability, the best single illustration of what the historical method can accomplish in a difficult and obscure field. The separation of the Gospels into their component parts has been only one part of that effort.

That they have a composite origin is beyond question. Expert authorities now generally agree that no narrative of Christ's life was written for more than thirty years after his death. The gospel was first preached to people who had seen Jesus, or had heard too much about him to be curious for details of his life, while the disciples looked forward to his second advent at an early date. Since Paul's Epistles, written about 50–60 A.D., make no reference to any of the four Gospels, it is a fair inference that they did not then exist. Tradition indicates that written accounts began to be set down between 60 and 70 A.D. The first of the four was probably the so-called Gospel of St. Mark, and can apparently be dated within a decade of Paul's martyrdom. For centuries the church regarded this Gospel as less important than the others, partly because Mark was not an apostle, and partly because Matthew and Luke are much fuller. But it is now believed that a good part of Mark's narrative may have been derived directly from the lips of Simon Peter, and is not merely an earlier story than the other two Synoptic Gospels, but in some respects more dependable. They are based largely upon it, or upon another narrative, now lost, which it most faithfully represents. Indeed, internal evidence suggests that Matthew and Luke lean heavily upon Mark. Some authorities believe that they lean also upon a lost Gospel, which German scholars termed the Q Gospel,[2] and which may have run fairly parallel to Mark. The Gospel of Matthew was perhaps written last of all, and could certainly not have been penned by the Apostle Matthew, though it may have been founded in part upon some of his recollections.

Let us concentrate, for the purposes of illustration, upon Matthew. It is incontestable, in the view of modern Biblical scholars, that this Gospel is a composite work, written from two main

[2] James Hall Roberts has written a superlative novel, *The Q Document,* on this question. In this book, and the more recent *February Plan,* Roberts shows himself to be the most literate of our present thriller writers. [Editor's note.]

sources which the author knew in Greek, and various minor sources. The two main sources are Mark, and an unknown work originally written in Aramaic. Scholars have accurately separated the two. For example, the matter from Matthew ix, 27, to the end of Matthew xi is taken from the Aramaic document; then comes a long section from Mark, but with additional data from some other source; and finally we have the author's own ending. A peculiar feature of the Gospel is the way in which the author has welded together a number of discourses, or collections of sayings, by Jesus, taking part of the material from statements which other sources attribute to Christ at other times and places. Thus Matthew introduces into the Sermon on the Mount some sayings which according to Luke were uttered elsewhere. The account in Matthew x of the address to the twelve disciples contains matter which Luke x, 1–16, states was delivered to a different group, together with various other sayings of which the precise occasion is unknown. Altogether, Matthew contains eight distinct discourses or collections of sayings, put together in more or less artificial fashion from Christ's utterances on various occasions. This artifice does some violence to history, according to the strict rules of the present day, but it offers a more effective presentation of Christ's doctrine.

The Gospel of St. Mark consists of an original text studded with later interpolations, which scholars have been able to identify with fair certainty, and which stand on a lower plane of credibility than the work in general. Thus from internal evidence it is regarded as probable that the two parables in Mark iv, 26–32, are insertions made in the original, which they do not precisely fit. It is believed also that the collection of Christ's sayings in Mark ix, 41–50, is interpolated; for the author of Mark does not elsewhere make up such discourses. Moreover, some of these particular sayings are given by Luke in different contexts. Such obvious inaccuracies occur in the account of Christ's crossing of the lake after the feeding of the five thousand, inaccuracies the more striking in a book remarkable for precision of topography, that this bit may also be an interpolation. It need not be said that the historical value of St. Mark's Gospel is impaired by these interpolations, and restored when they are struck out. Similarly, the historical authority of Matthew is compromised at various points by bits which the author has apparently derived from untrustworthy traditions. Among them is the story of the setting of the Roman guards at the grave, and their presence at the resurrection; the story of the silencing of this guard by the chief priest; the story of the testimony borne by the guard and the centurion who kept watch at the cross; and the story of Pilate's effort to throw the guilt of the crucifixion upon the Jews. Competent scholars regard these episodes, to quote one of them, as "legendary additions which had arisen through the desire to commend the Gospel to the Romans," and which the very late author of Matthew inserted along with his authentic materials. . . .

The integrity of written documents of all kinds has frequently been vitiated by censorships, political or religious. In many countries and in every century, texts have been mutilated, garbled, or rewritten by some tyrannical authority. No Italian, German, or Russian newspaper under the régimes of Mussolini, Hitler, and Stalin respectively could be regarded by careful students as an authentic presentation of what was originally written for its columns. Still less could it be regarded as what the journalists would have written had they been free! . . . Not even the greatest of authors have been respected. A student who uses foreign sources of a type exposed to censorship will sometimes save himself from grave error by studying the conditions of bureaucratic or ecclesiastical control for his period. He will then not assume that because a periodical is conservative or obscurantist in tone, its editors and contributors were antagonistic to liberalism; that every word printed is to be taken in its literal sense. . . .

Texts may also, as every reader of general literature knows, be corrupted by bad editing; by bad translations; by careless printing; and by sheer accident. The canons applied to the editing of manuscript sources for publication have become steadily more severe. Of course these canons are not rigid. According to the nature of the text, the editor may regard his work as primarily literary, intended for the lay public, or primarily historical, intended for general readers. John Evelyn and Philip Hone wrote their diaries with a broad appeal in view; to reproduce every archaic spelling or capitalization in Evelyn, every abbreviation, misspelling, or defect in punctuation in Hone, would be to repel the general reader. It would defeat the main purpose of the diary. So with volumes of letters expected to have a broad appeal. The editor is not merely justified, but required, to spell out awkward abbreviations, make capitalization and punctuation conform to present-day usage, and otherwise, without altering the sense, to render the text readable. The editor of Grover Cleveland's letters, with this end in view, was justified in even occasional changes in paragraphing. But where a text is intended primarily for the use of historical students, it should be reproduced precisely as it stands. The *Diary* of Edward Bates, Lincoln's Attorney-General, for example, has much value to the historian and no attractions whatever to the general reader; its editor rightly reproduced every letter, every comma, verbatim. . . . But the most courageous of editors dare not and should not publish a complete text of some writings. No useful purpose is served by concessions to mere pruriency. Beyond a certain line, such concessions indeed run afoul of the law. The completest edition of Pepys still omits a small number of passages of outrageous indecency. The editor of the fullest edition of Franklin remarks: "Unfortunately, it is impossible without offence to quote many of his briefer paragraphs. . . . He out-Smolletts Smollett in his letters to young women at home and experienced matrons abroad. Among the manuscripts in the Library of Congress, and in the columns of his newspaper and the introductions to 'Poor Richard,' are productions of his pen, the printing of which would not be tolerated by the public sentiment of the present age." Such productions, generally speaking, would be valueless to history. Their omission, properly indicated, does it no violence. . . .

Translations may be of all degrees of goodness or badness. . . . But it is important to remember that a translation, no matter how excellent, is always a change. It subtly alters the flavor of the original. Not a few historical works have been twice translated. Russian books, for example, have first been rendered into German or French, then into English. At least one important historical book is available to American readers only after passing through the medium of four languages. This is the autobiography of a young Chinese, Tan Shih-hua; dictated in Chinese to Professor S. Tretiakov, written by the latter in Russian, translated into German, and again translated into English! To suppose that the texture of Tan Shih-hua's thought was not transformed in these four processes is to suppose a great deal. One reason why a command of foreign tongues is valuable is that it dispenses with translation; and no man having such a command should be content with less than the original.

The garbling of texts by accident or negligence has sometimes led to grave results far outside the sphere of scholarship. A misplaced comma may cause a diplomatic crisis. In 1912 the misprinting of a single word involved a serious political issue in the United States. The official Democratic Textbook of that year published one plank of the party platform as declaring against "the Aldrich plan for a central bank"—which would have left the way open for another type of central bank. The error was multiplied by many copyings. But party leaders, referring to their records, established the fact that the plank as drafted had condemned "the Aldrich plan *or* a central bank," binding the party to a sweeping interdiction of all such banks; and President Wilson recognized this reading as valid. But the most interesting work of scholars in the correction of negligent texts lies in the field of medieval manuscripts and early printed books.

Particularly interesting, and full of lessons to the historian, is the immense labor expended upon the establishment of a correct version of Shakespeare's plays. The greatest monument ever erected to the cause of textual integrity is beyond question the New Variorum Edition of Shakespeare begun by Dr. H. H. Furness and carried on by other scholars. The lore of whole libraries, the cunning of the most ingenious minds, the sensibility of the most delicate ears have been utilized to make straight the thousand crookednesses of the early texts. . . . Beginning with Lewis Theobald and Alexander Pope, a long list of critics in many lands spent patient years to give the world just what Theobald entitles his book, *Shakespeare Restored*. It was Theobald who suggested the most brilliant conjectural emendation which has ever gained place in the text of an English classic. In Dame Quickly's immortal description of Falstaff's death, where the line "and a table of greenfield" had long puzzled readers, he substituted the sentence, "and a' babbled of green fields." He won equally universal acceptance for his recasting of Hermia's line, "Emptying our bosoms of their counsel swelled," into "Emptying our bosoms of their counsels sweet." He and his successors employed every possible instrument. One German scholar even spent a long period studying Elizabethan styles of chirography and orthoepy in the British Museum, and thus constructed an Elizabethan paleography which he applied to the problem. That is, he attempted to conceive what Shakespeare's long-vanished manuscripts, written like other Elizabethan scripts, must have looked like, and tried thus to puzzle out correct readings for some of the printer's misreadings. Still others have labored on the theory that the printers did not set type direct from Shakespeare's manuscript (perhaps much cut up for stage use), but had it read aloud to them.

By the use of varied instruments, Shakespeare's editors have unquestionably done marvels in turning a very corrupt text into one of fair integrity. One typical feat may be cited. By comparing the Quarto of *A Midsummer Night's Dream* with the First Folio, Dr. Furness took a passage which seemed suddenly to turn four fairies into eight—

TITANIA. — And I will purge thy mortall grossnesse so,
That thou shalt like an aerie spirit go.
Enter Pease-Blossom, Cobweb, Moth, Mustarde-Seede, and four fairies.
FAIRIES. — Ready: and I, and I, and I, where shall we go?

and converted this into the piquant and convincing fragment:

TITANIA. — And I will purge thy mortal grossness so
That thou shalt like an airy spirit go.
Pease-Blossom! Cobweb! Moth! Mustard-Seed!
Enter four fairies.
FAIRIES. — Ready; and I, and I, and I. Where shall we go?

11. A Medley of Mysteries:

A Number of Dogs That Didn't Bark

WE SHALL NOW GO, READY AND AYE, AS NAVY MEN ONCE said, to one more general treatment of the problem of evidence. Sherlock Holmes, it is true, did not read manuals on detection, although he wrote them (if a treatise on cigar ash may be referred to so slightingly), but it is well to know the rules of the game before we begin to violate them. There are only three books on historical methodology, the *hortus siccus* of the discipline, that are readable throughout. We have drawn excerpts from two of these—by Richard Altick and Allan Nevins—and in revered pedagogical fashion the best comes last. Jacques Barzun, until recently Provost of and now University Professor in Columbia University, and Henry F. Graff, Chairman of the Department of History at the same institution, combined to write *The Modern Researcher.* Their range is exceptional, for Barzun is a noted historian of European intellectual developments while Graff covers the American waterfront. Barzun, let it be added, is also one of the most attentive followers of detective fiction within the ivoried towers, as his (for I presume that it is his) recourse here to the words "mystery," "evidence," and "clues" should reveal. Whether he has written any mystery stories of his own, under a pseudonym, I cannot say. No matter: he has written some fine history.

♦ ♦ ♦

Every thinking person is continually brought face to face with the need to discriminate between what is true and what is false, what is probable and what is doubtful or impossible. These decisions rest on a combination of knowledge, skepticism, faith, common sense, and intelligent guessing. In one way or another, we decide whether the road to town is too icy for going by car, whether the child is telling the truth about seeing a burglar upstairs, whether the threatened layoff at the local steel plant will take place after all. Any adult has acquired techniques for verifying reports so that he can take appropriate action. He supplements his experience and learning with recourse to special sources of information—the broadcast weather report on the state of the road; the child's known habit of fantasy; or the word of the local magnate who has access to first-hand knowledge.

Few of those who run their lives in this way stop to think that in the first case they trusted a technical report which, though not infallible, is the only authority on the subject; that in the second case, the ground for judgment was observation and inference; and that the third resort was to a competent witness. It is sometimes possible to use all three kinds of aids to judgment, and others besides, such as the opinions of neighbors and friends, to say nothing of trial and error. All but the most thoughtless and impulsive will, in short, use their minds before giving credence to others' reports and try to collect evidence before trusting their own surmises. The world is too full of error and falsehood to make any other course mentally or physically safe.

The intelligent newspaper reader, for example, daily encounters "incredible" stories and tries automatically to "verify" them, first by "reading between the lines" and drawing what seems at the moment an acceptable conclusion, and later by looking for further reports.

For additional reading: A drier, but still valuable, primer in heuristics—as the professional jargon has it—is Homer Carey Hockett, *The Critical Method in Historical Research and Writing* (New York, 1955). It is now somewhat dated but no less good reading for that, just as Dorothy L. Sayers' *The Omnibus of Crime,* ably edited, speaks for its genus as of its publication date in 1929 (New York).

Limited as this effort is, one cannot always make it from an armchair.

Take the report that appeared under the headline: "CLARE LUCE'S ILLNESS IS TRACED TO ARSENIC DUST IN ROME VILLA."[1] According to the article, Mrs. Luce, at that time United States Ambassador to Italy, had in the summer of 1954 begun to suffer from symptoms of anemia and fatigue that disappeared when she was absent from her post in Rome, but recurred as soon as she returned to it. Hospital tests, it was said, disclosed that she was the victim of arsenic poisoning. Who was administering the poison? Investigation had brought out that the arsenic paint on the roses adorning her bedroom ceiling was the source of the poison. Minute flakes of the paint were dislodged by people walking in the laundry above and drifted down, to be inhaled by the Ambassador or swallowed with her morning coffee. Skillful detection by the Central Intelligence Agency was credited with finding the cause of the trouble; and it was announced that steps had been taken to remove it.

The immediate response to the story is, naturally, shocked surprise. But almost at once there begins the work of truth-seeking or verification. To begin with, one can think of no reason why the report should have been fabricated. Second, one notes that the events were first made known in a news magazine published by Mrs. Luce's husband: he has every reason to protect his reputation for accuracy. Third, one reflects that since the announcement was made by Mrs. Luce just before returning to her post, the incident is almost certainly true. What patriotic person would want to embroil Italian-American relations by raising even the possibility of a plot to poison the American Ambassador?

But in offset to these probabilities, the critical reader observes that there is no corroborative statement from either the Department of State or the Central Intelligence Agency—or from any Italian source. It is difficult, moreover, to imagine the United States Ambassador living in a house where the paint is so old as to flake off, and where the washing is done on a floor above the bedrooms. When the ordinary reader encounters a story of this kind and car-

[1] *New York Times,* July 17, 1956.

ries his speculation as far as we have supposed, he ends by doing one of several things: (1) he accepts it because it appeared in the *New York Times;* (2) he rejects it because it does not square with what he thinks likely; (3) he suspends judgment until more information appears;[2] or (4) he ignores the difficulty altogether.

A judicious reader will adopt 3, though there is nothing reprehensible about the other choices. But the researcher and historical reporter has a greater responsibility, which denies him the right to any of the four solutions. He may indeed come to rest on 3, but not until he has done a great deal of work; and except under certain conditions, 1, 2, and 4 go against his professional training and obligations. As the student of past events tries to answer the question What *did* happen?, he confronts the same uncertainties as the newspaper reader, but with this important difference: *the historian must try to reach a decision and make it rationally convincing not only to himself but to others. The steps by which he performs this task constitute Verification.*

Verification is required of the researcher on a multitude of points—from getting an author's first name correct to proving that a document is both genuine and authentic.[3] Verification is accordingly conducted on many planes, and its technique is not fixed. It relies on attention to detail, on common-sense reasoning, on a developed "feel" for history and chronology, on familiarity with human behavior, and on ever enlarging stores of information. Many a "catch question" current among schoolboys calls forth these powers in rudimentary form—for instance the tale about the beautiful Greek coin just discovered and bearing the date "500

[2] Subsequent reports confused the original story beyond hope of armchair unraveling; first, the Ambassador herself cast doubt on the chronology by putting the poisoning back one year; and then the U.S. pathologist who had been consulted at that time asserted that no tests for arsenic had been made. (*New York Times,* July 22 and November 20, 1956.)

[3] The two adjectives may seem synonymous but they are not: that is genuine which is not forged; and that is authentic which truthfully reports on its ostensible subject. Thus an art critic might write an account of an exhibition he had never visited; his manuscript would be genuine but not authentic. Conversely, an authentic report of an event by X might be copied by a forger and passed off as the original. It would then be authentic but not genuine.

B.C." Here a second's historical reflection and reasoning is enough for verification: the "fact" is speedily rejected.

The first sort of verification consists in clearing up the simple obscurities that arise from one's own or somebody else's carelessness. A good example is found in the following account of a copy editor's search, as reported by the publishing house where she worked:[4]

> In the bibliography of a manuscript there appeared this item: "Landsborous, A., and Thompson, H. F. G. *Problems of Bird Migration.*" In the line of duty, the editor queried the spelling of Landsborous, but it was returned by the author without change or comment. Not satisfied, she searched in various bibliographies and in two library catalogues for the name. She could find neither it nor the title of the book. Then she began to look for "Thompson, H. F. G.," but without success. Under the subject "Birds—Migration" she was referred to "Aves—Migration." There she found that an A. L. Thomson (without the "p") had written *Bird-Migration* (2nd ed.). Further research in the subject index of the British Museum Catalogue revealed that the first edition had indeed been entitled *Problems of Bird-Migration.* The proper entry then proved to be: "Thomson, Arthur Landsborough. *Problems of Bird-Migration.*" The initials following the name "Thompson" in the original version continued to puzzle the editor until someone suggested that they might indicate an honorary fellowship in geography. . . .

Not all uncertainties are so thoroughly grappled with and disposed of. Some are like prickly fruit: one does not know how to take hold of them. Others are plain enough but require enormous patience and tireless "legwork." No interesting or important question, though, can be settled without detailed knowledge, solid judgment, lively imagination, and the ability to think straight. What to do and how to go about it comes with practice; to enumerate rules would be endless and of little use. The best way to show in what the practice consists is to describe in some detail a variety of typical operations through examples taken from life.

[4] Columbia University Press, *The Pleasures of Publishing,* XIV (June 30, 1947), 2.

COLLATION, OR MATCHING COPIES WITH SOURCES

One of the fundamental ways of verifying complex facts is known as collation. This simply means "bringing together." Thus when a scholar has found a manuscript and is about to print it, he must collate the successive proofsheets with the original before he passes them for publication. Collating is best done with help: one person reads the text, punctuation included, while the scholar—who is known in this role as the "editor"—follows the printed version.

Many rules govern the form in which this kind of transfer from manuscript to type is to be made. They need not concern us here. But the principle of collation should be noted as being what, on a small scale and apart from work with manuscripts, is called comparison. It is by rapid singlehanded collation that you discover small discrepancies among authorities, and thereby create your own problems of verification, because it is important to stop error by getting small points right.

Suppose that you have at some time come across the interesting letter dated July 6, 1776, in which the composer Joseph Haydn gives a young lady a brief account of his life and career. You have cut out the article, with a facsimile reproduction of part of the document, and have set it aside for future use. Near the beginning of the letter Haydn says: "I was born on the last day of March, 1733." You have no reason to doubt so plain a statement, but you note that the magazine merely printed the letter, without any signs of scholarly editing. Your inclination may be to take Haydn's word for such facts as his birth date, the name of his birthplace, of his early patrons and teachers, and so on. But the titles of some unfamiliar works, as well as allusions to other composers, lead you to seek verification.

You begin by looking up Haydn in some reliable work of reference, such as *Grove's Dictionary of Music and Musicians.* You pull down Volume II of the Third Edition, flip the pages, and your eye falls on the running head "Haydn," page 590. You can see that you have hit on the end of the article, so you turn back a page, only to find "Haydn, Johann Michael," born 1737. This obviously is the wrong Haydn. You move forward again, since Joseph comes after Johann—or should, for he doesn't. Instead, you have landed in the middle of the article "Hayes." It is impossible that Joseph Haydn should not be in *Grove*. Back you go to Johann, in front of whose name you notice the figure (2). There must be a (1), who turns out to be "*Franz* Joseph, born in the night of March 31, 1732."

This is puzzling in two ways: whose is the misprint as to the year, and what is the meaning of "the night of March 31"? It may mean either the night from March 30 to 31 (which would accord with Haydn's phrase "the last *day* of March"); or it might mean the night of March 31 to April 1st. As it happens, you have brought your "original" with you to the library, including, you clearly remember, a fragment in facsimile. As you recall it, this was either the beginning or the end of the letter, to show off the salutation or the signature. By good luck it is the beginning, and you read plainly in Haydn's neat script: 173*3*.

Now there is no question but that a man is an eyewitness to his own birth. Yet it is an event about which he has to take other people's word for the rest of his life. He *may* therefore have erred about the date—or again he may have had reason to falsify it. Napoleon and two of his brothers did just that on the occasion of their marriages, with the result that the record shows all three to have been born within the same year.

You are still suspended in doubt about Haydn's dates. You turn to the end of the article in *Grove* for the Haydn bibliography, and incidentally to see who wrote the sketch you have been reading. "C.F.P." leads you to the key, which says: C. Ferdinand Pohl. This German name wakes an echo in your mind—perhaps you remember the writings of Richard Pohl about his contemporaries, Wagner and Berlioz. Ferdinand Pohl doubtless belongs to the next generation. The certainty comes over you that this article in *Grove's* third edition (1927, 1935) is an old one reproduced or recast from the original edition (1879, 1896). And from experience you know that the original tended to be more garrulous and thereby often more informative. It is at any rate worth a try. The library keeps both editions side by side on the reference shelf, the first having an invaluable index not repeated in the later one.

You confidently turn to "Haydn, J." only to find that he has again revolved around his brother Johann Michael, being listed here as plain Joseph. And the very first words solve most of your perplexities: "Haydn, Joseph, or, according to the baptismal register, Franz Joseph, the father of the symphony and the quartet, was born in the night between March 31 and April 1, 1732." Blessed garrulity! Here at last is a reporter—it is, we note, our same friend Pohl before he was cut down for the next edition—here is a reporter who professes to speak from the baptismal register, a better source than a middle-aged man's autobiographical letter to a Mademoiselle.[5] . . .

SKEPTICISM, OR SIFTING OUT THE FITTING FROM THE FALSE

It may seem more difficult to start questioning small details in genuine documents than to doubt a legend or anecdote that sounds too pat to be true, but Verification may be as laborious in the one case as in the other.

The doubtful anecdote you recognize immediately; it bears a family likeness common to the many that you know to be apocryphal. One such famous story has for its hero Stephen A. Douglas, the Illinois Senator contemporary with Lincoln. Tradition has it that on September 1, 1854, a few months after reopening the slavery question by introducing the Kansas-Nebraska Bill, the "Little Giant" stood before a hostile crowd in Chicago and attempted to justify his action. Booed, jeered, and hissed, Douglas held his ground for over two hours, determined that he would be listened to. Finally, so the story goes, he pulled out his watch, which showed a quarter after twelve, and shouted: "It is now Sunday morning—I'll go to church and you may go to Hell."

How does an historian verify his doubts of a "good story" of this kind? The steps taken by one scholar[6] to establish or destroy this legend were as follows: First, he searched through the Chicago newspapers of late August and early September, 1854, for some

[5] The latest *Grove* (5th ed.) gives: "born 31 March or 1 April, 1732."

[6] Granville D. Davis, "Douglas and the Chicago Mob," *American Historical Review*, LIV (April, 1949), 553–56.

account of Douglas' return from Washington. This, he found, had been regarded as a great event, impatiently awaited by the public and fully covered in the press. Next, he scanned the accounts of the meeting itself, looking for any reference to the scornful remark. He found none. Neither the newspapers nor the first biography of the Senator, which was published in 1860, reported the incident. So far the results of a good deal of work, being negative, seemed to justify the doubt.

Yet the search turned up on the main issue some positive though indirect evidence. Two papers, one in Chicago and one in Detroit, stated that Douglas had left the platform at ten-thirty. Moreover, the meeting had taken place on a Friday, not a Saturday night! Failing a dated newspaper, a perpetual calendar (every researcher should own one) will quickly establish the day of the week on which a date fell or will fall in any year of the Christian era. This is a fixed point: no doubt is possible about it, September 1, 1854, was a Friday.

But considering the simple ways of press reporting at the time, another possibility remains: perhaps in the uproar no newspaperman heard Douglas' emphatic remark. Of course, if we suppose this in order to support the story, we must also assume that Douglas was so rattled by the heckling of the crowd that he could neither read his watch correctly nor remember what day of the week it was. When the researcher finds himself multiplying hypotheses in order to cling to a belief, he had better heed the signal and drop the belief.

By now our scholar's curiosity was aroused and he wanted to know the full history of the anecdote. Where had it first appeared? Perhaps Douglas himself had uttered or recorded the statement after the incident. If this were so, his biographers would surely have discovered the starting point and noted it. What do they in fact quote from when they repeat the tale? From a volume written by Douglas' father-in-law, James Madison Cutts, and published in 1866, five years after Douglas' death. The work is entitled *A Brief Treatise upon Constitutional and Party Questions;* it contains so many half-truths and outright fabrications that it may be deemed generally untrustworthy. Only one small chance remains: that on this single matter, the book is accurate. True or made up after the event, the tale may have been told by Douglas to Cutts himself.

Beyond this the scholar cannot go. What certainty has he garnered for his pains? Enough to reward his labors. He now knows —as *we* know, thanks to him—that Douglas spoke on a Friday night, that he was not reduced to complete silence by the crowd, and that the meeting did not last past midnight. The probability is great that Douglas would not have mistaken the day and announced his intention of going to church on a Saturday morning. If he told his audience to "go to Hell," no contemporary seems to have noticed the words. The remark seems a trifle intemperate for a calculating politician who had his eye on the Presidency. Combining certainties with probabilities, the verifier reaches the inescapable judgment that the famous remark was never made. At best, it is what Douglas might have wanted to throw in the teeth of his hecklers but never did. . . .

EXPLICATION, OR WORMING SECRETS OUT OF MANUSCRIPTS

Young researchers who want to obtain their professional "license" by earning the Ph.D. degree often believe that the greatest proof of merit is to find a packet of letters in an attic. The implication is that historians value a new find of primary sources[7] above any other achievement of the human intelligence. This is not so. But new evidence is always interesting, and if it consists of manuscripts, it creates special problems for the verifier. Manuscripts often come to him in huge unsorted masses—the "papers" of a man or a family being the bulky leftovers of busy lives. Of such papers, letters are perhaps the most difficult to subdue: they must be made, in spite of slips of the pen, bad handwriting, or allusions to unidentified persons, to tell the exact story which the author intended and which the recipient probably understood.

In this kind of decoding and classifying no librarian can go very far in supplying help. It is an expert's job and no one is an

[7] In historiography, a primary source is distinguished from a secondary by the fact that the former gives the words of the witnesses or first recorders of an event—for example, the diaries of Count Ciano written under Mussolini's regime. The historian, using a number of such primary sources, produces a secondary source. . . .

expert until he has made himself into one. You learn your letter-writer's quirks and foibles from what he wrote and said; you date and interpret the documents by internal and external clues. To do these things, you shuttle back and forth between clear and obscure, dated and undated, pieces, acquiring information by which to pull yourself forward until gaps are filled and contradictions become intelligible. Dumas Malone, for instance, learned from long familiarity with Jefferson's papers that his subject's vocabulary grew more "radical" in writing to younger men. This was a sign not so much of Jefferson's eagerness for a new revolution as of his desire to awaken the coming generation to its responsibility for progress. This fact, once observed, becomes a test for the literalness of some of Jefferson's most advanced proposals. The point of this example is that only an expert—one might even say: only *the* expert—is in a position to make sound inferences from a given letter.

Dealing with letters, then, is not a sinecure. It requires an agile mind, or one made such by repeated bafflement and discovery. Consider the simplest of questions: When was this written and to whom? Unless the post office stamped the letter itself, or the envelope has been kept, or the recipient was a methodical person who "endorsed" each letter with the particulars of its date and bearing, the precious piece of paper may raise more questions than it answers.

For a pair of representative puzzles we may turn to the letters of the composer Hector Berlioz (1803–1869). These letters keep appearing on the market as the interest in his life and work steadily grows, and it becomes the scholar's task to fit them in among the hundreds already published. Before he can do this he must supply deficiencies of place, date, or addressee's name. Two forms that this operation can take may be briefly illustrated. The A.L.S. says, in French:

19 rue de Boursault,
Thursday June 23

Dear Sir:

Here is the Table of Contents of the book about which I had the honor of speaking to you. If you will kindly look it over, you will have a rough idea of the subjects dealt with and the general tone of the work. Till next Monday.

Yours faithfully,
Hector Berlioz

Now the address with which the note starts is in Paris, and it is one at which Berlioz resided from July 1849 till April 1856. (This knowledge comes from a table prepared by the researcher from a survey of all the letters extant.[8]) So the piece to be identified falls within those seven years. The next step is to the perpetual calendar, which gives Thursday, June 23, as falling in 1853. This seems to settle the matter, except that the only book Berlioz had in hand during those years was ready by May 1852 and was published the same December. We are forced to conclude that despite the "Thursday June 23" the note was written not in 1853, but in 1852. This is at once confirmed by the table of domiciles, which shows that in June 1853 Berlioz was in London, not Paris. We know from other instances that he frequently mistook the day of the week. Moreover, in June 1852 the twenty-third falls on a Wednesday; so that, assuming a mistake, his dating would be only one day off. Combining these likelihoods, and knowing also who accepted the book when presented, we conclude that the note was sent to Michel Lévy, a well-known publisher. An inquiry at the present offices of the firm showed that no records of the period were preserved. Internal evidence is therefore our only guide.

The subject of the note just examined was of small moment, but sometimes the identification and collation of an original will rectify a universally held opinion. Witness our second example. In 1846 when Central Europe was seething with nationalistic passion, Berlioz was giving concerts in Hungary and Bohemia and performing there for the first time his rousing *Rákóczy March.* Soon after the premiere, a German periodical got hold of one of his letters to a young Czech musicologist, who was also a patriot, and printed a piece of it as if it were the whole, garbling it in such a way as to turn the message into something of a political document. As late as 1940, when a Hungarian scholar quoted it again in the New York *Musical Quarterly,* no one questioned the letter, and its editor commented on the politico-musical passion it displayed.

Ten years later, in tracking down Berlioz letters in private collections, [Jacques Barzun] was given an opportunity to copy a long letter dated one day before the published one. Suddenly, in the

[8] For this table and examples of the dating technique, see Jacques Barzun, *New Letters of Berlioz* (New York, 1954), pp. 304–05 and 273 ff.

midst of it, familiar words appeared: they were part of the famous "political" letter, which the German paper had garbled and reduced to one paragraph out of eight. In the full text, all but half a dozen lines have to do with music, and these few lines show that the newspaper resorted to grave distortion, while also misdating the letter for reasons no longer ascertainable.

Each such correction may be small in itself, but the cumulative effect over a series filling several volumes may be very great. Moreover, the editor of a famous man's complete letters never knows when the rectification of a single date or name, unimportant from his point of view, may not resolve the difficulty of a worker upon another subject who is searching for the verification of *his* uncertain data.

DISENTANGLEMENT, OR UNRAVELING THE SNARL OF FACTS

Not every problem of textual verification is found in rare manuscript letters. Most researchers never use anything but printed sources. Yet these too are full of contradictions that have to be resolved, as are also the inferences from artifacts. Imagine, for instance, an observant foreigner who had noticed that the words "In God We Trust" appeared on some of our coins but not on others, nor on our paper money. Imagine him further as writing a textbook on American history, for which he wanted to verify his reasonable guess that the four words in question formed the official, yet seemingly optional, motto of the United States.

His first step might be to find out how early in our history the slogan was used on our coins. Thumbing through *The Standard Catalogue of United States Coins,* he would learn that the phrase is not to be found before 1864. It first appeared on the bronze two-cent pieces, and two years later on all gold and silver coins. The verifier would also observe that it disappeared from the five-cent pieces in 1883 and did not return till 1938. What is more, it was put on, then removed, from the newly designed gold coins that were issued in 1907. Clearly, the researcher would say to himself, this alternation of "now-you-see-it, now-you-don't" suggests either fickleness or the fact that inscriptions on American money are not ruled by settled official policy.

Noticing that the picture of Secretary of the Treasury Salmon P. Chase adorns the greenbacks, or paper money, issued during the Civil War, when the motto was first used, the historian might conclude that Chase had a special interest in the design of our money. The obvious course would be to seek more light in a biography of Chase. The surmise about Chase would be wrong but the upshot would carry the researcher one step forward. He would find that although Chase took no interest in the numismatic art, he was a religious man. He put "In God We Trust" on the coins to satisfy a crusading clergyman who thought it imperative. Next, from the disappearance of the motto in 1907 and its absence for a year, our foreign scholar would correctly conclude that the choice lay within the discretion of the Secretary of the Treasury. As for our present paper money, he would see that it is too richly decorated with signatures and serial numbers to leave room for the creed.

No sooner would he be confident that the motto had no official standing than he would read in the leading American newspapers about the decision of Congress—ninety-two years after Chase's—to make the words official and inscribe them on all our currency, both metal and paper.[9] . . .

CLARIFICATION, OR DESTROYING LEGENDS

The amount of verifying a researcher does depends not only on his own curiosity but also on the grasp of his subject that he possesses at the start. The more he understands at the beginning, the more he finds to question and ascertain. It is expected, of course, that the researcher into any subject will approach it with a well-developed sense of time—whether the time be the few weeks or months of a particular crisis or the centuries separating St. Augustine from St. Thomas. Thus the narrator of the French Revolution or the First World War proceeds by days in those fateful summer and autumn months, whereas the historian of Rome must without stumbling move across a span of twenty generations.

[9] Bill signed by President Eisenhower, July 30, 1956.

But the investigator's original fund of knowledge must embrace even more than a well-populated chronology; it must include an understanding of how men in other eras lived and behaved, what they believed and how they managed their institutions. This kind of mastery fills the mind with images and also with questions, raising many points to verify; in the end it makes for what we term depth. Meanwhile the funded information suggests the means for conducting the inquiry.

Consider the sort of inquiry that leads to the exploding of a legend. Legends abound and flourish despite the verifiers. But this does not lessen the importance of verification, for important new ideas are often made to rest upon pseudo-truths that "every schoolboy knows." For example, a reputable psychiatrist published in 1955 a volume embodying his clinical researches into the states of mind of dying patients.[10] In this work he draws conclusions affecting our present culture and he buttresses them with "well-known" historical generalities. Unfortunately one of these happens to be a myth: "When the first millennium after the birth of Christ approached its end, Occidental man was seized by the fear of and hope for the Lord's return. The end of the world was envisaged, which meant man's final end [*sic*] had arrived. With the approach of the second millennium, the conviction again has spread that the days of man are counted. . . ."[11] That this parallel is false in every respect will be clear if we retrace the path of the scholar who half a century ago disposed of this legend about the end of the world coming in the year 1000.[12]

His first step was to discover when the tale originally came out in print. He found that this was in a 1690 edition of a late-fifteenth-century chronicle. Thus the first public record of the story occurs about seven hundred years after the supposed date of doom. Seven hundred years is a long time—twice the span since Shakespeare's death, four times that since Cornwallis' surrender at Yorktown. By the eighteenth century, then, a period when the Middle Ages were in disrepute and instances of their superstition were gladly

[10] K. R. Eissler, *The Psychiatrist and the Dying Patient* (New York, 1955).

[11] *Ibid.*, p. 108.

[12] George L. Burr, "The Year 1000 and the Antecedents of the Crusades," *American Historical Review,* VI (April, 1901), 429–39.

seized on, the published tale of 1690 referring to an event seven centuries earlier was first widely circulated. Indeed, it became usual to ascribe the launching of the Crusades to the relief felt by the Christians when the end did not come in 1000. This emotion was also said to account for the remarkable increase in church building. Although these several explanations were discredited by nineteenth-century historians, at the turn of the new century educated people still believed the myth—they still do, as our example dated 1955 shows. The terror of the year 1000 was the core of many a piece of moralizing. Said one confident writer of the 1880's about the men of A.D. 999: "Some squandered their substance in riotous living, others bestowed it for the salvation of their souls on churches and convents, bewailing multitudes lay by day and by night about the altars, many looked with terror, yet most with secret hope, for the conflagration of the earth and the falling of the heavens."[13]

In the face of such vivid, though belated reports, what could make a thoughtful scholar suspect the truth of the whole episode? The answer is: his intimate knowledge of the Middle Ages.

He knew in the first place that the end of the world had been foretold so often that only the ignorant in the year 1000 would seriously believe a new rumor. Moreover, long before that year, it had become orthodox belief and teaching that if the end of the world were really to come no man would know the time in advance.

In the second place, he knew that however impressive round numbers based on the decimal system are to us, they had no such hold on the imagination of medieval man. The numerals of that era were the Roman *I*'s, *V*'s, *X*'s, *L*'s, *C*'s, *D*'s, and *M*'s. For the Middle Ages no magic property would attach to "the Year M." No doubt, mystery and significance would then have been connected with 3's, 7's, 12's, and their multiples. For these were the sacred numbers of the Jews, and the Christians had repeatedly used them for prophecy.

Thirdly, our scholar knew that the Christian calendar did not come into general use until after 1000. And even then there was no agreement on dating. Nor was this the only difficulty arising

[13] H. v. Sybel, *Geschichte des ersten Kreuzzugs* (2nd and revised ed., Leipzig, 1881), p. 150; quoted in *ibid.*, p. 429.

from the calendar. When did the year 1000 begin? At Christmas, at Annunciation, at Easter, on the first of March (as in Venice), at the vernal equinox (as in Russia), on the first of September (as in the Greek Empire), or on the first of January (as in Spain)? In such a state of things the world could obviously not end on schedule everywhere.

Fourth, our accomplished medievalist knew that bare numerical dates meant little or nothing to the ordinary medieval man. He guided his life by the feast- and fast-days of the Church, not as we do, by engagement books in which not only the days, months, and year are marked, but the hours and half-hours, A.M. and P.M. We carry watches and consult them every few minutes. Medieval time, differently divided, was of a different texture.

In short, it is profoundly unhistorical to read back our habits and behavior into an age many hundred years past, and the conclusion is plain: taking the lack of any contemporaneous evidence of panic together with the facts of daily life and thought in the Middle Ages, the scholar demolishes a legend whose effects, potent as they are, would be still more benighting if his work had not enlightened at least a part of the educated public.

IDENTIFICATION, OR ASCERTAINING VALUE THROUGH AUTHORSHIP

Sometimes a problem of verification is solved by reaching behind your desk and taking down the single reference book that contains the fact you need.[14] Sometimes a day or two in the library is required. More often the task becomes for a time one's central occupation.

This is almost sure to be true when the problem is to trace the authorship of a large and important source whose authorship is unnamed or in dispute. If there is no chance of examining and com-

[14] The researcher will soon discover that reference books frequently disagree. This does not always mean that all are wrong except one; what happens is that one book in giving, say, the date of a treaty will give the year of its signing, and another book the date of its ratification, months later. Similar disparities can and do occur about most events, private and public, so that the "right" date is frequently a conventional choice among several possibilities.

paring handwritings because the document exists only in print, the undertaking can be laborious indeed. Even with a manuscript original, such as that of a government document, one may be foiled by the fact that it is the work of an amanuensis.

One does not set out to discover the author as a pastime, but because important consequences follow: knowing who the author is will help establish responsibility for acts or words, it will identify persons, explain meanings, and clear up allusions throughout the text as well as in other places, and it may relieve other historical figures of malicious charges, false rumors, and silent imputations of error. The fact that John C. Calhoun, not James Monroe, was the author of the War Report of 1812[15] is a minor matter in our history, but it serves to strengthen the view that the "War Hawks," of whom Calhoun was one, helped precipitate the war rather than Secretary of State Monroe, to whom the warlike document was originally ascribed.

Of all the problems of authorship in American history, that of finding out who wrote "The Diary of a Public Man" has been the most gigantic. Indeed, the odyssey on which it took the chief investigator is unparalleled. The document first appeared in 1879 in four installments published by the influential *North American Review*. Covering the winter of Secession, 1860–1861, the diary consists of entries for twenty-one days between December 28, 1860, and March 15, 1861. A fact of great importance to the user of the diary and, as we shall see, to the verifier, is that on twenty of these days the author was in Washington; on one, February 20, 1861, he was in New York City.

The value of the document may be gauged from the fact that it is the only source for a number of incidents about Lincoln's acts during the crisis of the Union. Among its more picturesque revelations is the account of Douglas' conduct at Lincoln's inauguration which school children have learned ever since: "A miserable little rickety table had been provided for the President, on which he could hardly find room for his hat, and Senator Douglas, reaching forward, took it with a smile and held it during the delivery of the

[15] Charles M. Wiltse, "The Authorship of the War Report of 1812," *American Historical Review,* XLIV (January, 1944), 253–59.

address. It was a trifling act, but a symbolic one, and not to be forgotten, and it attracted much attention all around me."

Who then was "me"? Professor Frank Maloy Anderson [of the University of Minnesota] spent nearly thirty-five years trying to find the answer.[16] His undeviating persistence seems in retrospect to have been as single-minded and tireless as any in the history of verification. The fact that the question is still in dispute does not lessen the utility of his labors or their exemplary value for the researcher. Every attempt at verification advances knowledge and displays the technician's skill, whether or not luck seconds his attempt. . . .

[16] Frank Maloy Anderson, *The Mystery of "A Public Man": A Historical Detective Story* (Minneapolis, 1948).

12. The Case of the Mysterious Diary:

Evidence Over Time

PROFESSORS BARZUN AND GRAFF REFER TO ONE OF THE most fascinating cases of a scholar's single-minded pursuit of a number of missing links that American historiography has ever seen: Frank Maloy Anderson's *The Mystery of "A Public Man."* Anderson's approach was very much that of the detective, piecing together evidence from hotel registers, timetables, and old newspapers. For our purposes, the example deserves closer examination.

Not everyone was happy with Anderson's solution, although a great many agreed with his chief conclusion, that the famous diary was a mixture of fact and fancy. The most persuasive analysis of Anderson's methods was written by a graduate student at the University of Washington in Seattle, Roy N. Lokken. Trained in a seminar concerning historical research and writing introduced at Washington by Professor W. Stull Holt, a scholar who once had observed that history was "a damn dim candle over a damn dark abyss," Lokken won the Mississippi Valley Historical Association's Pelzer Award for 1953 as a result of his work. Holt had taught at the Johns Hopkins University, where he introduced such a seminar, somewhat after the German method to which the Hopkins was already amenable, and Holt's and Hopkins' students across the land have brought similar approaches to historical inquiry into the universities to which they have gone.

Lokken's essay is essentially an example of textual criticism used in the service of healthy skepticism. Its principal aim was to reopen the question of the diary's authorship. It is not entirely without its own faults, as Anderson's reply to it, which follows, will show. Nonetheless, it serves two useful purposes here—to carry the presentation of the methods of the historian a step further, and to provide one good example of the kind of essays that graduate schools encourage within their seminars. Lokken now teaches at East Carolina University in North Carolina; Anderson has died, and the debate cannot continue, at least in its present form.

♦ ♦ ♦

Frank Maloy Anderson's *The Mystery of "A Public Man"* . . . represented the culmination of a thirty-five-year effort to bring to a final solution a problem which had puzzled historians of the American Civil War since 1879. This problem involved the identification of the unknown author of a diary purportedly kept in Washington, D.C., from December 28, 1860, to March 15, 1861. Published anonymously in the *North American Review* in 1879, the diary had generally been accepted as authentic by historians and had been the source of several noted Lincoln anecdotes. Although many theories had been advanced since 1879 as to the identity of the diarist, none of them had been proved. Allen Thorndike Rice, publisher of the *North American Review* in 1879, who certainly

---

For additional reading: Two other entertaining essays on the subject are Evelyn Page, "The Diary and the Public Man," *New England Quarterly,* XXII (June, 1949), 147–72; and Benjamin M. Price, "That Baffling Diary," *South Atlantic Quarterly,* LIV (January, 1955), 56–64, which concludes unconvincingly that Henry Adams was the author. Hillary Waugh's *That Night It Rained* and *The Missing Man* deal with much the same problem in terms of detective fiction of the procedural school.

ought to have known, had refused to his death to disclose the name of the diary's author. The Boston *Herald* and the Chicago *Tribune* in 1879 had named as possible authors of the diary such varied personalities as Horatio King, postmaster general in the Buchanan administration, Charles Edward Stuart, United States senator from Michigan from 1853 to 1859, and Thurlow Weed, publisher of the Albany *Evening Journal.* Anderson himself had at various times held theories that the mysterious diarist might have been Henry S. Sanford, Lincoln's minister to Belgium, John W. Forney, editor of the Philadelphia *Press,* or Amos Kendall, the business agent of Samuel F. B. Morse, the inventor of the telegraph. All of these theories had been rejected for one reason or another.

The suggestion that the diary might be largely spurious had first been made by Edward L. Pierce in a paper read before the Massachusetts Historical Society in March, 1896. Pierce's doubts had been raised by entries which attributed cabinet-making activity to Charles Sumner. Pierce had questioned the description of a conference between Lincoln and the diarist on the afternoon of March 7, 1861, and he had doubted that Hiram Barney had attended breakfast at Moses Grinnell's on February 20, 1861, as indicated in the diary. His doubts, however, had been based on little direct documentary evidence and gave historians little reason to question the authenticity of the diary. Anderson himself had long believed that the diary was a genuine historical document and had rested his early investigations on that basic assumption. In his book published in 1948, however, Anderson finally reached the conclusion that the diary was largely spurious and that the author was none other than the once-celebrated "King of the Lobby," Sam Ward. . . .

Anderson became convinced that the diary was a spurious document when he failed to prove that Amos Kendall was its author. He advanced the Kendall theory at a meeting of the American Historical Association in Indianapolis in December, 1928, when he read a paper entitled, "Who Wrote the Diary of a Public Man? Amos Kendall, Henry Wikoff, or X?" At this time Anderson believed entirely in the genuineness of the document and was of the opinion that any solution to the mystery must rest upon the internal evidence of the diary itself. Accordingly, he examined the diary carefully and drew from it eighteen points of personality which he proposed to employ as criteria in an effort to determine the identity of the diarist.

While some of Anderson's criteria were well taken, some did not necessarily follow from the internal evidence of the diary. Most of them concerned the interests, sympathies, antipathies, and activities of the Public Man as revealed by the diary. The only physical description of the Public Man that Anderson could find was that he was a tall man. This criterion, however, appears to have been based on a none too careful reading of the passage in the diary wherein Lincoln asked the Public Man if he had ever "put backs with Sumner." Sumner was a tall man, and Anderson supposed that Lincoln's query indicated that the Public Man was also tall. The inference was not altogether justified, however, as the tone of the passage indicates that Lincoln was subjecting the Public Man to a little good-natured jesting. The diarist went on to say: "I suppose I looked as much surprised as I felt; but I laughed and said that I did not think I ever had done so. 'Well, I supposed not,' he [Lincoln] said." On the basis of this evidence a good argument can be made that the Public Man was short, and that Lincoln, who took great pride in his own height, was having a bit of fun with him on that account. Another criterion which is not a necessary conclusion from the internal evidence of the diary was that the Public Man was "of considerable acquaintance with the French language and literature." The few French words and phrases in the diary do not justify this conclusion, and there is no significant evidence in the diary to indicate that the Public Man had more than a superficial understanding of French political thought.

Probably the most objective criterion used by Anderson was the evidence of the diary that the Public Man was in New York City on February 20, 1861, and in Washington on each day specified in the diary between December 28, 1860, and March 15, 1861. During the course of Anderson's investigation this criterion became of key importance. For a time Anderson thought that Amos Kendall was the diarist, because the facts of Kendall's life fitted most of the eighteen points; but he finally and regretfully eliminated this prospect. Kendall, he found, could not have been the diarist, because external evidence indicated that Kendall was in New York

City on December 29, 1860, when the Public Man was in Washington, and that Kendall was probably not in New York City on February 20, 1861, when the Public Man was.

Anderson subsequently abandoned the date criterion altogether. His failure to prove the Kendall theory, because of the difficulty raised by the chronology of the diary, caused Anderson to re-examine the diary to determine whether or not it was authentic. During this re-examination he found numerous reasons for concluding that the diary was either a mere invention or had as a nucleus a genuine diary embellished with recollections and inventions. Anderson was convinced, however, that the diary was not a mere invention, because it was free of the anachronistic blunders into which the author of a fictitious diary would be likely to fall and because it reflected contemporary newspapers in a manner possible only to one who was reading them from day to day as they came from the press. He therefore decided in favor of the theory that the diary was basically genuine but embellished with recollection and fiction, and he accordingly drew up a list of thirteen points of personality to describe a man who had kept and transformed such a diary.

In his new list of criteria Anderson omitted eight of the original eighteen points, added three new ones, and modified several others. Anderson now believed it unnecessary to assess the diarist's political importance and experience in Washington, as he had done in the earlier criteria. He no longer cared whether the Public Man was tall or short. Such criteria as the Public Man's acquaintanceship with Sumner and Lincoln's knowledge of the diarist in 1848 no longer concerned Anderson. He remained interested in the diarist's sympathies and antipathies, but he was less concerned with the diarist's movements as described in the diary. He omitted the more objective of his earlier criteria, especially the diary's chronology which had given him the most trouble in his earlier investigations. Anderson now was looking not merely for a diarist but for a hoaxer, and what appeared in the diary might well be fiction or inaccurate reminiscences.

By drawing up this new list of criteria Anderson committed himself to the hypothesis that the diarist was the author of a largely spurious document. The validity of this hypothesis depended on the accuracy of Anderson's contention that the diary was not altogether authentic, that it was originally a meager diary which had actually been kept in Washington during the winter of 1860–1861, and that in 1879 it had been embellished with recollections and fictitious stories. Of the twenty-six proofs of the diary's unauthenticity advanced by Anderson four were based on documentary evidence, one appeared to have been based on direct evidence but was undocumented, two were based on the absence of corroborative evidence to support the diary, one was based on the doubtful validity of existing corroborative evidence, and seventeen were based on circumstantial evidence.

The four proofs based on documentary evidence were supported by the recollection of an old man, by contemporary newspapers, by the correspondence of William H. Seward, Lincoln's secretary of state, and by Lincoln's inaugural address. The first of these was the testimony of Hiram Barney in 1886 that he had not attended breakfast with Lincoln at Moses Grinnell's on February 20, 1861, as recorded in the diary. Anderson admitted that the memory of old men is not always reliable, but he could not see how Barney's memory could have failed on this particular point. Moreover, he could not find Barney's name listed in New York newspaper accounts of the Lincoln breakfast published on February 21, 1861.[1] Anderson overlooked the fact, however, that the diary does not specifically state "Hiram Barney." The diary refers to "Mr. Barney," without giving his full name. Barney is a common name. The New York *Daily Tribune* for February 21, 1861, mentions a "Councilman Barney" as having been present at Lincoln's reception in the Governor's Room in New York City from 11 A.M. to 1 P.M. on February 20. The only Barney who was a city councilman in New York City in 1861 was George A. Barney, a painter. There is evidence, also, that there was an Abram Barney in New York who was associated with the Grinnell group in a letter to Lincoln written after the attack on Fort Sumter.

[1] It may or may not be significant that New York newspaper accounts named only the most prominent men present. The New York *Daily Tribune* for February 21, 1861, named only sixteen of the thirty guests. It is possible, although only barely possible, that Hiram Barney was present but was not considered important enough by newspapermen to merit particular notice.

Anderson also cited as evidence the contemporary New York newspapers, the *Herald, Times, Tribune, Evening Post, World,* and *Daily News,* to prove his argument that the interview between the Public Man and Lincoln on February 20, as described in the diary, probably did not take place. He appears, however, to have consulted only some of the New York newspapers. Furthermore he failed to give the names of the Lincoln visitors listed in the newspapers and to explain why none of those visitors could have been the diarist. Anderson also stated that at a late hour in the afternoon "Lincoln was reported to have been resting and denying himself to all callers." He did not say what that hour was. The New York *Evening Express* for February 21, 1861, a daily that Anderson does not appear to have consulted, reported that Lincoln on February 20 received visitors from 2 to 5 P.M., including Simeon Draper, Sheppard Knapp, James R. Briggs, General James Watson Webb, Daniel E. Gavitt, Samuel Hottaling, and others whose names were not given. At 4:30 P.M. Lincoln received Dr. Lyman Beecher and his wife. After they left, a Captain Faunce of the United States revenue cutter *Harriet Lane* came in. At 6:45 Lincoln was entertaining Chauncey Schaffer and the speaker of the house of representatives of Massachusetts. When these visitors departed was not stated, but by that time the afternoon was over and evening had begun. Lincoln left for the opera at the Academy of Music at 8 P.M. The article stated nothing about Lincoln's resting and denying himself to callers. It showed that Lincoln was receiving visitors during the late afternoon of February 20. The diarist himself did not indicate at what hour of the day he visited Lincoln. He could have been any one of the callers named or not named in the newspaper accounts.

Anderson compiled a list of the persons who called on Lincoln at the Willard Hotel in Washington on February 28, 1861, based on an examination of the New York *Herald, Times, Tribune,* and *Evening Post,* the Baltimore *American,* the Springfield *Republican,* the Cincinnati *Commercial,* and all the Washington newspapers. As the result of this study he concluded that none of the listed callers could have been the diarist. At the time, however, Anderson was using the eighteen points of personality which he subsequently abandoned in favor of a revised list of criteria. He did not appear to have employed the thirteen points of personality in checking his list of Lincoln callers of February 28. Furthermore, he failed to name the persons that he listed as having called on Lincoln that day and to explain why none of them could have been the Public Man.

Anderson also contended that the diarist could not have had the interview with Seward on the evening of March 7, 1861, described in the diary. He based this conclusion on the evidence contained in a letter from Seward to his wife, dated March 8, 1861. In this letter Seward wrote:[2]

> I went to the office [at the State Department] on Wednesday [March 6] and for two days have attended at the department nine hours each. Last night [i.e., March 7] I broke down and sent for Dr. Miller. I have kept my chamber to-day except for an hour, when I went on a necessary errand to the White House.

Anderson argued, furthermore, that Seward could not have dropped in to see the Public Man on March 9, as the evidence showed that Seward was still unwell on that day. This evidence was contained in a letter from Alexander Rives, a Virginia Unionist, to Seward, March 9, 1861, and in a letter from Seward to Lincoln of the same date.[3]

There is evidence, however, that Seward may have used his illness from March 7 to March 11 for diplomatic purposes and that it may not have been as serious as appears on the surface. Seward at this time was stalling off the Southern commissioners, John Forsyth, André B. Roman, and Martin J. Crawford, possibly awaiting the return of his agent, Colonel Francis W. Lander, from Virginia.[4] Senator William M. Gwin of California in his "Memoirs," written

[2] Frederick W. Seward, *Seward at Washington,* 3 vols. (New York, 1891), II, 518.

[3] "I desired to present the enclosed letter to you in person; and to that end, called upon you at the Department and your residence; and was sorry to learn that you were too unwell to receive visitors." Alexander Rives to William H. Seward, Washington, March 9, 1861. . . .

[4] That Seward may have been awaiting the return of Lander from Virginia is indicated by the following undated note from Seward to Lincoln: "Colonel Lander failed to come but I shall see him this evening, and probably bring him over to see you." The date of this note is given on the Library of Congress catalogue card as March 10, 1861, but it is uncertain. Lincoln Papers (Library of Congress), No. 7959. . . .

long after the event, testified that in March, 1861, he was acting as Seward's intermediary with the Southern commissioners, especially with Crawford. Gwin, on March 7, conveyed a message from Crawford to Seward expressing the former's desire for "something more tangible than verbal communications," and Seward asked Gwin "to call at a certain hour the following morning, [Mr. Seward] desiring time for consideration for his answer." Gwin construed this incident as indicating that Seward was not as confident "of securing an amicable settlement between the North and the South as previously." Gwin returned the next morning, March 8, "and was informed that Mr. Seward the night before had had a severe attack of lumbago which rendered it impossible for him to leave his bed to transact any public business." The California senator interpreted Seward's sudden illness "as evidence of the fact that Mr. Seward could give no such guaranty to the South" as that desired by Crawford. Gwin, after notifying Crawford that he no longer considered himself an intermediary between Seward and the Southern commissioners, left that day for New York.

If Seward's illness had been "a severe attack of lumbago," it is unlikely that he could have left his chamber to go "on a necessary errand to the White House" for one hour on March 8. That Seward was still engaged in the administrative details of his department on March 8 is proved by a note from Seward to Lincoln of that date introducing a State Department clerk who took to Lincoln a draft for $5000 for his signature. . . . On March 9, Seward advised Lincoln that he was "yet kept indoors," but offered to ride to the White House any time if necessary. Nevertheless, he did not appear to have been too ill to receive visitors, as Lincoln asked him to "give Mr. [Carl] Schurz a full interview." It is evident that Seward's illness gave him an opportunity to turn away visitors he did not care to see. The Southern commissioners, Senator Gwin, and Alexander Rives were undoubtedly among those persons Seward was particularly anxious to avoid between March 7 and March 11, 1861. He had no reason, however, to avoid the diarist, with whom he was on friendly and confidential terms.

Anderson's final proof of the diary's unauthenticity, based on documentary evidence, was the alleged inaccuracy of Stephen A. Douglas' statement to the diarist on March 3, 1861, that Lincoln had inserted the words "hold, occupy, and possess" in his inaugural address after his arrival in Washington. Anderson cited several copies of the draft of the inaugural address showing the alterations made after Lincoln arrived in Washington. These copies are in the Robert Todd Lincoln Collection of the Papers of Abraham Lincoln which are preserved in the Library of Congress. The words, "hold, occupy, and possess," wrote Anderson, "were in the draft prepared before he left Springfield." There is other evidence, however, which indicates that Anderson may have misunderstood this passage of the diary. On February 12, 1861, Orville Hickman Browning parted with Lincoln at Indianapolis, as the president-elect proceeded on his journey to Washington. Before they parted Lincoln gave Browning a copy of his inaugural address and asked for his opinion of it. After reading the address, Browning wrote to Lincoln on February 17: "Would it not be judicious so to modify this as to make it read: 'All the power at my disposal will be used to hold, occupy, and possess the property and places belonging to the Government, and to collect the duties and imposts, etc.' . . . ?" The passage which Browning, on February 17, suggested that Lincoln modify in his inaugural address included the words, "hold, occupy, and possess," which Anderson claimed were already in the draft of the address before Lincoln departed from Springfield. After Lincoln arrived in Washington, the passage to which Browning had referred was subjected to considerable criticism and alteration. The original passage appears to have been as follows:

> All the power at my disposal will be used to reclaim the public property and places which have fallen; to hold, occupy and possess these, and all other property and places belonging to the government, and to collect the duties on imposts; but beyond what may be necessary for these objects, there will be no invasion of any State.

In Washington, Lincoln gave copies of the address to Francis P. Blair, Sr., of Maryland, and Seward and asked for their suggestions. Blair praised it without qualification. Seward, however, wrote out a list of alterations and amendments to the address, proposing that the whole passage quoted above be struck out and that the following substitution be inserted:

> The power confided to me shall be used indeed with efficacy, but also

with discretion in every case and exigency according to the circumstances actually existing, and with a view and a hope of a peaceful solution of the national troubles and the restoration of fraternal sympathies and affections.

At this time Lincoln appears to have received and agreed to Browning's letter of February 17, because there is another copy of the address in the Lincoln Papers with changes either in Lincoln's handwriting or that of one of his secretaries. The passage in question was so altered in this copy as to read as follows:

All the power at my disposal will be used [to reclaim the public property and places which have fallen;] to hold, occupy and possess the[se and all other] property and places belonging to the government, and to collect the duties on imposts. . . .

There is, in the Lincoln Papers, a printed copy of the inaugural address which appears to be the final edition of the text. In this copy the printed passage in question was cut out entirely and replaced by the following handwritten passage:

The power confided to me, will be used to hold, occupy, and possess the property, and places belonging to the government, and to collect the duties and imposts; but beyond what may be necessary for these objects, there will be no invasion—no using of force against, or among the people anywhere.

The words "hold, occupy, and possess" in this copy are not in print, but are handwritten; they are a part of the inserted passage. Douglas may well have seen this copy and have drawn the conclusion that the whole passage, including the words "hold, occupy, and possess," was a completely new insertion. It has that appearance, and Douglas can hardly be blamed for having drawn such a conclusion, especially if Lincoln did not go to the trouble of explaining every step of the process by which the passage, in its final form, was created. Both the diarist and Douglas supposed that Seward must have been responsible for the inserted passage, and they were partially correct. The words "the power confided to me" were Seward's, and the whole passage was modified and toned down in accordance with the advice of both Browning and Seward. . . .

One of Anderson's proofs of the diary's unauthenticity based on the absence of corroborative evidence to support the diary concerns so much of the entry of February 20 as described Lincoln wearing black kid gloves to the opera. Anderson examined more than a dozen contemporary newspaper accounts of Lincoln's attendance at the opera at the Academy of Music in New York City during the evening of February 20, 1861, and found nothing to support the story purportedly told the diarist by his "Cousin V——." It is true that the black gloves passed unnoticed by the majority of newspaper reporters present at the opera. They were observed, however, by the reporter for the New York *Dispatch* [for February 23, 1861], a weekly which Anderson does not appear to have consulted. In his account this observant reporter noted that Lincoln

> although not afflicted by a regular stage fright, was somewhat nervous; twitched and was restless, jerked at his beard and looked uneasy. He was followed by half a dozen men, none of them indicating in appearance or manner any familiarity with the etiquettes of the opera; one with a face like that of Henry Ward Beecher, his hair thrust behind his ears, dark gloves that he soon got tired of wearing . . . edged himself into the most conspicuous part of the box between Mr. Lincoln and the stage.

This account indicates that the diarist's "Cousin V——" was correct as to the black gloves (although "dark" may indicate dark blue or brown, as well as black) but that he was mistaken as to the owner. He did not himself know Lincoln by sight but had to have the president-elect pointed out to him. Since the owner of the gloves occupied the most conspicuous part of the box, he could easily have been identified as Lincoln by people seated on the opposite side of the auditorium, as was "Cousin V——." Anderson's further assertion that Lincoln could not have visited the director's room between acts, as related by the diarist's "Cousin V——," is supported by contemporary New York newspaper accounts which state that Lincoln left the Academy of Music soon after the second act. If it is true that "Cousin V——" did not know Lincoln from a man who looked like Henry Ward Beecher, however, it is likely that the diarist's informant erred on this point too. The inaccuracy of "Cousin V——'s" gossip does not constitute proof of the diary's unauthenticity.

Anderson also rejected the diarist's account of a visit to Lincoln made by a group of anti-Chase New York men on March 2, 1861, on the grounds that he could find no corroborative evidence to support it. Contemporary newspapers failed to report any such meeting, and a study of Washington dispatches to New York newspapers led Anderson to the conclusion that Lincoln had been so occupied that day that a conference of the nature described by the diarist could not have taken place. Anderson, however, did not state what contemporary newspapers he had examined and what other sources, if any, he had consulted in arriving at this conclusion. Moreover, he made no effort to determine the identity of the New York delegation, although the diary itself contains several pointed allusions.

In the entry of March 2 the diarist introduced the New York anti-Chase delegation story with the observation, "These New York men have done just what they have been saying they would do, and with just the result which I have from the first expected." This is an allusion to a passage in the entry of February 26 which states that the diarist was shown a letter[5]

> received a fortnight ago from Mr. Draper, in New York, expressing great anxiety as to Mr. Seward's position in the Cabinet in case of the nomination of Mr. [Salmon P.] Chase, and intimating an intention of visiting Washington with several other gentlemen for the purpose of making Mr. Lincoln understand that he must absolutely drop the idea of putting Mr. Chase into the Treasury. I told him that Mr. Weed had to-day expressed the same ideas to me, and I asked him if he did not know that a counter-pressure was putting on Mr. Lincoln to exclude Mr. Seward. "Suppose," I said, "they should both be excluded?"

The diarist, after he had learned of the New York anti-Chase delegation conference with Lincoln on March 2, observed that he could not "feel even sure now that Mr. Seward will be nominated at all on Tuesday: and certainly he neither is nor after this can be the real head of the Administration, even if his name is on the list

[5] "The Diary of a Public Man," *North American Review,* CXXIX (September, 1879), 263.

of the Cabinet." The two passages are in thought and expression so closely related that it is quite likely that the anti-Chase group mentioned in the entry of March 2 was that which Simeon Draper had in February announced that he would accompany in a visit to Washington. Frederic Bancroft, in his biography of Seward, cited Ward H. Lamon's *Recollections* as authority to support the statement that "a party of Seward's friends ventured, on March 2d, to inform the President-elect that Seward could not serve in the Cabinet with Chase," but he did not identify the "party of Seward's friends." Such a group might well have been led by Simeon Draper, as Draper was then the president of the Republican Central Club of New York City.

Although evidence existed confirming the diarist's account of Stephen A. Douglas holding Lincoln's hat at the presidential inauguration on March 4, 1861, Anderson doubted its trustworthiness. He cited in support of this doubt a letter by Gustave Koerner who stood next to Douglas during the inaugural ceremony but mentioned nothing about Lincoln's hat. Also, his examination of contemporary newspapers led him to believe that such newspapers as did refer to the hat incident based their accounts on a report published in the Cincinnati *Commercial* of March 11, 1861. This report was made, not by a journalist, but by a representative in Congress from Ohio. Since the representative's name was not given and since the Cincinnati *Commercial* was Republican, Anderson was inclined to believe that the report was either hearsay or an invention. Other accounts of the hat incident in memoirs, reminiscences, and other books he dismissed as having been written after the publication of the diarist's story in the *North American Review* in 1879 and therefore probably inspired by it. On the basis of such statements of probability Anderson arrived at the highly questionable conclusion that the story of Lincoln's hat was "almost certainly a myth." He gave no indication that he had made any effort to determine the identity of the representative in Congress from Ohio who reported the story to the Cincinnati *Commercial,* certainly a matter of key importance in this connection.

Seventeen of Anderson's proofs of the diary's unauthenticity were based entirely on circumstantial evidence and statements of probability. . . .

Anderson also asserted that the diarist erred in stating, on February 28, 1861, that Lincoln had not revealed the content of the inaugural address to Seward, because evidence indicated that Seward had seen the document as early as February 24. He based this criticism, however, on a misconstruction of the passage in the diary to which he referred. This passage is as follows:[6]

He [Douglas] told me he had urged Mr. Lincoln to recommend the instant calling of a national convention, upon which point Mr. Seward agrees with him, as his motion in the Senate shows today. But he admitted that he had no success getting Mr. Lincoln to a point on the subject, and this led to a question of what Mr. Lincoln really means to say in his inaugural. I found that Senator Douglas knew just as well as I knew that Mr. Lincoln has not confided this yet, even to Mr. Seward; but I could not get him to feel as I do how strangely compromising this is to all our hopes of a settlement through the influence of Mr. Seward.

The diarist did not say that Seward had not seen the inaugural address on February 24; he said that as of February 28 Lincoln had not confided to Seward what he "really" intended to say on inauguration day. Seward, on February 24, had suggested certain changes in the address. Between that date and March 4 Lincoln made several revisions, including part of an amendment suggested by Seward. According to the diarist, the final revision of the inaugural address was revealed to Douglas on March 2. . . .

How Anderson came upon the Sam Ward theory is itself a mystery. He attributed it to an instance of "serendipity"—"the faculty of making happy and unexpected discoveries by accident." At any rate, having made the discovery, Anderson studied the William H. Seward Papers and the family connections of Sam Ward. After fifteen years of research he obtained what he called "a decisive result." Although he did not state specifically what this "decisive result" was, it appears to have been an undated note from Ward to Seward which may be found in Appendix K of Bancroft's biography of Seward.[7]

[6] *Ibid.*, p. 268.

[7] Frederic Bancroft, *The Life of William H. Seward,* 2 vols. (New York, 1900), II, 542–43.

Samuel Ward was born in New York City on January 27, 1814, the son of Samuel Ward, head of the banking firm of Prime, Ward, and King, and brother of Julia Ward Howe, composer of the "Battle Hymn of the Republic." He graduated from Columbia College in 1831, traveled extensively in Europe, participated in the gold rush to California, engaged in an unsuccessful brokerage business on Wall Street, and in 1860 he was in Washington to represent the interests of claimants in land title disputes involving valuable mining properties in California. During the Civil War he accompanied the English journalist, William H. Russell, on a journey through the Southern Confederacy, but spent most of his time in New York, and was frequently in Washington. After the war he became so successful a lobbyist in Washington that he was known widely as the "King of the Lobby." He died in Italy in 1884.

The facts of Ward's life coincided with some of Anderson's thirteen points of personality. Ward was in Washington during the winter of 1860–1861 and was acquainted with many public men, including Seward. He had the diary habit. A man of the world of wide experience, Ward was conversant with the French language and literature. He was furthermore a New Yorker who was at least moderately interested in business affairs. Anderson did not prove, however, that Ward disliked Francis P. and Montgomery Blair of Maryland, Senator Edward D. Baker, and Edwin M. Stanton, as did the diarist. He failed to prove by documentation that Ward distrusted and feared extremists on both sides of the secession controversy and that he took personal satisfaction in casting ridicule upon Caleb Cushing, Pierre Soulé, and Charles Sumner. Hence, the thirteen points of personality did not prove conclusively that Ward was the author of the diary. There were many men in Washington during the winter months preceding the attack on Fort Sumter to whom most of those criteria could easily have been applied. Anderson needed more convincing evidence.

Such evidence Anderson attempted to supply by identifying five of the more than one hundred concealed identities in the diary. In the Seward Papers [then] in Auburn, New York,[8] and the S. L. M.

[8] The Seward papers have since been moved to the Rush Rhees Library at the University of Rochester. [Editor's note.]

Barlow Papers in New York City he found a series of memoranda written by Ward to Seward which established a connection between Senator Judah P. Benjamin of Louisiana, S. L. M. Barlow, a New York lawyer, William H. Aspinwall, a prominent New York business man, Senator William M. Gwin of California, and William M. Browne, editor of the official Buchanan administration newspaper. On the basis of this connection Anderson identified Mr. B—— in the diarist's entry of December 28, 1860, as William M. Browne, Senator —— in the same entry as Senator Gwin, and Mr. B—— in the entry of January 13, 1861, as S. L. M. Barlow.

That these people are to be found in the diary is not surprising; they were all interested, for one reason or another, in staving off civil war by achieving a peaceful compromise with the South. The efforts to achieve such a compromise constitute the theme of "The Diary of a Public Man." The identification of such people as Barlow, Gwin, and Browne does not necessarily prove that Ward was the diarist; it proves only that the diarist moved in the same circles as Seward, Gwin, Barlow, and the other *dramatis personae* of the diary. Moreover, Ward's memoranda reveal that only one of the three Southern commissioners in March, 1861, was named by Ward. That was Martin J. Crawford. The diarist, however, mentioned only John Forsyth by name.

Anderson also identified the diarist's "Cousin V——" in the entry of February 20, 1861, as Sam Ward's cousin, Valentine Mott Francis, and "——, at Augusta" in the entry of March 9, 1861, as Mrs. Eve, of Augusta, Georgia, supposedly an acquaintance of Ward's. These identifications, however, depended entirely on the validity of the Sam Ward theory.

On the whole, Anderson proved neither that the diary was a mass of reminiscence and fiction built up around a skeleton diary kept during the winter of 1860–1861 nor that the diarist was Sam Ward. Much of the evidence he presented was circumstantial, and where he did present direct documentary evidence there remained, nevertheless, an element of doubt. It appears from Anderson's own account of his historical detective story that he began his researches with a sincere attempt to find some objective basis for a solution of the problem. The transition from the eighteen to the thirteen points of personality was attended, however, by a certain selectivity which involved the rejection of certain portions of the diary as fictional —portions which only too obviously would have proved embarrassing to the Sam Ward hoax theory as a solution. One of the eighteen points was that the diarist was a tall man. Since Ward was a short man, the elimination of that criterion was an obvious convenience. Moreover, there was no evidence that Ward was a frequent visitor at the Senate chamber. A second criterion omitted by Anderson in constructing his thirteen points was that the diarist frequently attended Senate meetings during the winter of 1860–1861 and that he must have had a motive for it. Another important criterion omitted by Anderson was that the diarist had had "long experience of Washington." This was not true of Ward, who had spent much of his life prior to 1860 in Europe, California, and New York, but not in Washington. The date criterion served to eliminate Amos Kendall as the diarist. So might it have eliminated Ward, but the elimination of the date criterion proved convenient for the eventual introduction of the Ward theory. Yet it appears most singular that Anderson never explained why Kendall, Henry Wikoff, or someone else might not have been as satisfactory a hoaxer as Sam Ward.

Anderson was right in warning historians against accepting on faith the details in a document when the authenticity and authorship of that document are in question. He was not justified, however, in concluding on the basis of the evidence he presented that the diary is "a semi-fictional production . . . [which] ought not to be regarded as history." Moreover, he was too easily satisfied with the meager results he derived from his efforts to identify the concealed *dramatis personae* of the diary. My own researches have convinced me that the numerous lacunae in the history of the secession winter of 1860–1861 tend to obscure many of the events and unnamed persons to whom the diary refers. When the veil of mystery has been lifted from these lacunae, a combination of internal and external criticism should reveal the authenticity or unauthenticity, as well as the authorship, of the diary. Until then, the mystery of "A Public Man" remains unsolved.

Professor Anderson replied to Mr. Lokken as follows:

. . . In describing my book Mr. Lokken declares: "While the book affords an illustration of the way in which critical research has to be done, the conclusion that the diary was a semifictional production was not justified on the basis of the evidence presented. Likewise, the evidence advanced does not warrant the conclusion that Sam Ward was the author of the diary."[9]

The arguments put forth in support of this verdict are mainly of two sorts. One is that I have relied too much upon circumstantial evidence. For the other Mr. Lokken has made a careful selection of . . . incidents reported in the diary whose actual occurrence I have questioned. He then argues in effect that the incidents related could have happened as the diarist says they did.

In formulating his criticism that I have relied too much upon circumstantial evidence, Mr. Lokken quite overlooks the fact that it was necessary to make considerable use of such evidence if the problem of the authorship of the diary was to be solved. Careful reading of my book would have shown that I had searched far and wide for all the direct evidence obtainable but could find only a limited amount—not enough on that basis alone to warrant the drawing of definite conclusions. I therefore had to employ circumstantial evidence to considerable extent. Mr. Lokken's objection to the amount of circumstantial evidence—seventeen items, he says, out of twenty-six of all sorts—overlooks the common-sense consideration that where a considerable amount of circumstantial evidence is employed and all of it points to the same conclusion, the greater the amount of the evidence, the stronger the proof. All of the circumstantial evidence I have cited, impressive in quality as well as in amount, points to the conclusion that "The Diary of a Public Man" is in part fictitious and that Sam Ward was the author.

As to the second criticism, it is not possible in the space afforded . . . to give detailed consideration to all of the . . . incidents that Mr. Lokken has selected for discussion. As often happens in

[9] This is not a precise quotation: Lokker wrote "product" rather than "production" and "the arguments advanced in the book do not warrant" rather than "the evidence advanced does not warrant," an error in transcription that might lead some readers to doubt the exactitude of some of Mr. Anderson's other qutotations. [Editor's note.]

debate over controversial matters, refutation would require much more space than assertion. It is possible, however, to consider a few of the points that Mr. Lokken tries to make in the course of his arguments. Such an examination will throw a good deal of light upon his methods of handling historical evidence.

One of these incidents is reported as occurring in New York City on February 20, 1861, the day that Lincoln spent there on his way to Washington. The diarist reports: "Mr. Barney came to see me this morning at the hotel from breakfasting with Mr. Lincoln at Mr. Grinnell's, to see if I could fix a time for meeting Mr. Lincoln during the day or evening." In discussing the incident I naturally assumed that "Mr. Barney" was Hiram Barney. . . . Mr. Lokken questions the identification and suggests that the diarist's caller may have been somebody else by the name of Barney, as Barney was a rather common name. In support of that idea, he points to a letter to Lincoln, April 12-June 14, 1861, now in the Lincoln Papers at the Library of Congress. The letter is signed by a number of prominent New Yorkers. One of the signatures, Mr. Lokken says, is that of Abram Barney. On examining the document I find that the Barney signature is indubitably that of *Hiram Barney*. In this instance careless reading of the document is the sole basis for one of Mr. Lokken's arguments.

Shortly after William H. Seward became secretary of state he was absent from his office for several days, and there was public announcement that the absence was due to illness variously described as lumbago or pleurisy. Mr. Lokken questions the validity of the excuse. He asserts that "There is evidence, however, that Seward may have used his illness from March 7 to March 11 for diplomatic purposes and that it may not have been as serious as appears on the surface." Paying particular attention to March 8, he says: "That Seward was still engaged in the administrative details of his department is proved by a note from Seward to Lincoln of that date introducing a State Department clerk who took to Lincoln a draft for $5000 for his signature." Obviously the value of the note as evidence of what Seward did that day, or for the state of his health, depends upon the date when the note was actually written. Mr. Lokken would have been well advised if he had looked into the matter of the date as closely as possible. If he had done so, he would have discovered that the note was not written until a later time. In writing the note Seward put no date upon it. Somebody else has written upon the document in *pencil* "March 8, 1861 (?)." Mr. Lokken has completely disregarded the dubious character of the dating. The question mark, if nothing else, should have served to warn him that he was dealing with a document that called for most careful attention. The contents of the note show clearly that it could not have been written as early as March 8, 1861. In the note Seward gave the name of the man who took it to Lincoln, Mr. Baker, and described him as "disbursing Clerk to me." Baker, however, did not hold that post on March 8, 1861. He was appointed on March 12, when his predecessor was dismissed. It is therefore manifest that the note has no value as evidence for anything on March 8, 1861.

There is one piece of interesting and significant evidence bearing upon the character of the Seward illness on March 8, 1861, that Mr. Lokken has overlooked or disregarded. Two of the Confederate commissioners, Martin J. Crawford and John Forsyth, had already reached Washington. Their reports to the Confederate government at Montgomery are now in the Library of Congress. The one written on March 8 tells how their agent had gone to the State Department early in the day to get a memorandum that Seward was expected to have ready for them. Their report then continues: "On arriving there he learned that the Secretary of State was at home ill & that his physician had positively forbidden approach to him on any matter of business. Apprehending that it might be a *ruse* to gain time, we took every means to verify the fact of his illness & became satisfied that it was real & not feigned. Mr. Seward has caused his friends uneasiness by looking badly for some time past & is said to be now attacked with pleurisy."

One of the most intriguing incidents described in the diary is said to have happened on March 2, 1861. It has been often cited by historians and biographers of Lincoln. According to the diarist a group of Seward's friends had a meeting with Lincoln and made vigorous protest against any appointment of Salmon P. Chase as secretary of the treasury. As the diarist describes the meeting, Lincoln met the protesters in masterly fashion. In my book I have argued that almost to a certainty no such meeting took place. Mr.

Lokken argues that the meeting might have occurred as the diarist says it did.

Mr. Lokken in discussing the incident fails to see that the only basis for his argument is the diary itself and Ward H. Lamon's *Recollections of Abraham Lincoln.* The latter is represented as giving independent support to the former. Apparently Mr. Lokken did not make a personal examination of the Lamon book. Had he done so, he could scarcely have failed to discover that the author of the book has merely borrowed from the diary, copying from it almost word for word. Instead of two witnesses Mr. Lokken has only one and that one is the witness whose reliability is under discussion.[10]

Scattered through Mr. Lokken's arguments in regard to the . . . incidents are some surprising blunders. He puts Alexander Rives into a list of men that, he thinks, Seward was anxious to avoid meeting during the period March 7 to 11, 1861. If Seward was trying to escape meeting any of the men in the list, he was certainly not trying to avoid meeting Alexander Rives, for Rives, an influential member of the Virginia legislature, was a leader among the Virginia Unionists, a group of men with whom Seward was working hand in hand in his efforts to prevent the secession of Virginia. . . .

I regret to find that in one of his criticisms Mr. Lokken has resorted to a form of argument that I regard as unfair and highly deplorable. In the course of my search for the diarist I formulated and made some use of two lists of points of personality that the writer of such a diary would have possessed and which would in some degree be reflected in his production. One of the lists, consisting of eighteen points, was formulated and used during the early period of my search, and at a time when I still took the diary for what it purports to be. The other, of thirteen points, was used at a later period, i.e., after I had reached the conclusion that the diary is in part, at least, fictional. Mr. Lokken remarks in [a] footnote . . . : "A detailed study of the process by which Anderson transferred his criteria from the eighteen points to the thirteen is a

[10] Compare Ward H. Lamon, *Recollections of Abraham Lincoln* (Chicago, 1895), pp. 49–51, with the passage in the diary on which it is based. See Anderson, *The Mystery of "A Public Man,"* pp. 220–22.

revelation of his methodology. Lack of space forbids such a study here, but the reader will be well rewarded by an examination of *ibid.,* 52–60, 124–44." That is an argument by innuendo. It manifestly hints at some hocus pocus on my part, some serious departure from sound historical method. . . .

Mr. Lokken gives considerable space to Sam Ward but does not really come to grips with my arguments that Ward was the author of the diary. One of his arguments is that I did not make sufficient effort to discover friends and associates of Ward among the persons designated in the diary by symbols but not mentioned by name. He says there are "more than one hundred concealed identities in the diary." That is gross exaggeration. The actual number is about thirty-two or thirty-three. He must have made his estimate by counting the number of symbols, disregarding the numerous cases of repetition. His other contention is that mention in the diary of quite a number of persons on somewhat intimate terms with Ward merely showed that they and he moved in the same social circle. This overlooks the fact that the persons who can be identified as friends of Ward would not in all instances have been mentioned in the diary of anybody else. Some of them, of course, might have appeared in the diaries of other persons but not such a list as a whole. . . .

. . . Mr. Lokken's essay . . . does not put forward any good reason for questioning the validity of the conclusions at which I arrived.

Mr. Lokken also replied:

I am sorry that Dr. Frank Maloy Anderson has misunderstood the "tone and character" of my essay. My approach was that of a skeptic. In his book Dr. Anderson made positive statements about a subject important to students of the American Civil War. I attempted to show that many of his positive statements were open to question, that even "where he did present direct documentary evidence there remained, nevertheless, an element of doubt." I find nothing in his rejoinder that changes my mind.

Dr. Anderson accuses me of "argument by innuendo." Nothing was farther from my mind. The first draft of my essay was sixty-six pages long, and it contained a detailed analysis of the transition from the eighteen points to the thirteen points. In reducing this draft for publication, I reluctantly deleted the analysis, among other things, and substituted for it the footnote to which Dr. Anderson objects. That substitution was made against my better judgment.

Dr. Anderson introduces evidence which was not in his book—a letter from John Forsyth and Martin J. Crawford to Robert Toombs, dated March 8, 1861. This letter, hitherto unknown to me, does not prove, however, that Seward was too ill to receive visitors or to visit confidantes. In my essay I did not deny that Seward was ill. I suggested "that Seward may have used his illness from March 7 to March 11 for diplomatic purposes and that it may not have been as serious as appears on the surface." The Forsyth and Crawford letter includes hearsay evidence that Seward "is said to be now attacked with pleurisy." Pleurisy would not necessarily have prevented Seward from having visitors or going out on March 9. Evidence cited in my essay shows that he was not too ill to receive callers or to call at the White House on March 8 and 9. The date on the note from Seward to Lincoln, which I had no reason to question heretofore, is not essential to my suggestion that Seward might well have dropped in to see the diarist on March 9, for it was only one in a list of evidence cited by me in that connection.

Document No. 9002 in the Lincoln Papers was not "the sole basis" for my argument that the "Barney" in the diary was not necessarily Hiram Barney, as Dr. Anderson asserts. In my essay I suggested that George A. Barney, a New York city councilman, might also have been the diarist's "Barney." Ward H. Lamon, whose veracity Dr. Anderson questions, was a close associate of Abraham Lincoln in February and March, 1861. . . .

Dr. Anderson has given many years of meritorious service to the historical profession, and one of his contributions was to caution historians "against accepting on faith the details in a document when the authenticity and authorship of that document are in question." He went too far, however, when he claimed to prove that "The Diary of a Public Man" was a hoax perpetrated by Sam Ward. His rejoinder does not convince me that the mystery of

"A Public Man" is a finally solved research problem in the history of the American Civil War.

> The only verdict can be that of a Scots court, "Not proven." The escalation of care taken in the research into the identity of "A Public Man" nonetheless is a modern classic of its kind. Here the historian was as close to actual detective work as he is likely to come. Here his moments of triumph, hope, and woe, small as they were, and over an issue in itself perhaps small, are given homely testimony.

13. The Case of the Harried Scholars:

Of the World That Is Too Much with Us

ANOTHER SOURCE OF WOE TO THE SCHOLAR'S WORK IS the world. The world does not really care about history; scholars soon find that, like the men in Stephen Crane's "The Open Boat" who cursed the lighthouse that failed to help them, they must contend not so much with malevolence as with indifference. Most people do not care about historical research as such, although they may care about the economic value that attaches to some of the sources the historian must use. When economic value, disputes over some of man's most deeply held convictions, and international power politics all triangulate, as they did at the time of the discovery and first analysis of the so-called Dead Sea Scrolls, the historian still must contend with the minutiae of daily routines that have little to do with his research if much to do with his work. Some contend badly and some contend well, but it is safe to say that no scholar today can afford to live the abstracted and absent-minded life so often credited to him by that other group of hairy-chested writers, the Doers of Great Deeds (in fiction). The following selection speaks for itself on these points. It is from Millar Burrows' *The Dead Sea Scrolls,* on "the greatest manuscript discovery of modern times."

The scrolls have led to much rethinking of Old Testament problems and to wide speculation about the nature of early Christianity. Their story is an exciting one—one which this selection does not attempt to recount. I include the following passages, rather, to illustrate some of the practical problems that cross a scholar's path. The author was Director of the American School of Oriental Research in Jerusalem and, at the time he wrote, was also the Winkley Professor of Biblical Theology at Yale University's Divinity School. The essay serves to tell us something of the rôle of accident and the problem of communication in scholarship.

♦ ♦ ♦

If we had only known it when we went down to the shore of the Dead Sea on 25 October 1947, we could have walked to the cave where an extraordinary discovery of manuscripts had been made some seven or eight months earlier. Conducting field trips to study the archaeology and historical geography of Palestine was one of my duties as Director of the American School of Oriental Research at Jerusalem that year. This particular excursion, however, was not so much a scientific expedition as a pleasure trip and pilgrimage combined. At Kallia, near the north-western corner of the Dead Sea, some of our party took a swim in the thick brine before we proceeded to the traditional site of the baptism of Jesus and then back to Jerusalem by way of Jericho. In the party were two young scholars who will have a prominent part in this narrative, Dr. John C. Trever and Dr. William H. Brownlee, who were both students at our school that year on fellowships. At the time of our excursion the manuscripts, which were later to become famous, were already at Jerusalem in the possession of the Syrian Monastery of St. Mark and of the Hebrew University, but we at the American School of Oriental Research did not learn of their existence for another four months.

Because these manuscripts were found in a cave near the Dead Sea, they are commonly called the Dead Sea Scrolls. Father [R.] de Vaux of Jerusalem . . . protests that the scrolls did not come out of the Dead Sea. The name is convenient, however, and will be

---

FROM Millar Burrows, *The Dead Sea Scrolls* (New York: The Viking Press, Inc., 1955), pp. 3–17, 31–32.

used here. A more exact designation is the Wadi Qumran Manuscripts, but this does not cover the manuscript fragments found later at other places in the region.

Exactly when and how the first cave and its contents were discovered can hardly be determined now, though the discoverer, a fifteen-year-old boy of the Taamirah tribe of Bedouins, was identified and questioned about two years later. His name was Muhammad adh-Dhib. . . . It was probably in February or March 1947 that he found the scrolls. The Syrian Orthodox archbishop who sought some of them says that he first heard of them in the month of Nisan, which corresponds roughly to our month of April; and Father [J. P. M.] van der Ploeg of Nijmegen saw them at the Syrian Orthodox monastery late in July. According to one form of the story, Muhammad adh-Dhib was herding goats or looking for a lost sheep when he found the cave; according to another, he and one or two companions were taking goods, perhaps smuggled across the Jordan to Bethlehem. One story has it that they took refuge from a thunderstorm in the cave. Another story is that a runaway goat jumped into the cave, Muhammad adh-Dhib threw a stone after it, and the sound of breaking pottery aroused curiosity, whereupon he called another lad, and the two crawled into the cave and so found the manuscripts. . . .

Whenever and however the discovery came about, the cave, when first entered, contained several jars, most of them broken, with pieces of many others. Protruding from the broken jars were scrolls of leather wrapped in linen cloth. They were very brittle and rather badly decomposed, especially at the ends, but it was possible to see that they were inscribed in a strange writing. Muhammad adh-Dhib and his friends, the story goes, took these scrolls to a Muslim sheikh at their market town, Bethlehem. Seeing that the script was not in Arabic and supposing that it was Syriac, the sheikh sent them to a merchant who was a member of the Syrian Orthodox (Jacobite) community at Bethlehem, Khalil Eskander, who informed another merchant belonging to their church at Jerusalem, George Isaiah; and he in turn informed their Metropolitan-Archbishop, Athanasius Yeshue Samuel. In the meantime, if the late Professor [E. L.] Sukenik of the Hebrew University at Jerusalem was correctly informed, the great manuscript of the book of Isaiah, the largest and oldest of all the scrolls, had been offered to a Muslim antiquities dealer at Bethlehem for twenty pounds, but he, not believing that it was ancient, had refused to pay that much for it.

In the heart of the Old City of Jerusalem, just south of what the British and Americans call David Street, there is an interesting little monastery with a fine library of old Syriac manuscripts. This is the Syrian Orthodox Monastery of St. Mark. There is a tradition that it stands on the site of the house of Mark's mother, where the disciples were gathered for prayer when Peter came to them after his miraculous deliverance from prison (Acts 12: 12–17). A few years ago a Syriac inscription recording this tradition was found in the monastery. Here Khalil Eskander and George Isaiah brought one of the scrolls and showed it to Archbishop Samuel.

The archbishop recognized that the writing was not Syriac but Hebrew. After breaking off a little piece and burning it, he perceived by the odour that the material was leather or parchment. He told the merchants that he would buy the scrolls. Several weeks went by, however, before they could again get in touch with the Bedouins, who came to Bethlehem only for the weekly market on Saturday. It was not until the first Saturday of the month of Tammuz, which corresponds to July, that the Metropolitan received a telephone call from Khalil Eskander, the merchant in Bethlehem, saying that three Bedouins were there with the scrolls.

Even the archbishop did not see the Bedouins. Instead of coming with them, Eskander apparently sent them to George Isaiah, the Jerusalem merchant. He took them to the monastery but was refused admission, because the priest who met them at the door thought that their dirty, dilapidated manuscripts were of no interest. When the archbishop learned what had happened he telephoned in considerable perturbation to Eskander, who said that two of the Bedouins had returned and consented to leave their scrolls with him, but the third had decided to look elsewhere for a buyer and had taken his share of the scrolls to the Muslim sheikh at Bethlehem. It was presumably this portion that Professor Sukenik acquired in November for the Hebrew University.

Khalil Eskander told Archbishop Samuel further that when George Isaiah and the Bedouins were sent away from the monastery they proceeded to the square just inside the Jaffa Gate. Here they encountered a Jewish merchant who offered to buy the scrolls for a good price and asked the Bedouins to come to his office for the money. George Isaiah, however, persuaded them to refuse this offer.

Two weeks later the two Bedouins who had left their scrolls with Eskander at Bethlehem came back to his shop, and both he and George Isaiah went with them to St. Mark's Monastery. This time they succeeded in seeing the archbishop, and he bought the manuscripts still in their possession—five scrolls. Two of the five scrolls turned out to be successive portions of one manuscript, which had come apart. This was what I named later the "Manual of Discipline." The other three scrolls were the great manuscript of Isaiah . . . , a commentary on the book of Habakkuk, and a badly decomposed Aramaic scroll which at this writing has still not been unrolled. For some time we called this simply "the fourth scroll" (counting the two parts of the Manual of Discipline as one). After our return to America, Dr. Trever detached one column, and on the basis of its text identified the document tentatively as the lost book of Lamech; from then on we called it the Lamech Scroll.

At the suggestion of the archbishop, George Isaiah persuaded the Bedouins to take him to the cave, where he saw one whole jar and fragments of others, a mysterious piece of wood lying on a stone, and many fragments of manuscripts, as well as bits of cloth in which the scrolls had been wrapped. In August the archbishop sent one of his priests, Father Yusef, to examine the cave again. The idea of removing the whole jar still in the cave was considered but abandoned, because the jar was too heavy to carry in the intense summer heat of that region, more than a thousand feet below sea level.

During the course of the summer Archbishop Samuel consulted several scholars and showed his scrolls to a number of visitors at the monastery, hoping to gain accurate information concerning the contents, age, and value of the manuscripts. The first person consulted seems to have been a member of the Syrian Orthodox Church, the late Stephan Hannah Stephan, a well-known Orientalist, who was then working with the Department of Antiquities of

Palestine. He confidently pronounced the scrolls worthless. Since his special competence was in the field of Arab history rather than in Hebrew archaeology or paleography, his judgment in this case can only be attributed to general scepticism.

Archbishop Samuel also mentioned the scrolls to one of the scholars of the French Dominican School of Archaeology, Father A. S. Marmadji, another Arabist. It happened that an eminent biblical scholar from Holland, Father J. P. M. van der Ploeg, was then staying at the Dominican Monastery of St. Stephen, with which the School of Archaeology is connected. Father Marmadji therefore brought him to see the scrolls and the other manuscripts at the Syrian monastery. Father van der Ploeg at once identified the largest scroll as the book of Isaiah, being perhaps the first to make this identification.

Early in September, Archbishop Samuel took his scrolls to Syria and showed them to the Patriarch of his church at Homs. He tried also to consult the professor of Hebrew at the American University of Beirut, but found that he had not yet returned from his vacation. After returning to Jerusalem, the archbishop tried again to get information from Stephan Hannah Stephan, who at his request brought him some books about the Hebrew alphabet, but these did not give him much help. Still sceptical, Stephan offered to bring a Jewish scholar of his acquaintance, who, he said, was a specialist in such matters. Apparently this was Toviah Wechsler, who later took a prominent part in the public controversy concerning the scrolls.

Wechsler agreed with Stephan that the scrolls were not ancient. Archbishop Samuel quotes him as pointing to a table and saying, "If that table were a box and you filled it full of pound notes, you couldn't even then measure the value of these scrolls if they are two thousand years old as you say!" Later Wechsler decided that he had been misled by some marginal corrections in one of the manuscripts, which were written in ink still so black that he thought it could not be ancient.

Early in October, Archbishop Samuel showed his scrolls to Dr. Maurice Brown, a Jewish physician who had called at the monastery in connexion with the use of a building owned by the Syrian Orthodox community. Dr. Brown informed President Judah L.

Magnes of the Hebrew University, at whose request two men were sent to the monastery from the university library. After seeing the manuscripts, however, they suggested that someone from the university more competent than they were should be invited to examine the scrolls. Meanwhile Dr. Brown spoke to a Jewish dealer in antiquities named Sassun, who came and looked at the scrolls and suggested that pieces of them be sent to antiquities dealers in Europe and America, but this the Metropolitan was unwilling to do. . . . Sukenik, Professor of Archaeology at the Hebrew University, had been in America while all this was going on and did not hear of the manuscripts immediately when he returned to Palestine. On 25 November he was shown a fragment of a scroll by an antiquities dealer, who told him about the discovery of the cave and asked whether he would like to buy the scrolls. Although he naturally suspected forgery, Sukenik answered in the affirmative. Four days later he met the dealer again and bought from him some bundles of leather, together with two pottery jars in which the Bedouins claimed to have found the manuscripts.

On the very day that this purchase took place the General Assembly of the United Nations passed the fateful resolution recommending the partition of Palestine. Welcomed by the Jews but bitterly resented by the Arabs, this led to a rapid deterioration in the relations between Jews and Arabs, so that peaceful communication between them soon became impossible. Before this point was reached, however, Sukenik managed to bring his two jars from Bethlehem to the Jewish part of Jerusalem and to buy a few more portions of manuscripts. In this he was encouraged and assisted by President Magnes, who provided money for the purpose.

Up to this time Sukenik had not been informed of the scrolls acquired by the Archbishop Samuel. Early in December he learned about them from one of the men in the university library who had visited the monastery during the summer. Rightly supposing that these manuscripts probably belonged to the same collection as those he had purchased, Sukenik endeavoured to visit the monastery, but found that this was no longer possible. There the matter rested until the latter half of January, when he received a letter from a member of the Syrian Orthodox Church named Anton Kiraz, in whose property south of Jerusalem he had previously excavated an ancient tomb. Kiraz wrote that he had some old manuscripts which he would like to show to Sukenik.

Since by this time there was no going back and forth between the Arab and Jewish quarters, the meeting took place at the YMCA, located in what was then Military Zone B, to which passes could be secured for entry from other parts of the city. On seeing the scrolls, Sukenik recognized at once that they and the portions of manuscripts in his possession were indeed parts of the same collection. Kiraz admitted that they had been found in a cave near the Dead Sea, and said he had been to the cave. He offered to sell the scrolls to the Hebrew University and proposed a conference with the archbishop to discuss terms. Archbishop Samuel, however, says that all this was done without his consent or knowledge.

Kiraz allowed Sukenik to borrow three scrolls for two days, and Sukenik took this opportunity to copy several columns, which he later published, from the Isaiah manuscript. On 6 February, according to his account, he returned the scrolls to Kiraz and was shown two others, one or both of which belonged to the Manual of Discipline. It was agreed that there should be another meeting, and that President Magnes and Archbishop Samuel should be present, in order that negotiations for the purchase of the scrolls might be concluded. This meeting never took place.

Meanwhile Archbishop Samuel was making his own arrangements. One of the monks of St. Mark's Monastery, the late Butrus Sowmy, suggested that a trustworthy judgement concerning the scrolls might be obtained from the American School of Oriental Research. To this end he telephoned on 17 February to Bishop Stewart at the Collegiate Church of St. George and asked for the name of some person at the American School whom he might consult. I was absent from Jerusalem at the time, having left on the preceding Sunday for a visit to Iraq. It happened, however, that one of my students, Dr. William H. Brownlee, who was taking Arabic lessons at the Newman School of Missions, had found it necessary to obtain from a resident clergyman a statement certifying that he was a Christian, so that the Arab guards at the roadblocks would allow him to pass back and forth between our school and the Newman School of Missions. He had obtained this certificate from Bishop Stewart, who therefore thought of him at once and gave Sowmy his name, mentioning the fact that I had just left for Baghdad.

Accordingly on Wednesday, 18 February 1948, Butrus Sowmy telephoned to the American School of Oriental Research and asked for Brownlee. Shortly before the call came Brownlee had gone out to buy some wrapping paper for shipping his personal effects to America. The servant who answered the telephone told Sowmy, therefore, that Dr. Brownlee was not in the building, and that I was out of the city, but that Dr. John C. Trever was the Acting Director of the school in my absence. Trever was therefore called to the telephone and invited Sowmy to bring the manuscripts to the school the next day.

At two-thirty Thursday afternoon, as agreed, Butrus Sowmy and his brother Ibrahim came to the school with the scrolls. This time Brownlee had gone to the post office and had again been delayed through roadblocks, so that he missed this opportunity to meet the Syrians. Trever received them and looked at the scrolls, and with Sowmy's permission copied two lines from the largest scroll. Puzzled by the form of the Hebrew alphabet used in the manuscript, he compared it with the script of several old Hebrew manuscripts, as illustrated in a collection of Kodachrome slides which he had prepared. The manuscript whose writing seemed most like that of the scrolls was the Nash Papyrus, a fragment variously dated by different scholars from the second century B.C. to the third century A.D.

When Brownlee returned, Trever showed him the passage he had copied, which he had soon found to be the first verse of the sixty-fifth chapter of Isaiah. Others, as we have seen, had already identified this scroll as the book of Isaiah; one of the Syrians, indeed, said that he thought one of the scrolls was Isaiah, but Trever did not take the statement seriously because the Syrians could not read Hebrew, and he did not know then that other scholars had seen the manuscript.

The following morning Trever managed to get into the Old City and visit St Mark's Monastery, where Butrus Sowmy introduced him to the Archbishop Samuel. He was given permission to photograph the scrolls, and the archbishop and Sowmy agreed to bring them to the American School for that purpose. They also brought out the Isaiah manuscript, in order that Trever might see how much of the book of Isaiah it contained. Unrolling it with difficulty, he copied what seemed to be the beginning of the first column, which turned out to be the first verse of the first chapter of Isaiah.

The scrolls were brought to the school on Saturday, 21 February, and the two young scholars began the difficult task of photographing them. The following Tuesday afternoon, having completed the first stage of their task, Brownlee and Trever took the scrolls back to the monastery of the Old City. During the rest of the week the development of the negatives was completed, and prints were made from them. A few of the first prints made were sent to Professor William F. Albright of Johns Hopkins University, to get his judgement on the nature and age of the manuscripts. Prints of the Isaiah scroll and the two scrolls later identified as parts of the Manual of Discipline were made first. On Friday, 27 February, prints of another scroll were completed, which Brownlee discovered to be a commentary on the first two chapters of the book of Habakkuk. The contents of the other two scrolls were not determined until after I returned from Baghdad.

A complete set of the photographs was given to Archbishop Samuel. According to his account, it was after he received these that Kiraz asked his permission to show the scrolls to Sukenik at the YMCA. The Archbishop suggested, he tells us, that Kiraz take the photographs, but Kiraz protested that they were not large enough. This does not agree with Sukenik's statement that, after copying some of the Isaiah manuscript, he returned the scrolls to Kiraz on the sixth of February, three weeks before Trever's photographs were finished. How the discrepancy is to be resolved I do not know. In any case, Archbishop Samuel decided to retain possession of the scrolls and entrust their publication to the American School of Oriental Research, while Kiraz assured Sukenik that the Hebrew University would be given priority whenever the scrolls should be offered for sale.

Late Saturday afternoon, 28 February, our party returned to Jerusalem. To my relief I learned that there had been no trouble at the school during our absence, though there had been a frightful bomb explosion in the city, causing more than fifty deaths. My diary says: "Everything OK at the school, but John and Bill all excited over manuscripts at the Syrian Convent in script John thinks older than the Nash Papyrus, including the whole book of Isaiah, a text of Habakkuk with midrashic material in verse (so Bill says), and an unidentified composition resembling Wisdom Literature." The unidentified composition was, of course, the Manual of Discipline.

Monday morning, 1 March, I went with Trever to the monastery, after securing from the Arab Higher Committee a pass into the Old City, now carefully guarded at every entrance. At the monastery I met Archbishop Samuel and saw the scrolls. In a small fragment of the badly damaged fourth scroll which had come loose, my eye caught the word *'ar'ā,* and I remember exclaiming in surprise, "This is Aramaic!"

That afternoon we had our first class session on the Habakkuk Commentary. One of the courses I was giving was in epigraphy, and we agreed to devote the rest of our time in this course to the study of the scrolls.

The first photographs of the Isaiah scroll proved unsatisfactory because the limited amount of film at hand compelled Trever to photograph two columns on each sheet, and so the photographs were too small for adequate enlargement. It was therefore necessary to photograph the scroll again, but finding suitable film of the right size proved very difficult. The best that could be found was some outdated portrait film.

Under such circumstances it was remarkable that the photographs came out as well as they did. The plates in our subsequent publication of the Dead Sea Scrolls were made from these photographs. Critics of the publication who do not consider the reproductions satisfactory have not seen the manuscript itself. Some have said that the manuscripts should have been rephotographed after they were brought to the United States, but they were not then in our possession, and Archbishop Samuel was unwilling to have them photographed again.

Still the Aramaic scroll had not been unrolled. On Wednesday, 3 March, the archbishop gave Trever permission to attempt to open it; Butrus Sowmy, however, with some justification, was opposed to the undertaking, and it was postponed in the hope that it might be carried out later with better facilities in Europe or the United States.

On the morning of Thursday, 4 March, Mr. R. W. Hamilton, the Director of the Department of Antiquities, came to see me at the school. As I looked back on our conversation later, it seemed strange that the subject of the scrolls had not come up at all. Both Mr. Hamilton and I were just then much more concerned about other matters. The purpose of his call was to discuss plans for the administration of the Palestine Museum after the impending termination of the British Mandate.

The department, however, was not uninformed about the scrolls. It will be remembered that one of the first persons to see the manuscripts at St. Mark's Monastery was a member of the Department of Antiquities, Stephan H. Stephan. Mistakenly regarding them as useless, he apparently did not think it worth while to make any report to the department concerning them. Two years later Hamilton wrote to me that Stephan had never even mentioned the scrolls to him.

He was told about them by Trever, but at the time of their first conversation Trever did not yet know that the scrolls had been discovered within the past year. Archbishop Samuel and Sowmy, with characteristic caution, had talked vaguely at first about the manuscripts as being in the library of their monastery, leaving the impression that they had been there for about forty years, and Trever was still under the impression when he first discussed the scrolls with Hamilton. Not until 5 March was he told that the scrolls had been found in a cave only about a year earlier.

Soon thereafter this information was passed on to Mr. Hamilton. On 20 March Trever wrote to his wife: "I have already talked with Hamilton at the Museum about the proper procedure. He has given me permission to visit the place to gather up any loose materials left." On 27 February, the day before my return from Baghdad, Trever had spoken about the antiquities laws with the archbishop, who consequently relinquished a plan to visit the cave and assured Trever that he "would cooperate in every way possible with the American School of Oriental Research and the Department of Antiquities in carrying out the excavation of the cave."

My diary mentions a visit of Archbishop Samuel and Butrus Sowmy at the school on Monday, 8 March, after which I drove them back to the Allenby Square in the school's station wagon. My note continues, "Three or four cars, especially station wagons, have been stolen lately in broad daylight at the point of guns, though most politely, so we aren't eager to take ours out." Three days later the building of the Jewish Agency was damaged by explosives believed to have been brought in by an Arab using a car that belonged to the American Consulate.

Most of the entries in my diary during these weeks record shootings, explosions, and casualties in Jerusalem and in other parts of the country, with many rumours, like the one we heard on 15 March that our water supply had been poisoned. That same day, however, Trever received a reply from Professor Albright, confirming his judgement as to the age of the manuscripts and pronouncing the find "the greatest manuscript discovery of modern times."

On 18 March the archbishop called on me at the school, and Trever and I discussed with him several matters concerning the manuscripts. I expressed to him my conviction that the Isaiah scroll was the oldest known manuscript of any book of the Bible, and he was duly impressed. I also submitted for his approval a news release I had prepared. Having learned by this time that the manuscripts had been discovered in a cave near the Dead Sea, I felt that it would materially help us in establishing their age if we could visit the cave and find any remains of the jars in which they had been found. We therefore discussed with the archbishop the possibility of a trip to the cave. We talked also about plans for the publication of the manuscripts by the American Schools of Oriental Research.

My diary for 19 March says: "John saw the bishop again today and learned that Dr. Magnes was taking an interest in the manuscripts!" This was our first intimation of the negotiations between the Hebrew University and St. Mark's Monastery. We still knew nothing of the scrolls and fragments Professor Sukenik had acquired.

During the morning of the twentieth we went with guards sent by a good friend to the Haram, the sacred enclosure containing the Dome of the Rock. Here we met a man from the shrine of Nebi Musa, near the Jericho road, who said he could arrange for us a trip to the cave. We were to drive to Nebi Musa and proceed on foot to the cave, with a local Bedouin as guide. To our great disappointment, when the appointed day came the man who was to come for us did not put in an appearance. We were later told that the trip was considered too dangerous because Jewish troops were in training on the plain north and west of the Dead Sea. Who was really responsible for the frustration of our plan we shall probably never know, though we have our suspicions. We could not go by ourselves, and could not have found the cave if we had attempted it.

On 25 March, Archbishop Samuel told Trever that Sowmy was on his way with the manuscripts to a place outside Palestine. I myself had suggested that they were not safe in the monastery in the Old City, and Trever had mentioned the possibility of removing them to another Syrian Orthodox monastery down by the Jordan River. The soundness of these suggestions was demonstrated when St. Mark's Monastery was damaged by shell-fire and Butrus Sowmy himself was killed not many weeks later. The removal of the scrolls from the country, however, without an export licence from the Department of Antiquities, was illegal. How fully the archbishop realized this I cannot say; I know only that we tried to tell him. He had already, of course, taken the scrolls to Syria and back.

In all fairness it should be remembered that for many centuries Palestine had not had an independent government of its own, but had been ruled by one foreign power after another. Under such circumstances it was not unnatural that there was sometimes, even in high places, an attitude towards law which is not entirely unknown in the Western democracies. It should be said also, not as extenuating but as partly explaining what happened, that in March 1948 there was no longer any effective government in the country, and no peceptible prospect of any. The Department of Antiquities was still carrying on as best it could, but its major anxiety was to protect its treasures in the face of impending chaos. What the future would bring, both to Jerusalem and to the Dead Sea Scrolls, could not then be foreseen.

During the rest of the month of March we spent many hours in making arrangements for our trip home. Conditions were growing steadily worse. Facilities for transportation, communication, banking, and other needed services had reached a point where the word "facility" was no longer appropriate. On 27 March we held our last class, completing the first reading of the Habakkuk Commentary.

The next day, Easter Sunday, was one of the saddest days I can remember. An effort had been made to obtain a truce for the day, but it broke down completely. On Tuesday, 30 March, Brownlee departed for America. My wife and I left Jerusalem on 2 April but could not get away from Haifa for another two weeks. Trever, after a final conference with Archbishop Samuel and Butrus Sowmy on 3 April, went down to Lydda on the fifth and took a plane to Beirut. . . .

The discussion entered a new phase when the cave where the manuscripts had been found was rediscovered and excavated. Much of the controversy and doubt might have been obviated if the cave could have been immediately excavated or even inspected by competent archaeologists when the first scrolls were found. Not only was that impossible; the cave was visited several times by unauthorized and incompetent persons before any archaeologist knew of the discovery. In November or early December 1948, before order had been established in the country after the fighting of that year, unscrupulous individuals interested in nothing but plunder and gain cut a second opening into the cave, lower than the natural opening. They dug up the floor of the cave and threw some rubbish outside. An accurate description of the cave's condition and contents as first found by the Bedouins was thus rendered forever impossible.

"Forever impossible"; "forever lost"—these are among the saddest of refrains the historian can sing. Thankfully the limits of the impossible, and even of forever, are somewhat elastic. So, too, are the historian's methods, and the case studies of the applications of those methods are legion. We turn shortly to more of the best examples of those case studies, although a few general problems remain for exploration.

By now the message that the historian is by profession and probably by temperament a skeptic should be clear enough. This does not mean that he is a professional doubter, for if he did not believe that a strand of objective reality exists, he would scarcely continue to weave his tapestries. The historian does not bang his fist upon the table, only to shout that sense alone does not prove that the table is there, and he is a bit too unsophisticated to enjoy for long arguments about whether a falling tree makes any sound if no one but God is around to hear it. He can still be taken in, of course: not long ago an Ivy League university accepted a doctoral dissertation in American history, and an Eastern university press published that dissertation as a book, only to discover that the entire effort was a fabrication—evidence, footnotes, titles cited, all were awash in a sea of fiction. There were those in the guild who thought that the author, stripped of his degree, his book recalled from the stores by the press, and dismissed from his job, deserved a doctorate in creative writing as his least reward.

Of course, tastes change, in honesty as in obscenity and in historical interpretation. Immediately following the Civil War the victorious Northern historians ascribed the causes of that war almost entirely to the South and to the issue of slavery. Early in the present century and through the nineteen-thirties Charles A. Beard and others, under the impact of a growing awareness of the importance of economic forces in our history, said that the cause was the tariff, or Northern expansionism, or other drives less noble than a desire to free the slaves. By the late nineteen-thirties and through the forties, as historians discovered Freudian insights, they tended to hold the abolitionists—clearly fanatics ready to destroy an entire nation to accomplish their obsessive, ego-driven purposes—primarily responsible. Avery Craven, a distinguished historian of Southern birth teaching at the University of Chicago, was at the forefront of the attack. By the nineteen-fifties, however, as historians and the public at large became increasingly aware of the deeply entrenched patterns of discrimination practiced against the Negro throughout the nation, scholars began once again to emphasize slavery as the truly divisive issue. Arthur Schlesinger, Jr., demonstrated with crisp and aggressive logic[1] that one could factor out every other cause —the tariff, the abolitionists, the idea of a separate Southern national identity—and still argue that there would have been a Civil War. But one could not factor away slavery, the irreducible minimum to explain the pattern of causation. And now, as younger scholars discover that their commitments may not always lie parallel to those of their nation, as the civil-rights movements drain into the anti-Vietnamese War movement, there are those (brought together by Martin B. Duberman in his collection of original essays, *The Anti-Slavery Vanguard: New Essays on the Abolitionists* [Princeton, 1965]) who see the abolitionists not as fanatics but as courageous men who stood firm for their beliefs. Even Professor Craven, in a second look at his now classic work, *The Coming of the Civil War,* called *An Historian and the Civil War* (Chicago, 1964), has softened the harsh colors of his portraits.

Thus, as Allan Nevins has remarked, every generation must rewrite its own history, for each generation wishes to draw from the past meanings that will help bring some order into the chaos of the present. Evidence cannot, therefore, be considered as firm but only as indicative, for it may be read in several different ways—as Becker and Woodward warned us. Even so astute a historian as Allan Nevins can be hoist by his own petard, for elsewhere in the essay of his we have read he forgets that each generation will write its own history. On the question of obscenity he suggests that we need not read either Pepys or Franklin exactly as they wrote, for omitting their boisterous vulgarities "does [history] no violence." Yet those vulgarities now appear in the multi-volume edition of the Franklin Papers coming forth from the Yale University Press under the hands of Leonard W. Labaree, and no one blushes. Franklin stands forth, for our generation at least, as a

[1] See Arthur Schlesinger, Jr., "The Causes of the Civil War: A Note on Historical Sentimentalism," *Partisan Review,* XVI, (October, 1949), 969–81.

man of considerably more flesh and blood. Nevins probably was not envisioning the day when one could dull one's senses with *Myra Breckinridge, Portnoy's Complaint* (both, surely—despite the sentimentalism of those critics who must show that they, too, have hair on their chests, even though they may need to wear hair shirts to sustain the illusion—appallingly bad books), or with the crudities—to return, at least to the periphery, of detective fiction—of Mickey Spillane's Mike Hammer and Tiger Mann.

The historian cannot always go to the treasure house. Sometimes he must go to such dunghills, too. For what is obscenity to a judge in Boston may, sentimentalism aside, be merely another kind of evidence to the historian. Too often, otherwise realistic well-researched biographies read like those Victorian novels in which the heroine, with no reference to man's primal act, brings forth a child without apparent pregnancy during the preceding months. If some men are as harried and broken today by their sexual drives as they appear to be, or as novelists (and especially the new cult of spy-writers, such as Len Deighton and Noel Behn) would have us believe, then were Gladstone and Disraeli, Jefferson and Hamilton, Caesar and Alexander, without sexual selves? Caesar, after all, if we may except Venerable Authority, appears to have cared that his wife be pure. But what little that historians have written of the history of sex is poor, most of it properly to be sold by those tiny but thriving houses that specialize in "esoterica" in their book catalogues. There is no work of history yet (and I include Gordon Rattray Taylor's foragings) that need be mailed in a plain envelope.

How the historian can deal with man's sexual energies forms a theoretical chapter in itself, one not included here but worthy of comment. I should be as ready as any other emancipated American to provide an extract from the pornographers under the guise of scholarship, for Harper & Row is as eager to see sales thrive as I am, but while the provenance of pornography presents a legitimate historical question, and indeed so, too, does the material itself, a diligent (and on occasion pleasurable) search has revealed nothing quotable.

Some dirty books are merely dirty after all. These we may set aside, unless we are pretending to be students of the mind of our age, in which case we may justify reading the sports page of the newspaper, comic books, the *Blue Book* of the John Birch Society, the *Watchtower,* and the *American Scientist* as well. I know one historian who reads the *Yale Daily News* because, he says, he must keep alert to the mind of the student. One might have thought such alertness was best gained in the classroom, but one man's rationalization is another man's pleasure, and some dirty books also are fun (parts of Henry Miller, for example, or Chester Himes).

And some dirty books do tell the historian something of value. *The Memoirs of a Woman of Pleasure,* usually known as *Fanny Hill,* by John Cleland, contains not one offensive word and tells us quite a bit about the eighteenth century. H. Spencer Ashbee's (if it is his) *My Secret Life* is clearly obscene, but I know of no book which so reveals how sex was a commodity in publicly virtuous Victorian Britain, or which shows so nakedly the great gulf between the classes. Nor could we dismiss the value of the famous erotic carvings at Khajuraho, in India, any more than we can overlook the phallic carvings of the Maori, so revealing of their assumptions about the Creation, or the *linga* throughout South and Southeast Asia.

There are minds that would suppress these, however, and thus the historian is faced with yet another task: to hunt out the evidence for man's sexual and thus family mores without appearing to be merely another dirty old man in search of kicks. For while manuscripts and prints have been suppressed for many reasons, no other reason than obscenity has kept them suppressed. Heretical writings of a new religious order may be scourged from out of the land, but there will always be a monastery, or a believer, who will preserve them for posterity, one day to be dug up like the Dead Sea Scrolls. Pornography alone is most likely to be destroyed rather than kept, and those few who keep it are most unlikely to admit to the fact.

Of course, pornography, scatological political pamphlets, and heretical religious tracts are not the only kinds of material that have a tendency to disappear from the public eye. So, too, does junk, at least as the lay reader would interpret the term: old telephone directories, book dealers' catalogues, old cookbooks, high-school newspapers, the instruction manuals from old dishwashers. Such types of materials have their potential uses to historians, however, for the first two are organized around names—and often the historian has only a name to go on—while the third and fourth are organized in terms of activities which the historian may wish to reconstruct for a past age. The last will tell the historian of the future something of the domestic technology of the present. If only the men who set up the great stone statues on Easter Island, or the megaliths at Stonehenge, had left us with a manual! The historian, as a result, becomes something of a pack rat. He may not wish to keep such ephemera himself, nor may he want his own university library to be burdened with a 1936 telephone directory for Cut Bank, Montana, but he will hope that some library, somewhere, is specializing in just such material and publicizing the fact. A chief source of woe to the historian is the admittedly overburdened librarian who can see no reason at all to keep the 1936 sewer inspection report for Bishop's Stortford (Herts.), and therefore consigns it to a pulping machine. And therein arises the irrational, vital love-hate relationship between librarian and historian, between scholar and technology. There is the passion of the historian revealed: to preserve that he might know. "Forever impossible"; "forever lost"—much of the past will be lost as the dry selvages disappear behind us. Happily, however, much has not disappeared either, and more than enough work continues to greet the historian each day, as the following case studies will show.

PART IV

THE CASE METHOD

14. The Case of the Needless Death:

Reconstructing the Scene

TANGIBLE EVIDENCE, AS IT ARISES FROM DOCUMENTARY sources, must be read against the intangible evidence of a man's actions. Historians frequently caution their students, "Do not look alone at what a man says; look at what he does." The advice is simple enough, even simple-minded in the proper meaning of those much-abused words. The application is much harder, for it involves a series of tiny leaps of faith across often narrow but nonetheless deep chasms of supposition. So does any method of gathering and evaluating evidence, for our value judgments are shaped by our own experience with human nature. Trite phrases notwithstanding, human nature does change, so the historian must be slow to read into another age the motivations of his own—even the surfacing of biological urges, triggered by the cultural environment as they may be. To answer Who, What, When, Where, and How, the first five of the reporter's standard questions, is much easier than to tell Why, not alone because the five questions must be answered before the sixth can be raised.

Some historians balk at the jump between data and conclusion and are content, they say, to "let the record speak for itself." But no record, historian's or politician's, speaks for itself; the records are silent, and the historian who does not venture out onto at least the nearer shores of human motivation is little more than an antiquarian, a grubber after facts for their own sake. Most historians probably would agree with this. The question, then, is what limits does the individual historian place upon interpretation? How wide a gap between data and conclusion will his faith permit him to leap? And does his faith force him to distort, however slightly, the record itself or to play unfairly with the reader by suppressing some portion of the record, either his own or his subject's? The gap must not be too wide, of course, for one must argue from the evidence. Nonetheless, one must come to know the subject of one's study from within, living with the subject as intimately and as long as other sanctions will permit.

To me the following essay represents a brilliant example of just how far the historian can go in reconstructing the motivations behind past deeds. Professor J. C. Beaglehole, O.M. of Victoria University in Wellington, New Zealand, is the world's leading authority on the exploration of the South Pacific. He has devoted a major portion of his life to editing the journals of Captain James Cook, the great British explorer whose own detective work first opened up the major expanses of the Pacific to our knowledge. Cook died under somewhat mysterious circumstances on the fourteenth of February, 1779, while ashore on the main island of the present Hawaiian group. Beaglehole reconstructs the scene for us.

♦ ♦ ♦

On 9 October 1784 William Cowper wrote to his friend the Rev. John Newton. He had lately finished reading the three quarto volumes entitled *A Voyage to the Pacific Ocean . . . for Making Discoveries in the Northern Hemisphere,* which were at last in that year given to an impatient public. "The reading of those volumes afforded me much amusement, and I hope some instruction," wrote the poet. "No observation, however, forced itself upon me with more violence than one, that I could not help making on the death of Captain Cook. God is a jealous God, and at Owhyhee [Hawaii] the poor man was content to be worshipped. From that moment, the remarkable interposition of Providence in his favour was converted into an opposition, that thwarted all his purposes. . . .

Nothing, in short, but blunder and mistake attended him, till he fell breathless into the water, and then all was smooth again. The world indeed will not take notice, or see, that the dispensation bore evident marks of divine displeasure; but a mind I think in any degree spiritual cannot overlook them . . . —though a stock or stone may be worshipped blameless," concludes Cowper, "a baptized man may not. He knows what he does, and by suffering such honours to be paid him, incurs the guilt of sacrilege."[1]

It is unlikely that many will be prepared to accept this explanation of what seemed to contemporaries so tremendous an event; though it should be pointed out that to the servants in Hawaii of the American Board of Commissioners for Foreign Missions the Cowperian line of reasoning, independently adopted, was very persuasive. I admit for a beginning that I am not so persuaded myself, though if I were, I think I should have the reservation that Jehovah should have been a little more perceptive of the circumstances. For though the facts are fairly simple, the circumstances are extremely complicated. Circumstances are also facts. Circumstances indeed may become the essential facts.

What then were the facts, commonly considered? They are so well known that perhaps I should blush to recount them. On 17

FROM J. C. Beaglehole, "The Death of Captain Cook," *Historical Studies: Australia and New Zealand,* XI (October, 1964), 289–305. Reprinted with the permission of the author.

For additional reading: Perhaps the most obvious parallel to Cook's death, as a problem in historical reconstruction, is the massacre of General George Armstrong Custer at the Battle of the Little Big Horn in 1876, on which many books have been written, the best by Edgar I. Stewart, *Custer's Luck* (Norman, Okla., 1955). In a rather different vein, a striking work of historical reconstruction which is, in fact, "psychohistory," is Robert Jay Lifton's *Death in Life: The Survivors of Hiroshima* (New York, 1968). Since reconstructing the crime is the oldest form of mystery fiction known—from Edgar Allan Poe's "The Murders in the Rue Morgue" in 1841 to John D. Macdonald's *Pale Gray for Guilt* in 1968—it would be invidious as well as impossible to single out a presumed classic in the genre. An enjoyable—and unusual—recent book is *Murder's Burning,* by S. H. Courtier, set in a part of the Australian outback which I have visited. While the account collapses in the end, the first two-thirds are the best example of the detective as historian that I know.

[1] Thomas Wright, ed., *Correspondence of William Cowper* (London, 1904), II, 249–50.

January 1779, after a hard season on the north-west coast of America and in the Bering and Arctic seas, Cook put into Kealakekua Bay, on the western side of the island of Hawaii, for refreshment and the overhaul of his two ships *Resolution* and *Discovery*. He was enthusiastically received by the Hawaiians. He himself was at once the recipient of divine honours; he was granted the use of a *heiau,* or religious enclosure, for his observatory tents; his officers and men were popular and could wander and explore where they liked in perfect safety, and aided in every possible way; women were kind; there was great trade in every sort of provisions the island grew, at generous rates of exchange, ironware being the article most in demand on the native side. The only drawback was the assiduity with which the people stole—stole anything, but more particularly, again, anything of iron. The supply of provisions was not quite so lavish by the time the ships departed, on 4 February; for the British numbered 180, and they were no small eaters. Two days later, as they worked up the northern coast of the island, the weather turned squally, and on the 8th the head of the foremast was found sprung. After some deliberation about possible harbours for its repair Cook rather reluctantly—because he feared he might have outworn his welcome—decided to put back to the known convenience of Kealakekua Bay; and there he anchored again on the morning of the 11th. Greetings were not as warm as before, but they were warm enough. The mast was taken on shore. The struggle against theft was resumed. On the 13th there was a first scene of violence. During the succeeding night the *Discovery's* cutter was stolen. As this was a serious loss, Cook decided to get the ruling chief on board as a hostage for the boat's return, and went on shore with a body of marines early in the morning to do so. It could not be done; the Hawaiians took to arms in large numbers and on both sides tempers rose; Cook shot a man; and in walking down to his boat to re-embark he was himself killed.

A simple tale. No one can impugn its truth. But *why?* What were the circumstances? Cook had taken hostages before, repeatedly, peacefully, successfully; it was standard and proven practice with him, he had done it earlier on this voyage. When, once, he adopted a different policy, which involved much destruction of native property, some of his puzzled officers asked why: why did he not take a hostage, instead of doing such needless damage? Was this, asked those who had not sailed with him before, the Cook whose reputation for humanity stood so fabulously high? Why, again, now marines?—he had never used marines before. Cook had been annoyed with his own men the afternoon before at their getting into a mess: then why did he get into this fatal mess himself? Why, after spending so many energies on three long voyages on keeping his men out of situations in which bloodshed must be inevitable—why, after hammering into them elementary respect for native susceptibilities and elementary precautions against unpleasant surprise, should he himself misjudge precaution, fall victim to lack of foresight? Was lack of foresight the trouble, or did he fall victim rather to undervaluing a potential enemy . . . ? Are lack of foresight and undervaluing your potential enemy the same thing? Why did Cook lose his temper at the precise moment he did, and shoot a man at the most unfavourable of all times? Why did he lose his temper at all? Why, if he were looked on as a god, did the Hawaiians proceed to kill their god? Are we indeed absolutely certain of even our most elementary facts? I may point out that though we have a vast amount of reporting of that incident at Kealakekua Bay, we have only one report, a very brief one, from a person [Molesworth Phillips] who actually was with Cook, and that that person did not actually see Cook fall. "The business was now a most miserable scene of confusion," he said of it as it rose to its climax.[2] The historian's curse is upon us: we are faced by the old difficulty of seeing clearly the dramatic, the emotional, the critical, swift-moving moments in history. I add that we have no direct account from the Hawaiian side at all that we can repose faith in, and no traditionary account that was not given to the Hawaiians decades later by missionaries from Massachusetts. So if we say that a vast irony broods over the whole scene, as I have always thought, and still think, it is an irony of different sorts. . . . But let me now ignore the irony and the poetry, and the tears, and

[2] Molesworth Phillips, the lieutenant of marines, from his report as given in Clerke's journal, P[ublic] R[ecord] O[ffice, London], Adm[iralty] 51/1561, entry for 14 February 1779.

see if, in attempting to answer my own questions, I can make our simple tale really intelligible: see if circumstances do in any way become essential facts.

First, without taking my questions in order as I asked them, let us look at Cook himself. Obviously, at the moment of crisis, he lost control, and the reason for this loss must lie partly in his own character. He had, one must note, lost control on an earlier occasion, but this was in his prentice days as a diplomat, in Poverty Bay in New Zealand, October 1769. With the best will in the world, he had attempted to stop a canoe-load of fishermen, to make their closer acquaintance, but had miscalculated his means. Maoris had been killed, Cook had suffered much from remorse;[3] and from that time forward he doubled and redoubled his guard against bloodshed. When driven to hostilities, he preferred to inflict fright rather than death. He preferred to use small shot rather than ball; generally speaking, his men were under the most stringent orders in this matter. Disobedience incurred his rage, and his rage was formidable. The eighteenth century lower-deck seaman was no great respecter of the blood of other people, had no great plans in view, was not gifted with foresight, got into a scuffle with remarkable facility, had no sense of responsibility when it came to the transmission of the deadly disease he carried with him, no sense—one sometimes thinks—whatever. It is one of Cook's great achievements, therefore, though not a much publicised achievement, to have kept these men so much out of trouble. It is an important point, for trouble with them in any island entailed trouble with the islanders, and that sort of trouble might imperil a whole voyage. Cook's own first approaches to native peoples were perhaps not thought out as a system, but they were instinctively highly intelligent; he put weapons and companions behind him, was transparently friendly as well as interested, carried at once the air of authority and of goodwill. This is as true for his third voyage as for any time previously. But in other ways there is a change.

I think one can put it best by saying that on this voyage Cook was a tired man. He would himself undoubtedly have rebutted the remark, and none of his officers seems to have made it. I am there-

[3] *Journals of Captain James Cook,* I, ccx–ccxii, and 170–71 [edited by J. C. Beaglehole].

fore proposing the result of much reading between the lines. He may have seemed to those around him unchanged: his physique was magnificent, he had on this voyage none of the sickness of his previous one, which had caused his life to be despaired of; his conduct of the voyage, for its prime purpose of geographical discovery, his seamanship, under the difficult conditions of the American north-west coast and the ice-ridden arctic seas, seemed to those officers as admirable and masterly as ever. We have records of their admiration. Yet we can point to a time when the ships were saved from piling up on the Aleutian coast in fog only by startlingly good luck, after a piece of blind navigation that a modern commission of enquiry would examine with the most acute horror.[4] We have a man tired, not physically in any observable way, but with that almost imperceptible blunting of the brain that makes him, under a light searching enough, a perceptibly rather different man.

Consider Cook, in July 1775, at the end of that wonderful second voyage, in his forty-eighth year. For the last seven of those years he had been, we may say, at the full stretch of human endeavour—except for the leisure (we do not know how much it was, but it must have been little enough) he could snatch between voyages. The fitting out of the *Resolution* was in itself a matter of extreme worry. For years he had been subject to every possible strain of body and mind and spirit, varying from the demands of antarctic navigation to those of his relations with a whole series of hitherto unknown peoples; he had, to give a brief geographical judgment, got not merely New Zealand and Australia but most of the Pacific into order, and a good part of the South Atlantic as well. Sick or well, his faculties in the management of men had been drawn on to the utmost. He arrived home and was given a captaincy in Greenwich Hospital—"a fine retreat and a pretty income," he said[5]—which he accepted on condition that he would be called on for work whenever he seemed the right person for it. He never went to Greenwich: he had on his hands the publication of the journal of

[4] Cook's *Journal,* B[ritish] M[useum] Egerton MS 2177A, 26 June 1778. It was off the south-east end of Unalaska. Compare [Charles] Clerke's wry comment, P.R.O. Adm 55/23, for that date: "very nice pilotage, considering our perfect Ignorance of our situation."

[5] Cook to John Walker, 19 August 1775, *Journals,* II, 960.

his second voyage, and no one who has studied the manuscripts will deny the work entailed in that; and he had the preparations for the third voyage. Why, one is tempted to cry out in indignation, couldn't they leave him alone? If the North-west Passage had to be discovered, and Cook was the heaven-sent commander, could it not be left for a year or two? The Admiralty, in fact, did have some sense of shame. They could not in decency give an order, could not ask Cook to go out again at once—even if he had laid himself open to it. But they were not above plotting a stratagem, not above asking for advice from a man they were pretty certain could be made a volunteer. The famous dinner-party was held, the project was described, the advice was asked, the man volunteered.[6] No doubt, among the other aspects of the voyage touched upon, the £20,000 prize for the first ship to discover the Passage was mentioned; and it is certain that Cook, who lived on his pay, included in his duty his duty to his wife and family. It is doubtful if that was needed to move him, the case being put as it was.[7] So, to the labours of authorship . . . were added those of preparing his ship for another voyage; and if we consider what press of work there was in the royal dockyards in 1776, and the nature of their corruption, we do not need to be surprised that in that work there were inadequacies, whatever Cook's demands. I feel fairly certain, in sum, that Cook should have been forbidden to go on the voyage, or else the voyage should have been postponed.

There is no doubt about it—I make the point again—that this third voyage was technically a great achievement, though from the nature of things it was doomed to failure, and Australians and New Zealanders tend to think of it mainly as a frame for the last great picture, the slaying of Cook. Nonetheless its details are fascinating, however laborious to follow. Where is the significant detail, the evidence of what I have called the rather different man? I have

[6] Andrew Kippis, *Life of Captain James Cook* (London, 1788), pp. 324–25.

[7] "It is certain I have quited an easy retirement, for an Active, and perhaps Dangerous Voyage[.] My present disposition is more favourable to the latter than the former, and I imbark on as fair a prospect as I can wish. If I am fortunate enough to get safe home, theres no doubt but it will be greatly to my advantage." Cook to John Walker, 14 February 1776, Dixson Library [Sydney] MS.

given one little bit already. It would not be fair to adduce Cook's miscalculation of the winds after he left New Zealand at the end of February 1777, which cost him a whole season, because he was working on his previous experience, and his previous experience was simply not repeated. I cannot think that the Cook of the second voyage, however, if on the coast of Tasmania, would not have taken the chance to test [Tobias] Furneaux's conclusion, that Tasmania was joined to Australia—a conclusion different from that of more than one of Furneaux's subordinates.[8] Again, would the younger Cook, if at Tonga with plenty of time at his disposal, and hearing of the existence of Fiji and Samoa within three or four days' sail—seeing the so different Fijians among the Tongan crowd—have been content to take these islands on trust? Would he not at least have made an eager reconnaissance, got some valuable positions down on the chart, related the two groups to the rest of the island systems? Might he not—though I ask this with hesitation—have gained a little more clarity about some of the features of the American coast south of Nootka Sound? Certainly it was not his stated business to do so, but Cook had never been one to confine his attention to stated business. A piece of business, unfinished, and much more curious, was that over St. Lawrence Island, in the Bering Sea, first named by Bering himself. It is not a large island. Cook sighted it four times, in foggy and snowy weather, in August and September 1778, and thought it was three different islands, and possibly four. He does not seem to have suspected that any of his longitudes were wrong, in spite of the awful conditions for observation. Can anyone doubt that the Cook of four or five years earlier would have both suspected and solved the problem, whatever the conditions, as a matter of course?

What, you may ask, has all this to do with Cook's death? A good deal, I answer—if it is, as I suggest it is, evidence of a mind that has through weariness lost its finest edge. Let us turn to his dealings with men. One of the things that emerge clearly about him in his previous voyages is his understanding of the genus *Seaman,* his practical wisdom as a psychologist, his readiness to forgive and to expunge the record of offence. The evidence of this third voyage is not so clear. At Tahiti he made a tactful speech and got his crew's

[8] *Journals,* II, 153 and nn; 165.

willing agreement to do without their grog for the moment, so that they should not go short in the cold future. Few commanders could have registered that sort of success. But later on, tactful speeches gave place to the uncompromising order. There was, for example, the matter of walrus meat in the arctic. Fresh food it was, certainly; invaluable food; and unfamiliar. Cook could eat anything. His taste, thought one of his midshipmen, "was, surely, the coarsest that ever mortal was endued with."[9] Walrus, however, made some men vomit: very well, then, they could live on their scanty allowance of bread, and "complaints and murmurings" had to rise to a very considerable pitch before he would give them back their familiar salt beef. There was a fierce row over sugar-cane beer as a substitute for grog, off the Hawaiian islands in December 1778. The crew wrote Cook an expostulatory letter. Sugar-cane beer or water it was to be, said Cook, . . . and flogged the cooper, who had started a cask of the decoction which had turned sour.[10] He had found easier ways before out of such an impasse as this; conservative seamen had not before been so unequivocally referred to in his journal as "my mutinous turbulent crew." I have mentioned a flogging. It was a flogging age, and Cook was a man of his age. There is no burking the fact that Cook the humanitarian flogged. I have kept no statistics, but I have the very strong impression that he did so more severely on this voyage than before.

Certainly the islanders suffered more in this way; and for the old cause, theft. Polynesians thieved enthusiastically and with the utmost skill—by day, by night, surreptitiously, brazenly, by way of highway robbery mingled with assault or with a bold *insouciance* that almost calls forth admiration. In the Tongan islands they stole tools, muskets, a quadrant, all Captain [Charles] Clerke's cats. The things they stole, from New Zealand to Hawaii, are beyond computation. Other people stole too: at Nootka Sound Cook's gold

[9] James Trevenen, midshipman *Resolution,* note on *Voyage,* II, 457. This was one of a series of notes that Trevenen wrote on the *Voyage.* I have used the copy of these notes now among the MSS in the Archives of British Columbia.

[10] P.R.O. Adm 51/4559/212; 10, 11, 12 December 1778. For the 12th, ". . . At the same time ye Captn address'd ye Ships Company, telling them He look'd upon their Letter as a very mutinous Proceeding & that in future they might not expect the least indulgence from him." The letter was partly about short allowance of provisions, which Cook rectified.

watch went, but was recovered; at Prince William Sound they tried to steal the *Discovery.* To Cook, for some reason, these last seemed venial offences. Tongan and Tahitian offences he appears to have put in a different category, probably because they went on over so long a period, day after day and week after week. At Tonga in particular, Cook was irritated, exasperated—one might say, were one not trying to be scrupulously accurate in analysis, almost driven out of his mind. No careful forethought on his part, no stringent regulations for the conduct of his officers or punishment for careless men, could keep the robbers at bay. When they were taken he flogged: a dozen lashes were succeeded by two dozen, two dozen by three, four and five. He had arms slashed with a cross; he cropped ears. The humane among his own people were disquieted, and registered their disquiet in their journals. In spite of all this his relations with the ruling chiefs were on the whole excellent; with most of their subjects he seems to have got on well enough. He was "as ready to hear the Complaint of an Indian and to see justice done to him when injured, as he was to any of his own men, which equitable way of proceeding rendered him highly respected & esteemed by all the Indians," writes [David] Samwell the surgeon.[11] We have not a corresponding Tongan witness. When [Bruni] D'Entrecasteaux called at Tongatapu in 1793 and told them of Cook's death some wept; others, alas, remembered him for cruelty.[12] We can hardly regard as other than cruel his punishment meted out to the unfortunate people of Moorea for their failure to return punctually a wretched goat that had been stolen. The burning of houses, and far worse, of twenty-five great war-canoes may seem an immoderate measure to take: "a troublesome, and rather unfortunate affair," wrote Cook in his journal, after somewhat understating the destruction, "which could not be more regreted on the part of the Natives than it was on mine."[13] Once again some of his officers were disquieted.

Cook, we know, was a passionate man. He stamped and swore on his deck, and his midshipmen were accustomed to refer to his

[11] David Samwell, "Some Account of a Voyage to South Seas," B. M. Egerton MS 2591, f 61 v.

[12] J. J. H. de Labillardière, *Account of a Voyage in Search of La Pérouse* (London, 2nd ed., 1802), II, 149–50, 181–82.

[13] *Journal,* 10 October 1777.

rages as his "heivas," after the expressive Tahitian dance: "the old boy has been tipping a heiva" at someone. It is from the third voyage that we pick up this anecdote,[14] though in the captain's previous journals we can remark traces of annoyance, most of which has been scrupulously removed before the record has been submitted to the Admiralty. The evidence, I think, is of a man who knows his own failing, and is reluctant that others should suffer from it. Necessary naval discipline is another thing, and he is not upset that midshipmen should think him stern. He is determined to be just, even if he begins by being hasty. In technical matters he has been cautious and deliberate, taking risks only when he has had to, or when he has been able to calculate them professionally. Rage, on the other hand, is not a thing one can calculate. Under the strain of continued responsibility for his men, continued planning, continued wrestling with the fundamental problem of his voyage, continued meeting of geographical and nautical and human emergencies, Cook might, had his physical and mental constitution been less powerful, have gone limp. He did not go limp; but, I have argued, he was, perhaps without knowing it, tired. . . .

We may therefore return to Kealakekua Bay with all these considerations in mind, and look as closely as possible at the narrower circumstances of Cook's last hours. Before we do that, however, let me clear out of the way two or three misapprehensions that gained great currency during the course of the nineteenth century—largely, I think, from the somewhat anti-British, American-missionary writers who imposed a tradition on the Hawaiians themselves, or from students of Polynesian culture whose learning was not quite adequate enough. Cook has not, on the whole, had a very good press in Hawaii. It has been suggested, first of all, that somehow Cook became involved in the distress of the lower order of Hawaiians, that his fate was, to put it in rather dubious terms, a function of class-structure. The class-structure of Hawaii was one of chiefs, priesthood, and commoners, the last oppressed and exploited as commoners have always been. Cook came and was hailed as a god, by a priesthood always alive to the main chance; his presence played into their hands, and vast quantities of provisions were virtually extorted from a groaning populace to feed not simply the

[14] Trevenen, note on *Voyage,* II, 283.

stomachs of alleged deities, but the prestige of their professional servants. Naturally, in due course, when the oppressed ones saw the gods at a disadvantage, they rose; and Cook, having accepted undue and unexpected exaltation, incurred a just-as-little-expected retribution. The trouble about this theory is that there is no evidence to support it. It is true enough, I think, that Cook was taken for the god Lono. It would occupy too long a time to argue the matter; but I cannot see that the populace suffered in his presence, or in his return, an insupportable burden. Nor, in the end, were all the priests on his side, nor all the laity against him. Supplies of food were not a forced tribute; they were bought in fair enough trade. The theory omits the nature of the Polynesian mind: it is a liberal-European theory, circa 1830; or perhaps one might say, bearing in mind its inventors, a Jacksonian democratic theory.

Another attempt to account for the unpopularity, supposedly growing, of the visitors, is a more directly theological one. On 1 February, the *Resolution* being short of firewood, Cook asked Lieutenant [James] King to see if he could buy the paling round the *heiau* where the observatory was set up, a paling interspersed with carved images. King succeeded in doing so, and the paling, not in good repair, was taken off, together with a variety of these images. Now here was a shocking piece of vandalism, say the critics, a monstrous affront to Hawaiian religion, a deliberate overriding of *tapu,* a forcing of the people into a signal act of impiety. How could Cook make himself so guilty, or expect that such guilt could go unrequited by a people devoted to their gods?[15] The criticism is founded on ignorance. It was the paling Cook wanted, not the images, and Hawaiians themselves had been seen removing pieces of it. Neither this sort of fence nor an image that formed part of it was regarded by Hawaiians as sacred; either could be burnt. King was a tactful man and consulted the priests, and certain images from the *heiau* itself, which they regarded as important and were *tapu,* were carefully preserved. There was no affront to religion, there was indeed less destruction than the ordinary Ha-

[15] The origin of this theory seems to have been John Ledyard's book, *A Journal of Captain Cook's Last Voyage to the Pacific Ocean . . .* (Hartford, Conn., 1783), pp. 136–37. The thing is a worthless production which nevertheless managed to make a place for itself in American historical folklore.

waiians themselves were contemplating. On the same day William Watman, an old seaman devoted to Cook, died and was buried ashore on the *heiau*. It has been alleged that here was a revelatory thing, convincing the people that their visitors were after all not gods, and therefore it had some influence on the events that followed. Once again I can find no evidence to support the allegation. Certainly the Hawaiians took a great interest in the burial, and added their own ceremony to it in great form; but their behaviour was simply that of a friendly and sympathetic nation, who displayed no sense of surprise to see this intimation of a common mortality. Whatever they thought of Cook, there is no indication whatever that they endowed his followers with the attributes of godhead. It may seem sadly contradictory. We must accept the fact that they themselves were human beings, and had a quite human capacity for self-contradiction. I cannot see that the fate of William Watman had any connection at all with the fate of his captain.

It is true, I think, that familiarity with the seamen had bred among the people not contempt but, perhaps, a little boredom, a willingness to tease, a certain experimental attitude towards quarrelling, to see how far it could safely go. Something of the same sort had caused minor trouble in Tonga in 1777. This, added to the increased number of thefts, was only too likely to cause major trouble now. On the morning of 13 February the Hawaiians behaved so badly on board both ships that they were all ordered off. In the afternoon the carpenters were busy over the mast on the *heiau,* and at the other end of the little beach a party of men in charge of a midshipman were filling water for the *Discovery,* helped by natives who were paid for their assistance. Other natives began to be very troublesome in hindering this work, and the midshipman came to King, who was in command, to ask him for a marine as a guard. King sent a marine without a musket. The Hawaiians thereupon armed themselves with stones, the midshipman came to King again; and King, a highly respected person, took another marine, this time armed with a musket, and with his authority put an end to the trouble. At this moment Cook came on shore. King told him what had happened, and—I use King's words—"he gave orders to me that on the first appearance of throwing stones or behaving insolently, to fire ball at the offenders: This made me give orders to the Corporal, to have the Centries pieces loaded with Ball instead of Shot."[16] These words seem to me to be highly significant ones: they are, in fact, the first indication we have that Cook's patience was coming to an end. For ball could kill; small shot, as I have already said, only caused fright.

Late in the afternoon there was worse trouble. While a chief of some importance was calling on Clerke in the *Discovery,* a bold fellow managed to get up the side, ran across the deck, snatched the armourer's tongs and a chisel, and was overboard again before anyone had recovered from the surprise. A canoe took him in and made for the shore, fired at from the ship without effect. [Thomas] Edgar, the master of the *Discovery,* put off in the ship's small cutter in pursuit, so hurriedly that neither he nor his men had time to seize a musket or any other weapon; but the canoe outdistanced them and got safe to shore. Meanwhile Cook, inspecting the carpenters, heard the noise of firing and saw the chase, and calling to King, a corporal and a marine, ran to intercept the canoe. In vain; a great and noisy crowd gathered; Cook, King and the marines, leaving the canoe and hoping to catch the thief, were misled till dark; Cook's threats to shoot, at first taken seriously, in the end merely caused laughter; bodies of men kept on collecting, and Cook at last thought it best to return, though not in King's opinion "from the smallest Idea of any danger." While he was being misled, out of sight of the boats, something worse had happened. Edgar had reached the shore, and saw the men with the tongs hand them over to another canoe, which gave them back to him. He was about to make for the ship, well pleased, when he saw the *Resolution*'s pinnace pulling towards him, and Cook and King in full cry. An unhappy impulse determined him, with such reinforcements, to seize the thief's canoe, as it was paddling off, and take it on board. The men in the pinnace, all of whom were, like Edgar and his men, unarmed, did seize the canoe; but alas, it belonged not to the thief, but to a very friendly chief called Parea, who in his turn was just coming on shore. He seized back his own canoe; a fracas broke out, a man in the pinnace hit him on the head with an oar, the crowd stoned the pinnace so heavily that her men were forced

[16] *Ibid.,* f. 130.

to leap out and swim to a rock, Edgar and Midshipman [George] Vancouver were assaulted and beaten, and only through the efforts of the injured Parea were the boats able to get away with broken oars and battered men.[17] Cook, when he heard the gist of all this, was exceedingly angry with his own men for their folly in getting into the quarrel with no means of defending themselves. He was angry with the Hawaiians, and doubtless he was none the less angry at having been made a fool of. I quote King again: "In going on board, the Captn expressed his sorrow, that the behaviour of the Indians would at last oblige him to use force; for that they must not he said imagine they have gained an advantage over us."[18] And these again are significant words.

I have gone into that afternoon in a little detail, because its events, and their repercussions, are not detached and separate. Its hours are the first, in a period of less than twenty-four hours, that contains the climax of our story. We can, as it were, see the wave rising that is to break next day. In the night a few men crept about the base of the *heiau,* where King slept, and a sentry shot off his musket, but no harm was done. There was, however, the final theft. The *Discovery*'s large cutter had been submerged at a buoy between the ship and the shore to keep her planks from splitting. The moorings were cut and the boat taken away—a serious loss, as she was the only large boat the *Discovery* had. Her recovery seemed essential. As soon as Clerke heard of the theft, at daybreak, he went to the *Resolution* to tell Cook of it, and it was resolved—the plan was Cook's—to send boats to the two points of the bay to prevent any canoes from leaving; "for he said [I quote Clerke] he would seize them all and made no doubt but to redeem them they would very readily return the Boat again."[19] Clerke thereupon rowed back to his own ship to give the necessary orders, and the boats, well armed, shortly set off to their stations. Clerke, who was seriously unwell with the tuberculosis that killed him, could himself take no active part in any measure. He had no

[17] Edgar gives his own account of this incident in P.R.O. Adm 55/24, ff. 58v–59v.

[18] Adm 55/122, f. 130v.

[19] P.R.O. Adm 51/1561. Clerke's account of the incidents of 14 February and the week thereafter is in this volume, ff. 209–27; it is copied out, I think as a communication for the Admiralty, in Adm 55/124.

sooner left the *Resolution* than King came on board, and "found them all arming themselves & the Captn loading his double Barreld piece; on my going to acquaint him with the last nights adventure," writes King (meaning the disturbance round the *heiau*) "he interruptd me & said we are not arming for the last nights affairs, they have stolen the Discoverys Cutter, & it is for that we are making preparations."[20] Cook, that is, having dismissed Clerke, had had a further thought, or impulse: he had determined to make the Hawaiian king, Kalei'opu'u, his hostage for the return of the cutter, as well as to seize the canoes. For that purpose he was going on shore with an armed party of marines, their muskets loaded with ball. . . . We have no alternative to concluding, I think, that his patience had been tried beyond its limit; now, once and for all, he was going to put an end to the exasperations these people inflicted on him. And he, who had always calculated so coolly and carefully, made two miscalculations, one bad, the other fatal.

The first miscalculation lay in taking the marines. Hawaiians were used to marines, standing about as sentries, amiably hobnobbing or pursuing their women; but this was too obviously something different, a body of marines, a set piece of menace. There is no doubt that Cook on his own, at a more normal hour, could quite easily have got the chief on board. For tact he was substituting a threat; and threats, as he had already proved at Moorea, do not always work. They sometimes work in quite the wrong way. We may add that if he were going to take marines at all, and really anticipated having to use them, then the number he thought necessary—a lieutenant and nine men—was a melancholy underestimate. The total number in the ships was thirty-one. Some of these were with King, on ordinary guard-duty. How many were then actually on board the *Resolution,* and available, I do not know. Perhaps Cook merely thought in terms of more men than he had had with him the afternoon before. Or it may be an indication that not force but a slight show of force was all he had in mind; that he thought the threat would do his business. On that I have already commented. The threat in any case was not one the Hawaiians could clearly understand: they were not to know how the muskets

[20] Adm 55/122, f. 131.

were loaded. If your threat is ambiguous you are at a disadvantage as much as are those you threaten.

The second miscalculation was over the effect of muskets loaded with ball. I have already said, again, that Cook disliked firing at native peoples with ball, for he disliked killing. His hasty preparations this morning therefore themselves cast a light on the irritation of his mind. His officers did not all agree with his general theory; much better, some thought, to kill a man or two at once on the first sign of disagreement and make an example, prove your superiority, and save trouble in the future. Small shot was useless. This could be turned into a humanitarian argument; for saving future trouble, you might also save future slaughter. It is a nice point. Nothing could be more repugnant to the soul of Cook; but, with his own feeling, and some experience, he also overestimated the effect of musket-fire. . . . It was a ruinous [estimation]; and with this opinion, between six and seven o'clock on the morning of 14 February, he stepped into his boat and went ashore.

There were three boats, the men in them all armed—the *Resolution*'s small pinnace, small cutter, and launch. The cutter was sent to lie off the north-west point of the bay to keep the canoes from leaving. The village of Kaawaloa, where Kalei'opu'u had his habitation, lay just inside this point. The shore close to the village was then partly sand, partly an irregular lip of lava above shallow water; though the sand has gone, the line of the shore seems to have survived pretty well the earthquakes and tidal-waves that have altered so much the appearance of the rest of the bay, and if one thinks away the trees and the prickly American lantana and acacia that have spread over most of the place, it is possible to visualize there the events of the morning without great difficulty. Cook, the young Lieutenant Molesworth Phillips of the marines, and his nine men landed; and the two boats withdrew to keep off the bottom. For the story I now tell I follow the report made to Clerke by Phillips, who was with Cook till just before the climax; the journal of Clerke, who discussed the matter closely with Phillips, and knew Cook as well as anyone did; and a few sentences from the journal of King, who seems to have made a careful enquiry. A great deal of circumstantial detail reported by others, whether published or unpublished, we can afford to ignore. I think, in the light of the manuscript material we have, we can ignore the printed account of Lieutenant King, who certainly rewrote very carefully for official publication the account given in his journal; we can ignore what I may call the classic unofficial printed account, the pamphlet by Samwell, and even the longer one in the journal of Samwell, who went to immense pains to assemble a connected story. About much of this I feel as [James] Trevenen the midshipman felt about Samwell's pamphlet, "some things are represented . . . in situations which should seem to render minute detail impossible." Trevenen was aware of the historian's curse.[21]

[21] Molesworth Phillips kept a journal, which has now disappeared. Clerke incorporated the report in his own journal, Adm 51/4561, entry for 14 February. King has printed his in *Voyage to the Pacific Ocean* [London, 1785], III, 41–46. Samwell's pamphlet was *A Narrative of the Death of Captain James Cook. . .* (London, 1786); reprinted most recently by Sir Maurice Holmes (San Francisco and London, 1957); the corresponding portion of his MS journal is about 1000 words longer. His journal for 4 February to 22 February was printed, not with entire accuracy, in *Historical Records of New South Wales,* I [Sydney, 1893], part 1, 450–78. There are interesting passages in the logs or journals of Watts, Harvey (at the time midshipman *Discovery*), Edgar, [William] Bayly, the astronomer, [James] Burney (Mitchell Library [Sydney] MS), and some better marginal comments by [William] Bligh (who in his early twenties was master of the *Resolution*) in the Admiralty Library copy of the *Voyage*. R. T. Gould printed Clerke, Edgar and Bayly in his article "Some Unpublished Accounts of Cook's Death," in the *Mariner's Mirror,* XIV, ([October], 1928), 301–19, and Bligh in his "Bligh's Notes on Cook's Last Voyage," *ibid.,* 371–85, and more particularly 380–82. Dr. George Mackaness also has printed these notes in his *Life of Vice-Admiral William Bligh* (Sydney, 1951), pp. 20–25. The printed volumes of [John] Rickman (anonymous, 1781), [Heinrich] Zimmerman[n] (1781), [William] Ellis (1782), Ledyard (1783) cannot help being interesting in one way or another; but none of these men was on the spot, any more than the others I have referred to. Trevenen's remark comes from "A letter to a friend" quoted in Admiral Sir C. V. Penrose's memoir of Trevenen, Alexander Turnbull Library [Wellington] MS, p. 14. We have the point rammed home in one of the fragments of the MS "logbook" of Alexander Home, master's mate *Discovery,* now in the National Library of Australia [Canberra]: "I was not present in this Fray being Sick So this Account is Entirely from the Mouths of others Who were present. But these Differed greatly in their Relation of the same Matters So that what I have here said I do not Aver to be the Real truth in Every particul[ar] although in General it may be pretty Nigh the Matter. I have carefully Asserted such Relations as had the greatest appearance of Truth. But indeed they were so Exceedingly perplexed in their Accounts that it was a hard Matter to Colect Certainty, in particular cases or indeed to write any Account at all."

Cook and the marines marched into the village, where Cook enquired for Kalei'opu'u and his two lively young sons, who spent much of their time on board the *Resolution*. The boys soon came and took him and Phillips to their father's hut. After waiting some time Phillips went to bring out the just-awakened chief. It was obvious within a few words that he knew nothing of the stolen cutter, and he quite readily accepted the invitation to the ship. He started off for the beach with Cook and Phillips; one of the boys ran ahead and jumped happily into the pinnace. So far all was well; but near the waterside Kalei'opu'u's wife and two lesser chiefs came up, began to argue with him, and made him sit down. There was a change in the chief: he "appear'd dejected and frighten'd," says Phillips. Also a great crowd had gathered, rather clearly not well-disposed. So many muskets, "& things carried on in a quite different manner from formerly" (I quote King)[22] had caused alarm. Cook pressed the chief; his friends insisted he should not go; the noise increased. The few marines were huddled in the midst of the crowd: Phillips proposed to Cook that they should form a line along the lava rocks by the water, facing the crowd; Cook agreed, and the people quite willingly made way for them. A large body of marines, drawn up on favourable ground, and disciplined like the Guards at Waterloo, might now have been of some use. At the same time the Hawaiians were arming themselves with spears and stones—to repel any force that might be exerted on Kalei'opu'u, so Phillips thought—and many had daggers. Some of these daggers were iron ones obtained from the English, a favourite article of trade. Then, remarks Phillips, "an Artful Rascal of a Priest was singing & making a ceremonious offering of a Coco Nut to the Cap[t] and Terre'oboo to divert their attention from the Manoeuvres of the surrounding multitude." I confess I cannot understand this: Phillips does not mention any thing one can recognize as "manoeuvres"; and the priest, however artful, was not necessarily a rascal, or diverting attention. And if he was diverting attention, why Kalei'opu'u's attention? At any rate, Cook decided to abandon his plan, and said to Phillips, "We can never think of compelling him to go on board without killing a number of these

[22] Adm 55/122, f. 133.

People." These words I quote partly because they are, as far as I know, one of the very few remarks by Cook ever directly reported. Note that Cook still believed he had the initiative. Clerke agreed: there was nothing at this time to stop Cook, in spite of the clamour, from walking peaceably down to the boat and embarking; nothing to stop him from taking off the marines. He did begin to walk slowly down.

Two things now happened which I cannot put in order, nor is their precise order particularly important. One was, so far as Cook was concerned, a mere chance. At the other end of the bay, to keep a canoe from escaping, muskets had been fired, and a man killed. The man was a notable chief. Another chief hastening to the ships in passionate indignation to find Cook and tell him the story was disregarded, and forthwith made for the beach. It was Cook he wanted, not the crowd; but it was the crowd that got the news, spreading like wildfire, not Cook; and the news was enough, with the other thing, to carry them over the border-line of excitement into attack. The other thing was the culmination of all the wearing irritations and exasperations to which Cook's mind had been subject for so many months, as I have been at such pains to lay before you. As he walked down to the boat he was threatened by one of the mob with a dagger and a stone—perhaps out of mere bravado. Cook's temper boiled over. He fired one barrel of his musket, loaded with small shot, at the man; and at that moment he lost the initiative. The shot did no damage, even at close range, the man being protected by his heavy war mat—except that it further enraged the Hawaiians. Kalei'opu'u's young son in the pinnace was frightened and was put ashore; but even then the men in the boats saw no particular reason for alarm—even then, when the wave was about to break. It broke. A chief attempted to stab Phillips, stones were hurled, a marine was knocked down, Cook fired his other barrel, loaded with ball, and killed a man, Phillips fired, there was a general attack, Cook ordered the marines to fire, and the boats joined in. Phillips had time to reload his musket. The overwhelmed marines did not. Cook shouted "Take to the boats!," an order hardly necessary, as the unfortunate and ill-trained men were already scrambling into the water and towards the pinnace, "totally vanquish'd," as Phillips said. Phillips was knocked down by a stone and stabbed in the shoulder, shot his assailant dead and managed to get to the pinnace, and then out of it again to save the life of a drowning man. After being knocked down he saw no more of Cook. So much for the deterrent power of fire with ball.

The men in the pinnace, which had kept in as close to the shore as possible, saw Cook's last moments. He was close to the edge of the lava waving to the boats to come in when he was hit from behind with a club; while he staggered from this blow he was stabbed in the neck, or shoulder, with one of the iron daggers—a blow not in itself fatal, but enough to fell him, strong as he was, face down into the water. There was a great shout and a rush to hold him under and finish him off with daggers and clubs. The man who stabbed him was shot and killed. The overloaded pinnace pulled off, the cutter came round and fired till it was recalled, the *Resolution,* seeing trouble on shore, had fired some of its four-pounders. The launch had not gone in closer: it was commanded by a very peculiar and unpopular man, Lieutenant [John] Williamson; and Williamson, incomprehensibly mistaking the meaning of Cook's wave, had even rowed further out. Some people have therefore directly blamed Williamson for Cook's death. I find his personality distasteful, but can find no justification for this. As the boats pulled off to the ship, it was shortly after 8 o'clock.

Of the ten marines (including Phillips) four had been killed and four wounded. Of the Hawaiians, seventeen were killed; many others were badly wounded. Clerke could find no Hawaiian premeditation in the affair. He was clear that, at the end, Cook had acted unwisely. I have, I suppose, made clear my own hypothesis. One question remains: how, if Cook was deemed a god, could those who exalted him also kill him? The answer to this surely is that many savage peoples have not hesitated to beat or otherwise punish their gods when they have failed in their duty as gods; and Cook, a god who was not without marks of humankind, had given some provocation. He was mourned and honoured by the people who killed him, and a question asked more than once by them of his men was "When will the god—when will Erono—come again?" They were indeed somewhat shocked by what they had done.

In England also, to which I now return, though not to William Cowper, there was a sense of shock. "Dear Sir," wrote Lord Sandwich to Sir Joseph Banks, on 10 January 1780, "what is uppermost in our mind allways must come out first, poor captain Cooke is no more. . . ." A sense of shock: I can think of nothing in our history of quite the same order until the news came through in 1913 of Scott's death in the Antarctic.

One not only learns of Cook, and of the historian's methods, from this careful exercise in surmise: one also learns of New Zealand, for whom Professor Beaglehole speaks in his last sentence. Captain Robert Falcon Scott, the courageous explorer of the Antarctic, used New Zealand as his departure point, just as Sir Edmund Hillary, himself a New Zealander and the conqueror of Mount Everest many years later, was to use that country's Southern Alps for his training. Beaglehole writes, then, not only as historian, and as New Zealander, but with an implicit audience of like-minded listeners in mind—for his essay was first a public address read in Canberra, the Australian capital, in 1964. The reader should always put to himself the question For whom was this written? as he turns to any interpretive material, for it will enrich one's understanding of both subject matter and of the craft to do so. It is not irrelevant that the preceding essay began as a paper to be read aloud; its cadences, its turns, its repetitive structures would all tell us this, even were the author not to do so. The best writers remember that we learn with the ear as with the eye, and even when writing solely for the printed page, they read their material to themselves to root out ungainly constructions. They have it read back to themselves as well. The ear will catch the false note, the effect not achieved, the garbled syntax, the unintended repetition, the unconscious and unwanted alliteration, where the eye does not.

Nor can one stress too strongly the value of going over the ground of history. Perhaps I am deficient in character, for I cannot imagine a scene any more than I am able—unlike so many people, it would seem—to visualize what a man looks like from hearing his voice on the telephone.

I envy those scholars who, after one such talk, perhaps across a continent, can tell me that the man at the other end of the line was short, fat, asthmatic, and smoking Cuesta-Rey Earls. Being deficient in imagination, I must meet the man, stand on the spot—here, precisely *here,* is where Henri Mouhot first came upon the great ruins of Angkor—and drink the palm wine before I can write. The ground itself is a document which the scholar must not neglect.

15. The Private Eye:

Going Over the Ground

AESTHETICALLY THE MIND MAY BE THE BEST INSTRUMENT for grasping the precise dimensions of a well-wrought urn. The eye, the tongue, the ear, and the hand must be employed by most of us who, not being Ved Mehtas, cannot reconstruct the color of a man's coat from the odor of his tobacco. Increasingly, as research funds and time permit, the historian does realize the necessity to go over the ground of history. Francis Parkman and Henry Adams did, and they were the two greatest historians nineteenth-century America produced. Samuel Eliot Morison, the seafaring biographer of Christopher Columbus, John Paul Jones, and Stephen Decatur, informed his prose with nuance-precise knowledge not only by his long acquaintance with the sea but also by taking a ship roughly of the dimensions of the *Santa Maria* along the curves Columbus himself traced. I have argued before the necessity to go to the spot in order to capture those essential nuances, but I have not argued the equal necessity to go over the ground in the way in which one's subjects would have done so. Of course, chariots are not available for driving the Roman Road in Britain; feet must serve. The following short extract from a charming book by Ernle Bradford, *Ulysses Found,* tells how he came upon the land of the Laestrygonians, as he believes Ulysses did, "entirely by accident." There are few detectives, after all, who do not insist upon returning to the scene of the crime, and there are none who have not benefited from chance. Following upon Bradford's exploration is another, which also serves to illustrate the importance of archaeological work for the historian.

♦ ♦ ♦

On a summer day when a light easterly breeze was just stirring the sea, I sailed up the Straits of Bonifacio. Ulysses was far from my mind and I doubt whether I had glanced at the *Odyssey* for a year or more. I only found myself in that part of the Mediterranean by accident, having accepted a last-minute offer to help crew a friend's sailing boat to Corsica and Sardinia.

The wind died towards noon and we sat idly about the deck until, with the first cooling of the land towards evening, an offshore breeze sprang up from Corsica and shrugged impatiently in the white folds of our mainsail. We decided to put into Bonifacio for the night. It was a harbour that none of us had visited before, so we busied ourselves over the *Admiralty Pilot* and a large-scale chart of the area.

I suppose my reading of the *Pilot* should have given me the first clue. "Port de Bonifacio consists of a cove, from three-quarters of a cable to one cable wide, formed by the peninsula on which the town is built: it affords excellent shelter to small craft. The harbour is entered between Pointe du Timon, the south-western extremity of the peninsula, and Pointe de la Madonetta, the southern extremity of a small peninsula. . . . The entrance is difficult to distinguish from a distance." As we closed the Corsican coast I could confirm the accuracy of the *Pilot.* Even with the aid of binoculars, it was a long time before I could make out the break in the cliffs that marks the entrance to Bonifacio.

The wind was gusty now, spilling off the high cliffs and causing

---

FROM Ernle Bradford, *Ulysses Found* (New York: Harcourt, Brace & World: Harvest Books ed., n.d.) pp. 85–88, © 1963 by Ernle Bradford. Reprinted by permission of Harcourt, Brace & World, Inc. and Hodder and Stoughton Limited.

For additional reading: A similar book is Roderick Cameron's *The Golden Haze: With Captain Cook in the South Pacific* (London, 1965). For a particularly striking sense of place in detective fiction, see any of the books of John Buchan or Geoffrey Household.

us to tack constantly as we worked our way towards the land. It brought with it the scent of the *maquis,* that tangled undergrowth which carries the whole of the Mediterranean on its breath. I think it was not until we were right up to the entrance of the harbour that it dawned on me where I was. The cliffs stood high on either hand, and through the heart of them ran the knife-thrust of the sea. There were a few rocks offshore at the entrance to the harbour. We tacked, and came about again as we found ourselves at the mouth of the channel. Suddenly I recognized it—the place I had vainly sought in Sicily and Italy.

Bonifacio is unlike anywhere else in the Mediterranean. It would be an unique harbour in any country, but in this tideless sea where few rivers channel their way through the land, it is so rare a place that no sailor could avoid remarking on it. It is true there are other fine natural harbours—Grand Harbour in Malta for one, and Port Mahón in Minorca for another. But there is no other place like Bonifacio. I can think of only one other that remotely resembles it—the small harbour of Ciudadela in south-western Minorca. But Ciudadela, quite apart from its distance from Ustica, could never have been the home of the Laestrygonians. The creek which leads up to Ciudadela is no more than a channel winding through sandstone banks only a few feet high.

At Bonifacio, two bold headlands front one another and between them there is only this narrow channel. At the most, it is no more than 200 yards wide, and in places considerably narrower. So high are the cliffs on either hand that the channel appears even smaller than it really is. It is even more surprising to find how far back it winds into the land. The harbour itself, at the head of this channel, is indeed "closed in on all sides by an unbroken ring of precipitous cliffs." The channel bends round to the right, and once inside there is no sight or sound of the sea. This is truly a place where a vessel might lie and never be disturbed, whatever weather was blowing in the straits outside. This, I feel sure, was the harbour where the Greek squadron was ambushed by the Laestrygonians. This was the death-trap where Ulysses had lost all his other ships.

Later, when I read Victor Bérard's work on the *Odyssey,* I discovered that for quite a different reason he had come to the conclusion that the territory of the Laestrygonians lay in the Straits of

Bonifacio, but he placed it in a small cove on the Sardinian side. His reasons for this were philological not geographical—and geographically it does not fit the Homeric description. Bérard's theory was that Homer had based the wanderings of Ulysses on a Pilot, or *Periplous,* of Phoenician origin and whatever may be said for or against this argument, I find myself agreeing with one major point that he made: "To sum up, then, it would seem that Odysseus had ten important adventures in the seas of the West (the Phaeacians, the Lotus-Eaters, Cyclops, Aeolus, the Laestrygonians, Circe, the Land of the Dead, the Isle of the Sirens, the Island of the Sun, and Calypso); of these, seven take place in sea gates and all of them can be connected with these seven sea gates." I very much doubt whether Homer had any conception of where the Land of the Laestrygonians really lay. But what I do not doubt is that his description of the harbour was based on the first-hand account of someone who had been into Bonifacio.

It is known for certain that Corsica was inhabited long before the period when Homer wrote, and before the period that he was describing. There are numerous megalithic monuments in the island, and near Bonifacio itself a number of megalithic burial-places have been found. Under their slabs of stone lie the skeletons of the savage men who were to be immortalized as the cannibal Laestrygonians.

It was here, then, that the Greeks came after leaving Ustica. Previously I had been following the false trails of Leontini and Formia because I had been trying to be logical as well as to follow classical tradition. I had looked towards the east and the north-east, because I knew that it was in that direction Ulysses should have steered. I had never really considered that he might have made a north-westerly course. I feel convinced, at any rate, that the harbour which is described in the *Odyssey* is Bonifacio in Corsica. So perfect a natural harbour, moreover, at one of the main "sea gates" of the Mediterranean is certain to have been recorded by the first sailors who entered these waters. The Strait of Gibraltar, the "main gate" into the Mediterranean, is described, and so too that other important "gate" the Strait of Messina where Scylla and Charybdis lurk. At Bonifacio yet another of the most important Mediterranean "gates" is accurately depicted.

Bonifacio, almost exactly 240 miles north-west from Ustica, is within the radius of a vessel making one and a half knots from Ustica and arriving on the seventh day after a steady passage. The fact that the harbour of the Laestrygonians lies to the north-west, and not where I expected to find it, does not worry me as much perhaps as it should.

That night, with our boat lying safe and still beside the old wall in the harbour, I knew that I had found the place where the Greeks met their doom. Bonifacio is formed by nature not only as a safe shelter in all winds and weathers, but as an ideal trap in which to ambush a ship or a squadron of ships.

Above my head, and all the way down the channel-mouth to the invisible sea, ran the towering cliffs from which a man could easily drop a rock on to the deck of a boat below. The Greeks, who entered this channel unsuspecting, perished to a man when the Laestrygonians, "standing on the top of the cliffs began pelting the ships with stones."

Only Ulysses escaped, for he had moored to one of the rocks off the entrance to Bonifacio. When the trap was sprung on his companions, he had only to cut the hawser securing his ship and stand out into the safety of the sea. "With the fear of death in their hearts my men settled down to row. It was with a sigh of relief that we sped out to sea, leaving those frowning cliffs behind us. . . ."

Bradford, who has written of Malta, Constantinople, and other reaches of the Mediterranean, brings the expertise of the sailor to his work. The scholar's own expertise, often a kind of wise innocence, may not need to be either technical or practical; perhaps he need merely be a reasonably intelligent, dogged man who knows that not all materials rest in libraries and that not all ruins can be reached by automobile. One still approaches Petra on horseback, after all. The following essay is meant to complement the preceding one, to show that perhaps the historian's best ally is a strong pair of legs and an iron stomach. Written by Leo Deuel, the selection tells of Aurel Stein, who as a schoolboy dreamed of following in the steps of Marco

Polo, as Parkman followed the Oregon Trail, and who as a man opened up the interior of Central Asia to modern scholarship.

In the 1870's a schoolboy at a Dresden Gymnasium was captivated by the romantic epic of Alexander the Great. He read voraciously of his idol's lightning campaigns that swept over half the known world and subdued the proud empires of the East. Most of all he immersed himself in Alexander's thrust across the Hindu Kush into India. Here was high adventure after his own heart: unexplored, rugged mountains; physical courage and mental alertness; and a gateway that led deep into the exotic world of Asia. But when the boy sought information on the actual routes taken by Alexander, the passes he crossed, the sites where he fought some of the most crucial and brilliant battles of his career, the books failed to furnish him with sufficient answers. Right then he conceived the plan to follow Alexander, and to chart his exact route through ancient Bactria and his later retreat from the Indus delta to Persia.

For many years, even after he had grown to manhood and achieved international recognition, he was refused permission by the authorities of Afghanistan, the modern kingdom that occupies ancient Bactria, to carry out any investigations. Three viceroys of India intervened on his behalf. Once he sent the Afghan ruler a two-volume set of one of his masterly works on Asiatic exploration, but the king wrote back that he knew no English and would have to have the books translated before he would be in a position to express his appreciation, and this might take years. All seemed in vain. And then, in the fall of 1943, when Aurel Stein was past eighty, a personal friend from Harvard, at the time American minister at Kabul, was able to obtain the necessary permission. Within a few days Stein, as vigorous and enterprising as ever, left his favorite retreat high up in Kashmir and quickly made

---

FROM Leo Deuel, *Testaments of Time: The Search for Lost Manuscripts and Records* (New York: Alfred A. Knopf, 1965), pp. 425–31, 433–36. Reprinted, with omissions, by permission of Alfred A. Knopf, Inc.

his way to Kabul, where he stayed at the minister's residence. Two days after his arrival, he caught a chill on a visit to the local museum. A stroke and death followed in less than a week. Before the end, he told his American friend: "I have had a wonderful life, and it could not be concluded more happily than in Afghanistan which I have wanted to visit for sixty years."

In the sixty years between his youthful dreams and the threshold of their fulfillment, Sir Aurel Stein came to be regarded as "the greatest explorer of Asia since Marco Polo." Though he remained an admirer of Alexander all his life, the conqueror's route was only one of the royal roads into the mysterious continent. In later years Sir Aurel chose as guides his Venetian precursor, Marco Polo, and, above all, a seventh-century A.D. Chinese Buddhist monk, Hsüan Tsang, to whom he loved to refer as his "patron saint." Stein would never tire of invoking the memory of this pilgrim, an acute observer of Indian, Gandharan, and Turkestani sites. Hsüan Tsang led the way to Inner Asia. He was witness and symbol of the link between China and India, which Stein reconstructed in his explorations. Fittingly, Hsüan Tsang had ventured from China into India to settle obscurities and discrepancies in Buddhist texts. He returned years later with a load of sacred books. Proceeding in the opposite direction after an interval of twelve hundred years, Stein was to emulate his "gentle master."

Marcus Aurelius (later Sir Aurel) Stein was born in 1862 in Budapest. He came from a middle-class Hungarian-Jewish family of merchants and intellectuals, and he spoke German and Hungarian from childhood. After pursuing Oriental languages and archaeology at several universities on the Continent—culminating in a Ph.D. from Tübingen in Indo-Iranian studies at the age of twenty-one—Stein came to England in 1884 to continue research at Oxford and the British Museum. There intervened a year of military training in Hungary, during which he received valuable instruction in surveying and topography. Upon his return to England, which became his adopted country after the death of his parents and brother in Hungary, Stein gained the attention of Sir Henry Yule, the learned editor of Marco Polo's works, and Sir Henry Rawlinson, the soldier-scholar who helped to decipher cuneiform. To his English mentors Stein owed his appointment in

1888 as principal of Oriental College at Lahore and registrar of the Punjab University. So, at the age of twenty-six, Stein had found his way to Asia.

His stay in India brought Stein physically closer to the historical highways and byways which crisscrossed the continent's little-known interior. But for a long time he was tied down by official duties; and he began to doubt whether he would ever escape the drudgery of a career in education. Rare and brief were the intervals of hard-earned leisure which he could devote to antiquarian pursuits. And he had to do without public patronage or subsidy. That the Indian administration should support archaeological explorations was considered absurd at the time. Antiquarian investigation of Inner Asia or even of India was virtually nonexistent. To European officialdom and the general public, archaeology was almost synonymous with the excavation of Homeric Greece and Near Eastern sites linked to the Holy Scriptures. Troy and Knossos had Schliemann and Evans, men of wealth who could finance their own projects, and various societies for the promotion of Christian knowledge were dispensing funds liberally for excavations in the Bible lands. Stein's chosen area did not intrigue any of these. Then, when Stein was thirty-seven, his opportunity finally came.

Within a few years of Stein's arrival in Asia, several fragments of inscribed birchbark leaves had reached collections in the West and in India. Some had been purchased by the ill-fated French traveler M. Dutreuil de Rhins. Best-known and most extensive of all was the so-called Bower manuscript, named for L. H. Bower, the British officer who came into possession of it in 1890. It was actually a fairly voluminous package of fifty-one leaves, consisting of seven distinct, though incomplete, texts. The manuscript, first declared to be illegible, was deciphered by an Anglo-German Orientalist, A. F. Rudolf Hoernle, and was found to contain unknown tracts on medicine and divination. The script was of the Gupta variety of northern India, datable to the fourth to sixth centuries A.D. There was little doubt that the manuscript had been written by native Indians—possibly Buddhist monks—as the language, the writing, and the typical Indian *pothi* format (imitating the shape of loose talipot palm leaves) indicated. No written work of such antiquity had survived anywhere in India.

The surprisingly well-preserved leaves of the Bower manuscript, and others like it, had been acquired in the distant desert uplands of Chinese Turkestan through local treasure seekers or their intermediaries. A land capable of harboring such treasures for more than twelve hundred years surely deserved closer investigation, and Stein was the first to realize the full implications of these finds and to act on them. Modern travelers had entered Inner Asia, but no part of it had been scientifically explored. Stein was much encouraged in his plan to launch a large-scale expedition by the reports of visitors, such as Sven Hedin, that there were indeed ancient ruined sites in the region and that these were relatively accessible and could be excavated. Stein adroitly and persuasively presented his plan to the Indian government in 1898. It was finally approved, thanks largely to the intervention of the Viceroy of India, Lord (George Nathaniel) Curzon, himself an eager student of Asian history.

Luckily, Stein had at least one other objective besides archaeology, and that was geography. Even vigilant administrators would dispense government money for a project which promised to survey entirely uncharted mountains and plateaus in the Indian borderlands. Stein was fortunate enough, then, to be sponsored by the Survey of India. The assignments he carried out as a topographer in the heart of Asia were a labor of love as well as an important achievement. In order to gather all the geographical data he could, he made it a point never to take the same road twice from India to Turkestan or any other region. He traversed the Takla Makan Desert at its greatest width and climbed up and down the snow-covered massifs of the highest Asian ranges. Crossing passes above 15,000 feet became almost routine for him.

Stein was a wiry little man of incredible endurance and a frame of iron. Once he requested the government to assign to him a hardy native soldier for his surveys along the North-West Frontier. The request was passed on to the military authorities in the region, and they carefully selected a young Pathan tribesman from the hills. When the mission was completed, the Pathan soldier was asked by his superior officer how he fared on the journey. "Stein Sahib," exclaimed the young man, "is some kind of supernatural being, not human; he walked me off my legs on the mountains; I could not keep up with him. Please do not send me to him again, Sir." At that time Stein was well over sixty. Years earlier, in 1907, he had lost all the toes of his right foot to frostbite when mapping areas of the Kunlun, at an altitude of 20,000 feet. On another occasion he was severely lacerated when his horse threw him while crossing a river, and fell on him. He broke his collarbone several times, and barely escaped drowning in the Persian Gulf.

Stein avoided a large retinue and cumbersome equipment on his expeditions, and preferred the company of Sikhs and Pathans to Europeans. Invariably he took along Dash, his agile Scottish terrier, or rather, successive members of that species (numbered I to VII) who were temperamentally attuned to the nimbleness of their master.

The sandy, windswept waste of innermost Asia, which was the object of Stein's most vital archaeological explorations, comprises largely what is today Chinese Turkestan, or Sinkiang. The area stretches eastward for about 1,500 miles from the headwaters of the Oxus in the Hindu Kush to China proper, and is 500 miles at its widest. The drainageless Tarim basin and the Takla Makan Desert occupy the central part of the area. In the north it is bounded by the Tien Shan, the "Celestial Mountains," and in the south by the mighty Kunlun ranges, across which lies Tibet. In the west tower the Pamirs, "Roof of the World." Unless one is attracted to the metaphysical charms of endless undulating sand mounds and shifting dunes, one will be hard put to find appealing a series of windswept altiplanos. In the absence of moisture in the atmosphere, and almost total lack of salt-free water, human, animal, and plant life cannot be sustained there for any length of time except at a string of oases confined to a narrow fringe near the piedmont, which are watered by glacier-fed streams.

Artificial irrigation supports life in a larger area during times of political stability. Evidence points to progressive desiccation, however, which has led to the shrinking of most settlements and even to their abandonment to the encroaching desert sea. One frequently comes across shriveled whitish stumps and skeletal branches of dead trees, indicating past habitation and in shrill surrealistic accents suggesting the existence of sand-buried edifices nearby. Other characteristic landmarks of the dried-up oasis belt are tamarisk cones, accumulations of sand around decayed tamarisk shrubs, which through the years have been piled up to considerable heights.

Despite the visible advance of the desert dust bowl on villages and towns, there is no reason to assume that Chinese Turkestan, except for a marginal zone, was ever fertile enough for settlement. Nature has apparently raised here one of its most formidable bastions. But like any natural barrier—ocean, river, mountains—it is potentially also a bridge, and as such it has played a vital role in Asian history. It was never really inaccessible. Though forbidding, it served as a natural corridor between eastern and western Asia, with connecting links to Tibet in the south and, via the Gobi, to Mongolia and Siberia in the north. To judge by Paleolithic and Neolithic artifacts, the long trail across the desert may be one of the world's oldest roads, perhaps associated with the birth of Chinese civilization itself. Long before it became a silk road, it was a jade road, for over it jade may have reached Troy, thousands of miles away, in the second millennium B.C. Chinese Turkestan was also a source of the lapis lazuli cherished by Sumerians and Babylonians. . . .

Stein's foray [into this area] had one immediate purpose: to trace the source of the manuscripts which recently had reached the West, and possibly to add to their number. He also hoped that ancient documents would untie the skein of that region's tangled history and lead him to physical evidence of the cultures that once flourished there. The stage was thus set for what [Charles] Leonard Woolley has called "the most daring and adventurous raid upon the ancient world that any archaelogist has attempted."

From 1900 to 1916, Stein was engaged in three major expeditions into Central Asia, which kept him in the field for seven years. During the second, and perhaps most important, campaign, undertaken from 1906 to 1908, he was on the move for two and a half years. Altogether he covered, mostly on foot, some 25,000 miles. At least in a spatial sense, Stein practiced extensive rather than intensive archaeology. He did not concentrate on a single rich site, but searched out an entire civilization in its widest range and physical setting. Typically, Stein was absorbed in tracing the ancient routes—particularly those of Hsüan Tsang and Marco Polo—by which several civilizations met.

All three journeys covered roughly the same ground. Stein would set out from Kashmir, explore little-known valleys of the Hindu Kush and Pamir, and then follow the oasis belt from Kashgar in the west, along one of the two edges of the Takla Makan Desert. From present-day towns he would venture into the desert to abandoned sites, where he excavated. He visited several of these ruins on successive expeditions, and between seasons he undertook his cartographic surveys of the high mountains.

Stein's first journey, covering seven months in 1900–1, centered largely on the city of Khotan, the long-time capital of a native kingdom at the southern fringe of Eastern Turkestan. Stein was convinced that Khotan had been a significant link in the exchange of goods and cultural influences. He already knew of scattered passages in the Chinese Annals which mentioned Khotan as a way station on the road to the Oxus. During the Later Han Dynasty and the Tang Dynasty it was apparently under direct Chinese political control. Some artifacts (including manuscripts) which displayed affinities with ancient Indian objects had already been discovered in the Khotan area at the ruined sites by native treasure seekers. As most of these places had been thoroughly ransacked, Stein decided to move on to more remote areas on the ancient desert road to China. But there was a puzzling problem he had to answer first.

Since 1895, several paper manuscripts and block prints in strange and confusing characters had been purchased on behalf of the Indian government by its representative in Chinese Turkestan. Considerable quantities of documents of a similar kind had drifted into Russia and into public collections in Europe. Every one of these was supposed to have been excavated in the desert area near Khotan, and all of them could be traced to one man, a Khotan treasure seeker by the name of Islam Akhun. A few years earlier, the Indian representative had been able to persuade him to disclose the location of the sand-buried ruins from which he had allegedly obtained the manuscripts. Yet Stein had some doubts about the genuineness of these strange texts and he set himself the task, while he was still in India, of getting to the bottom of the mystery. He resolved to visit the old sites named by Akhun. On the road from Kashgar to Khotan he stopped at a place called Guma, which had been listed by the treasure seeker. Local dignitaries assured him that no "old books" had ever come to light there. Of the number of nearby ruins mentioned by Akhun, only two were known to them. They took Stein to these, but it was obvious that the ruins had been abandoned in relatively recent times. None could have furnished any antiquities whatsoever.

In Khotan, Stein vainly waited for a visit from Islam Akhun peddling his dubious ware, which he usually offered to recent arrivals. But the man, for reasons best known to himself, shunned prospective customers from India just then. Meanwhile Stein made the acquaintance of a Russian Armenian who was the proud possessor of a birchbark manuscript in the same writing. The Armenian, who had bought the book as a speculative investment, wanted to have it appraised. Stein could not be very reassuring, however; an examination of the book only increased his suspicions. None of the birchbark leaves had received the careful preparation known to Stein from his analysis of such materials in Kashmir. Neither was the ink of the type traditionally used for writing on bark.

Unfortunately there was still no sign of Islam Akhun. Every time Stein came back to Khotan from excursions into the adjacent mountains or desert, Akhun was absent. A confrontation took place finally, but only during Stein's last trip to Khotan at the end of his first expedition. Though the evidence of fraud was pretty conclusive, Stein was "anxious for a personal examination of that enterprising individual whose productions had engaged so much learned attention in Europe." The local Mandarin governor volunteered his assistance and Islam Akhun was at last seized.

At first the suspect presented himself as only the docile sales agent for other "old book" dealers, who conveniently had either run away or passed on to their just reward. Akhun seemed convinced that there was no direct evidence to implicate him in fraud and made a great show of his respect for the law. But he overreached himself. Not knowing that a report published in India contained in indelible print the account he had given to the British resident of his "discoveries," he now told Stein that he himself had never been to any of the places from which the books had supposedly come. Stein promptly put the report before him. And, as Stein wrote in an amusing chapter of his personal narrative on the rascal, "the effect was most striking. Islam Akhun was wholly unprepared for the fact that his lies told years before, with so much seeming accuracy of topographical and other details, had received the honour of permanent record in a scientific report to Government. He was intelligent enough to realize that he stood self-convicted, and that there was nothing to be gained by further protestations of innocence." Gradually the whole truth came out.

Islam Akhun had indeed once engaged in collecting genuine antiques from neighboring ruins. Then an Afghan trader alerted him in 1894 to the new lucrative market for ancient manuscripts among the "Sahibi" of India. It seems, "the idea of visiting such dreary desert sites, with a certainty of great hardships and only a limited chance of finds, had no attraction for a person of such wits as Islam Akhun. So in preference he conceived the plan of manufacturing the article he was urged to supply the Sahibs with." . . .

With little coaxing from Stein, the forger became rather voluble, and in fact boasted of his accomplishments. He even showed Stein one of his artful implements for the creation of fakes, about which Stein remarked: "How much more proud would he have felt if he could but have seen, as I did a few months later, the fine morocco bindings with which a number of his . . . forgeries had been honored in a great European library!" So pleased was Islam with himself that he considered his talents wasted in the Turkestan hinterland—he had the effrontery to ask Stein to take him to Europe. Stein on his part was well satisfied that he had solved the case without any "resort to Eastern methods of judicial inquiry." . . .

16. The Case of the Missing Telegrams:

Suppressing Evidence

MANY REPUTATIONS WERE AT STAKE IN 1897 WHEN A committee of inquiry in England investigated the events that lay behind the notorious Jameson Raid. Dr. Leander Starr Jameson, personal physician and assistant to Cecil Rhodes, the empire-building Premier of Britain's Cape Colony, led four hundred and seventy men on a raid from Bechuanaland into Paul Kruger's Boer Republic of the Transvaal on the night of December 29, 1895. Rhodes was determined that the Boers should not stand in the way of his, and British, expansion from the Cape toward Cairo, and he and Jameson thought that the raid would precipitate an internal uprising in the Transvaal by the *uitlanders* —British and other non-Boer settlers who had moved into the area—which would bring Kruger down. Neither Joseph Chamberlain, who had become Colonial Secretary in the ministry of Lord Salisbury, in London, earlier in the year, nor Salisbury himself had any official word of Rhodes's intentions, and the British government was able to dissociate itself from the raid.

Unofficial knowledge was a different matter. Certainly the High Commissioner and governor at the Cape, Sir Hercules Robinson, knew of Rhodes's plot, as he admitted to his secretary, but he learned of it in an unofficial capacity and fell back upon the moral fiction that as governor he had not been informed. The raid is the point at which many historians choose to begin the story of the Boer War, for it—like the sinking of the *Lusitania* or the explosion against the hull of the *Maine*—seemed to lead to an escalation of an already intense crisis. It was the Tonkin Gulf incident of Britain's most imperial war, and, like that incident, investigation began to reveal the several Chinese boxes of intrigue that nestled within each other.

To this day we do not have all the answers about the Jameson Raid. The Committee that inquired, in 1897, into the circumstances of the raid suppressed evidence. The papers of Chamberlain, of Rhodes, and of the latter's secretary, Sir Graham Bower, are not complete, and those of Robinson have never been found—another search for lost manuscripts well worth making. We do know that Rhodes, aware that the raid would fail, sent a telegram to Jameson to tell him to abandon the raid and that the telegram did not reach him; we know that Robinson sent a courier after Jameson to order him to desist, in the Queen's name, and that Jameson refused. Chamberlain denounced the raiders and telegraphed a repudiation to Kruger. The question, then, is how much of this anti-raid activity on the part of British officials was a cover, in the knowledge—transmitted to Rhodes by his agent in Johannesburg, Dr. Rutherfoord Harris, who had also tried to dissuade Jameson—that the raid would fail? The Boers contended that the British government was deeply involved; the government insisted that it was innocent.

The Select Committee of the House of Commons, which included Chamberlain himself as a member, together with powerful Opposition voices in Sir William V. Harcourt and Sir Henry Campbell-Bannerman, sat for five months, reporting in mid-1897 to censure Rhodes and to acquit Chamberlain. Two members of the Committee disagreed with the findings, for while the group had examined over forty telegrams that had been sent from London to Cape Town before the raid, they had failed to compel the production before the Committee of eight others that had formed a part of the same series of communications—eight telegrams that were expressly withheld on Rhodes's personal orders. The mystery of the missing telegrams continued to rankle and the Jameson Raid has remained a synonym in anti-imperial circles for the sinister machinations of the British in South Africa.

The entire affair is extremely complex and no short essay can do full justice to it. The literature on Rhodes, Jameson, and Chamberlain (although not on Robinson) is substantial, and the reader might wish to consult other titles, listed below. For our purposes, the best approach is through an article by C. M. Woodhouse, British historian and member of Parliament.

♦ ♦ ♦

A select group of people shared Rhodes's knowledge of the intended revolution in Johannesburg and the purpose for which Jameson had been placed on the border. Among them were Joseph Chamberlain, Secretary of State for the Colonies; his Under-Secretary, Lord Selborne, who was the son-in-law of the Prime Minister,

---

FROM C. M. Woodhouse, "The Missing Telegrams and the Jameson Raid," *History Today,* XII (June and July, 1962), 396–400, 403–04, 506–12, 514. Printed with permission of the author.

For additional reading: As evidence of the fascination the raid holds for historians, see Melvin G. Holli's article, "Joseph Chamberlain and the Jameson Raid: A Bibliographical Survey," *Journal of British Studies,* III (May, 1964), 152–66. Two of the best studies are those by Ethel Drus, "The Question of Imperial Complicity in the Jameson Raid," *English Historical Review,* LXVIII (October, 1953), 582–93, and "A Report on the Papers of Joseph Chamberlain, Relating to the Jameson Raid and the Inquiry," *Bulletin of the Institute of Historical Research,* XXV (May, 1952), 36–62. Most scholars agree that Chamberlain shared a high degree of responsibility, contrary to the views of his biographer, James L. Garvin, in *The Life of Joseph Chamberlain,* III (London, 1934). Also entertaining is Joseph O. Baylen, "W. T. Stead's *History of the Mystery* and the Jameson Raid," *Journal of British Studies,* IV (November, 1964), 104–32. Detective stories which combine the elements of the Jameson mystery abound. Among the best, each with a quite different approach, are Rebecca West's *The Birds Fall Down,* Freeman Wills Crofts' *Crime at Guilford,* and Michael Innes's *The Paper Thunderbolt,* which ends deep within the Bodleian Library at Oxford. While spy fiction often turns to Africa for local color, mystery writers seldom have moved below the Blue Nile. One book that does so is Elspeth Huxley's *Murder on Safari,* to be read with her *Murder at Government House,* both set in East Africa.

Lord Salisbury; and a number of his senior officials, particularly Edward Fairfield, who died, luckily for Chamberlain, before he could be publicly questioned. There were also the High Commissioner in Cape Town, Sir Hercules Robinson, and his Imperial Secretary, Sir Graham Bower, a retired naval officer. There was Flora Shaw, later Lady Lugard, the Colonial Correspondent of *The Times,* and the paper's Assistant Manager, Moberly Bell. There was Rhodes's solicitor, Bourchier Hawksley, and a number of his business and political associates, particularly Dr. Rutherfoord Harris, Alfred Beit, and Earl Grey.

Most of these eventually more or less admitted their degree of complicity, when it could no longer be concealed. But Sir Hercules Robinson and Joseph Chamberlain escaped scot-free. Robinson, the High Commissioner, did so by downright lying, supported by the loyalty of Bower, his Imperial Secretary. The latter took the blame on himself for having failed to tell his superior what he had learned from Rhodes of his plans, although he knew also that Rhodes had personally given the same information to the High Commissioner. Chamberlain's escape was luckier and not quite so dishonourable. He was able to say, without actually lying, that he had no prior knowledge of the Raid, because nobody had any prior knowledge of the Raid as it actually happened, not even Jameson until the day he started. Chamberlain was also protected by the general belief of his colleagues and even of his political opponents that he was innocent; and that even if he were not, the public interest required that he should not be exposed. But most of all he was saved by Rhodes's refusal to incriminate him, against the strong advice of Hawksley, his solicitor, and other colleagues; and therein lies the . . . mystery.

Apart from telling the whole truth himself, Rhodes had the means to incriminate Chamberlain through a dossier of telegrams, collected in the first place by Harris and later held by Bourchier Hawksley. The dossier contained a series of messages, probably totalling fifty-four in all, which had been exchanged between London and Cape Town in the months before the Raid. None of them had originated from Chamberlain himself, but they often referred to him; and even allowing for the reckless irresponsibility with which some of them were drafted, particularly by Rutherfoord

Harris, their publication would inevitably expose Chamberlain to exceedingly difficult questions, from which his complicity in the abortive revolution and the preliminaries to the Raid could not fail to emerge. Hawksley urged Rhodes to publish them, but Rhodes refused.

Chamberlain learned of the existence of the dossier from Hawksley a few weeks after the Raid. In June 1896, Hawksley allowed Chamberlain to see the telegrams, and Chamberlain, with the help of his staff, then wrote an elaborate commentary on them, which was in effect a brief for his own defence if they were published. Since he had already agreed, under pressure in the House of Commons, that there should be a Select Committee to investigate the Raid, publication must have seemed to him to be unavoidable eventually. Chamberlain thereupon offered his resignation to Salisbury, who refused it. Such was the government's confidence in Chamberlain that he was actually appointed a member of the Select Committee himself. Moreover, the Enquiry was successfully staved off until the beginning of 1897; and much might, and did, happen to confuse the situation in the meantime.

Every successive effort to throw light on the Raid during 1896 only served to veil it in deeper mystery. First, the Transvaal government published a collection of documents captured in the trunk of one of Jameson's officers (*"de trommel van Bobby White"*), which further damaged the reputation of Rhodes without directly implicating Chamberlain or the High Commissioner. Then the Legislative Assembly at Cape Town appointed a Select Committee of enquiry, which produced a report roundly condemning Rhodes and his entourage but acquitting almost everybody else. Lastly, at Christmas, the well-known journalist, W. T. Stead, published a semi-fictional account of the Raid, entitled *The History of the Mystery,* which was made still more mysterious by last-minute deletions, after the proofs had been passed, of passages incriminating Chamberlain. Stead clearly knew of the existence of the Hawksley telegrams when he wrote the *History,* but he had not seen them. The deleted passages, which nevertheless appeared unexpurgated in a review of the story published in Cape Town, had been removed at the request of Rhodes.

Rhodes was, in fact, determined to protect Chamberlain, and he continued to do so when he was called before the Select Committee at Westminster in February 1897. His reason is no longer in doubt. What he valued above all things was the Royal Charter under which the British South Africa Company was operating in the territory already known as Rhodesia. Any Colonial Secretary but Chamberlain would certainly have revoked that Charter after the implication of the Chartered Company in the conspiracy against the Transvaal. It followed, by Rhodes's reasoning, that Chamberlain must be kept in office at all costs to safeguard the Charter. Whether there was an explicit bargain between Rhodes and Chamberlain, by which Rhodes agreed not to incriminate Chamberlain and Chamberlain agreed not to revoke the Charter, is unknown and immaterial. Certainly there was at least a tacit understanding. This accounts for the peculiar tension between Chamberlain and Rhodes, nominally the interrogator and the accused, at the Enquiry by the Select Committee, which was observed but not understood by reporters at the time.

In spite of the indiscretions of Stead, the Select Committee took an inordinate time to ferret out the telegrams. Some thought its ineptitude was calculated: the Enquiry even came to be known derisively as the "Lying in State at Westminster." Rhodes was asked about the telegrams during his evidence, which came at the beginning of the Enquiry, but he refused to produce them, and the Select Committee did not press him. It was only after he had left the country and become apparently inaccessible—though still communicating with Hawksley from Central Africa—that the Committee began to demand the production of the telegrams more vigorously. Hawksley, on Rhodes's orders, then refused to produce them. Chamberlain, who had already seen them and had them copied at the Colonial Office, did nothing to facilitate the Enquiry in which he was supposed to be taking part.

All that the Committee could get out of Hawksley was the Chartered Company's cipher-book. But they also obtained forty-six of the fifty-four telegrams from the telegraph company which had despatched them. The telegraph company had destroyed, as a matter of routine, everything prior to November 1st, 1895, and this was the ostensible reason why the other eight telegrams were missing. The explanation is not quite watertight, because although five of the "missing telegrams" were dated before November 1st, 1895, two were dated later; and it is difficult to account for the disappearance of these two except by collusion. It is noteworthy that the deciphering of the available forty-six telegrams was done for the Select Committee by an employee of the Chartered Company—that is to say, a partisan of Rhodes. Moreover, there is evidence in the Rosebery Papers . . . that in 1898 Rhodes told Rosebery that the Chairman of the Select Committee, W. L. Jackson (later Lord Allerton), personally helped to deceive his colleagues by "severely editing" one or more of the telegrams presented; so that collusion is certainly not an impossibility. The Committee, however, had now at last got most of the contents of Hawksley's dossier, and the forty-six deciphered telegrams were duly published in appendices to their Report. They made further efforts, half-heartedly and without success, to extract the remainder from Hawksley, but eventually gave up—some say not very reluctantly—in order not to delay the completion of their work.

The eight "missing telegrams" form the last hard core of the mystery. Chamberlain saw them all, and made notes on them in his memorandum of June 1896. His memorandum, which survives, quotes parts of them *verbatim,* and has been generally taken by modern historians to be the only remaining evidence for their contents. Everyone who has written about the Jameson Raid hitherto has long since given up any hope of ever seeing the actual texts. It is known that the original Hawksley dossier was destroyed many years ago. Some say it was destroyed by Hawksley, some say by Rhodes's Trustees; the present Mr. E. D. Hawksley, grandson of Bourchier and now Secretary of the British South Africa Company, believes that it was done by his father or grandfather after the papers had been stored for many years in the cloak-room at Victoria Station. The copies retained by Chamberlain, and originally annexed to his memorandum of June 1896, have also disappeared. One of the missing eight, however, the earliest, now turns out to have been lying buried ever since 1895, along with four out of the forty-six that were eventually seen by the Select Committee, in Rhodes's papers. These papers are now at Rhodes House in Oxford. . . .

The first of the "missing telegrams," was drafted by Rutherfoord

Harris in London on August 2nd, 1895, despatched on the following day, and received by Rhodes in Cape Town on the 5th. It was sent after Rutherfoord Harris and Lord Grey had had an interview with Chamberlain about the Bechuanaland Protectorate. Chamberlain, who had become Secretary of State for the Colonies only a few weeks earlier, had already agreed to allow the Cape Colony (of which Rhodes was Prime Minister) to annex the Crown Colony of Bechuanaland, which adjoined it to the north. The Protectorate of Bechuanaland was distinct from the Crown Colony of Bechuanaland, and lay betwen it and Rhodesia, along the western frontier of the Transvaal. Rhodes had long wanted to acquire the Protectorate also, but he wished it to be brought under the administration of the Chartered Company rather than the Cape Colony: in other words, he wanted to annex it to Rhodesia. To this several of the Bechuana Chiefs objected, and with the help of sympathetic missionaries they took their objections to Chamberlain personally. The purpose of the visit of Harris and Grey to Chamberlain on August 2nd, 1895, was to persuade him to overrule their objections.

Rhodes wanted the Protectorate in a hurry, ostensibly in order to continue the construction of the railway line from the Cape Colony to the North, but in reality in order to provide Jameson with his jumping-off point. (This is not to say, of course, that Rhodes was not really interested in the railway as well: it was one of the passions of his life, but for the moment it was secondary.) If Harris and Grey could not get the whole Protectorate, which Rhodes maintained had been promised to him in principle for several years, then they were prepared to settle temporarily for a strip of it along the border of the Transvaal, which would be wide enough for the railway, and incidentally also for Jameson. The ostensible business of Jameson's force in the strip would be to protect the railway. Chamberlain refused their main request, but offered to compromise on the alternative.

How frankly Rhodes's motives were expounded to Chamberlain and his officials on August 2nd, 1895, was a matter of later dispute. Harris, who was a bad witness, said later that he spoke much more frankly than Chamberlain, who was a very skilful witness, would allow; and [E.] Fairfield, the principal official present, who was alleged to be rather deaf, was also dead by the time the Select Committee reached the crucial point. The nearest to an authentic account—subject to the qualification that nothing from Rutherfoord Harris could be quite authentic—was Harris's telegram despatched on August 2nd-3rd. The text was seen by Chamberlain in June 1896, and his memorandum contains all that has hitherto been known of it. The version given in the Chamberlain memorandum was published in part by J. L. Garvin in 1934 [(London)], in the third volume of his *Life of Joseph Chamberlain* (pp. 110–1), but more fully by Miss Ethel Drus in 1952, in the *Bulletin of the Institute of Historical Research*. . . . What Chamberlain wrote on the telegram reads as follows:

> Gives a substantially accurate account of the attempt of the Directors to obtain an immediate transfer of the administration of the Bechuanaland Protectorate and of my decisive refusal. But after recounting this the telegram continues:
>
> "We decided therefore inform Secretary of State for Colonies guardedly reason we wish to have base at Gaberones and advisable our presence in Protectorate. Secretary of State for Colonies heartily in sympathy with C. J. Rhodes's policy, but he would not on this ground alter decision with regard to Protectorate, but offered as alternate (alternative?) to justify residence B.S.A. Co. in Protectorate to consider favourable at once application for large land grant Protectorate in exchange Railway extension north. It is now C. J. Rhodes to decide whether large grant township sale of stands is practicable during the month of October appears only solution."

The words from "but he would not . . ." to the end were omitted by Garvin in his biography as "code jargon about matters in no way concerning the point at issue." He has been much criticized by later historians, who point out that they are in fact far from irrelevant. But he did hit upon one important point, which others have overlooked, when he called them "code jargon." Whatever that phrase may have meant, it is a fact that the version seen by Chamberlain is clearly not the original text as drafted in the head office of the Chartered Company in August 1895: not even Rutherfoord Harris could have produced quite such clumsy phraseology out of his own head. The most obvious explanation of the evident verbal corruptions would be that Chamberlain's text had been deciphered from an enciphered version. But that seems to be ruled out by the improbability that Harris and Hawksley should have had available to them in 1896 only the enciphered version of what had been despatched in August 1895, and not the plain-language original.

An alternative possibility is that there was an intermediate stage in the process of transmission between the original draft and the encipherment. The supposition is that a clerk prepared the original text for encipherment by translating or editing the text into "telegraphese," substituting, for instance, phrases which he knew to be in the cipher-book for those that were not, and so on. It seems perfectly possible that this "telegraphese" version should have survived in London, and that this was what Hawksley showed to Chamberlain in June 1896. Such a supposition would readily account for the obscure language of the last part of the telegram, which Garvin dismissed as "code jargon." . . . The supposition is borne out by comparison with the original text of this "missing telegram," for it now turns out not to be missing at all but buried in the Rhodes Papers at Oxford. By a fortunate chance, the Rhodes Papers contain both the original text as drafted by Harris in London and the deciphered version as received by Rhodes at Cape Town. This means that the earliest of the so-called "missing telegrams" is now unique in that we know exactly what was written at the despatching end, not merely what was deciphered at the receiving end. It has happened because, at the same time as Harris's telegram was despatched, a confirmatory copy was sent by post in a letter from the London Secretary of the Company, Mr. Herbert Canning. (The letter is actually dated a day earlier than the telegram.) This letter and the text as deciphered on receipt were filed together, the latter folded inside the former. . . . Words for which there was no cipher equivalent were sent *en clair* —a point which has an important bearing on some of the later telegrams in the series.

The letter from Canning reads as follows:

Dear Mr. Rhodes,

We sent you to-day the following private wire, which I confirm—

"Earl Grey & Dr. Harris saw Secretary of State for Colonies, he considers Crown Colony having been transferred to Cape Colony at moment entering office he has shown practical proof of sympathy with Mr. C. J. Rhodes policy; but although he is friendly very, considers cession Protectorate at any near date utterly impossible. His attitude on this point without compromise and decisive. He states presence C. J. Rhodes England will not alter his mind; that C. J. Rhodes must leave him alone for the present. In his opinion he acceded to transfer Crown Colony in order to ensure immediate further Railway Construction, and much upset that it was not the case because sale B. Ry. Co. to Cape Colony it had not taken place. Dr. Harris explained Parliament(ary) position & Sauers remarks to convince Secretary of State for Colonies no breach of faith on our part; but he still considers B.S.A. Co. if finance is favourable is obligated to proceed at once with Railway towards Palapye. We decided therefore to inform Secretary of State for Colonies guardedly reason we wish to have base at Gaberones, and advisable our presence in Protectorate. Secretary of State for Colonies heartily in sympathy with Mr. C. J. Rhodes policy, but he would not on this account alter decision with regard to Protectorate, but offered as alternate, to justify residents of B.S.A. Co. in Protectorate, to consider favourably at once application for large land grant in Protectorate in exchange for Railway Extension north. It is now for Mr. C. J. Rhodes to decide whether large land grant with formation Township and sale of stands is practicable for October.

"This appears to be the only solution."

This was a somewhat long cable to code, but I hope that it came to you in a clear form. The time will come no doubt. Believe me

Yours faithfully

Herbert Canning

It will readily be seen that the last four sentences correspond to the text shown to Chamberlain and quoted in his memorandum of June 1896. But there are certain small differences which are significant. One of them serves to show conclusively that the word "stands" is a noun (meaning "sites") and not a verb, as Lady Longford ingeniously conjectured in her attempt to reconstruct the meaning of the telegram from the version in Chamberlain's memorandum (Elizabeth Pakenham [Countess Longford]: *Jameson's Raid* [London, 1960], p. 178). Another important point follows from the fact that we know Canning's letter contains the authentic text as originally drafted by Harris, before encipherment. It is clear from the verbal differences in Chamberlain's text that what he saw was not the original version. This might well have been inferred from its confused phraseology, but for the fact that one instinctively expects Harris's phraseology to be confused. It is now a demonstrated fact.

The text received by Rhodes in Cape Town was the deciphered version, and likewise not the original. But how closely did it coincide with the version shown to Chamberlain? The question cannot be answered because of an extraordinary chance, which, like so many other episodes in the story of the Raid, serves to thicken the mystery in the very process of enlightenment. The surviving telegraphic text received by Rhodes was torn away, obviously deliberately; and the point at which it breaks off is precisely the point at which Chamberlain's version begins. There is no ground for thinking that this is anything more than a coincidence. It can hardly be, for instance, that the last part of Rhodes's text was torn off in order to be included in the dossier shown by Hawksley to Chamberlain, because it is clear from Chamberlain's memorandum of June 1896 that he saw the whole of this telegram and not merely the part that he quoted. It is therefore impossible to say whether the text seen by Chamberlain and the text seen by Rhodes were literally identical; and it is also impossible even to compare them, because, so far as the critical sentences are concerned, only the version seen by Chamberlain survives.

The foregoing argument applies, of course, only to the last four sentences of the telegram, from "We decided therefore . . ." onwards. The whole of the first part of the telegram, which was seen by Chamberlain but not quoted in his memorandum, now emerges into the light of day for the first time. It is unique among all the telegrams connected with the Jameson Raid in being now available both in the original and in a deciphered version. There are some verbal discrepancies between the two versions, but they are not significant. They serve simply to show, what might easily be expected, how minor differences could creep into the telegrams in the process of preparation for encipherment, transmission and decipherment; and that is useful because of the bearing it has on other telegrams in the Hawksley dossier or the Rhodes Papers. It remains only to assess the significance of the newly discovered texts for the study of the Jameson Raid and Chamberlain's rôle in relation to it.

The telegram confirms Chamberlain's own claim to have decisively refused the main request put to him by Grey and Harris. It adds nothing to the presumption of his guilty knowledge of Rhodes's conspiracy, though that is a presumption that hardly needs reinforcement at this date. One must in any case recognize the virtual impossibility that any of the telegrams in Hawksley's dossier should by itself literally and directly convict Chamberlain of complicity, since none of them emanated from him. What they did, in many cases, was to put words in his mouth that he may or may not have used; and the danger that they constituted to him was that of providing a basis on which awkward questions could be put to him at the Enquiry. So it would have been in the present case. For instance, he later pretended to have believed, as did Sir Hercules Robinson, that the purpose of Jameson's force was to guard the railway; but the newly revealed first part of the telegram of August 2nd-3rd now suggests that he already knew—and was indignant at the fact—that the stretch of railway which Jameson's men were supposed to be intended to guard did not exist. In any case the question remains, why, if he regarded his own rôle as innocent, did he take such pains to ensure that this telegram, with its companions, was withheld from the Select Committee?

The real importance of the new text, however, does not lie so much in the awkward implications that it might have had for Chamberlain at the Enquiry. Its importance is two-fold. Firstly, there is the simple fact that an historic document long written off for good as "missing" is missing no longer. Secondly, the fact that it survives in two versions, one as originally drafted and one as deciphered, serves to show that the version seen by Chamberlain was not the original text. This establishes a presumption that other telegrams in Hawksley's dossier, as shown to Chamberlain, may also have been different from the originals; and this presumption has an interesting bearing on other telegrams preserved in the Rhodes Papers.

. . . [S]everal different versions of each of the telegrams connected with the Jameson Raid have to be distinguished. To say this is not to presuppose that anyone deliberately tampered with any of the texts for nefarious purposes, though that is also in some cases probable on other grounds. The distinct versions that must have existed legitimately, as it were, may be labelled as follows:

I. the original draft by the initiator of each message;
II. the above as edited into "telegraphese" for encipherment and despatch;
III. the above as deciphered on receipt and presented to the addressee;

To these must also be added in the case of most of the telegrams, though of course not, by definition, in the case of the "missing telegrams," one more version:

IV. the text recovered from the telegraph office and deciphered for the benefit of the Select Committee in 1897.

The difference between version III and version IV was that the latter had not gone through the process of being telegraphed, and was deciphered by a different clerk in different circumstances.

Each of the above versions has an importance of its own. Version I represents, in each case, the *ipsissima verba* of the originator; but the formerly "missing telegram" of August 2nd/3rd, 1895, . . . is the only case in which it survives. Version II can safely be presumed to be, in each case, that which was preserved in Hawksley's famous dossier, and shown to Joseph Chamberlain in June 1896. Version III is that which was received by Cecil Rhodes in Cape Town in 1895 (or, in the case of telegrams initiated by him, received by his accomplices in London). Version IV is that which was shown to the Select Committee in 1897 and embodied in the Appendices to its Report. There is no case in which all four versions survive, but it is easy enough to deduce that all four must have existed, except for version IV in the case of the "missing telegrams." Several interesting questions then naturally arise.

The first is whether the Rhodes Papers contain any more of the "missing telegrams," in addition to that of August 2nd/3rd. The answer is that they do not, but they do contain four of the telegrams from Rutherfoord Harris to Rhodes, dated November 4th and 5th, which were eventually obtained from the telegraph company, deciphered and published by the Select Committee; and the versions that the Rhodes Papers contain are those received by Rhodes in Cape Town (version III). . . .

The second question is whether there are any significant discrepancies between the versions received by Rhodes (III) and the versions shown later to Chamberlain and the Select Committee (respectively II and IV). The answer is . . . that there are; and this leads to the third question, whether it is possible to throw any light on the discrepancies and to determine which version is correct. The answer to this last question lies in the code-book of the British South Africa Company, which fortunately survives in the National Archives of Rhodesia and Nyasaland at Salisbury. . . .

The . . . process of encipherment and decipherment has a particular relevance to some of the peculiarities about the telegram of November 4th. Thanks to the Select Committee of 1897, something is known about two other versions of this telegram: version II, which was shown to Chamberlain in June 1896 and indirectly quoted by him in his evidence to the Select Committee; and version IV, which was published in Appendix 14 to its Report. There are minor but significant variations between each of the three versions now extant.

The discrepancies will emerge most easily if the version presented to the Select Committee is given first:

J. Chamberlain he does not return London until to-morrow. I have spoken open E. Fairfield and I have accepted if Colonial Office (they) will transfer to us balance protectorate with police 7 Nov. we will agree to any liberal native reserves for native chiefs also remain under imperial rule for a period of years and we give up railway subsidy 200,000*l.* last bargain E. Fairfield he does press if you cannot approve let us know about this as soon as possible by telegram. We believe E. Fairfield will carry out promises. Regret to inform you that J. Chamberlain he does continue punching Consul General Transvaal with regard to drifts. E. Fairfield he is anxious Johannesburg if they take steps in precedence of. Dr. Harris[.]

The above telegram has always been one of the most controversial of all the documents connected with the Jameson Raid, much of it being very difficult to interpret. The controversy began as soon as it was seen by the Select Committee on May 18th, 1897, when Rutherfoord Harris was giving evidence. He was asked at

Q.[uestion] 8217 whether there was "any special significance" about the phrase: "I have spoken open E. Fairfield." He replied with a characteristically unhelpful rigmarole, the upshot of which was a refusal to reply on the grounds that Fairfield was not there to give his own version of the conversation. "If he was here I am sure we should not differ materially," he said—a rather oblique reference to the fact that Fairfield was actually dead. He agreed, however, that the words meant that he had "spoken frankly to Mr. Fairfield."

The Chairman proceeded to question him about the extraordinary jumble of words forming the last sentence of the telegram. Rutherfoord Harris was in the middle of another prevaricating reply when Joseph Chamberlain, the Colonial Secretary and himself a member of the Select Committee, intervened to give his own version of their meaning. He did so by reading out a letter that had been written to himself by Fairfield in June 1896, thus incidentally revealing that this was one of the telegrams in Hawksley's dossier that he had already seen. In commenting on this telegram, Fairfield had quoted a part of the text of it, and thus gave us version II of the final sentences:

> Regret to inform you Secretary of State for the Colonies is still punching Consul General of the Transvaal about the drifts. Fairfield he is anxious Johannesburg, they take steps in precedence.

It is clear enough from the verbal discrepancies between this version (which was read out by Chamberlain from a written document) and that contained in the Appendix that we have here two distinct texts (II and IV), though of course they have a common origin.

What did the telegram mean? The Select Committee spent many weary hours trying to find out. They knew, of course, that the second sentence referred to the negotiations between Chamberlain and Harris, acting on Rhodes's behalf, about the terms on which a part of the Bechuanaland Protectorate (the jumping-off point of the Jameson Raid) should be transferred from the Crown to the Chartered Company. They also knew that the reference to the "drifts" (which meant "fords") concerned the crisis caused in the summer of 1895 by President Kruger, when he prevented traffic between the Cape Colony and the Transvaal from fording the Vaal River—a crisis that had very nearly led to war three months before the Jameson Raid. But what did all the rest mean? And what had Harris "spoken open" about to Fairfield?

Chamberlain quoted Fairfield's explanation of the final passage, which Fairfield in turn was quoting from someone he had himself consulted—"a gentleman likely to know what was its meaning," who was never named. The anonymous gentleman thought it meant that Fairfield "did not agree with the policy of Her Majesty's Government, and thought that the grievances of Johannesburg had a prior claim to those of the Cape Railway Department on the diplomatic services of the Imperial Government." Fairfield did not seem to be very convinced by the explanation, if it can be called an explanation, and volunteered in his letter to Chamberlain the thought that he might have quoted to Harris the view of "a friend of the Transvaal" (who also remained anonymous) that

> it would have been more to the credit of the British Government if they had used their diplomatic influence to try and obtain redress for the dynamite, educational, and other grievances of the Johannesburgers, than to have taken up the drifts question at the bidding of Mr. Rhodes, so as to enable him to get the better of the Netherlands Railway Company in a purely local and commercial squabble.

Obviously these attempts at explanation impressed nobody. The Select Committee left the telegram on one side for the moment, but repeatedly returned to it. Sir William Harcourt, the Leader of the Opposition in the Commons, tried in vain to extract intelligible answers from Rutherfoord Harris, and so did the more hostile Radical M.P., [Henry] Labouchère. Chamberlain felt constrained to intervene again at Q. 8579, when he read out another letter that he had received from the late E. Fairfield. This new letter had been written on the very same day (November 4th, 1895) as the interview with Harris at which the latter claimed to have "spoken open." It gave a detailed account of the state of negotiations about the Bechuanaland Protectorate and appeared to contain no guilty secrets at all, except for one phrase: "Rhodes very naturally wants to get our people off the scene as this ugly row is pending with the Transvaal." The words might be construed as a reference to the conspiracy that culminated in the Jameson Raid eight weeks later, and that is how historians hostile to Rhodes and Chamberlain have taken it. Chamberlain himself tried to forestall the hostile interpretation by inserting his own gloss as he read: "that, of course, refers to the drifts."

Harris had no desire to help Chamberlain. When he was asked whether Fairfield's letter was a fair account of what he had said when he had "spoken open," he insisted that it was incomplete. "I cannot say that that is solely what I said to Mr. Fairfield," he said at Q. 8583, and again in answer to the next question: "It is within the knowledge of other gentlemen that I spoke more openly than that." He identified Bourchier Hawksley, Rhodes's solicitor, as having been present at the conversation, but under close questioning by Labouchère at the Committee's next session he admitted that he had jumbled up several meetings with Fairfield in his mind. It was never made clear whether Hawksley or any other witness had in fact been present when Harris had "spoken open." Harris was . . . a deplorable witness.

The Select Committee tried again to elucidate the incomprehensible telegram when Chamberlain submitted himself to questioning on June 1st, 1897. But Chamberlain could not help them any more than Harris, and with better reason: after all, it was Harris and not he who had drafted the telegram, and he had certainly not been present at the meeting between Harris and Fairfield. He did assert emphatically, however, at Q. 9566, that Fairfield was accustomed, as was his duty, to speak with complete frankness to himself; and that Fairfield had not on this occasion communicated (in the words of the questioner) "anything whatever of what is alleged to have been communicated to him." He added at Q. 9590 that there had been nothing in Fairfield's manner to suggest that he had been holding anything back.

It is typical of the atmosphere of pompous mystification in which the whole Enquiry was conducted that no one ever attempted to define what was alleged to have been communicated by Harris to Fairfield. Harris had "spoken open": that was all he would ever say. It was, of course, left to be assumed that what he had "spoken open" about was the plan to use Jameson's force, stationed on the borders of the Transvaal, to support a revolution against President Kruger's government in Johannesburg; but no one actually said this in so many words. It is hardly to be doubted now that both Fairfield and Chamberlain did, in fact, know what Rhodes's intention was in placing Jameson on the border (though his intention was by no means the same thing as what Jameson actually did). To that extent Chamberlain's complicity is nowadays generally accepted. But what was, and still is, at issue in considering Harris's telegram of November 4th is the extent to which, taken by itself, it bears upon the question of complicity.

That is the issue on which the discovery of the text as received by Rhodes (version III) now throws a new light. . . . Some of the discrepancies are of no importance, except in so far as they confirm the distinctness of the three versions: for instance, we find "Secretary of State for the Colonies" in version II, "Mr. Chamberlain" in version III, and "J. Chamberlain" in version IV. We also find that in the second sentence, version III uses the plural "we" whereas version IV uses the singular "I." Since both versions are presumed to have been deciphered from the same enciphered text —the only difference being that III had been transmitted by telegraph and IV had not—one cannot base any substantial argument (for instance, about the presence of other witnesses at the conversation) upon this discrepancy.

Two other minor discrepancies deserve to be mentioned before turning to the major problems. It will be seen that the version received by Rhodes agrees with that presented to the Select Committee in giving the date November 7th for the proposed transfer of the balance of the Protectorate with the police. November 7th was, in fact, the date on which Chamberlain's decision was formally put into writing. But it will also be seen [from the code book] that the code-phrase in the left-hand column opposite "7 November" is *stechheber;* and reference to the code-book shows that *stechheber* corresponds to "14 November," whereas the coding of "7 November" is *stecheiche*. It would be difficult to account for the appearance of "7 November" in both version III and version IV if it were in fact an error; so more probably the error is in the left-hand column. In either case, it is evident that the clerk who deciphered the telegram in Cape Town was grossly careless.

The same carelessness is evident later in the telegram, where the clerk in Cape Town has omitted the word "promises" at the end of the sentence: "We believe E. Fairfield will carry out promises." On the line below "he will carry out," the new version has: *murrsinne*—"Regret to inform you that." But *murrsinne* stands for "promises" in the code-book; and the coding of "regret to inform you that" is *oxyrrhodin*. . . . [T]he clerk . . . omitted *oxyrrhodin* from the left-hand column and "promises" from the right-hand column; and he . . . then moved one line up incorrectly on each side, thus aligning *murrsinne* with "regret to inform you that." It will therefore come as no surprise to find that he . . . committed even more glaring errors as well.

The major discrepancies affect the very passages of the telegram that caused the Select Committee so much worry. They occur at the beginning, in the second sentence; and at the end, in the last two sentences. The conclusion which they point to is in each case the same: if the telegram as received by Rhodes in Cape Town had ever been submitted to the Select Committee—and it was, after all, for practical purposes the effective version of the telegram—then everyone would have been saved a vast amount of trouble and Rutherfoord Harris would have been spared the necessity of a great deal of prevarication.

The first major discrepancy is the omission of the word "open." As Rhodes read the telegram, Harris never said that he had "spoken open" to Fairfield at all. He simply said that he had "spoken," a sufficiently innocuous expression which need never have provoked the flood of questions and evasions and half-truths that in fact occurred. Moreover, it is not difficult to guess how the word "open" crept into the version presented to the Select Committee. The practice in deciphering was . . . to write words which had been transmitted *en clair* straight into the right-hand column without making any entry in the left-hand column. It can be seen that this is what was done with the word "spoken." (Reference to the code-book has confirmed that it contains no coding for "spoken.") The cipher-clerk who deciphered the telegram for the Select Committee therefore saw at once that the word was *en clair;* and as it was the first word transmitted *en clair* in this particular telegram, he (or somebody else) indicated the fact by writing the word "open" alongside it. When it was copied out for presentation to the Select Committee, the word "open" was naturally but erroneously embodied in the text. It is a safe guess that the version shown to Chamberlain (version II) did not contain the misleading word.

The second major discrepancy concerns the phrase in the penultimate sentence, which is common to versions II and IV (those shown to Chamberlain and the Select Committee respectively) about the Secretary of State "punching Consul General [of the] Transvaal." Much argument has revolved about the word "punching," which seemed a curious expression even for Rutherfoord Harris. It will be seen that neither "punching" nor "Consul General" is to be found in the version seen by Rhodes in Cape Town. What does appear there, however, is the combination: *gunchina* (left-hand column)—"consult" (right-hand column). But there is no such word as *gunchina* in the code-book; and the cipher-clerk accordingly put a question mark alongside it. It is clearly a corruption of "punching," which was therefore equally clearly transmitted *en clair* because (as reference to the code-book has also shown) there was no way of enciphering it. It is thus established that "punching," peculiar though the expression may be, is correct.

What about the Consul General? If *gunchina* becomes "punching" and is transferred to the right-hand column, there is a gap in the left-hand column where the cipher-clerk (not for the first time) has omitted a phrase. It will be seen that "Consul General of" (versions II and IV) and "consult" (version III) are immediate neighbours in the cipher-book, being represented by *entlehnen* and *entleibung* respectively. One or other of these two phrases has been omitted by the Cape Town cipher-clerk. Oddly enough, the result which he has produced ("regret to inform you that Mr. Chamberlain he does continue consult Transvaal with regard to drifts") makes, on the face of it, better sense than the versions seen by Chamberlain and the Select Committee. Nevertheless, two facts are decisive in favour of "Consul General." One is that if "punching" is correct, the next word must be a noun; the other is that versions II and IV concur on this point. Harris was indeed depicting Chamberlain as punching the Consul General of the Transvaal, however ridiculous the activity may seem. The one important new point that emerges is that this picture was never conveyed by Rhodes. Thanks partly to the cipher-clerk's carelessness and partly to his guesswork, Rhodes received a seemingly meaningful but incorrect version instead of a correct but almost incomprehensible one.

The last major discrepancy concerns the final sentence which is common to versions II and IV: "E. Fairfield he is anxious Johannesburg if they take steps in precedence of," as it appears in II, slightly varied in IV. . . . [T]his sentence does not occur in version III at all: in other words, it was never seen by Rhodes. It is extremely difficult to say what can have become of it in the course of transmission to Cape Town. Yet it was certainly present in the version prepared for encipherment in London (which is assumed to be identical with that seen by Chamberlain in June 1896), as well as in the version deciphered for the Select Committee in 1897. One explanation that springs naturally to mind is that it was simply omitted by the clerk in Cape Town (who was, on this hypothesis, presumptuous as well as careless), on the grounds that the words were meaningless. But this explanation will not do if, as appears to be the case, the document now discovered in Rhodes House was the clerk's working copy; for he could not have seen that the words were meaningless until he had deciphered them, or at least some of them; and the corresponding code-phrases would therefore be expected to appear in the left-hand column. . . .

It does not seem possible to solve the mysteries of the telegram of November 4th completely. Various attempts have been made to reconstruct the meaning of the last two sentences, but none of them can be considered successful. The significant points that emerge from the discovery of the text received by Rhodes in Cape Town, however, seem to be three. In the first place, Harris seems not to have originally claimed any specially "open" character about his talk with Fairfield on November 4th. Whether or not he remembered in 1897 what he had written eighteen months earlier, he simply found it convenient to tease and mystify the Select Committee with innuendoes at the expense of a dead man's reputation. In the second place, the phrase about "punching the Consul General of the Transvaal," although part of the original telegram, was never seen by Rhodes before the Raid; so whatever its significance may have been, it had none for him. In the third place, the final sentence, which appeared to the Select Committee to have some reference to the projected rising in Johannesburg, was also never seen by Rhodes before the Raid, and can therefore have played no part in his calculations at the time. . . .

Ciphers and codes do have a way of standing in the path of the researcher today. In the nineteenth century and earlier most such devices were unsophisticated, as the preceding essay has shown us; they can be broken by any historian who has advanced even as far as Helen Fouché Gaines's *Elementary Cryptanalysis.* In the British Colonial Office papers for 1919, a body of material first made available to researchers in the spring of 1966, I found the following coded cable, sent from the Colonial Secretary to the Governor General of Canada in Ottawa, and with an endorsement indicating that the paper following upon it had been put "in Secret cupboard": "undejected acting miterone sluggard ticpolonga deplexam bootjack recent legislation recidiate reciprocal trade between Canada and Japan baptizing existing treaty expires orbibus jibcama exchange of note corbitatum sir edward grey alejaron jacksnipe megaphonie forthwith aleajar when such exchange spurcatori advice thereof be cabled." It would not, I suspect, take long to break this down. Fortunately for me, however, the recipient had broken security in the worst of all possible ways, just as in the affair of the Jameson cables—the encoded words were given their proper meanings on the copy of the cablegram itself. The message then reads, less entrancingly, "14 June. Acting Prime Minister suggests that in view of desirability of bringing into force recent legislation with regard to reciprocal trade between Canada and Japan before the existing treaty expires on the 19 June exchange of note contemplated by Sir Edward Grey and the Japanese Ambassador should be made forthwith and that when such exchange takes place advice thereof be cabled."

For additional reading: For an example of a *post-hoc* intelligence evaluation, see Paul W. Blackstock's treatment of the Zinoviev Letter of 1924 in his *Agents of Deceit* (Chicago, 1966). David Kahn, *The Code-Breakers: The Story of Secret Writing* (New York, 1966), is a massive but consistently interesting study.

17. The Case of the Very Minor Matter:

Inadvertent Error

To be misleading documents need not be forgeries, poorly edited versions of putatively reliable originals, or garbled decodings. With the best will in the world a scribe can introduce an error that proves crucial to later historical interpretation. Biblical scholarship, and virtually all history written on subjects pre-dating the Renaissance, are exposed to such problems aplenty. Josephine Tey—that is, Elizabeth Macintosh—a mystery writer of unusual ability, once turned one of her books, *The Daughter of Time,* on what historians, and what she herself acting as historian, could tell us of the character of Richard III. He was, as any reader of Shakespeare knows, short-lived and untrustworthy. So, too, was another Richard, the second, hysterical and treacherous. Let us look at the evidence for one of his outbursts, as examined by an English historian, L. C. Hector. The crucial passage stands here first in Latin, and it will do the reader no harm to be reminded that just as Georges Simenon's Inspector Maigret does his ratiocination in French, whatever the English editions may say, the historian also must know the language of those he would interrogate.

♦ ♦ ♦

"The character of Richard II has always been an enigma."[1] There has never been, perhaps there never will be, complete agreement

[1] Professor V. H. Galbraith, in *History,* n.s., XXVI [March, 1942], 224.

among historians about the answer to the riddle: it is therefore all the more desirable that there should be as little disagreement as possible about the admissibility of the evidence upon which are to be founded assessments and re-assessments of Richard's personality.

In this connexion a certain minor importance attaches to an episode which took place when Richard was at Salisbury for the parliament held there in April and May of the year 1384. The bare outlines of the story, which is familiar to all students of the reign, are as follows. The king had just heard mass in the apartment of the earl of Oxford when he was approached by the celebrant, an Irish Carmelite named John Latimer, who brought charges of treason (subsequently rebutted) against the duke of Lancaster, John of Gaunt. Pending the investigation of his charges, the friar was committed to custody but on his way to Salisbury Castle he was seized by a gang, who, in an endeavour to extract from him information about the sources of his story, subjected him to a series of tortures which were soon followed by his death.

Among the accounts of the incident to be found in contemporary chronicles [Thomas Frederick] Tout regarded that of the monk of Westminster as the most circumstantial. "The high character of this chronicler makes for its general accuracy, and in outline he is confirmed by the other writers, notably Monk of Evesham . . . and the two St. Albans versions. . . . But the Westminster writer was clearly doubtful as to details, presenting alternate versions of

---

FROM L. C. Hector, "An Alleged Hysterical Outburst of Richard II," *English Historical Review*, LXVIII (January, 1953), 62–65. Reprinted with permission.

For additional reading: The problem of inaccurate transcription is given further illumination in Howard K. Beale, "Is the Printed Diary of Gideon Welles Reliable?," *American Historical Review,* XXX (April, 1925), 547–52. I have attempted to show how misled some of us have been by what Harriet Beecher Stowe had to say, and did not say, about the origin of her Uncle Tom, in an introduction to a reprint edition of *The Narrative of Josiah Henson* (Reading, Mass., 1969). Again, this situation—the garbled transcription, the misplaced comma, the dying message improperly heard—is a cliché of detective and spy fiction. Among those who have used the device well are Ellery Queen, Simon Harvester, and Holly Roth.

some episodes and pointedly quoting Sir John Clanvowe, a knight of the king's chamber, as his source of information."[2]

After referring to the friar's celebration of mass and his obtaining leave to speak freely to the king, the text of this chronicle, as printed by [J.] Lumby,[3] continues:

frater praedictus ducem Lancastriae instanter impetiit et tam acriter processit quod rex sine examinatione ducem praedictum juberet occidi. Sed alii nobiles domino regi astantes id fieri omnino negabant asserentes iniquum fore ut quispiam sine judicio condemnaretur. His quoque auditis rex velut sapiens secundum consilium eorum se protunc facturum promisit. *Igitur secundum quod dominus J. Clanvowe praedixerat statim simulavit furorem exuit se capa sua et calciamentis suis eaque per fenestram ejiciebat ac ea quae furiosi sunt ipse per omnia agebat.* Et ulterius interrogavit saepedictum fratrem an foret aliquis hujus rei conscius vel ipse solus novit. Ad quem frater respondit. "Immo dominus Le Souche plenam noticiam haberet hujus materiae et bene cognosco me moriturum pro ista causa." Cui iterum ait rex, "Sume tibi parcamentum ac facias duas billas indentatas continentes omnia quae volueris objicere contra aliquam personam et tradas mihi unam et alteram habebis penes te, et tunc sciemus quid super hujusmodi faciemus." Sed frater quodammodo confusus erat eo quod dux Lancastriae ad objecta sibi imposita respondere deberet. Rex itaque haec videns jussit eum interim custodiri. . . .

It is reasonable to suppose that the passage here italicized has been generally regarded as evidence, for what it is worth, of the neuroticism of Richard II's character. The construction normally placed upon it is probably fairly represented in the following extracts from the work of distinguished historians published during the past sixty years:

Richard . . . accepted their advice, but as soon as they had left his presence, burst into hysterical fury, threw his cap and slippers out of the window, and flung himself about the room like a madman. Meanwhile the friar had been arrested. . . .

—G. M. TREVELYAN, *England in the Age of Wycliffe* [New York, 1929], p. 276.

[2] *Chapters* [*in the Administrative History of Mediaeval England*], III [Manchester, 1927], 392 n.

[3] Higden (Rolls Ser.), IX, 33.

Richard, nervous and highly strung at all times, now completely lost self-control. He behaved like a madman, took off his hat and shoes and threw them out of the window.

—S[YDNEY] ARMITAGE-SMITH, *John of Gaunt* [London, 1904], p. 283.

According to Malvern (Higden) Richard bellowed with maniacal fury at being thwarted, throwing his cloak and shoes out of the window.

—J. H. RAMSAY, *Genesis of Lancaster* [Oxford, 1913] II, 214.

But [the friar's] confident manner and earnestness seem to have convinced the king for the moment. He burst out into a sudden rage, hurled his hood and boots out of the window like a man distraught. . . .

—C. W. C. OMAN, in *Political History of England* [London, 1906], IV, 91.

One historian regards behaviour of this sort as habitual with Richard:

Unfortunately he expended much of his energy in ungovernable fits of temper, in which he would throw his hood or his boots out of the window, and behave in every respect like a maniac.

—K. H. VICKERS, *England in the Later Middle Ages* [London, 1903], p. 267.

The linguistic difficulties in the way of such constructions could not be expected to count heavily with any reader who came to the passage fresh from thirty-three pages of the chronicler's Latin. It remains none the less true that the use of *igitur*—"therefore"—to introduce a piquant contrast with what precedes it, smacks of a sophisticated humour not affected elsewhere in the chronicle; *statim* is poor warrant for "as soon as they had left his presence"; and the exact significance of *capa* clearly presents problems. But niceties of language apart, many readers must have been struck by the psychological and artistic implausibility of a narrative in which the king's behavior is made to pass with such bewildering abruptness from the rational to the irrational and back again. Tout's reservations, quoted above, and the omission of picturesque detail from his treatment of the episode may well be symptomatic of an uneasiness which has probably been widely shared.

It is therefore fortunate that the printed text of the chronicle can be shown to embody an egregious editorial blunder. The writer of the manuscript[4] from which Lumby was printing inserted, before

[4] Corpus Christi College, Cambridge, MS. 197, p. 142.

the word *Igitur,* a small letter *b*. If Lumby saw this letter, he was apparently unaware that in accordance with a common medieval scribal convention its presence is intended to warn the reader that there has been dislocation and that a complementary *a* and *c* must be sought in the neighbourhood, the three letters serving to indicate the order in which are to be read the passages to which they are severally prefixed. Very little scrutiny of the manuscript discovers the *a* and the *c* placed respectively before the sentences beginning *Et ulterius* and *Rex itaque*. . . .

All is now clear and logical; and in translation the whole passage would run somewhat as follows:

the friar pressed home his attack on the duke of Lancaster, running on with such vehemence that the king gave orders for the duke to be put to death without further enquiry, but the nobles in attendance on him flatly refused to allow this to happen, declaring that it was wrong for anybody to be condemned unheard. After listening to them, the king, like a sensible man, undertook to act in accordance with their advice. He proceeded to ask the friar whether there was anybody else who was privy to this matter, or whether he alone knew of it. To this the friar replied "No, lord la Zouche has full knowledge of the affair; and I am well aware that this thing will be the death of me." The king went on: "Take some parchment and draw up two indented bills containing all the charges you wish to prefer against anybody; hand one to me and keep the other in your own possession; and then we shall see what we shall do about this." The friar, however, was somewhat disconcerted by the prospect of the duke's replying to the charges brought against him. He therefore, according to a statement by Sir John Clanvowe, immediately shammed insanity, stripping off his cope and shoes and pitching them out of the window and generally producing the behaviour characteristic of a madman. On seeing this, the king ordered him to be kept in custody. . . .

On this evidence Richard cannot be charged with having exhibited anything more spectacular than youthful impulsiveness. The critical passage, in which all the words bear their normal literal meanings, is seen to refer to a ruse adopted by the friar to extricate himself from an awkward situation. . . .

Hector arrives at his conclusion by correcting a misread source. Increasingly, historians will find that they must acquire the knowledge with which they may correct a misread character, too. Making men immortal is not the historian's task; they do that for themselves through their deeds. But historians do have the obligation not to allow their mortal subjects to acquire false reputations on the basis of misunderstood motivations. Scholars must attempt to discover why the Hound of Heaven could torture one man and not another, why Sammy ran and Sambo did not. Members of the guild are coming to see that psychology, psychiatry, and psychoanalysis all may have something to offer them, even though few would permit their practitioners to call themselves scientists. Our next case study deals with the mystery of motivation in a way which Hector did not attempt.

18. The Case of the Feigning Man:

Medical-Psychological Evidence

ADDRESSING THE AMERICAN HISTORICAL ASSOCIATION IN 1957, the President, William L. Langer, designated the study of psychology as "the next assignment" for his listeners. Several have taken up that charge with gusto. Just as many of the most recent *police romanciers,* following upon the lead of Simenon, weave their intricate webs around Why? rather than Who?, some historians have been able to inject into their work a sense of suspense, of new and necessary depth, by using within the limitations permissible to the guild's rules of evidence some of the concepts of the psychologist. John A. Garraty, who teaches at Columbia, pointed out several legitimate approaches to the subject in his work, *The Nature of Biography* (New York, 1957). The following year a professional psychologist crossed his work with history and Erik H. Erikson's highly influential *Young Man Luther* appeared (New York). (A portion of that work comes later in this volume.) His son Kai Erikson has been equally successful in mixing his chief discipline, sociology, with history in *Wayward Puritans: A Study in the Sociology of Deviance* (New York, 1966). Not all have been so well received, of course—witness the silly and even pathetic collaboration between Sigmund Freud and William C. Bullitt which produced their alleged biography of Woodrow Wilson, also in 1966—but there has been enough important new work in the decade since Langer spoke to prove the utility of psychology to the historian.

An excellent example of the restrained way in which a master historian may employ the insights of psychology and also draw upon the harder data of medical evidence appears in David Donald's biography of Charles Sumner. Donald, now Professor of American History at Johns Hopkins University, has spent many years of his academic life with Sumner, the junior Senator from Massachusetts. Sumner, as a leading anti-slavery Northerner during the eighteen-fifties and through the Civil War, was an irritating thorn in the side of the South, for he was articulate and spoke at length, often, and with force on the floor of the Senate. In May of 1856, Senator Sumner delivered a particularly abusive oration, known to historians as "The Crime Against Kansas" speech, in which he denounced a South Carolinian, Andrew Pickens Butler, who was not present at the time. The result was a flow of events which form one stream in the many that merge to contribute to the outbreak of the Civil War. Donald unravels the events that follow for us with the care of a prosecuting attorney reconstructing the scene of a crime—not that against Kansas but one to come, against Sumner—and the historian then moves on to examine Sumner's reactions to those events.

♦ ♦ ♦

Along with many other representatives, [Congressman Preston S.] Brooks [of South Carolina] had gone over to the Senate chamber on May 19, when Sumner began his oration, and he remained long enough, apparently, to hear Sumner call Butler, who was Brooks's

---

FROM David Donald, *Charles Sumner and the Coming of the Civil War* (New York: Alfred A. Knopf, 1960), pp. 290–91, 293–97, 309–17, 322–33, 335–36. Reprinted, with omissions, by permission of Alfred A. Knopf, Inc.

For additional reading: Bruce Mazlish has edited a collection of essays on *Psychoanalysis and History* (Englewood Cliffs, N.J., 1963). Psychological thrillers are well represented in the notes to previous selections in this volume. To those already mentioned, one might add Kenneth Millar's *The Three Roads,* any of the books by Charity Blackstock or Jean Potts, and the spy stories of John Le Carré and Elliot West.

cousin [uncle], the Don Quixote of slavery. Of Sumner's remarks on the second day Brooks knew only by report, but that apparently was enough to convince him that the Massachusetts senator had "insulted South Carolina and Judge Butler grossly." By the code of Southern chivalry Butler, when he returned from South Carolina, would be obliged to flog Sumner. Realizing that his cousin [uncle] was old and that Sumner was "a very powerful man," Brooks concluded: "I felt it to be my duty to relieve Butler and avenge the insult to my State." But with curious deliberateness he waited until he could read the published version of Sumner's speech, on May 21, before definitely deciding to take action.

Finding the speech as offensive as rumor had reported, Brooks determined to proceed according to the Southern code duello. Though he believed Sumner's remarks clearly slanderous, he did not even think of bringing legal action. No Southern gentleman considered a law suit the proper redress for a slur upon his own good name or upon that of a member of his family. Though Brooks had fought a duel in his youth, he did not consider challenging Sumner to a fight. In the first place, he knew that Sumner would not accept, as "the moral tone of mind that would lead a man to become a Black Republican would make him incapable of courage." Secondly, he thought that Sumner might report the challenge to the police, in which event Brooks would become liable "to legal penalties more severe than would be imposed for a simple assault and battery." But chiefly Brooks refrained from challenging Sumner because, according to the code of the Old South, a duel must be between social equals; to call Sumner out to the field of honor would be to give him, in Southern eyes, a social respectability he could not otherwise attain.

"To punish an insulting inferior," the Southern code ruled, "one used not a pistol or sword but a cane or horsewhip." Brooks coolly explored these possibilities. "I . . . speculated somewhat as to whether I should employ a horsewhip or a cowhide," he declared later; "but knowing that the Senator was my superior in strength, it occurred to me that he might wrest it from my hand, and then . . . I might have been compelled to do that which I would have regretted the balance of my natural life." In other words, "it was expressly to avoid taking life that I used an ordinary cane." The instrument he selected was a gutta-percha walking stick, presented to him several months earlier by a friend. Weighing eleven and one-half ounces, the cane had a gold head; it tapered from a thickness of one inch at the large end to three quarters of an inch at the small, and had a hollow core of about three eighths of an inch.

Having selected his weapon, Brooks had merely to pick the time and place for chastising Sumner. . . .

At 12:45 [on May 22] the Senate adjourned, and most of the members left the chamber, though several stood talking in the vestibule and in the cloakroom. Sumner stayed at his desk, pen in hand, franking copies of his "Crime Against Kansas" speech. Several visitors tried to interrupt him, but he promptly and briefly dismissed them, declaring that he was busy.

Impatiently Brooks awaited his opportunity. Until the room could be cleared, he took a desk in the back row of the chamber, across the aisle and three seats removed from Sumner. . . . When [Representative Henry A.] Edmundson [of Virginia] came up and jokingly asked Brooks if he were now a senator, the South Carolinian, fuming with anger, replied that he could not approach Sumner while there were ladies present, and he pointed to a pretty but persistent female conversationalist who had taken a seat in the lobby not far from where Sumner was sitting. . . .

Finding the lobby at last clear of women, Brooks proceeded upon his errand. Operating, as he thought, "under the highest sense of duty," he approached the front of the desk where Sumner still sat behind a large pile of documents, "writing very rapidly, with his head very close to the desk," his armchair drawn up close and his legs entirely under the desk. With cool self-possession and formal politeness, Brooks addressed him: "Mr. Sumner."

Sumner did not get up, but merely raised his head to identify his visitor. Nearsightedness, for which he was too vain to wear glasses, made the figure before him indistinct, but perfect vision would not have warned him, as he did not know Brooks by sight.

"I have read your speech twice over carefully," Brooks began in a low voice. "It is a libel on South Carolina, and Mr. Butler, who is a relative of mine—"[1] As Sumner seemed about to rise, Brooks interrupted himself to give Sumner "a slight blow" with the smaller end of his cane. Stunned, Sumner instinctively threw out his arms to protect his head, and Brooks felt "compelled to strike him harder than he had intended." He began to rain down blows. . . . In the excitement, Brooks forgot that he had set out only to flog Sumner, and began to strike him on the head "as hard as he could."

Dazed by the first blow, Sumner of course could not remember that in order to rise from his desk, which was bolted to the floor by an iron plate and heavy screws, he had to push back his chair, which was on rollers.[2] Perhaps half a dozen blows fell on his head and shoulders while he was still pinioned. Eyes blinded with blood, "almost unconsciously, acting under the instinct of self-defence," he then made a mighty effort to rise, and, with the pressure of his thighs, ripped the desk from the floor. Staggering forward, he now offered an even better target for Brooks, who, avoiding Sumner's outstretched arms, beat down "to the full extent of his power." So heavy were his blows that the gutta-percha cane, which he had carefully selected because he "fancied it would not break," snapped, but, with the portion remaining in his hand, he continued to pour on rapid blows. . . .

As soon as Sumner was free from the desk, he moved blindly "down the narrow passage-way, under the impetuous drive of his adversary, with his hands uplifted." As "Brooks continued his

[1] It is difficult to determine precisely what words Brooks used. The version here given is that remembered by Sumner himself, who asserted that Brooks began striking while uttering these words; he also recalled that Brooks had used the phrase "old man." . . . Brooks claimed that he used more elaborate phraseology: "Mr. Sumner, I have read your Speech with care and as much impartiality as was possible and I feel it my duty to tell you that you have libeled my State and slandered a relative who is aged and absent and I am come to punish you for it." . . . I accept Sumner's version both because the senator's memory was remarkably precise and because the phrasing is shorter and less "literary." In any case, the difference is not great, for Brooks admitted that he struck before he ended his sentence.

[2] I have been permitted to inspect Sumner's desk and chair, which are preserved in the Massachusetts Historical Society, through the courtesy of the Director, Mr. Stephen Riley.

blows rapidly with the part of the stick he held in his hand," Sumner lost consciousness and "was reeling around against the seats, backwards and forwards." "His whole manner seemed . . . like a person in convulsions; his arms were thrown around as if unconsciously." Knocking over another desk, diagonally in front of his own, he seemed about to fall when Brooks reached out and with one hand held Sumner up by the lapel of his coat while he continued to strike him with the other. By this time the cane had shivered to pieces. . . .

The beating had taken place in less than one minute. The sound made by Brooks's cane had at once attracted the attention of everyone who remained in the Senate chamber, and most of them began rushing toward the fracas. Representatives Ambrose S. Murray and Edwin E. Morgan, who had been in conversation behind the screen that separated the Senate seats from the vestibule, were the first to arrive. While Morgan caught Sumner, Murray seized Brooks by the arm while in the act of striking, and tried to draw him back from his foe.

While Brooks struggled against this unexpected interference, the elderly Whig senator from Kentucky, John J. Crittenden, came up the aisle, expressed his "disapprobation of such violence in the Senate chamber," and warned Brooks: "Don't kill him." Brooks, apparently realizing that he had far exceeded his original purpose, muttered: "I did not intend to kill him, but I did intend to whip him."

Just as Crittenden was warning Brooks, [Laurence M.] Keitt [of South Carolina] who had been near the clerk's desk at the outset of the attack, bounded up the center aisle, with his "small cane . . . lifted above his head, as if he intended to strike." "Let them alone, God damn you," he shouted at Crittenden. . . .

In a few seconds, friends led Brooks off into a side room, where they washed a small cut he had received above his eye from the recoil of his stick. Minutes later he and Keitt were walking together down Pennsylvania Avenue. . . .

. . . While Brooks was being led off, Sumner, partially supported by Morgan, lay "at the side of the center aisle, his feet in the aisle, and he leaning partially against a chair." He remained "as senseless as a corpse for several minutes, his head bleeding copiously from the frightful wounds, and the blood saturating his clothes."

Within a few minutes Sumner regained consciousness. One of the pages gave him a glass of water, and somebody suggested that he should be carried to a sofa in the anteroom. Sumner said that he thought he could walk, requested that his hat be found and that the documents on his desk be taken care of, and, leaning upon Morgan and another man, stumbled into the anteroom. His face was covered with blood as he passed Louisiana Senator John Slidell, who "did not think it necessary to . . . make any advances toward him" or to express any sympathy. A few minutes later Dr. Cornelius Boyle, who had been hastily summoned, dressed the wounds, which were still bleeding profusely, and put two stitches in each. . . .

Before falling into a dazed sleep, Sumner remarked: "I could not believe that a thing like this was possible." . . .

In Southern parlance, Preston Brooks had inflicted a caning, or a whipping, upon that blackguard Sumner in order to chastise him for his unprovoked insults to the hoary-headed Senator Butler and for his foul-mouthed denunciation of South Carolina. There was no conspiracy, and Brooks had no coadjutors. He acted not for political reasons, but solely to redress a personal wrong. In caning Sumner, he neither violated the privileges of the Senate nor broke the Constitutional guarantee of free speech to congressmen.[3] His weapon was nothing but a common walking stick, such as gentlemen frequently use. After sufficiently warning Sumner, Brooks lightly struck him across the face with a blow that was but a tap, intended to put him on his guard. As Sumner promptly rose to defend himself, Brooks naturally applied the stick with more force. After the first blow, Sumner bellowed like a bull calf and quickly

[3] Though my purpose here is to show what men thought and felt, I am obliged to add that this contention was most dubious. Brooks's defenders argued that the Senate was not in session when he struck Sumner; that he chastised the senator not for words uttered in debate, but for libelous words printed in advance of delivery and read, not heard, by Brooks; and that in any event senatorial privilege, as guaranteed in the Constitution (Art. I, sec. 6) does not cover defamation of character. But American courts have consistently ruled (4 Mass. 27; 103 U.S. Reports 200; 341 U.S. Reports 367) that the immunity of congressional speech is absolute. . . .

fell cringing to the floor, an inanimate lump of cowardice. Though Sumner suffered only flesh wounds, he absented himself from the Senate because of mortification of feeling and wounded pride. Brooks, with conspicuous gallantry, promptly reappeared in the House of Representatives, ready to face all accusers.

In Northern language, the affair bore an entirely different aspect. Bully Brooks had made a brutal assault upon Sumner with a bludgeon. The act had no provocation; on the contrary, Sumner for years had silently endured a harsh stream of unparliamentary personalities from Butler and other defenders of the slave power. The alleged cause of the assault, Sumner's speech, was marked by the classic purity of its language and the nobility of its sentiments. The fearlessness of Sumner's ideas had, in fact, been what singled him out for assassination. Brooks was the mere tool of the slaveholding oligarchy. While fellow conspirators gathered around him to prevent interference, the South Carolinian stealthily approached Sumner and committed his brutal and barbarous outrage upon an unarmed man. Though Sumner courageously tried to defend himself, the ruffian took advantage of his defenseless position and of the surprise, beat Sumner senseless, and continued to strike him after he collapsed on the floor. . . . While Brooks's coadjutors triumphantly led their champion out of the Senate, Sumner lay prostrate and suffering, his head a mass of beaten flesh, a martyr to the cause of Liberty and Free Speech. . . .

When the two sections no longer spoke the same language, shared the same moral code, or obeyed the same law, when their representatives clashed in bloody conflict in the halls of Congress, thinking men North and South began to wonder how the Union could longer endure. "I do not see how a barbarous community and a civilized community can constitute one state," [Ralph Waldo] Emerson gravely declared. "I think we must get rid of slavery, or we must get rid of freedom." . . .

While Congress and the public were angrily debating the Brooks assault, Sumner was trying to regain his health. It was more than three years before he was able regularly to resume his Senate duties. During this unhappy period he wandered restlessly from one health resort to another, fretting impatiently at the slowness of his recovery and experimenting with any cure, however rigorous, that might promote it. These three years were filled with exciting developments in national politics: James Buchanan was inaugurated; the Supreme Court handed down the Dred Scott decision; [Stephen A.] Douglas broke with the administration over its Kansas policy; Abraham Lincoln challenged the "Little Giant" in his home state; John Brown's raid sent panic through the South. On all these subjects Sumner's voice was unheard in the Senate chamber. His only consolation for his enforced abstinence from politics was his conviction that "to every sincere lover of civilization his vacant chair was a perpetual speech."

When Sumner was led bleeding from the Senate chamber on May 22, 1856, nobody anticipated that his recovery would be thus protracted. To be sure, his injuries were painful. He had three wounds on his head: one very slight and requiring no medical attention; another on the left side, "two and a quarter inches long, cut to the bone—cut under, as it were, and very ragged"; and still another on the right side, "rather in front," not quite two inches long, cut also to the bone. In addition, he had bruises on both his hands, on his arms, and on his shoulders, and there was a heavy black bruise across his thighs, made as he wrenched his desk from its bolts.

During the first three days after the assault, Sumner seemed to be recovering rapidly. Though he remained in bed most of the time, under the care of his brother George, who hastily came down from Boston to act as nurse, Dr. Cornelius Boyle, his physician, thought that he was "doing very well." . . .

Dr. Marshall S. Perry, who was sent down from Boston by wealthy Republican manufacturer George L. Stearns so as to be sure Sumner would receive the best medical treatment, also found the patient in very satisfactory shape on May 25. . . . Troubled by "a pulpy feeling" on the right side of Sumner's head and by the senator's "unnaturally excited state," Perry recommended that he keep very quiet and get complete rest. . . .

[On the] evening [of May 27 Sumner] suffered a relapse. . . . Dr. Boyle decided that the patient's discomfort resulted from the "cuticle" (a solution of gun cotton and chloroform) he had applied to the wound on the previous day, and, removing it, found "about a tablespoonful of pus, . . . which had gathered under the scalp."

He then poulticed the wound, and Sumner, under an opiate, was able to get several hours of sleep.

At this point George Sumner dismissed Dr. Boyle. He felt that the treatment of his brother had been unskillful, and perhaps he was displeased when the doctor told congressional investigators that his patient suffered only "flesh wounds." Dr. Perry took complete charge of the case, and he promptly called in Dr. Harvey Lindsly, a Washington physician, as consultant. They permitted the wound to suppurate freely, and soon Sumner felt "very nearly free from pain in the head—more calm and composed than he had been." On May 29 George was able to write [H. W.] Longfellow: "The crisis has passed and our noble fellow is safe." . . .

. . . Anemia had probably followed his septicemia.[4] Sumner no longer complained of much pain from the wounds on his head, which were healing over, but he began exhibiting other, more disturbing symptoms. A neuralgic pain in the back of his head came on in paroxysms. He had "a feeling of oppressive weight or pressure on the brain," which he repeatedly described as "a 56-pounds weight" upon his skull. "Increased sensibility of the spinal cord, and a sense of weakness in the small of the back" made his walking so irregular and uncertain that "after slight efforts he would lose almost entire control of the lower extremities." . . .

It was clear that Sumner needed less exciting and more salubrious surroundings, and, after arranging his affairs in Washington, he left for the North. At Philadelphia he consulted the distinguished physician, Dr. Caspar Wister, who found that Sumner was in "a condition of extreme nervous exhaustion, his circulation feeble, and in fact every vital power alarmingly sunken." At Dr. Wister's advice, he went to Cape May, where for a week he seemed to do very well, though the water was too cool for bathing, but an unaccountable setback sent him seeking other remedies. In early August he found the secluded health resort of Dr. R. M. Jackson, high in the mountains at Cresson, Pennsylvania, where he was put on a regimen of "judicious diet, mild tonic agents, constant exercise in the open air on horse back or in a carriage." . . .

[4] For this diagnosis, as for much of the other medical opinion incorporated [here], I am indebted to Dr. Julia L. Schneider, of the Neurological Institute of New York.

With the invigorating mountain air, the exercise, and Dr. Jackson's mild remedies . . . outward symptoms gradually began to disappear, leaving Sumner to wrestle with more subtle and frightening warnings of illness. Walking (but not horseback riding) or the slightest mental exertion continued to produce the sense of pressure on the top of his head. His thigh muscles continued to be weak. When fatigued, he often involuntarily relived the trauma of the assault. His secretary described his symptoms: "At times he feels as tho' the blows were raining upon his head again; then will feel a numbness in the scalp; then again acute pains; then a sense of exhaustion that prevents any physical or mental effort."

Restless and unable to sleep at night, Sumner feared that these symptoms might mean that he was losing his mind. He had always dreaded incapacitating disease more than death itself. . . . George Sumner's indiscreet reminiscences of mental cases he had seen in Paris hospitals undoubtedly contributed to Sumner's state of mind. So did Dr. Wister's disclosure that he was uncertain as to whether Sumner's brain "was deranged *organically* or only *functionally*." . . .

In this state of anxiety, Sumner closely watched his symptoms, and every weakness, every ache, every bout of insomnia reinforced his troubled conviction that his brain was affected. After a month he found the isolation of Cresson unbearable and, against Dr. Jackson's advice, he returned to Philadelphia. He explained that he wanted to be nearer his Senate duties; perhaps he also wanted something to distract his mind. . . .

These sufferings, of course, did not go unobserved. Newspaper correspondents followed Sumner from one health resort to another and filled Northern newspapers with stories of interviews with "the Martyr Senator." So great was popular enthusiasm for Sumner that the New York *Tribune* and the Cleveland *Leader* urged that he be named as the vice-presidential candidate on the Republican ticket, along with John C. Frémont, who was slated to fill the first place. At the Republican national convention in June, Sumner received thirty-five votes in the balloting for vice-presidential nominees—a sizable tribute. . . .

If Sumner's health was of great concern to his friends, both personal and political, it was of equal interest to his opponents, who from the beginning found something suspicious about his invalidism. As it was part of the standard Southern interpretation of the assault that Brooks had only "chastised" Sumner with a "light walking cane," proslavery congressmen never accepted as a fact that Sumner had been seriously injured. Their suspicions were confirmed when Dr. Boyle testified to the House investigating committee on May 27 that Sumner's injuries were "nothing but flesh wounds." When Senator Butler spoke in defense of Brooks on June 12, he argued: "For anything that appears in that testimony, if [Sumner] had been an officer of the Army, and had not appeared on the next day [after the attack] on the battle-field, he would have deserved to be cashiered."

After Republicans made "Bleeding Sumner" one of the principal issues in the 1856 presidential campaign, supporters of both Buchanan, the Democratic nominee, and [Millard] Fillmore, the American candidate, openly charged that the senator was shamming. His wounds, they noted, offered a most convenient political martyrdom. As Sumner was not too ill in June to prepare a carefully revised edition of "The Crime Against Kansas," the Boston *Courier* decided that he was "playing the political possum." In July the Washington *Union,* the official organ of the [Franklin] Pierce administration, charged that Sumner's wounds were entirely healed, but that he stayed away from the Senate because of "his wounded pride and his irrepressible anger and indignation." The Boston *Post* suggested that Sumner's doctors were conspiring to picture the senator as an invalid until just prior to election, when he could reappear before the public and capitalize "very much upon the interest his protracted absence from public duty [would] excite to see and hear him, for party effect." By fall the Washington *Union* had uncovered an even worse plot: physicians were "nursing the disease, lest it should die a natural death," because Sumner was "resolved not to recover until after the next Senatorial election in Massachusetts." . . .

Sumner was furious over these accusations. "While thus suffering for more than four months," he exclaimed in September, "I have been charged with the ignoble deed of *shamming illness!* It seems to me, if any thing could add to the character of the original act it is this supplementary assault on my character." Republican politicians were also seriously troubled over these slanders, which seemed to attract much credence in the Northwest, and they urged Sumner to collect affidavits from his other physicians to counteract the influence of Dr. Boyle's damaging testimony. [Senator Henry] Wilson helped Sumner gather statements from Dr. Lindsly, Dr. Wister, Dr. Perry, and Dr. Jackson, all declaring that Sumner's brain had "received a shock from which it might not recover for months" and all emphatically affirming that Sumner was unable to resume his Senate duties. This combined medical statement, Sumner himself declared in private, "was specially intended for Indiana, where the calumny had been employed; and . . . it was necessary that it should be circulated before the Election. . . ."

The publication did not down the suspicion of fraud. Throughout the next three years, while Sumner was generally absent from the Senate, hostile newspapers carried occasional stories that he was "malingering" with a "sham sickness." Sumner, declared the New York *Atlas* in 1858, "is rapidly acquiring the reputation of a charlatan, who, preceded by his servant in motley, with a trumpet and drum, cries his injuries and sufferings in the cause of freedom as saleable wares, for the purpose of putting money in his purse." "This most ridiculous of humbugs," announced another editor, "fairly stinks in the nostrils of the American people."

This accusation, which has found some defenders among later historians of pronounced antiabolitionist sympathies, rests upon very flimsy evidence. The only medical testimony that supports it is the statement of Dr. Boyle, a Southern physician, strongly opposed in politics to Sumner and very friendly to both Senator Butler and Preston Brooks. Even if Dr. Boyle had been an unprejudiced observer, his testimony as to Sumner's superficial wounds, lack of fever, etc., would have only limited medical value, for it was given on May 27, before septicemia was apparent. In his frequently overlooked testimony on the following day, Dr. Boyle added that Sumner had begun to run a fever, that infection had set in, and that he had prescribed opiates.[5] If Dr. Boyle's testimony

[5] . . . When George Sumner peremptorily dismissed Dr. Boyle, the physician grew very angry at what he considered a slur upon his professional integrity, and tried to collect other evidence to prove that Sumner had not been dangerously injured. The best he could do was to get an offhand remark from Dr. Lindsly to the effect that there was "not much the matter" with Sumner—an opinion that Dr. Lindsley presently contradicted in an affidavit—and a letter from Dr. Thomas Miller, who helped drain Sumner's

is accepted in its entirety, it proves only what no one ever denied: that Sumner seemed to be recovering quite satisfactorily during the first few days after the assault, but that infection set in on the evening of May 27. . . .

There is a notable lack of evidence to support the theory that Sumner was pretending to be ill. Certainly not one word he ever uttered or wrote, even to his closest friends and to his brother, could be interpreted as lending support to such a charge. If there was a plan to have Sumner feign sickness until after the 1856 elections, somebody must have been in on the plot. But there is not a known scrap of evidence, in the correspondence of any of his friends, in the papers of any Republican leader, or even in any belated reminiscence, which lends credence to the theory. If there was a plot, it was one of the best kept secrets in American history.

Those who charged Sumner with shamming relied upon logic as defective as their evidence. If he was pretending invalidism in order to aid the Frémont campaign or to promote his own re-election to the Senate—and there is no question but that his illness was skillfully exploited for both purposes—surely by January 1857 the game should have been over and Sumner should have resumed his seat. In fact, Southerners were puzzled at his failure to do so. Recognizing that after 1856 neither Sumner nor the Republican party had anything to gain by continuing a charade of this kind, proslavery men changed their attack and, during the next two years, attributed Sumner's absence from Washington to embarrassment at having been detected in his sham or to cowardice.

If the charge that Sumner was malingering must be dismissed as illogical theorizing upon insubstantial evidence, it must be admitted that the precise nature of Sumner's ailment was mysterious.[6]

---

wounds on May 30, declaring that he did not think "Mr. Sumner in any danger." . . .

[6] In the following discussion of Sumner's medical problems, I have been fortunate to secure the advice of two leading specialists, Dr. Bronson S. Ray, of the Cornell Medical Center, and Dr. Julia L. Schneider, of the Neurological Institute of New York. Giving generously of their time, both Dr. Ray and Dr. Schneider read through a 30-page memorandum I had prepared, listing in objective fashion Sumner's symptoms and the treatments prescribed for them. The judgments of these two eminent specialists, made quite independently and without any consultation between themselves, coincided at every point.

He looked well in the face, his voice was as firm and manly as usual, his intellect was bright and strong; but, when he tried to rise from his chair, he had to reach out for support, and he "walked with a cane and quite feebly, instead of his peculiarly vigorous stride." His progress toward recovery was disturbingly unpredictable. "Sometimes I think at last it has come," he wrote in January 1857, "and then before the day is over I am admonished that I can do but little." . . .

He decided to go to Europe for his health. Delaying in Washington only long enough to be sworn in on March 4, the beginning of his second Senate term, he sailed from New York three days later. Though he was seasick, his other symptoms began to disappear. By the end of the voyage he could rise from a seat without difficulty, and, aided only by a cane, he walked the decks for hours. . . .

During the entire trip Sumner kept up a rigorous schedule of sight-seeing which would have exhausted a man half his age. Despite a cold that persisted for the two months he remained in Paris, he saw everything and everybody in the French capital. On May 24 he went on a tour . . . and visited Orléans, Blois, Chambord, Tours, Angers, Nantes, La Haye, Poitiers, Bordeaux, Bayonne, Toulouse, Lyons, and Dijon—as well as a number of intervening places—in something less than three weeks. Then followed two months of frenzied social life and sight-seeing in London. Returning to the Continent, Sumner then went to Rheims, Strasbourg, Basle, Berne, Lucerne, Turin, the Hospice of St. Bernard, Geneva, Heidelberg, Frankfurt, Cologne, Amsterdam, the Hague, and Brussels, all within a month and without missing one of the starred attractions in his Baedeker. Returning to London for a week in September, during which he had five dinner engagements, Sumner then traveled to Manchester, Leeds, Edinburgh, Glasgow, Aberdeen, and Llandudno before sailing from Liverpool on November 7.

The mere recital of this exhausting peregrination is enough to prove that Sumner, while in Europe, was not severely troubled by the effects of the Brooks assault. Though he occasionally complained that his health was "not yet firm" and that he had "a morbid sensibility of the spinal system," everybody reported that he looked remarkably well. Young Henry James never forgot his disappointment when Sumner turned up in Paris "with wounds by that time rather disappointingly healed," and not even the senator's "visible, measurable, unmistakeable greatness" could quite compensate for that defect.

Toward the end of his European tour, however, Sumner's health received a setback, which was of psychological rather than physiological origin. Convinced that he had received "injuries to the brain" during Brooks's assault, he was uncertain about whether he should resume his place in the Senate when the new session of Congress began in December. Instead of asking the advice of any of several distinguished British physicians, he solicited the opinion of George Combe, whose writings on phrenology he had at a much earlier day admired. Combe, who was not a doctor and who was now nearly seventy years old, wrote out an account of what he took to be Sumner's symptoms and submitted them to Sir James Clarke, the Queen's physician. Clarke, without making any examination himself—indeed, without even seeing Sumner—gave as his considered judgment: "I have no hesitation in affirming, that, if he returns to mental labor in less than a year from this time he will soon become a permanent invalid, if he does not lose his life." Passing the diagnosis along to the senator, Combe added his personal opinion that Sumner's "brain, although apparently functionally sound, . . . would give way under the pressure of public life in America."

Bearing these medical warnings always in mind, Sumner returned to America torn between conflicting desires. With all his conscious will he wanted to reappear in the Senate and further to expose the villainies of the slavocracy. From the very day after the Brooks assault he had expressed "the constant wish . . . that he might be speedily restored so as to take his seat again in the Senate, from which . . . he had never before been absent for a single day." . . . "If I ever get back to Washington," he promised Thomas Wentworth Higginson, "the speech that I shall make when I do get there . . . will be to my last speech in the Senate of the United States as first proof brandy to molasses and water."

Perhaps the very frequency and intensity of such statements

suggest the inner reluctances that Sumner also felt about returning to the Senate. The more Sumner committed himself to delivering another powerful attack on slavery, the less he could forget the likely consequences. All along he had been convinced that a new attempt would be made against his life. He believed such letters as that signed by "A South Carolina Plug Uglie," who wrote "to say if you value your life not to visit Washington the coming session. . . . You may take the whole of Boston as your body guard but it wont make a damn bit of difference I am willing to sacrifice my life for the honor of my native state." "I suppose I shall be shot," Sumner told Higginson as he talked of going back to his seat. "I don't see what else is left for them to do." Now to these fears the English physicians added another and, in his eyes, even greater danger—one that had never been entirely absent from his thoughts—the likelihood that if he returned to the Senate, it would be "at the peril of his intellect." . . .

Every time Sumner had to go to Washington, all his old symptoms returned. In February 1858 Wilson summoned him to the capital for a few days to vote against Buchanan's Army Bill, "giving soldiers to a wicked Government" for use in Kansas, but, though Sumner tried to spend most of his time in the Smithsonian Institution and in the Library of Congress, the strain was too great and he had to return to New York. Brought down again in April, he arrived too late to give his vote for the free-state cause in Kansas, but, during the several days he remained, the tense bitterness of the Senate debates once again affected him. Without warning his old enemy struck. While reading in the stacks of the Library of Congress, he was called to the Senate to cast a vote. Perhaps he rose too quickly or walked too rapidly to the Senate chamber, for the afternoon found him prostrate with exhaustion. For the next three or four days he suffered back ailments and could rise from his chair only with great difficulty. At Wilson's insistence, he again left Washington. "All my plans are clouded," Sumner gloomily wrote. . . . "Two years gone already! How much more!" . . .

. . . Unfortunately Sumner never had a complete neurological examination, for he never consulted Dr. S. Weir Mitchell, of Philadelphia, the one specialist in the United States competent to make such a study. As Sumner's friends refused to permit an autopsy of his brain and spinal cord after his death in 1874, the question of his injuries can never be settled with absolute certainty. Fortunately, however, Sumner kept such elaborate records of his health, his physicians' opinions, and even his medical prescriptions that modern neurologists and brain specialists can agree on the nature of his affliction.

These physicians declare that Sumner's reactions during the first few days after the Brooks assault were precisely what they would expect in a patient who had received a nasty blow on the head.[7] He did not have either a fractured skull or a concussion, for he did not suffer the severe headaches, changes in state of awareness, and somnolence which accompany brain traumas; instead, his condition was feverish and excited. Septicemia developed in his wounds and left him considerably debilitated, perhaps suffering from anemia. The symptoms of which he subsequently complained —pressure on the skull, weakness of the spine, difficulty in walking—could not, from a neurological point of view, possibly have been the results of blows he received on his head or even of a spinal lesion. The urinary condition that caused Sumner so much distress had no medical connection with the Brooks assault. At the same time no physician who has studied the voluminous medical documents in Sumner's case has the least suspicion that Sumner was malingering; his sufferings were intense and genuine.

The diagnosis, then, is that Sumner was not shamming, but that his ailments were not, neurologically, the result of Brooks's beating. Cases of this sort are far from rare in medical history, and modern specialists classify Sumner's illness as "post-traumatic syndrome," in which numerous symptoms without objective causes follow a traumatic experience, such as an accident (physical trauma) in which the patient is not seriously injured. The precise

[7] Sumner's remarkably complete medical record includes diagnoses by Drs. Boyle, Wister, Lindsly, Jackson, Perry, [C. E.] Brown-Séquard, and George Hayward; prescriptions and medical instructions given Sumner by Brown-Séquard, Hayward, Perry, and Jackson; and elaborate day-by-day accounts of Sumner's appearance and symptoms by Sumner himself, by interested friends, and by political and personal opponents.

nature of such a post-traumatic syndrome is not entirely clear; most neurologists believe it to be largely psychogenic. Patients suffering from such symptoms have great difficulty in reassuming their obligations to their families, their friends, and their employers.

In Sumner's case it is clear that the Brooks assault produced psychic wounds that lingered long after the physical injuries had disappeared. The pressure he felt on his head was a mental re-enactment of the beating. Bearing in mind that the attack occurred in 1856, one is not so puzzled that he felt the weight on his skull to be precisely fifty-six pounds. The pain in his thighs was reminiscent of his tearing up his desk as he sought to rise under Brooks's lashing. It is at least suggestive that the senator who had for years been demanding a political party with "Backbone" should suffer mysterious spinal complaints. All these symptoms occurred chiefly, though not exclusively, when Sumner turned his mind to public affairs or tried to return to his Senate duties. The incredibly unprofessional and unscientific warnings of his English physicians that mental exertion might permanently impair his brain added to his tension on these occasions, as did his strong belief that the Southerners would shoot him. Hitherto Sumner had driven himself with his inflexible will to maintain impossibly high standards, despite overwork and mental strain; now he was faced with rebellion on the part of his body and of an unconscious segment of his mind. . . .

> A man who has devoted all his time to regaining his lost health will, upon looking back, see the duration of that time differently from time passed in bursting good spirits. As he endures Time, he also will see each hour as a day, especially if the hour is painful. This is common sense and we all know it. Nor do we need to be reminded about relativity and human perception. What those who have not studied history sometimes do need to know, however, is that a historian's perception of time must, in a real as well as in a philosophical sense, differ from culture to culture and from period to period as he studies. Events of wide significance for the entire world have so multiplied and quickened during the twentieth century as virtually to tele-

scope time as a unit of measurement. It is true that, as British television had it recently, "This Hour Has a Thousand Days," while a thousand days in the tenth century may have been but an hour. Textbooks reflect this, of course; increasingly survey courses in American history, for example, move from 1492 to 1877, and even to 1898, in the first semester, leaving those events within the memory of people alive today for the entirety of a second semester. Time is the historian's staple, and he must know what to do with it.

Time also is the staple of detective fiction, for alibis, the moment of death, or the fateful arrival (or non-arrival) of the courier expected on the 9:02 from Geneva, are crucial to plot and to solution. One must have an alibi, of course, or be suspect: Arnold Toynbee once charged whole cultures with having no alibis and put the Jews and the Polynesians, among others, into historical niches for those whose growth had been stunted. What had those people been doing with all their time, when other societies were marching vigorously ahead? He has since reconsidered that rather too pat position and ceased to ask societies to alibi themselves. Yet some must, it is true, for a society that has a place for the innovator in its midst will change more rapidly, and have a different conception of what constitutes a "long time," than a people hostile to innovation. There are, in effect, intellectual site and situation factors, cultural bench marks, which the historian must not only use for his own chronology and gross measurements of epochs but which he must also understand in relation to the societies from which they grew. This is a nice philosophical and perhaps even theological point and the historian cannot finesse it.

In another sense, time is best grasped, as Alice knew, at the beginning and taken to the end, when one stops. But the historian also knows that it will no longer suffice to say that because we know that Karl Marx was born in 1818 and died in 1883 we have learned anything of value.

Increasingly historians are recognizing how important the early years of life are—how *that* time is more important than *this* time—and they are turning to closer study of childhood. In 1950 Erik Erikson, in *Childhood and Society,* showed ways in which historians could understand the significance to a subject's later life of his early development. Historians had known this but on the whole they had preferred to treat childhood as akin to man's sexual relations—not capable of documentation and too open to errors of interpretation to permit the scholar to comment with conviction or even credibility. In this last decade, however, historians have begun to recapture their and their subject's youth, to admit to having read Joseph Altsheler, or the Hardy Boys, or even Nancy Drew, not in themselves aberrant childhood reading choices, and confessing that in some cases precisely such early decisions led them into history. A French scholar, Philippe Ariès, in *Centuries of Childhood,* showed how schools influence the very duration of childhood, how the schools in turn respond to that duration, and how the idea of childhood has helped shape the functions of the family. A Swiss, Jean Piaget, in writing on the child's conception of the world, of number, space, and causality, has opened yet other doors. The 1966 American Historical Association, meeting in New York, showed just how far these interests had developed, for of seventy-six sessions, at which one hundred and forty-two papers were read, no less than thirty-five were given over to new, comparative, psychologically oriented approaches to history.

Time, then, the historian's staple, is changing. Chronology remains important, for without a sense of sequence no one can reconstruct causal patterns. But time itself, once amorphous, and always relative, now has a shape of its own which the historian also must study. Time which, in its finiteness, forces the statesman to dictate his autobiography, which leads the politician to seek out a ghostwriter, which compels the actress to pour out her social commentary to a hired hack for another "as told to" story—such time not only destroys the historian's sources but distorts them in the moment of their making. The historian needs allies for his protection.

For additional reading: On the problem of ghostwriting, see Ernest R. May, "Ghost Writing and History," *American Scholar,* XXII (Autumn, 1953), 459–65. On the influences of childhood in later life, see Gillian Avery and Angela Bull, *Nineteenth Century Children* (London, 1965). In *Yesterday's Children* (Boston, 1959) John Morton Blum, biographer of Theodore Roosevelt, brings together selections from *Our Young Folks,* that forerunner of *Children's Activities* and *Boy's Life* which helped teach T.R. how to behave in the adult world. George Kubler, an art historian, has explored *The Shape of Time* (New Haven, 1962), as have Stephen Toulmin and June Goodfield in *The Discovery of Time* (New York, 1965). In their classic volume on *The Evolution of Physics,* which many undergraduates of my generation and before devoured (New York, 1938), Albert Einstein and Leopold Infeld show how relativity applies to the historian's work, if the historian wishes to read their words that way. For an unconventional blend of science and detection, read Lloyd Biggle, Jr., *All the Colours of Darkness.*

PART V

ALLIES

19. The Case of the Grassy Knoll:

The Romance of Conspiracy

Some apparently simple events have been shown to be far more complex than at first imagined. The reverse may also be true, however, for the public mind enjoys the *frisson* of living next to a conspiracy. No better example of this psychological trait can be given than through an examination of the several counter-theories that have been produced to account for all the elements in the assassination, in Dallas, Texas, in November of 1963, of President John F. Kennedy. Many people have not been satisfied with the official report of the Warren Commission, which was established to examine all the evidence in relation to the shooting, and certainly there are elements in that report which are disquieting to anyone who has read it with care. The selective indignation of those who have attacked the report is no less disquieting, however, for while they zero in on apparent oversights and contradictions in the conclusions, they also overlook other evidence which runs counter to their own proposals.

The best analysis that I have seen of the several books on the assassination was written by a professor of law—a discipline in which many historians have been trained—from Stanford University, in an essay, "The Assassins." Here the historian would, were he to repeat the analysis, have to use the methods of the trial lawyer. This is precisely what Professor John Kaplan does in the selection that follows.

♦ ♦ ♦

The present furor over the assassination of President Kennedy and the work of the Warren Commission can best be understood as part of a four-stage controversy—of which we are now just entering the fourth stage. First, in 1964, just a few months after the assassination, Thomas G. Buchanan (*Who Killed Kennedy?*) and Joachim Joesten (*Oswald: Assassin or Fall Guy?*) put forth quite different theories which agreed that the President had been slain by a right-wing conspiracy. Although both books enjoyed large sales outside the United States and to some extent within it, the perspective of only three years has proven them so inept that it is embarrassing to read them. Second came the *Warren Commission Report,* followed shortly by its twenty-six volumes of documentation. Inside the United States, and to a markedly smaller extent abroad, the work of the Warren Commission received lavish, indeed uncritical, praise which quieted most doubts. Then in the spring of 1966 we reached the third stage, in which a second generation of unofficial inquiries into the assassination began to appear. Although these inquiries differ enormously, they have had a single impact on the public mind and have, at least for a substantial segment of the American people, cast great doubt upon the Commission's conclusions and upon the ability and integrity of the Commissioners themselves. Finally, in the past few months we have begun to hear not only more and more evidence tending to throw the Commission's conclusions into question but also, for the first time, demands for action from those who have the power to compel action.

FROM John Kaplan, "The Assassins," *Stanford Law Review,* XIX (May, 1967), 1110–151, and used with the permission of the author. This is an amended and corrected version of an article that first appeared in the *American Scholar,* XXXVI (Spring, 1967), 271–86, 288, 290, 294, 296, 298, 300, 302, 304, 306.

For additional reading: An equally brilliant analysis of the spate of books dealing with Kennedy's assassination appeared in the *Times Literary Supplement* in London on December 14, 1967. This article, "After the Assassination," was by John Sparrow, Warden of All Souls College, Oxford, and an acute critic who previously had written a series of acrid, fascinating *Controversial Essays* (London, 1965). His analysis of the Kennedy literature has since appeared as a book in the United States. Thrillers which turn upon assassination attempts are commonplace; few of them read well, although an exception is Adam Hall's *The 9th Directive,* which nicely captures the feel of Bangkok.

To understand how stage four has been reached, we must look carefully at stage three, the stage in which the first serious and specific criticisms of the Commission appeared. This stage consisted essentially of five books: *Inquest,* by Edward Jay Epstein; *Rush to Judgment,* by Mark Lane; *Whitewash: The Report on the Warren Report,* by Harold Weisberg; *The Oswald Affair,* by Léo Sauvage; and *The Second Oswald,* by Richard H. Popkin. Although these books differ greatly in detail and in thesis from one another, they all share two characteristics: first, they rely primarily on the Warren Commission's own testimony and exhibits; second, they agree that the Warren Commission, even in evaluating its own evidence, did at very best an incompetent job and at worst something that can only be darkly hinted at.

We must therefore draw a sharp distinction between the report of the Warren Commission and its twenty-six volumes of published hearings. Although the report is criticized on almost every conceivable ground, most of the ammunition for the attacks is contained in the evidence that the Commission itself published. It has only rarely been argued that the stenographers did not record what the witnesses actually said, that the physical exhibits were altered, or that the expert witnesses lied. And, equally significant, no one in the third stage has come up with any witnesses of importance whose statements were not before the Commission either through direct testimony or through interview reports. This is not to say that the authors in the third stage afford equal credence to the testimony that the Commission believed or that they view the weight of the evidence as did the Commission. To the contrary, in each of the books there is a rejection of those witnesses whom the Commission apparently believed, an acceptance of those whom the Commission discounted, and a drawing of entirely different conclusions from the same evidence.

Nor is it merely whim that made each of these authors accept witnesses and theories that the Commission had rejected. Each author argues that his account is unbiased and therefore completely rational and that the Commission's report is not completely rational since it was more interested in "political truth" than in the actual facts of the assassination. The theory is that the Commission thought that the most politically settling account the country could hear was that a lone assassin, unconnected with any power group and completely without political motive, had committed a hopelessly irrational act and had then died at the hands of someone equally alone and equally irrational. In light of the Commission's underlying motivations, they argue that no great dishonesty need be imputed to the Commission, but only a subconscious straining to find what it wished to find. Indeed, this theme is repeated so often throughout these books that one almost accepts it as an obvious truth.

However, when one thinks about it, it is hard to visualize a set of facts about the assassination which, if published, would afford no consolation to at least one of two such polar men as Earl Warren and J. Edgar Hoover. Moreover, although it sounds much nicer to say that the Commission need only have acted out its subconscious desires in order to have made the gross errors of which it is accused, one would have to distort the facts alleged in all of the books to conclude that this is a possibility. For their main theses to be at all valid, all of the books—with the possible exception of Epstein's—must imply that many people, including members of the Commission, had deliberately lied, suppressed evidence, and concealed the truth.

There are, of course, certain problems with the conspiracy-to-suppress-the-truth theory. The fact is that the Commission itself did relatively little of the work of collecting and analyzing the facts. In common with many other governmental commissions, the Warren Commission was chosen for its balance and its members' reputations for integrity. But even if both of these qualities were in fact lacking, the charges of fraud would be meaningless unless balance and integrity were similarly lacking in the staff—composed primarily of young honor graduates of the nation's leading law schools.

The argument that the Commission consciously or subconsciously suppressed the truth has, aside from the flat allegation of motive, two main prongs. The first is that the Commission got off on the wrong track by regarding Lee Harvey Oswald from the beginning of the hearings as the principal, and indeed the only, suspect. To evaluate the justice of this complaint, one must consider the physical evidence that greeted the staff and the members of the Commission when they began their work. The President was killed by a series of shots, of which at least two, judging from the resulting wounds and the marks on his limousine, appeared to have been fired from above and from the rear, the general location of the upper stories of the Texas School Book Depository. In the depository a rifle was found that not only bore a palm print of Lee Harvey Oswald, an employee of the depository, but was purchased several months earlier by Oswald under an assumed name. Moreover, shortly after the shooting, a bullet in almost perfect condition (the famous exhibit 399) was recovered, most likely from the stretcher of Governor Connally, and was identified positively as having come from Oswald's rifle. In addition, of the bullet fragments recovered from the Presidential limousine, two were identified positively as having come from Oswald's rifle, and the rest, though no positive identification could be made, were consistent with this theory of origin.

Even if this were the only evidence against Oswald, it would certainly justify a jury verdict against him. Cases have turned on physical evidence no better than this—for instance, the identification of a typewriter rather than a gun transmuted the testimony of Whittaker Chambers into a case strong enough to convict Alger Hiss, a far more attractive defendant than Lee Oswald.

But the use of Oswald's rifle in the killing was not the only evidence connecting Oswald with the crime. His subsequent behavior would be hard to explain to a jury on any theory other than his involvement in serious crime. Within forty-five minutes of the killing of the President, a Dallas patrolman, J. D. Tippit, was shot to death, and a few minutes thereafter Lee Oswald was arrested in a nearby movie theater. A revolver was found on his person, and, although the barrel was too large to allow conclusive identification of the bullets that killed Patrolman Tippit, several shell casings found at the site of the Tippit killing were unambiguously identified as having come from this gun. One need not assert that these facts prove Oswald's guilt beyond any possible doubt, or even—as is indisputably true—that any prosecutor having such a hard core of evidence would sleep quite comfortably before the trial. Rather, all that need be said is that this evidence gave the Commission a likely and proper starting point. An investigative body cannot collect facts endlessly without a working hypothesis to give direction to the investigation and to separate that which is relevant from that which is not. It would seem that the Commission used the most rational method of inquiry by starting with a working hypothesis that Oswald had a hand in the killing of the President and by attempting from there to find out, first, whether this was in fact so; second, whether, if so, anyone aided or conspired with him; and third, whether Jack Ruby had any connection with Oswald or with the assassination.

The second prong of the argument that the truth was suppressed by the Warren Commission is much more complicated. This prong is that the Commission should have treated the inquiry at least in part as a trial of Lee Oswald and should therefore have afforded him the benefits of the adversary system by appointing a lawyer to cross-examine witnesses and to protect his interests. (The Commission did appoint a lawyer to "represent" Oswald, but neither this attorney—then the president of the American Bar Association—nor the Commission took the appointment at all seriously.) It is argued that the failure to appoint an attorney not only was unfair to Oswald, but it contributed to the unreliability of the Commission's conclusions. It should be clear, however, that although a criminal trial of Lee Oswald might have been the best method of determining Oswald's guilt, it would have been one of the worst methods of deciding whether Oswald, if guilty, had been part of a conspiracy. For a host of reasons, evidence bearing on the question of a conspiracy would have been ruled inadmissible in such a prosecution, even if the parties felt that they were tactically better off by producing it. Furthermore, it is really quite unlikely that either side would have tried to produce it. Oswald's case would not have been improved by showing either that there was or that there was not a conspiracy; and while the government might perhaps have been marginally benefited by showing that a conspiracy did exist (if it had had such evidence), the chances of confusing the jury and leading them away from the basic issue of Oswald's guilt might very well have made such a course inadvisable to any confident prosecutor.

The lack of counsel for Oswald on the issue of his own guilt is another point entirely. Here I part company with the Commission and think that a competent, honest, and dedicated staff working solely to show that Oswald was innocent would have improved the reliability of the Commission's determination. On the other hand, it was hardly outrageous for the Commission to place on its staff the burden both of looking for exculpatory evidence and of cross-examining witnesses. These techniques did in fact reveal the unreliability of a great deal of evidence that might otherwise have been adduced against Oswald. Moreover, had Oswald been alive, he, presumably knowing the facts, would have been the most competent person to advise his counsel how to proceed. But since Oswald was dead by the time the Commission was created, his lawyer would have been put in the position of the famous advocate who is reputed to have defended a rape case by arguing first that the man never did it and second that the girl consented. The facts brought before the Warren Commission might support arguments, albeit very weak ones, that Oswald did not commit the crime, for, say, eight mutually exclusive reasons. Presumably, only Oswald would have known whether any of these reasons was true—and hence which was the one most likely to succeed. Any counsel who tried seriously to put forth all of the inconsistent defenses would only have succeeded in burying the valid one beneath many that turned out to be spurious. Moreover, any lawyer for Oswald would have been open, after the fact, to the charge, "Why didn't you show thus-and-so?" The answer, of course, might have been, "Because if I did, my witness could have been destroyed completely," or, "Thus-and-so was obviously not true." These might be good answers, but coming from the Commission's defenders they would not prove sufficient to allay suspicion, and it is unlikely that they would prove more so if they came from a "defense" lawyer.

The fact is that the death of Oswald made the work of the Commission vastly more difficult. If Oswald had been alive, his failure to point out any possible theories of innocence would have been taken as an admission that there were no valid ones, and his refusal to testify or provide any evidence—the highly artificial command of the fifth amendment notwithstanding—would have been taken as an effort to cover up guilt. With Oswald dead, however, the Commission was left to refute every possible argument that Oswald might conceivably have made—an almost endless task.

Although the five books of the third stage rely in part on general criticisms of the Commission to support their conclusions, it is on their discussions of specific items of evidence that they must stand or fall. For this reason, Epstein's book is the best with which to begin. Its exposition of the facts is the shortest; it is the clearest and least polemical; and it hits at what is probably the most difficult to justify of the Commission's major conclusions. Epstein does not deny that Lee Harvey Oswald took part in the assassination of President Kennedy. The thrust of his work is that the Commission, in concluding that there was no reason to believe that Oswald had not acted alone, accepted a hypothesis that on its own evidence was a most unlikely one and rejected persuasive evidence that Oswald must have had aid in firing at the President.

Although the evidence against Oswald was ample, the Commission, of course, was most interested in determining whether he was acting alone or in concert with others. While this task was central to the Commission's role, a little thought reveals just how difficult a problem the Commission faced. If the Commission could find enough evidence of a conspiracy, it could then prove—or at least assert with confidence—that one had existed. On the other hand, if it could find no evidence of a conspiracy, what would that prove? How would one ever prove that Oswald had *not* been part of a conspiracy? It was always possible that somebody had telephoned the night before and encouraged him; someone might have been waiting farther along the President's route prepared to fire had Oswald missed; it is even possible that Oswald fired after—or at the same time as—another attempt, which failed so completely that it did not even cause a disturbance. Certainly the failure of the Commission to find evidence of any of these things was only very weak proof that they did not happen. Therefore, a reasonable possibility that Oswald had conspired with others would remain regardless of the care and competence of any investigation which found no evidence of a conspiracy.

On the other hand, the Commission might be able to prove whether Oswald could have fired the shots himself. It thus became imperative to examine more closely the sequence of shots that struck the President and Governor Connally. In this task, the Commission was aided enormously by moving pictures taken by a clothing manufacturer named Abraham Zapruder. In determining the timing of the fatal volley the Commission began with the likelihood—not disputed by Epstein—that there were three shots. Since Oswald's view of the President would have been blocked by the foliage of a large tree between frames 166 and 210 of Zapruder's film, the first shot must have been fired either before frame 166 or after frame 210. The elimination of the period before frame 166 was fairly simple. President Kennedy's reaction to the first bullet wound appeared about frame 225, and his reaction time would have been inordinately slow—over three seconds—had he been struck at frame 166. The film not only fixed the President's first wound at sometime between frames 210 and 225 (because Zapruder's view was blocked briefly by a sign, the President disappeared from the film at frame 205 and did not reappear until frame 225, at which time he seemed to have been hit), but it also showed that Governor Connally had been hit before frames 235–40 and that at frame 313 the fatal bullet struck the President's head.

While one might initially conclude from Zapruder's film that the first shot hit the President in the neck, the second hit Governor Connally, and the third hit the President's head, another fact makes this reconstruction impossible. Oswald's single-action rifle could not be reloaded and fired in less than 2.3 seconds, or, in terms of Zapruder's film speed of 18.3 frames per second, 42 frames. As a result, even if the President had been hit at frame 210—the earliest point at which Oswald could have had a clear shot—it would have been impossible for another bullet from Oswald's gun to hit Governor Connally by frame 235. The Commission therefore adopted what has since become known as the "one-bullet" theory and concluded that the same bullet first passed through the President's neck and then struck Governer Connally. Moreover, since one bullet was fragmented when it struck the President's head and there was no sign of any other bullet mark on the limousine, the Commission concluded that one of the shots must have missed the Presidential car completely. With two bullets physically accounted for, exhibit 399 (the bullet found on Governor Connally's stretcher) had to be the "one bullet" that had struck both President Kennedy and Governor Connally. To reach this conclusion, the Commission had to answer three major questions:

(1) Is the one-bullet theory refuted by Governor Connally's testimony that he heard the first shot and had time to turn around before being hit by what he was certain must have been the second shot? (2) Could one bullet have inflicted both the wound in President Kennedy's neck and the wounds found in Governor Connally's rib cage (front and back), his wrist, and his thigh? (3) If one bullet had done all this damage, could it have remained in the almost perfect condition of exhibit 399?

The Commission felt that it had satisfactorily answered each of these questions. Governor Connally's testimony could be explained by the fallibility of memory and perception in time of crisis and by the fact that often there is a perceptible lag (here the lag would have had to be on the order of one-half of a second) between the time one is struck by a bullet and the time one realizes it. Although the photographic evidence did not show any obvious reaction by the Governor immediately after he was presumably hit, this too could be explained by a delayed reaction. As to the other two questions, the Commission felt that the physical evidence and the expert testimony before it fully supported its conclusion.

In this context Epstein's argument can be understood. First, he argues that since Oswald himself clearly could not have fired two shots as close to each other as the ones that struck President Kennedy and Governor Connally, the rejection of the Commission's one-bullet theory forces one to conclude that there must have been another assassin. Actually, of course, this is but one possibility; another and perhaps more likely possibility is that Oswald indeed fired his first shot before frame 210 while the foliage obscured his view (it was possible to see, although not well, through that foliage). This would account for Governor Connally's statement that he heard the first shot before he was hit. In that case exhibit 399 might be either the first bullet fired, which struck President Kennedy (and then somehow did no further damage either to itself or to the car), or the second bullet fired, which wounded Governor Connally. Although for various reasons each of these possibilities is unlikely, neither seems more so than Epstein's conclusion.

Despite Epstein's having leaped to the most sensational of the conclusions that follow from his own arguments, his attack upon the one-bullet theory deserves careful attention. It has two independent parts, either of which, if accepted, would be enough to demolish that theory. The first, and by far the most discussed, involves the nature of the wounds on President Kennedy's body. According to the Commission, the first bullet to strike the President hit him in the back of the neck-shoulder area, continued in a downward path, and exited from his neck below the Adam's apple. It then continued downward and struck Governor Connally, who was sitting in the jump seat ahead of the President.

This conclusion, however, had not been obvious from the beginning. The doctors at Parkland Hospital, where the President was first brought, noticed a wound on his throat below the necktie line, but since they did not turn him over, they failed to note the wound in the back of his neck-shoulder area. As a result, they concluded that the visible wound "could be" an entrance wound. They then cut through the throat wound as part of a tracheotomy, obscuring it completely. Later, when the body was flown to Washington for autopsy, the autopsy surgeons noted what they thought was clearly an entrance wound in the back of the neck-shoulder area. They could find no exit wound, however, and it was only the next morning, when they talked to the doctors who had treated the President at Parkland Hospital in Dallas, that the autopsy surgeons learned about the obscured wound in the front of the President's neck. Then it all became clear to them. The wound in the back, a bruise they had noted on the lung where it extends into the neck, and the obscured neck wound were all on a straight line extending slightly downward. From this they concluded that a bullet had been fired from above and had passed downward through the President's neck and out at an angle. The Commission concluded that the angle of the wound was consistent with a trajectory that would have enabled the bullet to strike Governor Connally in the rib cage, wrist, and thigh (all of these wounds being located on a straight line).

Epstein's argument with reference to the President's wounds is basically a twofold attack on this reconstruction. He concludes that the bullet that struck the President did not go through his body and further that the wound on the President's back was located much too low for the bullet to have described the path attributed to it by the Commission. In support of the former attack, Epstein cites an FBI report made at the time of the autopsy that stated, "[T]here was no point of exit, and . . . the bullet was not only in the body." A supplementary FBI report dated January 13, 1964, stated, "Medical examination of the President's body had revealed that the bullet which entered his back had penetrated to a distance of less than a finger length."

Certainly, if this were true, it would demolish the one-bullet theory. Epstein states: "Clearly, the FBI Summary and Supplemental Reports and the Warren Report give diametrically opposed findings regarding the President's autopsy. This presents a dilemma. . . . [I]f the FBI reports distorted such a basic fact of the assassination, doubt is cast upon the FBI's *entire* investigation. . . ." Actually, this is far from clear. The fact is that there are many errors in the FBI reports, as, for that matter, there would be in any large-scale investigation by any agency. That an agency is not infallible—and the FBI most certainly is fallible—does not "cast doubt" upon its entire investigation. The explanation that several of the Commission's staff have given is that an FBI agent left before the autopsy was complete and telephoned in his report before the doctors had determined the path of the bullet through the President's body. (Actually, even this explanation is unnecessary, for until they spoke to the Parkland Hospital doctors the next morning even the autopsy surgeons thought that the bullet had not passed through the President's neck.)

Nor is the fact that this statement was not corrected in the supplemental report, even though the FBI had the autopsy report by that time, grounds to imply, as Epstein does, that the infallible FBI was sticking to its guns despite a false autopsy report. First of all, anyone who has dealt with a governmental agency knows how information from a previous letter or report gets included in subsequent documents long after it has been shown to be wrong. Furthermore, even this aspect of Epstein's theory also involves fallibility on the part of the FBI since the proper course would have been to discuss and point out the error in the autopsy report. Finally, the assumption that the FBI did and does make errors does not, as does Epstein's theory, involve perjury on the part of at least the three autopsy surgeons (one of whom, Colonel Pierre Finck, did the one-bullet theory considerable damage in an entirely different connection). Not only did these doctors have no reason to lie, but, perhaps more significantly, at the time of the autopsy they had no possible way to know of the evidence disclosed by the Zapruder films and hence no possible way to know that this aspect of their testimony and report would prove so crucial.

Epstein's other argument concerning the President's neck wounds is that the downward course of the bullet as determined by the autopsy surgeons was impossible because the bullet wound in the President's back was lower than the wound in his throat. If this were so, the bullet which struck the President could not also have struck Governor Connally so as to cause his wounds, because his wounds clearly were made by a bullet which followed a downward path (the Commission calculated the angle at around eighteen degrees). Again, Epstein's case is based primarily on the reports of the investigatory agencies rather than upon those of the autopsy surgeons. Thus the FBI and Secret Service reports, respectively, state that the wound was in President Kennedy's "back . . . approximately six inches below the top of the collar," and "about four inches down from the right shoulder." Moreover (and Epstein regards this as crucial), the FBI reports show that the hole in the back of the President's jacket was 5⅜ inches below the top of the collar and that the bullet hole in the back of his shirt was 5¾ inches below the top of the collar. From this Epstein concludes that the actual location of the wound was "obviously inconsistent with the position of the entrance wound" according to the Commission. At first glance, anyone not familiar with anatomy would think this was so. But it just so happens that in humans the front of the neck extends considerably lower than the back of the neck —an anatomical fact which the reader is strongly urged to verify. In fact, if one raises one's right arm slightly, as if to wave to a crowd as the President was doing, one can discover that a point 5¾ inches below the top of the collar is slightly above a point on the neck just below the Adam's apple, where the exit wound was. Considering President Kennedy's exceptionally powerful shoulder development and allowing for about an inch of "riding up" by his shirt and jacket, as would be expected since he wore a brace, it is not unreasonable to assume the entrance wound would be approximately two inches higher than the exit wound, which would account for the eighteen-degree downward movement. Interestingly enough, the autopsy surgeons located the point of the entrance wound at fourteen centimeters below "the tip of the right mastoid process"—a place, depending on the length of President's Kennedy's neck, approximately two inches higher than the position of his exit wound. It is hard to decide which is more astounding—the fact that Epstein could have written the book without bothering to measure or the fact that this elementary point slipped by his reviewers.

The second major part of Epstein's assault upon the one-bullet theory concerns the condition of the bullet which the Commission concluded wounded both President Kennedy and Governor Connally. This argument is more difficult to answer than the first and perhaps has not had the full attention it deserves. Epstein's argument here is simply that the "one bullet," exhibit 399, is in too good condition to have done all of the damage to Governor Connally's rib cage, wrist, and thigh. Indeed, Colonel Pierre Finck, the only witness to state categorically whether exhibit 399 could have caused Governor Connally's wrist wound, concluded, "No; for the reason that there are too many fragments described in that wrist." Nonetheless, although the Commission's investigation would certainly have been more satisfactory if it had probed further into this testimony, there are reasons to believe that exhibit 399 could have done just the damage that the colonel denied.

First, Colonel Finck had not seen Governor Connally's wounds, and the description that he relied upon makes it quite clear that the fragments found in Governor Connally's wrist were minute. Dr. Charles F. Gregory, who actually treated Governor Connally's wrist, testified that the missile that struck Governor Connally's wrist "could be virtually intact, insofar as mass was concerned."

Second, the bullet that struck Governor Connally in the back of the rib cage made a most unusual wound. As one of Connally's physicians described it: "The wound entrance was an elliptical wound. In other words, it had a long diameter and a short diameter. It didn't have the appearance of a wound caused by a high velocity bullet that had not struck anything else. . . ." This kind of wound is typical of that made by a bullet that has already hit another object and is tumbling.

Third, there was expert testimony that a bullet striking Governor Connally's wrist without having gone through other objects would have done far more damage than actually occurred.

Fourth, exhibit 399 was damaged only on the rear end, as though it had hit bone rear end first—a condition consistent with the probable tumbling behavior of the bullet that struck Governor Connally. The refusal, then, to accept the one-bullet theory would have forced the Commission to explain what the bullet that struck Governor Connally had struck first to set it tumbling; what, other than Governor Connally's rib and wrist, exhibit 399 could have struck rear end first; and what happened to the bullet that exited from the President's neck still moving fast enough to damage both itself and anything that it struck.

The one-bullet conclusion is by no means obvious, especially since the crucial testimony—that of Governor Connally's doctors—contains many inconsistencies, some of which point away from that theory. On the other hand, in addition to raising all the above questions, the most significant of the alternative theories presupposes a second assassin who was firing from the same area as Oswald but who left no trace at all. Therefore, it was hardly unreasonable for the Commission to decide that the probabilities favored the one-bullet theory.

Although Epstein's first major substantive point is almost certainly wrong and the second is quite dubious, he spends most of his effort on what may well be a useful and reasonably accurate description of the Warren Commission's procedures. However, Epstein's treatment of the substantive issues, together with charges by many members of the Commission's staff that Epstein is guilty of flagrant misquotation, force one to withhold judgment on what might be the more significant aspect of Epstein's work.

However, one need not withhold judgment on the most interesting, and certainly the most publicized and profitable, of the revisionist works, Mark Lane's *Rush to Judgment*. It is a wide-ranging attack on almost every conclusion of the Warren Commission, and it at least initially leaves the reader thinking that if only a tenth of Lane's implications are true, he has more than made his case that the Warren Commission's performance is a major national disgrace. The problem is that if the reader (as, of course, few readers do) begins to check the assertions in *Rush to Judgment* against the evidence, he will find again and again that he has been expertly gulled. Though the book is cleverly constructed to make more use of implication and innuendo than of fact, nowhere near one-tenth of what Lane says stands up to careful scrutiny.

The book is not an easy one to demolish. The enormous range of his attacks on the Commission has allowed Lane to profit not only by the reluctance of book reviewers to dig deeply into the evidence, but perhaps also by the decision of many periodicals not to give the book the respectability that would come from discussing it in detail. Moreover, Lane's book is especially difficult to review because he presents no coherent theory about the assassination. He instead presents a long string of weakly connected points without formulating any one central point from which his assertions can be attacked. Proving his points insubstantial, therefore, is an almost endless task, and the complete demolishing of one point still leaves people—as, I regret to say, it will leave many readers of this piece—demanding why this or that point has not been refuted.

Lane's technique can best be appreciated by examining his effort to prove that the shots fired at the Presidential limousine came not from the sixth floor of the Texas School Book Depository, where Oswald's rifle was found, but rather from a grassy knoll in front of and to the right of the Presidential car. His argument makes two major points: first, that the noise of shots appeared to come from the area of the knoll rather than from the book depository, and second, that a puff of smoke was seen rising from the area of the knoll at about the time the President was shot. Indeed, he is able to make his case with a certain amount of persuasiveness—but only at the cost of completely distorting the evidence. Regarding the source of the noise, Lane convinces us that many (but by no means the preponderance he would imply) of those at the site of the assassination thought that the shots came from near the grassy knoll. Lane does not, however, bother setting out the highly relevant testimony of a railroad worker named Lee Bowers, although he relies on that witness for other points. Bowers testified that because of an echo in the area it was almost impossible to tell whether a noise came from the overpass near the grassy knoll or from the depository. Bowers had noted the echo before the assassination when the workers near the knoll could not tell whether noises originating in some work being done on the depository building came from that building or from the overpass nearby. Moreover, although there were certainly many witnesses before the Commission who thought that the shots came from the grassy knoll area, Lane is not content merely with their recorded testimony. He quotes his own interview with witness James L. Simmons in which Simmons said that the sound of shots "came from the left and in front of us, toward the wooden fence." But Lane does not mention that some two years earlier Simmons had stated to the FBI that he had the impression the shots came from the book depository.

Lane's argument about the smoke over the knoll is equally interesting. Actually, it was not disputed that there was a puff above the knoll; one witness described it as "smoke or steam," and another said it was "a puff of smoke . . . about 6 or 8 feet above the ground." The Commission did not attempt to deny this. Lane's sleight of hand is going from the smoke to the assumption that the puff came from a gun fired at the President. He quotes witness Clemon E. Johnson as saying that he saw white smoke, but does not go further to note Johnson's statement that he "felt that this smoke came from a motorcycle abandoned near the spot by a Dallas policeman." Moreover, unless the assassin fired a fifteenth-century harquebus it is hard to see how a shot fired at the President could have made as much smoke as Lane implies was visible. In addition, the area was teeming with people. It is conceivable that a man with a rifle might have escaped notice. However, not only is this most unlikely, but attempting to assassinate from the knoll would be so dangerous that it is hard to believe any assassin with even minimum rationality would have chosen such a spot. Finally, and most important, the physical evidence indicates beyond any reasonable doubt that the two shots that struck the President and the Governer were fired from the rear and from above; and though, of course, there might have been dozens of other would-be assassins firing and missing while concealed in other areas, we can say that, if so, they left no physical traces.

The question of the smoke over the grassy knoll further illustrates Lane's technique. He has excoriated the Commission both in his book and in innumerable public appearances for not calling witnesses who could have testified that a puff of smoke was seen over the grassy knoll. The implications are, first, that in this matter the Commission did at best a slovenly job in not calling those witnesses (whose statements to the FBI were before the Commission), and second, that this testimony would (or could) have changed the Commission's conclusions. The untruth of the second implication shows why the first is also false.

Nor can we assume, as might be charitable, that Lane's distortions are simply rooted in his ignorance of what we might find relevant. Lane's treatment of his own testimony before the Commission provides conclusive refutation of this. Lane made two appearances before the Commission and refused to make available to it two different items of evidence. In both instances the difference in treatment between the record of Lane's statements before the Commission and his own versions of his testimony is more than merely dramatic—indeed, the English language lacks a word for his colossal gall.[1]

One of the incidents involved Lane's refusal to make available a tape recording of a conversation he had with Helen Markham, who was also a witness before the Commission. At the hearing he defended his refusal on the ground that he had been retained by Marguerite Oswald, the mother of Lee Oswald, as an attorney for Lee, and that "I have an attorney-client relationship existing. The Commission is now asking for working papers of an attorney. The Supreme Court has been quite plain, I think, on the question of the sanctity of working documents of attorneys. And I think, therefore, that the questions are no longer in a proper area."

Lane's assertion that the *Hickman v. Taylor* doctrine barred the Commission from getting such a transcript of a conversation between a witness and an attorney shows such an appalling lack of legal skill that it is hard to believe he meant it as more than a joke.

[1] My colleague, Dr. George Torzsay-Biber, has informed me that the Hungarian *van porfja* would be appropriate here. Certainly the Yiddish *chutzpah* is appropriate. *Chutzpah* is usually explicated rather than defined; its classic illustration is the man who took a taxi to the bankruptcy court and invited the cab driver in as one of the creditors.

Indeed, any first-year law student putting forth the same proposition could be certain of getting no more than a "C" on his civil procedure exam. Lane apparently now realizes this since in his book he gives an entirely different story:[2]

> Had the Commission been motivated by an authentic desire to know the truth, surely it would have directed me to give the tape recording up. I was eager to furnish this evidence, but I was reluctant to break the law, for to make and divulge a recording of a telephone conversation may be a violation of the Federal Communications Act. I had made the recording; if I divulged it by presenting it voluntarily to the Commission, I could be tried in a court of law.

Not only is there no hint of this reasoning in Lane's testimony, but it is every bit as bad law as his first legal justification. The cases are legend that no criminal violation, or any other violation, of the Federal Communications Act inheres in a person recording a telephone conversation to which he is a party. Moreover, Lane's argument that he was hoping that the Commission would order him to give up the recording is hardly compatible with his answers to Commission questions such as "Are you refusing to disclose it, then?" Lane's answer was, "I have a specific direction from Mrs. [Marguerite] Oswald . . . not to discuss this matter publicly. . . ."

The second incident in Lane's testimony is even more remarkable. Lane testified before the Commission that he had a witness who could testify that a meeting had taken place before the assassination between Bernard Weissman (the author of a violently anti-Kennedy ad which appeared in the Dallas papers on the morning of the assassination), Patrolman Tippit, and Jack Ruby. Although the Commission was unable to find evidence that such a meeting had taken place—and indeed there is very good reason to disbelieve its existence—Lane refused to name his informant on the ground that he had promised not to. In discussing this in *Rush to Judgment,* Lane states: "But if the Commission had wanted his name, it need only have asked one of its witnesses, Thayer Waldo, a reputable journalist on the staff of the *Fort Worth Star-Telegram,* who was questioned by counsel in Dallas on June 27, 1964. Waldo, from whom I originally heard of the meeting, was well acquainted

[2] Lane, *Rush to Judgment* (New York, 1966), pp. 181–82.

with the witness. . . . Counsel, however, did not ask Waldo about the meeting."

The problem with Lane's handling of the issue is that nowhere in his testimony did he mention Waldo's name, or indicate to the Commission that Waldo might have such information. Nor was there any hint in Waldo's testimony before the Commission that he might have such knowledge. Indeed, while Waldo was not asked specifically whether he had any information on the meeting alleged by Lane, he did state that apart from the testimony that he gave (which was primarily about Jack Ruby's behavior in the Dallas jail the night of the assassination) he had nothing else to tell the Commission relevant to its inquiry.

Going through Lane's book piece by piece consumes so much time and space that, after this brief taste, it is more appropriate merely to classify his techniques of distortion. First, there is the rank distortion of witnesses' testimony. For example, to bolster his argument that the shots came from the grassy knoll area, Lane discusses the testimony of Lee Bowers:[3]

He told Commission counsel that "something occurred in this particular spot which was out of the ordinary, which attracted my eye for some reason, which I could not identify."

Q. You couldn't describe it?

Bowers: Nothing that I could pinpoint as having happened that—

Before Bowers could conclude this most important sentence, the Commission lawyer interrupted with an unrelated question. A little later Bowers was excused as a witness, leaving unexplained what it was in the area behind the fence that caught his eye at the moment the President was shot.

In a subsequent interview with me which was filmed and tape-recorded, however, Bowers offered more detailed information on this important point.

Bowers: At the time of the shooting, in the vicinity of where the two men I have described were, there was a flash of light or, as far as I am concerned, something I could not identify, but there was something which occurred which caught my eye in this immediate area on the embankment. Now, what this was, I could not state at that time and at this time I could not identify it, other than there was some un-

[3] *Ibid.*, p. 32 (footnotes omitted).

usual occurrence—a flash of light or smoke or something which caused me to feel like something out of the ordinary had occurred there.

Lane: In reading your testimony, Mr. Bowers, it appears that just as you were about to make that statement, you were interrupted in the middle of the sentence by the Commission counsel, who then went into another area.

Bowers: Well, that's correct. I mean, I was simply trying to answer his questions, and he seemed to be satisfied with the answer to that one and did not care for me to elaborate.

Lane's implication that the counsel for the Commission wished to avoid this revelation is typical of his approach. The dialogue just before the testimony which Lane quotes, however, casts a certain light upon what actually happened before the Commission:[4]

Mr. BALL. When you said there was a commotion, what do you mean by that? What did it look like to you when you were looking at the commotion?

Mr. BOWERS. I just am unable to describe rather than it was something out of the ordinary, a sort of milling around, but something occurred in this particular spot which was out of the ordinary, which attracted my eye for some reason, which I could not identify.

Moreover, eight questions earlier, the question and answer went as follows:

Mr. BALL. Did you see any activity in this high ground above Elm after the shot?

Mr. BOWERS. At the time of the shooting there seemed to be some commotion, and immediately following there was a motorcycle policeman who shot nearly all of the way to the top of the incline.

Finally, Lane does not set out the very end of Bowers' testimony—which hardly supports Lane's view that the Commission was trying to hide something:[5]

Mr. BALL. Is there anything that you told me that I haven't asked you about that you can think of?

Mr. BOWERS. Nothing that I recall.

[4] *Hearings before the President's Commission on The Assassination of President Kennedy* (Washington, 1964), VI, 288.

[5] *Ibid.*, pp. 288–89.

Mr. Ball. You have told me all that you know about this, haven't you?

Mr. Bowers. Yes; I believe that I have related everything which I have told the city police, and also told to the FBI.

The second technique Lane uses is the careful and factual presentation of one side of a case without indicating, in any way, that powerful reasons exist for rejecting the conclusion to which this side might point. Probably the best example of this technique is his discussion of the palm print on Oswald's rifle.

When Oswald's rifle was first sent from Dallas to the FBI for examination, the Dallas Police had indicated on it a number of possible fingerprints—none of which could be positively identified as Oswald's. Some days later, when Oswald's death had mooted Texas' case against him, all of the miscellaneous evidence against him not previously sent for examination was forwarded to the FBI. It was then discovered that among the miscellaneous documents and pictures was a piece of Scotch tape with a notation that on it was a palm print lifted from the rifle. This palm print turned out to be the only print on the weapon positively identifiable as Oswald's. The Dallas police officer who lifted the print stated that when the rifle was first sent to Washington he had not bothered noting that he had taken the print because he thought that enough of the lifted print was still identifiable on the weapon—an assertion which Lane calls "incredible" in view of the fact that the FBI expert testified that no such print remained.

With this evidence and the statement by Dallas Police Chief Jesse Curry that "[i]f we can put his prints on the rifle, why, it'll certainly connect him with the rifle and if we can establish that this is the rifle that killed the President, why—" Lane has a field day. Indeed, he makes a very persuasive case for the proposition that the "lifted" print was a fabrication by the Dallas Police after the rifle had been sent to Washington and that Oswald's prints had never been on the gun at all. Unfortunately, Lane does not choose to mention the only remaining piece of evidence on the issue. In response to a request from the Commission, an FBI fingerprint expert reexamined the lifted palm print and was able to determine that the interruptions in the print caused by the nicks and scratches on the surface of the material from which the print had been lifted exactly matched the nicks and scratches on Oswald's rifle—thus proving beyond question that Oswald's palm print had indeed been lifted from the rifle.

Lane's use of this technique does not always rise even to the level of one-sided truth. Thus, to make his case that the bullet that struck the President's head was fired from the right front rather than from the rear, Lane not only relies heavily upon the original impression of the doctors at Parkland Hospital, but he badly distorts their views as well. He vigorously disputes the assertion of the Commission that the bullet which struck the President in the head entered from the rear, making a small hole in the back of his head and a much larger one on the right front side (the President's head was turned to his left at the time the bullet struck). As evidence that no such smaller hole existed, Lane states that "eight doctors were unable to locate a smaller hole" and does not mention that the doctors in Dallas did not turn the President over either before or after their attempt to save him. Moreover, Lane does not set out the positive testimony of the three autopsy surgeons that the "coned out" inner surface of the rear of the President's skull established that the entrance wound was in the back of his head.

Lane's third basic technique is to set himself up as his own expert witness. Thus, his only mention of the two fragments found in the Presidential car is "two fragments which experts agree are hardly suitable for identification purposes." Lane later stated his expert opinion more flatly: "[T]he whole body of ballistics literature demonstrates that they are valueless for purposes of identification." Not only do the two fragments deserve far more attention than this since it is hard to see where they could have come from other than from the bullet that struck the President's head, but one would think that Lane should have pointed out that the two experts who testified before the Commission—and whose conclusions were supported by affidavits from two other experts—disputed his expert opinion and positively identified the fragments as coming from Oswald's rifle.

The technique of acting as one's own expert witness can be combined with the previously mentioned technique of leaving out crucial evidence. Lane does this when he insists that the famous picture of Oswald carrying a rifle is a composite of which only the head is Oswald's. Lane says he is led to this conclusion by his own observations of the shadows on the face and on the body. The reader can examine the picture for himself, but it does not appear to me that the picture is a composite. Of course, on this issue, I would rely neither on my own nor on Lane's observations. There is relevant expert testimony which Lane does not mention. An FBI photographic expert testified before the Commission that a microscopic examination of the picture led him to conclude that it was not a composite. Moreover, although the negative of the photograph Lane attacks was not discovered, the police found among Oswald's belongings the negative of another picture which also shows Oswald holding what is apparently the same rifle. An examination of this picture indicates that it was taken at the same time as its more famous companion (Oswald is wearing the same clothing and his hair is combed in exactly the same way in both photographs). As to this picture the evidence is overwhelming. The photographic expert testified that an examination of this negative and of Oswald's camera (which was also in evidence) showed not only that the negative was not a composite, but that it had been taken with Oswald's own camera.

The fourth of Lane's basic techniques involves the use of the gross logical fallacy. For example, he argues at some length that Lee Oswald was not a good enough shot to have assassinated the President in the way the Commission stated that he did and therefore implies that Oswald could not have been the assassin. At first glance the logical connection between the propositions seems apparent, but a little thought reveals that inability to perform a task means two entirely different things. First, one's inability to lift, without aid, a 10,000-pound weight or run a mile in two minutes is such that, regardless of any other evidence, we could conclude that such a thing just could not have happened. When we say, however, that someone is not a good enough shot to hit a given target two out of three times, we are speaking of an entirely different kind of inability. What we mean, of course, is that one is not good enough to do this consistently, and, although the chance of one's having made a particular shot becomes less and less as the shot becomes more difficult or as one's marksmanship ability decreases, it is always possible for one to have made a lucky shot or two.

Thus, the fallacy in Lane's argument is in asking whether Oswald was a good enough shot to have hit the moving targets twice in a given time, at a given distance, instead of asking whether the unlikelihood of Oswald's making those shots is enough to shake our conviction that he in fact did so. The latter, of course, depends upon the strength of the other evidence that Oswald was the killer—an inquiry which Lane does not undertake in this context. In fact, if I were to estimate the probabilities involved, I would have to say that, as an *a priori* proposition, the odds of Oswald's making the necessary shots were about one in fifty (although who can say to what extent it concentrates the mind to have the President of the United States in one's telescopic sights?). On the other hand, I would have to say that the other evidence, not counting that of Oswald's marksmanship, would lead to the odds of about one thousand to one that Oswald was the assassin. It may sound paradoxical, but a little thought reveals that the very best evidence that Oswald was able to make the shots is the mass of evidence that he in fact did so.

The remarkable thing about *Rush to Judgment* is that we have hardly scratched the surface in numbering and classifying Lane's distortions. There are more and more and more. Indeed, when one looks carefully at Lane's book and the evidence upon which he relied, it almost passes the point where one can call him fraudulent. Paradoxically, the very depth and thoroughness of the distortion in *Rush to Judgment* are perhaps strong evidence that Lane himself actually believes much of what he has written. While it is possible, of course, that he is secretly laughing all the way to the bank, it is hard to think of someone who just for the profit—admittedly considerable—could perpetrate as elaborate and tasteless a hoax as this.

Lane has defended himself on the ground that his book is not an objective analysis but more like a brief for Oswald. First of all, this defense comes only after Lane has been backed into a corner. Nothing in the book or in its publicity indicates to the uninformed reader that Lane is anything but objective—outraged, perhaps, by the dishonesty and deceit he finds all around him, but nonetheless objective. Furthermore, the idea that *Rush to Judgment* might merely be a brief for Oswald completely misconstrues the nature of a brief. True, an advocate has a certain latitude to emphasize some facts and deemphasize others. But Lane carries this far beyond mere advocacy. The fact is that any lawyer who carried this latitude to such an extreme and employed for a client the type and volume of misrepresentation that Lane does would be in danger of either disbarment or commitment.

We may pass over *Whitewash,* by Harold Weisberg, in just a sentence. It is the most strident, bitter, and generally irrational of all the attacks on the Commission. Out of charity, we shall mention it no further and move on to Léo Sauvage's *The Oswald Affair.* Sauvage, the American correspondent of *Le Figaro,* has written an absolutely bewildering book, which in some ways is very different from Lane's and in others quite similar.

As is true with Lane, the number and variety of Sauvage's objections to the Commission's version (and many of them are very different from Lane's) are so great that it is impossible even to begin to cover them all here. Sauvage's technique, however, is a fairly simple one. In discussing each question, he begins with the initial reports coming out of Dallas in the first hectic moments after the assassination. These were almost always so erroneous and garbled that they are sitting ducks now that a great deal more evidence has been made available. He then proceeds to discuss the reports and rumors that seeped out with all too great frequency during the Warren Commission investigation. On most occasions these turned out in one way or another to have been inaccurate too; and where they were not, Sauvage damns the Commission for allowing them to leak out at all. Finally, when he comes to the evidence presented by the Commission, Sauvage has the reader psychologically prepared to find that, like everything before, it is a tissue of lies.

Sauvage indeed seems convinced that America has another Dreyfus case (an analogy he uses on several occasions) and that Oswald had no hand whatsoever in the assassination. In Sauvage's words, "I find nothing to show that Oswald was the assassin of President Kennedy," and, "[I]t is logically untenable, legally indefensible, and morally inadmissible to declare Lee Harvey Oswald the assassin. . . ." Unlike Lane, who makes use of a broad range of tactics to attack the Commission, Sauvage concentrates primarily on just one: a refusal to accept the most likely thrust of the evidence because in his opinion it does not amount to a certainty.

Probably the most perverse of all of Sauvage's findings is that, as he has since phrased it, "there is no legally acceptable proof that Oswald had the revolver [ascribed to him] in his possession at the time of his arrest." Sauvage's reconstruction of the seizure of the revolver (exhibit 143) from Oswald is a virtuoso performance. He correctly points out what he considers to be an error in the testimony of Officer McDonald, the first policeman to approach Oswald in the Texas Theater following the slaying of Officer Tippit. McDonald, who identified exhibit 143 as the revolver he had taken from Oswald, could not of his own knowledge be sure that it was the same gun, since he had handed it to one Officer Carroll before his struggle with Oswald had ended.

Sauvage next moves on to the testimony of Officer Carroll. When asked by the Commission who had hold of the pistol at the time he took it, Carroll stated: "I don't know, sir. I just saw the pistol pointing at me and I grabbed it and jerked it away from whoever had it and that's all, and by that time then the handcuffs were put on Oswald." Carroll himself did not identify the gun but merely stated that he had given it to Officer Gerald Hill. Officer Hill then testified that he had kept the gun in his possession until he had time to scratch his name on it and was thus able positively to identify exhibit 143 as the gun that Carroll gave him.

Sauvage concludes from this testimony that "the testimony of the three policemen directly involved does not support the conclusion that a gun was taken from Oswald at the Texas Theater. . . ." The flaw he finds is that Carroll said that he did not know who had hold of the pistol and that "[t]he fact that McDonald stated that he had given the pistol to Carroll is utterly meaningless. Though neither [of the Commission attorneys] saw fit to ask any question to this effect, it is quite obvious that McDonald, fighting with Oswald and 'swarmed' by officers, could not have seen which one took the pistol, if he did give a pistol to someone." Actually, what is "quite obvious" to Sauvage is not at all clear. McDonald may very well have seen Carroll as he testified he did, even though Carroll did not know that McDonald was holding the other end of the gun.

But this is only the beginning. In addition to the testimony of the officers mentioned by Sauvage, it is interesting to note the testimony of others involved in the incident. Officer C. T. Walker testified:[6]

Mr. BELIN. When you saw Oswald's hand by his belt, which hand did you see then?

Mr. WALKER. He had ahold of the handle of it.

Mr. BELIN. Handle of what?

Mr. WALKER. The revolver.

Mr. BELIN. Was there a revolver there?

Mr. WALKER. Yes; there was.

Detective Paul L. Bentley stated: "Just as I entered the lower floor I saw Patrolman McDonald fighting with this suspect. I saw this suspect pull a pistol from his shirt, so I went to Patrolman McDonald's aid immediately." Patrolman Ray Hawkins stated: "Officer Walker and I ran toward the subject and grabbed him by his left arm. The subject had reached in his belt for a gun, and Officer McDonald was holding his right hand with the gun in it. Officer Hutson had entered the row behind the suspect, and grabbed him around the neck. . . ." Patrolman T. A. Hutson stated: "Officer C. T. Waker [*sic*] came up and was struggling with the suspect's left hand, and as Officer McDonald struggled with the suspect's right hand, he moved it to his waist and drew a pistol. . . ."

As if this were not enough, Oswald admitted to several police officers and federal agents that he had possessed a pistol in the theater, each time coupling it with a statement that that was all they had him for. Sauvage handles these statements with the assertion: "[T]he Commission notes that Oswald 'admitted nothing that would damage him but discussed other matters quite freely.' The fact of owning a revolver that the police said had killed Tippit would certainly tend to damage him. It would seem from the Report, therefore, that Oswald did not admit that."

Mr. Sauvage carries his perversity to extremes in this quotation.

[6] *Ibid.*, VII, 39.

Obviously, the reasonable construction of this sentence of the report is that Oswald admitted only that which he was completely convinced the authorities could prove. At the time, there was no ballistic determination of the gun used to shoot Officer Tippit, and Oswald obviously believed (and on the evidence one can hardly blame him) that his possession of the pistol could be conclusively established.

Finally, if exhibit 143 was not the gun that everyone saw Oswald draw, where did it come from? Sauvage concedes that it did belong to Oswald, having been purchased by him some half a year earlier. Could the gun have been brought into the theater by one of the police officers? If so, what was he doing with the gun that fired the shells found beside Officer Tippit's body, especially at a time when he could not have known of that evidence? Moreover, if exhibit 143 was not the gun Oswald drew, what happened to the gun he did draw? It apparently has disappeared completely. Perhaps Sauvage would suggest as the alternative explanation a complicated conspiracy among at least a dozen police officers, none of whom was near the assassination site and none of whom could, in any conceivable way, have known in advance where they would find Oswald. In the face of all this, a sufficiently desperate defense attorney might conceivably argue that it had not been proven conclusively that exhibit 143 was taken from Oswald at the theater, in order to take the prosecution's time and confuse the jury. But to say that the evidence "does not support the conclusion" is more than merely farfetched.

Although some of Sauvage's book could have been written by Mark Lane—Sauvage asserts "Lee Harvey Oswald did not have the skill required to commit the assassination"—for the most part their attitudes are quite different. Lane buries or omits any evidence other than that which leads his reader along his chosen path. Thus, Lane's only mention of the arrest is a passing reference on page 81; the reader who missed that might well conclude that Oswald had turned himself in to the police. Sauvage, on the other hand, generally mentions evidence he finds uncomfortable but applies his bewildering logic to minimize its effect or to turn it to his advantage.

A fine example of this is his treatment of the General Walker incident. The Commission concluded that one of the circumstances strengthening its belief that Oswald had killed the President was the fact that Oswald was the author of a previous assassination attempt on General Edwin A. Walker some seven months earlier. To be sure, on this issue Commission evidence, based in great part on the somewhat unreliable testimony of Marina Oswald, was not overly strong. During the investigation a note in Oswald's handwriting turned up that indicated that he had expected to be in some kind of trouble shortly. Marina Oswald told the Commission that her husband had left this note behind one night and explained that he had just attempted to kill General Walker. Sauvage spends some time demolishing this theory, pointing out that Oswald had not returned home with his rifle and that therefore it would have been necessary for him to stash it somewhere near General Walker's house. (According to Marina's testimony, Oswald told her he had buried it far from Walker's house.) Moreover, Sauvage points out that "the Dallas authorities never bothered to explain how Oswald got to Walker's house," since he had no car. Of course it is possible, Sauvage admits, that he took a bus. Sauvage asks us to:[7]

> Imagine Oswald with his rifle . . . under his arm, marching off to slay the general, and planning to return home the same way. . . . I doubt very much that a Lee Harvey Oswald, before reaching home "white and shaking," could make use of those buses and transfers, walk to and from the bus stops, wait at the bus stops for some time (the buses in Dallas, as elsewhere, do not run frequently at night), and do all this without being noticed by anyone.

Sauvage does point out a number of unlikely aspects of the story. On the other hand, we do know that among Oswald's possessions were found several photographs of General Walker's home, and since microscopic examination revealed that at least one was taken with Oswald's camera, we are not completely without evidence tying him to General Walker. Moreover, the dates involved may be relevant. One picture of the area by the house was taken between March 8 and 12, 1963 (this was determined from the progress on a building under construction shown in the background). On March 12 Oswald, under an assumed name, bought

[7] Léo Sauvage, *The Oswald Affair* (New York, 1966), pp. 155–56 (paragraphing omitted).

the money order which he mailed in to purchase his rifle; on March 20 the rifle was mailed out to him and on April 10 the attempt on General Walker's life occurred.

Sauvage's technique, however, requires him to mention the photographs, and he quotes the Commission as saying that "three photographs found among Oswald's possessions after the assassination were identified by Marina Oswald as photographs of General Walker's house." He concentrates, however, on pointing out an inconsistency he finds between this statement and an earlier statement of the Commission: "[U]ntil December 3, 1963, the Walker shooting remained unsolved." Since the pictures were found eleven or twelve days prior to this date, on November 22 or 23, Sauvage asks, "Wasn't it strange that the federal and local investigators who examined the pictures failed to identify them when they could have checked with the tourist bureau, the Chamber of Commerce, cab drivers, or Boy Scouts . . . ?"

It seems hardly strange at all to me that in the first eleven days after the assassination no one had identified the pictures of General Walker's house. Presumably, police were investigating many facets of Oswald and there was no reason at the very beginning of the investigation to think that those pictures might be significant. Indeed, considering the circumstances, the time lag of eleven days seems rather short.

Subsequently Sauvage is willing to assume for the sake of argument that Oswald did attempt to kill General Walker. In that case, however, he would regard this as evidence not that Oswald killed President Kennedy but that he did not. Here he reveals most clearly his talent for missing the point. Sauvage states: "I am ready to admit that Oswald was against fascists and that he might have been led to undertake some action against a Walker. Would the same reasoning have led him to kill a Kennedy?"

To me, evidence (though admittedly inconclusive) that Oswald had attempted to kill General Walker would be highly relevant to the question of whether he had killed President Kennedy. True, in a criminal prosecution such evidence would probably have been held inadmissible, but the reason for its inadmissibility would be not so much that it is not probative, but rather that it is, in a sense, too probative and therefore prejudicial. And though Sauvage, of course, is perfectly correct in stating that the absence of a motive to kill the President is some reason to believe that Oswald did not do it, it seems that the significant thing the attempt to kill Walker would indicate is that, in Oswald, we had a man who could try to kill from ambush a man who had done him no personal harm and from whose death he could not expect to profit.

We must be very careful not to use up all our synonyms for perversity on Mr. Sauvage's book lest we run out before coming to Richard Popkin's *The Second Oswald. The Second Oswald* is actually only a thin paperback that has had to be padded with nine appendices to make it as long as it is. The book is essentially Popkin's long and widely discussed review of the four previously mentioned books which first appeared in the *New York Review of Books* [July 28, 1966].

Popkin, chairman of the philosophy department at the University of California, San Diego, has grasped one of the great truths that has eluded most of the other critics of the Commission. It is one thing to attack the Commission's conclusion on this or that issue as not being based upon the evidence or as being the less likely of two possibilities. It is entirely different, though, to attempt to work all the evidence one accepts into a single coherent theory. Popkin understands the fallacy of agreeing with Epstein that there probably was a second assassin in addition to Oswald behind and above the President; with Sauvage that Oswald had nothing to do with the assassination; and with Lane that the fatal shots were fired not from the book depository but from the grassy knoll. Popkin realizes that if one agrees with Epstein that the autopsy doctors misplaced the President's wounds, one should be prepared to offer some explanation why they did this; that if one agrees with Lane that a bullet struck the President in the front of the throat, one should be prepared to explain what happened both to the bullet and to its exit wound; and that if one agrees with Sauvage that Oswald had nothing to do with the attempt on General Walker's life, one should offer an explanation of why he happened to have in his possession a picture of General Walker's house. The discipline required in formulating a theory rather than merely attacking on a large number of isolated points is that one's points and the evidence one accepts must then be consistent. Popkin, therefore, makes the effort, and his result is so silly that it is hard to believe that he is serious—which he very well may not be.

In many ways this is quite unfortunate, because several of Popkin's ideas might well have been made into a theory considerably more plausible than the one he finally chooses. Essentially, the problem which Popkin tries to explain and which throws his theory off is that several identifications of Oswald were made in testimony before the Commission that could not possibly have been correct since Oswald was undeniably proven to be elsewhere at the time. If Popkin had decided, as the Commission did, that these witnesses were either lying or unintentionally wrong, he would have had no further trouble. In fact, there is good reason to believe that at least one of the witnesses was lying in an attempt to gain publicity. If one accepts their testimony as true, however, as does Popkin, one has to conclude either that Oswald was in two different places at the same time or that there were two "Oswalds." Essentially, Popkin's theory is the latter; that the witnesses who identified Oswald as having been in places where he clearly could not have been were basically correct in their identification of an "Oswald," but were misled by an extremely complicated scheme to set up a false trail.

The crime was supposedly committed by both "Oswalds," with the rifle implicating Lee Oswald left at the assassination scene. The second "Oswald," who was a better shot and used a better gun than Lee, could then disappear. When the evidence all came in it would be so confused that it would be impossible to convict the actual Oswald.

In one of his chapters Mark Lane uses a variant of this theory in which Oswald was an innocent patsy. Under Lane's version, however, the incident in the Texas Theater becomes most difficult to explain. Moreover, framing poor Lee Oswald does seem a great deal of trouble for the conspirators to go to. For all they knew, by the time President Kennedy arrived in Dallas, Oswald might have either lost his job or gone to Mexico. And even if they could have been certain that Oswald would still be working at the depository, they could not possibly have known that he would not have been out in the street or elsewhere with a perfect alibi at the time of the shooting.

On the other hand, if Oswald was, as Popkin seems to assume, a willing party to the whole false-trail plan, one might point out that the trail would in great part not have been false at all. One might then ask what could have been Oswald's possible object in having the trail lead to himself, especially since he would end up being tried before a Texas jury that, having heard about his Marxist past, might not require a vast amount of evidence to give him the death penalty.

But the more basic problem with Popkin's conspiracy theory is that no sane or even mildly insane person would have done it the way Popkin has suggested. The scene as Popkin visualizes it has two men shooting with different rifles at the Presidential car. (Early in the book it seems that both are in the book depository—later Popkin either forgets this and places one on the grassy knoll or adds, without explanation, a third assassin at that site.) If it turns out—and they have no way of making sure it doesn't—that the identifiable bullet is fired not from Oswald's gun but from the other "Oswald's" gun, the entire scheme blows up completely. As it is, Popkin argues that exhibit 399 was planted beside Governor Connally's stretcher, presumably by someone who knew that there would be need for a bullet damaged only on the rear end.

One would think that if the second "Oswald" was able to get out of the book depository with his rifle without even being seen, there would be no reason to leave Lee Oswald behind as some kind of hostage. If Popkin's conspirators to assassinate President Kennedy from the Texas School Book Depository were as clever as he makes them out, they could have had Oswald, who worked there, and the other marksman fire their shots, put their rifles in a previously prepared box full of either high explosives or thermite, touch the thing off with a short fuse, and appear in the hallway asking what had happened. Since the murder weapons would then have been completely destroyed and there would have been no eyewitnesses, there would have been nothing against either man. Oswald could have said that he decided the best place to watch the parade was from a nearby window and that he had asked his friend, the marksman, to visit with him.

True, there are many ways one can suggest in which the crime, as reconstructed by the Commission, could have been better planned. Oswald obviously did not plan it well himself, and one would think that if he had help, that help was much more lucky than skillful. On the other hand, it is one thing to say that it was not well planned and a very different thing to say, as Mr. Popkin does, that it was planned without even a minimum of rationality.

The aforementioned five books, their publicity releases, and the public appearances of their authors constitute the great bulk of the third stage of inquiry into the assassination. The "mysterious death" issue, however, brought up after their publication (*Rush to Judgment* mentions it but gives it relatively little attention) also has to be accorded a legitimate portion of this stage. A number of magazines, the most publicized of which is *Ramparts,* have published stories commenting on and drawing the most sinister implications from the "mysterious" deaths of "witnesses" somehow connected with the assassination. Although this facet of the inquiry (like the curse of Tutankhamen of a few decades ago) has received a great deal of comment, even the most cursory examination of the stories shows how essentially foolish they are. A good many of the deaths hardly seem mysterious in that they were caused by auto accidents, heart attacks, and other phenomena that afflict our entire population. Moreover, before we could tell whether the number of these deaths is in any way unusual, we would have to know the number of equally "mysterious" deaths that occurred to people completely unconnected with the *Warren Commission Report.* But even apart from any statistical refutation, the theory that a set of conspirators is now devoted to wiping out a host of unimportant witnesses is almost too silly to be put forth. There is not the slightest indication that any of the "victims" have had anything to tell that they had not already told, and indeed the deaths seem concentrated among those who bore only the most peripheral relation to the assassination. When one stops to consider that almost each one of the "mysterious" deaths requires the recruitment of at least one and often several new conspirators, it would seem that, like the pyramid club, the conspiracy would be getting bigger and bigger rather than smaller. One would think that in light of what had happened to those who knew too much it would get very difficult to recruit new members into the conspiracy. Most important, however, it is hard to say why the supposed killers are taking whatever chances these murders entail when it is so obvious that, whoever the conspirators are, they have already gotten off scot-free.

In all probability the biggest question raised by the third stage of inquiry into the assassination has nothing whatsoever to do with any of the points that have been discussed here. Rather the question is, considering the abysmal quality of their thought and integrity, why the third-stage writings have attracted so much attention.

To my mind it is only a partial answer to rely on the dictum of P. T. Barnum. Three more basic reasons come immediately to mind. First, there really are doubts concerning the assassination of the President. This should hardly be surprising since even in a typical criminal case one cannot determine the guilt of a defendant beyond all possible doubt; this is why the jury is instructed that it need only be convinced beyond a reasonable doubt. But in the Warren Commission investigation there are other problems. Even if one concedes that Oswald was guilty beyond any reasonable doubt, a host of subsidiary questions still remain as to just how he committed the crime and whether he had help. In the typical criminal trial these questions, of course, would often not be answered beyond a reasonable doubt. The jury might well be completely undecided as to which of three or four different means the defendant employed and yet perfectly rationally believe that he had employed one of them.

Uncertainty about many issues is an inevitable by-product of any large-scale investigation, and where the issue is important there will of course be disputes. The evidence for the one-bullet theory is ambiguous, and, as often happens when ambiguity exists, some people assert one possibility while others disagree with equal fervor. In all probability we will never know, to a very high degree of confidence, whether the one-bullet theory is correct. If this thought is upsetting in the abstract, it is all the more so when one realizes that a completely competent investigation immediately after the assassination (and before the Warren Commission had come into being) might have given us the answer. Unfortunately, however, no one even realized that the one-bullet theory was an issue until after both the Zapruder film and Oswald's gun had been closely examined. By that time the autopsy on President Kennedy had been completed and his body was permanently out of the hands of the surgeons; Governor Connally's wounds were well on the way to healing; and, through an incredible bungle, the Governor's clothes had been cleaned, thus destroying any light they might have shed on the mystery.

The second reason for the great furor caused by the third-stage writings is the fact that, although the Warren Commission investigation seems on the whole a competent one, the actual report of the Commission shows two grave defects. The first defect is that it was obviously rushed out. Epstein gives a most plausible explanation why, and, although we can understand the Commissioners' desire to get the report published before the 1964 elections, their failure to have taken the necessary time shows up again and again in the quality of the report. Thus, the index to the twenty-six volumes and the citation of exhibits in the report are extremely inaccurate and incomplete, and there is a good bit of sloppiness which can be explained only by the pressures of time upon the staff. Despite the legitimate desire for speed, however, it was not necessary for the pressure to have compromised the work of the Commission. It would have made sense, considering the way in which the world awaited the report, for the Commission to have first put out what it did put out, or even something considerably more sketchy, as a preliminary report. The Commission could then have assembled its discussion of the evidence and its conclusions carefully and deliberately in the extra six or eight months this would have taken.

In all probability, however, a second basic decision of the Commission was even more detrimental to the report's ultimate value than the decision to get it out so quickly. This was the decision to write the report not as an impartial historian but, in many places, as an advocate. When I say that the Commission too often was an advocate, I do not mean to charge it with the distortions and misrepresentations that have characterized the third stage of inquiry. What the Commission did was to put the best face on the evidence it wished to use. Thus in its discussion of the one-bullet theory the Commission marshaled most of the evidence in its favor, but alluded only slightly to the opposing evidence and not at all to the possible importance of the issue. How much better it would have been had the Commission discussed the alternatives and then decided on the one-bullet theory as the most likely of the possibilities. It could have recognized fully the fact that the one-bullet theory was a likelihood on the basis of all the evidence—somewhat on the order of four out of five rather than, as it implied, ninety-nine out of one hundred. Having done this, the Commission could have discussed how the evidence could be rationalized were the one-bullet theory not true, instead of relying on what is perhaps a technically accurate but by no means obvious truth that the validity of the one-bullet theory was "not necessary" to any of the Commission's major conclusions.

The Commission's advocacy detracts from its discussion of other issues as well. It attempted to prove that Oswald's shots were not difficult ones and concluded, on the basis of his Marine record and several not very successful tests with his rifle, that Oswald "possessed the capability with a rifle . . . to commit the assassination." It would have been more candid to have pointed out that Oswald had probably just gotten off two "lucky" shots. The Commission's advocacy is visible at yet another point. Although it had what would seem to be sufficient proof that Oswald had slain Officer Tippit, the Commission nonetheless supported its view with a purported eyewitness identification by one Helen Markham, whose credibility had been completely destroyed during the hearings.

It is difficult to assess the blame for the Commission's failure to accord due respect to its historical role. Perhaps it lies in the fact that the majority of the Commissioners were lawyers and that lawyers, having reached a conclusion—even honestly and fairly—are accustomed to stating it in the form that most justifies their belief and that best convinces onlookers. Perhaps it is due merely to the time pressures that ruled out the longer and more careful discussion that would have been necessary had every point been given full consideration. Perhaps Epstein was partially correct, and the Commission, having decided that no conspiracy existed, tried to fulfill both its duty to its own integrity and its role as an organ of state by writing what it felt to be the truth in the most convincing form. Whatever the reason, however, the decisions to publish the report so hastily and from the perspective of an advocate were serious errors, and if the decisions are responsible for even a tiny part of the third stage, the Commissioners have suffered for them.

The third reason for the attention given the third-stage writings is the failure of the Commission to disclose the full contents of all the evidence before it. Although certain governmental privileges of secrecy do apply in a criminal trial, the strong presumption is nonetheless in favor of complete disclosure of all admissible evidence. The Warren Commission investigation was far different, however. Unlike the criminal trial, which is generally confined by the rules of evidence to a comparatively narrow range of facts bearing upon well-defined issues, the Warren Commission conducted the broadest possible inquiry into much less well-defined problems. As a result, controversy could arise over the disclosure of a great many bits of evidence that, not being admissible in a criminal trial, would have created no issue of disclosure there. Thus, reports on Oswald's behavior in the Soviet Union were at least peripherally relevant to the Commission's investigation. It is not too great a flight-of-fancy to believe that these reports would have revealed the names of confidential informers in the Soviet Union whose identity the CIA might reasonably prefer to have undisclosed. The question, then, is where the line should be drawn between the public's right to know and the legitimate demands of secrecy.

Although much of the material before the Commission as "evidence" was cleared for public access by the individual executive agencies which originated it, the Commission itself made no effort to determine which of the documents originating with the Commission, such as correspondence, minutes, and working papers, should and which should not be released to the public. Instead it turned over all of its documents to the National Archives, which, after initial confusion, asked the Department of Justice for help in determining which documents should and which should not be released. The Department of Justice, in consultation with the executive agencies involved, then worked out a set of general guidelines for this purpose, leaving the application of these guidelines, on a document-by-document basis, to the Archivists. These guidelines, as one might expect, were vague, providing that statutory restrictions and security classifications must be respected but at the same time calling on the agencies involved to reevaluate the security classifications to determine whether the information could be released.

As to unclassified material, the requirements were even more vague—although it is hard to see how one could have drafted specific requirements to cover the multitude of cases. The object was primarily to prevent the disclosure of documents that "[m]ight reveal the identity of confidential sources of information and [thereby] impede or jeopardize future investigations," or "[w]ould be a source of embarrassment to innocent persons . . . because [the documents] . . . contain gossip and rumor or details of a personal nature having no significant connection with the assassination. . . ." Although it may be argued that these directions are too inclusive, the guidelines also urged the Archives and the agencies involved to "weigh . . . [the] reason [for nondisclosure] against the over-riding policy . . . favoring fullest possible disclosure." Moreover, the classifications of documents are to be reviewed after five years, ten years, and every subsequent ten years to determine what documents may then be made available.

Although the standards for releasing documents seem completely reasonable, at least on the surface, there have been incidents of nondisclosure that cannot help but damage the public faith in the handling of the whole issue. Before the guidelines were worked out, the Archives refused to make available any documents without the Commission's approval. Unfortunately, by the time the guidelines were formulated the Commission had gone out of existence, and its general counsel insisted that he therefore had no jurisdiction to approve anything. Finally, the imbroglio was solved by the Attorney General's Office, which ruled that the Archives had "the authority and obligation to review that material and to determine which of it should be made available to, or withheld from, the public. . . ."

Far more important to the third-stage controversies, the X-rays and photographs taken at the autopsy of President Kennedy were not initially turned over to the Archives. Apparently—although this is far from certain—they were in the possession of the Kennedy family, which, considering matters of taste and the probable condition of the President's body, would have preferred not to release them at all. One positive result of the furor is that the exhibits are now at the Archives, and have already been made available to the autopsy surgeons (who have announced that their earlier conclusions have thereby been confirmed). Until those exhibits are made public, however, there will be many who feel that the photographs are being suppressed to cover the guilt of those who lied about the President's autopsy.

The problem of the autopsy photographs is a relatively easy one. If taste were the only reason for not releasing a document, it would be quite clear that all should be made public. Unfortunately, there are overriding security reasons for not releasing some of the documents; but clearly as long as any evidence exists that has not been made public, many Americans (especially those who do not recognize any distinction among governmental organs such as the Warren Commission and the National Archives) will view the restrictions as powerful evidence of a conspiracy.

Obviously, however, the lack of certainty, the defects in the report, and the nondisclosure of evidence by no means fully account for the violence and the number of attacks upon the Warren Commission and its investigation. The question then is, "What does?" One cannot, of course, know for sure, but I would suggest that one basic cause is the Vietnam issue. A major indication of this is that the great volume of both protest against the Vietnam involvement and complaint about the Commission has come from the left.[8]

[8] The widely publicized New Orleans investigation into a possible conspiracy to assassinate President Kennedy does not, of course, fit into this pattern. The fact that the case is now pending trial precludes comment on the strength of the prosecution's case. But even if the charge that Clay Shaw agreed with Oswald to assassinate the President were taken as true, the voluminous newspaper coverage indicates that it is hard to connect this agreement with the actual killing. First, there is no indication that the alleged agreement to have more than one person participate in the killing was followed. Moreover, at the time of the plot there was no way to know that President Kennedy would go to Dallas, where Oswald lived. And Oswald's job at the Texas School Book Depository was secured through means clearly unrelated to a conspiracy at a time when there was no indication that even if the President came to Dallas his route would take him past the depository. Second, this conspiracy seems completely unrelated to the kinds of conspiracies envisioned by those involved in the third stage. The New Orleans publicity has smacked far more of a conspiracy by sex deviates (with perhaps a slight touch of Castroite intrigue) than by the "racists" envisioned by Sauvage, the "Texas oil interests" envisioned by Buchanan, . . . or the "rightists" envisioned by Lane. Finally, the New Orleans in-

Hatred is not a pretty thing, and the hatred that the extreme left has developed for Lyndon Johnson, although it possibly matches that which the right wing had for Franklin D. Roosevelt, is something unparalleled in our time. In this context the attacks on the Warren Commission serve the function of blaming one more thing on Lyndon Johnson. After all, the Commission was a governmental body and Johnson not only heads the Government, he established the Commission and selected its members as well. Thus the widespread feeling, originating in the Vietnam issue, that the Government has forfeited the citizen's confidence in its integrity need only be extended somewhat to include the Commissioners within the ambit of those who have merely been loyal to the President in suppressing the truth.

Furthermore, in the background there is an even less pretty thought, one which is very rarely mentioned. Popkin slyly refers to those who see the assassination as "a subtle conspiracy, involving perhaps some of the Dallas Police, the FBI, the right-wing lunatic fringe in Dallas, or perhaps even (in rumors I have often heard) Kennedy's successor."

The Movement, the newspaper of the Student Non-Violent Coordinating Committee, in its November 1966 issue, points out: "Several commentators have remarked that the assassination must have been the act of one demented killer because it was not followed by a right-wing takeover. This explanation overlooks the fact that, in some policy areas, Johnson's accession to the presidency constituted a right-wing takeover." Although it is hardly clear in print, it should be clear that there is a sizable number of people in the United States who wish nothing more than to be able to pin the blame for President Kennedy's assassination on his successor. For them this would ease the frustrations of Vietnam involvement; avenge the death of one who after his death (although by no means before it) became a hero to them; and, finally, punish President Johnson for his transgressions.

---

vestigation sheds no real discredit on the Warren Commission, for the key witnesses of the new investigation, those who "heard" the plot, did not bother to tell anyone until three years after the assassination. [In March, 1969, a jury found Shaw not guilty.]

Nor is this hypothesis pure conjecture. Despite the fact that, from what we know of Oswald, a leftist conspiracy—if there was a political conspiracy at all—is far more likely than a rightist one, almost all the conspiracy allegations have been directed at the "Establishment" from the left. Men who deplored McCarthyism and all it stood for have been perfectly willing on the basis of incredibly flimsy evidence or no evidence at all to posit theories that Patrolman Tippit was a conspirator in the President's assassination; that the Commissioners lied and suppressed the truth; that a whole host of government officials perjured themselves; and indeed that a network of conspirators far surpassing anything charged during the "Who Promoted Peress?" days now pervades the nation. Even the most baleful excesses of the McCarthy era were not as unfair, irresponsible, and reckless as this.

To remark that these tactics can only do harm in the long run to the values that those who use such methods purport to support is beside the point. The fact is that they have been in some measure successful. We have already entered the fourth stage where the nation's opinion-makers are belatedly entering the picture.

The fourth stage, when organized mass media for the first time began paying serious attention to the outcries over the *Warren Commission Report,* began during the week of November 25, 1966. In the same week both *Life* and the *New York Times* demanded that something be done.

Life, which owns the original of the Zapruder film, reproduced (enlarged and in color) the crucial section, covering the period when the one bullet—or the two bullets—struck President Kennedy and Governor Connally, and entitled its feature story "A Matter of Reasonable Doubt." Although *Life* did not purport to draw any conclusions as to the validity of the one-bullet theory, the text included some of the arguments in its favor, as set out by one of the Commission's former staff members, Arlen Specter, along with a rebuttal by the *Life* staff. Certainly the piece leaves the average reader with the feeling that the one-bullet theory is the less likely of the two possibilities. There are, however, several things to note about *Life's* story and pictures. First, as *Life* points out, President Kennedy can easily be seen reacting before any reaction by Governor Connally is visible—almost half a second earlier according to the Governor himself. Interestingly, however, the frame the Governor chose as the one in which he was struck, frame 234, shows him very clearly holding his hand up and completely out of the path the Commission stated the bullet must have followed to strike him on the right wrist. *Life* explains it this way: "Nor can much importance be given to lining up Connally's three wounds—Specter's 'alignment of holes' theory. Hitting a rib would probably have deflected the bullet from a straight course; Connally's wrist could have been almost anywhere and still have been struck by it." *Life* may indeed be correct, but it is interesting to note that its staff missed a most relevant question and answer between Specter and Dr. Robert Shaw, who operated on Governor Connally at the Parkland Hospital:[9]

> MR. SPECTER. Would the shattering of the rib have had any effect in deflecting the path of the bullet from a straight line?
>
> DR. SHAW. It could have, except that in the case of this injury, the rib was obviously struck so that [a] not too dense cancellus portion of the rib in this position was carried away by the bullet and probably there was very little in the way of deflection.

In addition, the pictures reproduced by *Life* support the one-bullet theory in another way. If the "alignment of holes theory" is incorrect and if the Governor was hit at frame 234, the bullet that struck the Governor would have had to be deflected not only up to his wrist but back down to his thigh as well. Taken together with the other evidence, the pictures published by *Life* make it perhaps somewhat more likely that, despite his firm belief to the contrary, Governor Connally was struck before he lifted the hand visible in frame 234 and that his reaction was delayed half a second longer than President Kennedy's. (Anyone who has seen military combat can describe instances where reactions to or knowledge of wounds have been delayed considerably longer than this period.)

The *New York Times* also contributed relatively little in the way of enlightenment. It quoted one S. M. Holland, a railroad supervisor, who was standing on the overpass by the grassy knoll. "[T]here definitely was a shot fired from behind that fence [near

[9] *Warren Commission Hearings,* VI, 86.

the grassy knoll]." Holland's interview with the Warren Commission, however, cast some light on his views:[10]

Mr. STERN. You had no idea, I take it, that the shots were coming from your area?
Mr. HOLLAND. No.
Mr. STERN. It is your impression that they did not, could not, as far as the sound was concerned?
Mr. HOLLAND. As far as the sound was concerned they did not.

Moreover, Holland's answer to the usual final question, "Anything else occur to you?" was, "No, that is about all of it. If I have been of any help, I am tickled." And finally, Holland (who had attended the Commission's proceedings with a lawyer) was given and accepted the opportunity of reading over his full statement as transcribed by the stenographers before signing it as a true and correct copy.

The *Times* also quoted Malcolm Kilduff, former Acting Press Secretary to President Kennedy, to the effect that the one-bullet theory could not possibly be true because "Governor Connally still has a piece of the bullet in his leg." Unfortunately, Mr. Kilduff was not specific about the size of the fragment in the Governor's leg. However, Governor Connally's doctor, Dr. George T. Shires, testified before the Commission that there was indeed a remnant of the bullet in Governor Connally's leg but that its weight was "[i]n grains—a fraction of a grain, maybe, a tenth of a grain—very small." When one considers that there are 437.5 grains in an ounce and that the type of bullet used in the assassination weighed about 161 grains, it is hard to refute the one-bullet theory with a one-tenth-grain fragment.

Far more important than the new light *Life* and the *New York Times* have shed on the issues have been their calls to action. *Life* concluded its article: "The national interest deserves clear resolution of the doubts. A new investigating body should be set up, perhaps at the initiative of Congress. In a scrupulously objective and unhurried atmosphere, without the pressure to give reassurance to a shocked country, it should re-examine the evidence and consider other evidence the Warren Commission failed to evaluate." The *Times* editorial was less specific; it merely called on the members

[10] *Ibid.*, p. 245.

of the Commission and its staff to give "clarification and answers to unanswered questions." The *Times* asserted that the Commission's purpose "is being eroded a little at a time by the clamor" and that "merely more denials by the commission or its staff, are no longer enough."

By now it is clear that something will have to be done. But what?

Probably the most obvious measure would be to release the autopsy photographs and X-rays of President Kennedy. Certainly this should be done, but the trouble is that it will accomplish very little. The fact is that there is really no doubt as to what those pictures will show. Entirely apart from the photographs, the evidence that the autopsy surgeons were correct is overwhelming. Of course, the photographs should be examined, but if the surgeons were not correct, it is hard to see how they—after examining the photographs only very recently—could still have retained their bravado in the face of what might be imminent exposure.

More important, however, is the fact that the real controversy does not lie with the photographs themselves. Even though we might wish that the autopsy on President Kennedy had been done by more experienced forensic pathologists, that it was not can hardly be blamed on the Commission since the choice of the Bethesda Naval Hospital for the autopsy was made by the late President's wife before the Commission came into existence. In any case, the one-bullet theory will almost certainly not be disproved or even made less likely by anything we may now learn about President Kennedy's wounds. If the nature of wounds is to be investigated, Governor Connally's wounds are far more significant on the issue, and they are all healed.

This is not to say that a careful congressional investigation, choosing consultants who are experts in their field, could not in the first instance have put together a report better than that of the Warren Commission. But this is beside the point today. More importantly, today a congressional committee could and should call a host of witnesses who could tighten up a good many loose ends in the investigation. Some witnesses could be called to quiet doubts that already can be seen to be perverse. Others could be called to testify at length on issues about which the Commission assumed more knowledge than perhaps many laymen have—such as the fact that high-speed rifle bullets do not tumble in unobstructed flight. Still others could be called to examine with greater care the theories of the third stage—some of which the Commission could not have anticipated. But to move from the gathering of more evidence (which after all is what will be examined by future generations of historians) to selecting a group that would repeat anew the decision process would be a great—and unwise—step indeed. To say as *Life* does that the new investigators should "consider other evidence the Warren Commission failed to evaluate" is somewhat unfair. Although the Commission's report does not make this clear at all, there may well be no reliable evidence that it failed to consider. From all sorts of clues one can convince himself that the Commission evaluated far more evidence than appears at first glance. Certainly it should have made this more apparent, but the call for a formal reevaluation is a call for someone either to disagree with the Commission or to agree with it—and in either case a great number of problems are raised.

For instance, any new commission would have to decide whether to recall the witnesses. If it did not, it could not observe their demeanor—something lawyers regard as extremely important in passing upon credibility. And if it did call the witnesses afresh, time would have so dimmed their memory that, compared with the initial hearings, any second hearing would be more likely to misinform than to inform.

Furthermore, if such a commission is to second-guess the Warren Commission, it presumably would have to be composed of members whose reputation for integrity and prestige transcended that of the members of the Warren Commission. After U Thant, the Pope, and perhaps Arnold Toynbee, however, one has great trouble selecting mortals for this task. Moreover, the trail has gone cold. It is almost inconceivable that any new hard evidence will be turned up on the one-bullet problem, or for that matter on any other important issue in the case—though for a generation we will probably be treated to revelations by eyewitnesses, either to the assassination itself or to a conspiracy, who for some reason did not come forward during the investigation.

One should ask whether a whole new report and new evidence

produced by a new commission would quiet the critics of the third stage. My guess is that they would not, and for every point upon which one of those critics was satisfied, other critics would place the issues and the integrity of the investigators more in doubt. The fact is that any amount of evidence can be explained if one is willing to envision a big enough conspiracy; the mine of stories that have been given currency and swallowed is a good indication that this conspiracy can be extended as far as necessary. It is sad to acknowledge one more indication that political paranoia is not a monopoly of the far right.

Even apart from this, the hard fact is that the full truth about the assassination—in the sense that there is an objective and verifiable truth—will never be known. This is partly due to the death of Oswald himself—although if he had remained alive it would certainly have been to his interest to stave off execution by constantly hinting that he knew more than he had told. More to the point, the past may be as unknowable as the future. One may guess at what has already happened with greater and lesser degrees of accuracy, just as one may predict the future with greater and lesser degrees of accuracy. But in many of a nation's affairs, as in many of an individual's, truth can never be known, and even the important questions cannot be settled one way or another beyond a reasonable doubt. This is in many ways a most upsetting statement, and obviously the American people are upset by it. In one sense they have every right to be upset. But it is a sign of maturity to recognize that even the most important of issues often cannot be resolved to a certainty.

On Professor Kaplan's own showing there is one charge that would stick against the members of the Warren Commission: they failed in their historical rôle. They permitted themselves to be rushed into print, with a statement that could not be definitive by its very nature, under the pressure of immediate political events. They also allowed a credibility gap to grow between themselves, their own research staff, and their readers, by not explaining candidly just how they conducted their investigation, by giving the appearance that they had done the job in a way that almost anyone familiar with the intricacies of research would know they could not have done, and by not discussing all the evidence in such a way as to permit readers to make their own leaps of faith. The Commission wanted to wrap up the package and put a bow on it, and anyone who has ever attempted to answer the simplest of questions about the past should know that this cannot be done. Although there are historians who deeply distrust the report—Staughton Lynd in the United States and Hugh Trevor-Roper in England among them—in all probability the majority of historians, were they to be polled, would agree that the Commission arrived at the only creditable answers. The information was full and the evaluation accurate but the transmission was bungled.

20. The Roman Coin Mystery:

The Romance of Objects

THERE ARE MANY ALLIES FOR THE HISTORIAN. THE LAW is one. Art is another. Obviously enough, the historian of all periods must draw upon purely visual evidence for some of his data, for man has chosen to speak through pictures from the age of pictographs to that of the camera and the comic book. It is true that one picture is worth a thousand words, if it is the right picture—Andrew Wyeth's "Christina's World" can tell us as much about the twentieth century as Michelangelo's Sistine Chapel tells us about the sixteenth. One of the most important records of the Norman Conquest of England in 1066 is not a document at all, nor is it a painting. I refer, of course, to the great Bayeux tapestry. In fact an embroidery, the tapestry records the conquest by William; it is preserved in the Bayeux Cathedral Museum in Normandy. Five major books and many articles have been written on the tapestry; each shows just how much the trained observer can draw from pictorial evidence.

Such evidence naturally occurs in many ways. Historians, as we have seen in the example of the Horn Papers, draw upon artifacts no less than archaeologists do, if the need arises. Ancient historians will be especially conscious of the messages spoken by objects rather than by documents, since their written evidence is so sparse. There is something attractive, even romantic, about objects that we can hold and from which we must take messages that, themselves non-verbal, we must express in words. In "Ars Poetica" Archibald MacLeish described a poem as something that "should be palpable and mute/As a globed fruit/Dumb/As old medallions to the thumb/. . . ." This tactile sense is not to be scorned, as the numismatist knows. The scientific study of coins and medals, numismatics—like papyrology—is one of the necessary allies of the historian of the ancient world. The following essay will give at least a hint of what a scholar may do with coins (and why, therefore, the recent million-dollar theft of ancient coins from the Yale University Library was so disastrous a loss, or why so many thrillers have turned upon finding the Brasher doubloon). The selection comes from *Paths to the Ancient Past,* by Professor Tom B. Jones of the University of Minnesota.

♦ ♦ ♦

Numismatics . . . is one of the auxiliary sciences important to historical research. We [can imagine] the utility of numismatics in the solution of chronological problems, but its applications are much wider than this. Furthermore, it is especially in the reconstruction of Greek and Roman history that coins are most valuable and can be used in the greatest variety of ways.

A coin may be defined as a piece of metal of definite shape and fixed weight, bearing the mark or seal of an issuing authority as a guarantee of its purity and weight, and employed as a circulating medium (money). Coinage seems to have been invented or intro-

---

FROM Tom B. Jones, *Paths to the Ancient Past: Applications of the Historical Method to Ancient History* (New York: Free Press, 1967), pp. 175–87.

For additional reading: On the riches of Bayeux, read Sir Frank Stenton's *The Bayeux Tapestry: A Comprehensive Survey* (London, 1957), which contains essays by several scholars. Charles Gallenkamp, *Maya: The Riddle and Rediscovery of a Lost Civilization* (New York, 1959), parallels our earlier selection from Leo Deuel and tells us something of the problem of ancient history outside its usual context. Difficult, but valuable as evidence of how archaeologist, historian, scientist, and engineer may work together is J. E. Dixon, J. R. Cann, and Colin Renfrew, "Obsidian and the Origins of Trade," *Scientific American,* CCXVIII (March, 1968), 38–46. Dashiell Hammett's *The Maltese Falcon* is an obvious choice for parallel reading.

duced rather late in antiquity, certainly not before the end of the eighth century B.C. or perhaps even a century after that. Herodotus credited the Lydians with the invention of coinage, and the earliest coins known to us at present do indeed come from that part of western Asia Minor. Although metals had been used as media of exchange long before coins were devised, we do not know what first impelled people to adopt the practice of coining money. Some scholars believe that coins were found to be useful for the purposes of taxation or for the payment of troops; others have theorized that the attraction of coinage lay in the profits that accrued to the issuing authority from the seigniorage, or charge for minting. Until the end of the fifth century B.C., however, coins were used mainly in foreign trade as a convenient form of bullion.

Ancient coins were made of various metals and alloys. In Asia Minor gold, silver, and electrum (an alloy of gold and silver) were commonly used for the earliest Lydian and Greek coins. The Persians adopted coinage late in the sixth century, issuing pieces of gold and silver. The mainland and western Greeks ordinarily coined silver, rarely gold. Bronze (an alloy of copper and tin) came into general use in the latter part of the fifth century, and bronze as well as copper coins henceforth constituted the small change for everyday local transactions.

With regard to manufacture, the larger coins were cast in moulds, while the smaller ones were struck from dies. The earliest coins were rather crude—some were hardly more than bean-shaped lumps, but by the middle of the fifth century truly beautiful coins had begun to appear. The Greeks in particular became master die-cutters who had no close rivals in the ancient world.

Numismatics, like many other disciplines and sciences, has a vocabulary of its own, and a few of the most common terms should be defined at this point. We speak of the two sides of our coins as "heads" or "tails." The numismatist calls these respectively the *obverse* and the *reverse*. The *type* is the main device displayed on a coin, and the principal type occurs always on the obverse. The type on the obverse of our penny, or one-cent piece, is the bust of Abraham Lincoln, while the type on the reverse is the Lincoln Memorial. The inscription on a coin is called the *legend:* the legend common to all United States coins is UNITED STATES OF AMERICA which appears on the reverse.

On Greek and Roman coins a variety of types were used. For a long time the obverse types were the heads or busts of deities. Each Greek town chose to display its own particular protective deity: Athena at Athens, Artemis at Ephesus, the Sun God at Rhodes, and so on. The reverse type chosen might well be some symbol associated with the deity: the owl of Athena at Athens, the lyre or the tripod in the cases in which Apollo constituted the obverse type, the eagle of Zeus. The reverse often bore a legend giving the city name or an abbreviation of it. From the time of Alexander onwards the portraits of rulers became common obverse types; Julius Caesar and the Roman emperors displayed their portraits on the coins. Beginning with the Hellenistic period there was a great diversification of reverse types among the most common of which were monuments (temples and statues), personifications (Peace, Victory, Justice, Abundance, and so forth), and some purely ornamental devices.

Coins as historical evidence can be considered under two major headings: *1*] coins as artifacts, and *2*] coins as documents. As artifacts, we might put the coins in the same category and use them in the same way as we would employ the other material remains unearthed by the archaeologist: tools, weapons, pottery, terracottas, sculpture, jewelry, and architectural finds. Coins which could be assigned to known periods might help to date the various strata of a mound. An unknown townsite might be identified by the coins found there; for example, [Heinrich] Schliemann was sure that Hissarlik was the site of classical Ilium because the majority of the coins he found were of that town. Like pottery or any of the so-called "trade objects" the foreign coins found on a particular site provide an index to its trade relationships. Athenian coins and pottery occur together on many sites around the Mediterranean, and they tell us that the Athenians traded with these places. Sometimes commercial unions involving two or more states are suggested when the states in question are discovered to have used the same coin types and coin weights. Many of the colonies of Corinth issued coins which displayed the helmeted Athena and the Pegasus which were typical of the pieces from Corinth itself. The weight standards employed by the various states can sometimes be deduced from the coins, and the denominations of the coins themselves can often be identified. Although it is not as easy to establish as some people seem to imagine, the coins occasionally reveal something about economic conditions: prosperity, depression, rising prices, inflation, the changing ratio between gold and silver, etc. Quite apart from their monetary function, the coins may often qualify as objects of art, reflecting changing styles, and related, of course, to the art of gem-cutting. Famous sculptured works or temples and other buildings appear as coin types and may help us to identify unknown sculptures or to reconstruct temples and monuments. On Roman coins we may see the Column of Trajan, the tomb of Hadrian, or an arch or a basilica; the Zeus of Phidias appeared on many a Greek coin, and the people of Cnidus proudly displayed the Aphrodite of Praxiteles as one of their coin types.

As documents, the coins have a variety of uses also. The legends tell us something about language, vocabulary, and grammar, but the legends are valuable for epigraphy as well: the forms of the Greek and Roman letters change through the ages on the coins just as they do on the stone inscriptions; and the Cypriote syllabary and the strange scripts of Spain appear on the coins, too. The coin portraits are priceless. They show us the Roman emperors and their families, Hellenistic kings and queens, the Greek rulers of Bactria and India, and many others. Like the painted Greek vases, the coins abound in scenes from mythology and legend, of religious ritual and ceremony. They can sometimes tell us when and where a certain cult was popular and about its diffusion or decline.

More directly, some coins bear dates in the various systems of chronology we have already discussed: regnal years, the Seleucid era, city and provincial eras, and the like. Very often, especially in the Roman period, a dated coin will refer to or commemorate a specific event. Victories, accessions, birth, marriages, dedications of monuments, and the passing of an emperor can be dated by coins. Frequently, rather important happenings not mentioned at all in the literary sources are known to us only from the coins. It is furthermore not unusual for the numismatist to find a way to pinpoint chronologically a coin which does not bear a precise date. Again, in the Roman imperial period particularly, the coins reveal much about policy, for they were used by the Roman emperors as a medium of propaganda. On the coins an emperor could advertise his achievements in war and peace and drive home the ideas that he wanted to convey to his subjects. This is one reason for the great variety of reverse types which may occur during the reign of a single emperor. Vespasian celebrated the end of the Jewish War with coins which bore the legend JUDAEA CAPTA; Trajan advertised the *alimenta* program begun by his predecessor, Nerva; when Aurelian reunited the severed parts of the Roman Empire his coins referred to him as RESTITUTOR ORBIS.

Probably the best way to illustrate at least a part of what has been said above is to turn to a specific set of examples. [Coin evidence alone may] provide a brief . . . commentary on the career of Augustus, the first Roman emperor and founder of the Principate.

Gaius Octavius (Octavian), the grand-nephew of Julius Caesar, was born in 63 B.C. Following Caesar's assassination in 44, a reading of the dictator's will disclosed that Caesar had adopted Octavian as his son and heir. This inevitably matched Octavian against Mark Antony, Caesar's principal lieutenant who aspired to rule Rome now that Caesar was dead. By 43, however, Antony and Octavian had found it convenient to join forces, and together with Lepidus they formed the Second Triumvirate. The defeat of Brutus and Cassius at Philippi in 42 and the downfall of Sextus Pompey about five years later removed any reason for the continuance of the triumvirate; Lepidus was pushed aside, and Antony and Octavian became open antagonists once more. Octavian controlled the west, while Antony cast his lot with Cleopatra, the Ptolemaic queen, in the east. When Antony and Cleopatra occupied western Greece with a view to invading Italy, they were defeated at Actium (31 B.C.) by Octavian and his principal commander, Agrippa. After Octavian invaded Egypt, Antony and Cleopatra committed suicide, and the Ptolemaic kingdom was annexed by Rome (30 B.C.).

The victor, Octavian, returned to Rome in 29 B.C. to begin reconstruction and to repair the damage caused by the almost continuous civil war which had begun even before he was born. As the sole surviving strong man in Roman politics, he had very definitely a free hand to make what seemed to be necessary changes in Roman political and economic organization. Although he offered to relinquish his extraordinary powers in 27 B.C., he received instead a virtual mandate from the Senate and the Roman people to continue as their leader. At that time he was given the title of Augustus (the Revered) and proconsular powers with which to govern personally better than half the provinces of the empire. So began the reign of Augustus, as we shall henceforth call him, the first Roman emperor. During the next forty-one years he instituted the reforms that established the Principate, the new form of government that now replaced the Republic. Augustus died at a ripe old age in A.D. 14.

It is not a gross exaggeration to say that our main sources for the reign of Augustus are the biography by Suetonius in the *Lives of the Twelve Caesars,* the *Roman History* of Cassius Dio, the *Res Gestae,* and coins. Coins provide us with portraits of Augustus and his associates; they help us to date many important events of the reign; they commemorate the deeds of Augustus and they suggest to us, as they were intended to suggest to Augustus' subjects, the themes and ideas which he sought to publicize and popularize.

Augustus had not only to reconstitute the Roman economy, but also to reform the currency. He controlled directly the minting of gold and silver and indirectly the bronze, copper, and orichalcum (an alloy of copper and zinc) theoretically issued under senatorial auspices. Of the gold, the *aureus* was the basic coin. It was struck at 42 to the Roman pound, and an aureus was valued at 25 *denarii.* The denarius was the main silver coin minted at 84 to the pound. Thus, the gold-silver ratio was 12½ to 1. Earlier, under the Republic, the denarius had been equated to 10 copper coins, called *asses.* In the time of Augustus, however, 16 of the *as* coins equalled a denarius. The *as* was also minted in multiples and fractions: a large coin, generally of orichalcum, was the *sestertius,* equal to 4 *asses;* then, there was the *dupondius,* equal to 2 *asses;* and the *quadrans,* a small coin of which 4 equalled 1 *as.* The relationship of these denominations is summarized in the following table:

quadrans	1	4	8	16	64	1600
as		1	2	4	16	400
dupondius			1	2	8	200
sestertius				1	4	100
denarius					1	25
aureus						1

Official mints of the Roman government at Rome and elsewhere in the west undertook to provide the bulk of the coins which circulated in that half of the empire; and, as far as gold and silver were concerned, official issues supplied the east as well, but various Greek city states, Roman colonies, and provincial organizations in the eastern half of the empire were allowed to strike their own bronze coins. Nearly 150 such mint authorities are known from the reign of Augustus, while in Egypt a mint was established in Alexandria which issued a special currency intended only for circulation in that province. Occasionally, certain eastern mints were permitted to produce limited issues of silver.

A few of the coins illustrating the life and reign of Augustus may be [described here] . . . :[1]

1. A silver *cistophorus* (a Greek four-drachma piece equal to three denarii) [was] issued by the commune of Asia in 19 B.C. The head of Augustus appears on the obverse with the legend IMP(erator) IX TR.PO.V signifying that Augustus or his generals had won their ninth victory in the field and that Augustus was holding his fifth grant of the tribunician power. The tribunician power was conferred annually, and, since Augustus first received it in 23 B.C., we can date this issue in 19. On the reverse [is] the façade of a hexastyle temple with the inscription ROM. ET AVGVST (Rome and Augustus) on its architrave. This represents a temple dedicated to Rome and the genius of Augustus. This coin was probably struck at Pergamum, but . . . the *Res Gestae* was inscribed on the wall of a similar temple at Ancyra.

2. The obverse of a silver denarius display[s] the laureate head of Julius Caesar. The legend CAESAR DICT. QVART. indicates that Caesar was then dictator for the fourth time (45 B.C.).

3. A denarius with the head of Brutus on the obverse [shows] on the reverse . . . two daggers and a "liberty cap" with the legend EID. MAR. (the Ides of March). The coin celebrates, of course, Caesar's assassination on March 15, 44 B.C.

4. The obverse of a gold coin bear[s] the head of Lepidus. The legend reads M. LEPIDVS.III.VIR.R.P.C. Marcus Lepidus is thus one of the triumvirs for the reconstitution of the republic (*rei publicae constituendae*).

[1] The original text was accompanied with illustrations of each of these coins. The thirty-five illustrations, which are omitted here, were of thirty-one different coins, with obverse and reverse of four shown. The descriptions which follow are so full, including all that the illustrations themselves offered, that I have not found it necessary to reproduce the pictures here. [Editor's note.]

5. The reverse of another gold coin [shows] . . . the head of Octavia, sister of Octavian, who was married to Antony about 39 B.C. The legend mentions Antony as triumvir and consul designate, and his portrait appears on the obverse of [the] coin. . . .

6. The obverse of [a] silver coin bears the bust of Cleopatra; the reverse, the head of Antony. Cleopatra's title "Queen of Kings" dates this coin to about 34 B.C. when Antony had divorced Octavia, married Cleopatra, and divided the Roman possessions in the east among the children of Cleopatra (Donations of Alexandria).

7. The obverse of a bronze *as* of 23 B.C. show[s] the head of Agrippa; M. AGRIPPA L.F.COS.III (Marcus Agrippa, son of Lucius, consul for the third time) dates the coin to that year. Agrippa, the friend of Augustus and the greatest commander of the age, was the virtual colleague of the emperor, especially in the period 21–12 B.C. when he was married to Augustus' daughter, Julia. Agrippa died in the latter year.

8. Livia, empress of Augustus and mother of Tiberius and Drusus, is shown on [a] dupondius of Tiberius.

9. An *as* [shows] Tiberius, son of Livia and ultimately the adopted son and heir of Augustus. Tiberius reigned as sole emperor, A.D. 14–37.

10. A denarius bear[s] the head of Julia, only child of Augustus. The unfortunate Julia was regarded by her father as the key to the problem of the succession: since Augustus had no son of his own, Julia must provide him with a male heir. She was married first to Marcellus, her cousin, the son of Octavia. After Marcellus died, Julia was wedded to Agrippa. But Agrippa died, and Julia was given to Tiberius. The latter match was eminently unsuccessful—Julia was finally banished for adultery.

The first ten coins [described provided scholars with] portraits of Augustus and of the majority of his most intimate associates. At the same time, [they represented some of the] common denominations of coins . . . : for example . . . [aureus, denarius, *as,* dupondius, and cistophorus].

11. The . . . sestertius [is a sixth denomination]. An S.C. indicates that the coinage was issued by authority of the senate (*senatus consultum*), and the coin bears the name of one of the three mint officials (III *viri monetales*), Tiberius Sempronius Gracchus.

12. The reverse of a quadrans, [another denomination], bear[s] the S.C. and the name of the moneyer, Apronius Sisenna. As in the case [above], the title of the moneyer is given as triumvir A(ere) A(rgento)

A(uro) F(lando) F(eriundo), member of the board of three for casting and striking bronze, silver and gold.

13. The reverse of an *as* [shows] the S.C. and the name of the moneyer, C. Plotius Rufus.

14. The reverse of a cistophorus show[s] a sphinx, presumably in imitation of the signet ring of Augustus. The obverse . . . bears the portrait of the ruler.

Turning now to aspects of the reign as illustrated by . . . coins, we may [learn] the following:

15. The reverse of an aureus commemorat[es] the victory over Antony and Cleopatra at Actium. This is confirmed by . . . ACT appearing below the type, Apollo and his lyre. Other issues of denarii identify the deity specifically as Apollo of Actium.

16. The reverse of a denarius display[s] a crocodile and the legend AEGYPTO CAPTA. This commemorates the annexation of Egypt in the year following the Battle of Actium.

17. [The] reverse of a denarius show[s] Augustus and Agrippa standing on a platform, each with a roll in his hand. It has been presumed that the coin refers to the taking of the census in 28 B.C., but it is undoubtedly the later census of 13 B.C. that is commemorated . . . because of the known date of the moneyer, C. Marius.

18. Speaking of the events of 27 B.C., Augustus says in the *Res Gestae* (XXXIV): "I was given the title of Augustus by senatorial decree, and by public decree the doorposts of my dwelling were covered with laurel, and a civic crown was fixed over my door, and a golden shield was deposited in the Curia Julia. . . ." On the reverse of [a] denarius we [find] the laurel crown and a shield on which is inscribed S.P.Q.R. CL.V (clupeus virtutis), and the coin bears the legend OB CIVES SERVATOS.

19. Augustus narrowly escaped death in Spain when a bolt of lightning killed the man next to him. In gratitude for his escape he dedicated a temple to Jupiter Tonans in Rome in 22 B.C. . . . [T]he reverse of a denarius display[s] a temple within which is a statue of Jupiter. The legend is IOV(is) TON(antis).

20. In Ch. XXIX of the *Res Gestae* we read, "The plunder and standards of three Roman armies I forced the Parthians to return to me." The legend on the reverse of [a] denarius is SIGNIS PARTHICIS RECEPTIS. This was a great triumph for Augustus because the most important trophies returned were those which Crassus had lost at Carrhae in 53 B.C. The date of this major diplomatic success was 20 B.C.

21. In the same year Augustus significantly dedicated at Rome the temple of Mars the Avenger. The temple appears on the reverse of [a] denarius with the legend MARTIS VLTORIS.

22. In 19 B.C. when Augustus returned to Rome from the East, the Senate honored him by consecrating an altar to Fortuna Redux. The altar appears on the reverse of [a] denarius. The inscription reads FORT.RED.CÁES.AVG.S.P.Q.R.

23. The Secular Games, for which Horace composed the Carmen Saeculare, were celebrated in 17 B.C. These ceremonies were intended to herald the beginning of a new era, or *saeculum:* this, as Virgil had predicted, was to be a Golden Age. The Secular Games, like the return of the standards by the Parthians, served very well the campaign of Augustus to revive the morale and optimism of the Romans which had been sadly damaged by the civil wars. A *saeculum* was always heralded by signs and portents. A comet had appeared in 43 B.C., and normally the Romans would have begun the new era then, but the times were hardly propitious. When the comet returned in 17, the time was clearly ripe for the change. . . . [T]he comet [appears on a] denarius along with the legend DIVVS IVLIVS (the deified Julius). Caesar was associated with the comet because it had first appeared shortly after his assassination.

24. Referring to a decision of 16 B.C., the *Res Gestae* says, "The Senate decreed that every fifth year vows should be undertaken for my health by the consuls and priests. . . ." On the reverse of [a] denarius within an oak-wreath we [find] the legend: IOVI VOI. SVSC. PRO. SAL. CAES. AVG. S.P.Q.R. [The] coin has *pro salute* instead of *pro valetudine,* but other coin legends are known which follow the wording of the *Res Gestae* more closely.

25. In 12 B.C. after the death of Lepidus, who had been Pontifex Maximus since Caesar's assassination, Augustus was elected to that high religious post. [A] reverse shows a tablet or stele on which is inscribed C(omitia) C(aesaris) AVGVSTI. This refers to the vote of the assembly which elected Augustus Pontifex Maximus.

26. Augustus had hoped to establish his grandsons, Gaius and Lucius, as his successors. They were launched into public life and office-holding long before the customary age, and their grandfather took great pains to advertise their eligibility. The reverse of [a] denarius shows Gaius and Lucius, mere boys, at the very beginning of the Christian era. Within four years, both had died.

27. Statues and portrait busts of Augustus were everywhere in Rome. The one we know best is the standing figure of Augustus in military

costume with hand upraised. The same statue [was] portrayed on [a] coin.

28. The reverse of a denarius show[s] an equestrian statue of Augustus.

29. The reverse of an aureus shows a triumphal arch celebrating the Parthian victories.

30. Peace was a theme of Augustan propaganda. The dedication of the Ara Pacis in 13 B.C. was a piece of propaganda similar to the Ludi Saeculares of four years earlier. Pax (peace) also appears on [a] cistophorus from Asia.

31. Augustus, like Julius Caesar, was deified after his death. On the obverse of [a] dupondius [he is shown] with a radiate crown and the legend DIVVS AVGVSTVS PATER.

21. The Case of the Silent Witnesses:

The Romance of Gadgetry

TODAY MANY HISTORIANS ARE PREPARED TO PLACE A RADIate crown upon the computer, that new and highly sophisticated gadget which makes it possible for scholars of relatively modest mathematical expertise to pose questions and collect data in ways never before attempted. As conservative as he is likely to be in many of his personal tastes, the historian always has been prepared to make use of whatever machinery an increasingly technical world might give him—cameras and typewriters, tape recorders, microfilm readers, copyflow machines—all of which may be brought into the study, and now the magic of the computer, still too large and complex for home use. Beginning in 1966, special summer courses have been offered to advanced scholars who want to enter this new world of research, and even the most distinguished have been tempted to turn in the new direction.

Unquestionably, the computer has become one of the historian's most useful allies. He may use computers to organize and analyze data, saving himself months of arduous, mind-dulling labor. He need no longer pretend that he finds special virtue in having personally counted all the stars in his own firmament, a virtue to which he once professed merely because he had no other way of finding an answer than by counting. In those areas to which computer research is applicable—that is, where techniques of quantification may be used—the historian need no longer be an intuitivist to the degree necessary in the past. Lawrence Stone has used quantifying techniques to tell of the decline of the aristocracy in England; Lee Benson has applied such methods to an analysis of Jacksonian democracy in New York State; others have been able to tell us much about bureaucracies, about the nature of Colonial trade, and about the legal profession and its values. Studies by Bernard Bailyn, Samuel P. Hayes, and Richard Merritt have employed manifest lists, balloting, and word counts in Colonial newspapers to good effect, and many other studies are now in progress.

The computer can be especially helpful with problems of authorship. They have been put to good use on Homer, the Gospels, and *The Federalist* papers. Bayesian analysis applied by Frederick Mosteller and David L. Wallace, both mathematicians, has made it possible for us to know the average length of sentences that James Madison and Alexander Hamilton wrote, to learn the percentage of nouns, adjectives, one- and two-letter words, and of "the"s used by each, and to discover "marker words" for each author: Hamilton liked to use "enough" and "upon"; Hamilton used "while" where Madison would use "whilst." It may be argued that this is not much to know for the expenditure of a substantial amount of programming and machine time, and it may correctly be pointed out that a historian, Douglass Adair, already had found the "while"-"whilst" distinction. As Mosteller and Frederick Williams also discovered, Hamilton's average sentence length was 34.55 words while Madison's was 34.59 words, using the papers about which there was no doubt as to authorship, and they concluded, "These measures would be hopeless for discriminating between the two authors." Perhaps the question of the authorship of the twelve disputed Hamilton and Madison papers is not an important one in any case. But there are some things it is simply fun to know, even if it is not a matter of great significance; that, for example, upon completing their several tests, Messrs. Mosteller and

Wallace concluded that "we can say with better foundation than ever before that Madison was the author of the 12 disputed papers."

There are obvious dangers in computer research, and perhaps Mosteller and Wallace illustrated one of them without intending to. Faced with machinery capable of achieving in seconds computations that have taken previous generations of scholars years to perform, there is a temptation to think of things for the machines to do. They are expensive and should not be idle. Every computation helps tell us more about programming and the machine itself. All knowledge, useful or useless, is pure and therefore desirable, after all. Yet such machines may lead to much busy work which is of no greater significance than much that has been dismissed by professional historians in the past, save that the romantic glow of the machine itself will appear to give prestige to such work, raising it above the merely busy into the relevant. The historian may be tempted along the paths of those who, in nations poor in manuscript materials, chose to find sources first and then to determine what questions might be asked of those sources, surely scissors-and-paste history, as Collingwood defined it. For the pull of such glowing gadgetry may inveigle the historian into asking precisely those kinds of questions that one knows are capable of machine answers.

Nothing is wrong with this approach to history provided all remember that it is but one approach, an ancillary one at that, an ally to but not the substance of history. Data must not be made to conform to purposes that are quite other than those intended by the compilers of the data in the first instance; the historian must understand exactly under what conditions and for what purposes the data he is using were gathered. He must, if he begins with statistics compiled by others, test the accuracy of those statistics as he would test the mere notions of the past.

> . . . [M]any of the prevailing notions about steam shipping before 1860 need to be rather sharply revised. . . . [T]he general adoption of iron in steamship construction dates from

> the 1840's, more than a full decade earlier than the accepted estimates; . . . by the end of the 1850's most of the British steam merchant fleet was iron rather than wood; . . . the iron-screw steamer was predominant in new British steamship construction from at least 1851 onwards; . . . the 1853 trade boom together with the stimulus of the Crimean War demand for shipping were decisive in introducing the iron-screw steamer; . . . the iron-screw steamer very largely supplanted both wood and iron paddle steamers by the end of the Crimean War. . . . Britain's new steam merchant marine was a powerful influence in the development of Britain's exceedingly strong balance of payments position in the third quarter of the 19th Century.

Now these are important conclusions, for they revise backward some of our assumptions about the superiority of Britain's trading position during the Pax Britannica; precisely why they are important need not be argued here. The scholars who wrote these sentences in 1958 were two economic historians then at Purdue University, J. R. T. Hughes and Stanley Reiter. They used data concerning, as they entitled their article, "The First 1,945 British Steamships" in order to reach these conclusions.

The conclusions did not remain unchallenged, however, for in 1966 a young English economic historian, Robert Craig, argued that the raw material used by Hughes and Reiter did not claim to list all the steamships built and registered at British ports, but merely those that remained upon the registers at a specified date. "The general lesson to be learnt . . . ," Craig concluded, was "that statistical materials drawn up in the past for purposes quite other than those for which they may be presently utilized must be subjected, before being analyzed by computer, to the closest possible scrutiny. This requires that considerable attention be paid to the social, political and administrative nature and circumstances giving rise to the preparation of such material." In truth, this criticism was less devastating in the particular instance than it could have been, for Messrs. Hughes and Reiter had made it clear that they did not believe that they were dealing with all British steamships and the former argued in reply to Craig that the "missing numbers" might well make no difference, since the methods of statistical analysis used in data processing do not require more than a representative sampling. Right as the two historians no doubt are, Craig's warning is nonetheless valuable.

Statistics, some of us too often think, have a grasp upon reality that value judgments cannot have, since we presume them to be open to verification. But one need not work for the Bureau of Internal Revenue to learn to be skeptical of most statistics, especially if they imply a judgment of their own. Just how many Communists was it that Senator Joseph McCarthy found infesting the State Department? The number he cited in Wheeling, the number he cited from behind his Senatorial privilege in Washington, or some one other of his intermediate numbers? Is the crime rate rising or not? Do Washingtonians consume more alcohol per capita than other Americans or not? Are the glaciers in Alaska melting, and if so, at what rate? Just when may we expect to sink beneath the sea? Was the mechanic's estimate correct when you came to pay for that gouged fender? What time was it that your daughter came home last night? Are there more abortions in Sweden, more drunkenness in New Zealand, and more protein in Kellogg's K, or do you care? What, in fact, is a statistic?

The historian must ask the same questions of a statistic that he asks of any other datum. Where did it come from? Why was it provided? Upon what basis was it gathered? What value judgments may contemporaries have been tempted to draw from it? For what metaphor does it stand? Darrell Huff has shown, in *How to Lie with Statistics,* that one may fabricate such data. But what if those who employed the statistic in question had every reason to believe that it was accurate? What does this tell us about them, as well as about the figure itself? The statistic, then, becomes something rather different for the historian than for the mathematician, and the amount of work necessary to verify its base, to examine its social setting, and to explore its propaganda values may be far greater than the time saved once it has been accepted and fed into a machine for quite a different purpose.

"Figures alone put teeth into any . . . theory," writes Gerald Hawkins, an astronomer responsible for one breakthrough in that area where pre-history and history merge. Figures can be made to lie, as we know; they can also become abstractions for data particles which interact in too many ways for the human mind to grasp fully. Hawkins, then a professor of astronomy at Boston University, and now Dean of Dickinson College, turned to a computer to decode the mystery of Stonehenge, the thirty-five-hundred-year-old stone slabs on England's Salisbury Plain. Hawkins' solution is not entirely acceptable to other astronomers, however. The book from which the following selection was drawn was savaged by a British Stonehenge authority, R. J. C. Atkinson, in the British journal *Nature*, as "slipshod and unconvincing." A Cambridge archaeologist, Professor Glyn Daniel, was no less unhappy. Another Cambridge professor, however, Fred Hoyle (who is also known for his quite excellent combination of detective story and science fiction, *Ossian's Ride*), reworked Professor Hawkins' calculations and arrived at the same conclusion—that Stonehenge was an ancient astronomical observatory. Atkinson has used what he regarded as errors in the alignments of some of the fifty-six mysterious Aubrey holes at Stonehenge to challenge Hawkins, while Hoyle, also writing for *Nature*, in 1966, argued that the presumed errors were not errors at all but part of a system for marking crucial positions of the sun and moon at important times. Let Hawkins demonstrate his methods himself:

♦ ♦ ♦

As a boy in England I took little enough interest in my country's most famous ancient monument. I knew that it somehow pointed to midsummer sunrise, and I thought that the druids had built it, probably for human sacrifice, and beyond that my curiosity did not go. Actually, I grew up in Great Yarmouth, home of David Copperfield's Peggotty, and was much more curious about the mechanics of how the Peggotty family lived in that upturned boat.

Then I became an astronomer, and began to wonder about the midsummer sunrise alignment.

In 1953 I worked at the Larkhill Missile-testing Base just a mile north of Stonehenge. The idea of a missile-firing base so close to the stones naturally worried many people, but the missiles were always fired safely to the north. There is a story that during World War I a British airstrip commander had complained that the megaliths constituted a hazard to his planes, and formally requested that they be flattened, but I think that story is apocryphal.

From Larkhill I went often to Stonehenge, and soon became so interested that I took to reading about it. I quickly found that there is an immense amount of literature on the subject—so much that I would not presume to add to it now if I did not have new light to throw on the old mystery. Mythologists and sociologists and historians and other specialists as well as archaeologists—and poets—have written about the unique place, in many different ways. How-

---

FROM Gerald S. Hawkins, *Stonehenge Decoded* (Garden City, N.Y.: Doubleday & Co., 1965), pp. 89–94, 96–107, 111–18.

For additional reading: The work discussed above includes Frederick Mosteller and David L. Wallace, *Inference and Disputed Authorship: The Federalist* (Reading, Mass., 1964); J. R. T. Hughes and Stanley Reiter, "The First 1,945 British Steamships," *Journal of the American Statistical Association,* LIII (June, 1958), 360–69, and letters by Robert Craig and Hughes in the *Times Literary Supplement* for September 29 and October 13, 1966. I have examined another statistic to show both why it was in error and why the public chose to accept it in an article, "The Creation of a Myth: 'Canadian' Enlistments in the Northern Armies during the American Civil War," *Canadian Historical Review,* XXXIX (March, 1958), 24–39. Jerome M. Clubb and Howard Allen, "Computers and Historical Studies," in *Journal of American History,* LIV (December, 1967), 599–607, rather dryly summarize the present hardware situation. Martin Woodhouse, who has helped build computers, has written an espionage story which turns upon the computer—*Tree Frog*—although one learns surprisingly little about computers themselves from his book.

ever, my attention quickly focused on that one astronomical aspect, the fact, first noted by W. Stukeley in 1740, that the main axis of the monument was aligned to the midsummer sunrise. That seemed to me by far the most remarkable thing about the whole structure.

I was not alone, of course, in my interest in that alignment. The sad fact is that the fame, or notoriety, of viewing midsummer sunrise over the heel stone has grown to such proportions that thousands of people come each year to watch, and to carouse. Each June an increasingly carnival-like air pervades the site, beginning the night before the sunrise itself. So many merrymakers gather that occasionally the great event is marred by near-riot. . . .

The sunrise alignment has interested other astronomers. Since the line from the center over the heel stone does not *exactly* point to midsummer sunrise today, earlier astronomers assumed that the error had been caused by time—that is, by the slow drift of the horizon point of midsummer sunrise during the centuries since Stonehenge was built. Because the angle, or "tilt," of the earth's axis with respect to its orbit plane changes with time, the point on the horizon at which the sun rises on midsummer morning moves, very slowly. For the last 9000 years this movement has been to the right along the horizon at a rate of about 2/100 of a degree per century. Since this motion can be calculated very accurately, and since it seemed reasonable to suppose that the Stonehenge builders had aligned the monument to point exactly to midsummer sunrise, it was thought that the date of building might be deduced by determining when the axis had pointed to midsummer sunrise.

In 1901 the brilliant British astronomer Sir [Joseph] Norman Lockyer made such a determination, and arrived at an estimated Stonehenge construction date of between 1880 and 1480 B.C. . . . [T]hat estimated date was quite close to the actual date (circa 1850)—but Lockyer's result was discredited when it was announced, because two of his basic assumptions were not accepted as unique or even compellingly probable by archaeologists:

1) He assumed that "sunrise" was the first flash as the top of the sun appears over the horizon, but, the archaeologists pointed out, modern man does not know whether ancient man regarded sunrise as first flash; or midpoint, when the disc's center appears; or "last flash," as the whole sun lifts clear of the horizon. The dif-

ferences between the three positions are large—at Stonehenge, on midsummer day, the angular distance between the horizon points of first flash and final disc clearance, four minutes later, is almost a full degree.

2) Lockyer assumed that the Stonehenge builders had aligned the line from the center to the Avenue midpoint to point to the sunrise; if he had made the equally plausible assumption that they had intended the center-heel stone line to point to the first flash of the solstice sunrise, he would have produced an estimated construction date of about 6000 A.D.! . . .

Since Lockyer's time there had been little direct astronomical investigation of Stonehenge, although the problem of the solstice sunrise alignment continued to be of concern to those astronomers who interested themselves in the monument.

In 1960, I was writing a book on astronomy, *Splendor in the Sky*. In a discussion of eclipses, and the ancients' attitudes toward them (terror, mostly—even after the cause was understood), I wrote, "There must be a great deal of magic that has been forgotten in the course of time. . . . Stonehenge probably was built to mark midsummer, for if the axis of the temple had been chosen at random the probability of selecting this point by accident would be less than one in five hundred. Now if the builders of Stonehenge had wished simply to mark the sunrise they needed no more than two stones. Yet hundreds of tons of volcanic rock were carved and placed in position. . . . Stonehenge is therefore much more than a whim of a few people. It must have been the focal point for ancient Britons. . . . The stone blocks are mute, but perhaps some day, by a chance discovery, we will learn their secrets."

As I wrote those words I suddenly thought, "some day" perhaps is now—what better time for that "chance discovery"? I felt that the astronomic aspect of Stonehenge should be thoroughly explored.

By then I had gone from England to Cambridge, Massachusetts, to continue research and teaching. My wife and I made our plans, and the following summer we returned to England, like hunters stalking Stonehenge's celestial secret.

Like proper hunters, or explorers, we set up our base camp in a hotel in Amesbury, close by, and checked our equipment: cameras, compass, watch, binoculars, astronomical tables. Many people came that year to see the sunrise, but few could have prepared for it so meticulously. We had deliberately planned our visit for June 12, nine days before the solstice, because we feared that on the day itself the crowd would make it impossible to set up a camera on the correct alignment and have an unobstructed view, and from previous calculations I knew that the sun would then rise just one diameter to the east of its solstice position.

Dawn was to be about 4:30, daylight time. Among all our welter of preparations the night before we forgot two things: to pay our hotel bill, and to tell the manager that we would be going out so abnormally early. So feeling and looking like the archcriminals the authorities certainly would have branded us had they seen us . . . we furtively tiptoed down the long dark hall, no sound disturbing the silence except the soft ticking of the grandfather clock. . . .

Stonehenge stood black and massive against the lightening sky. From a distance it was most imposing. As we looked across the downs we saw not much evidence of dilapidation, and except for the modern road the time could have been June, 1600 B.C. A few hares were scampering around, starlings were chirping loudly, and it was quite cool. . . .

I set up my eight-millimeter movie camera with telephoto lens trained down the axis line so as to include in its field the sarsen circle archway through which the distant heel stone showed darker than the dark ground. We waited. Purple-tinged mist drifted across the valley, and we were apprehensive lest it creep up Larkhill and obscure the sun. Then suddenly, in the band of brightness to the northeast, we saw it—the first red flash of the sun, rising just over the tip of the heel stone!

It was a tremendous experience. The camera's whirring was the only reminder that we were not in the Stone Age; we experienced primitive emotions of awe and wonder.

Then, as I returned to the twentieth century and began to walk around, my astronomical sense reasserted itself. I felt strongly that the sunrise line had certainly been carefully planned, and that many other stones had also probably been laid out with alignment intended. Indeed, as I peered over and between the stones, I came to feel that *all* of them might have been placed according to some master plan; their relative positions seemed so carefully arranged. It was as if the stones were posing questions which called out for answers, like these:

1. On midsummer morning the full disc of the sun would rise over the heel stone so precisely that if I had been a Stone Age man I would have been delighted or frightened or comforted or awe-struck or whatever the priest-astronomers wanted me to be—that alignment had been beautifully established.

Why?

2. The trilithon archways are astonishingly narrow. The space between the gigantic pillars is so small that you can hardly poke your head through (I tried). The average width of the three standing archways is 12 inches, and the average thickness of the bordering uprights is 2 feet, so that when you look through two aligned archways your view is restricted to a very small angle. I felt that my field of observation was being tightly controlled, as by sighting instruments, so that I couldn't avoid seeing something.

What was I supposed to see?

3. The sighting-lines through the trilithon archways extend on through corresponding wider archways of the surrounding sarsen circle. But as I walked along the axis I noticed that those three sighting-lines flashed into view one after the other, and, as rapidly, out of view again. At no one spot could I stand and look down all of those double-archway-framed vistas. Viewing had to be from well-separated points. Such an arrangement is unusual. It violates customary architectural design which radiates vistas from a central single focus, and it somehow seems not "natural." I felt again that the placement had been deliberate, to stress the importance of the viewing.

Why was the viewing important?

4. The only two outer stones now standing, number 93 and the heel stone, are both of such a height that an average-sized man looks across their tops to the line of the horizon.

Why was there such precise arrangement of height?

5. The line joining corners 91–94 of the station stone rectangle lies just a few feet outside the stones of the sarsen circle.

Did they form a sighting-line which had been preserved?

Most of those questions, I felt, might somehow be answered by astronomy. Those precise alignments and controlled vistas, so carefully directing the eye to nothing now visible, might well have been sighting-lines for celestial events such as special rise or set points of those godlike forces of prehistory, the sun, moon, planets, and stars. Primitive men observed with apprehension the places where the great rulers of day and night entered and emerged from the dark earth. It would have been natural that the Stonehengers should mark those points by various means.

I thought immediately of the most obvious "God," the sun. As most schoolboys and all sailors, farmers, navigators and astronomers know, the sun moves from north to south as June moves to December. Only two days in the year—the spring and fall equinoxes—does it rise and set due east and west. Because of heavenly complexities involving factors like the obliquity of the ecliptic, . . . the sun swings annually from a summer declination (or celestial sphere latitude) of +23.5° (north) to a corresponding winter declination of −23.5° (south). That declination shift is a sizable 47°, but because of the facts of spherical geometry the angular variation in earthly viewing can be much larger. At the latitude of Stonehenge sunrise goes from a compass direction of 51°, almost northeast, at midsummer, down to 129°, almost southeast, at midwinter. That is an angular distance of 78° along the horizon, an average motion of more than 12° per month. If you have the habit of watching sunrises or sunsets, you will have noticed the astonishing rapidity with which the sun seesaws up and down the sky. And if it seems odd that in summer the sun, which everybody knows is always south of Florida and far south of England, rises to the north of an English viewer, remember that it seems to move in a small circle around the polestar once every 24 hours, and as one moves north on the earth the polestar is higher overhead. When the path of the sun is raised, it cuts the horizon closer to due north. . . . Therefore, the farther north you are, the more northerly is summer sunrise. Residents of Alaska see the June sun rise practically due north; within the Arctic Circle the sun rises and doesn't set for several days, and at the North Pole itself there is only one "day" a year, with sunrise in March, noon in June, and sunset in September.

By means of this north-south swing of the sun earthlings can follow the course of the year. If you are a sophisticated modern earthling, with knowledge of latitudes and declinations and great circles—and if you have some rather expensive equipment—you can use the sun as a cosmic calendar and tell the date to the nearest day. But if you were only a simple Stone Age man, you might regard yourself as fortunate if you could be sure of marking one special day every year, and you might well take great pains to mark it, because from such a known day you could reckon forward to the times for plantings and harvests, hunting, and other vital concerns for the whole year, until that day came again and the cycle was complete.

The Stonehenge builders had done that. Their axis pointed to the place of sunrise at midsummer. They had given themselves an accurate marker for midsummer day. What else had they done?

I thought of the sun, as its red disc moved rapidly away from the heel stone. Could Stonehenge have more solar alignments?

The noted archaeologist R. S. Newall once suggested that the axis reversed might point over some landmark, now lost, to midwinter sunset. There has even been a theory that the most important direction of Stonehenge was intended to be southwest, toward that midwinter sunset, rather than northeast, toward midsummer sunrise, because the Avenue entrance is from the northeast and most structures, like cathedrals, have the most important direction opposite the entrance. But that theory has not been proved. Nor has evidence ever been found that there was a marker on the axis extended toward the southwest.

Could there be alignments to celestial bodies other than the sun —to the stars or planets or moon?

The sun was moving eastward at such an angle that it was a full degree to the right of its first flash position when it finally lifted clear of the horizon. I marveled once more at the precision of placement of the axis and the heel stone, and at the whole precision of Stonehenge. I kept looking at those alignments formed by the ancient stones, and thinking of the many objects in the sky, and suddenly I felt defeated.

"It's no use just wondering," I said to myself. "To answer these questions—to find if these alignments have any celestial significance —we need precise measurement and comparison, a great volume of trial-and-error work—much more work than I can find time to do.

"We need the machine."

Computers are indeed wonderful things.

They are, of course, not new. For about as many ages as he has been Homo sapiens, perhaps for *exactly* as many ages, man has used things as tools to help him count. First there were fingers. Then, sticks, stones, scratches, any units which could be grouped and tallied. Then more elaborate devices like the sandglass, the running-water clock, the 2500-year-old abacus (which, in the hands of a good operator, is still faster than an electric desk calculator). The ancient Chinese also used small "counting rods," and the Romans made simple computations with little pebbles, or "calculi." The tenth-century Pope Sylvester II was credited with magical powers of divination, possibly because he mastered the abacus which the Saracens were then using. Three hundred years later the learned Roger Bacon developed many ingenious engines, some of them perhaps capable of performing calculations—he was popularly supposed to have obtained prophecies by means of a brazen head. In the sixteenth century Lord Napier, inventor of logarithms, apparently performed arithmetical and geometrical calculations with "certain pieces of wood or ivory with numbers on them, and these were called Napier's Bones." And in the seventeenth century the art of mechanical computing began to become a science.

In that century England's William Oughtred invented the slide rule. (Oughtred was the gentle cleric who taught Christopher Wren mathematics. . . .) France's Blaise Pascal designed a set of wheels "for the execution of all sorts of arithmetical processes in a manner no less novel than convenient." And Germany's Leibnitz made a crude device that could multiply.

At the end of the next century the French tried to make a monstrous calculating machine out of about a hundred human beings, but even Napoleon couldn't order that. In the nineteenth century the extraordinary Englishman Charles Babbage, responsible for dozens of innovations including flat-rate postage, skeleton keys and the cowcatcher, put together a "Difference Engine" which managed to compute simple mathematics tables. Then he dreamed, publicly, of an improved "Analytical Engine," capable of performing at the then alarming rate of sixty arithmetic operations a minute. . . .

But the "Analytical Engine" never got off the drawing board. After Babbage, there was little improvement in the machine calculation field; Victorian computers were turned by hand, at a suitably stately pace.

The really great advance took place in the 1940s. Howard Aiken of Harvard, employing some of the principles of the old "Analytical Engine," devised an automatic sequence controlled electromechanical computer. His "Mark 1" was completed in 1944. The next year John von Neumann proposed internal storage, and the race was fairly on. Now, a scant twenty years later, those early collections of vacuum tubes, switches and flashing neon bulbs have metamorphosed into transistorized magnetic tape giants, which shape the world of our time, and beyond.

A modern electronic digital computer like the IBM 7090 has 50,000 transistors, 125,000 resistors and 500,000 connectors, joined by some twenty miles of wire. Its successor, the 7094, has about 10 per cent more of those components, and is about a third faster in operation. The next generation of machines will be faster still. (And, oddly enough, the machines are growing smaller—because of increased use of transistors and other miniature parts, and more efficient circuitry.) . . .

[A computer] can perform 250,000 simple operations—additions, subtractions, trigonometric functions, etc.—per second, producing its answers in lines containing 26 5-unit "words" in figures or in alphabet letters or in any other code you choose, at the rate of 600 printed lines per minute. At those rates it could "read" the whole Bible in a minute, print it in some seven hours. It is uncomplaining, untemperamental, tireless—like that of mercy, its quality is not strained, nor is its capacity. Furthermore, it does not make mistakes.

In the early days of the model called "650" we were told that certain slight errors in a numerical check were caused by the machine's "warming up." We believed that. And we were wrong. The machine was trying to tell us that there was a significant error in the program that we had put into it; ultimately we had to recalculate the entire program. Nowadays if there is an error in the input program the computer not only detects it but gives the approximate description and location of the error and recommends procedure for correction. I am told that for new programmers this can be rather unnerving.

Computers are now being used for a wide range of tasks including such not obviously mathematical jobs as weather forecasting, diagnosis of illness, invention, literary composition and translation. In our space effort they are of course indispensable; without them there could hardly be a space effort. . . . Now there are some 500 man-made objects moving through space—all of them being tracked comfortably enough by the improved machines. The so-called Space Age might just as well be termed the Computer Age. . . .

Ours is becoming a computer world. University students are nudged into the computer room in their freshman year. To them, the machine is a way of life. Recently I asked a student to do a mathematical job worth about three pencil-hours. A week later she gave me the result. She had referred the problem to the 7090, which meant that for days she had to wait her turn for the use of a fraction of a second of the machine's time. In honest puzzlement I asked her, "Why didn't you use a desk calculator?" "I don't know how." "Then what about a pencil and graph paper?" "What's graph paper?" The moral, I suppose, is that one should keep one's problems hard.

Presently it is a popular occupation among the computer fraternity to compare their mechanism to the human brain. The conclusions are not disheartening—marvelous as the machines are, the brain seems still a good deal more marvelous. Like the mills of the gods, it grinds slow compared to the machines, but it grinds exceeding fine—it is original, imaginative, resourceful, free in will and choice. The machine operates at a speed approaching that of light, 186,000 mi. per sec., whereas the brain operates at the speed at which impulses move along nerve fiber, perhaps a million times slower—but the machine operates linearly, that is, it sends an impulse or "thought" along one path, so that if that path proves to be a dead end the "thought" must back up to the last fork in the road and try again, and if the "thought" is derailed the whole process must be begun again; the brain operates in some mysterious multipath fashion whereby a thought apparently splits and moves along several different paths simultaneously so that no matter what happens to any one of its branches there are others groping along. And whereas even a transistorized computer has a fairly modest number of components, the brain, it seems, has literally billions of neurons, or memory-and-operation cells. To rival an average human brain a computer built by present techniques would have to be about as big as an ocean liner, or a skyscraper. And even then it would lack the capacity for originality and free will. To initiate free choice in a machine the operator would have to insert into its program random numbers, which would make the machine "free" but uncoordinated—an idiot. . . .

In 1961, after I had decided that the problem at Stonehenge was worthy of a computer's attention, I had to fit that problem to the machine: feed it information it could digest, and ask it a question it could understand and answer. The machine requires definiteness. . . .

In this century there has been a great deal of conjecture, some of it very acute, about possible astronomic significance at Stonehenge. After Lockyer's 1901 attempt to date the monument by astronomic methods several qualified scholars have speculated about celestial orientations and significances. But their speculations lacked one thing—the calculation. Such theories should be tested mathematically. Figures alone put teeth into any astronomical theory—or, if the theorizer is unfortunate, take the teeth out.

For the machine, I needed something concrete; a well-defined problem, the best data available on Stonehenge, and a clearly stated question. Only with such input could there be effective output, and the question answered.

My question was definite enough: "Do significant Stonehenge alignments point to significant celestial positions?" The requirement of *significance,* on the ground and in the sky, was obvious. There are so many possible Stonehenge alignments—27,060 between 165 positions—that one could be found to point to practically anything in the sky, and, vice versa, there are so many objects in the sky—perhaps literally an infinite number—that hardly any line extended from earth could fail to hit at least one.

To answer that question, the machine needed pertinent information about Stonehenge and the sky.

We proceeded to give it that information.

First the programmers, Shoshana Rosenthal and Julie Cole (Judy Copeland joined us later), took a chart showing the 165 recognized Stonehenge positions—stones, stone holes, other holes, mounds—and placed it in "Oscar," an automatic plotting machine. Then they placed the cross hairs over each position and singular geometric point like the center and the archway midpoints, pressed the button, and "Oscar" punched each point's X and Y coordinates on a card. The X-Y intersection or origin was arbitrarily set well outside the charted area, in the southwest quadrant, so that all coordinates would be positive.

Then they went to the computer. They primed it with the geographic information—the latitude and longitude of "Oscar's" origin point, the compass orientation of the axes, and the scale—and they instructed it to do three things:

1) extend lines through 120 pairs of the charted points (some pairs, such as neighboring points, were judged valueless as alignment indicators),

2) determine the compass directions or azimuths of those lines,

3) determine the declinations at which those lines going out from Stonehenge would hit the sky. (If the heavenly bodies are regarded as lying in a hollow sphere enclosing the earth then the circles on that sphere corresponding to latitude circles on earth are called declinations.)

I hope this is clear. Perhaps it would help to put it this way: it was as if they told the machine to stand at each of the selected points, look across each of the other points to the horizon, and each time report what spot of the sky—the declination only—it saw.

This priming process, the programming of the machine, took about one day.

Then they gave the "Oscar" cards to a computer operator, who fed them into the machine. In a few seconds it transferred the card information to magnetic tape, scanned the tape, processed the information according to the programmed instructions, and shot forth its result—some 240 Stonehenge alignments translated into celestial declinations. (The 120 pairs yielded twice as many alignments because each line was considered as pointing in both directions.)

That task took the machine less than a minute. It would have kept a human calculator busy for perhaps four months. (To check the machine, Mrs. Rosenthal did one of the computations by hand. It took her four hours.)

And so we had half of the answer to our question. We knew where the important Stonehenge alignments met the sky, the declinations. The next part of the question was, "Were those declinations celestially significant? Did they mark special rise or set points of special heavenly bodies?"

We noticed at once that among the declinations which the machine had produced there was a large number of duplications. Figures approximating + (north) 29°, +24° and +19°, and their southern counterparts, −29°, −24° and −19°, occurred frequently. We decided to see what celestial bodies were close to those declinations.

Quickly we checked the planets. The closest one was Venus, but its maximum declination, ±32°, was not close enough. . . .

Then we ran through (nice phrase!) the stars. The six brightest stars are, in order, Sirius, Canopus, α Centauri, Vega, Capella and Arcturus. Of those, only Sirius, the brightest, was near. Sirius is at declination −16°39′ now, but in 1500 B.C. was at about −18°, according to Lockyer—the stars change declination at different rates, their positions as seen from earth being affected by their own actual motion, called "proper motion," as well as the motion of the earth's axis relative to the celestial sphere. . . . There seemed no probable significance to the possible star alignments; even if further calculation showed that Sirius worked exactly at some date in the past and one or two more alignments of fainter stars turned up, this is just what one would expect from pure chance. Furthermore even a bright star like Sirius can only be seen at rising under extremely favorable weather conditions. Fainter stars are totally invisible on the horizon. We decided to try the most obvious celestial bodies, those prehistoric deities, the sun and the moon.

This time the result was astonishing. Repeatedly and closely those declinations which the machine had computed seemed to fit extreme positions of the sun—which I had suspected that they might —and also—which I had *not* suspected—the moon. Pair after pair of those significant Stonehenge positions seemed to point to the maximum declinations of the two most significant objects in the sky.

I say "seemed" because at that stage we were using a preliminary search program of no great celestial accuracy. The stone alignments and resulting declinations as produced by the machine were as exact as the original chart allowed, but we did not then have correspondingly precise positions for the sun and moon as of the time of Stonehenge. We were using only rough approximations, gotten by mentally chasing those objects backward 4000 years in time. To verify the apparent correlations we needed precise sun-moon extreme positions as of 1500 B.C.

Back, of course, to the machine.

We gave it the present solar-lunar extreme declinations and the rate of change, and instructed it to determine what the extreme declinations had been in 1500 B.C. At the same time we programmed the machine to calculate the direction of rise and set of the sun and moon. Not knowing what the Stonehengers might have chosen we allowed three definitions: (a) sun just showing, (b) sun's disc cut in half by horizon, and (c) disc standing tangent on the horizon. There is about 1° difference between the direction of (a) and (c), which of course is not very great, but I wanted to determine if possible what the Stonehengers had chosen as their definition.

And now I must try the reader's patience with some more basic astronomy. I must explain a little about the moon.

I have explained that the sun moves from a northernmost maximum position of +23°.5 declination in summer to a corresponding −23°.5 extreme southern declination in winter. Just the reverse motion is true of the full moon. It goes north in winter, south in summer. And it has a more complicated relative motion than the sun; it has two northern and two southern maxima. In an 18.61-year cycle it swings so that its far north and south declinations move from 29° to 19° and back to 29°. Thus it has two extremes, 29° and 19°, north and south. This pendulumlike relative motion is caused by the combined effects of tilt and precession of the orbit and it is much too difficult to clarify quickly; even an astronomer has trouble visualizing the processes involved. Here it is only necessary to understand that the moon *does* have two extreme positions for every one of the sun.

To position the sun and moon as of 1500 B.C. took the machine a few more seconds. The declinations it reported were ±23°.9 for the sun and ±29°.0 and ±18°.7 for the moon. The most cursory glance showed us that those declinations were close, very close, to the ones determined by the Stonehenge alignments.

We compared the figures carefully. There was no doubt. Those important and often-duplicated Stonehenge alignments were oriented to the sun and moon. And the orientation was all but complete.

As I have said, I was prepared for *some* Stonehenge-sun correlation. I was not prepared for total sun correlation—and I had not at all suspected that there might be almost total moon correlation as well. For what the machine's figures showed was this:

To a mean accuracy of less than one degree, 12 of the significant Stonehenge alignments pointed to an extreme position of the sun. And to a mean accuracy of about a degree and a half, 12 of the alignments pointed to an extreme of the moon.

. . . [N]ot one of the most significant Stonehenge positions failed to line up with another to point to some unique sun or moon position. Often the same Stonehenge position was paired with more than one other to make additional alignments. And of the 12 unique sun-moon rise-set points, only two—the midsummer moonsets at −29° and −19°—were not thus marked.[1] . . .

It was an extraordinary correspondence.

And the precision of the alignments was noteworthy. The best fit was with the assumption of the sun or moon tangent on the horizon. . . . [T]he average accuracy of the sun lines was 0°.8 and the moon lines 1°.5. These average errors are caused to a large extent by two "bad" archways with errors of 3°.2 and 5°.4 on the western side. . . . Because of the slanting direction of sunrise, an error of 1° in the vertical direction corresponds to about 1°.6 in the horizontal, at 24°.

Usually a scientist does not discuss errors. When all precautions

[1] The stones which would complete these two alignments should by symmetry be near Aubrey hole 28, but this area beyond the ditch has not been thoroughly excavated.

have been taken, an error is recorded without comment because a second attempt might reduce the error and a third attempt cause it to be larger again. An error is an error is an error.

But at Stonehenge we might learn something by such discussion.

Firstly, . . . when I wrote [my] *Nature* article I had no information about actual skyline conditions around Stonehenge and had to assume a uniform skyline—afterwards I obtained a chart showing actual skyline altitude variations around the site. . . . However, neither the theoretical uniform skyline nor the actual skyline as of today would necessarily correspond to the skyline that circled Stonehenge in 1500 B.C. Trees growing then where now there are none could have elevated that ancient skyline by some 0°.2—which would mean that an error presently recorded at +°.2 might actually then have been 0.

Secondly, we found disagreement between one plan and another, and from the data available we were uncertain which plan was more correct. This gives an uncertainty in each figure of about ±0°.2. . . . This is annoying but not serious. Bear in mind that 0°.5 is a small angle for a naked-eye observer.

Thirdly, some of the trouble may have occurred when the priests were laying down the lines. The sun is easy to see during the several critical days at midsummer and midwinter, and sighting errors would be small. But the full moon had to be observed on *the* night of full moon at *the* particular year of a 19-year cycle. If it was cloudy, and the lines were set the night before or the night after full moon, the moon would not have been exactly at its extreme. When this happened, the error would have been positive when the moon's declination was positive and negative when the declination was negative. . . .

Fourthly, Stonehenge is not what it used to be. Stones have tumbled over to lie broken or to be re-erected by modern cranes. The worst errors involve stones that have disappeared long ago—24, 15 and 20. For these, I could only make an estimate of the original positions. Perhaps the errors for these three alignments should be left blank until the archaeologists can provide more information. Is there a hole beneath the turf near the expected position, is the hole a foot or two displaced from the estimates that I made? Furthermore, it is just possible that construction was deliberately halted at some stage of the work, because the builders realized that the design problem they had set themselves was insoluble. A completely symmetrical structure could not have exactly fitted the asymmetrical sky positions.

Finally, the most serious displacement of all may be due to modern man. . . . [T]he moonset archways 57–58, 21–22 . . . fell in 1797. . . . The Ministry of Public Buildings and Works pulled them up straight in 1958, but the stones were originally in shallow holes and it was difficult to reset them exactly. My calculations show . . . there is a horizontal displacement of 16 inches in one or the other of the archways; perhaps that shift has been caused by the re-positioning of these massive blocks.

Then again the sunset trilithons are presently in a sorry state. The great trilithon is broken, having fallen hundreds of years ago. Although 56 was re-erected in 1901, several authors have questioned the accuracy of the restoration; the stone is not perpendicular to the Stonehenge axis but is turned counterclockwise by several degrees. The summer sunset trilithon is half fallen and the corresponding arch marked by 23 is unreliable. Stone 23 fell, and was finally set in cement in 1964.

To support my suggestion that some of the errors are modern, note that the trilithons and archways which have never fallen are more accurately aligned.

The error for the most famous alignment of all, the midsummer sunrise as seen from the center over the heel stone, deserves particular discussion. At present a six-foot man looking from the center sees the top of the heel stone level with the distant skyline. In 1800 B.C. the first flash of the sun appeared about ¾ of a degree to the north, or left, and so the six-foot man standing in the center would have seen its lower edge pass just one-half of a degree above the top of the heel stone—*if* that stone had then been leaning at the angle it stands at today. But if the stone was upright in 1800 B.C., as I believe it was, it stood some 20 inches higher then, and the $0\overset{\circ}{.}5$ error registered by the machine for its present position would have been practically zero. I have calculated . . . on the assumption that the heel stone was upright, and the Stone Age viewer saw the solstice rising sun just graze the tip of the heel stone as it moved upward and over. Here there seems no doubt that the builders intended the disc of the sun to stand exactly on the marker.

Such precision of placement is, or was, astounding. To erect a boulder as irregularly shaped and ponderous as the 35-ton heel stone so that it was horizontally aligned to an accuracy of a foot was a task difficult enough; to sink that great block into the ground just so far and no further, so that its tip was also aligned vertically to an accuracy of inches, was an achievement requiring another whole dimension of skill. How, in fact, was it done? If, after erection, the stone had settled too deeply it would have been out of alignment—and how could it have been lifted? Of course, if it had not settled far enough its top could have been bashed away to lower it to the proper height—but the top was *not* bashed. Perhaps the heel stone was erected first, and the viewing point laid out afterwards?

So much for the errors.

Finally, in a consideration of these sun-moon alignments, it should be remarked how carefully those alignments were preserved, added to, and made more spectacular down through the successive waves of building. During the 300-year period of construction many people of many different thoughts and cultures came to Stonehenge. Different rulers, designers, priests and workmen set their brains and hands to the vast work of alteration, adaptation, change and creation. The great monument grew from a simple circle open toward the midsummer sunrise to a rectangle-within-a-circle to a massive and complex cathedral of stones standing in arched circles and horseshoes. Yet the oldest orientation of all, the axis alignment to summer solstice sunrise, was never lost; rather was it maintained, duplicated, emphasized. . . .

What the original builders had done was remarkable enough; to arrange a circle and a rectangle and six outlying stones so that between them, paired, they form 16 alignments on 10 of the 12 unique sun or moon points is very difficult. What the last builders did was even more remarkable; they duplicated 8 of those earlier, two-position alignments in archwayed vistas. Where the Stonehenge I and II people obtained their sighting directions by standing at one place and looking over another, the men of Stonehenge III saw

8 unique sun and moon risings and settings *through* tall stone arches. And the last builders, like the first, used one position for more than one sighting line. . . .

That final megalithic temple to the sun and moon required of its creators an absolutely extraordinary blending of theoretical, planning abilities with practical building skills. Consider the problem they set for themselves: to design and erect a circle enclosing a horseshoe in such a way that the units of both figures were regularly spaced and yet so arranged that the 5 narrow archways of the horseshoe aligned with 7 narrow archways of the circle to point to 7 of the 12 unique sun and moon horizon positions while the axis of the whole structure pointed through another circle archway to an eighth celestial position—all this to be managed with primitive tools, using "units" of stone, gigantic blocks weighing 30 tons or more. How well they solved that problem we see today.

The first builders—or rather we should say single designers with their groups of builders, because obviously there was directed planning before the construction gangs started work—needed intelligence, purpose and patience as well as physical skill and strength to create Stonehenge I. For Stonehenge II, more intelligence, and continuing purpose were required. To complete the great structure, incorporating the earlier works into a unified whole, a monumental temple with intricate celestial alignments concealed in apparent simplicity and symmetry of design—that required intelligence of a still higher order, a single purpose steadfastly maintained during three hundred years of changing populations, customs, and cultures, and varied skills beyond those possessed by many twentieth-century men. . . .

Once the machine had established that the Stonehenge builders had aligned their monument-temple to the sun and moon with such skill and persistence and impressiveness, the question of course arose, Why? Why had they gone to all that trouble? . . .

Only the archaeologists and other students of the past can ever answer that question. We astronomers with our computing machines can only provide facts for the trained fancies of those ancient-man specialists to play over.

But I would like to put forward this opinion.

The Stonehenge sun-moon alignments were created and elaborated for two, possibly three, reasons: they made a calendar, particularly useful to tell the time for planting crops; they helped to create and maintain priestly power, by enabling the priest to call out the multitude to see the spectacular risings and settings of the sun and moon, most especially the midsummer sunrise over the heel stone and midwinter sunset through the great trilithon, and possibly they served as an intellectual game.

To amplify a little on those three supposed reasons, let me state that it is well known that methods for determining the times of planting were of most vital concern to primitive men. Those times are hard to detect. One can't count backwards from the fine warm days, one must use some other means. And what better means could there be for following the seasons than observation of those most regular and predictable recurring objects, the heavenly bodies? Even in classic times there were still elaborate sets of instructions to help farmers to time their planting by celestial phenomena. Discussing the "deepe question" of the "fit time and season of sowing corne," Pliny declared, "this would bee handled and considered upon with exceeding great care and regard; as depending for the most part of Astronomie. . . ." Doubtless there are today many farmers who time their planting by the sky.

As for the value of Stonehenge as a priestly power-enhancer, it seems quite possible that the man who could call the people to see the god of day or night appear or disappear between those mighty arches and over that distant horizon would attract to himself some of the aura of deity. Indeed, the whole people who possessed such a monument and temple must have felt lifted up.

The other possible reason for the astronomical ingenuity and contrivance of Stonehenge is, I must admit, my own invention. I think that those Stonehengers were true ancestors of ours. I think that the men who designed its various parts, and perhaps even some of the men who helped to build those parts, enjoyed the mental exercise above and beyond the call of duty. I think that when they had solved the problem of the alignments efficiently but unspectacularly, as they had in Stonehenge I, they couldn't let the matter rest. They had to set themselves more challenges, and try for more difficult, rewarding, and spectacular solutions, partly for the greater glory of God, but partly for the joy of man, the thinking animal. I wonder if some day some authority will establish a connection between the spirit which animated the Stonehenge builders and that which inspired the creators of the Parthenon, and the Gothic cathedrals, and the first space craft to go to Mars.

In any case, for whatever reasons those Stonehenge builders built as they did, their final, completed creation was a marvel. As intricately aligned as an interlocking series of astronomical observing instruments (which indeed it was) and yet architecturally perfectly simple, in function subtle and elaborate, in appearance stark, imposing, awesome, Stonehenge was a thing of surpassing ingenuity of design, variety of usefulness and grandeur—in concept and construction an eighth wonder of the ancient world. . . .

Hawkins was writing, with the help of John B. White, for a lay audience, for he had presented his scientific findings to specialists in earlier journal articles. Such popular writing is not unlike a translation, in that it forces the scientist to use terms and comparisons which distort, however slightly. The late Anthony Boucher, who reviewed crime fiction for the *New York Times Book Review,* used to take his authors to task for their mangled efforts at putting Spanish or French into the mouths of their actors (revealing, incidentally, as if his own *The Case of the Seven of Cavalry* had not already done so, that he was a student of Romance languages at the University of California in Berkeley), and he was quick to scourge a bad translation of Simenon or Dürrenmatt. Boucher commented less frequently in his latter days, a sign that the standard of spoken Spanish had come up phenomenally among detectives or that the reviewer had given up the battle. (He reviewed favorably a book in which a feminine Sanch*o* Panza is permitted that masculine name.) Scientists do care about how they are translated, and time and again they comment on how a popularized version of an important piece of scientific research has lost one or more of its points. C. P. Snow, scientist, humanist, and author of detective novels himself, has shown us the obvious dangers arising from the gap between the two cultures.

We would be closer to historical truth if we read the scientific papers used by the scientists themselves as the basis for their discussion, but obviously few historians—excepting those historians of science who have taken advanced training in both disciplines—can do so. The historian, in his determination to avoid jargon and thus to be read, may have been too successful, for in the very readability of much that he has done, he has given many careless minds the impression that his discipline is less rigorous than the natural or even the social sciences. The next essay shows what may be done by a scholar from another discipline who recognizes the complexity of history and who does not conclude that it is simpler than his own area of knowledge.

For additional reading: Snow's *Death Under Sail,* although somewhat clumsy in construction, is worth attention, and his two novels in the Lewis Eliot cycle, *The Masters* and *The Affair,* both set in Oxbridge colleges, are closely allied to detective fiction in exposition, character, and resolution. The redoubtable seventh-century Chinese detective, Judge Dee, who appears in the books of the late Robert van Gulik, poses something of a translation problem at two levels. Van Gulik, who died in 1967, was a leading Sinologist whose work was as likely to appear in *Sinica Leidensia* as at your local drugstore; he drew upon authentic Chinese sources which he used in his scholarly writing to flesh out the adventures of his Ti Jen-chieh, or Judge Dee. These sources had to be translated into English and then the accounts had to be given authentic Chinese settings in which, despite distance and time barriers, the plot elements could be readily grasped by modern Western readers. From 1958, when *The Chinese Bell Murders* was published in England, van Gulik won an alert audience on both sides of the Atlantic. His first foray into such fiction, *The Chinese Maze Murders,* published in the Hague in 1956, is no less scholarly. I am the proud possessor of three of his novels, designated his New Series, which he published in Kuala Lumpur while serving as the Dutch Ambassador to Malaya. A near-closing line of one of these, *The Red Pavilion,* provides us with an exit line to the next selection, "Reputations are not always founded on fact!"

22. The Case of the Fit in the Choir:

The Application of Psychoanalysis

INCREASINGLY, AS WE HAVE SEEN, HISTORIANS ARE WILLing to use the insights of psychology and of psychoanalysis, valuable allies to anyone who wishes to understand human motivation. Just as computers may be abused, of course, so too may psychology become a source of error rather than enlightenment. David Donald, in his biography of Charles Sumner, made legitimate use of medical and psychological evidence, because he was firmly grounded in the discipline of history first and knew how to pick and choose among the glittering generalities offered up to him by psychoanalytic literature. A movement in the reverse direction is more difficult, as shown in particular by Sigmund Freud's famous analysis of *Leonardo da Vinci,* first published in German in 1910 and in an influential English translation in 1916. This book is still read in innocence by many undergraduates, for it is readily available in an inexpensive paperback edition, and the combination of two such culturally resonating names as Leonardo and Freud is difficult to resist in that first Freshmanly flush of desire to know all things. From the historian's point of view, however, the essay—famous as it is—was a bit of a fiasco, for Freud misread his sources, lacked the basic knowledge necessary to interpret the symbolism employed by Leonardo and his contemporaries, and ignored (sometimes intentionally, it would appear) evidence that ran contrary to his diagnosis of Leonardo's alleged homosexuality and artistic impulses. Not until 1956, however, did an art historian, Meyer Schapiro of Columbia University, a specialist in both medieval and modern art forms, demonstrate how disastrous to scholarship Freud's reasoning had been.

It is not to a negative demonstration of the pitfalls of psychoanalysis that we now turn, however, but rather to one of the relatively few applications of psychoanalytic insights to a historical problem of which historians have expressed widespread approval. Writing in 1958, Professor Erik H. Erikson, in *Young Man Luther: A Study in Psychoanalysis and History,* achieved what may be regarded as an academic breakthrough. Erikson, by training a psychoanalyst himself, and now Professor of Human Development at Harvard University, set out to examine the scholarship—by historians as well as theologians and psychologists—relating to Martin Luther and the birth of Protestantism. In doing so, he exposed the nerve ends of several earlier scholarly approaches and revealed a Luther who had at best been guessed at by earlier generations of students. Erikson's book was an able wedding of the two disciplines to which its subtitle referred, although clearly it was predominantly a work in psychoanalysis, and from this wedding came a renewed and growing respect among historians for the kinds of insights they might gain from a discipline of which they had been suspicious. Illustrative of Erikson's method was the second chapter of his work, "The Fit in the Choir," in which he described the available points of view on the young Luther's much-discussed (and perhaps only legendary) fit and then put forward a convincing analysis of his own.

♦ ♦ ♦

Three of young Luther's contemporaries (none of them a later follower of his) report that sometime during his early or middle twenties, he suddenly fell to the ground in the choir of the monastery at Erfurt, "raved" like one possessed, and roared with the voice of a bull: *"Ich bin's nit! Ich bin's nit!"* or *"Non sum! Non sum!*" The German version is best translated with "It isn't me!" the Latin one with "I am *not!*"

It would be interesting to know whether at this moment Martin roared in Latin or in German; but the reporters agree only on the occasion which upset him so deeply: the reading of Christ's *ejecto a surdo et muto daemonio*—Christ's cure of a man possessed by a *dumb spirit.* This can only refer to Mark 9:17: "And one of the multitude answered and said, Master, I have brought unto thee my son, which hath a dumb spirit." The chroniclers considered that young Luther was possessed by demons—the religious and psychiatric borderline case of the middle ages—and that he showed himself possessed even as he tried most loudly to deny it. "I am *not,*" would then be the childlike protestation of somebody who has been called a name or has been characterized with loathsome adjectives: here, dumb, mute, possessed.

We will discuss this alleged event first as to its place in Luther's life history, and then, as to its status in Luther's biography.

The monk Martinus entered the Black Monastery of the Augustinians in Erfurt when he was twenty-one years old. Following a vow made in an attack of acute panic during a severe thunderstorm, he had abruptly and without his father's permission left the University of Erfurt, where he had just received with high honors the degree of a master of arts. Behind the monk lay years of strict schooling supported only with great sacrifice by his ambitious father, who wanted him to study the law, a profession which at

---

FROM Erik H. Erikson, *Young Man Luther: A Study in Psychoanalysis and History* (New York: W. W. Norton & Company, 1962), pp. 23–48. Reprinted by permission of W. W. Norton & Company, Inc. First published in 1958 as the Austen Riggs Monograph No. 4. Also reprinted with permission of Faber and Faber Ltd.

For additional reading: The Schapiro essay referred to in the text above was "Leonardo and Freud: An Art-Historical Study," *Journal of the History of Ideas,* XVII (April, 1956), 147–77. For an adulatory article that compares badly with Schapiro, consult Erwin O. Christensen, "Freud on Leonardo da Vinci," *Psychoanalytic Review,* XXXI (March, 1944), 153–64. To see an exercise in detecting the detective, read Arthur Wise's *The Death's Head.* And for more of the work of Erik H. Erikson, see his equally provocative *Childhood and Society* (2nd ed., rev. and enlarged, New York, 1963).

that time was becoming the springboard into administration and politics. Before him lay long years of the most intense inner conflicts and frequently morbid religious scruples; these eventually led to his abandonment of monasticism and to his assumption of spiritual leadership in a widespread revolt against the medieval papacy. The fit in the choir, then, belongs to a period when his career, as planned by his father, was dead; when his monastic condition, after a "godly" beginning, had become problematic to him; and when his future was as yet in an embryonic darkness. This future could have been divined by him only in the strictest (and vaguest) term of the word, namely, as a sense of a spiritual mission of some kind.

It is difficult to visualize this young man, later to become so great and triumphant, in the years when he took that chance on perdition which was the very test and condition of his later greatness. Therefore, I shall list a few dates, which may be of help to the reader.

EVENTS OF MARTIN'S YOUTH

Born in 1483, Martin Luther	1483
entered the University of Erfurt at seventeen;	1501
received his master's degree at twenty-one, and entered the monastery, having vowed to do so during a thunderstorm.	1505
Became a priest and celebrated his first Mass at the age of twenty-three; then fell into severe doubts and scruples which may have caused the "fit in the choir."	1507+
Became a doctor of theology at the age of twenty-eight; gave his first lectures on the Psalms at the University of Wittenberg, where he experienced the "revelation in the tower."	1512+
At thirty-two, almost a decade after the episode in the choir, he nailed his ninety-five theses on the church door in Wittenberg.	1517

The story of the fit in the choir has been denied as often as it has been repeated; but its fascination even for those who would do away with it seems to be great. A German professor of theology, Otto Scheel, one of the most thorough editors of the early sources on Luther's life, flatly disavows the story, tracing it to that early hateful biography of Luther written by Johannes Cochläus in 1549. And yet, Scheel does not seem to be able to let go of the story. Even to him there is enough to it so that in the very act of belittling it he grants it a measure of religious grandeur: "Nicolaus Tolentinus, too," he writes, "when he knelt at the altar and prayed, was set upon by the Prince of Darkness. But precisely in this visibly meaningful (*sinnfaellig*) struggle with the devil did Nicolaus prove himself as the chosen armour of the Lord. . . . Are we to count it to Luther's damnation if he, too, had to battle with the devil in a similarly meaningful way?" He appeals to Catholic detractors: "Why not measure with the same yardstick?" And in a footnote he asks the age-old question: "Or was Paul's miraculous conversion also pathological?" Scheel, incidentally, in his famous collection of documents on Luther's development, where he dutifully reprints Cochläus' version, makes one of his very rare mistakes by suggesting that the biblical story in question is Mark 1:23, where a "man with an unclean spirit . . . *cried out*" and was *silenced* by Christ. However, the *surdus* and *mutus daemonius* can hardly refer to this earlier passage in Mark.

Scheel is a Protestant professor of theology. For him the principal task is explaining as genuinely inspired by a divine agency those attacks of unconsciousness and fits of overwhelming anxiety, those delusional moments, and those states of brooding despair which occasionally beset young Luther and increasingly beset the aging man. To Scheel they are all *geistlich,* not *geistig*—spiritual, not mental. It is often troublesome to try to find one's way through the German literature on Luther, which refers to various mental states as *"Seelenleiden"* (suffering of the soul) and *"Geisteskrankheit,"* (sickness of the spirit)—terms which always leave it open whether soul or psyche, spirit or mind, is afflicted. It is especially troublesome when medical men claim that the reformer's "suffering of the soul" was mainly *biologically* determined. But the *professor*—as we will call Scheel when we mean to quote him as the representative of a particular academic-theological school of Luther biography—the professor insists, and in a most soberly circumstantial biography, that all of Luther's strange upsets came to him straight down from heaven: *Katastrophen von Gottes Gnaden.*

The most famous, and in many ways rightly infamous, detractor of Luther's character, the Dominican Heinrich Denifle, Sub-Archivar of the Holy See, saw it differently. For him such events as the fit in the choir have only an inner cause, which in no way means a decent conflict or even an honest affliction, but solely an abysmal depravity of character. To him, Luther is too much of a psychopath to be credited with honest mental or spiritual suffering. It is only the Bad One who speaks through Luther. It is, it must be, Denifle's primary ideological premise, that nothing, neither mere pathological fits, nor the later revelations which set Luther on the path to reformation, had anything whatsoever to do with divine interference. "Who," Denifle asks, in referring to the thunderstorm, "can prove, for himself, not to speak of others, that the alleged inspiration through the Holy Ghost really came from above . . . and that it was not the play of conscious or unconscious self-delusion?" Lutheranism, he fears (and hopes to demonstrate) has tried to lift to the height of dogma the phantasies of a most fallible mind.

With his suspicion that Luther's whole career may have been inspired by the devil, Denifle puts his finger on the sorest spot in Luther's whole spiritual and psychological make-up. His days in the monastery were darkened by a suspicion, which Martin's father expressed loudly on the occasion of the young priest's first Mass, that the thunderstorm had really been the voice of a *Gespenst,* a ghost; thus Luther's vow was on the borderline of both pathology and demonology. Luther remained sensitive to this paternal suspicion, and continued to argue with himself and with his father long after his father had no other choice than to acknowledge his son as a spiritual leader and Europe's religious strong man. But in his twenties Martin was still a sorely troubled young man, not at all able to express either what inspired or what bothered him; his greatest worldly burden was certainly the fact that his father had only most reluctantly, and after much cursing, given his consent (which was legally dispensable, anyway) to the son's religious career.

With this in mind, let us return to Mark 9:17–24. It was a father who addressed Christ: "Master, I have brought unto Thee my son, which hath a dumb spirit. . . . and he asked his father, how long is it ago since this came unto him? And he said, Of a child. . . . Jesus said unto him, If thou canst believe, all things are possible to him that believeth. . . . And straightway the father of the child cried out, and said with tears, Lord, I believe; help thou mine unbelief." Two cures, then, are suggested in the Bible passage: the cure of a son with a dumb spirit, after a father has been cured of a weak faith. The possibility of an "inner-psychological" kernel in Martin's reaction to this passage will thus deserve to be weighed carefully, although with scales other than those used by Father Denifle—to whom we will refer as the *priest,* whenever we quote him as a representative of a clerical-scholastic school in Luther biography.

But now to another school of experts. An extremely diligent student of Luther, the Danish psychiatrist, Dr. Paul J. Reiter, decides unequivocally that the fit in the choir is a matter of severest psychopathology. At most, he is willing to consider the event as a relatively benign hysterical episode; even so, he evaluates it as a symptom of a steady, pitiless, "endogenous" process which, in Luther's middle forties, was climaxed by a frank psychosis. *Endogenous* really means biological; Reiter feels that Luther's attacks cannot "with the best of will" be conceived of as links "in the chain of meaningful psychological development." It would be futile, then, to try to find any "message," either from a divine or an inner source, in Luther's abnormalities other than indications of erratic upsets in his nervous system. Reiter considers the years in which we are most interested—when Luther was twenty-two to thirty—as part of one long *Krankheitsphase,* one drawn-out state of nervous disease, which extended to the thirty-sixth year; these years were followed by a period of "manic" productivity, and then by a severe breakdown in the forties. In fact, he feels that only a pitifully small number of Luther's years were really characterized by the reformer's famous "robust habitual state"—which means that Luther was like himself only very rarely, and most briefly. Reiter considers at least Luther's twenties as a period of neurotic, rather than of psychotic, tension, and he acknowledges the crisis of this one period as the only time in Luther's life when his ideological search remained meaningfully related to his psychological conflicts; when his creativity kept pace with his inner destructive processes; and when a certain "limited intellectual balance" was reached.

We will make the most of the license thus affirmed by the *psychiatrist,* as we shall call Reiter when we quote him as the representative of a medical-biological school in Luther biography. This class of biographers ascribes Luther's personal and theological excesses to a sickness which, whether "seated" in brain, nervous system, or kidneys, marks Luther as a biologically inferior or diseased man. As to the event in the choir, Reiter makes a strange mistake. Luther, he says, could not have been conscious, for he called out with "utmost intentionality . . . 'That's me!' " (*Ich bin's*)—meaning, the possessed one of the evangelium. Such a positive exclamation would do away with a good part of the meaning which we will ascribe to the event in the choir; however, three hundred pages earlier in the same book, Reiter, too, tells the story in the traditional way, making Martin call out: "That's *not* me."

And how about a psychoanalyst? The professor and the psychiatrist frequently and most haughtily refer to a representative of the "modern Freudian school"—Professor Preserved Smith, then of Amherst College, who, beside writing a biography of Luther, and editing his letters, wrote, in 1915, a remarkable paper: "Luther's Early Development in the Light of Psychoanalysis." I use the word "beside" deliberately, for this paper impresses one as being a foreign body in Smith's work on Luther; it is done, so to speak, with the left hand, while the right and official hand is unaware. "Luther," Smith claims, "is a thoroughly typical example of the neurotic quasi-hysterical sequence of an infantile sex-complex; so much so, indeed, that Sigismund [*sic*] Freud and his school could hardly have found a better example to illustrate the sounder part of their theory than him." Smith musters the appropriate data to show . . . that Luther's childhood was unhappy because of his father's excessive harshness, and that he was obsessively preoccupied with God as an avenger, with the Devil as a visible demon, and with obscene images and sayings. Smith unhesitatingly characterizes "the foundation-stones of early Protestantism . . . as an interpretation of Luther's own subjective life." Outstanding in Luther's morbid subjectivity is his preoccupation with "concupiscence" which Smith, contrary to all evidence, treats as if to Luther it had been a mere matter of sexual "lust." Smith in fact (while conceding that "it is to his great credit that there is good reason to believe he never sinned with women") attributes Luther's great preoccupation with concupiscence to his losing battle with masturbation.

It is instructive to see what an initial fascination and temporary indoctrination with "Freudian" notions can do to a scholar, in particular perhaps to one with a Puritan background: the notions remain in his thinking like a foreign body. In order to make the masturbation hypothesis plausible, Smith, obviously a thorough student of the German sources, flagrantly misinterprets a famous statement of Luther's. Luther reported repeatedly that at the height of his monastic scruples he had confessed to a trusted superior, "not about women, but about *die rechten Knotten.*" This phrase means "the real knots"; in the language of the peasant, it means the knotty part of the tree, the hardest to cut. This reference to real hindrances Smith suspects is a hint at masturbation, although the sound of the words does not suggest anything of the kind, and although at least on one occasion Luther specifies the knots as transgressions against *die erste Taffel* that is, the first commandment concerning the love of God the Father. This would point to Luther's increasing and obsessive-blasphemous ambivalence toward God, partially a consequence (and here Smith is, of course, correct and is seconded by the psychiatrist) of a most pathological relationship to his father; which in turn provides the proper context for Luther's sexual scruples. Professor Smith, incidentally, translates the reported outcry in the choir as "It is not I!"—words which I doubt even a New Englander would utter in a convulsive attack.

Although the professor, the priest, and the psychiatrist refer to Smith as "the psychoanalyst," I myself cannot characterize him in this way, since his brilliant but dated contribution appears to be an isolated exercise of a man who, to my knowledge, never systematically pursued psychoanalysis either in practice or in theory.

Why did I introduce my discussion of Luther with this particular event in the choir, whose interpretation is subject to so many large and small discrepancies?

As I tried to orient myself in regard to Luther's identity crisis by studying those works which promised to render the greatest number of facts and references for independent study, I heard him, ever again, roar in rage, and yet also in laughter: *Ich bin's nit!* For with the same facts (here and there altered, as I have indicated, in details precisely relevant to psychological interpretation), the professor, the priest, the psychiatrist, and others as yet to be quoted each concocts his own Luther; this may well be the reason why they all agree on one point, namely, that dynamic psychology must be kept away from the data of Luther's life. Is it possible that they all agree so that each may take total and unashamed possession of him, of the great man's charisma?

Take the professor. As he sifts the sources minutely and masterfully establishes his own versions, a strange belligerence (to judge from Freud's experience not atypical of the German scientific scene of the early part of this century) leads him to challenge other experts as if to a duel. He constantly imputes to them not only the ignorance of high school boys, but also the motives of juveniles. This need not bother us; such duels spill only ink and swell only footnotes. But the emerging image of Luther, erected and defended in this manner, assumes, at decisive moments, some of the military qualities of the method; while otherwise it remains completely devoid of any psychological consistency. At the conclusion of the professor's first volume, only a soldierly image suffices to express his hopes for sad young Martin behind whom the gates of the monastery have just closed: "Out of the novice Luther," he writes, "the warrior shall be created, whom the enemy can touch neither with force nor with cunning, and whose soul, after completion of its war service, will be led to the throne of the judge by archangel Michael." *Kriegsdienst* is the metallic German word for war service, and the professor makes the most of the biblical reference to God as El Zebaoth, the master of the armies of angels; he even makes God share the Kaiser's title *Kriegsherr*. Everything extraordinary, then, that happens to Luther is *befohlen,* ordered from above, without advance notice or explanation and completely without intention or motivation on Luther's part; consequently, all psychological speculation regarding motivation is strictly *verboten*. No wonder that Luther's "personality" seems to be put together from scraps of conventional images which do not add up to a workable human being. Luther's parents and Luther himself are pasted together; their ingredients are the characteristics of the ordinary small-town German: simple, hardworking, earnest, straightforward, dutiful folk (*bieder, tuechtig, gehorsam,* and *wacker*). The myth to be created, of course, is that God selects just such folk to descend on in a sudden "catastrophic" decision.

[Heinrich] Boehmer, whom I would place in the same school, although equally well-informed, is milder and more insightful. Yet for him, too, Luther's father is a harsh, but entirely well-meaning, sturdy, and healthy type, until suddenly, without any warning whatsoever, he behaves "like a madman" when his son enters the monastery. Boehmer acts as if such a childish explosion were a German father's prerogative and above any psychologizing.

Scheel's book is a post-World War I heir of two trends in the Lutheran writing of history, initiated by two men and never surpassed by others: the universalistic-historical trend of the great [Leopold] von Ranke, the "priestly historian," whose job it was to find in the conflicting forces of history "the holy hieroglyph of God"; the other, a theological-philosophical trend (sometimes fusing, sometimes sharply separating philosophy and religion) begun by the elder [Theodosius] Harnack. . . .

Denifle the Dominican priest, also an acknowledged scholar and authority on late medieval institutions of learning (he died a few days before he was to receive an honorary degree from the University of Cambridge), as well as a most powerful detective of Luther's often rather free quotations from and reinterpretations of theological doctrine, feels obliged to create a different image of Luther. To him he is an *Umsturzmensch,* the kind of man who wants to turn the world upside down without a plan of his own. To Denifle, Luther's protestant attitude introduced into history a dangerous kind of revolutionary spirit. Luther's special gifts, which the priest does not deny, are those of the demagogue and the false prophet—falseness not only as a matter of bad theology, but as a conscious falsification from base motives. All of this follows from the priest's quite natural thesis that war orders from above, such as the professor assumes to have been issued to Luther, could only be genuine if they showed the seal and the signature of divinity, namely, signs and miracles. When Luther prayed to God not to send his miracles, so that he would not become proud and be deflected from the Word by Satan's delusions, he only discarded grapes which were hanging as high as heaven itself: for the faintest possibility of any man outside the Church receiving such signs had been excluded for all eternity by the verification of Jesus as God's sole messenger on earth. . . .

Among all of Luther's biographers, inimical or friendly, Denifle seems to me to resemble Luther most, at least in his salt-and-pepper honesty, and his one-sided anger. "Tyrolean candor," a French biographer ascribes to him. The Jesuit is most admirable in his scholarly criticism of Luther's theology; most lovable in his outraged response to Luther's vulgarity. Denifle does not think that a true man of God would ever say "I gorge myself (*fresse*) like a Bohemian and I get drunk (*sauff*) like a German. God be praised. Amen," although he neglects the fact that Luther wrote this in one of his humorous letters to his wife at a time when she was worried about his lack of appetite. And he seriously suggests that the sow was Luther's model of salvation. I cannot refrain from translating here the quotation on which Denifle bases this opinion, which offers a contrast to Scheel's martial image and, as such, is an example of a radically different and yet equally scholarly suggestion for the real core of Luther's personality.

In an otherwise hateful pamphlet written in his middle forties, Luther relaxes into that folksy manner which he occasionally also used in his sermons. What he wants to make clear is that there is a prereligious state of mind. "For a sow," he writes,

> lies in the gutter or on the manure as if on the finest feather bed. She rests safely, snores tenderly, and sleeps sweetly, does not fear king nor master, death nor hell, devil or God's wrath, lives without worry, and does not even think where the clover [*Kleien*] may be. And if the Turkish Caesar arrived in all his might and anger, the sow would be much too proud to move a single whisker in his honor. . . . And if at last the butcher comes upon her, she thinks maybe a piece of wood is pinching her, or a stone. . . . The sow has not eaten from the apple, which in paradise has taught us wretched humans the difference between good and bad.

No translation can do justice to the gentle persuasiveness of these lines. The priest, however, omits the argument in which they appear: Luther is trying to persuade his readers that the as yet expected Messiah of the Jews could not make a man's life a tenth as good as that of a sow, while the coming of Christ has done more, has put the whole matter of living on a higher plane. And yet one cannot escape the fact that in Luther's rich personality there was a soft spot for the sow so large that Denifle correctly considers it what I will call one of Luther's identity elements. Oftentimes when this element became dominant, Luther could be so vulgar that he became easy game for the priest and the psychiatrist, both of whom quote with relish: "Thou shalt not write a book unless you have listened to the fart of an old sow, to which you should open your mouth wide and say 'Thanks to you, pretty nightingale; do I hear a text which is for me?' " But what writer, disgusted with himself, has not shared these sentiments—without finding the right wrong words?

The Danish psychiatrist, in turn, offers in his two impressive volumes as complete an account of Luther's "environment, character, and psychosis" as I have come across. His study ranges from the macrocosm of Luther's times to the microcosm of his home and home town, and includes a thorough discussion of his biological make-up and of his lifelong physical and emotional symptoms. But the psychiatrist lacks a theory comprehensive enough for his chosen range. Psychoanalysis he rejects as too dogmatic, borrowing from Preserved Smith what fragments he can use without committing himself to the theory implied. He states his approach candidly: it is that of a psychiatrist who has been consulted on a severe case of manifest psychosis (diagnosis: manic-depressive, à la Kraepelin) and who proceeds to record the presenting condition (Luther's acute psychosis in his forties) and to reconstruct the past history, including the twenties. He shows much insight in his asides; but in his rôle of bedside psychiatrist, he grimly sticks to his central view by asserting that a certain trait or act of Luther's is "absolutely typical for a state of severe melancholia" and "is to be found in every psychiatric textbook." The older Luther undoubtedly approached textbook states, although I doubt very much that his personal meetings with the devil were ever true hallucinations, or that his dramatic revelations concerning his mental suffering can be treated on the same level as communications from a patient.

Furthermore, when it comes to the younger Luther and the psychiatrist's assertion that his *tentationes tristitiae*—that sadness which is a traditional temptation of the *homo religiosus*—is among the "classical traits in the picture of most states of depression, especially the endogenous ones," we must be decidedly more doubtful. For throughout, this psychiatric textbook version of Luther does not compare him with other examples of sincere religious preoccupation and corresponding genuine giftedness, but with some norm of *Ausgeglichenheit*—an inner balance, a simple enjoyment of life, and an ordinary decency and decided direction of effort such as normal people are said to display. Though the psychiatrist makes repeated allowances for Luther's genius, he nevertheless demands of him a state of inner repose which, as far as I know, men of creative intensity and of an increasing historical commitment cannot be expected to be able to maintain. At any rate, he points out that even in his last years Luther's "psychic balance was not complete," his inner state only "relatively harmonious." Using this yardstick of normality, the psychiatrist considers it strange that Luther could not accept his father's reasonable plans and go ahead and enjoy the study of law; that he could not be relaxed during his ordination as other young priests are; that he could not feel at home in as sensible and dignified a regime as that of an Augustinian monastery; and that he was not able, much later, to sit back and savor with equanimity the fruits of his rebellion. The professor, too, finds most of this surprising; but he assumes that God, for some divine reason, needled Luther out of such natural and sensible attitudes; the psychiatrist is sure that the needling was done from within, by endogenous mental disease.

I do not know about the kind of balance of mind, body, and soul that these men assume is normal; but if it does exist, I would expect it least of all in such a sensitive, passionate, and ambitious individual as young Luther. He, as many lesser ones like him, may have had good inner reasons to escape premature commitments. Some young people suffer under successes which, to them, are subjectively false, and they may even shy away as long as they possibly can from what later turns out to be their true rôle. The professor's and the psychiatrist's image of normality seems an utterly incongruous measure to use on a future professional reformer. But then the psychiatrist (with the priest) not only disavows God's hand in the matter, he also disregards, in his long list of character types and somatotypes, the existence of a *homo religiosus* circumscribed and proved not necessarily by signs and miracles, but by the inner logic of his way of life, by the logic of his working gifts, and by the logic of his effect on society. To study and formulate this logic seems to me to constitute the task at hand, if one wishes to consider the total existence of a man like Luther.

I will conclude this review of a few of the most striking and best-informed attempts at presenting prejudiced versions of Luther's case with one more quotation and one more suggested Luther image. This image comes from sociology, a field certainly essential to any assessment of the kind to which our authors aspire. I could not, and would not, do without *The Social Basis of the German Reformation* although its author, R. Pascal, a social scientist and historical materialist, announces with the same flatness which we have encountered in the other biographers how well he could manage without me and my field. "The principle underlying [Luther's contradictions]," he states, "is not logical, it is not psychological. The consistency amid all these contradictions is the consistency of class-interest."

This statement is, perhaps, the most Marxist formulation in the economic-political literature of Luther's personality and his influence on the subsequent codevelopment of protestantism and capitalism. (The most encompassing book with this economic-political point of view is by Ernst Troeltsch; the most famous, at least in this country, those of [Max] Weber and of [R. H.] Tawney.) I am not smiling at it in superiority, any more than I am smiling at the statements of the dogmatic professor of theology, the Dominican scholar, or the "constitutional" psychiatrist. For each cites valid data, all of which, as we shall see, complement each other. It is necessary, however, to contemplate (if only as a warning to ourselves) the degree to which in the biography of a great man "objective study" and "historical accuracy" can be used to support almost any total image necessitated by the biographer's personality and professed calling; and to point out that biographers categorically opposed to systematic psychological interpretation permit themselves the most extensive psychologizing—which they can afford to believe is common sense only because they disclaim a defined psychological viewpoint. Yet there is always an implicit psychology behind the explicit antipsychology.

One of the great detractors of Luther, Jacob Burckhardt, who taught Nietzsche to see in Luther a noisy German peasant who at the end waylaid the march of Renaissance man, noted: "Who are we, anyway, that we can ask of Luther . . . that [he] should have fulfilled *our* programs? . . . This concrete Luther, and no other, existed; he should be taken for what he was" (*Man nehme ihn wie er gewesen ist*).

But how does one take a *great* man "for what he was"? The very adjective seems to imply that something about him is too big, too awe-ful, too shiny, to be encompassed. Those who nonetheless set out to describe the whole man seem to have only three choices. They can step so far back that the great man's contours appear complete, but hazy; or they can step closer and closer, gradually concentrating on a few aspects of the great man's life, seeing one part of it as big as the whole, or the whole as small as one part. If neither of these works, there is always polemics; one takes the great man in the sense of appropriating him and of excluding others who might dare to do the same. Thus a man's historical image often depends on which legend temporarily overcomes all others; however, all these ways of viewing a great man's life may be needed to capture the mood of the historical event.

The limitations of my knowledge and of the space at my disposal for this inquiry preclude any attempt to present a new Luther or to remodel an old one. I can only bring some newer psychological considerations to bear on the existing material pertaining to one period of Luther's life. . . . [T]he young monk interests me particularly as a young man in the process of becoming a great one.

It must have occurred to the reader that the story of the fit in the choir attracted me originally because I suspected that the words "I am *not!*" revealed the fit to be part of a most severe identity crisis—a crisis in which the young monk felt obliged to protest what he was *not* (possessed, sick, sinful) perhaps in order to break through to what he was or was to be. I will now state what remains of my suspicion, and what I intend to make of it.

Judging from an undisputed series of extreme mental states which attacked Luther throughout his life, leading to weeping, sweating, and fainting, the fit in the choir could well have happened; and it could have happened in the specific form reported, under the specific conditions of Martin's monastery years. If some of it is legend, so be it; the making of legend is as much part of the scholarly rewriting of history as it is part of the original facts used in the work of scholars. We are thus obliged to accept half-legend as half-history, provided only that a reported episode does not contradict other well-established facts; persists in having a ring of truth; and yields a meaning consistent with psychological theory.

Luther himself never mentioned this episode, although in his voluble later years he was extraordinarily free with references to physical and mental suffering. It seems that he always remembered most vividly those states in which he struggled through to an insight, but not those in which he was knocked out. Thus, in his old age, he remembers well having been seized at the age of thirty-five by terror, sweat, and the fear of fainting when he marched in the Corpus Christi procession behind his superior, Dr. [John von] Staupitz, who carried the holy of holies. (This Dr. Staupitz, as we will see, was the best father figure Luther ever encountered and acknowledged; he was a man who recognized a true *homo religiosus* in his subaltern and treated him with therapeutic wisdom.) But Staupitz did not let Luther get away with his assertion that it was Christ who had frightened him. He said, *"Non est Christus, quia Christus non terret, sed consolatur."* (It couldn't have been Christ who terrified you, for Christ consoles.) This was a therapeutic as well as a theological revelation of Luther, and he remembered it. However, for the fit in the choir, he may well have had an amnesia.

Assuming then that something like this episode happened, it could be considered as one of a series of seemingly senseless pathological explosions; as a meaningful symptom in a psychiatric case-history; or as one of a series of religiously relevant experiences. It certainly has, as even Scheel suggests, *some* marks of a "religious attack," such as St. Paul, St. Augustine, and many lesser aspirants to saintliness have had. However, the inventory of a total revelation always includes an overwhelming illumination and a sudden insight. The fit in the choir presents only the symptomatic, the more pathological and defensive, aspects of a total revelation: partial loss of consciousness, loss of motor coordination, and automatic exclamations which the afflicted does not know he utters.

In a truly religious experience such automatic exclamations would sound as if they were dictated by divine inspiration; they would be positively illuminating and luminous, and be intensely remembered. In Luther's fit, his words obviously expressed an overwhelming inner need to deny an accusation. In a full religious attack the positive conscience of faith would reign and determine the words uttered; here negation and rebellion reign: "I am *not* what my father said I was and what my conscience, in bad moments, tends to confirm I am." The raving and roaring suggest a strong element of otherwise suppressed rage. And, indeed, this young man, who later became a voice heard around the world, lived under monastic conditions of silence and meditation; at this time he was submissively subdued, painfully sad, and compulsively self-inspective—too much so even for his stern superiors' religious taste. All in all, however, the paroxysm occurred in a holy spot and was suggested by a biblical story, which places the whole matter at least on the borderline between psychiatry and religion.

If we approach the episode from the psychiatric viewpoint, we can recognize in the described attack (and also in a variety of symptomatic scruples and anxieties to which Martin was subject at the time) an intrinsic ambivalence, an inner two-facedness, such as we find in all neurotic symptoms. The attack could be said to deny in its verbal part ("I am not") what Martin's father had said, namely, that his son was perhaps possessed rather than holy; but it also proves the father's point by its very occurrence in front of the same congregation who had previously heard the father express his anger and apprehension. The fit, then, is both unconscious obedience to the father and implied rebellion against the monastery; the words uttered both deny the father's assertion, and confirm the vow which Martin had made in that first known anxiety attack during a thunderstorm at the age of twenty-one, when he had exclaimed, "I want to be a monk." We find the young monk, then, at the crossroads of obedience to his father—an obedience of extraordinary tenacity and deviousness—and to the monastic vows which at the time he was straining to obey almost to the point of absurdity.

We may also view his position as being at the crossroads of mental disease and religious creativity and we could speculate that perhaps Luther received in three (or more) distinct and fragmentary experiences those elements of a total revelation which other men are said to have acquired in one explosive event. Let me list the elements again: physical paroxysm; a degree of unconsciousness; an automatic verbal utterance; a command to change the over-all direction of effort and aspiration; and a spiritual revelation, a flash of enlightenment, decisive and pervasive as a rebirth. The thunderstorm had provided him with a change in the over-all direction of his life, a change toward the anonymous, the silent, and the obedient. In fits such as the one in the choir, he experienced the epileptoid paroxysm of ego-loss, the rage of denial of the identity which was to be discarded. And later in the experience in the tower . . . he perceived the light of a new spiritual formula.

The fact that Luther experienced these clearly separate stages of religious revelation might make it possible to establish a psychological rationale for the conversion of other outstanding religionists, where tradition has come to insist on the transmission of a total event appealing to popular faith. Nothing, to my mind, makes Luther more a man of the future—the future which is our psychological present—than his utter integrity in reporting the steps which marked the emergence of his identity as a genuine *homo religiosus.* I emphasize this by no means only because it makes him a better case (although I admit it helps), but because it makes his total experience a historical event far beyond its immediate sectarian significance, namely, a decisive step in human awareness and responsibility. To indicate this step in its psychological coordinates is the burden of [my argument].

Martin's general mood just before he became a monk, a mood into which he was again sliding at the time of the fit in the choir, has been characterized by him and others as a state of *tristitia,* of excessive sadness. Before the thunderstorm, he had rapidly been freezing into a melancholy paralysis which made it impossible for him to continue his studies and to contemplate marriage as his father urged him to do. In the thunderstorm, he had felt immense anxiety. Anxiety comes from *angustus,* meaning to feel hemmed in and choked up; Martin's use of *circumvallatus*—all walled in—to describe his experience in the thunderstorm indicates he felt a sudden constriction of his whole life space, and could see only one way out: the abandonment of all of his previous life and the earthly future it implied for the sake of total dedication to a new life. This new life, however, was one which made an institution out of the very configuration of being walled in. Architecturally, ceremonially, and in its total world-mood, it symbolized life on this earth as a self-imposed and self-conscious prison with only one exit, and that one, to eternity. The acceptance of this new frame of life had made him, for a while, peaceful and "godly"; at the time of his fit, however, his sadness was deepening again.

As to this general veil of sadness which covered the conflicts revealed so explosively in the choir, one could say (and the psychiatrist has said it) that Martin was sad because he was a melancholic; and there is no doubt that in his depressed moods he displayed at times what we would call the clinical picture of a melancholia. But Luther was a man who tried to distinguish very clearly between what came from God as the crowning of a worthwhile conflict, and what came from defeat; the fact that he called defeat the devil only meant he was applying a diagnostic label which was handy. He once wrote to [Philipp] Melanchthon that he considered him the weaker one in public controversy, and himself the weaker in private struggles—"if I may thus call what goes on between me and Satan." One could also say (and the professor has said it) that Martin's sadness was the traditional *tristitia,* the melancholy world mood of the *homo religiosus;* from this point of view, it is a "natural" mood, and could even be called the truest adaptation to the human condition. This view, too, we must accept to a point—the point where it becomes clear that Martin was not able in the long run to embrace the monastic life so natural to the traditional *tristitia;* that he mistrusted his sadness himself; and that he later abandoned this melancholic mood altogether for occasional violent mood swings between depression and elation, between self-accusation and the abuse of others. Sadness, then, was primarily the over-all symptom of his youth, and was a symptom couched in a traditional attitude provided by his time.

Youth can be the most exuberant, the most careless, the most self-sure, and the most unselfconsciously productive stage of life, or so it seems if we look primarily at the "once-born." This is a term which William James adopted from Cardinal Newman; he uses it to describe all those who rather painlessly fit themselves and are fitted into the ideology of their age, finding no discrepancy between its formulation of past and future and the daily tasks set by the dominant technology.

James differentiates the once-born from those "sick souls" and "divided selves" who search for a second birth, a "growth-crisis" that will "convert" them in their "habitual center of . . . personal energy." He approvingly quotes [Edwin D.] Starbuck to the effect that "conversion is in its essence a normal adolescent phenomenon" and that "theology . . . brings those means to bear which will intensify the normal tendencies" and yet also shorten "the period by bringing the person to a definite crisis." James (himself apparently the victim in his youth of a severe psychiatric crisis) does not make a systematic point of the fact that in his chapters on the Sick Soul, the Divided Self, and Conversion, his illustrations of spontaneous changes in the "habitual center of personal energy" are almost exclusively people in their late teens and early twenties—an age which can be most painfully aware of the need for decisions, most driven to choose new devotions and to discard old ones, and most susceptible to the propaganda of ideological systems which promise a new world-perspective at the price of total and cruel repudiation of an old one.

We will call what young people in their teens and early twenties look for in religion and in other dogmatic systems an *ideology*. At the most it is a militant system with uniformed members and uniform goals; at the least it is a "way of life," or what the Germans call a *Weltanschauung*, a world-view which is consonant with existing theory, available knowledge, and common sense, and yet is significantly more: an utopian outlook, a cosmic mood, or a doctrinal logic, all shared as self-evident beyond any need for demonstration. What is to be relinquished as "old" may be the individual's previous life; this usually means the perspectives intrinsic to the life-style of the parents, who are thus discarded contrary to all traditional safeguards of filial devotion. The "old" may be a part of himself, which must henceforth be subdued by some rigorous self-denial in a private life-style or through membership in a militant or military organization; or, it may be the world-view of other castes and classes, races and peoples: in this case, these people become not only expendable, but the appointed victims of the most righteous annihilation.

The need for devotion, then, is one aspect of the identity crisis which we, as psychologists, make responsible for all these tendencies and susceptibilities. The need for repudiation is another aspect. In their late teens and early twenties, even when there is no explicit ideological commitment or even interest, young people offer devotion to individual leaders and to teams, to strenuous activities, and to difficult techniques; at the same time they show a sharp and intolerant readiness to discard and disavow people (including, at times, themselves). This repudiation is often snobbish, fitful, perverted, or simply thoughtless.

These constructive and destructive aspects of youthful energy have been and are employed in making and remaking tradition in many diverse areas. Youth stands between the past and the future, both in individual life and in society; it also stands between alternate ways of life. . . . [I]deologies offer to the members of this age-group overly simplified and yet determined answers to exactly those vague inner states and those urgent questions which arise in consequence of identity conflict. Ideologies serve to channel youth's forceful earnestness and sincere asceticism, as well as its search for excitement and its eager indignation, toward that social frontier where the struggle between conservatism and radicalism is most alive. On that frontier, fanatic ideologists do their busy work and psychopathic leaders their dirty work; but there, also, true leaders create significant solidarities.

In its search for that combination of freedom and discipline, of adventure and tradition, which suits its state, youth may exploit (and be exploited by) the most varied devotions. Subjecting itself to hardship and discipline, it may seek sanctioned opportunities for spatial dispersion, follow wandering apprenticeships, heed the call of frontiers, man the outposts of new nations, fight (almost anybody's) holy wars, or test the limits of locomotive machine-power. By the same token it is ready to provide the physical power and the vociferous noise of rebellions, riots, and lynchings, often knowing little and caring less for the real issues involved. On the other hand, it is most eager to adopt rules of physical restriction and of utter intellectual concentration, be it in the study of ancient books, the contemplation of monkhood, or the striving for the new—for example, in the collective "sincerity" of modern thought reform. Even when it is led to destroy and to repudiate without any apparent cause, as in delinquent gangs, in colonies of perverts and addicts, or in the circles of petty snobs, it rarely does so without some obedience, some solidarity, some hanging on to elusive values.

Societies, knowing that young people can change rapidly even in their most intense devotions, are apt to give them a *moratorium,* a span of time after they have ceased being children, but before their deeds and works count toward a future identity. In Luther's time the monastery was, at least for some, one possible psychosocial moratorium, one possible way of postponing the decision as to what one is and is going to be. It may seem strange that as definite and, in fact, as eternal a commitment as is expressed in the monastic vow could be considered a moratorium, a means of marking time. Yet in Luther's era, to be an ex-monk was not impossible; nor was there necessarily a stigma attached to leaving a monastic order, provided only that one left in a quiet and prescribed way—as for example, Erasmus did, who was nevertheless offered a cardinalate in his old age; or that one could make cardinals laugh about themselves, as the runaway monk Rabelais was able to do. I do not mean to suggest that those who chose the monastery, any more than those who choose other forms of moratoria in different historical coordinates (as Freud did, in committing himself to laboratory physiology, or St. Augustine to Manichaeism), *know* that they are marking time before they come to their crossroad, which they often do in the late twenties, belated just because they gave their all to the temporary subject of devotion. The crisis in such a young man's life may be reached exactly when he half-realizes that he is fatally overcommitted to what he is not.

As a witness to the predicament of overcommitment, let me quote an old man who, looking back on his own youth, had to admit that no catastrophe or failure stopped him in his tracks, but rather the feeling that things were going meaninglessly well. Somehow events in his life were coming to a head, but he felt that he was being lived by them, rather than living them. A man in this predicament is apt to choose the kind of lonely and stubborn moratorium which all but smothers its own creative potential. George Bernard Shaw describes his crisis clearly and unsparingly:

> I made good in spite of myself, and found, to my dismay, that Business, instead of expelling me as the worthless imposter I was, was fastening upon me with no intention of letting me go. Behold me, therefore, in my twentieth year, with a business training, in an occupation which I detested as cordially as any sane person lets himself detest anything he cannot escape from. In March, 1876 I broke loose.

Breaking loose meant to leave family and friends, business and Ireland, and to avoid the danger of success without identity, of a success unequal to "the enormity of my unconscious ambition." He thus granted himself a prolongation of the interval between youth and adulthood. He writes: ". . . when I left my native city I left this phase behind me, and associated no more with men of my age until, after about eight years of solitude in this respect, I was drawn into the Socialist revival of the early eighties, among Englishmen *intensely serious* and *burning with indignation* at *very real* and *very fundamental evils* that affected *all the world*." (The words I have italicized in this statement are almost a list of the issues which dominate Martin's history.) In the meantime, Shaw apparently avoided opportunities, sensing that "Behind the conviction that they could lead to nothing that I wanted, lay the unspoken fear that they might lead to something I did not want." We have to grant some young people, then, the paradoxical fear of a negative success, a success which would commit them in a direction where, they feel, they will not "grow together."

Potentially creative men like Shaw build the personal fundament of their work during a self-decreed moratorium, during which they often starve themselves, socially, erotically, and, last but not least, nutritionally, in order to let the grosser weeds die out, and make way for the growth of their inner garden. Often, when the weeds are dead, so is the garden. At the decisive moment, however, some make contact with a nutriment specific for their gifts. For Shaw, of course, this gift was literature. As he dreamt of a number of professional choices, "of literature I had no dreams at all, any more than a duck has of swimming."

He did not dream of it, but he did it, and with a degree of ritualization close to what clinicians call an "obsessive compensation." This often balances a temporary lack of inner direction with an almost fanatic concentration on activities which maintain whatever work habits the individual may have preserved.

> I bought supplies of white paper, demy size, by sixpence-worths at a time; folded it in quarto; and condemned myself to fill five pages of it a day, rain or shine, dull or inspired. I had so much of the schoolboy and the clerk still in me that if my five pages ended in the middle of a sentence I did not finish it until the next day. On the other hand, if I missed a day, I made up for it by doing a double task on the morrow. On this plan I produced five novels in five years. It was my professional apprenticeship. . . .

We may add that these five novels were not published for over fifty years, at which time Shaw, in a special introduction, tried to dissuade the potential buyer from reading them, while recommending to his attention their biographical importance. To such an extent was Shaw aware of their true function and meaning; although his early work habits were almost pathological in their compulsive addictiveness, they were autotherapeutic in their perseverance: "I have risen by sheer gravitation, too industrious by acquired habit to stop working (I work as my father drank)." There is a world of anguish, conflict, and victory in this small parenthesis; for to succeed, Shaw had to inwardly defeat an already outwardly defeated father, some of whose peculiarities (for example, a strange sense of humor) contributed to the son's unique greatness, and yet also to that specific failure that is in each greatness. Shaw's autobiographical remarks do not leave any doubt about the true abyss which he, one of the shyest of religious men, faced in his youth before he had learned to cover his sensitivities by appearing on the stage of history as the great cynic ("in this I succeeded only too well"), while using the theatre to speak out of the mouth of the Maid of Orleans.

. . . Freud and Darwin are among the great men who came upon their most decisive contribution only after a change of direction and not without neurotic involvement at the time of the breakthrough to their specific creativity. Darwin failed in medicine, and had, as if accidentally, embarked on a trip which, in fact, he almost missed because of what seem to have been psychosomatic symptoms. Once aboard the *Beagle,* however, he found not only boundless physical vigor, but also a keen eye for unexplored details in nature, and a creative discernment leading straight to revolutionary insights: the law of natural selection began to haunt him. He was twenty-seven years old when he came home; he soon became an undiagnosed and lifelong invalid, able only after years of concentrated study to organize his data into a pattern which convincingly supported his ideas. Freud, too, was already thirty when, as if driven to do so by mere circumstance, he became a practicing neurologist and made psychiatry his laboratory. He had received his medical degree belatedly, having decided to become a medical scientist rather than a doctor at the age of seventeen. His moratorium, which gave him a basic schooling in method while it delayed the development of his specific gift and his revolutionary creativity, was spent in (then physicalistic) physiology. And when he at last did embark on his stupendous lifework, he was almost delayed further by neurotic suffering. However, a creative man has no choice. He may come across his supreme task almost accidentally. But once the issue is joined, his task proves to be at the same time intimately related to his most personal conflicts, to his superior selective perception, and to the stubbornness of his one-way will: he must court sickness, failure, or insanity, in order to test the alternative whether the established world will crush him, or whether he will disestablish a sector of this world's outworn fundaments and make a place for a new one.

Darwin dealt with man's biological origins. His achievement, and his sin, was a theory that made man part of nature. To accomplish this, and only for this, he was able to put his neurosis aside. Freud, however, had to "appoint his own neurosis that angel who was to be wrestled with and not to be let go, until he would bless the observer." Freud's wrestling with the angel was his working through of his own father complex which at first had led him astray in his search for the origins of the neuroses in childhood. Once he understood his own relationship to his father, he could establish the existence of the universal father image in man, break through to the mother image as well, and finally arrive at the Oedipus complex, the formulation of which made him one of the most controversial figures in the history of ideas. In *The Interpretation of Dreams,* Freud gave psychoanalysis its orientation as the study of unconscious motivation in the normal as well as the pathological, in society as well as the individual. At the same time he freed his own creativity by self-analysis, and was able to combine strict observation with disciplined intuition and literary craftsmanship.

This general discussion of the qualities of that critical area between neurosis and creativity will introduce the state of mind which engulfed Martin at the time of the fit in the choir. Even the possibly legendary aspects of this fit reflect an unconscious understanding on the part of the legend-makers, here Martin's monastic brothers, as to what was going on inside him. . . . [A] subsequent personality change . . . made it possible for the young man who in the choir was literally felled by the power of the need to negate to stand before his emperor and before the Pope's emissary at the Diet of Worms twelve years later and affirm human integrity in new terms: "My conscience is bound by God's words. Retract anything whatsoever I neither can nor will. For to act against one's conscience is neither safe nor honorable."

God's words: he had, by then, become God's "spokesman," preacher, teacher, orator, and pamphleteer. This had become the working part of his identity. The eventual liberation of Luther's voice made him creative. The one matter on which professor and priest, psychiatrist and sociologist, agree is Luther's immense gift for language: his receptivity for the written word; his memory for the significant phrase; and his range of verbal expression (lyrical, biblical, satirical, and vulgar) which in English is paralleled only by Shakespeare.

The development of this gift is implicit in the dramatic outcry in the choir of Erfurt: for was it not a "dumb" spirit which beset the patient before Jesus? And was it not muteness, also, which the monk had to deny by thus roaring "like an ox"? The theme of the Voice and of the Word, then, is intertwined with the theme of Luther's identity and with his influence on the ideology of his time. . . . [Y]oung Martin, at the end of a somber and harsh childhood, was precipitated into a severe identity crisis for which he sought delay and cure in the silence of the monastery; . . . being silent, he became "possessed"; . . . being possessed, he gradually learned to speak a new language, *his* language; . . . being able to speak, he not only talked himself out of the monastery, and much of his country out of the Roman Church, but also formulated for himself and for all of mankind a new kind of ethical and psychological awareness: and . . . at the end, this awareness, too, was marred by a return of the demons, whoever they may have been.

The historian has other tools with which to explore the origins of customs, beliefs, and institutions, of course. He will gladly borrow from sociology, anthropology, demography, linguistics, or any other source of knowledge. He knows the frustration of attempting to encompass all things, for no one can, and anyone who attempts to do so will never be able to conjure up the courage to add his own mite, on paper, to the sum of knowledge. But the historian is less guilty than most scholars of contemplating his navel, of being bedazzled by his own splendid methodology, in the way Freud so clearly was. Recently a graduate student in sociology defended to me a project I regarded as worthless—since he proposed to prove something historians had proved long ago—on the ground that while historians had to justify their existence by producing new data, sociologists justified theirs by testing their methodologies. This is, one hopes, not the whole of the truth, but it is a little part of it, for many social scientists seem to enjoy disputatious inquiries into their own methodologies without ever getting around to the delicate task of applying those methods to anything that ten sane men would regard as important. They enjoy packing their bags for trips they have no intention of taking, as one of their own number has remarked, and while knowledge of how to pack bags quickly is incontrovertibly useful in this jet age, knowledge of other aspects of the journey would seem of greater value. The historian, then, must borrow with extreme care and beware of "models" and "structures."

While I should have liked to demonstrate how other disciplines can work in alliance with history, space prevents my doing so. Two recent developments within the discipline, reinforced from without but nonetheless nicely housebroken to the historian's needs, must be mentioned, however. These are an increased use of oral tradition and oral history in reconstructing the past, and a growing willingness to argue by analogy.

"Oral source" means two quite different things which have in common only that the original source was not written down. As initially used, oral history arose among anthropologists, among those who pursued savage tribes into faraway places with strange-sounding names, to return with minute accounts of puberty rites in New Guinea and ritualist slaughter in Africa. Much of the pre-European history of Africa, for example, must come from oral traditions. Historians are learning Swahili, Yoruba, or Tutsi in order to interrogate natives and to draw from them oral accounts of past events, some buried many generations into that past and transmitted now as mythology and genealogy. Where historians have been able to verify such oral transmissions, as in several instances with the Maori of New Zealand, they have found them remarkably accurate. Once deciding to treat oral tradition as having a basis in fact, historians and anthropologists have slowly devised means for checking and double-checking the veracity of such history.

The second meaning given to oral sources applies to the recorded reminiscences of living figures. Begun by Columbia University's Oral History project some years ago, and now spreading throughout American universities and colleges, such methods will make available—usually upon the death of the person preparing the tape or recording—

lengthy and unedited statements of what the compiler wished to remember. Such reminiscences will have to be treated with the same caution as all memoirs, for memory falters, and personal animus, or the desire to give oneself an enlarged rôle in a historic event, will continue as before. A skillful interviewer often may draw from a subject much that he did not intend to say and may, by returning time and again to a central point, obtain needed clarification. There is, as one might expect, a substantial body of theoretical literature on how to conduct and to evaluate interviews. Such studies, combined with the growing awareness of the significance of kinesics and proximics, may give future historians many new windows onto the past.

An older window exists because of a growing willingness among historians to argue by analogy. In truth, historians always have done so, for an analogy is but another form of the leap of faith which historical analysis always demands of one. But the growth in comparative history has forced analogies upon historians who would have scorned them before. This is true even though America's most famous historian enveloped the whole of American historiography in a sweeping analogy three-quarters of a century ago.

The imaginations of the historians of the whole country were captured in 1893 by a young professor at the University of Wisconsin, Frederick Jackson Turner. After completing his doctorate at Johns Hopkins University, Turner—who had lived on what he regarded as a last vestige of the old Wisconsin fur trade frontier—rebelled against the "germ theory" approach to American institutions which he had been taught. At Johns Hopkins his professors had stressed how American culture had developed from European roots, arguing that democracy as we know it was an outgrowth from the forests of Germany and Britain. Turner felt that American culture was so different from European as to be virtually a new civilization, and he wished to find some single key to the problem of this evolution which had come to differ so much in degree as to have reached a difference in kind as well. Addressing the American Historical Association in Chicago in 1893, Turner proposed what across the years became known as the Turner thesis on "The Significance of the Frontier in American History."

Essentially Turner argued that environment so changes inherited cultural traits as to make the differences more important than the similarities. The Europeans acquired new habits of mind when they settled upon North America's Eastern seaboard, for they had to adjust to a new and raw environment. As each successive wave of settlers moved onto frontier lands, repeating the cycle of beginning again, they dropped certain cultural baggage suitable only to earlier conditions and took up new baggage. With each step Westward, more of the old was put down and more of the new taken up, so that democracy—in that Americans turned their backs upon feudal privileges, upon class warfare, and upon harsh exploitation of the worker by the employer—emerged from this movement across the land. This emergence was made possible, however, only because land was free; it was not encumbered by old titles, old customs, and old charges. A man could begin life anew on the frontier, and if he did not do so, the thought that he might turn Westward nonetheless invigorated him even as he remained bound to the East. The process was a dialectical one, Hegelian in concept, with the old cultural traits as the thesis, the new environment as the antithesis, and American democracy as the synthesis.

Turner's ideas were not quite so simple as this, of course, although some of his disciples came to make them so. He recognized that he was speaking in metaphor, and at least one of his students regards Turner more as a poet of the West than a historian. But in the last decade of the century American historians were hungry for something that would set their country apart from others, that would explain its uniqueness, as they saw it. The thesis was adaptable, it was open to many exciting research possibilities, and it was even patriotic. Some did not see the pessimism that lay within it as well, for Turner argued that the frontier had closed as of the last census report, that of 1890, and implied that whatever it had been that had worked to make America different no longer would be operative without artificial stimulus. The thesis was yet another example of that peculiar ambivalence in the historian which leads most, in this country at least, to be liberal in their politics but conservative in their history and in their private lives.

The frontier thesis was subjected to much heavy fire, but Turner's imagination had freed historians to think more and more along analogous lines. Some scholars demonstrated that Turner simply did not have his facts right in many instances and that he was statistically naïve. Others argued that true democracy came out of the city, out of contact with other people, rather than out of the forest—that it arose from asphalt, not from humus. Yet others showed that Turner's generalizations were too broad; perhaps he was correct for Indiana and Illinois, for example, but he was demonstrably incorrect for the Dakotas or for New Mexico, Utah, or California. The point at issue here is not whether Turner's thesis was correct or not, but rather that the thesis gave inspiration to hundreds of historians, and even as some chipped away at its edges, others found continuing value in its symbolic and metaphorical content.

The mysterious hold that Turner's Chicago speech has on historians has been well illustrated by two of the leading exponents of argument by analogy, Stanley Elkins and Eric L. McKitrick. These two men, representative of the newer breed of scholars, trained and well read not only in the traditional literature of their fields but in many supportive disciplines as well, had the imagination to see that Turner was right in many of his conclusions even while wrong in his argument. Writing in 1954, they asked why it was that, despite the evidence that the American forest did not create democracy, all observers would admit that "the development of political democracy as a habit" in

America was real. Drawing upon some of the findings of a sociologist, Robert K. Merton, they examined two communities, botn largely public housing projects and administered by the Federal Public Housing Authority, which were designated as "Craftown" and "Hilltown." In the first there had been a pervasive "time of troubles" when, faced with no municipal services, no schools, no churches, no grocery stores, a wave of vandalism, and an epidemic of poliomyelitis, the townspeople were driven to forming associations to do the work of government—that is, they behaved precisely as Turner had argued that frontiersmen had done, creating their own institutions in advance of the arrival of organized society, and thus making those institutions reflective of their will, their needs, and their work. Hilltown, on the other hand, experienced no "time of troubles" which bit deep into the community, and there was no widespread public participation in community affairs; " 'Democracy,' in short, was unnecessary there," they concluded.

Elkins and McKitrick thus forced historians to look again at the fast-receding applicability of Turner's thesis. They did so by drawing upon the research of sociologists, by seeing that Turner had been thinking in poetic rather than factual terms when he spoke, and by being willing to argue from a current situation back to one in the past, showing parallels between them. Elkins then went on, in 1959, to write the single best example of arguing by analogy yet seen in American historiography; this was his *Slavery: A Problem in American Institutional and Intellectual Life* (Chicago).

This book begins with some of the work done by social psychologists on the effects upon Jews in Nazi Germany's concentration camps of prolonged confinement, of brutalization, of being deprived of any capacity for making decisions because there were no decisions to be made. Elkins then applied this research to the conditions of pre–Civil War Negro slavery in the United States, to show how the conclusions of Eugen Kogon and Bruno Bettelheim, for example—conclusions written for a twentieth-century problem, Nazi concentration camps—might explain the development of the Sambo stereotype among plantation Negroes. The conclusion of Elkins' book was open to some highly important interpretations: that Southerners were wrong in thinking the Negro inherently inferior, for those traits he showed which were taken to prove his inferiority were culturally induced by a system that deprived him of any reason to exercise initiative; but that Northern liberal historians who argued that the black man was simply a white man with a black skin were also wrong, for the environment had, in fact, induced all the external behavior characteristics of infantilism. In short, while not inherently so, perhaps the Negro nonetheless was a very different person because of very different experiences. Some sociologists, and some Negroes, had argued this for many years, and the thesis was not entirely new. It was new to historians, however, and the method was different, since it involved not one but two leaps of faith—one to accept the legitimacy of the conclusions of such psychologists as Bettelheim and Kogon about the mechanism of adjustment to absolute power necessary to survival in a concentration camp, and a second leap to connect those conclusions to the slave experience. The leaps were too great for some scholars while others used them to reinforce the rapidly-growing field of comparative studies and to break down yet further the barriers that separated disciplines. The names of Elkins and McKitrick—the latter having gone on to write an equally significant, if less immediately controversial, study which also argued from analogy, on *Andrew Johnson and Reconstruction* (Chicago, 1960)—are thus closely associated with an important breakthrough in theoretical, rather than textual, criticism.

As the historian reaches out for yet other allies—as some, identifying themselves with the New Left, say that they must write scenarios of the past, and as others turn from the romance of objects to the romance of beauty, in sound as well as in visual images—the craft will change.

The historian will continue to set himself the task of "telling it like it is," but the methods of telling, and the conception of the truth of what it is like to have been a slave, or to be black, or to be a king, or to be hunchbacked, will change as our knowledge of economics, of race, of psychology, or of medicine grows. There will always be room for a hundred approaches to history, each valuable, one perhaps more fashionable than another under the pressures of the moment. The historian may still be found in the moment of his joy with discoveries that only he, *now, right here,* can find or explain.

For additional reading: On oral traditions, see Daniel F. McCall's *Africa in Time Perspective: A Discussion of Historical Reconstruction from Unwritten Sources* (Oxford, 1964). For a good essay demonstrating what one may do with oral history, read Francis W. Schruben, "An Even Stranger Death of President Harding," in the *Quarterly* of the Historical Society of Southern California, XLVIII (March, 1966), 57–84. Elkins and McKitrick's study of Turner appeared in two parts; the first, "A Meaning for Turner's Frontier; Part I: Democracy in the Old Northwest," in the *Political Science Quarterly,* LXIX (September, 1954), 321–53, is particularly good. Authors of detective fiction who have used the device of analogy to plot advantage include Raymond Postgate, William Hardy, Anthony Gilbert, and Ian Stewart.

PART VI

VERDICTS

23. The Strange Nature of Pure Joy:

The Historian's Pleasure Principle

SO FAR, HISTORIANS WHO HAVE CROSSED OVER TO BORrow from other disciplines have done better work than have those who have traveled the other way. An example of one such scholar is William B. Willcox, now Professor of History at the Yale University. Not long ago Willcox published a massive study of Sir Henry Clinton, the British General who was Commander in Chief of the Army during the American Revolution. The book is full of stimulating and suggestive observations about Clinton's penchant for failure, and the following essay tells us something of how the historian drew upon his reading of psychology to help him understand his subject better.

There is a dividend in this essay which deserves comment here. By now the reader will be aware that the historian obtains a peculiar pleasure from discovering unanswerable questions. Most people prefer answers; the historian agrees with Gertrude Stein, who is supposed to have said, on her deathbed, not "What is the answer?" but "What are the questions?" The historian is doubly peculiar in that he positively welcomes an increase in the work that he must do; rather than groaning over the discovery that there is yet another collection of newly unearthed manuscripts to be examined (or newly minted forgeries to be refuted), he takes pleasure in seeing the mountain of material grow before his eyes. Ph.D., some wits say, means "Piled higher and Deeper," and while the reference in its original form was more excremental than incremental, not too many of us would be inclined to disagree. There is a very real pleasure in knowing that one will never *know,* that one will never reach the other end of the sea, because it is endless. The vistas of the receding horizons bring more pleasure than those of the approaching journey's end, and here the historian, if he agrees with this sentiment, is a traveler in league with Robert Louis Stevenson, who in *Travels with a Donkey* said, quite correctly, that to travel is the thing; arriving is anticlimax. Getting there *is* half the fun, and more.

Professor Willcox's essay also affords an opportunity for a stylistic observation of some importance. Historians write for an audience. Sometimes the audience is very small indeed, a body of like-minded specialists who wish to solve the Case of the Unknown Date, or when Dionysius the Pseudo-Areopagite wrote. Sometimes the audience is more general, although still professional; sometimes it is thought to be lay, in that it consists of intelligent and inquiring minds not necessarily trained to think in historical patterns or sequences. On occasion the audience may be a governmental department or a burst of deans. Often it will consist of a broad public, not even necessarily college-educated or college-bound, for many professional historians also contribute to the making of grade and high-school texts, since theirs is a discipline that has little meaning unless its findings are communicated. For this reason, again, "publish or perish" may more legitimately be applied to a historian than, as an example, to a specialist in Malayo-Polynesian. Through style, the historian will show his conception of his audience, and will incidentally tell much about himself, for writing is a natural extension of one's personality; at the moment when the author lies, in T. S. Eliot's phrase, "etherized upon a table"—naked to one's reviewers—that personality may show very tenderly indeed.

Willcox's essay was first written for the University of Michigan's Office of Research Administration, to help show, largely to alumni, what it is that historians do. Several other essays in this volume were prepared, as we have noted, as speeches first, and their diction, rhythm, and patterns of presenting evidence therefore differ; one communicates the spoken word in ways which subtly alter the unheard inflections of the word that is to be read only. Does an author employ an Attic fall at the end of his essay? Then he probably read it first, and perhaps to an undergraduate audience. Does he weave in asides and repetitive phrases? Then again an audience of the ear rather than of the eye seems indicated. And since the method of presentation does differ, however slightly, from audience to audience, a reader is wise to ask himself, For whom was this MS. left in its bottle?

♦ ♦ ♦

Research in history, as in other fields, is hard work. It has its high moments, as teaching does, but exacts a much heavier price in drudgery and monotony. Why, then, are so many university teachers of history also researchers? Although they have many motives, the one that seems to me the strongest is curiosity. If the historian were asked why he wants to tackle a particular research problem, he might well answer in the often quoted words of a British mountaineer, when asked a generation ago why he wanted to tackle Everest: "Because it's there." The problem is there, and its mere existence is a challenge. The historian, like the mountaineer, must of course decide which of many challenges will be worth his time and effort; and here he has little information to guide him. His

---

FROM William B. Willcox, "The Psychiatrist, the Historian, and General Clinton: The Excitement of Historical Research," *Michigan Quarterly Review,* VI (Spring, 1967), 123–30.

For additional reading: Geoffrey Elton, *Essays on History* (London, 1967), are shrewd and entertaining. C. M. Woodhouse, whose essay on the Jameson Raid we have read, makes good use of modern psychology in his biography of *Rhodes* (London, 1963), written in collaboration with John Gibson Lockhart. Nicholas Blake, Mabel Seeley, and Ngaio Marsh are all pertinent here. See, in particular, Miss Marsh's *A Clutch of Constables.*

decision, for all the hard thought that goes into it, rests essentially on hunch. He cannot predict the size of his problem, or the extent to which it will be soluble, or the value of solving it. But uncertainty is the spice of research. Exploration means reaching into the unknown, and the explorer who knows in advance what he will find is not an explorer.

An aspect of the past may appear from a distance picayune, and prove on investigation to be quite the contrary. Take for example the way in which work horses were harnessed in Merovingian times, a subject that scarcely appears calculated to fire the imagination. But appearance is deceptive. From earliest times until the Dark Ages, research disclosed, the power of the horse to pull a wagon or plough had been limited by his harness, which pressed upon his windpipe; the harder he pulled, the smaller his air supply and the less his strength. In the Merovingian period some unknown genius designed a new kind of harness that put the strain on the horse's shoulders; the animal was then free to breathe, and his efficiency went up. A mere rearrangement of leather straps augmented the basic source of power on the land, increased agricultural productivity, and so contributed to the slow beginnings of medieval civilization.

This example suggests a number of points about the nature of research. One, already mentioned, is that the importance of a problem cannot be predicted in advance. A second is that the problem is almost never tidily solved: some questions, such as the identity of the man who designed the new harness, remain unanswered for lack of evidence. A third is that the subject under investigation has no inherent limits, and must be limited arbitrarily. The investigator in this case establishes that increased horsepower was a factor in raising agricultural yield; his next logical step is to consider what other factors were at work, how they were interrelated, and for how long they operated—in other words to explore the whole economic history of the Dark and Middle Ages. This is too large a field for intensive research. Somewhere a line must be drawn, but where?

The line does not draw itself, for history is all of a piece. Studying a particular fragment of it out of context falsifies the nature of the fragment, and studying the entire context is impossible.

Between the two extremes the researcher must find his own mean, by setting such limits as his interests and sense of feasibility suggest; but these limits are his own. They are not determined by any logic inherent in his problem, and they are likely to change as his investigation progresses and grows toward an end that he may never have anticipated. Take for illustration my own experience. It is with a narrow area of history, but one that I believe contains pitfalls and surprises that are not essentially different from those in many other areas.

The Clements Library of the University of Michigan has a large collection of manuscripts relating to the British side of the War of Independence. When I came to the University years ago, I knew next to nothing about the war; but the wealth of the Clements material and the fact that no one else had explored it were a challenge. From that mass of documents a subject or subjects for research would surely emerge. What form the research would eventually take was unimportant; all that mattered was to begin. I was like an archeologist who confronts a site, knowing approximately when it was inhabited but nothing more, and who cannot tell whether he will find disconnected fragments or the integrated complex of a city.

The more I learned about the British military effort in America, the subject with which most of the manuscripts deal, the more insistently one question obtruded itself: how did Britain manage to lose the war? She began it with many advantages—uncontested sea power, troops that were better than the American and generals that were at least no worse, a government that for all its muddleheadedness knew more than the Continental Congress did about how to conduct a war. Even French intervention in 1778 was not conclusive, and by the summer of 1781 the issue was still apparently hanging in the balance. Then the British suddenly blundered through to defeat at Yorktown, a failure that seemed to be anything but predetermined. What factors, then, brought it about?

The question in its entirety was too large, too ramified, for manuscript research. Such diverse factors were involved as American and French planning, the political weakness of Lord North's administration, the enormous logistic difficulties that confronted the bureaucrats of Whitehall; and these factors, along with many others of equal importance, I could not explore on my own. I had to depend on the often meager findings of those who had already explored them, and limit my search for original material to that which bore on the British war effort in America itself. This was both an arbitrary and a necessary limitation.

Even when the field was so narrowly circumscribed, however, it proved to be too broad for productive research. Such matters as the organization of the British army and navy, the details of tactics and logistics, and the administrative routine that engrossed the attention of headquarters should all have been grist for my mill. I knew nothing about them, however, and digging out the requisite information would have meant years of tedious work. I consequently restricted myself still further, to those factors that clearly affected the strategic planning of the British high command. I was no longer asking why Britain lost the war, but why her principal officers in America contributed as much to losing it as they patently did. Even though a definitive answer was impossible, the question was small enough to be explored. Such a partial study of the losers' side of the war could not be expected to produce dramatic results. It might, however, at least modify accepted views of the conflict as a whole.

Historical research rarely does more. In most cases it leaves the accepted views intact, but suggests their inadequacy by introducing alongside them some ingredient that they do not cover. Any subsequent interpretation of the events in question, if it is to include this new ingredient, must be a more complex synthesis than its predecessors, and hence may be expected to approximate more nearly the infinite complexity of the events themselves. The aim of historical research is not to upset the scholarly applecart, in short, but to go on adding to the number of apples in it, until someone is forced to design a bigger cart.

My own research soon produced a kind of apple that I had not anticipated. British strategic planning in America turned out to be not a single problem but two distinct problems, which had for their focus the two successive commanders in chief of the army, Sir William Howe (1775–78) and Sir Henry Clinton (1778–82). The two men were poles apart, but each in his way was an enigma; and the strategy of each was inseparable from his personality. To pursue my quest I had to become in some degree a biographer, and I had to decide which general to concentrate upon. The choice was obvious. Howe served for four years and then disappeared from the scene in 1778, and few of his papers have been preserved. Clinton served for seven years, as second in command under Howe and then as commander in chief, and few of his papers have been lost; they fill almost three hundred volumes in the Clements Library. A study of Sir Henry would cover the whole British side of the war, and could be amply documented.

Another consideration strengthened the case for focusing on Clinton. I had already discovered that one of Britain's serious difficulties in America was the feuding that went on between her senior officers, and that as an instigator of feuds Clinton towered head and shoulders over all his fellows. The record of his altercations is fantastic, and their effect on the war was incalculable. When he was commander in chief, to take the major example, he was progressively on worse and worse terms with his opposite number in the navy and with his own second in command, Lord Cornwallis, until by the summer of 1781 these two quarrels had paralyzed cooperation between the two services and disrupted the army command. Sir Henry was not solely to blame, for the officers with whom he tangled were no models of tact. But they did get on reasonably well with most other men most of the time, whereas he kept their animosity at fever pitch for months and even years on end. By doing so he helped to ruin his own career and lose the war for Britain.

Clinton thus became the focus of my inquiry. He offered an approach, in biographical and manageable terms, to the otherwise unwieldy problem of why the British failed. A biography, furthermore, might do more than merely exhume an obscure general: it could be a case study of personality as a causal factor in history. For Sir Henry was in himself a cause of Britain's defeat—not the sole or even the major cause, but one that was significant, that had not been seriously studied before, and for which the evidence was voluminous. It is obvious that great men, when they have power in moments of crisis, help to mold events. It is perhaps less obvious that in the same circumstances little men do the same, for the very reason that they are little: they fail to meet the demands that the crisis makes upon them, and their failure contributes to the outcome. Louis XVI's shortcomings, for example, affected the course of the French Revolution. Clinton's shortcomings affected the course of the American, in less important but equally real ways; and I set myself to define and evaluate those ways as best I could.

Although my field of inquiry was established and its limits apparently set, I soon discovered that research can develop as unpredictably as if it had a life of its own. Clinton's role in the war could not be defined, much less evaluated, without a clear understanding of why he behaved as he did; and some significant aspects of his behavior proved to be beyond my comprehension. His inveterate feuding, which time after time defeated his own best interests as well as those of the service, was only one case in point. Another was his ambivalence about sticking to his post: for more than four years he tried unsuccessfully to resign; and then, when he had permission and good reason to quit, he clung to the command as if his life depended on it—and at the same time refused to exert the authority that it gave him. He was the rationalist *par excellence* in some areas, such as military planning; in others he behaved with an irrationality that I could not understand.

These contrasting sides of his character came out in his handling of evidence. He left behind him lengthy memoirs of his campaigns, the only general on either side who did. In most of what he wrote he adhered scrupulously to the facts, insofar as they can be established from other sources; but at rare moments he took off into fantasy. The most striking example has to do with the British disaster at Yorktown. In his account of that campaign, written not long afterward and intended for publication, Sir Henry asserted that the government had ordered him not to interfere with Lord Cornwallis, but to support the Earl and his army in Virginia. To prove this assertion Clinton cited the specific words of the command that he said he had received from the King's Minister in Whitehall. Here was what looked like established fact, and for years historians accepted it as such.

Sir Henry's behavior during the actual campaign, however, suggested that he had received no such order. Until the eve of Yorktown he tried to interfere in Virginia, by withdrawing troops from there to New York; and neither his words nor his actions indicated that he was flouting a royal command. Where, furthermore, was the original command to be found? It was not in any letter from the Minister that Clinton kept among his papers (and this letter, of all others, he might have been expected to keep), or in the Minister's copies of his outgoing dispatches. This negative discovery posed a nice question: when is a fact in history not a fact? The Minister *may* have issued the order, which *may* be in a letter that is not extant or has not yet come to light; no amount of historical research can prove that a document never existed, and that a quotation from that document is false. But in this case the probability is overwhelming that Clinton, looking back on the campaign, manufactured out of whole cloth a command from his King.

Sir Henry, if so, was not merely misremembering the past, as other men have done, in a way that cleared him of blame for what had happened; he was introducing into the record a specific and cardinal charge against the government. He was also planning to publish the charge at a time when those whom he accused were still alive to refute him. If the accusation was false, in other words, he was planning to gamble his reputation on a foolishly palpable lie. Everything else that I knew of the man convinced me that he was neither a gambler nor a fool nor a liar. The only tenable explanation, therefore, was that he believed what he said—and what all the evidence indicated was untrue. Here was an impasse: either I was deceived in thinking that Sir Henry had fabricated his claim, or in some way that defied analysis he had deceived himself into thinking that his fabrication was fact.

The second alternative seemed much the more likely. I had already observed in Clinton a habit of self-deception, and I assumed that this episode was an extreme example of it. He was patently unaware that his quarrels, and his refusal to give up or exert the authority of his position, defeated his own best interests; he asserted instead that he had sound reason for what I was convinced was unreasonable conduct, just as he believed that he had received what I was convinced was a nonexistent royal command. His conscious self seemed to have put out a smoke screen of rationalization, behind which he acted from motives so far below consciousness that he could not even discern them, let alone understand them.

I could dimly discern, but was no more able to understand than he had been, for the historian is trained to hunt for motivation within the broad limits of the rational. He assumes that men acted from what by his as well as their lights was rational cause, and that if he has sufficient information he can formulate a highly probable conjecture about what the cause was. His psychological insight amounts to the application of common sense, and he is helpless when the men with whom he is dealing did not behave sensibly. He is not equipped to make even a conjecture about motives that were irrational and hence unconscious. If he does conjecture, with nothing to go on, he is indulging in mere guesswork. If instead he labels behavior as odd or aberrant and leaves it at that, he is confessing failure, because the whole purpose of this kind of research is to uncover the wellsprings of conduct.

The historical discipline as applied to biography has inherent limitations, which I was discovering by bumping into them. Just when my inquiry was far enough advanced to be exciting, it was unexpectedly demanding analytic tools that I could not provide. To continue the quest I had to have help, and I had the great good fortune to get it from Professor Frederick Wyatt, chief of the Psychological Clinic of the University of Michigan, a colleague with psychoanalytic training and a humanist's interest in history. We collaborated for a number of years on the puzzle of Clinton's behavior, in an effort to discover whether teamwork between our two disciplines could produce a fuller understanding of an historical figure than either discipline could produce alone.

We hoped to arrive at a theory of Clinton's personality that was plausible by our different canons, and broad enough to include the irrational as well as rational aspects of his conduct. Our evidence would not, we knew, permit us to build a theory that was not merely plausible but demonstrable; evidence in history, as in psychotherapy, is almost never so obliging. The most we could expect was to resolve the apparent contradictions in the evidence we had, by bringing all of it together into a single, consistent pattern of behavior. This pattern would be our theory, and it would "solve" the problem in the sense that it would establish a relationship between what had seemed to be disparate sides of Sir Henry's character.

Our methodological difficulties were considerable, and for me they were educational. My colleague, like any psychotherapist, wanted to probe into Clinton's childhood, a subject about which the manuscripts were almost silent. The little that they did tell us, Wyatt insisted, should be compared with the norms of child-rearing in aristocratic families of the time; what were those norms? Again I did not know, or know where to find out; I was learning how fragmentary is a specialist's information about his period. We were forced to abandon this line of inquiry and try another—to examine the adult Clinton, about whom we had abundant information, in search of grounds for inference about Clinton the child.

Here we made progress. Sir Henry as a middle-aged general manifested—in his quarreling, his refusal to resign, his illusion that the government had been to blame for Yorktown—a form of behavior that is familiar to the modern clinical psychologist. It was the behavior now recognized as typical of the man who has never outgrown his childhood conflict with his parents, particularly with his father. The unresolved conflict endures: the child as adult longs to exercise paternal authority himself, and at the same time dreads to exercise it because he is trespassing on his father's preserve. Sir Henry showed the symptoms of this conflict so clearly and fully that we did not need to know the childhood roots of the conflict itself; we could assume their existence. What mattered to us was not the cause but the result—the consistency with which the adult Clinton continued to act out his difficulties with parents who by then had long been dead. To certain situations he responded, not sensibly, but with an almost predictable regularity; and his way of responding indicated an ambivalence that he could neither recognize nor control.

This consistency provided us with a pattern, or theory, that satisfied the requirements with which we had begun. How it satisfied them cannot be explained in brief compass, but we found that virtually all the irrational aspects of Sir Henry's behavior could be related to his basic internal struggle about exercising authority. Elements in his character that had hitherto seemed to me irreconcilable, because some were highly effective and others were self-defeating, fitted together as parts of a whole; and a man who had looked like a bundle of anomalies became a coherent person. We do not yet claim to have resolved every contradiction, to know Sir

Henry through and through; such a claim would be ridiculous. But we do believe that he has become intelligible enough to us to permit an evaluation of the role he played.

This has been a long illustration, and what does it illustrate? In the first place, that historical research is fluid, especially in its early stages. The inquirer begins with unknown material and no idea of what will come out of it. Even when some salient questions emerge to provide him a focus, it is not yet precise; considerations of time and his own interests, as much as of the material itself, determine how his problem develops. After it seems to have taken final shape (as when I decided on a biographical study of Clinton), new and unexpected questions can change the shape again. This evolutionary process may not come to an end of itself; and in that case the researcher, unless he wants to spend his life on one subject, must choose the moment for calling a halt.

My experience illustrates, in the second place, the problem of selecting evidence. On the one hand no project, however ambitiously designed, can embrace all the available and relevant data; arbitrary limits must be set, and even within them much relevant material receives only cursory treatment. On the other hand, once these limits are demarcated, no amount of digging will unearth all the data that the researcher wants; some areas about which he is curious, such as Clinton's childhood, remain obscure and conjectural. Research involves a series of choices, to emphasize this and neglect that, to go on digging or to stop; and few of the choices are logically satisfying. The specialist is not, as the old cliché would have it, one who learns more and more about less and less. He is one who is able to work out his own criteria for finishing a particular job, and to make his choices accordingly.

I have tried to illustrate, in the third place, the elusive quality of evidence. Historical "facts" are not facts in the sense that they can be empirically verified; they are merely the testimony of one or more observers about what happened. All testimony is suspect, because it depends upon whether the person giving it was in a position to know, whether he was calm or intelligent or objective enough to report accurately, and so on. Some "facts" such as dates—when the Declaration of Independence was signed, or when the firing stopped at Yorktown—can be established beyond reasonable doubt because many observers agree. But these are the historian's rudimentary data, which are about as important to him as the multiplication table is to a mathematician. . . .

When the historian moves from considering people's actions to considering their motives for acting, he must become even more tentative. The reason lies not only in the nature of his evidence but also in human nature; for about motivation, of the living as much as of the dead, opinions always differ. Listen to a group of reporters today discussing what impels President Johnson or General de Gaulle to a given line of action, and you will hear as many interpretations as there are interpreters; or try to explain precisely why a friend reached an important decision, and see how many of his other friends will agree with you. When our contemporaries' reasons for acting as they do are controversial, sometimes even mysterious, to those about them, it would be surprising if the motives of historical figures were easier to penetrate.

The best evidence about the nature of motivation in a man long dead is what was said about him at the time. Most of what was said was not written down, and much of what was written down has not survived; mere chance selects for the historian a small fraction of the original evidence, and with this fraction he must work. It consists in comments, which are sure to be hard to interpret, on the behavior of the man in question. Comments that he made on himself are valuable, but have a built-in bias. Contemporaries' comments are also biased, and in conflicting ways: no two observers, in the past as in the present, who look at the same person see the same person. Clinton, for instance, changes slightly when he is viewed through the eyes of each of his few friends and admirers, and greatly when viewed through those of his numerous enemies; the motives that these men perceived in him run the gamut from whole-souled concentration on winning the war to pride, vanity, and a love for the fleshpots of power. The historian must move cautiously through testimony that is colored by the likes and dislikes of those who created it, and must weigh and evaluate, select and discard, to reach an opinion of his own. . . .

All this may sound as if historical research were merely a system of guesswork, which might be defined, like the famous definition of logic, as "an organized method of going wrong with confidence."

There is, however, another side to the coin. If the historian does not know the truth about the past—and he certainly does not—he should have a better approximation of the truth than contemporaries had. They were imprisoned in their time as we are in ours, and they could not fully grasp the significance of what was happening before their eyes; they were also imprisoned in space, and could not grasp the significance of distant events. Take Clinton for illustration. He never spoke of the American Revolution because he did not know that there was one; he could not see the rebellion as revolutionary. Neither could he see the far-away troubles in Whitehall that impeded the war effort; he believed that the government was willfully neglecting him. The historian does not wear such blinders but has a broad perspective, and it reveals to him developments in time and space that were hidden from the men with whom he is dealing. He can never be entirely sure of what they did, let alone of why they did it; yet he can have a deeper understanding than they had.

Understanding, which comes in part from the historian's remoteness in time, comes also from the nature of his concern with the past. That concern is a blend of involvement and detachment, and the first is harder to achieve than the second. Involvement means using his imagination to become engaged with the people he is studying, so that as far as he can he sees through their eyes and views their controversies as they viewed them. He rarely takes sides, if only because he sees both sides at once; but the issues and the protagonists are almost as real to him as those of his own day. Unless he can achieve this feat of imagination, can enter into his period even while he is remote from it, his perspective upon it may be worse than useless. Suppose, for instance, that he is utterly incapable of imagining himself into another era; he must then impose upon it, *faute de mieux,* the presuppositions, values, and standards of judgment of his own society. These are certain to be inapplicable, and any conclusions to which they lead him are certain to be askew.

Detachment without involvement, in such an extreme case, leads the historian to distort the past by fitting it to the measure of his present, much as Procrustes distorted guests by fitting them to the measure of his bed. But involvement without detachment can also lead to distortion, although of a different kind; and here the biographer is in particular danger. No man, the saying goes, is a hero to his valet; neither should any man be a hero to his biographer, who ought to know him as well as the valet does. The man's foibles and complexities, virtues and shortcomings, should become so familiar to the biographer that he sees his subject not primarily as great or small but as alive, a person in his own right. When a biographer succumbs instead to hero-worship (or, more rarely, the inverted form that might be called villain-worship), his involvement has triumphed over his detachment. Where he should have assessed the evidence in its entirety, with all its shadings from white to black, he has selected in a way to bring out only the whites or blacks; and the resultant picture has the unreality of the oversimplified. This is the art of the cartoonist, not of the historian.

Research is not the only way to discover how to blend detachment with involvement; a few historians understand their discipline by instinct. Most, however, acquire understanding through research. They learn that they cannot work their way laboriously into a period without discarding many of their twentieth-century preconceptions and modifying the others. The more ambiguities and pitfalls they find in their evidence, the more gaps in their knowledge of what they thought were familiar events, the more complexities in the process of causation, the safer they are from the temptation to treat the past in Procrustean fashion. They remain objective, but experience teaches them to be cautious and tentative in their conclusions. The thundering ultimates of a Spengler or a Toynbee are not for them.

Exploring the past is a never-ending activity. The historian in each generation hunts for new evidence and reinterprets existing evidence, to provide fresh details and a fresh perspective. However stimulating the perspective may be at the moment, it will not remain indefinitely fresh; it is based on incomplete and conflicting data, and is likely to contain at most a kernel of lasting value. . . . Any segment of history, no matter how narrowly defined in time and space, is set in a context that is limitless and therefore cannot be entirely known. Although each researcher hopes to know a little more of it, to throw a little more light on the mystery of why a particular set of men acted as they did, he realizes that the mystery will remain, and that for all his efforts he will find only a partial approximation of truth.

Yet he cannot let the mystery alone, and involvement with it brings its own reward. His research may be narrow in scope, transient in value, riddled with unanswerable questions; it is still inherently exciting. It has no scale: any problem offers as sure an approach as any other to the underlying historical process, and demands the researcher's full powers of analysis and empathy. In his analytic function he is the rationalist, perhaps even the scientist. In his empathic function he is the artist, and it is research as art that redeems the drudgery of data-gathering.

This form of art is as exigent as any other. It requires its practitioner to enter into the past, to meet people who are very much alive yet different from him in ways that he can imperfectly apprehend, to view them objectively for what they were, and then to portray them in all their vitality. This is so large an assignment that his reach, he knows, will exceed his grasp; and why should it not? Just as the subject matter of research fascinates him because he will never be able to do it full justice, so does the art of research. The requirements of that art are too stringent for his comfort: they deny him the illusion that he has nothing more to learn, and keep him always reaching for what he cannot quite grasp. His own particular creativity is therefore at full stretch, and that is perhaps as near to pure joy as an academic can come.

24. The Pleasures of Doubt:

Re-enacting the Crime

To reach for what one cannot quite grasp can bring only perverse forms of joy to most people, but as Professor Willcox has shown, the historian finds his pleasures in ways which many might find strange. They are no less genuine joys for that, and among them are the desires of doubt, those opportunities to prove to oneself again that the horizons do continue to recede. There are, I have always thought, New York City people—those who like to see man-made creations about them, to give them a sense of conquest over nature—and there are Grand Canyon people—those who admire and find pleasure in the incredible chaos of the natural world. The first should be political scientists, perhaps, dedicated to the proposition that the task of getting on with life may be a science, while the second may be historians, preferring to think of that task as an art form, a pastiche perhaps but with a certain shape that awaits detection. Robin Collingwood, from whom we drew the case of John Doe, is one of the leading exponents of the necessity for doubt, recognizing as he does that no one can ever eliminate the tiger in his own garden. In the essay that follows, taken from his inquiry into "The Limits of Historical Knowledge," Collingwood opens up for us the penultimate problem with which we must deal: presentism, relevance, and contemporaneity—not the same thing—in historical research and writing. His conclusion, that historical certainty must be renounced, is in the final analysis a heartening one. Those who do not find it so should seek refuge exclusively in the world of fiction, for at some point we must realize that while all detective stories must have their resolutions, most historical accounts are at best only tentative. He begins by analyzing the problem of historical skepticism:

♦ ♦ ♦

Now—and this is the root of historical scepticism—we only have a strictly limited quantity of evidence concerning any historical question; it is seldom free from grave defects, it is generally tendencious, fragmentary, silent where it ought to be explicit, and detailed where it had better be silent; even at its best, it is never free from these and similar faults, it only refrains from thrusting them indecently upon our notice. Hence the best may be the worst, because it lulls us into a false security and induces us to mistake its incompleteness for completeness, its tendenciousness for sincerity, and to become innocent accomplices in its own deceit. Indeed, the poetic inspiration of Clio the Muse is never more needed, and never more brilliantly employed, than by the task of lulling to sleep the critical faculties of the historical student, while she sings his imagination a Siren's song. But if he binds himself to the mast and refuses to alter his course, he ceases to be a dupe and becomes a sceptic. He will now say, "I know that my evidence is incomplete. I know that I have only an inconsiderable fraction of what I might

---

FROM Robin G. Collingwood, "The Limits of Historical Knowledge," *Essays in the Philosophy of History,* edited by William Debbins (New York: McGraw-Hill, 1966; first published by the University of Texas Press, 1965), pp. 92–103, an essay which first appeared in the *Journal of Philosophical Studies*—now called *Philosophy*—in 1920. Printed with the permission of the University of Texas.

For additional reading: In *The Nature of Historical Thinking* (Chapel Hill, 1967), Robert Stover makes a useful distinction between history as viewed from "the standpoint of natural order" and history as seen from "the standpoint of living in the world." Alan Bullock has written on "The Historian's Purpose: History and Metahistory," in *History Today,* VII (May, 1951), 18–21, while Morris R. Cohen discusses "Causation and Its Application to History" in the *Journal of the History of Ideas,* III (October, 1942), 386–94. The problem of the double and triple bluff is too well known to readers of detective fiction to require exposition here. One might begin with another novel by Francis Clifford, *The Naked Runner,* or any of the work of Ross Hunter.

have had, if fate had been kinder; if the library of Alexandria had survived, if the humanists had been luckier or better supported in their search for manuscripts, if a thousand things had happened which did not happen, I should have had a mass of evidence where now I have only a few shreds. The wholesale destruction of documents due to the French Revolution, and the holocaust of manorial records and title-deeds now going on in England since the passing of Lord Birkenhead's Real Property Act—tempered though it is by the efforts of historical societies and the authority of the Master of the Rolls—have blotted out irreplaceably a vast percentage of the once existing sources for mediaeval history in France and England; what is left will never be more than a fragment, never enough to form the basis for a complete history of the Middle Ages. But even had these catastrophes not happened, our sources, though more extensive, would still be incomplete. We should have more to study, but our results would not really be more certain, except in the doubtful sense in which a larger finite quantity approximates more nearly to infinity."

To say this may seem tantamount to renouncing historical certainty altogether. Yet it must be said. Only by shutting our eyes to the most familiar and obvious facts can we fail to see that the evidence to the whole of which we always appeal when we decide a debated historical point is a mere fragment of what we might have had, if our luck had been better. . . . We toil and sweat to get the last ounce of inferential knowledge out of the sources we possess, whereas if we could acquire only a few more, our inferences would be confirmed or overthrown by the merest glance at the new documents. Only actual experience, or, failing that, a careful study of the history of research, can show how utterly the historian is at the mercy of his sources and how completely an addition to his sources may alter his conclusions. No doubt, the scientist may be no less profoundly affected by a new experiment; but this gives him no deep sense of impotence or futility, because it is his business to invent the crucial experiment and his fault if he does not; whereas the historian, however hard he works at the discovery of sources, depends in the long run on the chance that someone did not break up the Monumentum Ancyranum to burn in a limekiln, or light the kitchen fire with the Paston Letters.

And this, perhaps, is the real sting of historical scepticism. Doubt is a disease endemic in human thought; if history is doubtful, so is science, so is philosophy; in every department of knowledge, everything is doubtful until it has been satisfactorily settled, and even then it becomes doubtful again unless the doubter can settle it afresh for himself. In mathematics, we are not plagued by the doubtfulness of our theorems, because if we feel unhappy about the axiom of parallels we can think it out on our own account and arrive at an independent opinion; in physics, if we doubt the accepted view about falling bodies, we can climb a tower and test them. But the sources of history we must take or leave. They are not, like scientific or philosophical theorems, results of processes which we can repeat for ourselves; they are results, but results of processes which we cannot repeat; hence they are a solid barrier to thought, a wall of "data" against which all we can do is to build lean-to sheds of inference, not knowing what strains it is capable of bearing. The peculiar, the disastrous doubtfulness of history lies not in the fact that everything in it is dubitable, but in the fact that these doubts cannot be resolved. Everywhere else, it seems, knowledge grows by a healthy oscillation between doubt and certainty: you are allowed to doubt as much as you like, to say, like [Thomas] Hobbes on first looking into Euclid, "By God, it is impossible!" because it is by facing and answering these doubts that you acquire knowledge; but in history we must not doubt; we dare not doubt; we must assume that our evidence is adequate, though we know it to be inadequate, and trustworthy, though we know it to be tainted, for if we did not, our occupation as historians would be gone. . . .

This feeling, that in historical studies the mind is bound hand and foot by an act of irrational acquiescence, whereas in science and philosophy it is free to question everything, to reject everything that it cannot substantiate, and assert nothing that it cannot accept on the authority of its own thinking, seems to be what [Bernard] Bosanquet has expressed [when he says that history is "the doubtful story of successive events"]. Now it is easy to reply that this is hypercriticism; that such doubts do not affect actual historians in the actual course of their work, but only fastidious and probably unsympathetic spectators of that work; and that in point of fact, so far from its being true that history is unable to bear inspection, it is constantly being revised by enormous numbers of intelligent people, who actually all come to very much the same conclusions—that Charles I was beheaded, that Charles II was a ladies' man, that James II fled the country, and so on through a catalogue which may or may not be small beer, but is at least not found doubtful by anyone who takes the trouble to inquire into it.

Such a reply, I must confess, brings a breath of fresh air into an argument which had begun to smell stuffy. It is always with a sense of relief that, after arguing the hind leg off a donkey, one goes out into the field to look at the animal for oneself; and hypercriticism is no doubt the right term for an argument which proves that history, or religion, or politics, is an impossible or idiotic pursuit, when all the time one is aware that plenty of intelligent people are pursuing it in an intelligent spirit. But you cannot dispel an argument by calling it hypercritical. If your donkey has four visible legs, and you can prove that it ought to have three, the discrepancy is a reason not for ceasing to think about the donkey's anatomy, but for thinking about it again: revising, not merely ignoring, the original argument.

It is important to recognise this principle in the interest of all sound philosophical inquiry. People are often tempted to argue thus: "Such and such a view, if pressed home, leads to scepticism. Now scepticism is a self-contradictory position, because it materially claims to possess the knowledge which formally it denies; therefore whatever leads logically to scepticism leads to self-contradiction and is false. This is a sufficient refutation of such and such a view, which accordingly we hereby dismiss from further consideration." This type of refutation, though logically valid, is always unsatisfactory. . . . The critic has made a debating point against the view in question, and has left its advocate silenced but unconvinced; aware that his argument has not received justice, but has merely been bludgeoned into momentary submission. The bludgeon of a coarse common sense is a very necessary part of the philosopher's armoury. . . . But if one makes up one's mind to be permanently stupid, as those would have us do who teach their disciples . . . the exclusive use of the common-sense bludgeon, one is merely condemning oneself to learn nothing. When you have clubbed the sceptic into silence, get out your scalpel and dissect him; and you may be able to pick his brains to some purpose.

The contentions of historical scepticism—to take up the scalpel —are by no means the mere product of an unintelligent inspection of historical work from the outside. In the preceding paragraphs the writer has stated them altogether as the fruit of his own experience in historical research, and could enlarge on the topic considerably without for a moment ceasing to give an accurate description of that experience in one of its most prominent features. In reading history-books and memorising their contents, and even in teaching history to students, this feature sinks into the background and may be altogether lost to sight. But when one takes up the study of some difficult historical question as yet unsettled, and enters with well-equipped and honest opponents into . . . learned controversy, there is one thing which one cannot fail to observe. This is the existence of what I may call rules of the game. One rule—the first—runs thus: "You must not say anything, however true, for which you cannot produce evidence." The game is won not by the player who can reconstitute what really happened, but by the player who can show that his view of what happened is the one which the evidence accessible to all players, when criticised up to the hilt, supports. Suppose a given view is in fact the correct one, and suppose (granted it were possible) that all the extant evidence, interpreted with the maximum degree of skill, led to a different view, no evidence supporting the correct view: in that case the holder of the correct view would lose the game, the holder of the other view win it. Not only is this rule accepted by every player of the game without protest or question, but anyone can see it to be reasonable. For there is no way of knowing what view is "correct," except by finding what the evidence, critically interpreted, proves. A view defined as "correct, but not supported by the evidence," is a view by definition unknowable, incapable of being the goal of the historian's search. And at the same time, every historian actually engaged in such work keenly recognises the limited character of his sources, and knows very well that it is no more in his power to add to them than it is in the power of a chess-player to conjure a third bishop into existence. He must play the game with the pieces that he has; and if he can find a new piece—quote a hitherto unexploited source of information—he must begin a new game, after putting it on the table for his opponent to use as well as himself. Everyone who has any experience of first-hand historical research, especially in the sharpened form of historical controversy, is thus perfectly familiar with all the topics of historical scepticism, and is not in the least perturbed by them. In fact, experience shows that the people who are scared by them are never the practised historians, who accept them as a matter of course, but the philosophers of schools committed to theories which they seem, rightly or wrongly, to contradict.

But, I shall be told, I have frankly reduced history to a game. I have deprived its narratives of all objective value, and degraded them to a mere exercise in the interpretation of arbitrarily selected bodies of evidence, every such body being selected by the operation of chance and confessedly impotent to prove the truth.

It is time to drop the metaphor of a game. The so-called rules of the game are really the definition of what historical thinking is; the winner of the game is the historian proper—the person who thinks historically, whose thought fulfils the ideal of historical truth. For historical thinking means nothing else than interpreting all the available evidence with the maximum degree of critical skill. It does not mean discovering what really happened, if "what really happened" is anything other than "what the evidence indicates." If there once happened an event concerning which no shred of evidence now survives, that event is not part of any historian's universe; it is no historian's business to discover it; it is no gap in any historian's knowledge that he does not know it. If he had any ideas about it, they would be supernatural revelations, poetic fancies, or unfounded conjectures; they would form no part whatever of his historical thought. "What really happened" in this sense of the phrase is simply the thing in itself, the thing defined as out of all relation to the knower of it, not only unknown but unknowable, not only unknowable but non-existent.

Historical scepticism may now be seen in its proper function, as the negative side of the definition of historical knowledge. There is a permanent tendency in all thought—it is sometimes called the plain man's realism—to think of the object as a "thing in itself," a thing out of all relation to the knowledge of it, a thing existing in itself and by itself. From that point of view, the object of history appears as simply "the past"; the sum total of events that have happened; and the aim of the historian appears as the discovery of the past, the finding out of what has happened. But in the actual practice of historical thinking, the historian discovers that he cannot move a step towards the achievement of this aim without appealing to evidence; and evidence is something present, something now existing, regarded as a relic or trace left by the past. If the past had left no traces, he could never come to know it; and if it has, so to speak, inextricably confused its own traces, all he can do is to disentangle them up to the limit of his own powers. The past simply as past is wholly unknowable; it is the past as residually preserved in the present that is alone knowable. The discovery that the past as such is unknowable is the scepticism which is the permanent and necessary counterpart of the plain man's realism. It is its counterpart, because it asserts the exact opposite; the one asserts that the past as such can be known and is known by history, the other, that it is not known by history and cannot be known. It is a permanent counterpart, because wherever historical thinking is actually done, the discovery which is the basis of historical scepticism is invariably made. Date and Dabitur really are twins. It is a necessary counterpart, because without qualification by historical scepticism, historical realism is wholly false, and must lead to absurd misconceptions of the limits of historical knowledge.

Historical realism by itself implies that whatever is included in the sum total of events that have happened is a possible and legitimate object of historical knowledge. . . . Every historian as such ought to know the whole past. That being impossible owing to human frailty, the best historian is the one who knows the largest amount of the past; and the more information he can acquire, the better historian he becomes. This leads to countless absurdities. Every historian knows that to be an historian one must be a specialist, and that the historian who tries to know everything knows nothing. But historical realism would imply the reverse. It would imply that historical knowledge is to be reckoned by the quantity of facts with which acquaintance has been scraped, and that the greatest historical writer is the writer of the longest history of the world. Again, every historian knows that there are some questions—pseudo-questions rather—into which it is not his business to inquire, because there is no available evidence towards their answer; and that it is no shame to him to be ignorant by what name Achilles was called when he was disguised as a maiden. But historical realism would imply that this is incorrect; that there are no limits whatever to historical knowledge except the limits of the past as past, and that therefore the question what Julius Caesar had for breakfast the day he overcame the Nervii is as genuinely historical a problem as the question whether he proposed to become king of Rome. Again, historical realism involves the absurdity of thinking of the past as something still existing by itself . . . a world where Galileo's weight is still falling, where the smoke of Nero's Rome still fills the intelligible air, and where interglacial man is still laboriously learning to chip flints. This limbo, where events which have finished happening still go on, is familiar to us all; it is the room in the fairy-tale, where all the old moons are kept behind the door. . . . It is the land east of the sun and west of the moon. Its prose name is Nowhere. . . .

. . . It is enough for the present to have stated the general thesis that all historical thought is the historical interpretation of the present; that its central question is: "How has this world as it now exists come to be what it is?" and that for this reason the past concerns the historian only so far as it has led to the present. By leading to the present, it has left its traces upon the present; and by doing that, it has supplied the historian with evidence concerning itself, a starting-point for his investigators. The historian does not first think of a problem and then search for evidence bearing on it; it is his possession of evidence bearing on a problem that alone makes the problem a real one.

It thus appears that history is not doubtful at all. It seemed doubtful, to say the least, so long as we imagined its object to be the past as past; but though the question "what really happened," where "what happened," and "what the evidence proves" are assumed as distinct, is necessarily doubtful, the question "what the evidence proves" is not doubtful. Granted a training in historical methods, and equipment of historical scholarship, without which no one can fairly judge,[1] it is possible to take a particular problem, to study the solution of that problem advanced by a particular historian on a particular review of the evidence, and within the limits of this problem, as stated, to raise the question whether he has or has not proved his case. That question can be answered, by a competent scholar, with no more doubt than must attend any man's answer to any question that can be asked in any department of knowledge. And in the certainty of that answer lies the formal dignity, the logical worth, the scientific value in the highest sense of that word, of historical studies.

[1] It may be worth while to point out that even a rigidly cogent historical argument always seems to contain loop-holes of doubt, to a critic unfamiliar with the matter in hand; a reader, *e.g.*, who does not know enough numismatics to know what the possible alternatives in a given case are, cannot judge the solidity of an expert numismatist's discussion of that case, because he will see that certain alternatives are tacitly ruled out, without knowing why. Had the numismatist been writing for beginners, he ought to have explained why; not otherwise. One might have supposed that the logic of an historical argument could be judged by one ignorant of its subject-matter; that is not the case. . . .

25. The Problem of Hope:

Contemporary History

DESPITE COLLINGWOOD'S SOMEWHAT OLYMPIAN VERDICT, most Americans want their history to be relevant to present problems and to be seen to be relevant. There is no reason why it cannot be, of course, although this must not be the historian's primary purpose in research or writing. One asks different questions of events just past, and of the data relating to those events, from those one asks of the Roman Empire, for the effects of the answers one gets will be immediate. One guards against bias more carefully, and for different reasons. One becomes alert to "slow and fast time"—to an "increase in the velocity of history," as Arthur Schlesinger, Jr., says in the selection which follows. As he suggests, contemporary history raises important methodological questions for the future.

Not all will agree with the essay. As a participant in the events of the administration of President Kennedy, as the author of a best-selling contemporary history of that administration, and as an outspoken liberal, Schlesinger is suspect to some readers, who exercise their proper right to make their own historical evaluations. But he is a master of his craft, one of the most thoughtful as well as prolific of American historians. Having won a Pulitzer Prize when he was twenty-eight for his portrait of *The Age of Jackson,* having written on such diverse figures as Orestes Brownson and Franklin Delano Roosevelt, having taught generations of graduate students at Harvard and now his first generation at the City University of New York—and having also taught, one suspects, many White House technocrats—Schlesinger is uniquely qualified to answer the questions: When do contemporary affairs become history? What are the limits in time forward, rather than time backward, to the historian's sphere? What is the rôle of history (and by implication of the historian) in public policy? With these questions we leave utterly the realm of the detective and turn to that of the judge, of the man who must seek verdicts, not upon history (for there are none) but upon the discipline. The following attempt at some answers is from Schlesinger's essay, "On the Inscrutability of History"—the greatest mystery of all.

♦ ♦ ♦

However hard it may be to define with precision the role of history in public policy, it is evident that this role must stand or fall on the success of history as a means of prediction. This is a point, it should immediately be said, on which professional historians, on the whole, have few illusions among themselves. They privately regard history as its own reward; they study it for the intellectual and aesthetic fulfilment they find in the disciplined attempt to reconstruct the past and, perhaps, for the ironic after-taste in the contemplation of man's heroism and folly, but for no more utilitarian reason. They understand better than outsiders that historical training confers no automatic wisdom in the realm of public affairs. Guizot,

---

FROM Arthur Schlesinger, Jr., "On the Inscrutability of History," *Encounter,* XXVII (November, 1966), 10–17. Printed with the permission of the author. This essay also appeared, in somewhat altered form, in Professor Schlesinger's *The Bitter Heritage: Vietnam and American Democracy, 1941–1966* (Boston: Houghton Mifflin Co., 1966), pp. 80–98.

For additional reading: Schlesinger has other useful things to say to us in "On the Writing of Contemporary History," an address read before the 1966 meeting of the American Historical Association, and published in the *Atlantic Monthly,* CCXIX (March, 1967), 69–74. An example of good contemporary history is James W. Silver, *Mississippi: The Closed Society* (rev. ed., New York, 1966). An example of poor contemporary history is William Manchester, *The Death of a President* (New York, 1967), which falls into the Grapefruit School of writing: the assumption, perhaps taken from *Time* magazine, that we need to know what a man eats for breakfast if we are to understand him. For contemporary detective stories, consult the front page of your local newspaper.

Bancroft, Macaulay, Thiers, Morley, Bryce, Theodore Roosevelt, Woodrow Wilson: one cannot say that their training as historians deeply influenced their practice as politicians; and the greatest of them—Roosevelt and Wilson—were harmed as politicians by exactly the moralism from which the study of history might have saved them. But then neither was a particularly good historian.

Yet historians, in spite of their candour within the fellowship, sometimes invoke arguments of a statelier sort in justifying themselves to society: particularly the argument that one should study history because knowledge of yesterday can provide guidance for tomorrow. . . . In what sense is this true? Why should history help us foresee the future? Because presumably history repeats itself enough to make possible a range of historical generalisation; and because generalisation, sufficiently multiplied and interlaced, can generate insight into the shape of things to come.

Many professional historians—perhaps most—reject the idea that generalisation is the goal of history. We all respond, in Marc Bloch's phrase, to "the thrill of learning singular things." Indeed, it is the commitment to concrete reconstruction as against abstract generalisation—to life as against laws—which distinguishes history from sociology. Yet, on the other hand, as Crane Brinton once put it, "the doctrine of the absolute uniqueness of events in history seems nonsense." Even historians who are sceptical of attempts to discern a final and systematic order in history acknowledge the existence of a variety of uniformities and recurrences. There can be no question that generalisations about the past, defective as they may be, are possible—and that they can strengthen the capacity of statesmen to deal with the future.

So historians have long since identified a life-cycle of revolution which, if properly apprehended, might have spared us misconceptions about the Russian Revolution—first, about its goodwill and, later, when we abandoned belief in its goodwill, about the fixity and permanence of its fanatical purpose—and which, if consulted today, might save us from the notion that the Chinese Revolution will be forever cast in its present mould. . . . In fact, communism has come only to nations in a relatively early stage of development, like Russia and China, and it has come to such nations precisely as a means to modernisation, not as a consequence of it. Instead of being the climax of the development process, the end of the journey, communism is now revealed as a technique of social discipline which a few countries in early stages of development have adopted in the hope of speeding the pace of modernisation. Instead of the ultimate destination towards which all societies are ineluctably moving, communism now appears an epiphenomenon of the transition from stagnation to development. Modernisation, as it proceeds, evidently carries nations not towards Marx but away from Marx —and this would appear true even of the Soviet Union itself.

History thus far has refuted the central proposition in Marx's system of prediction. It has also refuted important corollary theses —notably the idea that the free economic order could not possibly last. Far from obeying dogma and perishing of its own inner contradictions, free society in the developed world has rarely displayed more creativity and vitality. It is casting as powerful a spell on the intellectuals and the youth of the communist world as the communist world cast on us during the Depression thirty years ago.

Why did Marx go wrong here? His forecast of the inevitable disintegration of free society was plausibly based on the *laissez-faire* capitalism of the mid-19th century. This devil-take-the-hindmost economic order did very likely contain the seeds of its own destruction—especially in those tendencies, pronounced irreversible by Marx, towards an ever-widening gap between rich and poor (alleged to guarantee the ultimate impoverishment of the masses) and towards an ever-increasing frequency and severity of structural economic crisis (alleged to guarantee the progressive instability of the system). This may indeed be a salient example of the "paradox of prevision"; for the Marxist forecast unquestionably stimulated progressive democrats to begin the reform of classical capitalism through the invention of the affirmative state. "The more we condemn unadulterated Marxian Socialism," Theodore Roosevelt used to say, "the stouter should be our insistence on thoroughgoing social reforms. . . ." The combination of the affirmative state with the extraordinary success of the free economic order as an engine of production—a success which, contrary to *laissez-faire* dogma, government intervention increased rather than hampered—eventually thwarted the Marxist prophecy.

In the end, the Marxists were undone by Marxism. Ideology told them that those who owned the economy *must* own the state, and the state could therefore never act against their desires or interests. Yet fifteen years before the *Communist Manifesto* an American President, Andrew Jackson, had already suggested that the state in a democratic society, far from being the instrument of the possessors, could well become the means by which those whom Jackson called the "humble members of society" might begin to redress the balance of social power against those whom Hamilton had called the "rich and well-born." Thus, in the 20th-century developed world, the economic machine drowned the revolution in consumers' goods, while the affirmative state, with its policies of piecemeal intervention in the economy, brought about both a relative redistribution of wealth (defeating Marx's prediction of the immiseration of the poor) and a relative stabilisation of the economy (defeating Marx's prediction of ever-deepening cyclical crisis). The last place to look for a Marxist victory is precisely the place where Marx said it would come first—*i.e.,* in the most developed countries.

So the Marxist prophecy of a single obligatory destiny for mankind has missed in both its parts: in its prediction of the irresistible breakdown of the free economy, and in its prediction of the irresistible triumph of communism as the fulfilment of the development process. In spite of many subsidiary insights and successes, Marxism must surely stand in our time as the spectacular flop of history as prophecy. The failure, indeed, has been so complete that contemporary Marxists revile each other in seeking the true meaning of the most elementary doctrines; the more fanatical stand Marx on his head, rejecting his basic theory and arguing that communism will come "out of the countryside," not the city.

Yet the democratic world is hardly in a position to take too much satisfaction from the intellectual collapse of Marxism. It is true that our philosophical heritage—empirical, pragmatic, ironic, pluralistic, competitive—has happily inoculated us against rigid, all-encompassing, absolute systems of historical interpretation. But, though we may reject the view of history as metaphysically set and settled, we seem at times to embrace our own forms of historical fatalism—even if we invoke history less as theology than as analogy. This is only a marginal advantage. The argument by metaphor can generate a certitude almost as mischievous as the argument by determinism.

For democratic policy-makers, history generally appears as a "negative" rather than a "positive" model. It instructs us, not like Marxism, in the things we must do, but in the things we must *not* do—unless we wish to repeat the mistakes of our ancestors. The traumatic experience of World War I thus dominated the diplomacy of World War II, at least as far as the United States was concerned. So the American insistence on the doctrine of "unconditional surrender" in 1943 sprang from the belief that the failure to get unconditional surrender in 1918 had made possible the stab-in-the-back myth and guaranteed the revival of German nationalism. The American obsession with the United Nations came from the conviction that the failure to join the League of Nations had opened the way to the second World War. . . .

The second World War, then, provided a new traumatic experience. In the years since, the consciousness of policy-makers has been haunted by the Munich and Yalta analogies—the generalisation, drawn from attempts to accommodate Hitler in 1938, and Stalin in 1945, that appeasement always assures new aggression. Of these analogies, Munich, as the more lucid in its pattern and the more emphatic in its consequence, has been the more powerful; Yalta, indeed, figures rather as a complicated special case. I trust that a graduate student some day will write a doctoral essay on the influence of Munich analogy on the subsequent history of the 20th century. Perhaps in the end he will conclude that the multitude of errors committed in the name of "Munich" may exceed the original error of 1938.

Certainly Munich was a tragic mistake, and its lesson was that the appeasement of a highly wound-up and heavily-armed totalitarian state in the context of a relatively firm and articulated continental equilibrium of power was likely to upset the balance and make further aggression inevitable. But to conclude from this that all attempts to avert war by negotiation must always be "Munich"s goes beyond the evidence. No one understood this better than the greatest contemporary critic of Munich. An historian himself, Winston Churchill well understood the limits of historical analogy. So he defined the issue in his chapter on Munich in *The Gathering Storm:* . . .

> Those who are prone by temperament and character to seek sharp and clear-cut solutions of difficult and obscure problems, who are ready to fight whenever some challenge comes from a foreign power, have not always been right. On the other hand, those whose inclination is to bow their heads, to seek patiently and faithfully for peaceful compromise, are not always wrong. On the contrary, in the majority of instances, they may be right, not only morally but from a practical standpoint. . . .
>
> How many wars have been precipitated by fire-brands! How many misunderstandings which led to war could have been removed by temporising! How often have countries fought cruel wars and then after a few years of peace found themselves not only friends but allies!

Sixteen years after Munich President Eisenhower wrote Churchill, "If . . . Indochina passes into the hands of the Communists, the ultimate effect on our and your global strategy and position . . . could be disastrous. . . . We failed to halt Hirohito, Mussolini and Hitler by not acting in unity and in time. That marked the beginning of many years of stark tragedy and desperate peril. May it not be that our nations have learned something from that lesson?" Eisenhower was invoking the Munich analogy to persuade the British to join the Americans in backing the French in Indochina. Churchill remained unmoved by Eisenhower's argument. He saw no useful parallel between Hitler, the man on the bicycle who could not stop, a madman commanding vast military force and requiring immediate and visible success, and the ragged bands and limited goals of Ho Chi-Minh. Nor could he see any useful parallel between Europe—a developed continent with well-defined national frontiers, interests, and identities and a highly-organised equilibrium of power—and South-East Asia, an underdeveloped subcontinent filled with fictitious states in vague, chaotic, and unpredictable revolutionary ferment. Churchill rejected Eisenhower's analogy—which did not, of course, prevent Churchill's successor as Prime Minister two years later from seeing Nasser and the Middle East in terms of 1938 and committing his nation to the Suez adventure. This time it was Eisenhower who rejected the Munich analogy.

Today the same analogy pursues us again, echoing in the corridors of Washington, with China now cast in the role of Nazi Germany.

"In the 'forties and 'fifties," President Johnson has said, "we took our stand in Europe to protect the freedom of those threatened by aggression. Now the centre of attention has shifted to another part of the world where aggression is on the march. Our stand must be as firm as ever." The instrument of this aggression, we are told, is the communist-instigated war of national liberation. If this technique is permitted to succeed in Viet Nam, it will be tried elsewhere. If it is defeated in Viet Nam, the Chinese will know that we will not let it succeed in other countries and they will have to reconsider their policies. . . .

This is not the place to comment on the Viet Nam riddle—except to suggest that it is not to be solved by bad historical analogies. It may seem a little forced, for example, to equate a civil war in what was up to a dozen years ago the single country of Viet Nam with Hitler's invasion of Austria and Czechoslovakia across well-established national frontiers. And if Mao rather than Ho has now become the equivalent of Hitler, the U.S. State Department has yet to produce evidence that the Viet Cong of South Viet Nam are only the spearhead of a premeditated and co-ordinated conspiracy of Chinese aggression. Nor do the Chinese themselves have the overwhelming military power nor, evidently, the pent-up mania for immediate expansion which would substantiate the Hitler parallel. . . .

The fact that the Munich analogy is invalid does not necessarily invalidate the Viet Nam policy. There is much to be said for the proposition that a negotiated settlement in Viet Nam will be impossible so long as the other side thinks it can win; and this offers a strong argument for a holding action in South Viet Nam, though hardly for widening the war in the north. The point here, however, is not to assess American Viet Nam policy but to illustrate the depressing persistence of the mentality which makes policy through stereotype—through historical generalisation wrenched illegitimately out of the past and imposed mechanically on the future. Santayana's aphorism must be reversed: too often it is those who *can* remember the past who are condemned to repeat it. . . .

I well remember President Kennedy expressing to me after the Cuban missile crisis in 1962 his fear that people would conclude from his victory that all we would have to do thereafter in dealing with the Communists was to be tough and they would collapse. The missile crisis, he pointed out, had three distinctive features: it took place in an area where we enjoyed local conventional superiority, where Soviet national security was not directly engaged, and where the Russians lacked a case which they could convincingly sustain before the world. Things would be different, he said, if the situation were one where the Communists had the local superiority, where their national security was directly engaged, and where they could persuade themselves and others they were in the right.

Kennedy, who, like Churchill, had the mind of a first-class historian, was without illusion about the infallibility of historical analogy. The point is not terribly complicated, even for village idiots. Burke long ago warned against the practice of viewing an object "as it stands stripped of every relation, in all the nakedness and solitude of metaphysical abstraction. Circumstances (which with some gentlemen pass for nothing) give in reality to every political principle its distinguishing colour and discriminating effect." Even Toynbee, the magician of historical analogy, has remarked that historians are

> never in a position to guarantee that the entities which we are bringing into comparison are properly comparable for the purpose of our investigation. . . . However far we may succeed in going in our search for sets of identical examples on either side, we shall never be able to prove that there is not some non-identical factor that we have overlooked, and this non-identical factor is not the decisive factor that accounts for the different outcomes in different cases of what has looked to us like an identical situation but may not have been this in truth.

Or, as Mark Twain put it, somewhat more vividly, in *Following the Equator:* "We should be careful to get out of an experience only the wisdom that is in it—and stop there; lest we be like the cat that sits down on a hot stove lid. She will never sit down on a hot stove lid again—and that is well; but also she will never sit down on a cold one. . . ."

One cannot doubt that the study of history makes people wiser.

But it is indispensable to understand the limits of historical analogy. Most useful historical generalisations are statements about massive social and intellectual movements over a considerable period of time. They make large-scale, long-term prediction possible. But they do not justify small-scale, short-term prediction. For short-run prediction is the prediction of detail and, given the complex structure of social events, the difficulty of anticipating the intersection or collision of different events and the irreducible mystery, if not invincible freedom, of individual decision, there are simply too many variables to warrant exact forecasts of the immediate future. History, in short, can answer questions, after a fashion, at long range. It cannot answer questions with confidence or certainty at short range. Alas, policy-makers are rarely interested in the long run—"in the long run," as [John Maynard] Keynes used to say, "we are all dead"—and the questions they put to history are thus most often the questions which history is least qualified to answer.

Far from offering a short-cut to clairvoyance, history teaches us that the future is full of surprises and outwits all our certitudes. For the study of history issues not in scientific precision nor in moral finality but in irony. If twenty-five years ago, anyone had predicted that before the end of the decade of the 'forties Germany and Japan would be well on the way to becoming close friends and allies of Britain and the United States, he would have been considered mad. If fifteen years ago, as the Russians and Chinese were signing their thirty-year pact of amity and alliance, anyone predicted that by the end of the 'fifties they would be at each other's throats, he too would have been considered mad. The chastening fact is that many of the pivotal events of our age were unforeseen: from the Nazi-Soviet pact and the Tito-Stalin quarrel of years ago to such events in today's newspapers as the anti-communist upsurge in Indonesia and the overthrow of Nkrumah in Ghana (and his resurrection in Guinea).

Occasionally one reads in the U.S. press that leading political figures in Washington are shaping their actions today by calculations with regard to the Democratic presidential nomination in 1972. I am sure that the men mentioned in such stories are themselves under no delusion about the hopelessness of such an undertaking. 1972 is today as far away from us as 1960, and no one reflecting on the unpredictability of the last six years in the United States could sensibly suppose that the next six are going to be any more predictable. I have often thought that a futurist trying to forecast the next three American Presidents in early 1940 would hardly have named as the first President after Franklin D. Roosevelt an obscure back-bench senator from Missouri, anticipating defeat by the governor of his state in the Democratic primaries; as the second, an unknown lieutenant-colonel in the United States Army; and, as the third, a kid still at college. Yet that sequence began to unfold in less time than between now and 1972.

The salient fact about the historical process, so far as the short run is concerned, is its inscrutability. One must bear this in mind, I believe, when asked to accept drastic decisions now on the basis of someone's speculation as to what the behaviour of Communist China will be a dozen years from now. In its coarsest form, this is the argument that "we must have a showdown with China before it gets the bomb." Here is the old preventive-war thesis we used to hear so often in the late 'forties: yet I do not think anyone can rationally contend that the world would be better off today had we dropped the bomb on Russia twenty years ago. Having been wrong so often in the past, how can we be sure we have achieved such infallibility now that we would risk the future of mankind on a guess?

Who can possibly predict the course the Chinese Revolution will take in the years ahead? The study of revolution has shown us that the emotional and doctrinal pitch of revolutions waxes and wanes; that, while revolutions at first may devour their children, in the end the children sometimes devour the revolutions; that even totalitarian revolutions fail at total mass indoctrination; that a successful revolution begins to develop a stake in the *status quo;* that post-revolutionary generations have their own identities and aspirations; that the possession of a major nuclear arsenal has thus far had a sobering effect on the possessor; that nations follow their historic interests rather more faithfully than they do their ideologies; and that there is no greater error than to try and deduce the policy of future from the rhetoric of the present. Nor does the example of Hitler and *Mein Kampf* change this. Hitler was indeed the man on the bicycle; he had to keep moving. The Nazi revolution never got beyond the first messianic phase; its nature condemned it to *Götterdämmerung*. We must not forget that the Chinese revolutionary régime has already lasted five years longer than the whole life of the Third Reich. And we have seen in the case of the Soviet Union the permutation and erosion time and national interest have worked on what were once thought to be final motives and permanent objectives. With an equation so overflowing with variables, how can anyone forecast now the behaviour of China twenty years from now?

History, in short, does not furnish the statesman with a detailed scenario of particular relationships or policies. Too often it equips his decisions with good rather than real reasons, holding out a mirror in which he fatuously sees his own face. This is not an argument against the knowledge of history: it is an argument against the superficial knowledge of history. The single analogy is never enough to penetrate a process so cunningly compounded not only of necessity but of contingency, fortuity, ignorance, stupidity and chance. The statesman who is surest that he can divine the future most urgently invites his own retribution. "The hardest strokes of heaven," Herbert Butterfield has written, "fall in history upon those who imagine that they can control things in a sovereign manner, playing providence not only for themselves but for the far future—reaching out into the future with the wrong kind of far-sightedness, and gambling on a lot of risky calculations in which there must never be a single mistake."

What then has history to offer the statesman? Let me suggest first that the way to protect the policy-maker from the misuse of history is not to deprive him of historical knowledge altogether. This is the practice customarily adopted in totalitarian states, and the results invariably show the melancholy consequence when politicians believe their own propaganda. Can one infer from this that it is short-sighted for democratic governments, as, for example, in Great Britain, to withhold from its Parliament and people cautionary tales of governmental folly? Happily, we have had in the United States the full benefit of the Bay of Pigs—an event which took place five years after the British adventure in Suez but which has been discharged a good deal earlier from the cosy bondage of official secrecy. Does the British government really regard the protection of the reputation of politicians as the primary function of history? Naturally such a theory has a strong bi-partisan appeal, but it is surely injurious not only to history but to democracy itself. The acquiescence of the British people in the denial to themselves of facts indispensable to the judgment of their masters is one of the masochistic curiosities of our age.

The only antidote to a shallow knowledge of history is a deeper knowledge—the knowledge which produces not dogmatic certitude but diagnostic skill, not clairvoyance but insight. It offers the statesman a sense, at once, of short-run variables and long-run tendencies, and an instinct for the complexity of their intermingling, including the understanding that (as Rousseau once put it), "the ability to foresee that some things cannot be foreseen is a very necessary quality." Indeed, half the wisdom of statecraft, to borrow a phrase from Richard Goodwin, is "to leave as many options open as possible and decide as little as possible. . . . Since almost all important policy judgments are speculative, you must avoid risking too much on the conviction you are right."

Of course keeping too many options open too long may paralyse the lobe of decision and lose the game. There *does* come a time when accommodation turns into appeasement. This is the other half of the wisdom of statecraft: to accept the chronic lubricity and obscurity of events without yielding, in Lincoln's words, firmness in the right as God gives us to see the right. In deciding when to decide the criterion must be the human consequences—the results for people, not for doctrine. . . .

. . . Far from unveiling the secret of things to come, history bestows a different gift: it makes us—or should make us—understand the extreme difficulty, the intellectual peril, the moral arrogance of supposing that the future will yield itself so easily to us.

"I returned," *Ecclesiastes* reminds us, "and saw under the sun that the race is not to the swift, nor the battle to the strong, neither yet bread to the wise nor riches to men of understanding, but time and chance happeneth to them all." The Old Testament carries the case against historical generalisation to the extreme. But, without going so far, we can agree that history should lead statesmen to a profound and humbling sense of human frailty—to a recognition of the fact, so insistently demonstrated by experience and so tragically destructive of our most cherished certitudes, that the possibilities of history are far richer and more various than the human intellect is likely to conceive. This, and the final perception that while the tragedy of history implicates us all in the common plight of humanity, we are never relieved, despite the limits of our knowledge and the darkness of our understanding, from the necessity of meeting our obligations.

26. Conclusion:

A Letter to Groucho Marx

WE NEED NOT TAKE THE TRAGEDY OF HISTORY SO SERIously as to forget our obligation to laugh as well. Perhaps the humor of history is black, a discipline of the absurd to match the world's stage on which the theatre of the absurd plays to standing-room-only audiences, but the humor is there nonetheless. Let the final word here be given to a man who represents those historians of the moment, newspaper reporters, those men who give most Americans all the history they will ever read once they have left school, and all that they have ever read with pleasure. Russell Baker, a columnist for the *New York Times,* reminds us of Carl Becker's message, that Everyman will be his own historian.

♦ ♦ ♦

Washington,
March 27 ——

DEAR GROUCHO [MARX],

The Groucho Letters is (are?) a delight for all us F.B.I. types who like to read other people's mail, but you're probably going to find, next time you face a piece of stationery, that publication was a mistake.

Once you start letting letters get into print, you tend to get confused when you sit down to write a note to Aunt Hannah. The problem is whether you're writing for Aunt Hannah's benefit or

---

for the 300,000 people who are going to gobble up your next book of letters.

One of those moderately notorious characters in which Washington abounds lives down the street here, and a few years ago he agreed to give some university out West all his correspondence, on the theory that the documentation of American history would be incomplete without a record of his notes to the milkman.

The trouble is that ever since he committed himself to writing letters to posterity he hasn't been able to write a line. Sometimes when you drop in at his place he'll have thirty or forty quarts of milk in the kitchen because he hasn't been able to rephrase "No Milk Today" with the felicity that will satisfy Edmund Wilson when his correspondence is published.

He's an extreme case, admittedly, but not the worst example of what happens to people when they realize their letters are being mailed over the heads of their correspondents for ultimate delivery to the *New York Review of Books*. The worst is the sort of thing that happened to a certain novelist, formerly of Possum Gap, Tenn., now of New York who hit it big with his first book and, after yielding to the inevitable pressures to publish his letters, began worrying about his literary reputation.

His mother passed through Washington not long ago and dropped by the office. "How's Al?" I asked her. "He writes all the time but he don't say," she said. "It's gotten so I hate to see the mailman coming up the hollow on account of I know it's going to be another one of those eight-page letters from Al telling me about how wrong some fellow named Eliot was in comparing Henry James and Turgenev."

All his mother wanted to hear, of course, was that he was making a mint and eating high on the hog, but having committed his letter to print, Al felt he'd be destroying his literary reputation unless he poured it on her about subjects that book reviewers think a real artist ought to talk about to the old mom. His mother, naturally, assumes he has become unhinged.

This is known in medicine as the Lord Chesterfield reaction. You, as a father, know as well as I do that all Chesterfield's son wanted from the old boy was a few lines ending with, "Enclosed find check for the amount you requested." Instead, Chesterfield battered him with volumes of advice on how to get on in the world, which was obviously meant to show posterity what a keen bird old Chesterfield himself was.

We can assume as a matter of course that the boy thought the old man, at best, daft.

At that, Chesterfield was a more entertaining writer of letters for the public than most men who do.

Now that you're stuck with writing letters to posterity, you're going to have problems. Take your letter to Norman Krasna in which you review *The Balcony* by Jean Genêt. A splendid letter because it was written without posterity peeping over your shoulder.

Not expecting any literary critics to intercept your mail, you could easily write, "If this is show business, I'm glad I'm getting out."

But suppose you were writing to Krasna in your new manifestation as Groucho, Man of Letters, vulnerable to assault by Jean-Paul Sartre. Knowing that dismissal of a Genêt work as a "turkey" (your word) is an offense punishable by character assassination, you would probably take 6,000 words to say it and end up sounding like Marcel Proust.

Or take "Last Night I saw a broad we had both pursued during moments of our more active lives." Marvelous. But are you still going to be able to come up with a line as free-spirited as that now that you know your mail is likely to wind up on shelves between Lord Chesterfield and Mme. de Sévigné? There's the frail germ of a joke there, but I'll leave the punch line to you. These days you never can be sure your mail isn't being delivered direct to the printer.

As ever,

[Russell Baker]

As George Savile, Marquess of Halifax, a seventeenth-century moralist, politician, and author of political works important to historians, once noted, "There is no stronger evidence of a crazy understanding than the making too large a catalogue of things necessary." From here the reader may make his own catalogue.

Bibliography

The literature on historical method is large. In one sense, all written history is a part of the methodological literature, for all books are examples of research methods in practice. Some authors are more self-consciously committed to setting out how evidence was collected and evaluated than others, but one can usually assess a book fairly quickly by reading any bibliographical essay or note on sources that it may contain, together with the preface and the footnotes. Such reading does not provide the reader with the substance of the book, of course, merely with the foundation. Nor does the present collection of essays do more than help establish a few badges of identity for the historian, so that the wary reader may recognize when the scholar is writing history and when he is writing some grade of *haute* journalism. Especially provocative are J. H. Plumb's *The Death of History* (1969) and David Hackett Fischer's, *Historians Fallacies: Toward a Logic of Historical Thought* (1970).

For further reading in methodology and theory, the reader should turn to Homer Carey Hockett, *The Critical Method in Historical Research and Writing* (New York, 1955), which contains an excellent bibliography. The books excerpted here—Altick, Nevins, Barzun and Graff—also should be read in their entirety. A recent book, which contains an excellent example for the beginning student of *explication de texte,* something which most historians do in their classrooms, is *How to Study History* (New York, 1967), by Norman F. Cantor and Richard I. Schneider. Many years ago everyone read Charles V. Langlois and Charles Seignobos, *Introduction to the Study of History* (New York, 1912), in a translation from the French by G. G. Berry; conversations with graduate students would indicate that it is little read now, having been replaced, quite rightly, by two rather different books, Marc Bloch, *The Historian's Craft* (New York, 1953), and E. H. Carr, *What Is History?* (New York, 1962). Carl Gustavson, *A Preface to History* (New York, 1955), is interesting, and if one really needs to begin at the beginning, A. L. Rowse's *The Use of History* is well suited to a high-school audience.

To see a master historian at work, especially one whose prose style is justly admired for lean informality, read J. H. Hexter, *Reappraisals in History* (Evanston, Ill., 1962). His essay "Storm Over the Gentry," which first appeared in *Encounter* X (May, 1958) and which is reprinted in *Reappraisals,* should have been included here. A very useful but sometimes quite untrustworthy little book, at least as it applies to the United States, is Philip Hepworth's *How to Find Out in History* (Oxford, 1966). *Generalization in the Writing of History,* edited by Louis Gottschalk (Chicago, 1963), is immensely helpful. Historiographically, John Higham, Leonard Krieger, and Felix Gilbert, in *History* (Englewood Cliffs, N.J., 1964), have provided an excellent point of departure. Daniel F. McCall, in *Africa in Time Perspective: A Discussion of Historical Reconstruction from Unwritten Sources* (Oxford, 1964), mentioned in Part V, writes of "the heritage of the ears" and of how changes in the structure of language can help the historian. To discover what the econometric approach to history is all about, see Robert Fogel's summary in the *Economic History Review,* XIX (December, 1966). The best statement of another theoretical and time-related problem with which the historian must deal appears, oddly enough, in an issue of *Yale French Studies* (Nos. 36–37, 1966) devoted entirely to "Structuralism." "The Problem of the Christian Historian," by E. Harris Harbison, which appeared in *Theology Today,* V (October, 1948), raises a number of important questions. Perhaps the best book of all, which discusses several distinguished historians in highly personal terms, is Ved Mehta's *Fly and the Fly-Bottle: Encounters with British Intellectuals* (London, 1963), a series of essays which first appeared in *The New Yorker.* Mehta does not always make the historian attractive but he does make him real.

Many case studies are listed under the *For additional reading* sections in this volume. Other books and articles, which I was forced to omit but which belong on any "short list" of detective stories in history, are John Chadwick, *The Decipherment of Linear B* (Cambridge, 1958); R. W. Southern, "The Canterbury Forgeries," *English Historical Review,* CCLXXXVII (April, 1958); and K. B. McFarlane, "Henry V, Bishop Beaufort and the Red Hat, 1417–1421," in the same journal, LX (September, 1945), which is a classic of its kind, although only for the initiated. Three good methodological inquiries which raise questions not taken up in the selections are Christopher Hawkes, "Archeological Theory and Method: Some Suggestions from the Old World," *American Anthropologist,* LVI (April, 1954); Ian Grosart, "Writing the History of Papua and New Guinea," *Journal of the Papua and New Guinea Society,* I (Summer, 1967); and D. P. Singhal, "The Writing of Asian History," *Hemisphere,* VII (July, 1963). The last two are cited for their strengths, and also to show again that good things may appear in obscure places, and that the historian must attempt to keep abreast of a wide range of such journals.

This listing could be made longer, of course, but the original footnotes to some of the articles printed here should also help lead the reader, now versed in the ways of research, down those paths he wishes to follow. However, since few of the essays really deal with what might be called the moral dimension—to publish when publication will hurt someone, or to withhold publication; to use but render anonymous sources which do not wish to be used; to publish accurately researched conclusions which run directly contrary to the immediate public good —I would suggest that two other essays might be read together. They raise once again the interesting question posed by the famous exchange between Jared Sparks and Lord Mahon. Richard C. Vitzthum, writing on "The Historian as Editor: Francis Parkman's Reconstruction of Sources in Montcalm and Wolfe," in the *Journal of American History,* LIII (December, 1966), showed that Parkman often was careless or distorted documents in order to give them greater artistic impact, since time had diluted their immediacy. Vitzthum concluded that Parkman was guilty of little more than "deviations from a respectable scholarly norm" and that some changes were of no factual importance and did make Parkman's story more comprehensible. Writing three years earlier, Francis Jennings concluded, in "A Vanishing Indian: Francis Parkman Versus His Sources," in the *Pennsylvania Magazine of History and Biography,* LXXXVII (July, 1963), that Parkman "edited his sources not just for rhetorical effect, but to falsify facts clearly stated in the sources."

There are, as is indicated by Helen MacInnes's title *The Double Image*—which turns upon the ability of a professional historian to keep his eye on history while reasoning through to the final capture of a former S.S. colonel—two sides to every question of evidence. A trite conclusion, but true, and that is what much of history must be. History is, as James Malin once remarked, like nailing jelly to a wall. But someone must keep trying.